# A
# Spiritual
# House
# Preserved

# A
# SPIRITUAL
# HOUSE
# PRESERVED

*A Century in*
*the River's Bend*

1916-2016

*Edited by* CALVIN KALSBEEK

REFORMED
FREE PUBLISHING
*ASSOCIATION*
Jenison, Michigan

© 2016 Reformed Free Publishing Association

Scripture cited is taken from the King James (Authorized) Version

Reformed Free Publishing Association
1894 Georgetown Center Drive
Jenison, Michigan 49428
www.rfpa.org
mail@rfpa.org

Cover design by Christopher Tobias / www.tobiasdesign.com
Interior design by Katherine Lloyd / www.theDESKonline.com

ISBN 978-1-944555-06-1

LCCN 2016937536

# Contents

## Chapter 3: HOPE'S BUILDINGS:
### DEDICATED TO THE SERVICE OF GOD ............ 77

## Chapter 4: HOPE'S INVOLVEMENT IN THE
### CONTROVERSIES OF 1924–25 AND 1953.......... 103

## Chapter 5: PERSPECTIVES OF HOPE'S FORMER MINISTERS .... 131

# A House Built by Christ

*Rev. David Overway*

To whom coming, as unto a living stone, disallowed indeed of men, but chosen of God, and precious, ye also, as lively stones, are built up a spiritual house, an holy priesthood, to offer up spiritual sacrifices, acceptable to God by Jesus Christ.

1 PETER 2:4–5

THANKS BE UNTO GOD! AND THANKS BE unto his Son, Jesus Christ our savior, who gathers, defends, and preserves us! For he has built us and preserved us for one hundred years as a church, as a congregation, as a spiritual house for himself!

All the praise and thanksgiving must be directed unto God in Jesus Christ, for he is the one who has built us up and preserved us. We have not built ourselves. We have not been preserved by our own doing. On this one-hundredth anniversary of our existence as a congregation, we are not lifted up with pride in ourselves. Nor will we praise our forefathers or ourselves as if the spiritual house of our church has been built and preserved by men. But Christ must receive all our praise, for he alone has built us up and preserved us to be a spiritual house for his Father.

A house of God is what he has made us to be. The church is a house wherein God dwells. So says Ephesians 2:22: "Ye also are builded together for an habitation of God through the Spirit" (cf. 1 Cor. 3:16). This is also the idea of 1 Peter 2:5, as it speaks of our being built up as a "spiritual house." As a church we are a spiritual house, a house within which God dwells by his Spirit.

He dwells within us as our covenantal God. He reveals himself within us and unto us as our covenantal Father and friend. He communes with us, speaking to us and listening to us as he dwells within us as a congregation and graciously causes us to enjoy the fellowship of his family friendship.

As a spiritual house we are also a living house. 1 Peter 2:5 says that we are "lively," or better, "living" stones. Each member of the church is a living stone, arranged together to form a living house. We are a house of God that is alive with a spiritual life by virtue of the Spirit's dwelling within us.

Although this spiritual house is made up of many stones, yet it is one house. Each stone is so united to each and every other stone that one united house is formed: many stones, yet one house; many members, yet one church. This is true of our congregation at any point in time. This is also true of our congregation over the generations, even over the past one hundred years: many members, indeed, but all sharing such a unity that we have been, and are, one house—"*a* spiritual house" of God.

All of this is because we have been built by Christ. The verb in the original for "built up" in 1 Peter 2:5 is passive, indicating that the church does not build herself, but is built by another. Christ identifies himself as the builder in Matthew 16:18: "I will build my church." He established the legal right to build us into the house of God through his suffering and death on the cross. By the cross he also gained for us the right to be used as living stones in Hope church.

That we are built by Christ, then, means that we are built in grace. Everything about his building us to be a spiritual house is gracious. Since his grace is always sovereign, particular, and almighty, so also is his building of us into a spiritual house. What a comfort!

Graciously and mightily he builds us upon himself, for he is the cornerstone of the church. Verse 4 refers to him as a "living stone," while verses 6 and 7 make clear that this living stone is also the "chief corner stone." He is the foundation of the church, the unmovable, solid rock upon which the universal church and every congregation within her is built.

We are established upon Christ, the cornerstone, because we are established upon his word (Eph. 2:20). Christ has built us up by establishing us upon the truth and a strong confession of that truth. The apostle Peter, as he wrote the words of this text, certainly remembered Jesus' instruction to him, when upon his confessing the truth of Christ, the Lord had said to him, "Upon this rock I will build my church" (Matt. 16:18). So must we remember how precious the truth of Christ is to us as a church, for it is our very foundation, the rock upon which we are built. We stand as a church today because Christ has built us upon the truth, and we have been preserved for one hundred years because Christ has faithfully maintained us upon the cornerstone of his truth.

Upon this foundation of truth he has built us up as living stones, adding stone upon stone, generation by generation. According to his covenantal promise, he has added to our number over the years the elect children of covenantal believers, even while gathering the previous generation to take their place in that spiritual house of many mansions in glory. He has also added others who have joined our congregation over the years, and he has fit them into the spiritual house and remembered his promise to them, too, to save believers and their seed in their generations.

His building us up has included not only adding to our number but also adding to our strength. The verb for "built up" in 1 Peter 2:5 also carries the meaning of "to strengthen." How marvelously Christ has strengthened us. He has led us through many trials, difficulties, and sorrows. All the while and even *through* those trials, he has strengthened us. He has taught us to cling ever more tightly to the truth about himself as our only comfort in our pilgrim journeys. By his Spirit within us and among us he has worked in us a growth in our knowledge and love of this truth. Thereby he has strengthened us.

Christ is continuously building his spiritual house. Never does he rest; always as the faithful servant of God and savior of the church, he builds. The verb in the original also indicates this ongoing activity. In our past Christ has built us up. In the present he is building us up. This is our comfort for the future, too, for he will continue to build us up as a spiritual house unto God.

Therefore we have been preserved. All the opposition of the gates of hell have not prevailed against us (Matt. 16:18), because Christ has built us, and Christ has preserved us as a spiritual house of God upon the Cornerstone of his saving truth. We are a house built by Christ!

Thanks be unto God! Thanks be unto his Son and our savior, Jesus Christ! For he has built us and preserved us! To him be all the praise!

# Editor's Comments

## A Baby is Born

In the fall of 2014 the council of Hope Protestant Reformed Church asked the congregation for volunteers to serve on the one-hundredth anniversary committee. On December 1, 2014, those who volunteered met and decided to divide into two committees, one to plan the activities for the celebration and one to plan a commemorative book. The two committees continued the evening by meeting independently to formulate initial plans of action to meet the council's mandate, that is, "as a committee [to] decide how you will handle the celebration." This mandate was the *council's* mandate, and as such it served as a reminder to the committee members that we were accountable to the council. Therefore, the committee regularly reported its progress and received in return the council's approval of the work.

The four members of the commemorative book committee (Susann Grasman, Calvin Kalsbeek, Evelyn Langerak, and David Moelker) considered the council's mandate with the result that the volume the reader is now holding, *A Spiritual House Preserved: A Century in the River's Bend*, was conceived. Little did we know at the time the monstrosity that would be born after a trying, sixteen-month pregnancy. But born it is and monstrous it is too.

It did not take the book committee long to figure out that publishing a fairly comprehensive book about Hope's one-hundred-year history in sixteen months was much more than the four of us could handle. Thus we enlisted help—lots of help. Once we determined what we thought needed to be included in the book, we enlisted an army of willing writers. Upon reception of their contributions, the committee added a multitude of pictures, picture captions, and sidebars that related to their writings. Throughout the pregnancy, however, it was not uncommon for the committee members to think of something else to include in "the book" or to receive new ideas from the congregation. Fueled by those ideas, the committee members would ask at our next meetings, "What about this?" or "What about that?" or "Shouldn't we include a chapter on...?" or...? And without fail we answered, "Yes, we should include that; the book will not be complete without it."

So you see this monstrous baby is not all our fault. If the prospective writers had not been so willing, if the congregation had not been so free in sharing its ideas and memories, if our members had not been so willing to share their pictures; much of this would not have happened. But happened it has, and grateful we are for all the contributions.

The good thing is that as a congregation we can truly say, "This book is OUR baby!" And the story it tells is, by the grace of our faithful heavenly Father, ours too. Thanks be to him!

## Acknowledgments

Many contributors to A Spiritual House Preserved deserve recognition for their valued writing. Their names are found along with their contributions. These include seven former ministers who in ignorance believed their work at Hope was finished when they took a call to another congregation; eight busy sons of Hope in the gospel ministry who without complaint agreed to make contributions; and at least thirty members of Hope church whose fingers have "touched" these pages, some in very significant ways. Three of them willingly used their photography and photo editing skills to enhance the book.

There are also many others who deserve our expressions of appreciation.

Gerald Elders and Hope Christian Reformed Church willingly shared the translated Dutch minutes of the early years of Hope church and permitted us to use interview quotes from their seventy-fifth anniversary book, The History of Hope 1916–1991.

Grandville Historical Commission was very accommodating in providing pictures relating to early transportation on the Grand River.

Dick Harms and the personnel of Calvin College Hekman Library cheerfully gave of their time and expertise to locate and allow us to use pertinent pictures and documents relating to Hope's history.

Gordon Mast and First Jenison Christian Reformed Church researched their early minutes at our request.

Tom and Bonnie Moelker of Moelker Orchards repeatedly responded to our requests for pictures relating to Hope's early history. The best pictures of Hope's early buildings were received from them.

James Morren and Walker United Reformed Church provided pictures and information relating to Hope's beginnings and to Hope's charter members who came from the Walker church.

Gerald Roberts, who lives in the old Pelton house on the corner of Kenowa and Luce, shared pictures and information relating to the early history of River Bend.

Fourteen people, whose names are listed in chapter 7, courageously submitted to interviews and provided pictures for the book. Charles Terpstra submitted for this chapter the interview he conducted with his uncle, Dewey Engelsma, in the 1980s.

Daughter congregations, Faith, Grandville, and Grace, readily submitted to mother Hope's requests for histories of their congregations and appropriate pictures.

Philip Harbach was very gracious in submitting family photos and writing and submitting for publication a record of his father's work as a missionary of Hope church.

Charles Terpstra and the Protestant Reformed seminary upon request tirelessly answered many requests for information from the archives of the Protestant Reformed Churches.

On every page of this volume is evident the expertise of Katherine Lloyd, the typesetter. We thank her for the professional design, typesetting, photo editing, and photo placement. Her ideas, advice, accuracy, and timeliness were invaluable, along with her willingness to typeset and to "develop" the book chapter by chapter with the committee.

Thanks also to the many members and former members of Hope church and others whose contributions of pictures and memories added some spice where it was needed.

The anniversary book committee must be commended (even though that includes the editor) for its excellent work while under a lot of pressure because of time constraints. Busy they were deciding book and chapter titles, layout, researching historical documents and minutes, writing, gathering pictures and quotes, copyediting, proofreading, and a multitude of other tasks connected with the book. When you ask them about it, they will tell you that it was enjoyable work, but it was *work,* and lots of it, nonetheless. Thanks for a job well done!

Much could be written concerning what Hope's one-hundredth anniversary committee has experienced and accomplished over the past eighteen months, but we chose not to bore the reader with the details. We would all agree on this however that when we started, we did not really know what we were getting into. But get into it we did; and survive, even thrive, we did as well. As the chairman of the committee, words fail to express adequately my appreciation for their dedicated focus, energy, and exceptional faithfulness in carrying out the work assigned us by Hope's council. Thank you, one-hundredth anniversary committee!

Anniversary committee back left to right: David Moelker, Hank Vander Waal, Clare Kuiper; middle: Brenda Bomers, Evelyn Langerak, Deb Vander Waal, Cal Kalsbeek; front: Susann Grasman, Erin Rutgers, Valerie Van Baren, John Van Baren, Linda Kalsbeek

Members of Hope Protestant Reformed Church are encouraged, when occasion permits, to express their thanks to those listed above for their valuable contributions to this volume and the anniversary celebration.

# Editor's Foreword

THE STORY OF HOPE PROTESTANT REFORMED CHURCH is only a tiny chapter in the massive, unfinished book that encompasses the history of the entire body of Christ.

> This Church hath been from the beginning of the world, and will be to the end thereof; which is evident from this, that Christ is an eternal King, which without subjects He cannot be...
>
> Furthermore, this holy church is not confined, bound, or limited to a certain place or to certain persons, but is spread and dispersed over the whole world; and yet is joined and united with heart and will, by the power of faith, in one and the same Spirit.[1]

In other words Hope Protestant Reformed Church does not stand alone. Using the inspired words of the apostle Paul, she is "built upon the foundation of the apostles and prophets, Jesus Christ himself being the chief corner stone" (Eph. 2:20).

Hope's spiritual lineage therefore begins with Adam and flows through the patriarchs and Old Testament Israel. Furthermore, she traces her new dispensational bloodlines through the apostolic church and the Roman Catholic Church. Following the great Reformation of the sixteenth century, her tradition is that of the decisions of Dordrecht and the Reformed churches of the Netherlands. As a result of the *Afschieding* (Secession) of 1834 in the Netherlands, Hope's spiritual ancestors came to America in 1846 under the leadership of Rev. Albertus Van Raalte and settled in dense forests of western Michigan. After a brief time in the Reformed Church of America, in 1857 four small

---

1 Belgic Confession 27, in *The Confessions and the Church Order of the Protestant Reformed Churches* (Grandville, MI: Protestant Reformed Churches in America, 2005), 58–60.

xix

congregations formed what is today the Christian Reformed Church of America, and in this small denomination Hope was born on June 8, 1916.

During the centennial anniversary of Hope Protestant Reformed Church, we do well to pause, if just briefly, to consider what the Lord did for us at each of these junctures in our spiritual lineage.

We are not Jews, yet the Lord was pleased through the history of Old Testament Israel to reveal himself as a covenantal God who would deliver his people from their sins by means of the Head of the covenant, his only begotten Son, Jesus Christ. His atoning death on the cross fulfilled all of the Old Testament sacrifices and ceremonies.

At Pentecost Christ poured out his Spirit on his church. This opened the way for us as Gentiles to be incorporated into Christ's church. Then by means of the Spirit-lead apostles the New Testament church received the fundamentals of the Christian faith as revealed in the New Testament scriptures. After the death of the apostles, false teachers arose to challenge many of the apostolic teachings, including the very divinity of the Lord himself. These challenges were purposeful, however, as they would lead Christ's church to make those challenged apostolic doctrines their own by means of church decisions and creeds. For example, at Nicea in 325 the church wrote the Nicene Creed to confirm the truth that Christ is not merely a creature of God, but that Christ himself is God. In 431 the church condemned the errors of Pelagius and established the truth concerning man's original sin and total depravity and thereby demonstrated man's need of a savior that is both God and man, "because the justice of God requires that the same human nature which hath sinned should likewise make satisfaction for sin."[2] These precious truths continue to be preached and taught in our midst.

The development of errors in the church of our spiritual lineage persisted, however. In what became known as the Roman Catholic Church, during the late ancient period and the Middle Ages, many new false teachings arose. In addition to establishing the unbiblical, hierarchical

---

2   Heidelberg Catechism A 16, in ibid., 88.

form of church government in which the pope ruled and was made the head of the church, Rome promoted the worship of saints, the adoration of Mary, and the worship of relics. While many other errors developed, two of the most notable were the false doctrine of transubstantiation (the belief that the bread and the wine of the Lord's supper are changed into the flesh and blood of Christ) and the teaching that one is justified by faith and works. Hope Protestant Reformed Church and all those who trace their spiritual ancestry to the sixteenth-century protestant Reformation were by God's grace delivered from those errors through the faithful labors of Martin Luther, John Calvin, and John Knox.

After the great Reformation, Hope's spiritual lineage is traced to the reformational branch most influenced by John Calvin. Our forebearers in the Lowlands (Belgium and the Netherlands) adopted as their own two protestant creeds: the Heidelberg Catechism and the Netherlands (Belgic) Confession. This action would prove very costly as Roman Catholic Spain (ruler over the Lowlands) employed every means at its disposal (including the Spanish Inquisition) to extinguish all the Protestants there. Spain's goals, however, were contrary to our Lord's wisdom. When the dust settled, the Lowlands were divided into Spanish Roman Catholic Belgium and an independent protestant Netherlands under the leadership of William of Orange.

Since this conflict with Spain connected the protestants in the Netherlands (church) with William of Orange (state) against their common enemy (Roman Catholic Spain), understandably these beginnings in the Netherlands led to a very close affiliation between the church and the state. This would not bode well for the church. Over time there developed in the Netherlands what could be called a state church. Resulting from this situation was a church that was rapidly corrupted by state interference in church affairs. The government in the Netherlands even determined if and when church synods could meet, with the result that false doctrine could be taught without fear of discipline. The errors of the Arminians were addressed by the Synod of Dordrecht (1618–19) only because Prince Mauritz favored those who supported orthodoxy. Through the work of this synod, Hope inherited the doctrinal riches of the well-known five points of Calvinism. In the end however false doctrine prevailed in the Dutch Reformed churches until 1834 when under the leadership of Hendrik de Cock a secession (*Afscheiding*) occurred, which was the next step in Hope's spiritual succession. However, this secession was strongly resisted by the state church. As a result, those who left the state church were persecuted by being fined, imprisoned, and restricted in their worship.

Consequently some of the leaders and people of the Secession of 1834 left the Netherlands and came to America beginning in 1846. Men such as Rev. Albertus C. Van Raalte (Holland, Michigan) and Rev. Cornelius Vander Meulen (Zeeland, Michigan) led the way. Their followers would experience many difficulties in western Michigan, but none greater than the internal conflict that divided them in 1857. In that year four small congregations separated from their union with the churches known today as the Reformed Church of America because in that denomination lodge membership was accepted, the Heidelberg Catechism was no longer preached regularly, changes were made in the Church Order and creeds, and hymns were allowed in the churches. When the dust settled those four churches began what today is known as the Christian Reformed Church of America. Hope Protestant Reformed Church began in 1916, just forty years later, in the Grand River's bend in what today is Walker, Michigan, with the name Hope Christian Reformed Church.

This abbreviated story of Hope's spiritual ancestry makes clear that there is no room for Hope's members to boast: what we have is the result of God's gifts to us though a "great cloud of witnesses" (Heb. 12:1). It also demonstrates that the existence of Hope Protestant Reformed Church for one hundred years is by the grace of God "a spiritual house… acceptable to God" not because of anything special about Hope, but because she is "chosen of God, and precious" in his sight (1 Pet. 2:4–5).[3]

This book is Hope's meager, but heart-felt, expression of gratitude for God's faithfulness. All thanks and praise to him!

---

3   1 Peter 2:4–5 is the text Rev. John R. Brink preached on at Hope's organization, and it is the theme of Hope's centennial celebration.

# Part One

## The History
### of a
## Spiritual House
## Preserved

# Editor's Introduction
## to Part One

Astounding it is to consider what God has done by incorporating us into his universal church.

Equally astounding it is to consider his faithfulness in gathering, defending, and preserving Hope as a local manifestation of the body of Christ in the Grand River's bend. No doubt, Hope's founders understood what it meant to be a local manifestation of the body of Christ, and were well aware of and committed to living that truth as it is expressed in the Belgic Confession:

> We believe, since this holy congregation is an assembly of those who are saved, and out of it there is no salvation, that no person, of whatsoever state or condition he may be, ought to withdraw himself to live in a separate state from it; but that all men are in duty bound to join and unite themselves with it, maintaining the unity of the church; submitting themselves to the doctrine and discipline thereof; bowing their necks under the yoke of Jesus Christ; and as mutual members of the same body, serving to the edification of the brethren, according to the talents God has given them.[1]

Part one clearly demonstrates that Hope's founders and membership throughout her one-hundred-year history were committed to the duty to "join and unite themselves" to the true church. They understood that to do otherwise is to "act contrary to the ordinance of God."[2] At times this would prove costly. Yet they counted the cost and by the grace of God were found faithful.

Part one further demonstrates Hope's firm resolve in "bowing their

---

1  Belgic Confession 28, in *Confessions and Church Order*, 60–61
2  Belgic Confession 28, in ibid., 61

necks under the yoke of Christ" and separating "themselves from all those who do not belong to the church," as is abundantly clear in her history during the controversies of 1924 and 1953. While the controversies were costly in the loss of buildings, members, and friends, the losses were of little consequence when compared to what they retained by "submitting themselves to the doctrine and discipline" of King Jesus.[3]

Humbling it is to consider that our majestic, mighty King has been pleased to work this wonder of his grace in a tiny corner of western Michigan nestled in a hook-like bend in the Grand River.

He alone is worthy of our thanks and praise!

---

3   Belgic Confession 28, in ibid., 60–61.

# Chapter 1

## HOPE'S BEGINNINGS IN THE RIVER'S BEND

*Calvin Kalsbeek*

1916 MARKED AN *END* AND A *BEGINNING* in the Grand River's bend located in what today is Walker, Michigan.

*Ending* was the steamboat era that had begun in 1837 with the launching of the steamboat *Governor Mason*. *Governor Mason* soon had competition from the *Owashtonong*, which sported the first steam whistle to be heard in the Grand River Valley.

Sternwheel steamboat on the Grand River

These forerunners to steamboat traffic on the Grand were soon followed by a host of others. However, the whine of the first train whistle in Grand Rapids on June 27, 1858, spelled the death knell of the

5

riverboats. Although the riverboat traffic on the Grand River gradually declined, it hung on for another fifty years; but just barely.

"Some school children were afraid to go to school when they first heard the [steamboat's] whistle, because they "thought it was a panther howling in the woods."[1]

*May Graham* was the last steamer to pass through the swing bridge in Eastmanville, and maybe, just maybe, Hope charter member, Jantje (Jennie) Engelsma, heard that last mournful whistle blast of the *May Graham* as it quietly navigated the river's bend near the Engelsma's farm where Kenowa Avenue dead-ends to the Grand River.

THE MAY GRAHAM
Last Steamer to ply the Grand River

The *May Graham* was the last riverboat to travel on the Grand River.

*Beginning* in the river's bend in 1916 was a newly instituted church of our Lord Jesus Christ. During the years prior, its founders had little interest in forming a new congregation, but a decision of the Michigan State Highway Department would change that.

---

1    *Grand River Scrapbook* (1894), quoted in Don Chrysler, *The Story of Grand River: A Bicentennial History* (n.p.: Don Chrysler, 1975), 11.

In 1912 the State Highway Department built a ferry to cross the river between River Bend and Jenison. Christian Reformed families [north of the Grand River] began attending the Jenison Christian Reformed Church instead of churches in Grand Rapids. However, the Highway Department abandoned the ferry service in 1914 leaving the people who had been attending the churches in Jenison to decide whether to return to the Grand Rapids churches or to form a church of their own.[2]

The existence of the ferry had made it possible, though challenging, for Jenison Christian Reformed Church to provide for the spiritual needs of the believers trapped in the river's bend: "The good pastor was given permission to hire a horse and buggy one half day of each week to make pastoral calls, including [to] those who lived beyond the river and came to Church by means of a Ferry Boat."[3]

The ferry was located at the south end of Kenowa Avenue.
It enabled people in River Bend to get to Grandville and Jenison.

---

2   Grandville Historical Commission, *Bend in the River: The Story of Grandville and Jenison, Michigan 1832–1972*, ed. John W. Mc Gee (Grand Rapids, MI: William B. Eerdmans Publishing Company, 1973), 242.

3   *Seventy-fifth Anniversary of the Jenison Christian Reformed Church 1875–1950*, 12.

## Map of River Bend

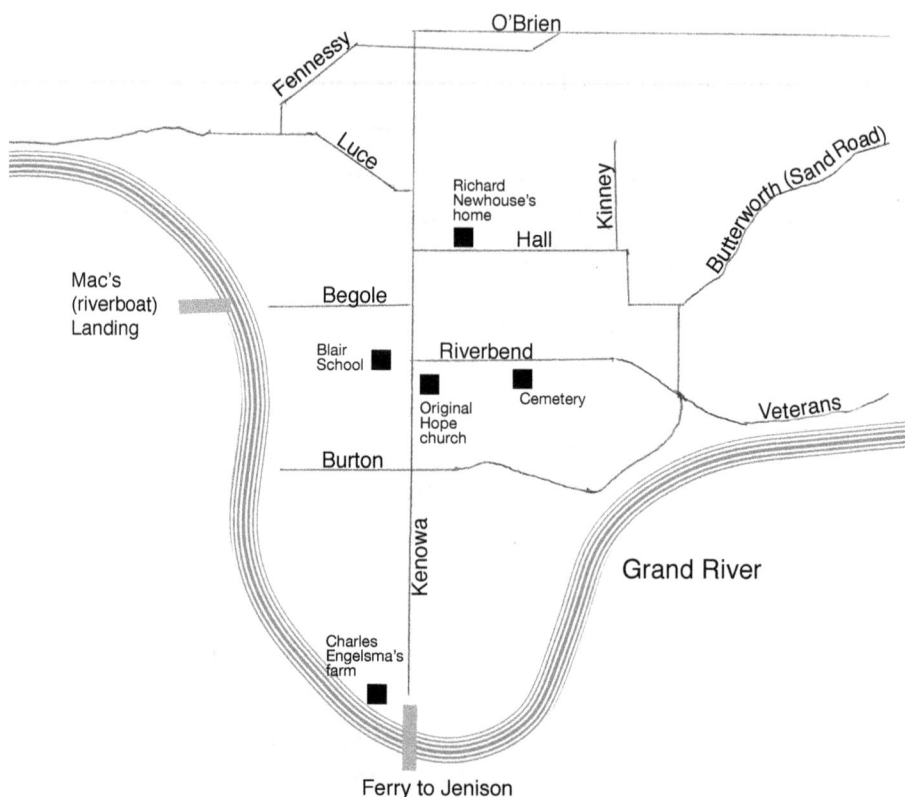

O'Brien

Fennessy

Luce

Richard
Newhouse's
home

Hall

Kinney

Butterworth (Sand Road)

Mac's
(riverboat)
Landing

Begole

Blair
School

Riverbend

Original
Hope
church

Cemetery

Veterans

Burton

Kenowa

Grand River

Charles
Engelsma's
farm

Ferry to Jenison

## Trapped in the River's Bend

Believers in "the bend" were cut off from Jenison Christian Reformed Church by the Michigan State Highway Department's decision to discontinue the ferry. Furthermore, distance, poor roads (if they could be called roads), and lack of good transportation (mostly horse driven) made it very difficult for Reformed believers in "the bend" to regularly attend the churches in Grand Rapids.

"I can remember one time in the winter they came to church with a team of horses and a sleigh. The snow was so deep in the road they had to go out into the field. The snow was right up to the horses' bellies. So they had all they could to get home from church. That wasn't funny either. They never cancelled church—nobody had a phone. It was unheard of."[4] —Celia Bergman

Providentially, a group of Christian Reformed believers about four miles to the north of River Bend were facing a similar problem. They "had difficulty getting to town on Sundays and also during the week to have the children catechised."[5] Their solution to these problems was to organize as a new congregation near Walker Station (intersection of Kinney and Remembrance) under the leadership of Rev. John R. Brink, home missionary of the Christian Reformed Church. They organized as the Walker Christian Reformed Church on November 18, 1912. Among their fourteen charter member families was Mr. and Mrs. Richard Niewenhuis (Newhouse). At that meeting Richard was elected as one of Walker's first deacons. Others trapped in the river's bend would soon follow Newhouse's lead and join Walker Christian Reformed Church.

Gridley's hill was on Riverbend Drive between Butterworth and Kenowa. The picture faces west toward Kenowa Avenue and Blair School.

The locals called Butterworth Drive Sand Road.

---

4   *The History of Hope 1916–1991* (Grandville, MI: Hope Christian Reformed Church), 7
5   City of Walker Historical Committee, *Echoes of the Past: A Bicentennial History of the City of Walker, Michigan,* ed. Warren Versluis (1976), 82.

Some of Hope's charter members came
from Walker Christian Reformed Church.

The stay at Walker church of some of those trapped in "the bend" looked to be short-lived, however, as Rev. Brink's memoirs make clear.

In the winter of 1916 I received a telephone call from a person [Richard Newhouse] living about two miles north of Jenison and about seven miles west of Grand Rapids. He wanted to know whether it would be possible to start a mission in his neighborhood, a rural community where several Christian Reformed families were living. As I had a number of fields under my care and was busy every Sunday, I agreed to come over on Wednesday evenings to preach for them. The man who called said that we could use his home as a meeting place. I soon found out that these people were hungry for the gospel message. There were also a goodly number of children at the meetings. The attendance grew, and soon we were compelled to move. A public school hall [Blair School, site of the present Riverbend Public School on Kenowa Avenue] was used, and soon Sunday services were started.[6]

---

6    J. R. Brink, "Memoirs of Rev. J. R. Brink," ed. Ralph V. Brink and Ruth Brink Hoeksema (private collection, 1985), 69.

Blair School was located at the intersection of Kenowa Avenue
and Riverbend. The congregation of Hope worshiped
there when it did not have a building of its own.

But sparks flew when home missionary Brink reported to Classis
Grand Rapids West of the Christian Reformed Church concerning that
work. Brink explains what transpired at that classis.

> When the report of these services came to Classis there was
> strong opposition. The argument was that they were located
> only a little over a mile from Jenison. They could easily go
> to the Jenison church, across the river. However, this com-
> ment overlooked two things: the old ferry, which had plied its
> way across the river at Grandville, had stopped running; the
> nearest bridge was at Wealthy Street in Grand Rapids, a trip
> of at least thirteen miles to get to the Jenison church. Also
> several of the people attending the services were not mem-
> bers of Jenison; some were "nominal" members of churches
> in Grand Rapids, many had not been attending any church
> for some time, and several were unchurched. So, after a lot of
> wrangling at Classis, to which I had become accustomed by
> this time, Classis finally allowed this to become a mission of
> our church.[7]

7   Ibid., 69. See Rev. J. R. Brink's report, "Hope, Grandville, Michigan," in appendix 1.

Apparently Rev. Brink had a sense of humor as the unedited version of his memoirs record his thoughts in response to those at classis who thought the people in River Bend could attend Jenison Christian Reformed Church: "As far as going to Jenison is concerned, it would be an easy matter to attend there provided those people had airplanes, which none owned."[8]

The April 27, 1916, *Banner* reported as follows concerning those interesting developments with respect to the mission endeavors of the Christian Reformed Church in River Bend:

When, therefore, urgent and repeated requests came from our people, and not knowing whether prospects were favorable or not, the missionary [Rev. Brink] went out to preach for them on Wednesday, January 25.[9] A fairly good number had gathered at the home of Mr. Newhouse, and interest shown from the very beginning was very noticeable. In order not to take any time from the other fields, this midweek service was continued for three weeks, each time succeeded by an after-meeting where plans for the future were discussed. It was decided to choose a location for a church building, and Mr. John Moelker was generous enough to donate a parcel of ground for the erection of a church building.[10] A building committee got a plan

Rev. John R. Brink

8   J. R. Brink, "Hope—Grandville" (unpublished and unnumbered memoirs).
9   The date of Hope's first worship service is in question. Rev. Brink reported the date as Wednesday, January 25. That day did not exist because January 25, 1916, was a Tuesday. Hope's minutes record the date as Sunday, January 23, 1916.
10  Subsequent events indicate that Hope did not build its first building on that parcel of ground. Article 4 of the minutes of the September 12, 1916, congregational meeting reads: "A committee, consisting of two members, R. Niewenhuis and I. Korhorn, is appointed. This committee is mandated to purchase an acre of land from C. Korhorn

ready according to which a complete church building could be put up for some $500 by buying lumber from the Grand Rapids Salvage Co., and doing most of the work themselves. Presumably this will be carried out next fall and winter. At the present time one service is held in the schoolhouse and the other at the home of Mr. Newhouse. Like in Walker, one service is held in the English language.

There are about 24 families in this district, of which a few families belong to Jenison, a few to city congregations and two to Walker. For several months, however, the Grand River, which lies between Jenison and Tallmadge [River Bend], is impassable. The distance to the city churches is too far to attend regularly, and so this community was rapidly developing into the "unchurched" class. By Sunday services, soon to be followed by catechism classes and Sunday school, this deplorable condition is checked. Some who had not attended church services for years, have already started again, and so the compliance with the command of Christ, "Go ye," is already bearing fruit. The people are enthusiastic about their successful beginning; our students are full of hope for its future, and if the Church at large has anything in common with her Master, whom she professes to follow, there is reason for rejoicing that the light of God's indispensable Word is shedding its radiant and benevolent beams into this region also.

Will the mission station develop into a congregation? We dare not prophesy and are not called upon to do so.[11]

While the author of this *Banner* report was in doubt about the future of that endeavor, clearly the families in "the bend" were not, as their plans for a church building predated their organization as a congregation of our Lord Jesus Christ.

---

(northwest corner)." The reference is to the northwest corner of C. Korhorn's property on the southeast corner of Kenowa Avenue and Riverbend Street.

11  J. R. Brink, "A Mission Station in Tallmadge," *Banner* 51 (April 27d, 1916):273.

## Escape in the River's Bend

Before 1916 the Grand River isolated the founders of Hope from meaningful life in the church of Jesus Christ. Led by the Spirit of Christ, their solution to this intolerable situation was to bring the church of Jesus Christ *into* the river's bend. The steps they took to accomplish this are found in the records they kept from the time of their first meeting on January 23, 1916, to the time of their organization on June 8, 1916.[12]

After the worship service in the home of Mr. and Mrs. Richard Newhouse (on Hall Street, one-eighth mile east of Kenowa Avenue) lead by Rev. John R. Brink on Sunday, January 23, the twenty-one people present agreed that "it would be advisable and necessary to establish a Mission Station in the vicinity of River Bend" because the distance to the Walker church and the churches in Grand Rapids made it almost impossible for them to regularly attend church. Consequently they "passed unanimously" a proposition "to call into being a Mission Station."[13] After choosing Charles Bouwman as secretary and Richard Newhouse as treasurer, they appointed a committee and gave them the mandate to "investigate the cost of a church building, and to find a suitable place (location) where such a building could be erected." The committee consisted of John Moelker, Jacob Zaagman, Mathys Van Eeuwan, and Richard Newhouse.

Former home of Richard Newhouse where worship services were held before the church was built

---

12  See Hope's Preorganizational Record in appendix 2.

13  Unpublished consistory minutes of the Mission Station of River Bend (January 23, 1916). These and subsequent minutes to January 1921 were translated by Rev. Sebastian Cammenga, a former minister of Hope Christian Reformed Church. All references in *A Spiritual House Preserved* to consistory and congregational minutes prior to June 8, 1916, are to the unpublished records of the Mission Station of River Bend.

They next met one week later in the home of Newhouse on Wednesday, February 2. Rev. Brink led twenty-five attendees in a divine worship service, after which "J. Moelker present[ed] a plan for the hopefully soon to be built church building," the dimensions of which would be 32' x 40' and "would be erected as practical as possible for this purpose." Article 4 of their record states:

> Since brother elders from the Walker congregation are present at this meeting, it is suggested by one of those brethren, to join ourselves as a Mission Station of River Bend, with one or the other churches. If we then needed help or support, one could apply to one of those churches. If we would place ourselves under Classis West, we would be acknowledged as a Mission Station.

Subsequently they decided to join themselves "as a Mission Station to the congregation of Walker," and they appointed as "delegates to the Classis, the brethren C. Bouwman and R. Nieuwenhuis."

The following Wednesday, February 9, another divine worship service led by Rev. Brink was held in the home of Newhouse. After the worship service, the fifteen members present decided to erect the church building on a piece of land "given gratis by J. Moelker" and to "request Classis for a $300 loan" for the building to be constructed. It was also decided to "conduct an English service in the forenoon; a service in the Holland language in the afternoon."

---

"We used to have church sometimes under the big tree in Richard Newhouse's yard on nice summer afternoons. One time Seminarian Monsma was preaching...He stopped in the middle of the sermon and he said, 'Do you think that storm's going to bother us? Is it going to rain?' Richard Newhouse said, 'No. I think it's going over. You just go ahead and preach.' Sounds funny now, doesn't it? I didn't think it was funny...It didn't rain. Richard was right."[14] —Celia Bergman

---

14  *History of Hope 1916–1991*, 2.

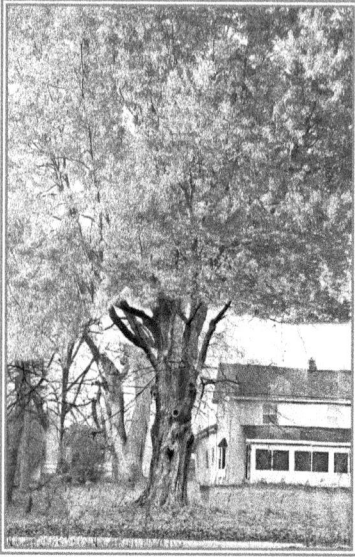

This tree in the front yard of Newhouse's house on Hall Street witnessed some of Hope's early worship services.

During a meeting held on April 25, 1916, in the home of Richard Newhouse, those present decided "that, since the summer is at hand and the [theological school] gives its students vacation, to have a student here during the next three months regularly." Most importantly, they "decided to request Classis West for permission to be organized as the Christian Reformed Church of River Bend."

Following the approval of Classis Grand Rapids West, and in the presence of a committee from West Leonard Christian Reformed Church, Hope organized on Thursday, June 8, 1916, in the home of Richard Newhouse. Rev. J. R. Brink preached on 1 Peter 2:4–5: "To whom coming, as unto a living stone, disallowed indeed of men, but chosen of God, and precious, ye also, as lively stones, are built up a spiritual house, a holy priesthood, to offer up spiritual sacrifices, acceptable to God by Christ Jesus."

"I was 14 when we moved to River Bend and there was no Hope church yet. We didn't go to church—just stayed home. Then a few people started the church. Korhorns, Moelkers, Kuipers, and others. They used to get seminarians with a horse and buggy from Grand Rapids."[15] —John Riddering

Article 2 of the organizational meeting that followed the sermon of Rev. Brink informs us of those who presented membership papers at

---

15  Ibid., 1.

that meeting. Coming from Walker Christian Reformed Church were Charles (Charley) Bouwman and his wife, Adrian Heyboer, Rijtse (Richard) Nieuwenhuis and his wife, Pieter Ruiter, Jan (John) Moelker with his wife and eight baptized children, Jantje (Jennie) Engelsma, and Wietse Visbeck who came as a baptized member. Joining from Coldbrook Christian Reformed Church were Jacob and Jacoba Zaagman with five baptized children. Pauline Ploegstra came as a baptized member from Grandville Avenue Christian Reformed Church. Johannes Van Dyke came from the Netherlands Reformed Church, and his wife, Jacoba Maria Wilhelmina Bating, and their four baptized children came from the Reformed Church (*Gereformeerde Kerk*) in the Netherlands. After reviewing those membership papers, the committee from West Leonard "approve[d] and accept[ed]" them. Then followed the election of office-bearers: John Moelker (president) and Charles Bouwman (clerk) were elected as elders and Richard Newhouse as deacon.

Mr. and Mrs. Richard Newhouse

Jan (John) Moelker, his wife, and eight oldest children were charter members of Hope

Jantje Engelsma

The minute of Classis Grand Rapids East in which Rev. Brink informed the classis of the organization of Hope. Prof. Herman Hanko gave the gist of the minute as follows:

> Rev. Brink reported on his missionary work in the... [cannot read the word, but it has something to do with progress]; received with thanks. Rev. Brink also read a report of the organization of the Tallmadge congregation (article 24 of the preceding minutes), saying that this church had been organized [literally, came to revelation] on June 8, [1916]. Ten households with seventeen confessing members [literally, Lord's supper goers] organized with twenty-nine baptized members, for a total of forty-six souls. The committee was thanked.

Article 4 of the record of Hope's birth concludes: "Candidate Terpstra speaks a few words to the congregation after which the above named brother closes with prayer after we had sung Psalm 122:1. The benediction is pronounced over the youthful congregation by Rev. J. R. Brink."

It would not be until four months later that this new manifestation of the body of our Lord Jesus Christ would be given an official name. With little fanfare article 5 of the October 5, 1916, minutes record, "The church at this place was given as its name, 'The Hope Christian Reformed Church of River Bend.'"[16]

## A Place for Worship in the River's Bend

Initially worship services were conducted in the home of Richard Newhouse. Later arrangements were made to use Blair School (Riverbend Public School) for worship in the mornings.

However, the schoolhouse was not available in the afternoons because some Methodists in the area used it at that time. The activities of the consistory and the congregation to provide a place for worship are recorded as follows:

---

16  Unpublished consistory minutes of the Hope Christian Reformed Church of River Bend (October 5, 1916). All references in *A Spiritual House Preserved* to consistory and congregational minutes from October 5, 1916, to January 24, 1925, are to the unpublished records of the Hope Christian Reformed Church of River Bend.

The need for a more proper and permanent house of worship continued to occupy the minds of the young congregation, and it was towards that end that much time and effort was put forth. On the evening of June 25, 1917, the consistory presented the congregation with building and financial details previously worked out in committee and consistorial sessions. Several proposals preliminary to building were adopted first: —to put a steeple on the church—to put wooden shingles on the roof—to face the area above the entrance with cement, etc. Understandably, concern was expressed for the congregation's ability to pay for the proposed structure. Then with knowledgeable faith, the decision was made to proceed with building the church at the estimated cost of $2,300...

Volunteer labor was used extensively, holding labor costs to a minimum...Mr. C[harles] Bouwman, I[saac] Korhorn, and C[harles] Engelsma landscaped the area around the building; Claus Hoeksema of Grandville Avenue Christian Reformed Church painted the new building inside and out, free of charge. Mr. Hoeksema used his

Hope church built in 1917

God-given artistic talents ably by also painting the picture of an open Bible on the interior front wall of the church inscribed with the words, "Choose You This Day Whom Ye Will Serve."

"The building was very plain. There was no heat in the basement. The inside was very drab. (We had) individual seats."[17]
—Celia Bergman

17  *History of Hope 1916–1991*, 6.

"The old church had a full basement...the furnace was on the Kenowa Road half and the east side had two rooms—a consistory room and a kind of ante room...for Sunday School classes. High ceilings, high windows, cold and drafty. There was no running water or anything, just an outhouse."[18] —Walter Bergman

Later, when necessity arose and money allowed, a room was prepared in the basement for catechism, a new organ was installed, new gasoline lights were added, and siding was put on the horse barn.[19]

"It had about eight stalls, didn't it? Cold in the winter time. It was to get the horses out of the wind while people were in church. People were concerned about their animals."[20] —Dewey Engelsma

"Every church had a horse barn. The one for Hope church was right behind church. The horse barn was a shed with a roof that kind of came up on the open end. It had maybe, less than ten stables."[21] —John Riddering

---

18  Ibid.
19  Richard Bloem, "A Brief History," in *Hope Protestant Reformed Church, Walker, MI: Fiftieth Anniversary* (1968), 3. See also *Hope Protestant Reformed Church, Walker MI: 75th Anniversary 1916–1991* (1991), unnumbered pages.
20  *History of Hope 1916–1991*, 2.
21  Ibid., 3.

River Bend den 23 Januari 1916

Den 23 Januari 1916 werdt er een Goddienst oefening
gehouden ten huize van R Nieuwenhuis, De bediening der
werdt verricht door D^m J R Brink En deze bij een Somi
waren er 21 toe hoorders aanwesig.
Na de Goddienst werd er een vergadering gehou:
den om eenige verbetering aan te brengen op
Kerkelijk terrein in de omgeving van River Bend.
Art 1   Als Pres voor deze vergadering werd D^m J R Brink
        gekozen.
Art 2   De Pres. vraagt zou het wenschelijk en nood
        zaakelijk zijn om en de omgeving van River
        Bend, een Zending Station op te rigten ten
        eersten zou het wenschelijk zijn om deze reden
        daar het geregeld ter Kerk gaan hier in deze
        omgeving bijna onmogelijk is Daar, de Kerk
        van Wolker en die van Grand Rapids te ver
        zijn van ons verwijderd zijn om die geregeld
        te bezoeken en vooral, voor de kinderen en
        ook voor de volwaschen Personen opdat de
        Cathegeties aan die zouden kunnen gegeven
        worden.
Art 3   Na dat dit alles in bespreken werdt gebracht
        en het noodzaakelijke van te hebben gezien om
        voor te gaan en te trachten onder den zegen
        des Heeren alhier een Zending Station in
        het leven te roepen, Het welk dan in steming
        werdt gebracht en met algemeene stem
        werd door de vergadering werd een Zending
        Station in het leven geroepen
Art 4   Als Scriba werd C Bouwman gekozen en als
        Penningmeester R Nieuwenhuis
Art 5   Daar hier in deze omgeving van River Bend
        geen gebouw is om geregeld Gods dienst in te houden
        werd er een Commissie benoemt die op gedragen
        werd om te onderzoeken wat een Kerkgebouw zou
        kosten en een gewenschte plaats te vinden waar
        zulk een gebouw zou kunnen worden opgetrokken
        om daar geregeld te vergadering De Comm bestaande
        uit de volgende vier personen J Wolker, J van Eeuwen
        J Zaagman en R Nieuwenhuis als deze Comm
Art 6   Na rondvragen werd deze vergadering op verzoek
        van D^m Brink gesloten met Dankzegging door J Kuipers
                                J R Brink V. Pres
                                C Bouwman Scr

First consistory minutes of Hope church

Home missionary, J. R. Brink, wrote about the dedication of the new church building in the *Banner* under the heading "Hope Church at River Bend."

> December 5 [1917] will long be remembered by the members of the above named congregation, formerly called Tallmadge.
>
> Upon the evening of that day a goodly number of people gathered to commemorate the goodness and mercy of God, "the Giver of all good and perfect gifts," to dedicate their new house of worship...
>
> A corner lot of one acre gives abundant room for church buildings, stables, and all the other buildings necessary in course of time, if the church grows stronger.
>
> The church is of very substantial construction, being built of cement blocks. Although not large, it has a very neat appearance, both within and without, and the whole, including lot and opera chairs, cost about $2,000.
>
> La Grave Avenue furnished the pulpit and carpet which formerly covered its church auditorium. A splendid pulpit Bible was given by Mr. and Mrs. C. Bouwman, and a complete communion set by the consistory of the First Church of Kalamazoo...
>
> The program did not contain very many numbers, but the whole was gratefully received by the people and visitors, the chocolate milk and cake at the end of the meeting not excepted.
>
> Several American people showed their interest by attending the service and joy was manifested on the faces of all those present.
>
> From the report of Mr. R. Newhouse we noticed that $500 was received from the Church Erection Fund, and another $500 was taken up on a note. The rest of the money was all paid by our people, with the exception of a few bills, which will be paid in the near future. Not a bad record for a church only a year and a half old...

River Bend is a good field, far enough away from other congregations, and our church is the only one in this community… one church for a community, using both languages, and not overburdened with debt, can accomplish a great deal of good and is a real necessity, worthy of our support.

It has already accomplished much good by saving some people who were in grave danger of drifting away from the church, and by feeding the "lambs of the flock."

May the great Shepherd bless this church abundantly and cause it to be a blessing in its community.[22]

## Thriving in the River's Bend

Hope's consistory was busy in those early years accepting new members. Consistory minutes tell the delightful story:

- July 11, 1916, article 2. "The church membership of Gelke De Jong and wife, and Hendrik Goeree and wife are accepted."
- July 11, 1916, article 6. "Three persons appear to make profession of faith. They include Mr. and Mrs. Goeree and Mr. Jan Dyke."
- August 11, 1916, article 4. "Mr. and Mrs. I. Korhorn made confession of faith at this meeting."
- August 29, 1916, article 4. "Confession of faith is made by Mr. and Mrs. J. Van Dyke."
- April 3, 1917, article 3. "Elder Bouwman is mandated to pay a visit to Mr. and Mrs. Bergman, since that brother and sister were new members coming from the Walker congregation."
- June 2, 1917, article 2. "Confession of faith was made by Mrs. K. Byl."
- June 4, 1918, article 5. "Confession of faith is heard before the consistory by Miss Celia Zaagman."

Mr. and Mrs. Isaac Korhorn

---

22  J. R. Brink, "Hope Church at River Bend," *Banner* 52 (December 13, 1917):798.

- July 2, 1918, article 3. "Confession of faith was made before the consistory by Mr. and Mrs. C. Korhorn."
- July 1, 1919, article 2. "Confession of faith is made by Mrs. H. Heiboer, nee Jinnie Schelhuis."
- August 4, 1919, article 3. "The following persons appeared to make confession of faith: Mr. and Mrs. J. De Jong, Mr. and Mrs. C. Engelsma, Mr. A. Schut, Mr. L. Fichbeek, Mr. A. Snip, Mrs. J. Haggerty (nee F. Fichbeek), Mr. H. Moelker, Mr. J. Kuipers."

Mr. and Mrs. Charles Engelsma

But thriving under the preaching of their own minister is another story. Although never mentioned explicitly in the consistory's minutes, it appears that the church fathers of Hope did not believe they could support a minister of their own in those early years. Apparent this is from article 6 of the August 11, 1916, consistory meeting: "We accept for information that, in case the Walker congregation should extend a call to a minister, Mr. Bouwman is to write the called minister regarding the congregation here at Hope."[23]

At its August 29, 1916, meeting the consistory voted to call a congregational meeting for September 12 at which meeting the congregation would be asked to decide "what the congregation of Hope shall pay for the work the minister of Walker will do here, when and if Walker is supplied with a minister." Sadly, article 2 of that congregational meeting leaves us hanging in limbo with this: "The question regarding Rev. [Peter] Hoekenga, since he has accepted the call of the Walker church, is postponed until a following meeting."

There was a following meeting, but there was no further mention of obtaining the services of Rev. Hoekenga. The one-hundredth

---

23  J. Brink and C. Bouwman, unpublished consistory minutes of the Christian Reformed Church at River Bend (August 11, 1916). References in *A Spiritual House Preserved* to consistory and congregational minutes from June 8, 1916, to October 5, 1916, are to the unpublished records of the Christian Reformed Church at River Bend.

anniversary book of Walker United Reformed Church supplies the likely reason the idea of obtaining assistance from Rev. Hoekenga was aborted:

Rev. Hoekenga's ministry at Walker lasted only seventeen months... Only a few months before coming to Walker, he needed a life-saving operation in Chicago, which prevented him from continuing his mission there [Chicago]. At Walker, he spent several weeks bed-ridden, and according to Dr. Henry Beets...he was near death. Although he recovered, his weak health forced him to resign from Walker in February 1918.[24]

Rev. Peter J. Hoekenga, minister of Walker Christian Reformed Church from 1916 to 1918

In March 1918 Rev. Jacob W. Wyngaarden accepted the call to Walker Christian Reformed Church and was appointed by classis as Hope's moderator. Hope's consistory enlisted his services for a few years to teach catechism on Saturday mornings.

Also, the consistory often arranged to utilize the services of Christian Reformed seminary students. Getting them to River Bend was not always so simple, however. Often horse and buggy transportation was used, at other times they came to Grandville via the interurban and then rowed by boat across the Grand River to River Bend. Utilizing seminary students when available, however, resulted in some unusual scheduling for catechism at times. The June 2, 1919, consistory minutes relate that arrangements were made to have seminary student John C. Medendorp at Hope for the summer months. Thus it was "decided to conduct two catechism classes, Wednesday evenings for the young people above sixteen

Rev. Jacob W. Wyngaarden

24  Walker United Reformed Church, *Celebrating Our 100th Anniversary, 1912–2012*, 10.

years; and Sundays, after the afternoon service, for the married members, especially for those who as yet have made no confession of faith." Concerning student Medendorp's labor at Hope the *Banner* reported:

> The little River Bend church, also called "Hope"...has been benefitted greatly by the service of student John Medendorp who labored here during the summer vacation. Over a dozen of people have confessed the Lord as Savior, among them a number who formerly cared little or nothing for God and his service. No wonder the "Hope" people are full of courage for the future.[25]

The fact that the consistory decided in April 1919 to "allow $10 for use of an automobile for Missionary Brink" demonstrates that Hope relied heavily on his assistance during those early years as a congregation. The minutes also make clear that the consistory was busy standing in the gap when seminarians and ministers were not available.

Finally, after limping along that way for five and a half years without a pastor of its own, the congregation decided at a June 14, 1921, meeting to call a minister and gave the consistory the right to make a trio. It is not surprising that the first call was extended to Candidate John C. Medendorp, since by that time they knew him well from his work among them. After he declined the call, a new trio was formed consisting of Candidates George M. Ophoff and Jacob Van Dyke and Rev. Dirk Jonker, from which Candidate Ophoff was called.

George Ophoff's acceptance of Hope's call and his subsequent installation opened a new chapter of Hope's preservation in the river's bend.

Rev. John Medendorp

---

25   A. Peters, "Grand Rapids Notes" *Banner* 54 (September 18, 1919):590.

*Chapter 2*

~~~ ◦◦ ~~~

# A BRIEF HISTORY OF HOPE
## FROM 1922 TO 2016

Richard and Betty Bloem

The history from 1922 to 1991 is based on the work of Richard Bloem, a deceased former member of Hope church. He wrote the history for Hope church's fiftieth anniversary in 1968 and the seventy-fifth anniversary in 1991.[1] The history since 1991 was written by the editor.

## Rev. George Martin Ophoff:
## January 26, 1922, to September 29, 1929

The task of caring for the spiritual needs of a congregation without an undershepherd is a difficult one indeed. For five and a half years the concerns of the young congregation had fallen heavily on the shoulders of the consistory made up of men spiritually able but young in experience. Therefore, a prayer of thanksgiving arose from the hearts of the members and joy filled their souls when Candidate G. M. Ophoff accepted the call they had extended to him to "come over and help us."

Minister-elect Ophoff was examined by Classis Grand Rapids West on January 17, 1922, and by unanimous vote was admitted to the gospel

---

1 Bloem, "A Brief History," in *Hope Protestant Reformed Church…Fiftieth Anniversary*, 2–11 and in *Hope Protestant Reformed Church…75th Anniversary 1916–1991*, unnumbered pages.

ministry. He arrived in "the bend" with his wife, Jane (Boom), and a fervent resolve to hold fast to the truth once delivered to the saints, to proclaim it faithfully, and to teach it to the generations following.

Rev. Edward J. Tanis installed Ophoff into the gospel ministry in Hope Christian Reformed Church on January 26, 1922.[2] Rev. Wyngaarden preached the sermon, and Rev. J. R. Brink charged the congregation.

This photograph of Rev. Ophoff, his wife, and child taken at least a year after his arrival at Hope demonstrates their adaptation to the rugged life in the river's bend.

The congregation had prepared to provide for the earthly wellbeing of a minister and his family by deciding in 1920 to build a parsonage and "to borrow $1,000 from Classis with the rest of the money to come from the congregation.[3] After rejecting a proposal to purchase the Peck farm and house,[4] the members chose a site on the east side of the church building for the new parsonage.

---

2   In 1922 Rev. Tanis was the minister of First Christian Reformed Church in Grand Rapids, Michigan. Later Tanis would vigorously defend and promote the theory of common grace in the Christian Reformed Church and oppose Henry Danhof and Herman Hoeksema. Rev. Tanis was also incensed when the two as yet-Christian Reformed ministers began the *Standard Bearer* magazine to explain their doctrinal views on the grace and covenant of God.

3   *History of Hope 1916–1991*, 6.

4   The Peck property was located on the northeast corner of Burton Street and Kenowa Avenue.

"When we built the parsonage we had a lathing bee—put on wood lathes at nights and on Saturdays. I helped some, but it wasn't much. I was only 12 or 13."[5] —Walter Bergman

The parsonage was located next to the church
on the southeast corner of Riverbend and Kenowa.

The new minister was not only to live in a new parsonage, but also he was to be paid $1,200 a year.

"On October 3, 1922, the members of Hope church were 'given the right...to start a singing school.'"[6]

On November 30, 1922, the congregation decided to buy an auto for the pastor to "ease" his errands on their behalf. The money was raised by periodically canvassing the congregation for funds and by borrowing the balance needed, all the while increasing their debt.

Cleanliness being a trait of people of Dutch descent, it was fitting that the consistory decided on November 13, 1922, to hire a janitor at $50 a year to clean the church building. This assured the congregation a

---

5    *History of Hope 1916–1991*, 6.
6    Ibid., 19.

warm building in the winter and a clean one at all times. Isaac Korhorn took over the task that previously had been done by volunteers.

No doubt Isaac and his wife shared those janitorial duties.

Although bound to pay its debts, early on the congregation had also accepted responsibility to assist others in their needs. Special collections were taken for many worthy causes, such as Grand Rapids Christian High School[7] and foreign missions. In 1923 a decision to have all special collections taken at the door of church was put into effect, while congregational giving for the poor was collected by the deacons during the worship services.

On July 3, 1923, "the consistory agreed to 'reimburse Rev. G. M. Ophoff for what money he paid out for labor and grass seed for the parsonage grounds.'"[8]

Between the years 1916 and 1924 the congregation experienced normal growth, and by 1924 it

had grown to 24 families, totaling about 125 members...Sunday School and catechism classes met on a regular basis. A singing society, a Bible class, a men's society and a missionary

---

7    Grand Rapids Christian High School was founded in 1920.
8    *History of Hope 1916–1991*, 19.

society were formed. Hope Church had picnics and occasional special programs such as a Christmas program. Hope Church helped draw the residents of Riverbend together as it put down roots in the small farming community.[9]

Rev. Henry Beets, editor of the Christian Reformed periodical, the *Banner*, reported on Hope's early years and the advancement of the congregation.

> Some years ago Home Missionary J. R. Brink started work there. We well remember the small beginning of the work. [Some of] the people living in the territory…attended church at Jenison, across the river. But it was not always possible to get across in winter time. The result was a somewhat neglected and church-neglecting people—barring exceptions…
>
> But there was a loyal remnant. Men like the brethren Newhouse and Moelker and Korhorn kept the home fires burning. Missionary Brink started services during the morning in the schoolhouse and during afternoons at Brother Newhouse's home. Then a church was organized. Not a foot of ground was owned when work was begun. But behold what, with God's blessing on consecrated efforts, a few years have wrought in the way of steady progress.
>
> We met with the Hope church people last Sunday. Some of the roads were still unbroken—people snowbound. But at night the church was nearly full. A good, substantially built church it is, with basement and superstructure. Only the steeple is still absent. Next to it is a comfortable manse occupied by the Rev. George Ophoff and family. And—the whole nearly paid for, except $1,400.[10]

Although the congregation had built a church and a parsonage and hired a full-time minister, it had "become self-supporting" by 1924.[11]

---

9  Ibid., 7.
10  Henry Beets, "Hope Church Advancing," *Banner* 59 (February 29, 1924), 136.
11  *History of Hope 1916–1991*, 7.

Most of Hope's members had little of this world's goods, but they were willing to make personal sacrifices to pay off the debt for the church and parsonage. They were also able to save $500.

"A congregational meeting was called for May 19, 1924, to vote on 'filling in on the west side of the church grounds to make a suitable parking place [for automobiles].' (Not many horses anymore!)"[12]

On July 10, 1924, "a motion was made and accepted to give the minister a two-week vacation."

In 1924 the unity of the Christian Reformed Church was divided, both in doctrine and church organization, as Classis Grand Rapids East deposed Rev. H. Hoeksema, the pastor of the Eastern Avenue church in Grand Rapids, Michigan, and his consistory for refusing to declare agreement with the three points of common grace as adopted by the mother church at its synod of Kalamazoo on July 7, 1924.

The causes and effects of those decisions were far-reaching, affecting also the life of the small congregation of Hope. True to his calling, Rev. Ophoff openly espoused the cause of the truth and zealously defended it. He became one of the editors of the *Standard Bearer*, a publication begun in October 1924 to combat the lie of common grace and to explain the truth regarding particular grace and the covenant of God.[13]

Hope's consistory and congregation in turn largely supported Ophoff's position, and although the doctrinal decisions of the Christian Reformed synod were binding, no protest or complaint had been made against Rev. Ophoff or his consistory.

Classis Grand Rapids West of the Christian Reformed Church, of which Hope church was a member, convened on January 13, 1925. Although no protest had been received against him, the classis discussed

---

12  Ibid., 19.

13  For more on the purpose and content of the *Standard Bearer*, see Henry Danhof and Herman Hoeksema, *For the Sake of Justice and Truth*, in *The Rock Whence We Are Hewn* (Jenison, MI: Reformed Free Publishing Association, 2015), 277–90.

the "heretical" position of Rev. Ophoff and drew up a twofold demand for dealing with him and the consistory.

On January 19, 1925, a special consistory meeting was held to address a letter from Classis Grand Rapids West that read as follows:

> To the consistory of Hope Christian Reformed Church
> at River Bend
>
> Dear brethren,
>     The Classis Grand Rapids West hereby requires you to require of your minister:
>
> 1.  That he declare himself unequivocally whether he is in full agreement, yes or no, with the three points of the synod of Kalamazoo (*Acta Synodi 1924*, articles 132, 145–47).
> 2.  An unconditional promise that in the matter of the three points he will submit (with the right of appeal) to the confessional standards of the church as interpreted by the synod of 1924, that is, neither publicly nor privately to propose, teach, or defend either by preaching or writing any sentiments contrary to the confessional standards of the church as interpreted by the synod of 1924. In case of appeal that he in the interim will acquiesce in the judgment already passed by synod of 1924.
>
>     The classis further requests you to furnish the classis by 10:00 a.m. Wednesday morning, January 21, 1925, with a definite written answer of your pastor to the twofold requirement of the consistory.
>
>     Fraternally yours,
>     Classis Grand Rapids West
>     w.s. W. Stuart, president
>     w.s. J. P. Battema, secretary

With firm resolve, Rev. Ophoff expressed his negative answer to the classical demands, after which the vice president asked the consistory what the individual members would do with the three points. Article 3 of that consistory meeting informs us that R. Newhouse, I. Korhorn, and G. De Young felt that they could not abide by the decisions of classis and the synod of 1924.

Hope's deposed officebearers
from left: G. De Jong, R. Newhouse, Rev. G. Ophoff, I. Korhorn

On the evening of January 26, 1925, at a congregational meeting held in the parsonage, the congregation was informed of the consistorial action. Rev. Ophoff gave a historical sketch of the events leading up to the consistory's decision, explained the doctrinal situation in the Christian Reformed Church, and presented his position and that of the elders.

Most of the congregation and the three elders agreed with Rev. Ophoff. They made the momentous decision to promote the continuation of the true church of Jesus Christ. John Moelker and Charles Engelsma were elected to replace the two deacons who agreed with the decisions of classis. Then the nucleus of the present-day congregation, united through division, tried but not found wanting, went home.

On January 29, 1925, the consistory of Hope attended a meeting with the consistories of Eastern Avenue Christian Reformed Church and of

First Christian Reformed Church in Kalamazoo, Michigan, which also had been expelled from the mother church. At a meeting on March 6, 1925, the three consistories "decided to form a temporary organization, pending the appeal to synod, consisting of a union of combined consistories and on the basis of an *Act of Agreement*."[14] The group adopted the temporary name Protesting Christian Reformed Churches.[15]

> "Division or settlement on the property hadn't taken place yet...Division among the people...had taken place, but Rev. Ophoff was still the minister here...He had not been denied the pulpit by the elders, so he was preaching...I suppose the other elements decided they were going to get their own preacher for that Sunday and therefore the conflict."[16]
> —Dewey Engelsma (Hope PR)

Hours of discussion, many frustrations, and momentous decisions faced the congregation that had been numerically reduced and financially decimated as a result of the struggles of 1924–25. Sadly, the mother church even took the meager $500 savings the congregation had managed to accumulate. All the difficulties facing a new congregation had to be dealt with plus issues of property settlement and membership that resulted from the doctrinal conflict.

> "They came marching in right down the aisle when Rev. Ophoff was preaching, and he didn't stop. They walked back out. I thought there were only two."[17]
> —Cornelia (Korhorn) Kuiper (Hope PR)

---

14  Herman Hoeksema, *The Protestant Reformed Churches in America: Their Origin, Early History and Doctrine* (Grand Rapids, MI: First Protestant Reformed Church, 1936), 250.
15  Ibid., 252.
16  *History of Hope 1916–1991*, 14.
17  Ibid., 14.

"My dad did mention to me...that there was physical violence...On a Sunday morning both groups wanted to use the
church and a couple [of] people stood at the door and threw
the other ones away...My dad did mention a gun...I think
there was an actual scuffle."[18] —Corneal Korhorn (Hope CR)

At the consistory meeting of July 7, 1925, "a committee was
appointed to see what can be done in regard to our church building if
there is a chance to retain the building so it would not get in the hands
of the classis west. R. Newhouse and G. De Jong were appointed as
committee."[19] Since it was apparent that any possibility of retaining the
buildings was very remote, an alternate plan was made at that same
meeting. "It was then agreed upon to start services at 10:30 a.m. and
7:30 p.m. in the Blair Schoolhouse."

"Walter Bergman [my dad] and Henry Goeree, the deacons
[that left Ophoff], hired a lawyer...so that we could get the
church...The lawyer said, 'Possession is nine points of the
law. You get in that church, stay overnight and the church is
yours.' Well the men were working and couldn't stay over the
night in the church basement so...two girls...spent the night
there without heat, light, or running water. The next morning
the lawyer came and explained to the faction that they were
expelled and the church belonged to the Christian Reformed
denomination."[20] —Celia Bergman (Hope CR)

Sadly the church property was lost on July 7, 1925.

---

18  Ibid., 13.
19  Article 4 of the unpublished consistory minutes of the Protesting Christian Reformed
    Church of Hope (January 5, 1926). All references in *A Spiritual House Preserved* to
    consistory and congregational minutes from January 29, 1925, to November 1926 are
    to the unpublished records of the Protesting Christian Reformed Church of Hope.
20  *History of Hope 1916–1991*, 13.

"I remember the sheriff coming over to our house on a Saturday afternoon and told us that we can't use the church anymore if we go with Ophoff...The sheriff went around to all the families that were with Reverend Ophoff."[21]
—Dewey Engelsma (Hope PR)

On January 5, 1926, after the consistory received a "notice from the lawyer to vacate the parsonage, a committee [of De Jong, Korhorn, and Newhouse] was appointed to look for a house for the minister."[22]

"The...judge in Grand Rapids ruled that the buildings belonged to the denomination. The people (the majority who went with Ophoff) figured that since they built the building, it belonged to them. That's why they had the trouble."[23]
—Walter Bergman (Hope CR)

Although the church and parsonage properties were lost, the church as an organization remained intact and functioning.

At the February 2, 1926, consistory meeting a "report was given that a house had been rented for the minister for $40 a month...On account of some circumstances the house was given up, but the house next to it was rented for the sum of $38 a month from the same party."

Rev. Ophoff and the consistory of Hope took an active part in the formation of a new denomination. At a November 1926 meeting the consistories of Eastern Avenue, Hope, and Kalamazoo formally organized as a classis and adopted the name Protestant Reformed Churches.[24] Thus Hope Christian Reformed Church became Hope Protestant Reformed Church.

The early years after 1925 were financially trying for the remnant congregation. Mostly poor farmers, they struggled to maintain their existence.

---

21  Ibid., 14.
22  Ibid., 12.
23  Ibid., 13.
24  Hoeksema, *Protestant Reformed Churches in America*, 278.

Typical farming activities in the river's bend

Article 2 of the August 23, 1926, congregational meeting reveals that Hope's continuation as a congregation was hanging in the balance: "The question was asked if we were going to continue as a congregation, and the answer was yes." That key decision, which passed by one vote, was followed in the same meeting by the decision of article 3 "to try and arrange a meeting with the consistory of Hudsonville and see if consolidation of the two congregations would be advisable." However, the idea to consolidate with Hudsonville apparently was rejected, as article 1 of the January 31, 1927, consistory minutes makes clear: "The committee that was to visit the consistory of Hudsonville was discontinued."[25]

---

25  Unpublished consistory minutes of Hope Protestant Reformed Church (January 31, 1927). All references in *A Spiritual House Preserved* to consistory and congregational minutes since November 1926 to the present are to the unpublished records of Hope Protestant Reformed Church.

No longer the owners of a sanctuary or a parsonage, the consistory also pursued other options for a church building, one of which was "to look for a building spot somewhere on Bridge Road" (March 11, 1926, article 1). Also a committee was appointed to investigate a "schoolhouse on West Leonard Road" (April 12, 1927).

Rev. Ophoff served the congregation for seven years and eight months, faithfully proclaiming the truth of God's word and providing able leadership during the difficult period of 1924–25.

On September 29, 1929, he preached his farewell sermon after accepting a call from the sister congregation in Byron Center, Michigan.

> Rev. Ophoff left Hope church but not before he led the consistory to "go on record as condemning the labor unions for the reason that they do not recognize God but depend on the arm of flesh" (June 3, 1929).

## Seven-year Vacancy:
## September 30, 1929, to November 1936

The loss of the church building in the division of 1925 was keenly felt by the congregation. Almost immediately ways and means were discussed to bring about the building of another place of worship. Property on the West Beltline owned by Isaac Korhorn was made available, financial assistance in the form of gifts and loans were promised, plans were reviewed, and bids were taken. On March 31, 1930, for the second time in its short history the congregation made a decision to construct a church building.

Significant to the location of Hope's new church edifice was the recently constructed West Beltline (Wilson Avenue). Furthermore, with the completion of the Grandville bridge over the Grand River in the early 1930s, new opportunities presented themselves for the people of Hope; one of which was Christian education for their children at Jenison Christian School. Several of Hope's families took advantage of this precious opportunity.

Wilson Avenue bridge over the Grand River under construction

The new house of worship did not deter the church fathers from assisting in the financial burden of God's servants. On December 2, 1930, the consistory decided to pay $7 per Sunday or $4 per service for preaching supply. To ensure that the new house of worship would be a clean house of worship, on January 6, 1931, the consistory decided to pay $25 per year for janitorial work.

Charles and Lena Engelsma

Another significant change was made about this time: no longer would Hope have one service each Lord's day conducted in the Dutch language. Beginning in February 1931 both worship services were in English. While this decision caused a degree of inconvenience for some of the older members, it did serve the best interest of the congregation as a whole.

During the seven years Hope waited for another undershepherd, the elders faithfully did what they could to nourish the congregation spiritually by providing reading services and teaching catechism.

"My folks [Charles and Lena Engelsma] left Hope for a few years [to attend Roosevelt Park Protestant Reformed Church], when Hope discontinued the Dutch service, because my grandma didn't understand English. We children stayed at Hope. This was in the early 1930s." —Johanna Bomers

"I went to church three times a Sunday for a long time... I took my grandmother and parents to the Dutch service in the afternoon and stayed there myself, because my father didn't drive. That's when I really learned the Dutch... When my grandmother died in 1936, we went back to Hope."
—Dewey Engelsma

Sister and brother: Johanna Bomers and Dewey Engelsma

The services of Seminarian J. G. Kooistra were obtained from September 1934 through June 1935 to labor in the congregation for $8 a week.

On August 31, 1936, from a nomination of three, Candidate Hubert De Wolf was chosen to receive the call as minister of the word and sacraments.

Seminarian J. G. Kooistra, later served as minister in Kalamazoo Protestant Reformed Church from 1935 to 1940

## Rev. Hubert De Wolf and a One-year Vacancy: November 1936 to October 18, 1941

Candidate De Wolf's acceptance of the call glad-dened the hearts of the whole congregation. On November 2, the consistory received the membership papers of Mr. and Mrs. Hubert De Wolf, and on January 4, 1937, he was elected as president of the consistory.

Even before Rev. De Wolf accepted the call, however, the consistory placed new emphasis on the necessity of building a parsonage to replace the house taken from the congregation in 1925. Travel was still difficult in those days, so having the pastor living away from the immediate locale of the church building would be inconvenient. For that reason on September 9, 1936, the consistory decided to look for ways and means to build a parsonage, but that turned out to be a long drawn-out process.

It was late in 1939 before plans and costs were obtained and the building committee could reach an agreement. The committee even looked into the possibility of buying back the former church and parsonage, but to no avail. On September 30, 1939, the congregation rejected a bid of $3,442 on a plan for the parsonage submitted by Division Avenue Lumber Company. Finally, on November 24, 1939, the congregation approved a plan for the parsonage submitted by Walter Bergman and accepted his bid of $2,800 for construction of the parsonage. Completed in May 1940, the new manse was financed by pledges, collections, and a mortgage on the church property.

The labors of Rev. De Wolf in Hope ended upon his acceptance of a call and his departure in October 1940. He had served the church faithfully for four years and the congregation had been blessed by his ministry.

The congregation was not without an undershepherd for long. Only three times its calls received negative answers. Then Candidate John A. Heys was chosen from a nomination that included Rev. John Vanden Breggen and Rev. John De Jong to receive its call.

## Rev. John Heys and an Eight-month Vacancy: October 19, 1941, to September 27, 1955

God inclined the heart of Candidate John Heys to heed that call, and he was ordained on October 19, 1941, beginning a ministry in Hope that spanned thirteen years.

"We had catechism in the basement with Rev. Heys. He would walk back and forth through the whole hour of catechism while he was teaching us. Even when he asked us our questions, he didn't look at us, but he would just go back and forth. That was just him. We knew our catechism because my dad always asked us every Friday night, and we had better know it." —Clara (Veenstra) Van Den Top

The following decade was peaceful for the congregation. Under the leadership of Rev. Heys spiritual life flourished and the joy of salvation was evident in the various activities. The consistory met and resolved the customary problems of a healthy church.

Prior to 1945 Sunday worship services had been held in the late forenoon and early afternoon to provide the farmers, who constituted a majority of the membership, opportunity to do the necessary farm chores at the proper times. As more members left farm work for factory jobs, the congregation desired to hold an evening service in place of the one in the early afternoon.

Rev. John A. Heys

On November 22, 1945, a proposal was adopted to hold Sunday evening services at 7:00 during the months of June, July, and August. This continued until November 24, 1947, when it was decided to hold evening services during the months of December through April. On November 28, 1949, afternoon services were discontinued.

> "I never saw Rev. Heys without a white shirt and a tie, and Mrs. Heys always went to church with a hat on. I don't remember her with a bare head." —Clara Van Den Top

Rev. Heys and the consistory with the Wilson Avenue church building
as the backdrop; from left: Richard Newhouse, John Lanning,
Dewey Engelsma, Rev. John Heys, Isaac Korhorn, John Moelker

Three elders and two deacons constituted the consistory of Hope for many years, but due to congregational growth, one deacon was added to its number in October 1946. In January 1953 it was decided that the deacons should be separately organized. The number of men in the consistory remained at three elders and three deacons for the next eleven years. Prior to January 1950 the oldest elder automatically became the vice president of the consistory by reason of his age.

Richard Newhouse with Etta and Sharon Kuiper (1953)

During the period of Rev. Hey's ministry in Hope, the consistory was also active in its witness of the truth of God's word in pamphlet form. The members of the consistory began to distribute through the mail the pamphlets published by the Protestant Reformed Sunday School Society. Names furnished by the congregation made up the mailing list. Discontinuation of this work came in January 1949 because of a lack of response.

"We had a single cup at communion, and everyone tried to be up in the front because we had a member with a long beard, and part of his beard hung in the cup." —Johanna Bomers

Since Hope's organization in 1916 the sacrament of communion has been faithfully administered and attended. The form read at the administration of the sacrament of the Lord's supper has always been the same, but one change in the partaking of the wine was made on

December 1, 1952. Individual wine glasses were instituted for use in observing the sacrament instead of the one or two large cups, which all communicants drank from by turns.

> "I remember as a young girl the celebration of the Lord's supper in our congregation. There was a change in the partaking of the wine. They went from the one large cup, which all the confessing members drank from, to individual cups. In the Bible and in the form for the Lord's supper we read this: 'The cup of blessing which we bless is the communion of the body of Christ.' It speaks of one cup, not many cups, and that bothered me as a child." —Clara Van Den Top

During the late 1940s and early 1950s threats to the peace and unity of the Protestant Reformed denomination arose. Some ministers and others in the Protestant Reformed Churches were promoting the lie of a conditional promise to all infants at baptism and related untruths. Hope's consistory approved the Declaration of Principles, a statement of the basic truths, or principles, of the Reformed confessions concerning God's covenant that was provisionally adopted by the synod of the Protestant Reformed Churches in 1950 and decisively by the synod of 1951.[26]

Highlights of congregational activities during the 1941 to 1952 period were sending clothes and money to brethren in the Netherlands who were in need due to the ravages of World War II, participation in March 1950 in the twenty-fifth anniversary celebration of the existence of the Protestant Reformed Churches, and the purchase in November 1951 of an electronic Hammond organ at a cost of $2,466 (paid for entirely by gifts). The organ was dedicated at a special program on February 29, 1952.

As the congregation grew, the individual financial burden decreased so that on November 22, 1945, a budget was adopted that for the first time

---

26  For the history of the adoption of the Declaration of Principles, see David J. Engelsma, *Battle for Sovereign Grace in the Covenant: The Declaration of Principles* (Jenison, MI: Reformed Free Publishing Association, 2005).

since 1925 did not necessitate financial subsidy from synod. But membership growth also creates the need for more seating, and the congregation was compelled in April 1948 to approve a proposed addition to the church auditorium at a cost of $4,000. Once again Hope had a debt to pay.

Because Hope Protestant Reformed Christian School was experiencing its own growth problems, in 1950 the congregation agreed to allow the school to use the church basement for some of its classes.

"We lived two and a half miles from school. We walked to and from school every day and to and from catechism on Saturday mornings." —Clara Van Den Top

In 1951 the first church membership directory was published. It listed a total of thirty-five families with a budget assessment of $2.75 per family per week and an assessment for the building fund of $2 a month for each family.

1951 CHURCH DIRECTORY

SERVICES

Morning — 9:30          Evening — 7:00

Consistory meetings are held the 1st or 2nd Monday evening of the month as announced on the bulletin.

CONSISTORY

Pres. Rev. John A. Heys,

Elders:                    Deacons:

R. Newhouse (Vice Pres.)   G. Moelker (Treas.)
A. J. Kuiper (Clerk)       T. Howerzyl
M. Veenstra                R. Bloem

BUILDING COMMITTEE

A. J. Kuiper        M. Veenstra        T. Howerzyl

CATECHISM CLASSES

Saturday, 9:30 A.M...................Boys and Girls 8-10 years
Saturday, 10:15 A.M..................Boys and Girls 5-7 years
Saturday, 10:45 A.M..................Boys and Girls 11-13 years
Wednesday, 7:15 P.M..................Young People 14 and older
Wednesday, 8:15 P.M..................Confessing Young People

SCHEDULE OF MEETINGS

Sunday, 11:00 A.M...................................Sunday School
Sunday, 2:00 P. M. ......................Young People's Society
Alternate Monday evenings at 7:45...................Men's Society
Alternate Tuesday evenings at 7:45.........Ladies' Aid Society

All announcements for the bulletin must be in the hands of the Pastor or Clerk by Friday evenings.

Those desiring a call from the Pastor or the Elders please inform either the Pastor or our Clerk.

Hope

Protestant Reformed Church

1539 Wilson Ave., S.W.

GRAND RAPIDS, MICHIGAN

Enter into His gates with thanksgiving, and into His courts with praise. — Psalm 100:4

REV. JOHN A. HEYS — PASTOR

1551 Wilson Ave., S.W. R. 5        Phone ARdmore 6-9851

MR. A. J. KUIPER — CLERK

1811 Wilson Ave., S.W., R. 5        Phone ARdmore 6-3498

1951 church directory

Hope's first membership directory also included a "Division of Districts." Each elder was given supervision over a certain district. One who desired help of an elder was to call the elder given supervision over the district in which that person lived.

The Choral Society was formed in 1952 and received approval of its constitution on November 3 of that year. Surely, the years of the forties and early fifties were blessed years for Hope.

```
               Congregational Statistics

     Families                                    35
     Individuals                                  5
     Souls                                      188
     Communicant members                         88
               Division of Districts

     Each elder is given supervision over a certain
     district. If you desire the help of an elder,
     please call the elder given supervision over
     the disctrict in which you live.

     District 1.                    Elder A.J.Kuiper
        All the territory south of River Bend Dr.
        including the south side of River Bend Dr.
     District 2.                    Elder M.Veenstra
        All the territory north of River Bend Dr.
        including the north side of River Bend Dr.
        and up to Lake Michigan Dr.(M.50.) but west
        of Wilson Ave. including the west side of
        Wilson Ave.
     District 3.                    Elder R.Newhouse
        All the territory north of Lake Michigan Dr.
        all east of Wilson Ave. including the east
        side of Wilson Ave. and up to River Bend Dr.


               Budget Information

        The weekly assessment per family is $2.75.
        The monthly assessment for the Building
        Fund debt is $2.00 per family.

            Committees of the Consistory

     Building Committee
        T. Howerzyl      A.J.Kuiper      M.Veenstra
     Pulpit Committee
        R. Bloem         G. Moelker      R.Newhouse
```

1951 church directory showing congregational statistics, budget, and the elders' districts

The church of Jesus Christ must never become complacent, for the devil and his hosts are always lurking about and seeking to subtly destroy. Such an attack came in 1953, when some were lured away from the truth by the supposition that all children born in the covenant are regenerated and do receive the promise of salvation at baptism. Certain ministers and laymen caused a schism in the Protestant Reformed Churches.

Throughout this trial the Lord graciously preserved Hope as a church of Christ, but its membership significantly diminished. From November 1953 through early 1954 no less than fifteen families, from a membership of forty families in early 1953, left Hope. During the 1953 schism the consistory received some letters of dissent, but no formal protests against the truth were lodged to further plague the congregation. While litigation over the property was a possibility for a time, none was forthcoming. Once again the Lord had preserved his church.

During the last two years of the pastorate of Rev. Heys in Hope, a Mr. and Mrs. Society was formed, and its constitution was given consistorial approval on December 21, 1954.

Toward the end of Rev. Heys' pastorate Hope's deacons reported their contact with a student at Calvin College, Rev. Ban-zig Hong, who was a pastor of a Korean Presbyterian church. As a result of his request, Rev. Heys wrote two meditations, one of which was "Rest for the Weary," a portion of which is pictured below.

### REST FOR THE WEARY

Are you, dear reader of these lines, weary and eager for rest? Do you come home from your daily toil tired and with a deep longing to rest?

There is nothing strange about it if you do feel that way. So it is with all men. And the older we get, the sooner we become tired and the more we long for rest. Presently our hearts will also become weary with all its years of beating and stop to beat no more. And then we die!

But are you spiritually weary? Do you feel the awful load of sin which is upon you?

Every day, every minute of the day we are adding to our load of sin and guilt. We sin and sin and sin against our Maker. We walk on His earth. We breathe His air. We use His rain and sunshine. We eat His food and drink His water. Yet we forget all about Him and use His creation to rebel against Him. We behave as though He does not exist. And yet He brings up His sun in the East every morning and sends to us the rain that is so necessary for our food. To deny that He exists is more foolish than to deny that the sun rises every morning in the East. Yet we are so foolish that we refuse to serve and obey Him.

Do you know that guilt? Does that burden bother you? Do you find yourself laboring, working hard to get rid of that burden of guilt? Do you desire to be restored to His favor? Do you desire to be able to serve Him and to be pleasing in His sight? Then the Scripture have a word of comfort for you. Jesus Christ Himself, the eternal Son ...

The meditations were translated into the Korean language and distributed to the people of Korea through Rev. Ban-zig Hong.

Korean translation of part of "Rest for the Weary"

Rev. Heys accepted a call from the congregation of Hull, Iowa, in January 1955 and made his departure after more than thirteen years of faithful labor at Hope.

The period of being without an undershepherd was a relatively short eight months.

## Rev. Herman Hanko and a Four-month Vacancy: September 28, 1955, to May 25, 1963

From a trio of Candidate Herman Hanko, Rev. George Ophoff, and Rev. Gerrit Vos, Candidate Hanko received the call to become Hope's fourth pastor. On September 28, 1955, he was ordained and installed.

Recent improvements to the parsonage, including a 10' x 13' enlargement of the living room would welcome Rev. Hanko and his family.

Rev. Herman Hanko and his wife, Wilma

Although the congregation had been reduced in numbers by the schism of 1953, under Rev. Hanko growth revived, and by October

1957 Hope constituted thirty-four families. Consequently the consistory deemed it wise to increase the number of elders from three to four.

The coming of Rev. Hanko seems to have marked the beginning of a new era in the history of Hope. The burdens and cares of the congregation had long been the responsibility of older faithful leaders who had maintained the truth through doctrinal debate and denominational division. During the pastorate of Rev. Hanko, a new generation grew to spiritual maturity and was ready to assume leadership in the church of Jesus Christ. This internal development can be seen by examining the catechism attendance records of those years. The year 1955, Rev. Hanko's first year, shows 40 catechumens while 1963, the year Rev. Hanko terminated his work at Hope, lists 110 in attendance. Possessing boundless enthusiasm and energy and deep spiritual motivation, Rev. Hanko was instrumental in providing basic religious instruction during the formative years for many children of the covenant in Hope.

The church of Jesus Christ continually desires to bear witness to the truth.

Contact with the Korean Presbyterian church in Korea, begun at the end of Rev. Heys' ministry, continued. A September 4, 1957, report to the congregation indicated that

> our contact with these brethren in Korea has…been limited [because of] the language barrier…We know that the Lord has his sheep everywhere, and when an organized body of individuals manifest themselves as believing in the same Lord and show forth His love in them by refusing to be conformed to the world, have the proper administration of the sacraments, and as far as can be determined, embrace the pure preaching of the gospel, then let us show them that same redeeming and sanctifying spirit of our Lord who is operative in us, and has wrought such great things for us, does also cause us to be mindful of the needs of our fellow Christians in far off Korea.

The consistory on February 6, 1958, decided to investigate the possibility of the congregation's sponsoring a radio broadcast of its own origin. After a year of inquiry and consideration, the idea was abandoned in favor of pamphlet publication and distribution.

Within another year a mailing list of nominally Reformed people was compiled. A series of pamphlets entitled *The Covenant Witness* was planned. The purpose of the series was to set forth truths and doctrines distinctive to the Protestant Reformed Churches. The first pamphlet was mailed in June 1960, along with introductory letters, to 219 persons. Written by Rev. Hanko and published bimonthly, the pamphlets have been a source of instruction for many people in the doctrine of the covenant of grace. Many letters of comment, favorable and unfavorable, have been received and answered.[27]

Roger Kooienga

September 1960 saw the formation of the Hope Heralds, a male singing group dedicated to the heralding of God's praises in song. While the Hope Heralds continues as a group of more than sixty members from many Protestant Reformed congregations in the Grand Rapids area, they no longer are under the supervision of Hope's consistory.

> "I have fond memories of both the Choral Society and Hope Heralds. When I went to Choral Society, the men would take turns driving Roger Kooienga to society as well as home. We would stop at Big Boy for a hamburger afterward. Both groups were enjoyable to sing in and gave me an appreciation for good Reformed music that I still have today."
> —Chester (Skip) Hunter Jr.

In January 1963 church membership had increased to fifty-five families, and the deacons' representation in the consistory was raised to four.

---

27  Rev. Herman Hanko wrote thirty-seven pamphlets in *The Covenant Witness* series, some of which were later published as Herman Hanko, *God's Everlasting Covenant of Grace* (Grand Rapids, MI: Reformed Free Publishing Association, 1988).

Rev. Hanko's departure in January 1963 to our sister church in Doon, Iowa, saddened the entire congregation. His labors had borne much fruit.

## Rev. Herman Veldman and a Two-month Vacancy: May 26, 1963, to November 5, 1966

God continued to richly bless Hope by providing her another undershepherd after only one declined call. From a trio of Rev. Cornelius Hanko, Rev. John Heys, and Rev. Herman Veldman, Rev. Veldman was called to come over and help us. Upon his acceptance of the call extended to him, he was installed on May 26, 1963, to become the congregation's fifth pastor.

Faithful to his calling, he fed the flock from Sunday to Sunday with spiritual food both nourishing and easy to digest. His God-given ability to make plain the truths of scripture from the pulpit served to make his labors in Hope spiritually beneficial for the whole congregation.

The numerical growth of the congregation during Rev. Hanko's pastorate had begun to stretch the limits of Hope's church building. Although reluctant to have the congregation commit to a heavy financial burden, the consistory felt that the need for space was real and the time to build was economically right. Consequently the consistory proceeded with plans to build a new house fit for the worship of God.

30th Wedding Anniversary
Redlands, CA.

Rev. and Mrs. Herman Veldman came to Hope church from Hope Protestant Reformed Church in Redlands, California.

It was December 15, 1963, when the congregation approved preliminary building plans and a method of financing. In addition, a property trade agreement with the board of Hope school gave Hope church adjacent school property in an even trade for part of the church property on Wilson Avenue. It was not until after working drawings were complete, bids were taken, and exact costs were established, that final congregational approval was given to proceed with construction. That decision was made the evening of September 29, 1964. Ground was broken just two days later on October 1, 1964. Construction of the new church edifice was completed and ready for use eight months later. On Sunday, May 16, 1965, the first worship services were held in the beautiful new structure. Significant it was that it was a Sunday when the congregation celebrated the sacrament of the Lord's supper, which made the solemnity of the day complete.

Original church edifice on the corner of Riverbend and Ferndale

The new church building was dedicated to the worship of God in a special public gathering on June 12, 1965, with fitting speeches and greetings by former pastors.

Before ending his work at Hope, Rev. Veldman also witnessed the addition of two more elders to the consistory, one each in 1964 and 1966, to carry the additional work brought on by membership growth. Significant also was the decision made on February 10, 1966. Article 15 of the consistory minutes reads: "A motion to meet as full Council (elders and deacons) at 7:30 and the consistory afterwards." From this time to the present Hope has had consistory meetings, deacons' meetings, and council meetings.

The departure of Rev. Veldman in September 1966 for our sister church of Hudsonville, Michigan, closely marked the milestone of fifty years of the existence of Hope Protestant Reformed Church. Fittingly, the congregation gathered for an evening of thanksgiving. The program included greetings from past ministers and a speech by son of the congregation, Rev. David J. Engelsma. The celebration echoed in word and song the quote from 1 Samuel 7:12 that was on the cover of the fiftieth anniversary booklet: "Ebenezer, hitherto hath the LORD helped us."

After only a two-month vacancy, from a trio of Rev. Cornelius Hanko, Rev. Jason Kortering, and Rev. Marinus Schipper, God sent Rev. Jason Kortering to shepherd the congregation.

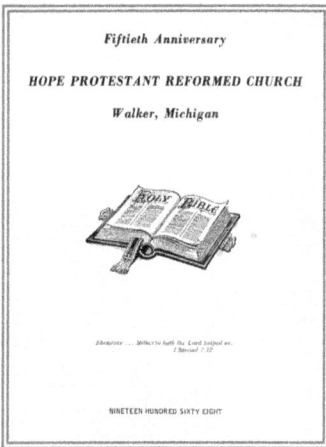

*Fiftieth Anniversary*

HOPE PROTESTANT REFORMED CHURCH

*Walker, Michigan*

NINETEEN HUNDRED SIXTY EIGHT

Cover of the anniversary booklet

---

### *Fiftieth Anniversary Program*

| | |
|---|---|
| Organ Prelude | Mr. John Moelker |
| Opening Prayer and Scripture Reading | Rev. Jason Kortering |
| Congregational Singing | |
| Greeting by Past Ministers | Prof. Herman Hanko<br>Rev. Herman Veldman |
| Organ and Piano Duet | Lois Engelsma<br>Bonnie Meulenberg |
| Anniversary Speaker and Son of the Church | Rev. David J. Engelsma |
| Mass Choir composed of Hope Heralds<br>and Choral Society | |
| Closing Remarks and Prayer | Rev. J. A. Heys |
| Congregational Singing | Doxology |
| Postlude | Mr. John Moelker |

Fiftieth anniversary program

## Rev. Jason Kortering and a Two-year Vacancy: November 6, 1966, to October 5, 1972

Rev. Kortering was installed on November 6, 1966, as Hope's sixth pastor.

The shepherding of Rev. Kortering followed closely the work of Hope's two previous pastors in tending particularly to the spiritual needs of the youth of the church. The fruit of his labors was evident when on the evening of November 7, 1968, thirteen young people made confessions of their faith in Christ. A blessed evening that was!

> "My first memory of Hope church other than visiting on Sunday evenings before we were members was catechism with Rev. Kortering. I was in ninth grade and therefore in the Heidelberg Catechism class. We had a gray folder with outlines. We had to know that material as well as the questions and answers for tests given periodically. Those tests were very comprehensive." —Chester (Skip) Hunter Jr.

Due to a significant increase in the membership of the Mr. and Mrs. Society, in 1965 the society decided to divide into two. The older members began meeting separately and called themselves the Senior Mr. and Mrs. Society. What was left of the existing Mr. and Mrs. Society took the name Junior Mr. and Mrs. Society.

Hope's written witness through the medium of pamphlets continued as Rev. Kortering authored pamphlets in *The Covenant Witness* series titled, *Try the Spirits, Our Life after Death, Evidence of Our Lord's Return, The Four Horseman, The Sealing of the 144,000, The Locust out of the Abyss*, and *The Eating of the Little Book*. In 1994 the Reformed witness committee published the pamphlets in a booklet entitled *A Study in Eschatology*. It was distributed by the committee, which was made up of members of the congregation and members of the council.

A Study in Eschatology

"We remember a Sunday morning during the time Pastor Kortering was minister at Hope. Someone in the front row of church suddenly got sick and threw up. The janitor quickly came to the rescue and sprinkled a powder on the mess to mask the smell. We all thought that he was finished, but then we saw him come down the side aisle with a snow shovel, and then he proceeded to finish cleaning up the mess. During all this commotion Rev. Kortering continued to preach. But then from the back of church we heard the janitor again, this time rolling a squeaky mop bucket down the side aisle. At this time Rev. Kortering decided it would be a good time to sing until the janitor was finished." —Bill and Carol Huber

Significant during this period of Hope's history was a letter from the liturgy committee of the denomination informing Hope's consistory "of a proposed new revision of the Heidelberg Catechism" (April 13, 1967, article 11). The consistory decided that the elders would study the proposed revision individually and then discuss their findings at a special consistory meeting. Apparently their individual studies resulted in some second thoughts regarding their role in this project. Article 5 of the June 29, 1967, minutes tells the story.

Concerning our study of the Heidelberg Catechism the following:

A motion is made that a committee of elders be appointed to draft a letter to the Professors Hoeksema and Hanko suggesting that the Catechism, as revised by them (by mandate of synod), be submitted to synod for study and approval.

Ground: 1. The elders are not qualified to make a study and evaluation because knowledge of the German language is necessary.

This matter carries.

On September 10, 1970, a ministerial certificate of dismissal was reluctantly granted to Rev. Kortering upon his acceptance of a call from our sister church in Hull, Iowa.

Shortly after Rev. Kortering's departure the consistory made several decisions regarding the liturgy of the worship services. The minutes of the February 24, 1971, meeting record those decisions:

> Article 9: when making public confession of faith each person answers separately.
> Article 10: when the sacrament of baptism is administered, each set of parents answers "yes" separately.
> Article 12: that the minister continues to read the Apostles' Creed as we are presently doing.
> Article 13: that the morning doxology remain unchanged and that the evening doxology be changed to "May the Grace of Christ our Savior."

Rev. Jason Kortering

For two long years the congregation continued the process of the Church Order and called men to come over and help. Ten times Hope's calls were not to the man of God's choice. The eleventh call was to Candidate Ronald Van Overloop.

## Rev. Ronald Van Overloop and a Two-year Vacancy: October 6, 1972, to March 5, 1981:

God led Candidate Ronald Van Overloop to accept Hope's call and sent him to lead the congregation for the next six and a half years. Minister-elect Van Overloop was ordained and installed as Hope's seventh pastor on October 6, 1972. Prof. Herman Hanko read the Form for Ordination of Ministers of God's Word, and Rev. Herman Veldman preached the installation sermon.

On October 15, 1972, over the signature of Hope's clerk, David Meulenberg, Professor Hanko was sent a letter from the consistory that included the following special words of thanks for his valued and capable assistance during the two years without an undershepherd:

> Many times we have called on you for advice and help, many times you have helped members of the congregation with

council [*sic*] and advice. We are truly grateful for these labors…
We thank you for your concern for the sheep of Christ and your
untiring labors on their behalf.

Rev. Van Overloop preparing a sermon

The membership records of January 1971 show a count of 92 families, including 178 catechumens in Hope. Continued growth resulted
in a full church every Sunday and a very full load of pastoral work for
the new, young undershepherd.

"Ushering was a challenge, as we knew which large families were going to be coming last. The ushers hoped there
was room for them so that we did not have to scatter them
throughout the congregation, especially if they had very small
children." —Chester (Skip) Hunter Jr.

Thus it was with good reason that on November 6, 1972, a public
meeting was held to determine if there was enough interest in organizing a new Protestant Reformed congregation in the western Grand
Rapids area. The meeting showed that an enthusiastic group of younger
families favored such a move. This resulted in a January 1973 classical
decision to delegate Hope church to be responsible for organizing a
new congregation in Jenison, Michigan.

On February 14, 1973, ten families with children requested the
consistory to transfer their memberships to the newly formed Faith
Protestant Reformed Church.

Due to the growth and expansion of Hope Protestant Reformed Christian School in 1970, the parsonage area on Wilson Avenue soon became used as part of the school's ground. Since the school could use the building and property to good advantage, plans were prepared in early 1973 to build a new parsonage on land north of and adjacent to the church sanctuary on Ferndale Avenue. On July 23, 1973, the congregation approved the construction of a parsonage at a cost of $41,055. On August 9, 1973, the house and land on Wilson Avenue was sold to Hope school for $12,000.

Always desiring the best way to worship the God whom we serve, in January 1975 the consistory instituted a significant change in Hope's order of worship. The change resulted in the following order of the beginning of our worship: votum, salutation, benediction, and doxology. Grounds for the change were the following:

1. It is proper that the service begin officially with the minister declaring the votum and not the organist moving from prelude to the giving of the cue for the doxology as has been our custom.
2. This change will add to the dignity and solemnity of the service.

During Rev. Van Overloop's pastorate in Hope, its members, consistory, and pastor had considerable interest and activity in home and foreign missions.

> "Rev. Van Overloop was still with us when I left the congregation to go to Doon. We young people appreciated his work with us and especially our post-confession class that was started with us." —Chester (Skip) Hunter Jr.

In 1974 Hope was named the calling church for a Protestant Reformed home missionary. In God's good time Rev. Robert Harbach accepted the call to labor in missions for God's church. Subsequently, Rev. Harbach was sent to Houston, Texas, where Trinity Protestant

Reformed Church was organized in 1977. Rev. Harbach later labored in the areas of Vancouver and Abbotsford, Washington, and Victoria, British Columbia.

Rev. and Mrs. Robert Harbach

On October 12, 1977, the consistory was confronted with an unusual request. Article 14 of the minutes explains: "A letter is received from the Committee of Contact with Other Churches. They request that we send our pastor to labor in the Orthodox Presbyterian Church of Christchurch, New Zealand, and in the OPC of New Zealand generally for a period of up to one year." Subsequent meetings with the committee resulted in a consistorial decision to agree to this request.

As a result from December 1977 to August 1978, Rev. Van Overloop labored in the Orthodox Presbyterian Church of Christchurch, New Zealand.

Rev. Houck 1980 in the Lansing mission

In 1979 Candidate Steven Houck accepted a call from Hope to labor in the area of Lansing and Charlotte, Michigan.

The mission labors of these messengers of God gave the Hope congregation a clearer vision of Christ's great commission to preach and baptize.

The urging of the Spirit created a strong desire in Rev. Van Overloop to serve the needs of the saints elsewhere than in an organized Protestant

Reformed church. On April 18, 1979, he accepted a call from the South Holland, Illinois, church to become home missionary of the Protestant Reformed Churches. On May 1, 1979, he preached his farewell sermon to the congregation of Hope. His six and a half years at Hope were memorable and profitable years indeed.

During the period of vacancy, the consistory decided to change its method of fulfilling article 23 of the Church Order "to visit the families of the congregation." Rather than to conduct family visitation with all the families in the fall of the year, the consistory decided "that ¼ of the families be visited prior to each communion service" (July 9, 1980, article 13).

On October 31, 1980, Hope church had a commemorative program and open house to celebrate Professor Hanko's twenty-five years in the gospel ministry. His father, Rev. Cornelius Hanko, spoke on "Father and Fellow-Minister." Hope church and the Protestant Reformed denomination has been richly blessed by Professor Hanko's many years of faithful service.

During the next two years nine calls were extended to men of God to come over and help the Hope congregation.

```
        PROGRAM AND OPEN HOUSE
    COMMEMORATING TWENTY-FIVE YEARS          Remarks               Mr. D. Engelsma
         IN THE MINISTRY                        Member of Congregation
       OF PROFESSOR HERMAN HANKO
      OCTOBER, 1955 - OCTOBER, 1980        Primary Section of the Sunday School
                                             Psalter # 53, The Lord Our Shepherd
                                             Psalter # 266, The Holiness of God
                                             Psalter # 400, Trust and Praise
 Organ Prelude          Mrs. D. Moelker        Mrs. D. Hop, Accompanist

 Opening Prayer         Mr. J. Buiter       Audience Singing          Psalter 241

 Solo                   Mr. A. Dykstra      Closing Prayer         Mr. J. Kalsbeek
   "O God Our Help In Ages Past"
     Mr. C. Kuiper, Accompanist             Postlude               Mrs. D. Moelker

 Piano-Organ Duet       Mrs. L. Garvelink
                        Mrs. I. Veenstra
      "To God Be the Glory"
 "Variations on the tune of Psalter #241"   Refreshments will be served in the basement

 Audience Singing        Psalter # 290      after the program.
                         Psalter # 383
     Mr. C. Kuiper, Leader

 Quartet from Hope Heralds   Psalter # 241
                        Arrangement, Psalm 23
 D. Dykstra, M. Lotterman, L. Meulenberg,
 D. Rau. Mrs. D. Pastoor, Accompanist

 Remarks               Rev. C. Hanko
     Father and Fellow-Minister
```

Program celebrating Professor Hanko's twenty-five years in the gospel ministry

## Rev. Richard Flikkema and a Three-month Vacancy: March 6, 1981, to December 1986

On March 6, 1981, Hope welcomed Rev. Richard Flikkema as our eighth pastor. After the two-year vacancy, his presence once again gave the members of Hope the awareness of a shepherd's loving care.

Flikkema family in 1983
back from left: Tammi, Marcia, Rev. Flikkema; front: Heidi, Tricia

"I remember the extremely hot summer evening worship services during the early 1980s. Air conditioning had not yet been installed. Our church was extra crowded with people before Grandville PR Church was organized, so the temperature during the worship was extremely hot and muggy. My family sat toward the front. Sweat would literally roll down my face. Large floor fans about six feet high would often be whirling at full speed in the back of church, pushing all the hot air around." —Keven Moelker

"Due to the extreme heat, I remember that Rev. Gritters took off his suit coat before he started preaching. This was the only time I ever saw a minister preach without a suit coat at Hope PR Church." —Keven Moelker

Breaking ground for the future Grandville Protestant Reformed Church building

Ten years after the organization of Faith Protestant Reformed Church, Hope found its membership numbers again stretching its facilities. In September 1983 two members made a request to have Sunday worship services held in Grandville, Michigan. This request was granted, and in January 1984 Grandville Protestant Reformed Church was organized. Its charter members numbered twenty families, three individuals, and forty-seven children from Hope. As appreciation for their past support and to assist them with their heavy financial burden, Hope pledged to give the Grandville congregation $80,000. The organization of the Grandville church again showed God's covenantal faithfulness to his people.

During the late 1970s and early 1980s six of the old guard of faithful ministers of the word and sacraments in the Protestant Reformed Churches left full active duty, and a new generation of young men took their place. It is interesting to note that in the same period five young men from Hope entered the gospel ministry, namely Rev. Kenneth Koole, Rev. Ronald Hanko, Rev. Kenneth Hanko, Rev. Russell Dykstra, and Rev. Charles Terpstra. Rev. David Engelsma had entered the gospel minister prior to that in September 1963. This contribution to the church of Christ in its gospel ministry is reason for humble gratitude.

Praising God with the voice of singing accompanied on an organ has been one of Hope's great joys and means of collective musical expression. The Hammond organ purchased in 1951 needed constant repairs. Already in 1976 collections began for the funding of a new organ. On June 10, 1984, a committee was appointed to come with a recommendation for the consistory to consider. On November 28, 1984, the congregation approved the purchase of the chosen model, an Allen electronic organ at a cost of $21,225.

In September 1986 Rev. Flikkema heeded God's call to labor for his people in Covenant Protestant Reformed Church in Wyckoff, New Jersey. His five and a half years in Hope proved to have been a period of quiet trust in God and continued spiritual growth.

In contrast to the previous two vacancies, the period of being without an undershepherd was short.

## Rev. James Slopsema and a Five-month Vacancy: December 1986 to November 25, 1995

Three months after Rev. Flikkema's departure Rev. James Slopsema came to Hope from our sister church in Randolph, Wisconsin. He moved into the parsonage with his wife, eight daughters, and one son in December 1986. He became Hope's ninth pastor.

Slopsema family in 1987; back: Sara, Crista, Shelly;
middle: Carla, Rev. Slopsema, Joan, Paula;
front: Debra, Gary, Brenda, Bethany

"On Sunday, weather permitting, my family would typically walk to church for the worship services. Other neighbors would also walk to church. Looking back in hindsight, it was a clear visible reminder of leaving home and possessions behind for the heaven that awaits the Christian pilgrim."
—Keven Moelker

Early in Rev. Slopsema's ministry Hope's consistory became concerned about the heavy workload of its pastor. Consequently the elders took action to relieve the pastor of some of his responsibilities. In a March 23, 1988, decision the consistory approved a letter to the congregation informing them of the duties of their assigned elders and encouraging Hope's members to contact their district elders rather than the pastor with respect to these duties.

Over the years these duties have changed somewhat. Presently they are the following:

1. Early in his term each elder is expected to establish contact with those of the congregation to whom he has been assigned, and to periodically, on an informal basis, keep in regular contact with them. These contacts will serve:
   a. to establish a rapport with those to whom he has been assigned;
   b. to inform them of his position as their assigned elder;
   c. to encourage them to contact him in times of need.

2. The elders are to take an active role in the comfort and counseling of God's people in their district by visiting the sick in the hospital and those who grieve over the physical and/or spiritual loss of loved ones.

3. The elders are to visit the widows and the widowers and those in institutions of mercy as scheduled.

4. The elders, if they are called upon by those who are distressed or those with marital problems, etc., should consider visits of this nature a part of their work.

5. The elders are to confer with the pastor concerning bulletin announcements relative to their assigned families.

6. The elders are to keep the consistory informed concerning the specific needs of those to whom they have been assigned. This will be important when other elders and/or the pastor visit families in his district for family visitation.

7. Anytime an elder will be unavailable for a period of more than two days, it is his responsibility to inform his alternate.

8. The elders are also responsible for the distribution of the following books to members in their district that qualify:
   a. *Bound to Join* on the occasion of graduation from high school.
   b. *Marriage: The Mystery of Christ and the Church* on the occasion of marriage.
   c. *Believers and Their Seed* and *Reformed Education* on the occasion of the baptism of a first child.

Note: Prior to distribution the district elder is to inscribe the book with an appropriate scripture passage, sign it, and have the minister sign it. (The clerk is responsible to have an adequate supply of these books on hand.)

First council of Grace Protestant Reformed Church
back from left: John Kuiper, Donald Lotterman, Gerrit Van Den Top
front from left: Gilbert Schimmel, David Hanko, Gerald Dykstra

Although it had only been five years since the birth of Hope's daughter, Grandville Protestant Reformed Church, the congregation had to use the basement for seating for communion services. It is not surprising therefore to find an October 1989 minute that requested "the consistory to actively propose the organization of a daughter church." That beginning ended with the organization of Grace Protestant Reformed Church six years later on Thursday evening, July 6, 1995.

Also significant during the years of Rev. Slopsema's pastorate was the beginning of something new for Hope. A letter dated May 14, 1991, from the denominational contact committee over the signature of H. Hanko came with a request concerning a minister-on-loan to Singapore: "The Contact Committee has decided to recommend to Synod that Hope Protestant Reformed Church be appointed the calling church...It is our hope and prayer that you will be willing to assume this responsibility." The council's favorable response over the signature of clerk, Peter Koole, resulted in Hope church being the calling church for ministers-on-loan to Singapore for fifteen years. From August 1991 to September 2002 Rev. Kortering served in that capacity and Rev. den Hartog did so until 2005.

Rev. J. Kortering, Jean Kortering, Evelyn Langerak,
Harry Langerak in front of Kortering's house in Singapore

Rev. A. den Hartog with daughter, Laura, and wife, Sherry

In the 2003 pictorial directory of Hope church Rev. den Hartog wrote,

> We are thankful to God to have served as your assistant pastor in the capacity of minister-on-loan to Singapore for almost two years already. Because we spend most of the time in Singapore, there are…many members of Hope…whom we do not even know personally.…We desire to be part of the communion of the saints among you…We will find this book [the pictorial directory] helpful as we read the church bulletins sent to us by email every week, [as they] mention your names. We want to be able to rejoice with you in the goodness and mercy of the Lord in your lives and also to pray for you in your trials…
>
> We covet your continued prayers on our behalf. We hope that our regular letters will keep you informed about what is happening in the churches in Singapore where we serve the Lord by His grace…We hope that you will…think about us as we do…you and pray for us as we are far away from you on the other side of the world working among God's people of a different, race, culture and background than you are. So may God bind us together in faith and love as we serve Him together each in our place and calling.
>
> We are always greatly helped and encouraged by knowing

that you support us in your prayers in the glorious work of the church and kingdom of the Lord Jesus Christ here in Singapore and also in the trials we sometimes face.

The years of Rev. Slopsema's ministry also included the significant milestone in 1991 of seventy-five years of Hope's existence as an organized church of Christ. Graciously God was with her, and graciously he provided for her throughout that time. Rev. Slopsema's message in the seventy-fifth anniversary booklet, based on the theme "Great Is Thy Faithfulness," included the following words of encouragement:

God is faithful!

God has eternally chosen to Himself a church in Jesus Christ. In love He has promised to form His covenant with her...in which He will save her from all her sins, live with her in sweet fellowship, protect her from all her enemies, [and] provide for her every need...

To keep his covenant promises require[d] of God the ultimate sacrifice—the death of His own Son...

The church which He saved and draws into His own covenant life is often unfaithful...Yet God in His love always brings them back in Jesus Christ, forgives them, and restores them to His covenant[al] friendship...

In response the church has learned to adore the great faithfulness of her covenant God...

In the 75 years of our existence we have enjoyed the great blessings of God's covenant. God has graced us with His salvation in Jesus Christ. According to His promise, we have seen salvation come to our children and our children's children. Over the years God has given us faithful office bearers. He has preserved us in the truth of His Word. He has caused us to multiply numerically. More importantly we have grown spiritually in His grace.[28]

---

28 James Slopsema, "Pastor's Message," in *Hope Protestant Reformed Church...75th Anniversary.*

75 Years
Anniversary Program
Hope Protestant Reformed Church
October 25, 1991  7:30 PM

Organ Prelude ........................... Marilyn King

Prayer and Scripture Reading ............ Rev. J. Slopsema
Jeremiah 31: 1-14

Congregation Singing .................... #269, all verses
#354, verses 1,2,6

Hope Heralds .................... How Firm a Foundation
Psalter #241

Speech ............................... Rev. K. Koole
Great Is Thy Faithfulness
Jeremiah 31:3

Organ Solo ........................... Clare Kuiper
An Arrangement of Psalter #116

Greetings From Our Former Pastors .... Rev. R. Van Overloop
Rev. R. Flikkema

Choral Society ................. O God How Good Thou Art
The Heavens Are Telling

Congregation Singing ............. Great Is Thy Faithfulness

Closing Remarks & Prayer ................ Prof. H. Hanko

Postlude ........................... Bonnie Moelker

Refreshments will be served in the fellowship room.

**Great Is Thy Faithfulness**

Great is Thy faithfulness, O God my Father!
There is no shadow of turning with Thee;
Thou changest not, Thy compassions, they fail not:
As Thou hast been, Thou forever wilt be.

Great is Thy faithfulness,
Great is Thy faithfulness,
Morning by morning new mercies I see;
All I have needed Thy hand hath provided--
Great is Thy faithfulness, Lord unto me!

Summer and winter, and springtime and harvest,
Sun, moon, and stars in their courses above,
Join with all nature in manifold witness
To Thy great faithfulness, mercy, and love.

Great is Thy faithfulness,
Great is Thy faithfulness,
Morning by morning new mercies I see;
All I have needed Thy hand hath provided--
Great is Thy faithfulness, Lord unto me!

Pardon for sin and a peace that endureth,
Thine own dear presence to cheer and to guide,
Strength for today and bright hope for tomorrow--
Blessings all mine, with ten thousand beside!

Great is Thy faithfulness,
Great is Thy faithfulness,
Morning by morning new mercies I see;
All I have needed Thy hand hath provided--
Great is Thy faithfulness, Lord unto me!

Seventy-fifth anniversary program celebrating God's covenantal faithfulness to Hope church

## Rev. Russell Dykstra and a One Year Vacancy: November 26, 1995, to September 1997

After a short vacancy due to the departure of Rev. Slopsema in the summer of 1995, Hope called home a son as our tenth pastor. Rev. Russell Dykstra left the shadow of the water tower in Doon, Iowa, to bask once again in the familiar confines of the "Hope ghetto."

Dykstra family in 1996
back from left: Chris, Rev. Dykstra;
middle: Nathan, Heidi, Jordan, Ryan;
Front: Emily, Carol, Holly, Courtney

Rev. Dykstra was installed on November 26, 1995, by Professor Hanko, and a welcome program on December 1 soon followed. Little did one of the young ladies (Rebecca Vermeer) who played *The Holy City* in an instrumental duet for that program know that eighteen years later she would be welcomed in like fashion as the wife of Hope's twelfth pastor, Rev. Overway.

However, Rev. Dykstra's stay as the pastor in Hope church would be short-lived: the Protestant Reformed synod of 1996 saw to that by calling Rev. Dykstra to serve in the Theological School of the Protestant Reformed Churches. It was a call that when he accepted it changed the title of Hope's son from Reverend to Professor.

"I remember well a very special and exciting time in my life during the pastorates of Rev. Slopsema and Rev. Dykstra in Hope church. I had just met my boyfriend, Jim Geerlings, who is now my husband of almost nineteen years. Jim had a Reformed background, but had not been baptized or had much catechetical instruction. He started attending catechism classes taught by Rev. Slopsema. Later, when Rev. Slopsema accepted the call to First Protestant Reformed Church in Grand Rapids, Jim continued his instruction with Rev. Slopsema. Hope then called Rev. Russell Dykstra, and he was Hope's minister for a short time before he accepted the call to be professor in the Protestant Reformed seminary. But before Rev. Dykstra left Hope, he administered adult baptism to Jim, and Jim and I both made confession of faith that same evening. Rev. Dykstra preached on 2 Timothy 2:3–7, "Enduring Hardness as Soldiers of Christ." We then took marriage counseling under Rev. Dykstra, and he married us about six months later. Both Rev. Slopsema and Rev. Dykstra played very important and special roles in our lives."
—Sara (Langerak) Geerlings

Though busily seeking a replacement for Rev. Dykstra to fill Hope's pulpit, the consistory did find time to make the then-serving communion committee happy (and every communion committee thereafter) by deciding to use disposable communion cups. Depending on how much care is exercised, washing glass communion cups can be rather tedious.

In the meantime Hope had her eye on a member of Hope who was also a promising seminary student.

## Rev. James Laning and a Three-year Vacancy: September 1997 to April 13, 2013

Following the passing of his 1997 synodical exam and receiving Hope's call, Candidate James Laning accepted Hope's call, moved into the parsonage, and in the worship services catapulted from pew to pulpit. At his installation service minister-elect Laning and the congregation were exhorted by Prof. David Engelsma to "Hear the Voice of God." And under Rev. Laning's faithful preaching we did indeed hear the voice of God.

Not only did Hope welcome a new pastor to her pulpit, but she also welcomed a new doxology to her number board. At the December, 17, 1997, meeting the consistory changed the closing doxology from "May the Grace of Christ Our Savior" to psalter number 197. Four grounds supported that change:

Rev. James Laning

1. It is proper to sing a doxology at this place in our worship service.
2. Psalter 197 is a doxology while "May the Grace of Christ our Savior" is not.
3. Psalter 197 is a psalm and therefore in keeping with article 69 of the Church Order.
4. Psalter 197 is God centered. It is proper for our worship services to begin and end with our attention focused on God.

The membership of Hope remembers well the series on Solomon that Rev. Laning preached early in his ministry at Hope.

Hope's consistory went on record as supporting the reading of good Reformed literature way back in 1964 by presenting newly married couples a one-year subscription to the *Standard Bearer*. Once again they demonstrated this support by deciding in May 2005 to give books published by the Reformed Free Publishing Association to members who reached the milestones of "high school graduation, marriage, and baptism of a first child." No doubt Paul's instruction to Timothy in 1 Timothy 4:13 to "give attendance to reading" entered into the discussion. Any remaining doubts about Hope's commitment to encourage her members to read were dispelled in 2006 when a church library was organized and housed in the basement room next to the kitchen.

While room was found for books in 2006, the following year would find a lack of room for people in Hope's sanctuary. Just twelve years after daughter Grace Protestant Reformed Church had been organized

David and Bonnie Moelker

to solve Hope's overcrowding "problem," on May 2, 2007, the council decided as recorded in article 17 of their minutes "to put up to thirty members in the basement to relieve the crowding in the auditorium." Proposed solutions to this "crowding in the auditorium" continue to be considered.

"I was a member of Hope church for thirty-three years. I remember my dad as a long-serving officebearer. My mom played the church organ at Hope since she was fifteen years old, for fifty years of service to Hope church. Rev. Van Overloop baptized me on November 25, 1973. I remember all the ministers from Rev. Van Overloop through Rev. Laning. At one point in the late 1970s, I remember Rev. Van Overloop went to New Zealand to preach." —Keven Moelker

Also of significance during the pastorate of Rev. Laning was the beginning of Hope's work with Rev. Titus and the saints in the Protestant Reformed Churches in Myanmar.

John Van Baren and Rev. Laning (back left) and Rev. A. den Hartog (back right) with the saints in Myanmar; Rev. Titus is the fourth from the right in the front row.

Hope said farewell to the Lanings in June 2010, but not before son Ben plugged up the tub drain with the sand he had cleaned out of an aquarium he was preparing to sell on craigslist. The Lanings were sent on their way to Hull, Iowa, with a kitchen table and a bag of leaves: leaves they would see precious few of in Iowa and that would at the same time remind them of what they had left behind in Michigan.

The Laning family toward the end of their time at Hope; from left: Samuel, Olivia, Peter, Benjamin, Rev. Laning, Margaret, Heather, Amy, Michael, Julianne

A three-year vacancy followed the departure of the Lanings. Much appreciated by the consistory and congregation was the willing, faithful labors of Professor Cammenga who provided excellent Heidelberg Catechism preaching and of Professor Hanko who preached series sermons on Galatians, James, and 1 Peter.

This lengthy time without a pastor also gave consistory members more than ample opportunity to hone their teaching skills, as the bulk of the catechism instruction fell upon their shoulders.

## Rev. David Overway: April 14, 2013, to the present

In April 2013 Hope welcomed Rev. David Overway; his wife Rebecca; and their three children, Joseph, Elena, and Benjamin, into her midst. With Rev. Overway's installation by Professor Hanko on April 14, Hope's lengthy vacancy came to an end.

The Overway family (2013); back from left: Joseph, Rebecca
front: Elena, Rev. Overway, Benjamin

Once again Hope is blessed through the faithful labors of the undershepherd. The pure word is preached by her pastor. The sacraments and church discipline are faithfully administered, and the children of the covenant are given sound catechetical instruction. The 150 psalms, the Lord's prayer, the Song of Mary, the Song of Zacharias, and the Song of Simeon are sung in worship services. The three forms of unity based on the word of God set forth the doctrinal confession of the church.

Congregational life flourishes, as indicated by the 2015 statistics in the 2016 church directory: 88 families; 77 confessing individuals, including those living with their families; 217 members by baptism, for a total membership of 470; 9 elders and 6 deacons; 166 catechumens; 99 Sunday school students; 23 in Men's Society; 27 in Ladies' Society; 36 in Junior Adult Bible Society; 62 in Senior Adult Bible Study Society; 30 in Senior Young People's Society; 23 in Junior Young People's Society; and 32 in Young Adults' Society.

In the days of the prophet Jeremiah, God's people were warned by the prophet to serve the Lord and to serve him only for then only would he bless them. May that warning also be heeded by God's people in Hope Protestant Reformed Church as we experience the great mercies and faithfulness of God. "It is of the LORD's mercies that we are not consumed, because his compassions fail not. They are new every morning: great is thy faithfulness" (Lam. 3:22–23).

Conscious of his faithfulness we can be confident that we are today, and will continue to be in the future, what our centennial anniversary theme expresses: "A Spiritual House Acceptable to God."

# Chapter 3

## Hope's Buildings: Dedicated to the Service of God

*David Moelker*

Take heed now; for the LORD hath chosen thee to build an house for the sanctuary: be strong, and do it.
—1 Chronicles 28:10

FINDING A CHURCH IN THE CITY OF Grand Rapids would have been easy in 1916. There were approximately 130 churches of many different persuasions, with the Dutch Reformed already having a strong presence at that time. Grand Rapids has often been called "the city of churches." The Reformed community was second only to the Roman Catholic community, which was often the case in the northern United States. So why desire that a mission be established in the countryside of such a thriving church community?

### Obstacles Faced in the River's Bend

To someone living in the river's bend in 2016, Grand Rapids proper is at most only ten minutes away. It is an easy commute perhaps accomplished a number of times in a day. But life in 1916 was at a different pace. Not many people had automobiles, and the horse and buggy was a common means of transportation, especially in an outlying farming community. And why not attend church in Jenison or Walker, only a couple of miles away in different directions?

Finding a church close to home and convenient to get to was difficult in rural, outlying Grand Rapids. There were barriers to easy traveling. The Grand River, a natural barrier, cut the people off from Jenison and lack of easy travel made a trip to Walker Station, as it was called, not a first choice. There was no West Beltline between Grandville and Walker to serve as a bypass and no bridge in Grandville over the river until both road and bridge were completed in the early 1930s.

These geographical difficulties were in mind already at the first gathering of the little group for worship near the river's bend on Sunday, January 23, 1916. At that time the United States was midway through World War I, the war to end all wars. On that day the temperature fell one hundred degrees in twenty-four hours in Browning, Montana, and set a record that has not been matched or broken as of 2016, one hundred years later. It can easily be concluded that it was a bitterly cold winter in the bend of the Grand River on that Sunday, when after a cold journey a meeting was held in a warm farmhouse on a little-known dirt road called Hall Street that cut through a swamp. At that meeting Christian Reformed missionary pastor, J. R. Brink, preached a sermon. We can believe that he said to the twenty-one souls gathered there on that cold winter day, "Grace, mercy, and peace be multiplied unto you," which must have been comforting words for that small, isolated group of believers.

After the worship service a meeting was held with the stated purpose of "bringing about various improvements regarding ecclesiastical matters in the vicinity of River Bend." Included in these improvements was the desire to have a permanent, visible meeting place.

The first improvement appears to have been choosing Rev. Brink as the little group's president, as article 1 of the January 23, 1916, minutes makes clear. The next order of business was to decide if it was advisable and necessary to establish a mission station in the vicinity of what was known as River Bend. After a unanimous vote was recorded, the group chose Charles Bouwman as secretary and Richard Nieuwenhuis (Newhouse) as treasurer.

Many of Hope's early church meetings were held in the home
of Richard Newhouse located at 4551 Hall Street SW.

## Early Building Considerations

Mr. Bouwman recorded as article 5 an almost surprising decision
for such a fledgling group.

> Since, in this vicinity of River Bend, no suitable building to regu-
> larly hold divine services is available, a committee is appointed.
> This committee is given the mandate to investigate the cost of
> a church building, and to find a suitable place (location) where
> such a building could be erected, to meet there regularly. The
> committee consists of the following four persons: J. Moelker,
> J. Zaagman, T. [Mathys] Van Eeuwen, and R. Nieuwenhuis to
> serve as Building Committee.

The fourth item of business for that newly organized mission, in
the middle of a world war and in a year of record winter weather, was
the building of a visible place of worship, God's house!

Article 2 of the February 2, 1916, minutes reads: "A report of the
Building Committee. Mr. J. Moelker presents a plan for the hopefully soon to be built church building if no suitable location is found

elsewhere." The plan was for a 32' x 40' building that would be erected as practical as possible for this purpose.

On June 8, 1916, the group was organized into an instituted church. Article 5 of the July 11 consistory meeting reads: "It is decided to extend freedom to the consistory, when the need arises, to purchase one thing or another for the new church building."

On August 29, 1916, the consistory of Hope Christian Reformed Church held its meeting in the home of R. Nieuwenhuis. In article 3 the consistory "decided to encourage the stirring up of interest to make better progress with the new church building." There must have been a knock on the door to interrupt the meeting, since article 4 gives evidence of a spiritually growing congregation when it records that Mr. and Mrs. J. Van Dyke confessed their faith. Then the consistory returned to the business at hand and recorded in article 5: "The building committee is instructed to determine of what building material the proposed church building will be constructed and...what the cost will be."

The congregation decided at a meeting held September 12, 1916, to construct a church building of cement blocks and to mandate a committee consisting of R. Nieuwenhuis and I. Korhorn to purchase an acre of land from C. Korhorn. It was also decided that the members of the congregation should construct a horse barn as soon as possible.

Apparently a higher value was placed on the comfort and protection of one's horse than on oneself in those years, as the congregation built a horse barn before they built the church building.

The congregation also decided that the dimensions "of the church building shall be 40' x 30'" (article 9). The windows were to be purchased from Rev. Brink, who had somehow come upon them and had saved them someplace.

On September 26, 1916, the consistory decided "as quickly as possible to canvass the congregation in order that the members may pledge over their signature, toward the new church building."

At the next consistory meeting, the minutes indicate that a few members of the congregation were present. The consistory decided to purchase the cement blocks on Walker Avenue from J. Weller for 9.5¢ each. "The cement (mortar) for the blocks is to be of the best and most economical." At that meeting the committee that had been mandated to purchase an organ reported that "the purchase was made for $5."

At the November consistory meeting the land acquisition committee had done its work. The committee reported that an acre of land on the corner of Riverbend and Kenowa should be purchased from C. Korhorn for $150. An interesting note is that the corner of Riverbend and Kenowa had a distinct *Y* configuration, as if traffic did not have to stop and could merge, much like today on our modern freeways.

Advertising by signage was already in vogue.
There was a Universal Car and Service Company
sign in front of the church building.

With a loan of $500 from classis taken out of the fund for needy churches, Rev. Brink purchased wood and gave it to the congregation for building the new church. At that same meeting proposals were passed to use "wooden shingles on the roof of the new church building…to place a tower (spire) on the church, [to make] the church building…as rounding as possible [refers to the inside ceiling], [to leave] the storm house...as it now exists, and [to trim] the windows with cement above them." No architectural fees were included, and Mr. L. Bergman would proceed to build the church building, apparently for the stipulated $1,500.

"The windows from Rev. Brink were stained glass, at least on the west and north sides of the building. The windows he supplied on the east side were a frosted type. The platform on the south end of the auditorium went all the way across the thirty-foot width with a notch cut out for the pump organ. The floor was wood with gasoline lights suspended from the ceiling. There was a covered entry area before the main door to the auditorium with three steps up to the door of the sanctuary. Immediately to the right of the entry door was the stairway to the basement." —Johanna Bomers

The new building for Hope church became a destination for some of the folks in River Bend.

Charles Bouwman, Isaac Korhorn, and Charles Engelsma were given the responsibility to "see to it [that] trees are brought around the church building, and also to make the ground level." Charles Bouwman and Henry Goeree made plans to "cover the vicinity of Butterworth Road, and J. Moelker and R. Nieuwenhuis [to cover]...the immediate area, to collect the promised money for the church building." From this bit of information we learn the approximate area in which the congregation lived.

The love of that new congregation was evident in acts of liberality. In one such act in the rural, post-World War I economy was a gift for the new building. Mr. and Mrs. C. Bouwman gave a *Staten Bijbel* for the pulpit along with the stipulation that if the congregation joined another fellowship the Bible had to be returned to the donors.

Following a consistory meeting on September 3, 1918, the congregation met to consider the matter of a furnace for the new church building. Article 2 of that meeting reads: "A committee is appointed to purchase this furnace which the members had looked at." The committee was given power to act, if necessary, to purchase said furnace "for $75 delivered and installed." It was decided to collect money for the furnace and as long as the congregation was met together, it was also decided to paint the church. Apparently some matters were decided spontaneously at early congregational meetings. This again points to the smallness and closeness of that community of believers.

At a congregational meeting held March 20, 1919, the committee responsible for the purchase of a furnace reported "that the furnace is too small for the church building." Occupation of the new building for worship services was placed on hold because of the small furnace. In October 1919 a larger furnace adequate to heat the building was purchased for $165 installed. Then a decision was made to finish off a room in the basement of the church that "can be used for a variety of purposes." The room was "to be finished off with plaster board," and a glass window was to be placed in the door to the all-purpose room. During this time C. Korhorn, a member of the building committee, was paid $10 to serve as janitor.

Later a house was built on the site where the church had been standing, using part of the walls for the foundation. The basement that contained the all-purpose room still can be seen, at least from the outside.

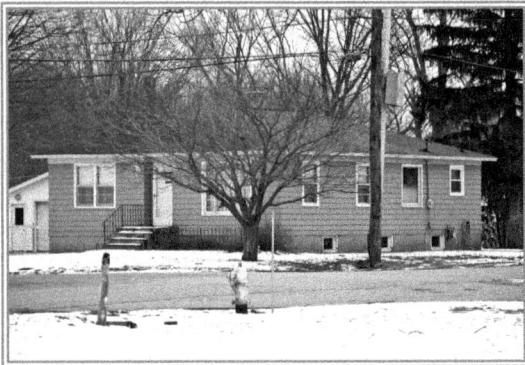

The picture shows that the foundation and windows are those of the church building. The original cement blocks and the basement windows are in their original places. The mortar that was to be the "best"—well it must have been just that, since it is still holding the blocks together after one hundred years!

Corner of Riverbend and Kenowa showing
parsonage, church, and Blair School

Corner of Riverbend and Kenowa in 2016 showing parsonage and
house erected on the foundation of the Hope church building

The record is not clear whether the consistory brought all these matters to be discussed and voted on or if they arose from the floor of that congregational meeting. What is plain is that at the end of the meeting each one was asked in turn if there was anything he wanted to bring up. The congregational meeting was then closed with thanksgiving. The work of the Lord was being done by the small band in the river's bend, even if it appears somewhat informal to us compared with our present way of doing things.

On April 20, 1920, another organ arrived. There is no record of what happened to the first one. It was decided to place the new organ on a platform in the auditorium. Apparently there was an unwritten qualification for an organist already at that time of not being bothered by stage fright. However, somehow the platform must have presented a problem for the consistory, because at a congregational meeting on August 2, 1920, the making of the special platform for the organ was ruled out.

At the same meeting the congregation decided to purchase a gasoline light for the church building. The small congregation made another major and significant building decision: "A motion is made and supported to build a new parsonage next to the church" (article 7). The congregation accepted that motion. Discussion was held regarding purchasing the farm of Mrs. Peck on Burton Street. After discussing the matter the congregation decided not to go in that direction. Instead a parsonage would be built next to the church, and money would be raised by canvassing the congregation. The money would be "written (pledged)" to be paid quarterly if possible. The building committee was empowered to borrow $500 for building materials and to request $1,000 of classis from its church-help fund.

The evidence of a small congregation and how it worked in unity is evident again in the last article of that congregational meeting and the reference to what was used at consistory meetings as well—"the circuit question." "After the circuit question is asked, the meeting is closed with the singing of Psalm 133:3 [at that time there were no printed English psalters] and thanksgiving prayer by Rev. J. R. Brink" (article 15).

The years 1924 and 1925 had more than doctrinal ramifications for the church in the river's bend. The church building became a part of the division of 1925. At the consistory meeting of July 7, 1925, a committee was appointed to see if it was possible to retain the building. To prepare for a possible negative outcome, it was also decided to hold worship services in Blair School beginning at 10:30 a.m. and 7:30 p.m. the next Sunday. The property was lost. The loss of the church building was keenly felt by the congregation more than in just the loss of real estate. The two congregations would now be worshiping fifty yards apart from each other across Kenowa Avenue. The fourth priority of the organizational meeting in 1916 had been a building. That priority would have to be set aside for a time. Although it is important to a congregation to have a church building as a meeting place in a community, the congregation had to go forward in the knowledge that even without a building a church continues to exist.

At what must have been one of the lowest points in the life of the small congregation, a congregational meeting was held on April 27, 1927, in the home of Deacon Moelker. The meeting was opened with singing verse 3 of Psalm 119 and prayer by the president, Rev. Ophoff. The minutes of that meeting are as follows:

> Article 1. Rev. Ophoff gave a short talk in which he explained the object of the meeting which was that our finance was nearly exhausted and to see if some means could be provided by which we could continue as a congregation.
>
> Article 2. A motion was then made and excepted [*sic*] to try the budget system which will amount to $4 a week [per family] for six families. Namely J. Kuiper, R. Newhouse, I. Korhorn, C. Engelsma, J. Moelker, and G. De Jong.

The budget collections would have raised $24 per week. In an attempt to gain more members, the congregation enlisted the use of a schoolhouse on Leonard Road to the north and purchased a lantern for use in the schoolhouse. Apparently, the hope was to increase numbers by church extension, thereby also increasing financial strength to be able to continue as a congregation. The record shows that on May 24, 1927, a decision was made to hold services in the schoolhouse one more week, and if no interest was shown to discontinue them. History is silent as to the outcome. The small beginning of June 8, 1916, in the river's bend appeared to be floundering.

## New Church and Parsonage Construction
## on the West Beltline

At the same May 24, 1927, congregational meeting the minutes show optimism. Ways and means were discussed to bring about the building of another place of worship. A motion was made and accepted "to build a small church building and to ask classis to get permission to hold collections in the different churches of our denomination for that purpose" (article 3). The building committee was also directed to borrow $1,000 and not to exceed 7 percent interest.

The bridge over the Grand River in Grandville was being built in the early 1930s. The proposed road over the bridge was first referred to only as the "bridge road." Later the highway department named the road the West Beltline after the purpose for which it had been created.

This new road cut past the edge of Isaac Korhorn's property. The minutes record that he owned property that he would make available for purchase by the congregation.

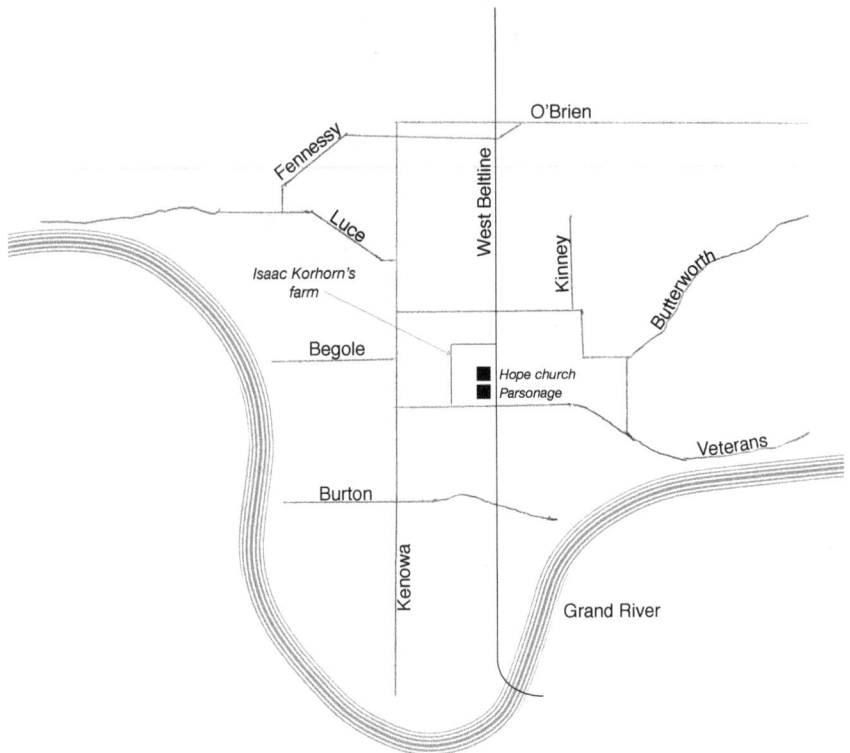

Map of Walker Township showing proposed West Beltline and bridge over the Grand River and Hope's future church building and parsonage

Financial assistance in the form of gifts and loans was promised, plans were reviewed, and bids were taken. On March 31, 1930, for the second time in its history, the congregation formally made a decision to construct a church building by accepting L. Bergman's bid of $2,095. The approximate measurements were 35' x 60'. It would not be the end of construction around this building site.

The new house of worship was first occupied the latter part of June 1930. A letter of thanks was sent the following month to the River Bend school board for the use of its building (Blair schoolhouse) for four and a half years.

Original Wilson Avenue church building

By 1936 the consistory decided to look for ways and means to build a parsonage. Travel was still difficult, and the parsonage was a rented house some distance away on Jackson Street. It was late in 1939 before plans and costs were obtained and the building committee could reach an agreement. On November 24, 1939, a low bid of $2,800 was accepted for a new parsonage. The house next to the church was completed in May 1940.

Although the parsonage debt was paid by December 1941, in the spring of 1940 the consistory was concerned about finances and on April 22, 1940, decided "to announce again to the congregation that we are still running behind financially and to warn the congregation if matters do not get better the consistory will have to use other means to get the money" (article 3). Also noted in these minutes is that screens were being made for the parsonage, including a screen door for the kitchen.

The consistory assumed that a new preacher would have a car and on November 4, 1940, made and passed the following motion: "that we go through the congregation to collect money to build a garage." The size was to be 10' x 20' x 8'. Building a garage must have proved uneconomical during those World War II years. On September 29, 1941, "a motion carried to approve the action of the committee in buying a garage complete at the price of $60" (article 2). And "a motion carried to pay A. J. Kuiper the sum of $8.96 for moving the garage on the church property" (article 3).

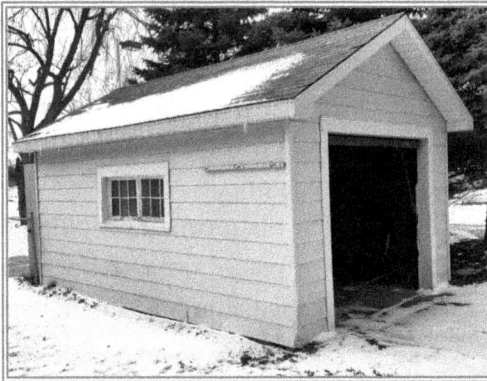

Garage of Wilson Avenue parsonage

The new preacher did eventually come—an energetic candidate, John Alexander Heys. In August 1941 a motion carried to buy paint for the kitchen in the parsonage. Heys would donate the labor.

Hope church has always been a singing church. This was again made evident when on June 2, 1941, the Ladies Aid Society came

with a request to the consistory for the permission to buy a new organ to replace the old organ in the church auditorium. The Ladies Aid assumes full responsibility of the cost of the organ and further asks the permission to canvass the congregation for donations and also if necessary to ask for help from the church fund.

The consistory delegated John Moelker and Harry Bloem as the committee to buy this organ.

To accommodate the growing congregation, an addition was constructed in 1948 to the south and west sides of the church that contained two bathrooms, a hall, and a stairs to the auditorium. Prior to that time there was only the common outside facility found in those days, except for the short time Hope School's bathroom facilities were available and used by Hope's congregants.

## Solutions to New Growth Concerns

About this same time the seating in the auditorium was modified to provide more seats by removing the center aisle and filling it with more folding seats. In the 1950s changes continued to accommodate growth. A row was also installed across the back under the windows and was usually occupied by some of the young, single men of the congregation.

Eventually those measures proved to be inadequate, and a flat-roofed addition that measured approximately 20' x 10' was built on the west side of the auditorium. The platform for the pulpit filled the space, so that *this time* the organ *was* placed on a platform far to the south side. There was a window directly behind the organ bench.

At one worship service during a raging thunderstorm while the congregation was singing, John G. Moelker was seated at the console playing the organ. A bolt of lightning struck so near the building that he reported later that it had caused the hair on his neck to stand. But Hope, being the singing church that it was, didn't miss a beat.

This addition allowed for two more rows of seats to be installed in the front of the sanctuary. The consistory minutes indicate that the Men's Society was given the right to build a coat rack in the rear of the auditorium. Finances must have again come through, and the balance of $28.50 on the note to Old Kent Bank was paid from the treasury.

Interior of the Wilson Avenue church building occupied
by children of Hope school

Later Hope school was granted permission to use the church base-ment for extra classrooms. An entrance to the basement was made on the north, front corner of the building. It consisted of a long, gradual, dark stairway that entered into a small society and catechism room in the basement.

> One catechumen in this room recalls Rev. Herman Hanko, teaching catechism and taking collection in his hand. To the young student his wide, deep, and cupped hand appeared to take on the look of a large soup bowl.

Eventually Hope school tore down the church building and turned the land into a parking lot.

> "I felt really bad when that little white church was torn down, because that was where I was taught most of my life in church and catechism." —Clara Van Den Top

The front edge of the present parking lot is where the front door and stairway to the "narthex," under the belfry had been.

One memory of this entrance is the ledge alongside the stairway. Cigar smoking was in vogue then, and it was common
to find the ledge being a repository of a number of partially
smoked cigars. They were carefully placed there in a row waiting for their owners to return.

One wonders if a mischievous young person ever changed their
order, or if the owners even remembered which cigars were theirs when
they exited the auditorium.

The Young People's Society met on Sunday afternoons then. More
than once the young men attending college engaged Rev. Hanko in
spirited debates on any number of subjects while the younger members
listened and learned.

## Plans to Move to Ferndale Avenue

The numerical growth of the congregation during Rev. H. Hanko's pastorate began to tax the facilities of the church building [on
Wilson] heavily. Although enlarged twice, the sanctuary was…
filled to overflowing, and the many societies were hard pressed to
find room for all their midweek meetings. Those activities which
attracted a greater number of people had to be held elsewhere.

In 1961, plans detailing a major enlarging and remodeling of
the existing church building were presented for congregational
approval and rejected as being inadequate and impractical. In
1962, a proposed purchase of properties adjacent to the existing
church property was also rejected as providing too unwieldy an
area for efficient use.[1]

In February 1964, to alleviate overcrowding in the auditorium, which
sat approximately two hundred, basement seating was necessary. Since
basement seating was a reality then, too; John Moelker installed speakers, and Jacob Kuiper Sr. prepared the east basement room for worship.

---

1    Bloem, "Brief History," in *Hope Protestant Reformed Church…75th Anniversary*,
     unnumbered pages.

Those were happy times for the congregation as she experienced stabilization through growth. Another chapter in the history of the small congregation in the river's bend was being written.

## Construction and Occupation
## of the Church Building on Ferndale

The congregation had voiced its desire to relocate. To that end in January 1963 the congregation approved the purchase of three lots on Ferndale Avenue at Riverbend Drive, about a city block west of the Wilson Avenue church building.

Although the consistory was reluctant to have the congregation commit to a heavy financial burden, the need for a larger place of worship was keenly felt, and the economic climate was right for building. With a great desire to build a house fit for the worship of God, the consistory proceeded with plans to do so.

On December 27, 1963, the congregation approved preliminary building plans, method of financing, and a property trade agreement with Hope Protestant Reformed Christian School that gave the school adjacent property in an even trade for part of the church property on Wilson Avenue. Proposed cost of the new church was $75,000. The motion to build a new church carried by a vote of 37 to 21.

At a special congregational meeting held September 29, 1964, the congregation voted to go ahead with yet another building plan. Article 2 of that meeting was recorded by the clerk, John Kalsbeek:

A motion is made and supported to approve Proposal 1 regarding the building project as submitted by the

general chairman of this year's drive. *Grandville Star* *10/8/64*

## New Structure
## To Seat 400

Construction has been started on the new Hope Protestant Reformed Church on Riverbend Drive. The site consists of three lots of the Fenske Plat of the old Korhorn farm and approximately one-half acre of school property owned by the church. The present church at 1545 Wilson Ave. is east of the new site.

The central room of the new church will have an arch construction with a wood deck and will seat 400. The kitchen, meeting rooms, and Sunday School rooms will be in the basement. Cost of the brick structure is estimated at $102,000.

Ten Horst and Rinzema are the contractors. Completion date is set for July.

Richard Bloem is chairman of the building committee. Assisting him are John Kuiper, Jr., Dick Kooienga, Louis Elzinga, Lammert Lubbers, and David Meulenberg.

consistory, quote, "That the maximum cost of the new church building be $100,000 instead of the $75,000 previously approved. The revised cost figure to provide a church building ready for use including seating, parking, and landscaping." Motion carries.

Two days later, on October 1, the ground was broken. Construction began, and the new edifice was completed and ready for use eight months later.

A committee had been appointed to determine what would go into the building's cornerstone, which has the date 1965 inscribed on it. The article of the consistory minutes reads: "The committee re document box reads a report of their work…The box will include a brief history of our church, copies of the current *Standard Bearer, Beacon Lights*, and church directory, and a Bible and a Psalter."

"The architecture of the building was contemporary, designed by architect James K. Haveman. Its beauty is in its simplicity. Total seating capacity in the sanctuary was 400."[2] —Richard Bloem

The final cost of the new church, including furnishings was $105,000. The congregation passed several proposals of interest regarding furnishing the new building: 100 Bibles at $1.45 each; 100 folding chairs at $4.15 per chair; 15 banquet tables for $27.95 each; a folding chair rack for $33.52; $237.65 worth of kitchenware. The cost of those items was to be paid out of the general fund.

The new edifice was soon used for special events, such as, weddings, society and young people's banquets, anniversary celebrations, and the like.

"The new church building was dedicated to the worship of God in a special public gathering on June 12, 1965, with fitting speeches and greetings by former pastors."[3] —Richard Bloem

---

2   Ibid.
3   Ibid.

1965 Hope church building

Memories of worship services in the first years in the new auditorium are many and varied. Those were the golden years for Richard Newhouse who had attended the first worship service of Hope church in his living room. You could find him usually sitting about four rows from the front on the south side of the aisle in front of the elders. Having been in the office of either deacon or elder at Hope throughout all of her history, he may have decided to sit in that spot out of habit or possibly because "the doors [were being] shut in the streets, when the sound of the grinding is low" (Eccl. 12:4). One thing is sure, the little Dutchman wanted to focus on the preaching. It was always expected that when the congregation sang his favorite psalter number, he could be heard clearly singing, "Gracious Lord remember David / How he made Thy house his care, / How he vowed to seek no pleasure / Till Thy house he should prepare."[4] That, after all, was what Mr. Newhouse had made his lifelong care, too.

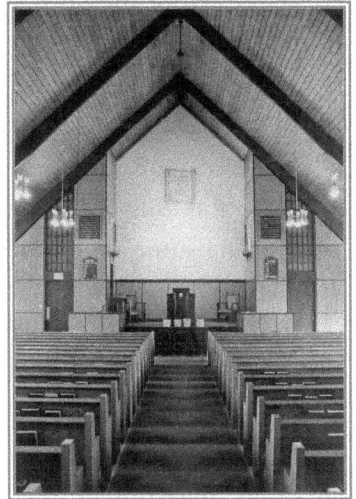

"How amiable are thy tabernacles, O Lord of hosts" (Ps. 84:1).

---

4    No. 367:1, in *The Psalter with Doctrinal Standards, Liturgy, Church Order, and added Chorale Section*, reprinted and revised edition of the 1912 United Presbyterian *Psalter* (Grand Rapids, MI: Wm. B. Eerdmans Publishing Co., 1927; rev. ed. 1995).

When this picture of Richard Newhouse was taken
in 1968 for the fiftieth anniversary of Hope church,
he was the only remaining charter member.

The 1960s and early 1970s was a time of undeclared war for our country in Vietnam. The congregation's young men were affected. When each took his turn leaving for the Army, an announcement was made and the congregation would send the young man off by singing psalter 345: "To the hills I lift my eyes, / Whence shall help for me arise?/ From the Lord shall come my aid/ Who the heav'n and earth has made. He will guide thro' dangers all, / Will not suffer thee to fall; He Who safe His people keeps/ Slumbers not and never sleeps."[5] With that song still ringing in their ears as they left for basic training, many eighteen- and nineteen-year-old young men would soon gain a new understanding of the meaning of those words.

The summers in the new auditorium proved to be an experience all their own. Without any fans, at first, the windows provided the only means of ventilation. They could be cranked open to catch the passing breeze if there was one. Usually, the breeze carried more than just hoped for cool air. Michigan in the summer has more than its fair share of southwesterly breezes, since much of our weather comes from that direction in the summer. It also happened to be that the neighborhood chicken farmer lived slightly to the southwest of the church building and across Riverbend Street. It must have been hard for the janitor to

---

5    No. 345:1, in ibid.

decide which complaint he wanted to hear—the one about the heat after he closed the windows or the one about the smell when he left them open. Those who remember the heat in the pews of Hope church of those days can hardly forget the rivulets of sweat, the white shirts sticking to the pews, and the great appreciation for the wall fans that were installed later to bring some relief.

On July 23, 1973, the congregation of Hope approved the plans presented by the parsonage building committee to build a new parsonage across the parking lot to the north of the church at a cost of $40,680. $12,000 was to be raised by the sale of the Wilson Avenue parsonage. $6,180 was to be taken from the building fund, and $22,500 was to be financed through a bond for a ten-year period at 8 percent interest, which would amount to a monthly payment of $272.99. The new house was finished in March 1974, and Rev. Ronald Van Overloop and his family were the first occupants.

An open house was held for the congregation on May 2 to see the finished product. The sale of the old parsonage was made known throughout the denomination. Eventually, Hope school purchased the parsonage as a home for its administrator. The school retains ownership of it at the present time.

Ron Koole, administrator of Hope school, lives with his family
in the former Wilson Avenue parsonage.
From left: Zachary, Derek, Ron, Sherry, Austin, Emily

## The 1991 Church Remodel

When the church building on Ferndale was dedicated in 1965, there were 60 families, 317 members, and 120 catechumens. In 1991 the congregation was still growing after two daughter congregations had been started from the membership. This growth and also the need for accommodations for a physically handicapped member caused the congregation to make a decision to expand the narthex to more than double its original size. Air conditioning, two bathrooms, an elevator to access the basement, and a society room under the new narthex were added to the building.

John Kuiper on the right conferring with the workers

Ron Kuiper on the ladder with Fred Huizinga looking on

The addition of another and larger bathroom and an elevator was needed because of a specific event. On March 31, 1972, Kristina Moelker was born. She was the first member born into the congregation with a physical handicap known as cerebral palsy. When it was no longer possible for her to be carried or for her wheelchair to be carried to the basement for catechism, the building committee recommended the addition of a handicap accessible bathroom and an elevator.

We can learn this part of history from Kris' own memories of Hope church.

As a lifelong member of Hope church and the first member born with physical disabilities, I have many memories of attending worship services, Sunday school, catechism, and society with my fellow saints. I have not always used a wheelchair at church: Hope church has not always had a ramp outside the main entrance, and Hope church has not always had an elevator.

Until my teenage years, I was able to be carried and then with adult assistance stand and walk into church most of the time. Until we moved out of the "Hope ghetto" during the summer of 1999, there were many Sundays when my family would enjoy walking to and from church. My dad or mom pushed me in a stroller or a wheelchair on those Sunday morning and evening walks. Then we would leave the stroller or wheelchair in the coat room. At first my dad or mom would carry me to a pew; but later with their assistance and the help of special shoes and braces, I was able to stand up and walk to a pew.

During the summers when I was five or six years old, I started using a wheelchair when we walked to church. About that time, I think a ramp was installed. There was still one step up to the front porch, which I needed assistance with to walk up and down it or being wheeled up and down.

Over time it became more difficult for me to handle walking into church, and then sitting in a pew became a challenge.

Eventually a section of the last pew on both sides of the sanctuary was removed so I could sit in my wheelchair in the sanctuary. A few years ago, the entire back pew on the south side was removed to enable more people with special needs to sit comfortably in the sanctuary.

Kris Moelker

When the addition on the building was completed in 1991, I was excited. Since the ramp had been added on to, no longer did I have to tackle the front porch step. The elevator ended the days when I had to be lifted up and down the basement stairs in my wheelchair. I was able to use my power wheelchair at church! (Since then, there have been a few occasions when I and a heavy, power wheelchair have been carried down and up the stairs due a malfunctioning elevator.) There was also a wheelchair accessible restroom I could safely use!

2016 Hope church building

### Planning for the Future

Because of steady membership growth, overcrowding in the auditorium, and the continual need to use the basement for seating, the council decided in 2013 to appoint a special building expansion committee.

Part of the congregation worships in the basement each Sunday.

The committee was to investigate first all possibilities of expanding the present facility. The committee was also to look for a possible building site to purchase for a larger church edifice.

Recall again the early parts of this chapter. Hope has not forgotten the conviction of the men who founded the congregation to have an adequate meeting place. Hope does not regret the fact that its congregational life is virtually the same as when it began. Her strength has been, by God's grace, in her "sameness," still enjoying stability, believing that it is not something to be feared, and having a simple worship service with preaching at the center.

In all the agony of consideration in dealing with size, Hope church is much aware of the leading of God as he has caused her to consider again her calling to maintain a visible presence in the community at the bend in the river. By God's grace Hope church is given the continued calling to preach the pure doctrine of the call of the gospel by her presence in the river's bend to those outside as well as to new generations born within.

This brief history of the buildings used by the Hope congregation in the last one hundred years illustrates a material aspect of its presence in the river's bend. The church, called by the name of *Hope* existed when there was no formal meeting place. But from the very beginning of the Mission Station of Hope in 1916, there has been the desire to make the church called *Hope* a visible testimony that the people of God do not neglect the gathering of themselves together in public, corporate worship on the Lord's day. Although they used houses when necessary, the goal has always been to have a visible place in the world in which to worship the only true and living God. This has been done at great personal sacrifice. Recall once again the labor of love that went into the first church building and later a parsonage as well, only to lose them both and to go back to meeting in a school. Or recall the cold, drafty building without an adequate furnace when the congregation could have met in a member's house and have been more comfortable. But like the rebuilders of Jerusalem in Nehemiah's day those simple folk had "a mind to work" (Neh. 4:6). Recall their resolve when the congregation's finances were exhausted and they struggled to continue. Or recall the loss of the church building after 1924. They went forward confessing "hitherto hath the LORD helped us" (1 Sam. 7:12).

May God grant the coming generations the resolve to have a mind for the work as did the little congregation in the river's bend on January 23, 1916.

*Chapter 4*

~~～◦◦◦～~~

# Hope's Involvement in the Controversies of 1924–25 and 1953

*Prof. Herman Hanko*

## Introduction to the Controversies

Two major controversies concerning the truth of scripture created and shaped the Protestant Reformed Churches: the controversy concerning common grace versus particular grace and the controversy concerning an unconditional covenant verses a conditional covenant of God.

The first controversy concerned the question whether God gives his grace to every man or limits it to the elect. The second controversy concerned the question whether God sovereignly and unconditionally establishes and maintains his covenant with his elect, or whether God promises salvation to every baptized child and requires the child to fulfill certain conditions before he or she is incorporated into God's covenant and remains in it.

The first controversy resulted in the formation of the Protestant Reformed Churches. The second controversy split the Protestant Reformed denomination and resulted in the loss of about 60 percent of the denomination's membership.

It is not the purpose of this chapter to enter into all of details of the controversies and thoroughly discuss them. The Reformed Free Publishing Association has printed a number of books dealing with both

103

controversies, and the available literature is vast.

This chapter in *A Spiritual House Preserved*, a book that records for posterity the goodness of God toward Hope Protestant Reformed Church for one hundred years, will deal only with the involvement of Hope congregation in both controversies.

The roles of Hope church in those controversies demonstrate that God in his gracious providence gave to Hope church the right man at the right time to preserve the congregation from the deadly errors of universal grace and conditional theology.

One was a minister who was an eccentric, theological genius with twenty years of formal education. The other was a Dutch immigrant, a fiery, simple elder who never finished grade school, and a charter member of Hope church in whom the waters of sovereign grace ran deep.

All this is in no way intended to place Hope church in the fore-front of the battles in 1924–25 and in 1953. The major roles in the first controversy over common grace were played by Herman Hoeksema, minister of the Eastern Avenue Christian Reformed Church in Grand Rapids, Michigan, and Henry Danhof, minister of First Christian Reformed Church of Kalamazoo. Michigan. In 1953 other Protestant Reformed congregations, including First church in Grand Rapids, were very deeply involved in the struggles and even suffered a great deal more than Hope church in the split that followed. But in commem-orating the anniversary of Hope church, the part that she played is of immediate interest in this chapter.

## Early History of the Common Grace Controversy

We must go back to the history of the Christian Reformed Church in the late eighteen hundreds and the early nineteen hundreds to pick up the first distant rumblings of the thunder that would crash over Hope Christian Reformed Church.

God had sent two reformations to the Reformed churches in the Netherlands. Hendrik de Cock led the *Afscheiding* in 1834, which was composed chiefly of simple, poorly educated, but humbly pious

Christians. Abraham Kuyper led the *Doleantie* in 1886, which was composed chiefly of the more educated people in the Netherlands. Immigrants from both reformations came to America and most of them joined the Christian Reformed Church.

The seeds of what was to become the controversy that roared in Hope Christian Reformed Church and throughout the Christian Reformed denomination in 1924–25 were sown in those immigrations. Some people of the *Afscheiding* held to a grace of God that was common to all men. This grace was an attitude of kindness and love that God showed to all men, especially by his well-meant, gracious offer of the gospel. He showed his favorable and loving attitude toward all men in the preaching of the gospel, because the gospel told everyone who heard it that God loved them, wanted to save them, and wished them to believe in Christ so they could be saved. God even gave them grace to know that God was sincere and to believe the gospel if they chose. This notion left the final decision for salvation with man, who had to accept or reject God's earnest pleas.

The immigrants of the *Doleantie* disdained such a well-meant, gracious offer of salvation to everyone. But they were followers of Kuyper, who in his later reformatory work developed another and very strange idea of common grace. He gave common grace a different name in Dutch, because he opposed the view of the well-meant offer. Kuyper's idea of common grace was that God in his favor toward all men gave his Holy Spirit to all men. The Holy Spirit kept men from sinning as much as they wanted to and enabled totally depraved men to do good deeds that met with God's approval, although the men themselves were not regenerated and saved. Kuyper maintained that one could find an enormous amount of good among wicked men that mightily pleased God and that God and his church could use for God's purposes.

Why Kuyper developed a strange and novel idea of common grace remains something of a mystery. Earlier in his ministry he had vigorously and with complete faithfulness to scripture defended the truth of sovereign and particular grace in his book *Dat de Genade Particulier*

*Is.*[1] It is likely true that the explanation lies in Kuyper's resignation from the gospel ministry to take up a career in politics and in his need of Roman Catholic support to become prime minister of the Netherlands. His large treatise on common grace was probably his theological justification for that attempt.[2]

## The Struggle in America

The two groups of Christian Reformed members, some from the *Afscheiding* and others from the *Doleantie,* did not get along very well. I studied Dutch under a Calvin College professor, an ardent and passionate believer in Kuyper's view of common grace, who frequently spoke of the bitterness of the controversy. He often talked of a book he wanted to write in which he would expose the shenanigans and corrupt political maneuverings of the followers of De Cock. The controversy had the potential to split the church.

Ralph Janssen, a learned and popular professor of theology in Calvin Theological Seminary in the early 1900s. He was publicly criticized by four fellow professors for his teachings and was disciplined by the Christian Reformed synod of 1922.

Eventually the dispute over common grace had to be settled by synod. The opportunity for synod to deal with the matter arose in connection with the Ralph Janssen case in 1922. The history is of great importance.

Ralph Janssen was a gifted professor in Calvin Theological Seminary who attracted many students. He taught higher critical views of the Old Testament scriptures, denied miracles, repudiated the divine authorship of some books in the Old Testament, and held dubious views of creation and revelation. His colleagues in the seminary criticized his views, and eventually his views came for judgment before the synod.

---

1    The book in English translation is Abraham Kuyper, *Particular Grace: A Defense of God's Sovereignty in Salvation,* trans. Marvin Kamps (Grandville, MI: Reformed Free Publishing Association, 2001).

2    Abraham Kuyper, *De Gemeene Gratie* [Common grace] (Amsterdam: Höveker & Wormser, 1902–4).

**SYNOD CONFRONTS VEXING PROBLEMS**

Janssen Case and Question of Iowa Support of Calvin Among Issues.

**MEETS IN ORANGE CITY**

(by Staff Correspondent)

Orange City, Ia., June 11.—Christian Reformed biennial synod will hold its meeting this year in First Christian Reformed church of Orange City beginning next Wednesday morning. On its previous meeting Rev. W. P. VanWyk, pastor of Oakdale Park Christian Re-

**JANSSEN CASE NOT ENDED BY SYNOD'S DECISION, IS BELIEF**

Action Brings Widespread Comment Following Adjournment.

**PROFESSOR IN PROTEST**

Student Notes Unfair Basis for Condemnation He Charges.

**SYNOD STILL BUSY ON JANSSEN CASE**

Has Heated Debate on Doctrine in Church Periodicals.

**JANSSEN OUSTER PROTEST BRINGS BREEN TO TRIAL**

Christian Reformed Synod Investigating Deposed Professor's Backer.

The Rev. G. Breen, pastor of Twenty-fifth Street Christian Reformed church of Grand Rapids, perhaps the foremost of the upholders of the views of Prof. Ralph Janssen in regard to his dismissal and excommunication from the denomination, and now the subject of an investigation.

**JANSSEN AGAIN REFUSES TO APPEAR.**

Orange City, Ia., June 28.— Prof. Ralph Janssen of Calvin college refused Tuesday for the second time to defend himself against the charge of "heresy" made by some members of the Christian Reformed denomination. Rev. D. Krommínga, Janssen's defender, refused to act as advisor in the case unless given a declaration by synod in regard to the professor's refusal to appeal.

What made that an interesting and important part of the history of Hope church was that Janssen defended his views on the grounds of Kuyper's view of common grace. Janssen argued that because grace was given to all men, the Bible-denying views of the higher critics were correct, for those views were the fruit of common grace.[3]

A committee was appointed to study the matter and to bring a report with recommendations to synod. For one reason or another, the committee decided not to bring Janssen's defense of his views with an appeal to common grace to synod, but chose to judge his views on their own merits or lack thereof. The committee recommended condemning Janssen for his higher critical views, and synod adopted that advice. Rev. Hoeksema was on that committee, and he was the chief author of the report that synod adopted.

---

3  For a study of the relationship between the views of Ralph Janssen and the doctrine of common grace, see Herman Hanko, "A Study of the Relation between the Views of Prof. R. Janssen and Common Grace" (master's thesis, Calvin Theological Seminary, 1988).

Rev. Herman Hoeksema in his study when he was the minister
of Eastern Avenue Christian Reformed Church.

The Christian Reformed Church had many Janssen and Kuyper supporters who were furious with Rev. Hoeksema because of his key role in Janssen's condemnation. Subsequent history points to the almost certain fact that Janssen's supporters decided to do everything they could to get Herman Hoeksema out of the church. I say history points in that direction, because the church political errors that led to Hoeksema's condemnation were of such a kind that any genuinely Reformed church would be ashamed of them, not to speak of any worldly court of justice.[4]

## Ophoff's Early Conviction concerning Common Grace

My thesis is that Hope church played a major role in the controversy that resulted in the establishment of the Protestant Reformed Churches in general and in Hope as a Protestant Reformed church in particular. Hope played a major role in the common grace controversy because God had made George Ophoff her pastor in 1922.

---

4    On the history of the Janssen case in the Christian Reformed Church and its relation to the attacks on Hoeksema by the advocates of common grace, see Hoeksema, *Protestant Reformed Churches in America*, 17–26.

The history behind Rev. Ophoff's role has one interesting feature. He was not confronted with the issue of common grace for the first time when the Christian Reformed Church was on its way to ridding the church of the opponents of common grace. He had confronted the issue in his days as a student in Calvin Theological Seminary.

His son, Herman, tells the story.

People ask me sometimes, "How did your dad become acquainted with this whole thing of common grace?" He was four years behind Rev. Hoeksema in the...[Christian Reformed] seminary, and common grace was in its early years of discussion. It wasn't at that time yet accepted, because this was perhaps four years before...1924...When my dad was in the seminary, he was asked, as an assignment, to give a paper on the biblical proof of common grace. Now, no one really understood yet at that point just exactly the fine points of common grace. It was too early—it was in the discussion stage. So my dad accepted that. He too wanted to learn. So he went home that day from the seminary, and he struggled with that. He had to give that paper in two months. He struggled and struggled and struggled. He could not see where common grace could be "friendly," as he put it, with the scriptures. And he struggled till the time finally came that he had to give that paper. But he yet wasn't prepared. He was not at peace with it.

On the way to the meeting (it was kind of a large gathering—all the students), there was a serious thunderstorm. It was so serious that lightening hit the electrical system where they were meeting. The lights went out, and they stayed out.

Now, this sounds a little bit superstitious, but it isn't. The lights stayed out long enough that they dismissed to come back a month later.

Well, that gave my dad some extra time. You know, no matter where you turn, you see the hand of God in everything...

So he went back and struggled with that and struggled with that. Finally he woke up at three o'clock in the morning and got to thinking... Finally it dawned on him. He said, "I'm going to treat this as if there is no common grace." Then the light came on, and he built his whole paper opposing common grace.

Now here's the punch line. He got to that meeting finally, and the moderator (one of the professors) and all of the students were sitting there. He had to give his paper, but it was in opposition to common grace. Now it hadn't been accepted then yet, but nonetheless, there were some serious thoughts in that direction. When he got all through, it was quite clear, at least in his mind, [that] there could not possibly be the theory of common grace. The moderator of the meeting got up after [Dad] had done his speech, and said, "Are there any questions from the student body?" Well, there may have been, but the professor referred to the student body as "victims." "Are there any more victims?"

This was four years before meeting Rev. Hoeksema. [Dad's] mind was solidly stayed on the fact, through that experience, that there could not possibly be a common grace. And from there on he did not struggle with that any more. There was still the battle of denial—that is to say, of those that still adhered to and wanted the common grace theory...But his own personal battle was over, and he never again questioned even the remote possibility of there being a common grace.

Your grandfather [Rev. Hoeksema] had his own way of coming to that conclusion...He was in seminary (...four years ahead of my dad). But even that space is an important thing because they both did not leave the seminary at the same time. They both had their own time of preparation...

They didn't say, like two people meet after school, "Hey, I think we really got something here." No. That wasn't it. They didn't even know each other then. But Dad learned of your grandfather by his reputation and his writing[s]. He read those, and that added fuel to his conviction.[5]

---

5   Herman Ophoff, interview by Mark Hoeksema, March 24, 2008, "Interview with Herman Ophoff," *Beacon Lights* 75, no. 1 (January 2016):8–10.

## Involvement of Hope Church
## in the Common Grace Controversy

As far as I know there is no record of Hope church from her organization in 1916 to the ordination of Rev. Ophoff in 1922 that gives insight regarding the theory of common grace. One elder told me that before Rev. Ophoff came to Hope seminary students and professors preached for the congregation. Especially one professor was emphatic in his preaching on sovereign and particular grace, but none of the students or professors openly made an issue of the subject in the preaching.

Nor is there any record that Rev. Ophoff brought the subject into his preaching. But we may judge from subsequent events that the doctrines of sovereign and particular grace were preached. And the pastor clearly and boldly preached them, for when the issue finally confronted Hope Christian Reformed Church the members were aware of the issues and for the most part had made up their minds. Most of them stood with their pastor.

The issue of common grace was brought to the synod of the Christian Reformed Church in 1924 by protests against the preaching of Rev. Herman Hoeksema. In spite of many church political irregularities and errors, the synod took up the matter and adopted the well-known three points of common grace.[6]

From one point of view, the three points were a masterful product, for it combined into one decision the common grace of the gracious, well-meant offer of the gospel and the common work of the Holy Spirit that restrains sin in the unregenerated and gives him spiritual strength to do works that God can use in his own work. The three points settled the bitter controversy that raged in the Christian Reformed Church and that threatened to split it.

The three points were part of a sloppy and amateurish synodical decision on a crucially important doctrinal issue. Today some members of the Christian Reformed Church are critical of that decision. What is

---

6   For the history of the common grace controversy, see Hoeksema, *Protestant Reformed Churches*, 11–282. The three points are on pages 84–85.

significant for this chapter is that the synod did not warn against opposition to its decision and, in fact, called for further discussions of the
subject of common grace. Nor did synod require any form of discipline
against objectors but actually did the opposite: it defeated a motion to
discipline opponents of common grace.[7]

But classis did what synod refused to do. Classis Grand Rapids East
and Classis Grand Rapids West forced discipline against those who dis-
agreed with common grace. Classis Grand Rapids East took the lead
and required Rev. Hoeksema and his consistory to express agreement
with the doctrinal formulation of common grace made by synod or
face deposition. They were deposed, and because almost the whole
congregation supported its minister and consistory, they became part
of a new denomination, the Protestant Reformed Churches in America
that came into existence.

It was well-known that Rev. Ophoff, minister of Hope church, and
Rev. Henry Danhof, minister of First Christian Reformed Church of
Kalamazoo, also maintained that common grace was not biblical or
confessional. Rev. Ophoff had made his position clear by preaching
in Rev. Hoeksema's church, Eastern Avenue Christian Reformed, after
Rev. Hoeksema's deposition. Ophoff preached with the permission of
Hope's consistory and in defiance of what Classis Grand Rapids East
had done.

Furthermore, the men who knew and understood that common
grace was heresy and that its adoption spelled disaster for the church
had formed the Reformed Free Publishing Association. The association began the publication of the *Standard Bearer* with the first issue in
October 1924. This was done because the church papers of the Christian Reformed Church had been closed to Herman Hoeksema and
Henry Danhof to defend their positions against common grace.[8]

---

7    For the synodical decision, see ibid., 85–91.
8    For the history of the beginning of the Reformed Free Publishing Association and the
     publication of the *Standard Bearer*, see Henry Danhof and Herman Hoeksema, *For the
     Sake of Justice and Truth*, in *The Rock Whence We Are Hewn* (Jenison, MI: Reformed
     Free Publishing Association, 2015), 277–90.

Rev. Ophoff joined the association and became one of the faithful editors of the paper. He thus announced to the whole church world of his day that he wanted no part of common grace. He "heartily and openly espoused the cause of the truth as it was presented by Reverends H. Danhof and H. Hoeksema, and zealously defended it."[9] The defenders of Janssen's heresies and of common grace turned their sights toward Rev. Ophoff and his consistory and Rev. Henry Danhof and his consistory.

Classis Grand Rapids West convened on January 13, 1925. The work of the classis was without precedent and violated almost every rule of Reformed church polity and brotherly charity in the church of Christ. In all of the dealings of classis with the matter, it was obvious that the one goal, already decided, was to rid the church of any dissenters who dared to raise their voices against common grace.

There was no reason for classis to take up the matter, for no charges had been brought against Rev. Ophoff, no reasons for discipline had come before the body, and no charges of evil-doing on the part of Rev. Ophoff had come to classis. All that came to the floor were a few overtures from a few consistories, asking that classis require Rev. Ophoff and his consistory to express full agreement with the three points of common grace adopted by the synod of Kalamazoo in 1924.

An extensive correspondence resulted between the classis and Hope's consistory. The classis wanted only one thing: a statement from Hope's minister and elders that expressed their complete agreement with common grace. The consistory pointed out the church political errors and irregularities, as well as the doctrinal errors of common grace, but classis would not listen or even permit a discussion of those matters on the floor of its meetings. Without any discussion of the issues, without any opportunity to defend themselves, without any consideration at all of the arguments of the consistory, the classis said as it were, "Sign the three points of common grace or else!"

It was brutal, to say the least, for one's church, one's spiritual mother, to treat a child of her heart in such a way. To this day it remains

---

9    Hoeksema, *Protestant Reformed Churches*, 230.

a towering disgrace. One could only say with Joseph, "Ye thought evil against me; but God meant it unto good" (Gen. 50:20).

The *Grand Rapids Press* reported on and quoted from Rev. Ophoff's final word to classis. It is part of the annals of Hope Protestant Reformed Church and stands as a monument to the power of God's grace in one man, without whose testimony the congregation would not be celebrating its one-hundredth anniversary in 2016. Under the heading, "Ophoff Prefers Death: Local Pastor Tells Christian Reformed Body He Will Not Subscribe," the article reads in part:

### Pastor Is Confronted

The reply of Mr. Ophoff's consistory was judged by the committee to be definite enough to warrant specific recommendations among which was the advice that the pastor be confronted on the spot by Chairman William Stuart, pastor of Lagrave-av. Christian Reformed church, with the request that he conform to the synodical interpretation of the three points. Classis approved the committee report and Chairman Stuart presented the proposition to Mr. Ophoff.

Very evidently stung to the quick by the scant consideration the special committee gave the very carefully constructed reply from his consistory, Mr. Ophoff launched into an impassioned answer that left no doubt of where he stood. He stressed particularly the reference to his carefully worded document as one of "copious arguments."

Rev. Paul De Koekkoek of Comstock Park and Rev. H. J. Mulder of Burton Heights sought to temper the recommendations of the committee and give the pastor another day to consider his position. Mr. Ophoff rejected any suggestion of leniency… [and] begged for four minutes to make reply.…

"My soul is in a strange state," he began. "I am glad it has come to this, and yet I am sad. I am sad because the committee spurned my arguments. It was because the arguments were too deep for them. It was because they couldn't comprehend them. I declare, the arguments I gave are sound and the committee is afraid to meet them."

### *Defies the Classis*

"I am going to speak. I am going to preach. I am going to write as long as God gives me life and breath. If the classis will not hear the denomination will. Those copious arguments refuted the contention that the three points are fundamental and interpreted to be so by the synod. That is why they remain unanswered.

"Mr. President, if you were to place me before a gun to be shot or before me the three points to adhere to I would choose the former. I can't sign the three points. If I did I would be tearing the Bible into shreds. I would be stamping the Word under foot. I would be slapping God in the face."[10]

The committee took his reply under advisement, recommended deposition of Rev. Ophoff and his elders, and classis adopted the recommendation.

Rev. Ophoff described what took place between a committee of the Christian Reformed Church and his elders at Hope.

In the evening of our deposition, my consistory was invited to meet a committee of the classis. The invitation was accepted. The meeting took place. I, however, was barred. Until three o'clock in the morning that committee was at work with members of my consistory in the attempt to induce them to attach their signature[s] to the new doctrine. According to their own

---

10  *Grand Rapids Press*, January 23, 1925.

admission, their policy is one they term *dood-zwijgen* [dead silence]. In their private assemblies, behind the closed door, they are most bold. In public, however, they maintain a profound silence. The objective has been gained. He whom they hated—the Rev. H. Hoeksema—was gotten rid of.[11]

Spiritually and theologically, it was not an auspicious beginning for Hope Protestant Reformed Church when it was only a little over eight years old. The church had grown to about twenty-four families at the time of the troubles over common grace, and the deposition of Rev. Ophoff and his elders and the subsequent split in the congregation left the congregation with thirteen families. But the truth is more important than numbers, and the congregation felt deeply the words of Zechariah 4:10: "For who hath despised the day of small things?"

## Later Events in Hope Church

Hope church lost its church and parsonage to the Christian Reformed Church. The congregation met in Blair School, just across Kenowa from the church building and parsonage, while houses were rented for Rev. Ophoff and his family about six miles away in the area of John Ball Park in Grand Rapids, Michigan.

Blair School on Kenowa Avenue, showing in the background the church and parsonage Hope church lost to the Christian Reformed Church in 1925

---

11 George M. Ophoff, "The Way They Work," *Standard Bearer* 6, no. 5 (December 1, 1929):119.

One more event of interest should be included in this history. The event occurred in 1929, just before Rev. Ophoff left Hope church to become minister in Byron Center Protestant Reformed Church. I will let him tell the story.

On the last night of my catechetical labors in Hope, River Bend, it happened that as I approached the school house, where we were wont to assemble, I discovered a goodly number of my catechumens grouped about Rev. Vande Kieft (the pastor of the portion of my flock, who, at the time of the rupture continued as the Hope Christian Reformed Church at River Bend) in conversation. Having been notified of my arrival, the gathering broke up, and the aforesaid catechumens came to class. After the hour of instruction, they told me that Vande Kieft, in view of the fact that I was about to leave [Hope church for Byron Center] had sought to induce them to attend his catechism class. His argument was that they would be much benefited, as our instruction had been faulty, deficient, in that our thought-structure was of a kind from which the doctrine of human responsibility had been nearly crowded out by the doctrine of the council [sic] of God. By means of this outrageous piece of slander, Vande Kieft sought to destroy my catechumen's confidence in my instruction. Of course, they knew better and told him so, adding that, whereas he was addicted to the theory of common grace, they would have nothing of him as a catechism instructor.

Of course, the above-cited fiery dart cannot be one fabricated by Vande Kieft.

The point is that the argument, by which he sought to slay us, is an invention of those higher up—the H. J. Kuipers, the Berkhofs, and the G. Hoeksemas, and the like. Vande Kieft was merely repeating what he had heard, and thus acting the part of a sort of parrot...When my catechumens let him know that, whereas the theory of common grace is also his, they would not be able to receive his instruction, Vande Kieft, wonderful to say, assured them that in their presence he would forever refrain from as much as broaching the hated subject.

My readers, let this spectacle capture your imagination. To begin with, the contemplated scheme was as dark as the night under whose cover it was being executed. The appeal was made, further, behind the back of the shepherd whose flock was being assailed. The shepherd was being stabbed in the back, and the weapon used, a piece of slander hatched out under the impulse of a powerful grudge. In his zeal to attach to his person the coveted sheep, Vande Kieft did not recoil from denying the very doctrine which he is duty bound to publicly defend. Such are his methods...

Having heard what had happened, I resolved to pay Vande Kieft a visit immediately. I did so, taking with me my catechumens. We knocked at Vande Kieft's door and were admitted. I called his attention to the charges he had lodged against us. He admitted that these charges had been made. Thereupon I offered to debate with him the issues at stake in the presence of my catechumens. He refused, saying that I was no gentleman. My insistence that his conduct of the night out of doors had been that of a crook had offended him. Thereupon we left, after assuring him that our one source of comfort in the present situation is the knowledge of the approach of the judgment day, that, further, we would dread to be standing in his shoes, then, and in the shoes of that clique responsible for our deposition...[12]

Apparently, the story became public knowledge with the additions, inaccuracies, and false charges that accompany such stories. Rev. Ophoff had set the record straight and then concluded with the following:

---

12  Ophoff, "The Way They Work," 118–19.

Why do we place this article? Because our experiences with Vande Kieft have become the talk of many. Let such know what actually happened. Because, in the second place, Vande Kieft's methods are typical of that group to which he belongs[13]

Rev. Henry D. Vande Kieft, minister in Hope Christian Reformed Church from 1927 to 1934. At the time he tried to recruit Hope's catechumens, he lived across the street from Blair School in the parsonage Hope church had lost to the Christian Reformed Church in 1925. Rev. Ophoff was living in Grand Rapids about six miles away.

Without the courage and faithfulness of Hope's pastor, consistory, and young people, there would not be a Hope Protestant Reformed Church today. While the pastor and consistory are now in heaven, our calling is to be faithful to the truth for which they fought and suffered.

Although Hope was then a small struggling congregation, the split reduced it to thirteen families. But no one in the congregation thought the price was too great to maintain the truth of God's sovereign and particular grace.

## Introduction to the
## Conditional Covenant Controversy

The second major controversy that involved the Protestant Reformed Churches was the conditional covenant controversy that took place from about 1948 to 1953.[14] It was a battle against the false doctrine of a conditional covenant and for the gospel of grace with specific reference to the covenant of God.

This controversy affected Hope church, as it did all Protestant Reformed churches. Hope played an important role in the outcome of the controversy. It is an important part of God's work through the congregation that is worth knowing, and it is part of Hope's heritage that we ought not to forget.

---

13  Ophoff, "The Way They Work," 119.
14  For the history of this controversy, see David J. Engelsma, *Battle for Sovereign Grace in the Covenant: The Declaration of Principles* (Jenison, MI: Reformed Free Publishing Association, 2013).

Knowledge of some of the background to the controversy will help us understand it and appreciate its importance.[15]

After the struggles, sufferings, and hardships of 1924 and the formation of the Protestant Reformed Churches, the flag flown above the denomination that marked its identity had on it the words "the greatness of God's sovereign and particular grace." Those words identified the denomination's chief characteristic and told the world God's truth for which it stood.

Strangely enough, less than twenty-five years after the denomination was formed, some in the denomination wanted to pull down the flag and write on it "God's conditional salvation," and thus make the Protestant Reformed Churches an entirely different denomination—one that flatly opposed the truth expressed in the first flag, for conditional salvation is the opposite of salvation by sovereign and particular grace.

The event that gave momentum to the movement was a visit to the United States by the Dutch theologian, Dr. Klaas Schilder. I knew him.

Klaas Schilder, founding father of the Reformed Churches in the Netherlands (liberated) and proponent of a conditional covenant

He stayed at our house. I saw him, talked with him, smelled the smoke of his cigars, admired his paunch, and was amazed at his enjoyment of a glass of wine. I understood nothing he said in Dutch, for his speech sounded to my seventeen-year-old ears like a man talking with a mouthful of hot potatoes.

He was an extremely influential theologian whose teachings can still be heard in countless churches around the world. Sad to say, he also influenced many Protestant Reformed ministers and people.

---

15 For the preliminary history to the schism of 1953 and the history of the schism, see Herman Hanko, *For Thy Truths Sake: A Doctrinal History of the Protestant Reformed Churches* (Grandville, MI: Reformed Free Publishing Association, 2000), 277–315.

"Protestant Reformed ministers...who defend[ed] the covenant doctrine of Klass Schilder...had become enamored
of this doctrine of the covenant at least in part by the per-
suasive presentation of if by Schilder...In the fall of 1947,
at the invitation of the Protestant Reformed Churches, he
had spoken on the covenant at conferences with Protestant
Reformed ministers, he had preached his covenant conception in the churches, and he won them over by personal
conversations."[16] —Prof. David J. Engelsma

One of the more interesting aspects of the whole controversy was
its relationship to the truth of God's covenant. It is not an exaggeration
to say that the doctrine of the covenant lay at the heart of the Protestant Reformed Churches' emphasis on sovereign and particular grace.
It came under fierce attack in those years of controversy.

The truth of God's sovereign grace in the establishment and maintenance of God's covenant was in the process of being developed by
Protestant Reformed ministers, officebearers, and people, for advances
in doctrine are made as Christ's Spirit leads the whole church, organically, into the truth. While the truth of God's covenant was being
developed among Protestant Reformed people, it was basically an
"old" doctrine in the Reformed churches in Europe and particularly
in the Netherlands since the sixteenth-century Reformation. All those
theologians who held without compromise to God's sovereign and particular grace also held to a covenant and a salvation that God works as
his own work without conditions.

Schilder wanted conditions, preached conditions, emphasized
conditions, and influenced others to take his side in that centuries-old
conflict. Conditions or no conditions: that was the heart of the controversy that filled the pages of the church papers and occupied discussions
in consistory rooms and peoples' homes.

The question was crucial. It involved not only the integrity of the

---

16  Engelsma, *Battle for Sovereign Grace*, 20.

Canons of Dordt; it was not only a battle in the Protestant Reformed Churches between sovereign grace or rank Arminianism; but also, at bottom, it was a battle over whether the Protestant Reformed Churches had the right to exist as separate churches. Were the spiritual fathers of these churches right in their denial of common grace, and was God pleased that those spiritual fathers formed a new denomination rather than submit to a destructive heresy? I may put it differently: is the truth of an unconditional covenant sufficiently important for one to be willing to be shot by a firing squad rather than to deny it? Common grace was, in Rev. Ophoff's opinion, such an issue. Conditional theology is equally important.

## Form of the Conditional Covenant Controversy

In these questions just asked and answered, I have done more than compare common grace and a conditional covenant with each other *as far as their importance for the Protestant Reformed Churches* is concerned. I also have claimed that the issues over which these churches were split in 1953 were basically the same issues as in 1924. Common grace—especially the main point of the first point, the well-meant, gracious offer of the gospel—is identical to a general, conditional covenant. A well-meant offer and a general promise are characterized by one difference: the general promise is limited to baptized babies; a well-meant offer concerns everyone who hears the gospel. A general promise claims that God promises salvation to every baby at the moment of baptism; a well-meant offer claims that God promises salvation to everyone who hears the preaching.

It will be worthwhile to compare the two errors, in order to grasp the connection between 1924 and 1953.

Common grace teaches that God wants everyone to be saved; a general promise at baptism states that God wants every baptized baby to be saved.

Common grace teaches that God loves all men without regard to election and reprobation; a general promise to all baptized children teaches that God loves all babies who are baptized regardless of election and reprobation.

Common grace teaches that Christ died for all men; a general promise at baptism teaches that Christ died for all the children of believers who are baptized, because God cannot promise to anyone a salvation never earned by Christ.

Common grace teaches that God gives grace to all men so they have the spiritual ability to accept or reject God's expression of his desire to save them; a general promise at baptism teaches that every baptized child receives grace to accept or reject God's promise.

Common grace teaches that many are not saved because they reject God's expression of love for them and his merciful longing to save them; a general promise teaches that some baptized children are not saved because they reject God's promise to save them.

That is, in both cases, the saved have met the conditions God lays down for salvation; while the unsaved have failed to meet the necessary conditions to be saved. In other words, God has done everything he can to save everyone he addresses with the gospel, but man has the deciding vote.

It is not so surprising, therefore, that when the whole matter made its way to the higher ecclesiastical assemblies of the Protestant Reformed Churches, it came in a way that identified the well-meant offer of the gospel with God's general promise to all. Both speak of a general promise, the one in baptism and the other in the preaching.

## History of the Conditional Covenant Controversy

At the 1950 synod of the Protestant Reformed Churches, which met in Hull, Iowa, the denominational mission committee requested synod "to draw up a form that may be used by those families requesting organization into a Prot. Ref. congregation. We believe that this would serve to remove all misunderstanding and aid toward unity."[17] In response to that request for a "form," synod drew up "A Brief Declaration of Principles of the Protestant Reformed Churches."[18] This document specifically and completely proved from scripture and the Reformed

---

17  *Acts of Synod, Protestant Reformed Churches of America, 1950,* 54.
18  Ibid., 83.

confessions that the salvation of the elect in general and the establishment of the covenant of grace in particular were unconditional works of God that required no assisting contribution from man, but were gifts freely and graciously given through Jesus Christ only to the elect. Thus the promise of salvation that God announced in the preaching and in the sacrament of baptism was made only to God's elect.[19]

"George M. Ophoff, with his colleague in the Protestant Reformed seminary, Herman Hoeksema, was the main proponent and defender of the Declaration and its theology of the covenant. The fiery Ophoff was, if anything, a fiercer foe of the theology of a conditional covenant than was Hoeksema."[20]
—Prof. David J. Engelsma

The provisional adoption of this important document by the synod of 1950 raised a storm of protests in the churches. Emerging from this storm in April 1951 was a lone voice in the cacophony: Rev. Hubert De Wolf in a sermon preached on Luke 16:19-31 in First church. In that sermon Rev. De Wolf made public that he stood on the side of conditionality. He said, "God promises every one of you that, if you believe, you will be saved."[21]

Rev. Hubert De Wolf

The statement was cleverly worded so that it sounded Reformed. If De Wolf had said, "God promises salvation in Jesus Christ to everyone who believes," he would have taught what Canons 2.5 teaches: "Moreover, the promise of the gospel is that whosoever believeth in Christ crucified shall not perish, but have everlasting

---

19  See Declaration of Principles of the Protestant Reformed Churches, in *Confessions and Church Order*, 412–431. For a "Brief Commentary on the Declaration of Principles of the Protestant Reformed Churches," see Engelsma, *Battle for Sovereign Grace*, 221–267.
20  Engelsma, *Battle for Sovereign Grace*, 60.
21  *Acts of Synod, 1954*, 54.

life."[22] Even if he had said, "God promises salvation to all believers," he would not have erred. His error lay in those few, seemingly innocent words, "every one of you." By those words De Wolf meant, "Every one of you here tonight, believers and unbelievers alike, as well as everyone everywhere who hears the gospel, has God's promise." But, De Wolf also meant to say, "You will not be saved, even if God promises you salvation unless you fulfill the condition of faith." The statement was calculated to deceive, and it successfully deceived many.

In September 1952 from the same pulpit, Hubert De Wolf made clear what he meant. In a preparatory sermon on Matthew 18:3 he said, "Our act of conversion is a prerequisite to enter into the kingdom."[23]

The words were different from his earlier statement, but the meaning was the same. Instead of salvation in general, De Wolf preached about the specific blessing of being in the kingdom of Christ. Instead of making faith the condition to salvation, he made "our act of conversion" the condition for entrance into the kingdom. Man has to fulfill the condition of becoming like a little child before he can claim citizenship in the kingdom of Christ. Both teach a conditional salvation. Both make salvation dependent on what man does. God is dependent on man to fulfill his purpose in Christ.

These statements became the topics of a two-year debate in the consistory of First Protestant Reformed Church where Hubert De Wolf was a member. In the spring of 1953 the whole matter was finally brought to classis for adjudication.

## Hope's Role in the Conditional Covenant Controversy

At this point Hope Protestant Reformed Church became decisively involved in the controversy. I do not mean to imply that before that Hope church had stood on the sidelines with nothing to say and with a determined effort to keep the controversy outside its church doors. The very opposite was true. Hope's pastor was Rev. John Heys, who in

---

22  Canons 2.5, in *Confessions and Church Order*, 163.

23  *Acts of Synod, 1954*, 54.

his own right was a gifted instructor and able preacher, who also wrote in the *Standard Bearer.* At every occasion Rev. Heys vigorously fought against conditional salvation and gave sound, positive instruction from the pulpit, in the catechism classes, on family visitation, and in his writings about the truths of sovereign and particular grace. It was evident from the passion with which he spoke and wrote that he was determined to "go down fighting" if necessary for the cause of the truth. He guided the congregation through a critical time in its history. Obviously, Hope church was caught up in the controversy and deeply affected by it.

However, I am referring to the more decisive action of the classis that settled the issues once and for all.

At the beginning of this chapter I mentioned that Hope's involvement in the common grace controversy was primarily through a learned, educated, and articulate minister of the gospel and professor of Old Testament.

Much of Hope's involvement in the conditional covenant controversy was through a relatively uneducated immigrant, a fiery, red-headed man who never reached five feet seven inches and never attained 150 pounds. Yet he knew from personal experience what it meant to fight for the truth and to be faithful to it at any cost. He had been an elder in 1925 and had been deposed from office by Classis Grand Rapids West along with Rev. Ophoff. He had served many terms as elder in Hope church and was elder there when I took up ministerial labors in Hope in 1955, as well as in subsequent years. I think Richard Newhouse did not realize that all his life God had been preparing him for the major role he would play in the controversy of 1953. If he had thought about it at all, I know he would have regretted his lack of education and his humble and poor upbringing.

Richard Newhouse.

But God uses men of his choice. He calls them by Christ, the head of the church, and qualifies them to work in the kingdom. Richard Newhouse knew and understood and, more importantly, loved the Reformed faith with all its emphasis on God and his glory. I do not know how many times in my stay at Hope church he quoted to me, in Dutch, what seemed to be his favorite scriptural passage: "For my thoughts are not your thoughts, neither are your ways my ways, saith the LORD" (Isa. 55:8). He was curt and blunt—some would say he had no love—with those who befuddled people with sweet and ambiguous talk that took away the sharpness of the truth. He could cut a man off with a stinging rebuke. He did not know the niceties of diplomatic and tactful speech.

In the providence of God, Richard Newhouse was delegated to the meeting of Classis East at which the protests of Rev. H. Hoeksema and Rev. G. M. Ophoff against their consistory (First Protestant Reformed Church) in the De Wolf matter would be decided. In the providence of God, Newhouse was appointed to serve on the committee of preadvice that would study De Wolf's statements and bring recommendations to classis. The committee was composed of five members: Rev. Edward Knott, Rev. George Lubbers (brother of Elder Peter Lubbers), Rev. Richard Veldman, Elder Peter Lubbers, and Elder Richard Newhouse.

It did not take long in the committee meeting for Elder Newhouse to sense which way the wind was blowing. The three ministers were intent on justifying De Wolf's statements by excruciatingly painful verbal legerdemain. The ultimate recommendations that the three minsters submitted to classis were longer than the sermon in which De Wolf's statements had been made.[24]

Elder Newhouse saw that the ministers were going in the wrong direction, and he informed the committee that he was leaving the deliberations, because he had heard nothing with which he could agree. He left the committee, and Elder Lubbers soon followed. It was two elders against three ministers.

---

24  The report was forty pages long and can be found in Herman Hanko, *For Thy Truth's Sake: A Doctrinal History of the Protestant Reformed Churches* (Grandville, MI: Reformed Free Publishing Association, 2000), 481–501.

"We...cannot agree with the necessity nor with the contents of the long document which precedes the advice given by the other members of our committee. Neither can we sign the advice that they have drawn up."[25] —R. Newhouse and P. Lubbers

The report of the two elders was just a bit longer than one page. They had written it with the assistance of Rev. Heys, and it was adopted by classis. The key words of the report were "both...statements are literally heretical regardless of what the Rev. De Wolf meant by them, regardless of how he explains them."[26] It was the expression of the two elders in their firm convictions that the grace of God is unconditional and given to the elect only.

Peter Lubbers

Their report was also an act of courage—of the courage of faith. Two elders—one a brother of a minister on the committee, and the other, a poorly educated farmer—dared to stand against three ministers of much learning. They dared to take a stand against men educated and ripened in the ministry of the gospel by constant study of Reformed theology. The elders did not have the wherewithal to draw up a minority report, but they knew the truth. They were willing to stand for it. God used them to vindicate his truth and to preserve it in the Protestant Reformed Churches.

It is the end of the story. The classical decision forced ministers, office-bearers, churches, and members to take a stand for or against sovereign grace. The churches were split: two denominations emerged. The one, defenders of conditional theology, went back to the Christian Reformed Church where they found a theology more congenial to their own.

---

25  R. Newhouse and P. Lubbers, "[Minority] Report of the Committee of Pre-advice in Re Protests of the Revs. H. Hoeksema and G. M. Ophoff against the Consistory of First Church," in ibid., 502. See the report in appendix 5.

26  Ibid.

Although in the years between 1925 and 1953 the congregation of Hope had grown to about forty families, it shrunk again in size. About fifteen families left; the congregation was brought down to about twenty-five families, although a few other families also joined the church shortly after the split. But as was always true and remains true today, it is better to be small and faithful to the truth than large and apostate. No price is too great to pay for the sake of God's truth.

Hope Protestant Reformed Church and the denomination to which she belongs were kept faithful by elders who were not afraid of men and feared God. Except for their godly courage, Hope would not be celebrating its one-hundredth anniversary in 2016. In God's mercy toward us we praise him for his faithfulness. May our covenant God give us a deep sense of thankfulness for men whom he sent to the church to preserve his truth, so that we, their children, may fight as they did for the great glory of our sovereign God.

# Chapter 5

~⌒◯◯⌒~

# Perspectives of Hope's Former Ministers

## Editor's Introduction

Our Lord Jesus Christ is the king of the church. As king he sends his messengers to bring his good news to his church. According to his sovereign rule King Jesus has faithfully provided for his spiritual house at Hope the ministers we have needed, when we have needed them. During Hope's one-hundred-year history, there also have been times of vacancy in our pulpit. We know that these times too were according to his sovereign good pleasure and in his love for Hope. In thankfulness we review in this chapter God's faithfulness to Hope in his provision of twelve former undershepherds to lead us in the green pastures of his word.

In the following pages Hope's former ministers provide biographical sketches and perspectives of their ministries at Hope. For the former pastors who are now in the church triumphant, we have employed the capable services of others to fulfill this task. Their names are written under the titles of their contributions.

The timeline below provides the order of these biographical sketches as well as the times when Hope's pulpit was vacant.

| | |
|---|---|
| 1916 to 1922 | Vacant |
| 1922 to 1929 | Rev. George Ophoff |
| 1929 to 1936 | Vacant |
| 1936 to 1940 | Rev. Hubert De Wolf |

| | |
|---|---|
| 1940 to 1941 | Vacant |
| 1941 to 1955 | Rev. John A. Heys |
| 1955 to 1963 | Rev. Herman Hanko |
| 1963 to 1966 | Rev. Herman Veldman |
| 1966 to 1970 | Rev. Jason Kortering |
| 1970 to 1972 | Vacant |
| 1972 to 1979 | Rev. Ronald Van Overloop |
| 1979 to 1981 | Vacant |
| 1981 to 1986 | Rev. Richard Flikkema |
| 1986 to 1995 | Rev. James Slopsema |
| 1995 to 1996 | Rev. Russell Dykstra |
| 1996 to 1997 | Vacant |
| 1997 to 2010 | Rev. James Laning |
| 2010 to 2013 | Vacant |
| 2013 to the present | Rev. David Overway |

## Rev. George Martin Ophoff

### Prof. Herman Hanko

Although there are a few members of Hope Protestant Reformed Church whose relatives knew Rev. Ophoff as their pastor, there are no current members who were old enough at that time to remember much about his ministry in Hope church. Since I knew him as one of my professors in the Protestant Reformed seminary, I was asked to write about his ministry in Hope church. I studied under Rev. Ophoff about thirty years after he served as pastor in Hope.

Compared with the violence found in the nations today, the times during which Rev. Ophoff served Hope church were relatively quiet. World War I had ended in 1918. However, not all was well in the world. Germany—angry that the country was under the heavy yoke of the Treaty of Versailles that had concluded World War I—was beginning to stir in preparation for another war. Hitler, the chief engineer of World War II, was starting his rise to power, although it would be several years before he attempted to expand his empire.

Life in the 1920s was not plagued with modern inventions. Horse and buggy were the preferred means of transportation within a given locale. Electricity could be found in the cities, but not in the country. Radio had been invented but was available to only a few people. The rutted dirt and sand roads around River Bend were suitable for horse and buggy, but useless for cars most of the year.

"Sand" Road.

Sand Road (Butterworth Drive)

No nearby bridge spanned the Grand River. The only way to travel to Grand Rapids from River Bend was the approximately eight-mile trip to the bridge over the Grand River on Wealthy Street. The trip was so long that those who came to minister to the new congregation of Hope arrived on Saturday and returned to town on Monday.

During the pastorate of Rev. Ophoff, Hope was a small, rural church established in River Bend six years before Rev. Ophoff was ordained as its first pastor. Rev. Ophoff came to Hope congregation with his wife, Jane, after his graduation in 1921 from Calvin Theological Seminary in Grand Rapids, Michigan. Hope church was Rev. Ophoff's first charge.

## OPHOFF IS INSTALLED
## BY RIVERBEND CHURCH

Candidate George M. Ophoff, who successfully passed his examination before Classis Grand Rapids West last week, was installed as pastor of Hope Christian Reformed church at Riverbend Thursday afternoon. Three pastors took part in the services.

Rev. J. Wyngaarden of Walker preached the ordination sermon; Rev. E. J. Tanis, pastor of Bates-st. Christian Reformed church, read the form, and Rev. J. R. Brink, home missionary for Classes Grand Rapids East and West, charged the congregation.

Mr. Ophoff will be the first pastor of the church, which was organized six years ago. A new church edifice was built two years ago and a new parsonage has just been completed.

A notice in the *Grand Rapids Press* dated January 26, 1922, announced Ophoff's ordination and installation as Hope's first minister.

The new minister had met and married Jane Boom during his seminary training. They moved into a new parsonage on Riverbend Street and took up their labors in Hope church.

Jane Boom 1920

George Ophoff, seminary graduation 1921

Today Hope members, John and Ashley Cleveland and their children,
live in the former Hope parsonage on Riverbend Street.
Back from left: Olivia, John, Ashley, Emily; front: Isaac, Evan, Emmitt, Ian

For Rev. Ophoff it was the beginning of a life's work. Perhaps most of his early life he had looked forward to that moment. It is certain that he had never seriously considered any other vocation. His heart had been set on the gospel ministry for years. There had been hardships and interruptions of his schooling along the way. There had been times when the goal seemed unreachable and years when he wondered whether the Lord had really called him to the gospel ministry. But the time had come for him to assume his labors as a pastor of one flock in the sheepfold of Christ.

Taking up his work in the peace and quiet of a small, rural church was part of the preparation that the Lord would use for a far greater work.

> "Rev. Ophoff would come over to our place on the farm and visit us on Monday mornings, since he wanted to talk with my old grandmother and see how his sermons were coming across." —Dewey Engelsma

Rev. Ophoff showed already in those early years the character traits that remained with him all his life. They soon became obvious to those who knew him. Even before the issue of common grace was on the agenda of the Christian Reformed Church, Ophoff was wholly committed to the truth of sovereign and particular grace. He had a bulldog-like tenacity, which served him well in the theological battles of 1924–25, but was sometimes an obstacle to close fellowship with the members of his congregation. When his mind was engaged in some activity or in theological studies, he was completely oblivious to what was going on around him. This included the passing of time. He was often late for scheduled engagements and frequently could not get to the pulpit by the time worship services began. Sometimes as people were arriving at church and it was nearly time to start the service, they saw Rev. Ophoff heading for the outside privy without his dress shirt and with his suspenders hanging. When he was on time and came to the consistory room, he frequently engaged in such heated conversations with one or more of the elders that their voices could be heard in the auditorium and the time to enter the auditorium was forgotten. When these discussions spilled over into the normal time to start worship, a brave man from the congregation would leave his seat, knock on the consistory room door, and shout, "It's time, brothers." When the consistory members became impatient with their pastor's tardiness in arriving at church, an elder would start the services without him. This did not please the minister, but it did solve the problem, at least for a few weeks.

Rev. Ophoff never hedged with words and sometimes spoke vehemently when he should not have done so. The consistory minutes record an instance when the elders reprimanded him for saying something better left unsaid. When he did wrong, he apologized for what he had done, thus showing that he was a humble man. One of Rev. Ophoff's most ardent admirers confided to me that Rev. Ophoff sometimes overdid his apologies. Yet no one could ever doubt the meaning of what he said, for he was straight to the point and blunt.

A reading of the consistorial minutes of those years indicates that the congregation under his ministry was a soundly Reformed congregation that showed the three marks of a true church. Rev. Ophoff faithfully preached the word of God, and there is no trace in the minutes of any dissatisfaction with his preaching. Catechism classes were held regularly, and the children and the young people were well taught. Family visitation was carried on, and the reports of visits were made to the consistory and duly recorded in the minutes. Problems in the congregation were dealt with firmly. Consistorial committees were appointed to deal with problems.

> "Rev. Ophoff said [something] in a sermon [that] made an impression on me. When I was about eleven or twelve years old, I looked at myself and thought, 'I'm kind of pretty.' Well, one Sunday Rev. Ophoff had a sermon on the devil. Sitting there in church, all of sudden I heard him say, 'You look like the devil, and you act like the devil.' I thought, 'I can never think of myself as being someone important.' He sure put me down. But that's how he was." —Johanna Bomers

In those days small, rural, Dutch communities were often outside the reach of the law and the courts, except in cases of major crimes. The result was that property disputes and financial disagreements were often brought to the consistory for adjudication. If these types of complaints would come before a consistory today, the elders would rebuke those involved with the words of Jesus when a man wanted Jesus to force the man's brother to divide their father's inheritance: "Man, who made me a judge or a divider over you?…Beware of covetousness."

One example of such a disagreement is a member of the congregation who loaned a team of horses to a fellow member for a duly-agreed price. At the end of the month, the member returned the horses, and the farmer who had loaned the team of horses demanded payment. The borrower refused payment on the grounds that the team was not used every day of the month. He also insisted that the negotiated price was too high because he had used the horses only half the time, and when he was not using them he had to feed them and shelter them in his barn. The case went on for a year and was finally resolved after repeated visits by a committee of elders. The amount of money at issue was $5.

The consistory had to deal with some difficult problems. One problem was that the older and mature baptized members refused to make confession of faith because they were not assured of their salvation. That problem was more or less found in many Christian Reformed congregations. I am convinced that the problem was the result of a faulty conception of God's covenant. Although the consistory labored mightily to instruct the people on that matter, it was not until the Reformed doctrine of the covenant was developed and taught in the Protestant Reformed Churches that the problem was solved.

Another problem was poor church attendance on the part of a few members who gave the elders various reasons or excuses for their negligence. The consistory labored patiently and faithfully with those members. But the consistory would not indefinitely allow poor church attendance and when necessary placed such people under censure.

It is interesting to note in the minutes that the first part of the Form for the Administration of the Lord's Supper, which deals with self-examination, was read the Lord's day before the Lord's supper—as is still done in some Protestant Reformed churches today.

Rev. Ophoff was extremely busy during his years in Hope.

After the split in 1924 Rev. Ophoff continued to labor fruitfully with the flock that remained. The congregation lost the parsonage as well as the church, so Rev. Ophoff had to move his family to other locations. The first residence was 1925 Watson Street, just off Butterworth Drive, in the vicinity of John Ball Park. The second residence was 1100 Jackson Street.

During those years three sons—Fred, George, and Herman—were born to Rev. Ophoff and his wife, Jane. Edward, a fourth son was born in 1930.

After his expulsion from the Christian Reformed Church in 1925, Rev. Ophoff taught Wednesdays and Fridays in the Protestant Reformed seminary. He concentrated on Hebrew and Old Testament subjects and also taught church polity, church history, and practice preaching. This required enormous amounts of time, for his insistence on sovereign and particular grace required him to develop his subjects from entirely different viewpoints than were common in the Christian Reformed denomination and seminary. Belief in common grace or a denial of it makes a considerable difference in one's approach to teaching seminary subjects.

Since the bridge in Grandville across the Grand River had not been built, Rev. Ophoff had to travel to the seminary in First Protestant Reformed Church in Grand Rapids via Butterworth Avenue (Sand Road) and Fulton Street.

Rev. Ophoff was also a regular contributor to the *Standard Bearer* magazine, which was begun in 1924 by the Reformed Free Publishing Association. For a while, he and Rev. Hoeksema filled nearly the entire paper.

All these obligations had to be worked into the life of an already busy pastor. The habit of long hours and little sleep stayed with him and his colleague all their lives.

Rev. Ophoff left Hope church in 1929 to take up congregational labors in Byron Center Protestant Reformed Church. He continued to write and to teach in the seminary. He became emeritus in 1959 and died on June 12, 1962.

Prof. George M. and Jane Ophoff, circa 1955

I have often looked back on my years as a professor in the Protestant Reformed seminary and pondered the influence of Rev. Hoeksema and Rev. Ophoff on me and my life as a pastor and seminary professor.

There can be no doubt that the teaching of Rev. Hoeksema gave me all the fundamentals of Reformed theology as they are found in Reformed theologians from John Calvin through Herman Bavinck and Abraham Kuyper to the theological genius of Rev. Hoeksema. But more importantly, he instilled in my heart a deep love for theology in general and for a theology that was in every respect God-centered. He made the study of theology an exciting adventure. I cannot repay that debt.

I recall that Rev. Ophoff did not make giant strides in the progress of a seminary course.

A recollection from Rev. Cornelius Hanko is that "the seminary students spent more time at Mount Sinai than the children of Israel did."

Rev. Ophoff was not known for systematic instruction. However, by his own methodical treatment, he taught his students how to exegete the Old Testament scriptures. The basic scheme used in the *Unfolding Covenant History* series came from him.[1] Rev. Ophoff divided all Old Testament history into six dispensations. In each dispensation God revealed, or unfolded, to his people additional truths of his covenant established with Christ and the elect in Christ. As far as I know, his work of explaining the whole of Old Testament history in the light of God's covenant, revealed first in the "mother promise" of Genesis 3:15, was original with him.

Rev. Ophoff also left two indelible marks on me that remain to this day.

---

1    *Unfolding Covenant History* is a series of books published by the Reformed Free Publishing Association that explains Old Testament history. Five volumes are completed. They cover creation through the history of Ruth.

One is so important that one ought not to be a minister of the gospel without it. It is a total and all-consuming love for and determination to defend the Reformed faith in everything one does. Ophoff and his colleague, Rev. Hoeksema, gave themselves totally to the ministry of the gospel of Jesus Christ. They spent themselves in their callings.

The other mark Ophoff left on me was of a different kind. I cannot speak for the other students, for I never talked with them about it and only came to appreciate it gradually. For some inexplicable reason Rev. Ophoff would not, at certain times, speak on the topic of the lesson he and we had prepared for; but he would launch out on a subject that was totally unconnected with anything we were studying. Such off-the-cuff speeches were more like reminiscences or spells of thinking aloud and were completely spontaneous and unprepared.

I am sure they were the fruit of hours and hours of thought on the part of the professor, but they held me spellbound. I was so completely absorbed in what he said that I did not even remember to take notes—much to my regret. But to this day I can quote almost verbatim large sections of those extemporaneous thoughts.

The strange part of it is that Rev. Ophoff, who was naive to the extreme in personal contacts with people, had a profound understanding of human nature in general—human nature created good, human nature fallen, and human nature redeemed. In all my reading and studying in this area, I have never, not anywhere, found anything approaching those "talks." Such subjects as the psychological aspects of hardening, the operations of the human conscience, and the mental and spiritual development of a baby, to name only a few, would put modern psychologists to shame.

Those talks formed the basis for my pastoral work over the years and still, to this day, give me food for thought. They were gifts from God through a most unusual man and a faithful servant of Christ.

It is not, I think, an exaggeration to say that Rev. Ophoff also made a mark on Hope church that remains to this day.

## Rev. Hubert De Wolf

*Tom De Vries*

Rev. Hubert De Wolf came to the Hope congregation in 1936. This was after a lengthy vacancy, Rev. Ophoff having left in 1929. There is little

Rev. Hubert De Wolf, minister at Hope from 1936 to 1940

remembered of him as Hope's pastor, since most who could have any memories have gone to glory. At the time of his pastorate the congregation was very small, consisting mainly of the Engelsma, Moelker, and Korhorn families.

This much is remembered. Rev. De Wolf was born in Iowa and came to Grand Rapids, Michigan, as a young man to attend the Protestant Reformed seminary. He graduated in 1936. His years of service to Hope church, 1936 to 1940, were during the height of the Great Depression. He was very poor, and the congregation did its best to help. Many members were farmers who supplied him with fresh fruits and vegetables. Meat was provided as farmers did their butchering.

"He [Rev. De Wolf] was a very good preacher...He came almost every Friday to the farm for food. He was dirt poor." —Johanna Bomers

"Rev. De Wolf got to be a good friend of the family. We babysat his kids and gave him produce and fruit when he was minister at Hope." —Donna Moelker

His vehicle was an old roadster, able to hold only two people. Two men of the congregation added a rumble seat to the rear, so that two more passengers could be accommodated in good weather.

At this time Hope church was a small, white, frame building located on Wilson Avenue, which at that time was a graveled, country road. The church was located just about where the front parking lot of Hope school is located today. The congregation had no parsonage then, so the church rented the upstairs of a two-story home for Rev. De Wolf's family. It was located near the corner of Leonard Street and Remembrance Road. During his ministry Dutch services were discontinued.

Rev. De Wolf was very much a likeable man. His sermons were appreciated in Hope.

> "Rev De Wolf was popular. There is no doubt about that... well-met and articulate." —Dewey Engelsma

He was by all accounts a very good catechism teacher. His sermons were solidly Reformed. They showed no signs of the teachings that later got him into great difficulties in First Protestant Reformed Church in 1953. His name is still remembered in the Protestant Reformed Churches because of his false teaching and preaching of a conditional covenant.

He was finally suspended from his office and left the Protestant Reformed Churches with a number of other ministers to form a new denomination. Many members of the Protestant Reformed denomination followed those false teachings, leading to a bitter schism. The new denomination lasted for a few short years, until most of the ministers, Rev. De Wolf included, and most of the members who had left with him, returned to the Christian Reformed Church.

## Rev. John A. Heys

### Tom De Vries

Rev. Heys came to minister to Hope church in October 1941, after just a short vacancy. Two months before his installation, he had married his wife, Esther Van Baren. His three children, Ardess, John, and Joyce, were born while he was Hope's minister.

"One wintry day when [John Heys] was shoveling snow at First Protestant Reformed Church in Grand Rapids, he encountered the Rev. Herman Hoeksema. When HH asked him what he hoped to do, he said that he was thinking about being a teacher. Hoeksema is reported to have asked, 'Why not become the ultimate teacher?' John took the suggestion, studied in the seminary under the tutelage of HH, and began his public ministry of the Word and sacraments in Hope."[2]
—Rev. Barry Gritters

Rev. and Mrs. Heys with their daughter Ardess

He was a good minister and had a great love for Reformed doctrine.

"Rev. Heys was a good leader, and he kept on top of the issues. He set them forth plainly, too, so that we knew what the differences were." —Dewey Engelsma

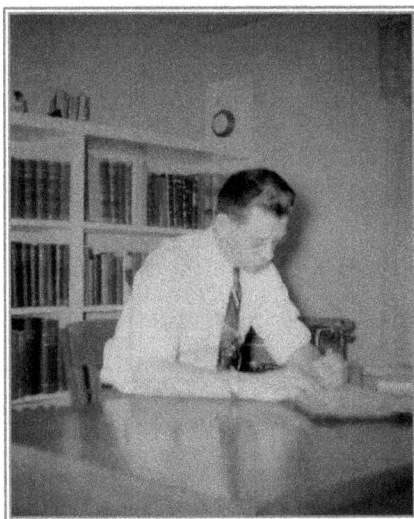

Rev. Heys, preparing a sermon in the study
of the Wilson Avenue parsonage

"In the early 50s, Rev. Heys was asked to teach a course in the seminary in Homiletics, the art of constructing a sermon." One minister related that Rev. Heys would say, "When the minister makes a sermon...he must put a cross at the top of the outline, to remind him that Christ must be central in every sermon."[3] —Rev. Barry Gritters

Rev. Heys' love for the truth carried over to his love for children and Protestant Reformed schools. He was instrumental in starting Hope school. He is remembered as working to build the school with the other men of the congregation. On a Saturday afternoon, he was seen on the new roof, coating it with tar and covered with tar himself, but he appeared on Sunday morning, completely scrubbed and ready to preach.

He was of a very sober character; a person did not often see him smile. However, he had a keen sense of humor and was very kindly disposed. He was a picturesque writer and teacher, making him very

---

3    Gritters, "The Rev. John A. Heys," in ibid.

effective in catechism classes. Rev. Heys was always dressed in a white shirt, no matter what he did.

"As a young child, I used to think Rev. Heys had no sin. I'd look at him and think that he must never sin because he was always dressed up in a shirt and tie." —Donna Dykstra

He is remembered as the umpire of the softball games at church picnics, dressed in a white shirt and bow tie. It would be difficult to argue with the ump when he is the minister of your congregation.

Dewey Engelsma and Rev. Heys with their children
at the 1951 church picnic

Young People's Society was held in the study in the parsonage.

The phone rang during one of those society meetings. Rev. Heys answered the phone, listened to the message, and told the young people that Pearl Harbor had been bombed and that there was to be war with Japan. He then ended the meeting and dismissed the young people.

Rev. Heys and the Young People's Society back from left: Ira Veenstra, Rev. J. Heys, John Huizinga, Jay Veenstra, Andy Sjoerdsma, John Kuiper, Duane Mensch, Ernie Korhorn; middle: Jim Lanning, Lou Boogaard, Geraldine Boogaard, Marge Kooienga, Marian Moelker, Henry Kuiper; front: Donna Kooienga, Eileen Engelsma, Annette Kuiper, Roger Kooienga, Connie Kuiper, Ann Veenstra, Helen Veenstra

"Either in catechism or society some boys played a trick on Rev. Heys, secretly putting a thumbtack on his seat. Rev. Heys had a good response. He sat down on it, then, of course, he got up suddenly and informed the kids, 'I will not stay on that point any longer.'" —John Kuiper

His term of service in Hope ended in 1955 when he left to serve in Hull, Iowa. He served Hope the longest of all its ministers.

Rev. Heys is still remembered in the Protestant Reformed denomination. He was a regular contributor to the *Standard Bearer*, beginning in the October 1, 1944, issue with an article about current events. For many years he continued his colorful and clear writing for the rubric, "The Day of Shadows."

Rev. Heys had a love for music and was an accomplished musician and organist. He composed the music and made the arrangements of the Lord's prayer in psalter numbers 433 and 434.

Heys' arrangements of the Lord's prayer

Rev. Heys playing the new Hammond organ

Many of the older members in Hope church think of him as they sing these two numbers and are thankful for him as a composer and as an upholder of the truth.

Long after Rev. Heys' departure as Hope's pastor, the consistory expressed its appreciation of his faithful labor by reading the following letter at a 1980 retirement gathering:

The Consistory of Hope Protestant Reformed Church is happy tonight to extend the congratulations and best wishes of the congregation to Rev. Heys and his wife on this occasion.

We would like to recall for you some of the history and highlights of his ministry in Hope, where he served as our pastor for more than 13 years, more than a third of his 39 years in the ministry.

It was in the year 1941 that Rev. J. A. Heys graduated from the Protestant Reformed Seminary and was declared a candidate for the ministry of the Word in the Protestant Reformed Churches. Hope Protestant Reformed Church, being vacant at this time, extended a call to Candidate Heys, and the Lord led him to accept this call, and he was subsequently ordained as a minister of the gospel in Hope Church. This was in October 1941.

Rev. Heys' installation took place only two months before the Japanese attack on Pearl Harbor. The first four and a half years of his pastorate at Hope, therefore, was a time when the world was aflame with the destruction and horrors of war. Young men also from Hope Church were called to leave their homes and church to serve in the armed forces for months and even years.

To be sure these boys and young men were a real concern to the new pastor and he bent every effort to keep in contact with them. Many letters were sent to our servicemen and many prayers were brought to the throne of grace on their behalf. In fact, Pastor Heys faithfully sent a summary of the Sunday evening sermon each week to each man in service. Two of the recipients of this correspondence, when they were far from home and church, are still members of the Hope congregation at the present time.

Another aspect of the labors of Rev. Heys we wish to share, concerns the beginning of Hope Protestant Reformed Christian School. Rev. Heys was a strong advocate of Covenant and Christian instruction, and this in the light of the Reformed faith, which the Lord our Covenant God gave us as a precious heritage. By means of the preaching and teaching of Rev. Heys, the Lord laid it upon the hearts of the members of the congregation to establish and maintain a day school, where these distinctive truths might be taught our covenant children. And thus, with the able counseling and guidance of Rev. Heys, within a year after the war ended, a school society was formed, out of which a board was chosen and commissioned to go forward, with a view to the construction of a building and the selecting of a teaching staff and all that this implied. In September of 1947 the school for which Rev. Heys had worked so hard opened its doors to two teachers and 52 pupils. Rev. Heys was chosen to be its first spiritual advisor. From this small beginning in 1947 we have today [1980] a school with 14 teachers and almost 300 children.

The final aspect of Rev. Heys' pastorate in Hope to which we call special attention is the 1953 schism.

The controversy period in the Protestant Reformed Churches in the early 1950s also involved the pastor and congregation of Hope. The older generation at Hope has not forgotten the strong leadership of its pastor during this period of heresy and schism. The congregation did not have to doubt their pastor's stand on the important doctrinal issues of that day. The sound of the trumpet was loud and clear. No uncertainty or vacillation whatever on the part of the pastor.

[His calling attention in the preaching] to the heresies that were plaguing our denomination provoked criticism by some. In response, one Sunday morning, before delivering his sermon, he answered these criticisms by reading Article 55 of the Church Order. We do well to quote this article here, so that we may the better understand the deep concern Rev. Heys had for the cause of Christ and the spiritual welfare of his congregation. Article 55 reads: "To ward off false doctrines and errors that multiply exceedingly through heretical writings, the ministers and elders shall use the means of teaching, of refutation, or warning, and of admonition, as well in the ministry of the Word as in Christian teaching and family visiting."

How true it was, as was also uttered by an elder in a consistorial prayer, when he thanked the Lord, that our pastor was indeed, "a workman that needed not to be ashamed, rightly dividing the Word of truth."

In conclusion, we want everyone here tonight to know, and we want you, Rev. Heys, to know that we are thankful to our Heavenly Father that He in His good pleasure sent you to serve and labor faithfully in the congregation of the Hope Protestant Reformed Church as a minister and pastor during those 13 years from 1941 to 1955.

Our prayer is that though you will no longer be a pastor of a local congregation, you may nevertheless still serve the churches in the capacity of an emeritated minister of the gospel.

May the Lord bless you and your wife, who has faithfully stood at your side all these years, in the remaining days of your earthly pilgrimage.

In the Name of the Congregation of Hope,
w.s. John Kalsbeek

## Rev. Herman Hanko
### *Prof. Herman Hanko*

The years God called me to be minister of Hope Protestant Reformed Church were years that proved to be a watershed in the history of our country and of the congregation.

In the United States seeds were sown that have serious consequences as Hope celebrates one hundred years of God's care of the congregation. In 1956 Dwight Eisenhower was elected to his second term and proved to be almost the last of good presidents. In 1960 John F. Kennedy was voted into office in a corrupt election. He set the country on an entirely different course and steered it on a downward course of immorality that continues to this day. An immoral man, he erased moral standards as qualifications for men occupying the highest office in the country, and thus he opened the door to the moral corruption that pervades our nation. The Civil Rights Movement gained momentum during his presidency, and, while in itself it was not wrong, he began a process of the adoption of antidiscriminatory laws that have condoned and protected the very worst sins committed by men and opened the door to grave threats to Christianity. He also began an era of space exploration in 1961 when the first manned space capsule was launched into space.

Rev. Herman Hanko, minister at Hope 1955 to 1963

The year I came to Hope, 1955, was also a year of change in the Protestant Reformed Churches. The effects of the shattering schism of 1953 were still present. The Lord had brought reformation to the churches in general and to Hope church in particular. Rev. John Heys had brought Hope safely through the gigantic struggle by pointing the church away from the heresies that had risen and were threatening the very existence of the Protestant Reformed Churches.

The time had come to put the agony of 1953 behind us and to move forward in the pursuit of the truth of God's sovereignty in the work of the establishment and maintenance of his covenant. A congregation cannot exist only by continuing to fight the battle against conditional theology; the congregation must move forward and develop the great truth God entrusts to her care. The Lord made this possible in various ways. Although the council was small, consisting of only five men, all were veterans in the responsibilities of working in the congregation. On the whole they were not men with college degrees and vast learning, but they had total commitment to the truth and vast experience and had fought for the cause of Christ in the past and were prepared to do so again.

In those days the deacons also served as elders. At the first consistory meeting I attended, the first item on the docket was a motion by one of the elders that all the minutes and all the subsequent motions and discussion be in the Frisian language—which all of them, I think, were able to speak. It was intimidating to me who was barely able to handle the Dutch, much less Frisian. The elders relented, and our relationship was off to a good start. I leaned heavily on my consistory those first years and thanked God for men to lead me through what for me were thickets of church polity and pastoral work.

One incident that stands out in my mind was an elder's observation that the fundamental error of the Netherlands Reformed Congregations was its wrong conception of the covenant. Although at the time I did not think he was correct, further reflection on the matter convinced me that he was right. His astute observation led me to write a series of pamphlets on the doctrine of the covenant. These writings were later published by the Reformed Free Publishing Association in my book, *God's Everlasting Covenant of Grace*.

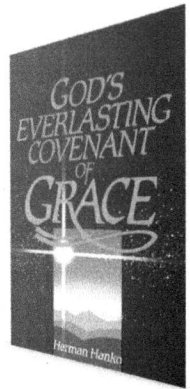

I had a catechism class of young adults who were qualified to become leaders in the churches, and under God's blessing many became teachers in Protestant Reformed schools, elders and deacons in the churches, and a minister of the gospel. When Southwest church did not have a minister, the young adults from that church attended the catechism classes at Hope. The discussions were animated and sometimes debates were exciting, so that I had little to do but steer the discussions, sum up the arguments, and direct the class in the path of the truth.

"When Rev. Hanko was our pastor, I remember him, walking in front of our seats taking catechism collection with his very large cupped hand. He would then slip all the coins into his suit coat pocket." —Bonnie Moelker

Because the congregation was small, consisting of about thirty-five families, the minister with an elder visited every family in the congregation each year. Family visitation was not conducted then as it is now, for careful inquiry was made into the spiritual lives of each member of the family, although the inquiry was centered on a particular topic. Family visitation was, on the whole, a delight for me.

In the six years of my ministry in Hope, I had no funerals, although I had three graveside services for infants who had died either at or shortly after birth.

The years God called me to minister in Hope church were also years of growth. The reason was that it was becoming increasingly difficult to find affordable housing on the east side of Grand Rapids, where three Protestant Reformed churches were located. Another reason was that Hope Protestant Reformed School had been established in 1947 on Wilson Avenue behind Hope church. There was also talk that a high school would soon be built near Hope church. As a result there was a westward movement of families into the Riverbend and Hudsonville areas. The congregation doubled in size in six and a half years, and the church building on Wilson Avenue was enlarged.

Hanko boys from left: Steve, Ken, Ron, and Neal, and Marcia at the piano

"Rev. Hanko had four little boys. One Sunday his wife was at home and the boys sat by themselves. I remember Rev. Hanko told them right from the pulpit, 'Boys, settle down!' He stopped the sermon and gave them a sermon."
—John Kuiper

"I remember while Rev. Hanko was preaching he stopped and said to his oldest son, 'Ron, shape up.' Ron didn't move a muscle the rest of the service." —Harry Langerak

God answered the prayers of his people as expressed in Psalm 122:6–9, verses on which I based my inaugural sermon: "Pray for the peace of Jerusalem: they shall prosper that love thee. Peace be within thy walls, and prosperity within thy palaces. For my brethren and companions' sakes, I will now say, Peace be within thee. Because of the house of the Lord our God I will seek thy good."

So far as I can recall, the consistory had to treat only two cases of importance. One was a case in which there was some disagreement over whether the weekly budget had to be paid in the amount that had been approved by the congregation at its annual meeting, or whether the budget fell under the principle of giving as the Lord has blessed you.

The other case involved the deaconate. Unknown to the deaconate one family was living in abject poverty. When the deacons discovered this and inquired of the family the reason they had not sought help from the deacons, the answer was that the deacons had to come to the poor and not the poor come to the deacons. The argument was that Christ comes to his people, and his people do not come to Christ, for that is Arminian doctrine. It took a little while for the elders to show convincingly that God's people do come to Christ in their need.

We came to Hope in 1955 with one child; God blessed our home with four more children in the years we stayed in Hope.

They were good years and the patience and long-suffering of the congregation were helpful to me to develop in the responsibilities of my calling. They were for me formative years that bore their fruit in the remainder of my ministry.

## Rev. Herman Veldman

### Tom De Vries

In the early summer of 1963, Rev. Veldman came from Hope Protestant Reformed Church in Redlands, California, to be pastor of Hope church in Walker, Michigan. Rev. Veldman was a nephew of Rev. Herman Hoeksema, and he apparently confided in Hoeksema and often asked him for advice. When he received Hope's call, Rev. Veldman contacted his uncle, who told him that he should go to Hope because it was a very solid congregation. Rev. Hoeksema told his nephew that he did not always have to go where there was trouble; that Hope would be an easy congregation for him.

Rev. Herman Veldman, minister at Hope 1963 to 1966

Rev. Veldman had been ordained into the ministry in 1932, just about the same time he married his wife, Flora. During his time in the ministry, his wife was pressed into service as a teacher in the Free Christian School in Edgerton, Minnesota, at Hope, and at Adams in Grand Rapids, Michigan.

> Rev. Veldman's daughter recalls, "Dad had taken the call to the Protestant Reformed church in Hamilton, Ontario. We moved to another country—Canada! We lived only a short distance from the Niagara Falls…We arrived at church one morning in 1951 to find that Dad had been banned from preaching, so he sat in the audience. We returned to Grand Rapids, Michigan." —Elaine (Veldman) Van Dyke

A difficult time in Rev. Veldman's life was his deposition as minister by the consistory of the Hamilton Protestant Reformed Church in Ontario, Canada. He had been there for just a short time, and almost immediately he discovered that most of his congregation were immigrants from the Netherlands who had been members of the Reformed Churches of the Netherlands (liberated), founded by Klaas Schilder.

The Consistory
of the
Protestant Reformed Church at Hamilton, Ontario Canada

Consistory of Hamilton (1950) back from left: T. J. Hart, S. Reitsma, L. Van Huizen; front: J. Ton, Rev. H. Veldman, L. Klapwyk

For two and a half years Rev. Veldman had no call. For most of that time he was a teacher at Adams Protestant Reformed School.

Rev. Veldman          Flora Veldman
They both taught at Adams during the school years 1951–53

There are many things that the older members of Hope remember about Rev. Veldman. He always entered the sanctuary with the elders. He then stood in front and prayed before climbing the stairs to the pulpit. He was a man who enjoyed preaching. He also enjoyed being with people; those times he always had a broad, beaming smile. He had a tremendous memory and on the pulpit used only a tiny note for sermon divisions and psalter numbers. Everything else he memorized. He enjoyed preaching and volunteered to preach in other churches when he came to synod. He readily agreed to preach after his retirement when asked to do so.

"Rev. Veldman took one small piece of paper with him when he preached and referred to that paper for the psalter numbers we were to sing. He ended his sermons, leaning over the top of the lectern, smiling at the congregation, and saying, 'And that's the way it is!'" —Bonnie Moelker

The last time he preached for Hope congregation as our pastor his text was 1 Corinthians 12:13: "For now we see through a glass darkly; but then face to face." When he came up to the pulpit, he had his usual smile; it could be seen that he was happy to be with us again. Before he began his sermon he smiled again and said, "You sure sing nice." In the beginning of his sermon, he paused and asked, "Now how am I going to get you people to understand what 'a glass darkly' means?" By the time he was done with his sermon all of us understood.

"Catechism was in the small room (now part of the consistory room). As we would file into the room, Rev. Veldman sat at a little table facing our rows of chairs. He would be leaning forward, arms resting on the table. His pipe would be on the table in front of him." —Bonnie Moelker

He preached so that all—young and old—could understand. He was very conscious of time when he preached. In the morning services he finished his first point at 10:30, the second point at 10:45, and he finished the sermon at 10:55. When done with his sermon, he turned to the side of the pulpit area and drank the water, finishing the glass in one long draft.

Hope was Rev. Veldman's shortest charge.

"He thoroughly enjoyed his time at Hope." —Elaine Van Dyke

He left in 1966 to take the call to Hudsonville.

"Oh, we just loved that man...I remember when he took the call to Hudsonville. I wasn't there at church; I was home with the little kids. He called me the next day, and he was crying, he couldn't even talk to me." —Donna Dykstra

"Rev. Veldman said to me, 'Harry, I have to go.'"
—Harry Langerak

After retirement he lived in Sunset Manor. He passed away in January 1997. It must be said of him that he was "a good and faithful servant."

However, Rev. Veldman's faithful service to Hope did not end with his acceptance of the call from our sister congregation in Hudsonville. Thirteen years later he returned during our 1979 to 1981 vacancy to provide Hope with some more of his excellent Heidelberg Catechism preaching for our morning worship services.

"Rev. Veldman was preaching for Hope during a vacancy in the late 1970s. At the time the PA system had a little microphone that clipped around the pastor's neck, and the jack was in the floor next to the pulpit. Rev. Veldman sat in one of the chairs behind the pulpit while the offering was being taken, and he began to twirl the cord as though it were a jump rope. After doing this for a while, some of us noticed and wondered what he was doing. There's not much going on during the offering so anything different, especially when it's moving, is quite noticeable. After several seconds of twirling the cord, Rev. Veldman said in Dutch, 'I feel like a puppy!' The older members who knew Dutch, and a very few of us who were studying Dutch in college, had a hard time keeping their laughter under control." —Brian Dykstra

## Rev. Jason Kortering

In early November 1966 we arrived at the parsonage on Wilson Avenue before our furniture arrived. We camped on the living room floor for one night with our four girls—Lori, Sharon, Joann, and Ellen.

We sent Lori and Sharon off to Hope school the next day, so they could begin acclimation to their new school (and be out of our way when we unloaded). We were excited about school, since it was our first experience with a Protestant Reformed school. The girls came home and couldn't talk fast enough as they told us all about school and their new teachers and friends. Our appreciation for the school increased daily.

The Kortering girls back from left: Ellen, Joann; front: Sharon, Lori

On Friday night the congregation welcomed us with a special program, our first exposure to the musical talent of Hope. This struck us as very special all during our stay—good congregational singing that was enhanced by voices trained by singing in Hope Choral Society and the Hope Heralds. Special musical programs were a regular treat at Hope.

It's funny what comes to mind when I recall meaningful events.

The birth of our last daughter, Carol, had its moments. My wife, Jean, went into labor Saturday evening. Ruth Elzinga came over around 10:00 to stay with the girls as we headed for Butterworth Hospital.

Carol was born at 12:05 Sunday morning. I was scheduled to preach in Holland that morning, so I got four beautiful gals ready for church and off we went. Rev. Veldman was scheduled to preach in Hope, so he announced the birth of our newborn. In typical Veldman style, with a big smile on his face, he informed the congregation that the Korterings had another baby during the night, and then he lowered his voice and said, "Another girl!" Everyone smiled.

Very soon after our arrival at Hope, I realized my need for an electric typewriter. For six years at Hull, I had used a portable, Smith

Rev. Jason Kortering, minister at Hope 1966 to 1970

Corona, manual typewriter. Work demands made it clear that I needed more than that. I shopped around and eyed a Royal, electric, office typewriter. But, how was I to pay for it? Almost immediately the *Reformed Witness Hour* committee asked if I would speak for the radio program. They agreed to pay me for speaking, but I do not even remember how much. So I prepared and delivered enough radio messages to cover the cost of the new typewriter. This worked well with the fancy, Gestetner, silk-screen mimeograph that the church owned. This was a huge step up from the old way of duplicating on a diapered drum on which ink was painted with a brush and stencils applied.

But alas, I had all the equipment only to learn that I did not even have to type and print the weekly bulletin. Jo Dykstra was already serving well in that capacity. So I concentrated on making catechism material, tests, society lessons, sermon outlines, and the like. The typewriter and mimeograph still got plenty of use.

Josephine (Jo) Dykstra served as the bulletin secretary from 1966 to 2010.

Most outstanding, and important to me, was to learn how a well-organized council (minister, elders, and deacons) functioned.

I knew very little of the work each officebearer did and how the officebearers assisted each other. The practice in Hull was that the minister literally did everything. This indicated the degree of disarray in the Protestant Reformed Churches following the schism of 1953. I lacked training, the officebearers had few role models, and the congregation in Hull lacked a church building and a parsonage, so everything was in disarray. When we came to Hope, the order of the meetings of the council, consistory, and deacons impressed me. The elders had their work to do, even family visiting two-by-two and not an elder just accompanying the pastor. Elders without the minister made discipline visits. The elders by rotation attended deacons' meetings, and I also attended deacons' meetings for the first time in my ministry. I thank God for this learning experience; it opened my eyes to see how a good Reformed church functioned. When we returned to Hull four years later, I shared with the elders and deacons that knowledge, and we set up similar arrangements there to the benefit of the church.

"Jo Dykstra began making the bulletins in late 1966. Prior to that, the bulletins were produced by our pastors.

This change took place when the doctor told Rev. Kortering that, for health reasons, he should have his workload decreased. Rev. Kortering did not tell the consistory this, but the consistory learned it by way of the "grapevine." I brought this information to the consistory, and suggested that the easiest thing to take off his plate would be the bulletin. I mentioned that First church had the clerk take care of the bulletins. Our clerk at that time literally jumped out of his seat and said, "Well, this clerk isn't going to do that!" So we decided it would be wise to appoint an assistant clerk who could take on that duty. Because I had brought up the idea, I was nominated and received every vote except my own. I stated my willingness to take that responsibility, but said it would be necessary for my wife to be the person doing the typing; otherwise the bulletin would not be readable! So a motion was made to ask Jo to take care of producing the bulletin for $250 a year.

Why should any minister do clerical work? It is never mentioned in any call letter, as Rev. Veldman was fond of reminding us. Yet, action was never taken until Rev. Kortering was our pastor.

One can receive some strange requests to be placed in the bulletin. An example of this was a letter listing a series of four detailed and wordy announcements promoting a particular event. These were to be placed in Hope's bulletins seriatim. It was meant to be a serious effort to convince the readers that they would not want to miss that event! I am not making this up. The writer was my sister! Jo and I got quite a laugh out of it, and, needless to say, Jo did quite a bit of editing on those announcements! Of course, editing announcements was something that was frequently necessary, just not usually to that extent!"
—John J. Dykstra

During our stay in Hope we were disturbed when one of the members of the congregation made himself worthy of Christian discipline by publicly writing evil things about the leadership of the Protestant Reformed Churches. It was the first time I was called on to read the Form for Excommunication. It did not help that a member sat in the first row during the service and held up a microphone attached to a tape recorder just to intimidate me. The Lord was good through all that trouble. He preserved the church, and the consistory stood united. What a blessing for me as pastor.

One final observation: during our brief stay of four years, we cancelled the evening service twice. I reflect on this and find it a bit amusing because Hope church hardly ever cancels church today. The first instance was for a tornado warning. Late one Sunday afternoon a warning came out that a tornado was sighted in the Holland area and was traveling toward Grand Rapids. The elders acted wisely on that and cancelled the evening service. In those days we only had radio, so we listened to radio. From reports the tornado was in the vicinity of Hudsonville, so our family went to the basement for safety. For those who remember the parsonage in those days, the basement was half concrete walls and floor and the other half was a typical Michigan basement.[4] While we were in the basement a torrent of rain fell. Right under the steps that led to the basement, it looked like a fire hydrant had been opened and water poured right into the area where we were sitting. The girls came out of there looking like a family of sewer rats. Once the storm passed (too late for church), the sky cleared and beautiful weather prevailed. Extensive damage was done in south Grand Rapids.

The second instance was a request from the Kent County sheriff, I think, responding to the civil unrest taking place in Grand Rapids and surrounding suburbs. The racial unrest was full-blown, and we were advised that it was unsafe to hold a public gathering. A blockade was in place on Wilson Avenue in Standale, about two miles away. The elders canceled that evening service as well. I recall a bit of fear, wondering if any gangs of thugs would travel down Wilson Avenue and harass us. But the Lord kept us well protected.

I recall many special pastoral needs that required work, which also led to spiritual bonding. I learned that the needs of each congregation lead to growth for both pastor and congregation.

"Russ was in bed at home for three months after a back surgery, and he couldn't get out of bed. Rev. Kortering would come and do catechism with him." —Donna Dykstra

---

4   A Michigan basement is a term for a crawlspace that was excavated to the depth of a basement. The area is usually shallower than the normal basement and requires the occupant to duck to avoid banging his/her head on the floor framing or furnace ducts above. The floor and the side walls of the excavation sometimes remain as exposed dirt, but are usually covered with a coating of concrete or cement. Or the side walls of the excavation may be finished with brick or block.

What a day it will be when we will be part of Christ's perfect church, no need to grow anymore, but only to rejoice in our heavenly Father who gave his Son that we might be united together as the eternal family of God. To Him is the glory forever. —Rev. and Mrs. J. Kortering

## Rev. Ronald Van Overloop

Greetings in our savior and Lord.

Sue and I rejoice with you on the occasion of the one-hundredth anniversary of Hope Protestant Reformed Church as an instituted congregation. It is a testimony of the grace of our heavenly Father that he has used sinful men and women whom he made to be faithful in the desire to uphold and maintain the Reformed faith as presented in our creeds. This reflection on what God has graciously done in the past is always accompanied with the prayer that he will not cut us off in our generations.

God graciously gave to me a special love and appreciation for Hope church—for both the members and the congregation as a whole—partly because Hope was my first charge as a minister of the word and sacraments. There I served from the fall of 1972 until the summer of 1979.

The Van Overloop family back from left: Sue, Kevin,
Rev. Van Overloop; front: Jared, Rhonda

"This memory is from long ago when I was a young, Saturday morning catechism student of maybe seven- or eight-years old. Lenora (Kalsbeek) Hoekstra and I would wait outside Rev. Van Overloop's study door and eagerly watch for him to cross the Hope church parking lot after he had spent a long morning teaching catechism. We would ask him if we could come in and look at the fish in his fish tank. I'm sure he had work up to his ears, and was probably hungry too, yet he would kindly let us in and patiently point out the various fish in his tank and tell us other fascinating fish facts. I'm not sure how many times we did this, but after a while he must have wondered if we were ever going to tire of seeing his fish."
—Brenda (Langerak) Bomers

The church was willing to take an inexperienced, young man fresh out of seminary to be its pastor. This it did even though it was at that time the second largest congregation in the denomination. The 1972 *Acts of Synod* reports 480 members, comprising ninety-seven families.

The church patiently bore with this young pastor and all his weaknesses for seven and a half years. It upheld him as he learned the real practical reality of what it means to make and deliver two sermons a week, to teach catechism, and to lead Bible studies for every age. It supported him as he learned to lead council and consistory meetings. And it was among them that he learned what it is to be a pastor: to visit in homes and hospital rooms, to baptize babies (94), to hear confessions of faith (69), to perform weddings (31), and to conduct funerals (16, 4 in the first year).

"One service when Rev. Van Overloop was our minister, there were boys sitting in the back goofing off. Rev. Van Overloop said, 'Would you boys in the back there behave?' When the consistory went out, he said, 'It's your son; it's your son...' Some were elders' children." —Donna Dykstra

This church taught him to give self-sacrificially when it loaned him for eight months to a congregation in Christchurch, New Zealand, at the request of our denomination's committee for contact with other churches.

Not for a moment did this young minister and his wife and children experience anything but love and care.

Though the memories of what transpired during those seven and a half years (it was "only" forty-three years ago) have somewhat faded, the recollection of the people and experiences is always accompanied with fondness and appreciation.

Rev. Ronald Van Overloop, minister of Grace Protestant Reformed Church

I thank God often for what he taught me through his use of Hope Protestant Reformed Church.

In Christ's and your service,

Pastor Ronald Van Overloop

## Rev. Richard Flikkema

Dear congregation in our Lord Jesus Christ,

I was asked by the anniversary committee to contribute to the book commemorating your one-hundredth anniversary, since I had the privilege of serving as one of your former pastors.

I served as your pastor from February 1981 to October 1986. I received your call while laboring in my first pastorate in Isabel, South Dakota. Interestingly, the congregation in Isabel also had the name Hope Protestant Reformed Church. And even more interesting is that while considering your call I received a call from the Hope Protestant Reformed Church of Redlands, California—calls from three Hopes.

The Lord placed before me the question, which Hope to serve? My first love was the Hope in Isabel. My wife and I were very happy there and loved the saints in that congregation very much. My heart was also drawn to the Hope in Redlands, having had the privilege of serving a classical appointment in their midst and getting to know the people while I was there. In the end the Lord led me to accept your call. I could not in good conscience say no. Since you had been vacant for over two years, your needs weighed heavily on me. So in the assurance of hope that the Lord would sustain me as your pastor, I left Hope to come to Hope.

The Lord did not fail. He enabled me to perform the work even though the work was difficult and taxing. There were the catechism classes. Initially, I taught them all—four on Saturday mornings and four on Monday nights. There were the society meetings. Initially I led three: Young People's Society, Junior Mr. and Mrs. Society, and Ladies' Society. There were the council and consistory meetings. I believe there was one council meeting a month and two consistory meetings a month and sometimes special meetings besides. There were the many pastoral visits that I had the privilege of making. And, of course, the chief task of making sermons and preaching twice on the Lord's day.

While I was in your midst, Hope served as the calling church for the mission field in East Lansing, and Rev. Houck served as the missionary. Subsequently that field was closed, and Rev. Houck went to labor in Modesto, California, under the oversight of Hope Redlands. Another milestone was the organization of Grandville Protestant Reformed Church as a daughter congregation. I had the privilege of installing her first minister, Rev. Kortering, who also was a former minister of Hope.

If memory serves, I believe I had over one hundred baptisms while at Hope and almost as many confessions of faith. There were many marriages that took place and several funerals—mostly of the aged saints, but also of people of various ages, including a funeral of a child who never saw the light of day on this earth, but who

Flikkema family 1986
back: Tammi; middle from left:
Rev. Flikkema, Tricia, Marcia;
front: Heidi, Kyle

awoke to see the light of the eternal day in glory. There were not only many joys, but also many sorrows.

But that is the life of the church of Christ in the midst of this world. The Lord in his blessing gives us many joys—the joy of salvation and the joy of seeing his covenantal faithfulness manifest in children's children, seeing them born, making confession of faith, and marrying in the Lord—but also the sorrows of seeing loved ones taken to glory in death. And yet those sorrows are never the sorrows of those who have no hope. We have hope in life and in death, the certain assurance of the Lord's blessing, grace, and peace.

That hope belongs to the congregation of the Hope Protestant Reformed Church. It is your name. It has been your experience for one hundred years, all of the years that you have been a congregation. And it will be your experience in the future.

For almost six years I had the privilege of laboring as your pastor. I labored in the same hope that you share. I labored in love for you and love for the Lord who called me to serve in your midst.

It is my prayer that the Lord will continue to bless you.

Your former pastor,

Richard Flikkema

## Rev. James Slopsema

My wife and I arrived at Hope in the cold and snowy December of 1986 with our nine children from the ages of fifteen years to three weeks. I still cannot believe that I put my wife though a move from Randolph, Wisconsin, with a three-week-old baby boy. We were a rather unusual family—eight daughters and one son. We filled the parsonage to overflowing. The neighbors remarked that the whole house was lit up at night, like a city on a hill that cannot be hid.

Our stay at Hope for eight and a half years was a very blessed one. We were embraced by the congregation. Our children were able to attend our own Christian schools—Hope and Covenant. In fact, they could even walk to school, although once in high school some of the children thought the long block to Covenant was way too far to walk.

The Slopsema family 1992
back from left: Crista, Sara, Paula;
middle: Debbie, Brenda, Rev. Slopsema,
Joan; front: Bethany, Gary, Shelly, Carla

Our children found a multitude of neighborhood friends with whom they went to church, catechism, and school. We did not fully realize what a great blessing that was until we moved away to another church and neighborhood. The years in Hope were an especially busy time for me. Hope church numbered about 125 families at the time, four times the size of my previous charges. I had to get used to the idea of not being directly involved with every part of church life, as I had before. I also had to learn to say, "No, I don't have the time for that." That was extremely hard at first.

My wife, Joan, and I rejoiced at the large number of very godly, stable families in Hope, often families that had many children. As a pastor I was also thankful for the elders and deacons that the Lord had given to Hope. They were dedicated and gifted men.

"Custom dictated that he remove his shoes before he entered the building. Perhaps this was one way this small congregation attempted to bring a high and mighty Dutchman down to earth." —*Edgerton Enterprise* writing about Rev. Slopsema's trip to Singapore

Joan Slopsema, Reverend's wife, plays the piano, organ, marimba, and accordion.

The children are musical too.

Here are a few things that may amuse you. There were two marriage proposals on the front porch of the parsonage during our stay, and one did not involve one of our children. The yard became a shortcut for the Hope school children to get to and from school. It was not uncommon in the morning for a few friends of our girls to come into the front door and leave with our children out the back slider or even through my study door. Within a year after we moved into the parsonage the septic tank and drain system had to be replaced. We took a lot of good natured ribbing for some time. "How large a family do you have? How many girls did you say you have?"

"Edgerton's Thrifty Acres had a pair of tennis shoes that had been on their shelf for many years because they couldn't find anyone with big enough feet—until Jim Slopsema came along while attending the 1963 young people's convention in Edgerton. The store manager made them his gift to the fourteen-year-old Slopsema boy. They were size fifteen."

Rumor has it that Rev. Slopsema was asked while in Singapore, "Are you the tallest man in the world?"

Our family thanks God for the time we had at Hope church. It was a great blessing for me personally as well as for my family.

Congratulations on your one-hundredth anniversary. May the Lord keep you and our denomination faithful until the Lord comes again! —Rev James Slopsema

**Program**

Organ Prelude .................................. Bonnie Moelker

Opening Prayer & Remarks ....................... Alvin Rau

Congregational Singing ........................... Psalter #162

Sunday School
Upper Grades
*When We Walk with the Lord*
Psalter 266, vs. 1 & 3
Acrostic Reading: FAREWELL
Lower Grades
*The Wise Man & the Foolish Man*
*Jesus Loves Me*
Upper & Lower Grades
Psalter 197, vs. 1 & 2
Psalter 60, vs. 3

Instrumental Duet ........ Melinda & Tamara DeMeester
*The Guardian Care of God*, Psalter 52

Instrumental Solo .................................. Daniel Kleyn
Psalter #247
Psalter #370

Poem ............................................. Connie Meyer
*We, Like Sheep*

Vocal Duet ...... Melva Mastbergen & Steve Lotterman
*God Hath Not Promised*
*Blest Be the Tie That Binds*

Vocal Quartet ............... Dan DeMeester, John Dykstra
Roger King, Harry Langerak
*The Mercy of God Besought*, Psalter #110
*God the Highest Good*, Psalter 27

Congregational Singing ........... Psalter #250, vs. 1, 4, 5

Presentation of Gift ............................... Jim Koole

Remarks & Closing Prayer ............... Prof. H. Hanko

Refreshments will be served following the program.

Farewell program for the Slopsema family

## Rev. Russell Dykstra

Accepting the call to Hope in 1995 meant coming home, and yet, obviously much had changed. I was now her pastor.

The congregation received us well. One of the issues with which I struggled in considering the call from Hope was Jesus' warning about a prophet's not being honored in his own country. I was returning to my "own country." However the congregation was quite different from the Hope where I grew up. Most of my generation had gone to one of Hope's three daughter congregations: Faith, Grandville, or Grace. Few of my relatives remained. I believed that Hope had a high enough regard for the minister that a lack of honor in one's own country would not be a problem. That was confirmed by our experience there. The congregation gave due respect to the office and received the preaching and instruction well.

**Program**

Organ Prelude ............... Bonnie and Kolleen Moelker

Opening Prayer & Remarks ...................... Prof. Hanko

Congregational Singing ............................ Psalter #407

Sunday School

    Lower Grades (Preschool - 1)
      *O Be Careful Little Eyes What You See*
      *That Man is Blest*

    Upper Grades (2 - 7)
      Psalm 100
      *The Lord's My Shepherd*

    Entire Sunday School
      Psalter #425:5

Instrumental Duet ................................ Rebecca Vermeer
                           Tamara DeMeester
            *The Holy City*

A Welcome Letter .................................... Kathy Knott

Violin and Piano Duet ...................... Marilyn DeVries
                           Kristen DeVries
            *Calvary*

Vocal Trio ............. Sharon Kamps, Elizabeth Langerak
                         Margaret Laning
            Psalter #50

Vocal Solo ............................................. Arnold Dykstra
            Psalter #397

Congregational Singing ......... Psalter #277, vs. 1, 2, 6, 8

Closing Prayer ..................................... Rev. R. Dykstra

Refreshments will be served following the program.

Welcome program for the Dykstra family

Certain events in a congregation can strengthen a bond between a pastor and the congregation: deaths, personal struggles, and pastoral counsel. In the providence of God, little of that happened in our short ministry in Hope.

And short the pastorate surely was. The year after we came to Hope, the synod of the Protestant Reformed Churches appointed me to the seminary. It was more than a shock to me. When I came to Hope, I had assumed that I was not even eligible for such a call, since the Church Order requires that a minister not be called for a year after accepting a call. Synod apparently did not believe that rule applied to synodical appointments to the seminary.

Convicted of the call of Christ to this new labor, I bid farewell to Hope after only eight months. At my request we never had a formal farewell. For another year we lived in the parsonage during which time I preached the Heidelberg

Rev. Dykstra and Carol 1996

Catechism and taught the catechism classes. When Candidate James Laning accepted Hope's call in 1997, we moved a couple of blocks and gladly continued as members.

Living in that area was a blessing—within walking distance of the church and the schools. Only after all of our children were out of the home did we consider moving, and that was given significant impetus from another young family who desired the same benefits we had enjoyed. With the purchase of a new home within walking distance of Faith Protestant Reformed Church, our latest stay in Hope came to an end. But the memories and the effects remain with us, and will, all our days.

We thank God for Hope church and pray that God will continue to keep her faithful. —Prof. Russell Dykstra

| Program | | | |
|---|---|---|---|
| Organ Prelude | Bonnie Moelker | Mr. and Mrs. Societies | |
| | | Poem: | Sherry Koole |
| | | *God's Providing Hand* | |
| Opening Prayer | Vice President, Alvin Rau | Men's Society | |
| | | Quartet: | Dan DeMeester, John Dykstra, |
| | | | Jim Huizinga, Harry Langerak |
| Introductory Remarks | Rev. James Laning | Psalter # 124 | |
| Congregational Singing | Psalter # 375:1,2,3,5 | Ladies' Society | |
| | | Piano Solo | Marilyn DeVries |
| | | *Medley: Seek Ye First the Kingdom, How Great Thou Art* | |
| Sunday School Primary Grades | | | |
| Psalter #1:1,3 | | | |
| Psalm 23 | | Congregational Singing | Psalter # 404:1,2,4,5 |
| Poem: | | | |
| *A pastor's like a shepherd, And we are like his sheep.* | | | |
| *With God's Word he feeds us, And gently leads us.* | | Closing Prayer | Rev. James Laning |
| Psalter # 53:1,2,5 | | | |
| Psalter # 213:1,3 | | | |
| Young Peoples' Society | | | |
| Piano and Organ Duet | Kolleen Moelker, Bonnie Moelker | Refreshments will be served following the program. | |
| | *Holy Art Thou* | | |

Welcome program for the Laning family

## Rev. James Laning

Our whole family has fond memories of our days at Hope Protestant Reformed Church. From the day that Margaret and I moved to Michigan with young Benjamin, we were warmly welcomed by the congregation. You helped us greatly through those pre-seminary and seminary days, and we quickly felt a family tie with our brothers and sisters at Hope.

The broad support throughout our days in the pastorate was a wonderful testimony of the work of the Spirit in your midst, and it is with joy that we reflect a bit on some of what the Lord did during that time.

If you would ask us what especially we remember, it would not take long for us to respond. The true communion we had talking with you about the things of God, the joy we had learning together with you, and growing more to know you as dear friends—that we remember most. Hearing about the things you were reading, discussing spiritual things not only at the well-attended society

Rev. James Laning, minister at Hope 1997 to 2010

meetings, but also after the worship services and in your homes—those moments we remember well, and the matters we discussed often come to our minds still today.

There were, of course, many lighter matters that we would not be able to forget. The difficulty keeping the children out of the creek on Sunday, the perplexed children trying to figure out how to work the rotary-dial phone in the church basement, people dialing in to listen to the worship services by phone and not realizing that their lines were connected to the line of someone else who could hear quite clearly anything they started talking about, and all the effort spent trying to get that system to function properly, only to have God take out the system with a lightning bolt after it finally worked. We think also of the time when one of the elders came up to the pulpit to shine a flashlight in front of my face during one of the rather frequent power outages, and the entertainment we provided with our miserable attempt at vegetable gardening that was clearly on display right next to the church parking lot. These are but a few of the many memories we have of those days.

Thinking back we also remember the church picnics. Each year much effort was put into this annual event. From the candy hunt in the kiddie swimming pool to adults on tricycles to guessing the combined weight of the men on the council, every age group had a fun event in which they were involved. The large number of people who came made the picnics a great joy, and they testified of the unity we experienced as a gracious gift from our heavenly Father.

During Rev. Laning's pastorate, he preached over one thousand sermons, seven times through the Heidelberg Catechism. He baptized about 150 children, conducted about 130 confessions of faith, and preached part of one sermon by flashlight.

Then there were the catechism classes. It is hard for me to express the great joy I had with the children of the church, and how much I have missed them all since we have left. Seeing the attentiveness in the classes, hearing the children singing the psalms, and engaging with them in back-and-forth discussions that showed the love the children had for the truth, were experiences I will never forget. Now as these children have been growing older, we very much enjoy having opportunities to see them from time to time.

Only one minister served Hope for more than Rev. Laning's thirteen years; that was Rev. Heys who was at Hope for fourteen years.

Margaret and I and our entire family give thanks to God for you saints at Hope church. By his grace you show your love for God and his people not only by your confessions, but also by your daily lives. We love you very much and rejoice with you as you celebrate your one-hundredth anniversary. May the Lord continue to bless you richly, strengthening you by his Spirit to glorify the God who has given you so much. —Rev. James Laning

## Chapter 6

# Minutes of Interest in Hope's One Hundred Years

## Editor's Introduction

"The consistory shall see to it that the record books are at hand for the inspection by the visitors." This decision of the synod of the Protestant Reformed Churches pertains to article 44 of the Church Order.[1] The "visitors" in the decision refer to the church visitors assigned by classis to visit the councils of all the churches in the classis each year for the purpose of providing their assistance to "help direct all things unto peace, upbuilding, and greatest profit of the churches."[2] The church visitors *do* inspect the record books of the elders, deacons, and council during their visits. Clearly the churches believe the preservation of accurate records is important. Experience demonstrates it. Not infrequently do diaconates, consistories, and councils find it necessary to refer to past decisions to assist them in the process of taking new decisions.

Thankfully Hope's consistory has kept an accurate record for one hundred years. This chapter demonstrates the consistory's diligence in this task, and at the same time it provides an inside look at some interesting matters addressed throughout the past century. While care needed to be exercised to leave out minutes of discipline cases and

---

1 Decision adopted by classis of June 6–7, 1934, and by the synod of 1944 in articles 66–67. See *Confessions and Church Order*, 394–95.
2 Church Order 44, in ibid., 394.

other sensitive issues, the minutes included will be informative and interesting.[3]

## A Word about the Records

*David Moelker*[4]

Record keeping is not something new. The storage of and the retention of records is mentioned in the Bible most notably in 2 Kings 22. There we read that Hilkiah found the book of the law and gave it to Shaphan the scribe to read. The record of the law that Shaphan had read, he then read to good King Josiah. Another time records are mentioned is in Ezra 4, where we are told that the records of a wicked kingdom were used to persecute the church. Then there is the account in Esther 6, where out of boredom the king of Persia had the record read to him one sleepless night.

I can identify with both Hilkiah and Shaphan in providing the following information. Although I knew where all the records were, and of course it was not the law, it would still be with a bit of excitement to go to the editor of this book and say, "You should read this!"

*A Spiritual House Preserved* reveals that in one hundred years an enormous amount of record-taking and record-keeping was done. What is even more amazing is that the records remain intact and still valuable after one hundred years. There is also the almost overwhelming thought as I researched the minute books that I was holding in my hands not only countless hours of consistory meetings, but also a history of how God was working to preserve his church called Hope in the river's bend.

When one researches records sometimes only small clues are given as to where to start to look for information. This happened countless times as the minutes were researched for this book. What is even more amazing is that the many clerks over the past one hundred years were

---

3    Apparently the clerks were not always careful to include the outcomes of motions. Motions listed without an outcome carried.

4    David Moelker is the 2016 clerk of Hope Protestant Reformed Church.

used by God to give an accurate account of each meeting that was then adopted as the official record of each consistory meeting.

Something else became evident through the reading of the historical record. It was apparent that the consistory meetings from the beginning, including the few as a mission station, were conducted faithfully in a timely way; the meetings were conducted with good order; the meetings were done with the welfare of the congregation uppermost in the mind of the consistory.

The lesson we can learn from the history embodied in all the records is that nonessential matters can and do change and that essential matters when carried on faithfully will, like salt to food, add flavor and have a preserving influence to God's glory.

## The Minutes

February 2, 1916, article 4: Since brother elders from Walker congregation are present at this meeting, it is suggested by one of those brethren, to join ourselves as a Mission Station of River Bend, with one or the other churches. If we then needed help or support, one could apply to one of those churches. If we would place ourselves under Classis West, we would be acknowledged as a Mission Station.

February 9, 1916, article 4: A motion is accepted to take an extra collection (offering) every last Sunday of each month when no more than $1 is contributed.

June 27, 1917, article 3: It was decided to place a tower (spire) on the church.

April 2, 1918, article 3: The consistory decided to conduct the worship services at 9:30 a.m. and 2:30 p.m.

October 19, 1919, article 7: The idea is accepted to place glass (a window) in the door to the basement all purpose room.

April 20, 1920, article 2: The new (organ) which was placed in the church by the committee was accepted by the congregation.

February 1, 1921, article 4: Motion was made and accepted not to pay the students or ministers on Sunday.

August 1922, article 4: Announcement to be made from the pulpit that the box in the church at the door is for the poor and that the congregation should try to give regularly for the poor.

November 7, 1922, article 4: Mr. J. De Jong was given the right to go and see another party about the furnace in the parsonage to see if the study room can be heated directly from the furnace.

December 5, 1922, article 4: A motion was made and accepted that the parents shall notify the consistory when they want their children baptized.

February 6, 1923, article 9: A motion was made and accepted to have a silent moment while the collections are taken.

September 5, 1923, article 10: A motion was made and accepted to have all special collections taken at the door except the collection for the poor.

October 2, 1923, article 6: A motion was made and accepted to buy five tons of coal for the church.

December 4, 1923, article 2: Try and get someone to look after the furnace and see if heat could not be made to enter the main floor a little farther north.

December 4, 1923, article 7: A motion was…made to allow some men to come here and show some slides about the heathen world.

July 10, 1924, article 5: A motion was made and accepted to give the minister two weeks of vacation and to suspend the catechism classes for two months.

December 2, 1924, article 10: A motion was made and accepted to give some of the young ladies of the congregation a chance to play the organ at the services.

January 19, 1925, article 1: The request from Classis West to the consistory was read, which contains a certain demand that the consistory put the minister, G. M. Ophoff, to test whether or not he is willing to submit to the Cenodical [sic] interpretations formulated by Cenod [sic].

January 19, 1925, article 2: After discussing the three points, the vice-president asked the consistory what they would do in regard to those three points.

January 19, 1925, article 3: The three elders, Newhouse, Korhorn, and De Jong did not feel it their duty to ask of their minister to submit to the three points laid down by Senod [sic]. The two deacons, Goeree and Bergman, felt that they should abide by the demand of classis.

A congregational meeting was held in the parsonage on January 26, 1925.

A talk was given by the Rev. G. M. Ophoff, in which he explained the present situation existing in the Christian Reformed Church, namely, that the Christian Reformed Church has wandered away from the Calvinistic doctrine. Proof for this was amply given (article 3).

A short talk was given by Mr. J. Kuiper, in which he explained that common grace as it is preached in our day is not the fundamental doctrine (article 4).

November 10, 1925, article 2: A motion was made and accepted to have the Thanksgiving service in the Holland language.

January 5, 1926, article 5: A motion was made and accepted to buy a book in which to put down the minutes and also a Holland psalm book for the church.

At a congregational meeting held August 23, 1926, "the question was asked if we were going to continue as a congregation, and the answer was yes (article 2).

May 3, 1927, article 3: A motion was made and accepted to build a small church building and to ask the classis to get permission to hold collections in the different churches of our denomination for that purpose.

May 3, 1927, article 4: A committee was appointed to look around for a suitable building spot somewhere on O'Brien Road, east of the county line but not further east than Mr. Steven Kuiper's crossroad. Committee: Mr. I. Korhorn, Mr. J. Moelker, and J. De Jong.

September 5, 1928, article 3: Catechism classes for the children will be held in the afternoons [on] Sundays after the service, starting Sunday, September 9.

February 12, 1929, article 2: A motion was made and accepted that every family pay $1.25 per week, and that the young unmarried pay $1...per week. This was agreed upon with the understanding that if anybody should be unable to pay they should notify the consistory.

June 3, 1929, article 3: The consistory went on record as condemning the labor unions for the reason that they do not recognize God but
depend on the arm of flesh.

At a congregational meeting held on September 11, 1929, a motion
was made and accepted to buy an acre of land of Mr. I. Korhorn on the
[West] Beltline on the front five acres, excluding the corner acre, for the
consideration of $200 (article 4).

November 4, 1930, article 5: Service to be held Thanksgiving Day
morning in the Holland language.

Mr. and Mrs. I. Korhorn

May 5, 1931, article 5: A motion was
made and accepted that the congregation
rise during the singing with the exception
of the song being sung while collection is
taken.

May 3, 1932, article 4: Motion was
made to have Prayer Day services Monday
evening, May 9, at 7:45.

On July 5, 1932, a consistory meeting
was held in the church basement. This
meeting was opened with reading Luke 20
and prayer by the president, J. Moelker. At this meeting no business was
transacted. The meeting was closed by Deacon J. Kuiper.

May 1, 1934, article 1: The minutes have been mislaid but will be
brought before the next meeting, if found.

At a September 10, 1934, congregational meeting, a motion was made
to ask student Kooistra to labor in the congregation for four months at $8
per week. This motion was seconded and carried (article 2).

October 30, 1934, article 6: A letter was read before the consistory,
which was sent by the treasurer of the missions in regard to money
owed to the mission by the congregation. This letter was tabled.

At a July 15, 1935, congregational meeting, a motion was made
and supported to call a minister for $800 a year with free house rent.
Motion carries.

February 4, 1936, article 8: A motion was made to incorporate the

Hope Protestant Reformed Church in Walker Township on the West Beltline.

April 21, 1937, article 2: Motion was made to start Sunday morning services at 9:00 starting the first Sunday in May. Motion carried.

April 4, 1938, article 5: Motion to give the [Ladies'] Society per-

Articles of Association of Hope Protestant Reformed Church

mission to buy a piano and place it in the church building with the understanding that the organ retains its place.

September 6, 1938, article 5: The consistory wishes to announce to the congregation that we are sorely in need of money so much so that we are unable to meet our obligations and are gradually running behind. The consistory therefore comes to the congregation with the urgent request that we all do our utmost best. We urge those who cannot do much to make an effort to do as much as they can and those who are able to give more to do that. Remember that we must give as the Lord has blessed us. Let us do so gladly, seeing it is our God-given duty to do it.

July 11, 1939, article 3: A writing from the RFPA asking for a collection was received for information.

July 24, 1939, article 2: A motion carried to buy an electric carpet sweeper in case someone will accept the work of cleaning the church building at the present rate of $35 per annum. If no one accepts this after announcement by July 29, a congregational meeting will be called the 7th of August to decide on either of two propositions: that each take a turn in cleaning the church building or raise the janitor's salary to $52 per annum.

March 19, 1940, article 3: Mr. and Mrs. Newhouse were appointed as delegates from the consistory to the banquet of the Ladies' Aid and the Men's Society.

February 3, 1941, article 6: A motion carried to institute a Christian instruction fund to be used for aiding parents in need of financial aid of our Protestant Reformed denomination. A collection will be taken during church services once every two months and once every two months for the poor fund.

February 2, 1943, article 10: New form for worship was accepted as follows: doxology, blessing, singing a number from the psalter, then service will continue as formerly until after the last psalter number is sung, at which time…two verses of the psalter number 197 will be sung and followed by the benediction.

October 5, 1943, article 3: A motion carried to type carbon copy bulletins for announcements to be made to the congregation. Rev. Heys will type the bulletins for which he will receive $10 plus material cost per annum.

November 3, 1943, article 11: A motion carried to propose to the congregation to stipulate a set amount of $25, which the consistory may spend at any one time without calling a congregational meeting, not to exceed $200 per year.

On the editor's actual birthday, October 1, 1945, a motion was made that we remain in our seats during communion except the consistory (article 13).

August 4, 1947, article 9: The Hope Protestant Reformed School board comes with a request to use the church if the school is not completed. Their request was granted.

April 6, 1948, article 13: Motion was…made and carried that Rev. J. Heys pay for the pulpit supplies when he has his operation for his tonsils, that is, when other ministers are here to fill his pulpit. This motion was made at the Reverend's own request.

March 28, 1949, article 12: A motion carried to place the following in our church bulletin:

> The consistory wishes to announce for the sake of our congregation that the young man whose behavior required a rebuke from the pulpit two weeks ago, was not a young man of our congregation. However this is not to excuse some of our own young people whose behavior in church is far from that which becomes a child of God and MUST be improved or their names will be mentioned from the pulpit.

December 5, 1950, article 13: A motion carried to discuss the "Brief Declaration of Principles" of the Protestant Reformed Churches. After some discussion due to the late hour, it was decided to call a special consistory meeting on Monday, December 11. (Due to unforeseen circumstances the meeting was held on December 18, 1950.)

1950 consistory back from left: Richard Newhouse, Jacob Kuiper, Ted Howerzyl, Arend J. Kuiper; front: Gerrit Moelker, Rev. John Heys, Dewey Engelsma

December 18, 1950, article 1: After more discussion a motion was made to present reasons as formulated[5] to [the] January classis for adopting the "Principles." An amendment was made to leave out "c" under "3." The amendment carried, and the motion with the amendment carried.

July 28, 1952, article 7: A motion to instruct the building committee to arrange a way to cool the church auditorium for services carried.

November 3, 1952, article 11: A motion to propose at the congregational meeting the institution of the individual communion cup carried.

July 28, 1953, article 14: A letter from the consistory of the First Protestant Reformed Church regarding the suspension of Rev. H. De Wolf was read. A motion to receive for information carried.

At a December 6, 1954, congregational meeting, the consistory presented the following proposal: That the congregation authorize the consistory to take a loan to purchase other seats for the auditorium without calling a congregational meeting in case we are able to obtain such seats at a reasonable price.

July 1, 1955, article 6: Propose to the congregation to build an addition to the north side of the parsonage to enlarge the living room; size of the addition will be about 8' x 13' at the approximate cost of $1800.

July 1, 1955, article 7: Motion made to accept amendment to make this 10' x 13'; this to include a door from the upstairs for airing deck. Both carried.

September 4, 1956, article 12: Motion made to place application for private telephone line to the parsonage. Carried.

November 7, 1957, article 13: The deacons submitted the budget for the coming year, which totaled $9,157. Motion carried to receive for information.

November 21, 1958, article 5: Rev. Hanko reports on mimeograph machines and prices quoted by two different firms.

November 21, 1958, article 6: A motion is made and supported to purchase a used machine costing approximately $50 carries.

September 10, 1959, article 23: A motion is made and supported

---

5    This is a reference to the document, "Hope Consistory's Response to the Declaration of Principles," in appendix 4.

that the congregation sing an appropriate psalter number after each baptism ceremony. Carries.

June 7, 1960, article 17: A motion is made and supported to send a letter of thanks to H. Meulenberg and Son for the new collection plates they have donated to our congregation. Carries.

In addition to the collection plates, Henry Meulenberg (right) and his son, David (left), made the pulpit furniture Hope currently uses.

April 10, 1961, article 15: The building committee submits a sketch of an addition to our present building. The consistory took no action on this because only one estimate has been given to date.

March 8, 1962, article 10: Motion carries to have the building committee investigate the lots of H. Fenske for a church building site.

March 8, 1962, article 11: Motion is made and supported to instruct the building committee to investigate the possibility of increasing the seating capacity in the church auditorium with the use of pews.

At a special congregational meeting on December 27, 1963, the clerk reads proposal 1 as adopted by the consistory, namely, "that a new church building be constructed on our Ferndale Avenue property for an approximate cost of $75,000 and according to the plans submitted by James K. Haveman, architect." A motion is made and supported to adopt proposal 1. Motion carries by a vote of 37 to 21 (article 2).

April 9, 1964, article 26: A motion is made and supported that the consistory presents newly wedded couples in the congregation with a one-year subscription to the *Standard Bearer*. Motion carries.

November 12, 1964, article 36: The committee to formulate regulations for wedding ceremonies held with a divine worship service recommends the following rules (supp. 3):

1. Anyone desiring a church wedding (solemnized in a divine worship service) shall request the consistory of same at least thirty days prior to wedding date.
2. Preferably this service should be held in our own church building.
3. The ideal is that these ceremonies be held at a regular Sunday worship service, although weekday services are not to be condemned.
4. The Lord's prayer should not be sung as part of the Form for Confirmation of Marriage, as this prayer is part of the divine service.
5. All songs sung during the worship service shall have consistorial approval.
6. We recommend that the congregation be informed of these regulations and that mimeographed copies be made available. A motion is made and supported to adopt the advice of the committee. Carries.

August 12, 1965, article 24: A motion is made and supported to donate the seating in the old church to Hope school as recommended by the building committee. Carries.

September 8, 1966, article 10: A motion carried to fill out the attached questionnaire of the Red Cross to be returned to them and to grant their request for use of our church building in the event of disaster.

November 8, 1966, article 5: The committee to study and advise regarding the proposal of the Mr. and Mrs. societies to establish a "nursery" gave its report (supp. 2). A motion was made and carried to receive for information.

February 9, 1967, article 13: A motion is made and carried to reinstate singing at the beginning of our council meetings and the end of the consistory meetings.

1967 council back from left: Arnold Dykstra, Louis Elzinga, John J. Dykstra, John Kuiper, John Kalsbeek; front: Peter Koole, Joe King, Rev. Jason Kortering, Dewey Engelsma, David Meulenberg, Peter Zandstra

January 9, 1969, article 10: A motion is supported to adopt the recommendation of the committee to introduce an offertory into our worship service. Motion carried.

September 23, 1970, article 18: Motion is made to instruct the music committee to work with a Choral Society committee to promote interest and/or enthusiasm for good music in the church. Motion carries.

February 24, 1971, article 9: Motion is made to adopt recommendation 2 of the committee regarding family visitation reports... Recommendation 2 is "when making public confession of faith each person answers separately." Motion carries.

April 26, 1972, article 16: A letter from Larry Meulenberg is read (supp. 5). A motion is made and supported to grant the request of Larry Meulenberg, that is, to have a divine worship service on June 16. His marriage to Judy Ondersma will be solemnized at this service. Motion carries.

August 8, 1972, article 11: John Cleveland and Carolyn Kamps appear at our meeting requesting a divine worship service for their wedding on September 29, 1972, at 7:30 p.m. in the First Protestant Reformed Church. They have asked Prof. H. Hanko to lead this worship service. A motion carries to grant this request.

August 8, 1972, article 12: A motion is made and supported to have a committee to study the regulations concerning weddings at divine worship services. Motion carries. Committee is Jon Huisken and D. Meulenberg.

February 14, 1973, article 7: The committee to study church wedding regulations reads its report (supp. 2). A motion carries to adopt this committee's report of change in church wedding regulations.

1. Marriage is a beautiful picture of the relationship of Christ and the church as groom and bride and as such should be witnessed by the church at a divine worship service.
2. The divine worship service at which the marriage takes place is no different from any other worship service. The preaching of the word must retain its central place and should not be minimized. Flowers and other wedding paraphernalia are not forbidden but they should not be allowed to detract from the centrality of the word.
3. Ideally, marriages should be solemnized at a regular Sunday worship service but weekday services are not forbidden.
4. It certainly may be announced to relatives and others that the marriage of two children of God will occur at a specific divine worship service but the congregation especially should be present to witness the marriage.
5. If the marriage ceremony is to be held at a divine worship service the following limitations will also apply.

a. The request for a divine worship service must come to the consistory at least thirty days prior to the wedding date.
b. Any deviations from the normal order of worship must be submitted to the consistory for approval at least thirty days prior to the wedding date.
c. The Lord's prayer should not be sung as part of the marriage form since this prayer is part of the worship service.
d. The service must be held in our church building.

November 27, 1974, article 12: A letter from the fiftieth anniversary committee requested that we officially observe the fiftieth anniversary of our denomination on Sunday, March 2, 1975. Motion to observe the fiftieth anniversary celebration on Sunday, March 2, 1975 as requested. Carries.

January 30, 1975, article 3: A motion that the congregation rise at the beginning of the worship service. Carries.

1975 council back from left: Ira Veenstra, Peter Knott, Donald Lotterman, Rev. Ronald Van Overloop, David Moelker, Arnold Dykstra, Harry Langerak, Milo De Wald; front: John Kalsbeek, Peter Koole, John N. Dykstra, Dick Kooienga, Charles Kalsbeek, Herman Van Dyke (Fred Huizinga and Vern Klamer absent)

May 9, 1979, article 14: Motion to approve the beginning of church extension work in the Allendale and Coopersville areas and to ask the Reformed witness committee to implement this action. Carries.

April 23, 1980, article 14: Mr. Don Lotterman enters the meeting.

Mr. Lotterman explains that he has an interest in involving our young people (those who are in their last year of Sunday school) in a new society that would cover the age group between the end of Sunday school and the beginning of society. This group would be the thirteen-year olds or eighth grade. They would expect to study the present Sunday school material but meet more like the present young people's societies do.

April 23, 1980, article 15: A motion to treat the above request at our next meeting is made and supported. Carries.

May 14, 1980, article 13: The matter of article 14 of the April 23, 1980, meeting is on the floor. A motion is made and supported to approve of the proposal, in essence, of Don Lotterman. The clerk will write to Don and also discuss the consistory's feelings on the matter. The motion carries.

December 28, 1981, article 6: Motion that our consistory draw up an official letter of greeting and congratulations to the newly to be instituted church to be called the Evangelical Reformed Church of Singapore is supported and carried.

October 26, 1983, article 15: Our pastor presented a request from Marcia Hanko for a divine worship service wedding ceremony during a Sunday evening service. A proposed order of worship and ceremony is read and filed (supp. 5). A motion is made to approve the request and the proposed order of worship and ceremony and the requests attached. Supported.

An amendment is made that the pulpit be left in the center of the platform for the sermon and moved to the rear immediately after the sermon. Supported and carried.

A second amendment is made that the consistory leave the auditorium before the presentation of the couple. Supported and carried. The motion as amended twice is voted on and carried.

May 15, 1986, article 19: A letter from Mr. Don Lotterman regarding the Bible study class is read. It is moved and supported to approve having this class.

December 14, 1988, article 11: A letter from Sybil Engelsma resigning as organist after fifty years is read and filed (supp. 4).

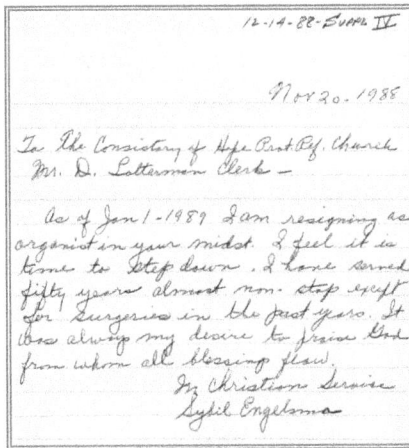

October 25, 1989, article 16: A proposal requesting the consistory to actively propose the organization of a daughter church is read. A motion to table is supported and carried.

February 24, 1993, article 15: Motion to place an announcement in the bulletin stating that those who would like to be served communion should be in the auditorium or the basement worship room so this can be done. Carries.

February 23, 1994, article 11: Motion to adopt the advice that only the believing parent be allowed to stand when their child is presented for baptism. Carries.

December 18, 1996, article 14: Motion is made and supported to use disposable communion glasses. Carries.

1996 council back from left: John N. Dykstra, Gordon Terpstra, Rev. Russell Dykstra, John De Vries, Harry Langerak, Martin De Vries, Harry Rutgers, Vern Klamer, Alvin Rau; front: Gary Nienhuis, Michael Bosveld, Timothy Bomers, John Cleveland, Timothy Koole, James Koole

June 3, 1998, article 15: A motion is made and supported that we make an announcement that the congregation is not to reserve seats and that the ushers are instructed not to respect reserved seats. Carries.

1999 council back from left: Daniel De Meester, Marinus Kamps, John J. Dykstra; middle: Timothy Bomers, Michael Rau, Jeffrey Kalsbeek, Robert Vermeer, Bruce Klamer, Steve Langerak, Jonathan Engelsma; front: Cal Kalsbeek, Tom De Vries, Rev. James Laning, Clare Kuiper, John Buiter, David Moelker

November 1, 2000, article 8: A motion is made that we include in the bulletin an announcement on the Sunday in which communion is administered as to our policy on close communion. Motion carries.

January 17, 2001, article 14: A motion is made and supported to allow the formation of a post-confession Young Adult Bible Society and to put an announcement in the bulletin. Carries.

December 4, 2002, article 7: Recommendation that a letter be addressed to the congregation to make known the need for organists and that the letter also encourages the young people to use their talents to be organists. It is moved, supported, and carries.

May 5, 2004, article 13: Elder _____ proposes by motion that the consistory at various occasions in the lives of the members of Hope church gives fitting books from the Reformed Free Publishing Association. These occasions would be high school graduation, marriage, and the baptism of a first child. Motion carries.

August 3, 2005, article 17: The original motion to recite the Apostles' Creed in unison during our evening worship service is now on the floor. The motion is voted on and fails.

May 2, 2007, article 16: A motion is made and supported to put up to thirty members in the basement to relieve the crowding in the auditorium. Carries.

August 5, 2009, article 10: A letter is read from Professor Hanko (supp. 6). He informs us that he will no longer be able to lead his Monday Night Class. He has asked Professor Dykstra to take his place. Motion to approve Professor Dykstra as replacement for Professor Hanko and ask him officially to take on this work. Carries. Clerk to contact Professor Dykstra. Assistant clerk to thank Professor Hanko by letter for thirty years of labor.

September 7, 2011, article 15: The minutes and archiving committee presents their report (supp. 11). They bring a detailed report regarding their study of the concept of minute-taking practices and archiving minute practices.

March 26, 2013, article 8:

1. Motion to upgrade our Sermon Audio account to include video webcasting and make the purchases necessary to enable us to stream video with four grounds. Carries.
2. Motion that we begin archiving sermons to our Sermon Audio website for download with six grounds. Carries.
3. Motion that we add audio recordings of our past lectures (and any future lectures that we may sponsor) to our website with two grounds. Carries.

2013 council back from left: Jon Rutgers, Timothy Bomers, David Moelker, Ken Engelsma, Hank Vander Waal, Joel Vink, David Kamps, Daniel De Meester, James Koole; front: John Van Baren, Michael Engelsma, Harry Langerak, Jeffrey Kalsbeek, Rev. David Overway, Daryl Bleyenberg, Gary Nienhuis

December 4, 2013, article 16: A book title to give at confession of faith, *For Thy Truth's Sake*, is chosen by carried motion.

July 2, 2014, article 5:

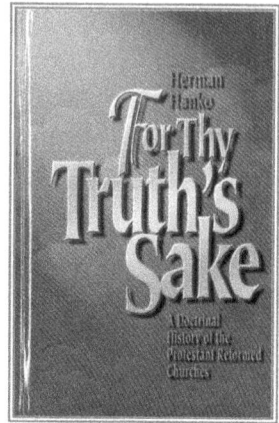

For Thy Truth's Sake

1. A motion is made that the congregation of Hope church recite the Apostles' Creed aloud, standing, and in unison with the minister when the creed is used in its ordinary manner, as a confession, in our worship services. The congregation will not recite the Apostles' Creed aloud in the prayer in the Form for the Administration of the Lord's Supper. With three grounds. Motion carries.

2. A motion is made that this will begin on September 7, 2014, at the evening service. Motion carries.

2014 council 4th row from left: Timothy Bomers, Jonathon Kamps, Daniel De Meester, David Moelker; 3rd row: Gary Nienhuis, Ken Engelsma, David Kamps, Michael Engelsma; 2nd row: Daryl Bleyenberg, Joel Vink, David Jessup, Vance Grasman; 1st row: Rev. David Overway, Harry Langerak, Steve Langerak, Neil Meyer

April 1, 2015, article 7: A motion is made to adopt a recommendation from the Reformed witness committee that the consistory give approval to the Reformed witness committee to fund the upfront costs of funding a PRCA church app (supp. 4). The money required to purchase the app is about $1000. The evangelism committee of Georgetown PR Church has already approved to split the costs with our committee, leaving each committee to spend $500. There are reoccurring monthly costs for the app that the Protestant Reformed domestic mission committee will cover.

Grounds:

a.  The increased use of smart phones.
b.  The app will provide a wealth of good, Reformed resources for mobile device users.
c.  It can be used to promote various events of the Protestant Reformed Churches. Motion carries.

June 17, 2015, article 15: A motion is made and supported to have a committee investigate ways and means to provide legal protection for Hope church in the area of abuse and to provide a plan in the event of a distruption to our worship services by outside influences. Motion carries.

2015 council back from left: Timothy Bomers, Alex Kalsbeek, Jonathon Kamps, David Jessup, David Moelker, Ken Engelsma; middle: Harry Langerak, Neil Meyer, David Kamps, Daniel Van Uffelen, Vance Grasman; front: Cal Kalsbeek, Rev. David Overway, Steve Langerak, Richard Peterson, Jonathan Engelsma

# Chapter 7

---∽ ୨୧ ∾---

# ORAL HISTORY
# ACCOUNTS OF HOPE

## Editor's Introduction

It goes without saying that the history of Hope Protestant Reformed Church involves the experiences of those who lived in the river's bend during the one-hundred-year existence of Hope. In his faithfulness to his spiritual house at Hope, our Lord raised up those who would serve to bring about the reality of Hope as an instituted church. This chapter presents an up-close-and-personal look at Hope through the eyes of some of the past and present members of Hope and of some nonmembers who have their roots in River Bend.

Readers should take into account that oral history is not an exact science. Its accuracy can be skewed because of challenged memories and different viewpoints of those being interviewed. Consequently, if there are some discrepancies between the accounts recorded in this chapter, or as recalled by some readers, please exercise a spirit of Christian charity.

To capture a little bit of the flavor of the experiences of those living in the river's bend as connected to Hope church, interviews were conducted with Betty Bloem, Johanna Bomers, Arnold and Donna Dykstra, Prof. David Engelsma, Dewey Engelsma, Prof. Herman Hanko, Roger Kamphuis, John Kuiper, Harry Langerak, Donna Moelker, Gerald and Clara Van Den Top, Lynn Wells Jr., and Lynn Wells Sr. The order of presentation in this chapter is alphabetical according to the last names of those interviewed.

## Interview with Betty (Korhorn) Bloem

Betty is the youngest daughter of Isaac Korhorn, an elder in Hope church in 1924. She was raised in a farmhouse located a few hundred feet west of the present location of Hope church on Ferndale Avenue.[1]

Betty Bloem
(Elizabeth Korhorn)

Korhorn family back from left: Bert, Betty, Gary;
front: Alice, Mrs. Korhorn, Nelo, Henrietta

CK: Betty, first would you tell us a little bit about your family, your brothers and sisters?

BB: There were six siblings: Alice (Veenstra), Gary, Bert, Cornelia (Nelo) (Kuiper), Henrietta (Velthouse), and me.

CK: You had an uncle Cornelius Korhorn who lived in the neighborhood?

BB: He was my dad's brother. He lived across the street from our house on the south side of Riverbend Street.

CK: You lived pretty much where Jim Koole's house is now?

BB: That's right.

CK: Didn't the house where you grew up burn down?

---

1   Betty Bloem was interviewed by Cal and Linda Kalsbeek on March 3, 2015.

BB: One Sunday I looked out of the window and said, "Our house is burning." Rich [Betty's husband] was there, and I said, "Go tell the folks not to come down [from their present house]. I don't want them to see their old house burning." It turned out it was empty at the time, although a man was living there off and on. He was smoking in bed, and that started the fire. He pulled his bedding out on the porch and watered it down. Then he went to sleep in the barn (laugh). Obviously, he didn't water the bedding good enough.

CK: So your family didn't live there anymore?

BB: That happened years after the family had lived there. Hope church was already on Wilson Avenue.

CK: Do you remember any of the charter members of Hope church? Were some of them still around that you remember?

BB: I remember Rich Newhouse. John Moelker was around for a little while.

CK: Do you remember anything about the building of the Wilson Avenue bridge?

BB: No, the bridge went up when I was about seven years old, so I don't remember anything before that or even the building of the bridge.

CK: What kind of work did your dad do?

BB: My dad worked in the plaster mills. He worked nights as the boss for quite some time. During the day he worked the farm.

CK: Tell us a little about your life on the farm.

BB: Yes, I remember that. We had a barn that was in the back and a lot of other buildings, such as a chicken coop.

CK: So you had animals? Did you have cows to milk?

BB: Dad did the milking, but I would have to go get the cows. They would be over by the main highway [Wilson Avenue]. The creek ran through the pasture land.

CK: So the cows would be where the church parking lot of Hope church is today?

BB: Yes.

CK: So, what kept those cows out of the road? Was the pasture fenced?

BB: Yes, it was fenced.

CK: So your property went up to Wilson Avenue. How far did it go to the north?

BB: To the woods, where the woods are today.

CK: Was that land all cleared? What did your family raise on it?

BB: We raised potatoes and everything.

CK: So you remember when they still used horses?

BB: We had a team of horses.

CK: When you were a little girl on the farm, what did you do for fun?

BB: The neighbor across from us was Uncle Cornelius Korhorn. They had a daughter who was my age. She would come over and we played jump rope, tea party, and things like that.

CK: Now that family [Betty's uncle] left Hope church in 1924 right?

BB: Oh, yes. We didn't see much of them after that. They weren't too friendly after that.

CK: What about the Moelker family? How were they related to you?

BB: They were my uncle and aunt. Mrs. Moelker was my mother's sister.

CK: Do you have any memories of past ministers?

BB: Not too much. But I do remember that Ophoff would always lay over the pulpit and sometimes he'd be hanging on to it. Once he said, "You should nail this thing down."

CK: What did you do for school?

BB: I started at Riverbend Public School. It was torn down, and the new building is now in its place [on Kenowa Avenue]. Some of the parents got together and the parents started bringing their children to Jenison Christian School. I must have been quite young because I hardly remember going to Riverbend. We went with the Ponstein, Kooienga, and Kievit children. The parents took turns bringing us to Jenison. They had automobiles then. That was the closest Christian school.

CK: Did anyone in your family go to high school?

BB: No, I don't think so.

CK: You must have had some grapes on the farm? When I went to Hope school, after school in the middle 1950s we would go pick them. I think they were there until the housing plat of Fenske was put in.

BB: Yes, on the fence between us and the neighbors on the west side. The grapes were there for years.

CK: Didn't your dad give the land for the church and school?

BB: Yes, that was all our land. The farm went all the way to the highway [Wilson Avenue].

CK: Did he ever retire?

BB: He worked in the plaster mines and the farm, and he painted houses. He painted with his brother when he was available. I remember he papered our living room. He put up two ladders with a board in between. I had to hold the bottom of the long piece of wallpaper. He would put the paste on, and I held the paper.

CK: When you were older do you remember some of the other members of the church?

BB: I remember the Kooienga, Kievit, and Engelsma families. The Engelsma family lived way down Kenowa [to the south]. We did not see them too much. Charles was the father.

CK: Here is a picture of an old church picnic. Why is your husband, Rich, way over here and not by you?

BB: Every time we had a picture taken at a church picnic, he would call the fella who took the picture and make the arrangements for him to come. Rich would help get the people to stand where they had to, and then at the very last he would run around to get in the picture. Every year the picnic was in Johnson Park.

CK: Do you remember anything about the Depression? Did it have an effect on your family?

BB: I didn't pay much attention. We grew our own food so we always had something to eat.

CK: When you were first married where did you live?

BB: We built a garage house right next to where I grew up. Then Rev. Mensch moved from across the street [at Riverbend and Moelker] to go out West. He sold his house to us. It was a good deal we couldn't pass up. So we moved there.

CK: Well Betty, thank you for allowing us to interview you. If other memories come to mind, let me know, and we will include them.

## Interview with Johanna (Engelsma) Bomers

Johanna is a daughter of Charles and Lena Engelsma and granddaughter of charter member, Jantje (Jennie) Engelsma.[2]

Johanna (Engelsma) Bomers

---

2    Johanna Bomers was interviewed by Cal and Linda Kalsbeek on March 17, 2015.

CK: I would like to begin by asking some questions about your family. Could you tell us about the siblings of your family?

JB: My sister Jen was the oldest then came Harry, Ted, Winnie, Dewey, Sadie, George, Melvin, Sybil, myself, and Eileen: six girls and five boys.

CK: What do you remember about your grandparents?

JB: My dad's mother [Jante] lived with us always. My grandma named all the children except Eileen.

CK: Your grandma named you? She had the right to do that somehow?

JB: My parents let her (laugh). My sister Jen was named after her, and the next one was named after my mother's family; every other one, [alternating between my dad's family and my mother's family].

CK: So there was an established rule about naming the children?

JB: There must have been. She was a very saintly woman, but she was always right. She was very domineering. How my mother put up with it all those years I don't know.

CK: So how long did she live with you?

JB: It began soon after my mother and dad got married. They were eighteen and nineteen when they got married.

CK: Let's now turn our attention to where your family lived. At what point did your parents move into the Hope area?

JB: After they were married. I think my dad lived in that area before he met my mother. My mother did house work in East Grand Rapids.

CK: Was the first place they lived in River Bend on the farm where Kenowa runs dead into the Grand River?

JB: Yes, and my grandmother had a room on the side [of their house], but she always ate with us. She slept in our part of the house. But to say that she was in her room so much I can't say that. She was more in my mother's house.

CK: How much land did your dad farm and what did he raise on the farm?

JB: He had ninety-five acres. He mostly grew feed for the cows, and he had a garden. We had raspberries, strawberries, and a lot of beans. Then he decided to try pickles. We thought, "Oh, not pickles." But they didn't grow well, so he never tried that again.

CK: So the children would help around the farm?

JB: Oh yes, we had to.

CK: So in what year were you born?

JB: 1925.

CK: And you said you were baptized by Rev. Ophoff?

JB: That's what I'm told (laugh).

CK: How long did you live on the farm?

JB: They sold the house before I was married. Then we lived on Hall Street, where your dad [John Kalsbeek Sr.] used to live. Dewey owned the house, and mom, Sybil, Eileen, and I lived in a trailer in the backyard. We had electricity, but no bathroom.

CK: I knew Dewey owned that house, but I didn't know there was a trailer in the backyard at one time.

JB: Sybil, Eileen, my mother, and I lived there until my mother's house was built on Riverbend. It's the second house, west from the cemetery. It's still standing. We [Johanna and husband Jay] lived in the house next to the cemetery.

CK: So your father had died by that time?

JB: Yes, he died in 1943 when I was eighteen years old.

CK: How much later did your mother die?

JB: Bruce [Johanna's son] was four years old. He was born in 1948, so she died in 1952.

CK: So you built the house on Riverbend next to the cemetery right away when you got married?

JB: Yes, because my mother needed help. Gordy [Terpstra] put a wire from her house to our house so that if she needed anything she could buzz us, and I would run over there and help her. She also had a wire from church so she could hear the sermons. Every Monday Rev. Heys came to see her. Every Monday morning about ten o'clock he'd walk over.

CK: Let's go into some of the charter members of Hope. I have a book here that has a list of the charter members in 1916. Now, of course, you were not around then, but I wonder if some of them were still around in later years that you would remember them. How about Charles Bouwman? Did you ever hear of him?

JB: Yes, I heard my folks talk about him, but that was it.

CK: How about Adrian Heyboer?

JB: I remember them. I knew who he was but that was it. They lived down Kenowa across from Tanis' storage [near Burton Street] in a big farm house.

CK: How about Peter Ruiter?

JB: I remember my folks speaking of him, that's about it.

CK: John Moelker, his wife, and eight children?

JB: They lived in the house on Kenowa that was and still is on the property of Moelker Orchards. I knew all their children.

CK: How about Jacob and Jacoba Zaagman?

JB: They lived on the east side of Wilson Avenue [south of Riverbend]. The house is still there. They added to the house. I want to say he worked at a feed mill, but I am not sure.

CK: How about Wietse Visbeck?

JB: I know who he was. He did not stay in the church that long.

CK: How about Johannes and Jacoba Maria Wilhelmina (Bating) Van Dyke and four children? You don't remember them?

JB: No, I don't. But you don't have any Korhorns on the list.

CK: No, they must have joined later.

JB: I remember Ike and Ricky lived across Ferndale from the present Hope church building where Jim Koole lives. His brother and his wife lived across [Riverbend Street]. After the split in 1924 when we started school there was so much bickering it was terrible. I was told I could not play with Dorothy [daughter of Cornelius Korhorn]. Dorothy was my best friend. How can you tell children they can't play together? So I came to school and said to Dorothy "I mayn't play with you," which was hard.

CK: How old were you at the time?

JB: We were in first or second grade. She asked me, "Why not?" I said, "Because you left the church." She did not know anything more than I did about it, you know. Then I came home from school one day and I said to my dad, "How can you stop me from playing with her, she's my best friend?" Well, he gave in a little bit. I could play with her at school, but she could not come over to my house. Then at that time her mother had triplets. Dorothy said to me, "You may come over and see the triplets." They were about three months old. Her mother would not let me in the house because we had had the split. So I never did see the triplets.

CK: Really! So the split not only affected the grown-ups but very much affected the children also?

JB: It was instilled in us that we could not have anything to do with those people.

CK: I suppose the parents were afraid that you would eventually go to their church or something?

JB: In those days if we asked anything about what went on in the church, we were told not to talk about that. Now today it's all out in the open right away.

CK: What about school? Where did you go to school?

JB: I went to Riverbend Public School through the seventh grade. When I was in the seventh grade, the Kooienga family and the Ponstein family moved out here, and their kids hated it at Riverbend. They had always gone to a Christian school. Dick

[Kooienga] got us to go to Jenison Christian School. He wanted to know how many would go there. Well, it was the families of Engelsma, Korhorn, and Kievit and that was all. We took turns driving to school.

CK: The Wilson Avenue bridge in Grandville was there, so then you drove into Jenison every day?

JB: Yes, every day we had a different driver. Kievit had the oldest car, and no one wanted anyone to see us in that car (laugh). So we always managed to be on the bottom and have someone sit on our lap.

CK: Do you remember when Hope school was started?

JB: I remember Rev. Heys on the roof tarring on a Saturday. I thought, "Is he going to be clean by tomorrow?"

CK: Okay, I would like to ask about a few specific memories you have of Ted Kievit. They didn't always live in that house on Hall Street [that was formerly the house of Rich Newhouse]?

Ted and Anna Kievit

JB: No, they lived around here, but they didn't live on Hall Street right away. I remember that Mr. Kievit didn't make confession of faith until his daughter, Evelyn, was about twelve or fourteen years old. He came to church all the time. I remember when he came and made confession of faith. I can still see him standing up there.

CK: And they farmed that land on Hall Street?

JB: They had nothing. My dad gave them raspberry bushes and they grew good, but otherwise there was not much that he could grow there.

CK: Let me ask you some questions about Rich Newhouse. Do you remember his wife? What was her name again?

Isaac and Henrietta Korhorn and Susie and Richard Newhouse

JB:  Oh, yes, Susie. She died when she was quite young. I would say she was close to sixty. She was very meek.

CK: I heard that Rich lived with the Ike Korhorn family where Michael Bosveld now lives on Kenowa?

JB:  He lived there after his wife died.

CK: I've heard that he lived in a trailer by Cliff Tanis on Burton Street. Is that right?

JB:  That also was after Susie died. I think he was more or less retired. He helped Cliff quite a bit on the farm.

CK: Let's turn our attention to some of Hope's ministers. Do you remember Rev. Ophoff when he was a minister here?

JB:  Yes, I remember him preaching. He preached here quite often.

CK: That must have been after he was no longer Hope's minister?

JB:  Yes, he didn't have a church when he was teaching in the seminary. I know Hoeksema had a church. Ophoff was a kind man, but you never knew how to take him (laugh).

CK: Betty Bloem remembers him, shaking the pulpit.

JB: He almost knocked the pulpit over. He stopped all of a sudden and said, "You men gotta nail this down sometime."

Another thing Rev. Ophoff said in a sermon made an impression on me. When I was about eleven or twelve years old, I looked at myself and thought, "I'm kind of pretty." Well, one Sunday Rev. Ophoff had a sermon on the devil. Sitting there in church, all of sudden I heard him say, "You look like the devil, and you act like the devil." I thought, "I can never think of myself as being someone important." He sure put me down. But that's how he was.

CK: After Ophoff left, Hope had student Kooistra for a while. Could you mention some of the things you remember about him?

JB: He spoke with the same tone of voice. When he taught catechism, he had his eyes on his notes, and the boys were monkeying around like mad. The girls usually sat in front.

CK: Is there anything else you can say about his catechism instruction?

JB: I would always know my catechism. But I knew what verse and what question I was going to get. He always went alphabetically. He never looked up; he just went down the list. But one time he skipped Betty and asked me, so I didn't know the answer. I thought, "There…" My dad always asked us our questions. If we learned the answers quickly, we could say them, but by the time we got to church we had forgotten them. Well that taught me a lesson. I had better know all the answers (laugh).

CK: So eventually Hope church got Rev. De Wolf. What do you remember about him?

JB: He was a very good preacher. Very nice and he came almost every Friday to the farm for food. He was dirt poor. He had an old car that had a rumble seat in it. We took care of Hubie [Rev. De Wolf's son, Hubert] every other Tuesday night during Ladies'

Aid Society. They brought him over, but he was scared to death of Dad. Hubie would stand in the corner all night.

CK: Hubie was a son of Rev. De Wolf?

JB: Yes, the oldest son. He didn't like my dad. My dad had a low voice. He'd say, "Come, Hubie, let's play." But he just stood in the corner. When he heard his dad's car drive in the driveway, he was out of that corner and to the door.

CK: Hope's next minister would have been Rev. John Heys. You remember him, working on the roof of Hope school?

JB: Yes, he was behind that school 100 percent. He was a real pusher for the school. I remember that his kids always played with our kids. Well, on Halloween we let our kids go to Howerzyl's house, Korhorn's house, and to my mother for a treat. Rev. Heys' daughter, Ardess, came over and said, "May I go with you?" Jay [Johanna's husband] said, "You have to go home and ask your dad if you may go." So she went and was back quite soon. She said she could go. When she came home with all that candy, Rev. Heys called Jay. He said, "Why did you give her permission to go?" Jay said, "I didn't, I told her she had to ask her dad and mother if she could go." Oh, he was so mad (laugh)! She was grounded for quite a while.

CK: Is there anything else you remember about Hope church that you recall or remember your parents talking about?

JB: I remember years ago when John Moelker was here. He was a farmer and was busy in the summer. When he got older he went to Florida for four weeks, and his name was up for elder. There was quite a stir at that time. We didn't know much about it because we weren't supposed to know. But, he did get in the consistory.

CK: So that created a little tension?

JB: Yes, it did, especially with relation, because the Korhorns and the Moelkers were related. Mrs. Korhorn and Mrs. Moelker were sisters.

CK: Anything else? Do you remember your folks talking about worshiping in Mr. Newhouse's house?

JB: I remember my folks talking about it. They would go to his house with a horse and buggy.

CK: Who, in your opinion, were most influential in Hope in those early years?

JB: The three main families were Korhorn, Moelker, and Engelsma, and they all had large families.

CK: Well, thanks for the interview. If any other interesting memories come to mind let me know.

Later Johanna related these additional memories:

1.  Rev. McCollam could not think of the benediction and looked at Sybil, who played the organ, to help him. She did.

2.  We had a single cup at communion and everyone tried to be up front because we had a member with a long beard, and part of his beard hung in the cup.

3.  My folks [Charles and Lena Engelsma] left Hope for a few years when the Dutch service was discontinued, because my grandma didn't understand English. We children stayed at Hope. That was in the early 1930s.

4.  John De Jong lived on Fennessy and had a long beard. He thought he was always right.

5.  John Kuiper, grandpa of John Kuiper, also had a long beard.

## Interview with Arnold and Donna Dykstra

Donna is the daughter of Dick and Sadie Kooienga who were long-time members of Hope church. Arnold and Donna are the parents of Prof. Russell Dykstra.[3]

Arnold and Donna Dykstra

JK:  Who were your mom and dad?

DD: Dick and Sadie Kooienga.

Dick and Sadie Kooienga

JK:  How and when did they come to Hope church?

---

DD: They lived in Byron Center. They moved to the Hope area in 1937 when I was three years old. Hope church was in existence already, just a real small church.

JK: Why did they move to this area?

DD: I think my dad was interested in this land.

AD: He had to clear it.

JK: Your dad had a brother Jake. Who are some of his children?

DD: Floyd, Will, Gerald, Les...

AD: Floyd lives right over here on Kenowa. His wife died a couple of years ago.

DD: Les would be Rog's age [Donna's brother]. They also had Ron and Marge and Jan. They all went to Hope church at one time. I was a friend of Les' wife when they got married, but when they left the church, I just kind of lost track of them. I think my dad was the only one who stayed in the Protestant Reformed Churches of all his family and all of my mother's family [Windemulder]. They were in Holland church.

AD: They all left except Sadie, who was married already [in 1953].

AD: Dick built the house on the east side of Wilson that Al Rau later purchased and where Dave Rau lives now.

JK: So he was a farmer then?

DD: Yes. Your dad and uncles worked there at times. Probably weeding or harvesting onions.

JK: Yes, I heard some stories about them and your brother, Rog. Rog was their straw boss. Tell me about your siblings.

DD: Yes, they were Joanne and Lois, Rog, Judy, Don, and Betty. There were seven of us, and we all went to Hope church. Joanne and Bob went to Hope church for a while, and then they had all kinds of issues so they left. And Lois left when she got married. And Rog of course stayed, and I did, and Betty. Don left when he got married, and Judy left when she got married.

JK:  How long did your family stay on that farm?

DD: That's where we all grew up. After we were all married, my parents sold the farm to Al Rau. They moved near Hope church.

AD: On Riverbend.

DD: Yes, that little green house. And then they moved across from church [Jim Koole's house].

JK:  What are some of your earliest memories of Hope church?

DD: I remember as a little girl we were sitting in church, and I had to go to the bathroom. My mother whispered, "Just go to the car when you're finished," because the service was almost over. So I sat in the car and I tooted the horn and kept tooting the horn. My dad came out and angrily put me in the back seat. I didn't even know what I was doing wrong. Under the window in back of the old church, there was a long row where all the young guys sat.

JK:  What was that white church like?

DD: When we got crowded, they'd put chairs up by the organ, right underneath the window. In the winter it would be so cold. I sat there one time with Russ, and I took psalters and put them up there so the wind wouldn't get in my neck. But it was a nice building. We kind of hated to see it torn down.

JK:  Others have said that too.

AD: One time Donna went to church and I stayed home to take care of the kids. While Donna was in church, we had eleven inches of snow. It was the second Sunday of April. We had a little German car with front-wheel drive, the only car with front-wheel drive. Donna was the only car to get off the churchyard without getting stuck.

JK:  I only remember your dad in his old age. Did he do anything like lead societies, things like that? Was he an elder?

DD: I can remember his being an elder most of the time. He also sang in the Hope Heralds, one of the first ones to get that started.

JK:  What do you remember about Mr. Newhouse?

DD: He was such a nice old man. One time he was over here for dinner on Sunday. After we were through eating, our boys all got up and cleared the table because they always did that. No girls in the house. He just kept remarking about that.

When Mrs. Miedema died, I remember Mr. Newhouse, walking down the aisle and reciting verses in Dutch out loud the whole time he walked down at the funeral. That's what he did. He was a strong Christian man, and his wife was little just like him, just a little lady.

AD: I used to visit Rich when he lived in the trailer back at the Tanis Orchard. He had his rocker or chair up on a pedestal so he could look out the window toward the road past the barn. I'd cut his hair and talk with him. I would always go to the nursing home too and cut his hair.

JK: Do you remember anything about the [Isaac] Korhorn family? Didn't they live right around here?

DD: Yes.

AD: Where the Bosveld family lives now on Kenowa.

DD: When Ike died, Mrs. Korhorn came to church faithfully every Sunday. She lived to be in her nineties. And she never stopped coming to church that I can remember. She'd come in with a hat on all the time.

JK: Who was the first minister that you remember at Hope church?

AD: De Wolf, wasn't it?

DD: Yes, Rev. De Wolf and then Rev. Heys.

JK: Do you remember much about De Wolf?

DD: They were good friends with my mother and dad. They came over in the summer and got celery, onions, muskmelons, and watermelons. Of course, when De Wolf became involved in 1953 that was hard on my dad, because they were good friends.

AD: Your dad [Dick Kooienga] used to say to me that, Rev. De Wolf had a good personality. He would come in the house, open the refrigerator, and grab something to eat, just like he was part of the family. That's the kind of person he was.

DD: I remember Rev. Heys as being my minister when I was growing up and his catechism teaching.

JK: What was he like?

DD: As a young child, I used to think Rev. Heys had no sin. I'd look at him and think, "He must never sin because he is always dressed up in a shirt and tie."

AD: That's how he went to the beach also.

JK: He even wore a tie to the church picnic.

DD: You never saw him anywhere without a white shirt and a tie.

AD: I remember him at Ottawa Beach; he was there just like that—white shirt, tie, and dress pants.

DD: Yes, we did like him. I used to babysit for him. Eileen Terpstra and I used to babysit when they'd have Ladies' Society.

DD: Mrs. Heys was a real quiet lady.

JK: All the ladies would wear dresses at the church picnic. Didn't they make pants for ladies yet?

Ladies at the 1946 Sunday school picnic back from left: Mary Howerzyl, Jean Korhorn, Mrs. Korhorn, Bess Moelker, Donna Moelker, Gert Wierenga, Bernice Kuiper, Nelo Kuiper, Betty Moelker, Flora Ponstein; front: Dena Engelsma, Hattie Lanning, Sadie Kooienga, Grace Engelsma, Kay Mohr, Anna Kievit, Lena Engelsma, Mrs. Boogaard, Esther Heys

DD: We had pants to work in the field. I remember buying a pair of jeans one time and my mother took them away from me because girls just didn't wear blue jeans.

JK: What do you remember about the split?

DD: It was just turmoil. My dad would talk to so many people, and it was a troubling time. For the family too. We felt it in the house that things weren't right.

JK: How old were you?

AD: You were nineteen. I wasn't around; I was in Germany in the Army. All I knew about the split was from Rev. Vos. He wrote to me.

DD: I think Rev. Heys handled it really well. I don't remember anything troubling about what he talked about. Because of him, I think most of the people stayed.

JK: Was there turmoil in your family?

DD: Just different families that would come over and try to talk my dad into leaving and because all of my mother's family left and my dad's too except Aunt Hattie [Lanning]. So it was a hard time for my dad and my mom too.

AD: But they were plenty happy that they stayed. I had nice talks with Donna's dad, and he'd talk about it. They couldn't persuade him to leave.

JK: After that, was he cordial with other family members?

DD: Up to a point. Sometimes he'd get started on something and then it was time to go. My dad couldn't leave it alone either. Right or wrong, I don't know, but he brought things up. That's what I mean about turmoil. They were our aunts and our uncles, we loved those people.

JK: And then on top of that, De Wolf was a good friend.

DD: Yes.

AD: A lot of it was personality in First church. De Wolf had a blossoming personality, he could talk to anybody. That's what some of the people liked. He was friendly. Hoeksema was kind of staunch, and everybody thought that he was hard to talk to. But he wasn't; I knew him. I talked to him a little later, of course.

JK: What do you remember about Mr. and Mrs. Kievit?

DD: Oh, Mrs. Kievit, she was such a dear lady. She really was. I used to love to go over there.

AD: One time Rev. Hanko, now professor, went to the Kievit's house on family visitation. He asked Mrs. Kievit if she had a Bible. She responded, "Well, what would you say if I didn't?" That's the way she was.

DD: Yes, she was a nice lady. Mr. Kievit was real quiet, but she made up for it.

JK: So Rev. Heys took a call, then who was your minister?

DD: Then we had Rev. Hanko. We really liked him.

AD: He was here in 1962 when Carl died.

DD: Yes, we had a baby die, that's why Professor Hanko is so special to us. Carl was our fourth boy, born between Brad and Mark. He was born with a bad heart.

AD: He lived two months, one month at home and one month in the hospital.

DD: You get real close to your minister when you go through something like that.

DD: I remember your grandma, Henrietta (Net) Kalsbeek. She and John went on a trip with my mother and dad, and the next morning after they returned she was killed in a car crash.

John and Henrietta Kalsbeek with grandchildren, Jeff, Jay, Jori, and Lenora

JK:  I didn't know that. What trip did they go on?

AD: Out East somewhere for a couple of weeks.

Sadie Kooienga, Net Kalsbeek,
and John Kalsbeek on their trip East

DD: Your grandpa called my mother and said, "Sadie, Net's gone," and my mother said, "Well, where'd she go?" She didn't catch on, you know.

JK:  When you married, did you become members at Hope?

AD: No, we went to Creston first. We moved here after one year and then came to Hope.

AD: Just about right now it would be about fifty-six years ago.

JK:  And that was in 1959 then?

AD: 1959, yes.

JK:  Do you have any memories of Rev. Veldman?

DD: Oh, we just loved that man. He was just so good. He had some quirks, you know, but...I remember when he took the call to Hudsonville. I wasn't there at church, I was home with the little kids, and he called me the next day, and he was crying, he couldn't even talk to me.

DD: When they read the form when he was installed here, then the minister says, "Yes, truly with all my heart." He was all choked up you could tell it on his voice, he could hardly get that out.

AD: But he knew his sermons all by heart. He didn't have anything in front of him.

DD: He was especially good on the catechism.

AD: He didn't stay very long. We moved into the new church [on Ferndale] when he was here. They built the parsonage when Rev. Van Overloop was here. Rev. Hanko was by us in the fall of 1955 to 1963, and then we had Veldman for three years only, 1963 to 1966. Then 1966 to 1970 was four years for Rev. Kortering. Then we had Rev. Van Overloop from 1972 to 1979, then Flikkema from 1981 to 1986, then Slopsema, and then Russ [Rev. Dykstra] for a few months.

JK: What do you remember about Rev. Kortering? Your boys were starting to go to catechism then, right?

AD: It was the fastest four years of our lives.

DD: We liked him so well and then he's gone again, so fast.

JK: Between 1957 to 1967 that's when your brother [Roger Kooienga] had his accident, right? What was that like for you, for the family, and for the church?

DD: He had just become a deacon when that happened. We had no idea. Well, I didn't anyway, that the accident was going to be a life-changing event. I just thought someday he'll be better, but he never did get better. That was hard, hard on my mother and dad too. But his wife, Lou, I can't say enough about her, because she brought those kids up and look how they all turned out.

Roger Kooienga

AD: All in the church.

JK: Tell me about the accident.

AD: A truck driver pulled into his lane on Route 16 by Fruitport.

Rog's truck after the collision

Nunica newspaper article

**Crash Hurts 5 in Ottawa**

Coopersville— (AP) —Five persons were hospitalized Friday, state police said, after the near head-on collision of two trucks on US16 between Nunica and Coopersville.

Jose Suarez, 28, of Okeechobee, Fla., driver of a semitrailer truck, was the only one to escape injury in the crash. Albert Rimmer of Dandridge, Tenn., a passenger, was admitted to Hackley hospital in Muskegon.

Their truck, police said, collided with an aluminum frame-loaded van truck driven by Roger Dale Kooienga, 37, of Grand Rapids. Passengers with Kooienga were his three sons, twins Ronald and Douglas, 6, and Michael, 3. All four were transferred to St. Mary's hospital at Grand Rapids following emergency treatment at Municipal hospital in Grand Haven.

State police said the eastbound semi-truck swerved across the center line of the highway to avoid a car which turned suddenly into a driveway. It careened into the path of the west-bound Kooienga vehicle. Officers said a slippery road, rather than excessive speed, was a crash factor. All occupants of both vehicles reportedly were thrown out upon impact.

AD: It was a two-lane road, and it was kind of snowy that morning. The truck driver got too close to a car ahead of him, and he couldn't stop, so he pulled out into oncoming traffic, hitting Rog.

DD: And he had three of his boys with him.

AD: They flew out in the field into the snow.

DD: Yes, no seatbelts back then.

AD: They had to pry Rog out of there. You wondered how he ever made it when you saw the cab of that truck.

I was the first one to get to the hospital. He was taken from Grand Haven Hospital to Butterworth because they knew he needed a better hospital. Then Donna called me at the barber shop and I went right to the hospital. When they took Rog in, oh he was so bad. I didn't think he was going to live.

JK:  What were the boys like?

DD: One had a broken leg and some cuts and bruises, but they weren't hurt very bad.

JK:  So then Rog was probably hospitalized for months.

DD: Yes, then he went to Pine Rest. He was there a long time. He lived with a broken body for forty-seven years.

DD: At one nursing home he was at we went to see him and he said, "Donna there is nothing to do here, nothing."

AD: That was on Leonard Street. He walked all the way home from Leonard Street once or twice.

DD: He came home from Pine Rest many times; we don't know how he got here. One time I was in the basement, I heard someone come in, and I looked up and there I saw a man's legs. I thought, "What in the world?" Well, I had to go look, and there stood Rog. He said he had walked home, I don't know how he got there from Pine Rest, but that's what he said. I still don't know to this day how he got here.

AD: I'm pretty sure he walked.

DD: I had to bring him back, I felt terrible, but I had to bring him back.

JK:  What do you remember about the Langerak family?

AD: I had a lot to do with Tony. I would go with his little Volkswagen and pick up hats. In those days people wore hats and they'd have them cleaned. I'd go pick them up for Tony on my day off.

JK:  He had a store in Standale right?

AD: Yes, Hi-Tone Dry Cleaners. That's why it's called Hi-Tone because his name is Tony. People would say, "Hi" to him when they came in, so he named it that.

AD: You probably don't remember that, but in those days a business like that picked up people's clothes from their houses. For instance, you would have something in your window that he could see. If you had something, he would pick it up.

DD: They did that for ice too when we were kids. All had their ice boxes.

JK:  And milk?

DD: And milk. John Dykstra was our milk man.

JK:  What did you do for work?

AD: Cut hair.

JK:  And it seems that on your days off you did other things.

DD: He used to be a brick layer too.

AD: I did cement work too.

DD: There's nothing he won't try.

AD: And I did plumbing because of your grandpa. Part time, I'd help him, especially when they were doing an addition on the Christian Rest Home. George Kamps [brother of Evelyn Langerak, Dorothea Kalsbeek, and Carolyn Cleveland], who was killed in an accident out East, he worked there then too.

AD: That's how I got to know George. And then he moved out East and got killed. That was a shock.

JK:  Did you ever have an idea that your son was going to go into the ministry?

DD: Oh no, not a minister. He wanted to be a teacher. I said to him one time when he felt the call to the ministry, "How is it, Russ, that you didn't feel it before?" He said, "All my life I wanted to be a teacher, and I would put that aside, I just didn't want to think about it because I wanted to be a teacher."

AD: People talked to him when he was in Hull, that he should go to the seminary.

DD: Russ was in bed at home for three months after a back surgery, and he couldn't get out of bed. Rev. Kortering would come and do catechism with him. So he would talk to Russ about that too, but he wanted to be a teacher.

DD: Of course that was during the school year. We had a box that was hooked up through the telephone to Hope school. His cousin, Ron Kooienga, would carry it from room to room [at Hope school]. In this way Russ kept up with his studies.

JK: Did you say that Kortering would tell him already at that age he ought to be a minister?

DD: Yes, when he would come and talk to him, he didn't say it every week, of course. He told me that I had better encourage him to do that because he has the qualifications.

JK: Arnold, why did you come to the Hope area?

AD: Because I married Donna.

DD: We moved back here when Russ was just starting school.

JK: That would be a good reason to come.

AD: We were both happy about that; it was a problem solved.

JK: Transportation problems?

AD: A lot of people who had school children moved in the area.

JK: And then when Covenant started, that really started bringing people to the Hope area.

DD: Right.

JK: So then the new church was built?

AD: When Rev. Veldman was here.

JK: Any other memorable experiences?

DD: One service when Rev. Van Overloop was our minister, there were boys sitting in the back goofing off. Rev. Van Overloop said, "Would you boys in the back there please behave?" When the consistory went out, he said, "It's your son; it's your son..." Some were elders' children.

AD: That was the end of their sitting by themselves.

JK: That's probably a good thing.

DD: Yes. It wasn't good that the kids sat together. They've got to sit with their families.

JK: What was it like for Hope during the Vietnam War? Men were getting drafted?

DD: Yeah, Larry Koole was and so was Mike Engelsma.

AD: Bob Miedema of Bob and Joanne.

DD: They all went to our church at that time.

JK: Your generation has lived to see the decline of our country.

AD: Yes.

DD: And you would despair if you weren't a Christian. You pray for your children and your grandchildren.

## Interview with Prof. David J. Engelsma

Professor Engelsma is the son of Dewey Engelsma, grandson of Charles Engelsma, and great-grandson of Hope charter member, Jantje (Jennie) Engelsma.[4]

Prof. David J. Engelsma

CK: Have you ever heard River Bend called "the devil's elbow"? I came across at least two, maybe three, people who recognized

---

4   Prof. David Engelsma was interviewed by Cal Kalsbeek on June 5, 2015.

that terminology of the devil's elbow. I have seen Rex Robert's stuff. He is quite educated and has a degree in agriculture from Michigan State University. He is also a poet. One of his poems refers to some of the families that settled in the devil's elbow. So I started asking around, Wells and Roberts and so on. They say it was called that because they believed that the topography of the land in the bend in the river diverted the rainfall such that they received less; thus the name the devil's elbow.

DE: I never heard that, but I remember Rex Roberts and his wife lived on the corner of Kenowa and Hall. In the fall I would pick up potatoes [Cal did that too] in their field.

I spent most of my time as a youth working days. After we gave up the old farmstead on Kenowa, I worked for Tony Tanis. I picked apples, did farm work, and milked cows, so I knew the Tanis family better than any of the old timers, although we would run across [the street] to the Wells now and then.

DE: Did the Wells have some interesting tidbits?

CK: Yes, they did. Lynn Sr. remembered you Engelsma kids when you lived on the Weller place [at the end of Kenowa] and walked to catechism on Saturday mornings.

DE: Well, we also walked to school every day. I checked the distance and it's close to two miles one way. But my parents were poor and we had one car, which my dad had to take to Keeler Brass to work. So fall, spring, and winter we walked both ways.

CK: His son (Lynn Jr.) gives your dad credit for getting him a job at Keeler Brass. I don't know how that worked out. Your dad was working there, and Lynn was looking for a job. Somehow your dad put in a good word for him. I heard another interesting thing. Your grandfather, Charles, sent tobacco to his family in the Netherlands. One time (at least Lynn says this) your grandfather was a little upset when whomever he was sending the tobacco to asked for cigarettes instead of tobacco (laugh). Lynn says that was the end of your grandfather's sending tobacco over there.

DE: I remember that my grandfather, Charles, died young of a heart attack in 1946 when I was six or seven years old. But every summer I would spend a couple of weeks on his farm because Aunt Eileen was there. She was the youngest child, and we were pretty close in age. She would dress me up as a baby and play house with me.

CK: We were at Hannah Bomers' house and she has a nice wedding picture of them. You may remember that, they were a good looking couple.

DE: I remember that picture. They had a big family. They went through the hard times, never had much money. But if you lived on the farm you had food during the Depression. It gladdened my heart to hear that even though they didn't have a lot themselves, Charles would give milk and eggs and whatever to people who were poorer than he was.

David Engelsma with his
Grandfather Charles and Aunt Eileen

David Engelsma with his
Grandmother Lena and Aunt Eileen

CK: I guess one of the main things I wanted to ask you about was Mr. Newhouse? You had a lot of contact with him. I know about him when he lived on Hall Street, but where did he come from? He was a charter member of Walker Christian Reformed Church when it started in 1912. He is on the membership list. When Hope started he became a charter member of Hope. Apparently in the meantime he had moved or somehow he came to live on Hall Street.

DE: I don't know if there were stops in between, but very early on after the Protestant Reformed Churches started in 1924 he lived either near or with Isaac Korhorn. Isaac lived on Kenowa just a little bit south of Riverbend [Bosveld's house]. But when I knew Richard he was living in a trailer on the farm of Tanis and caring for apple trees. He was basically Cliff's salesman on the market selling Cliff Tanis' fruit. Then the arrangement was that he could live on that property.

Richard Newhouse with Isaac and Henrietta Korhorn
in front of Rich's trailer

CK: I heard he had a store at one time. Did he ever say anything about a store in town?

DE: I don't know anything about a store, but I know he was what they called a string butcher.

CK: Do you know where that term came from?

DE: He must have worked in a store in the meat department and cut up animals. But where the term "string" came from I don't know.

CK: Lynn Wells said Newhouse would buy cattle at the auction and before the auction he would go in the pens and nudge the cattle to determine if they carried calves. Then that would be a good buy, but I didn't ever hear that he raised calves.

DE: But that would tie in with his working in a meat market or owning a store.

CK: I also heard that Rich resigned from the consistory in the 1930s because of travel. He must have moved to town.

DE: That was probably connected with the store. But I did not know he resigned from the consistory. Generally what I know about his early history is that he was always a prominent figure in the beginning of Hope church. He was in the consistory in the earliest days as an elder and continued to have the prominent position virtually up to the time he died.

CK: Was he in a trailer at the Tanis farm until he went to the rest home?

DE: Yes, I believe so. That would be a number of years. I searched my memory due to your coming here. He was certainly in that trailer when I was in my last year at Calvin, so that would have been 1959–60. And he was in that trailer all the while I was in seminary, so that would go through 1963. I am pretty sure he stayed there until it became impossible for him to live by himself. Then I was gone, of course, to Colorado so I didn't see much of him.

My next memory of him is when he was in the rest home in Allendale. I would go there with my dad. I don't know if I wrote this or someone else told me, but I have one outstanding memory typical of Richard Newhouse. It was in the summer and I was on vacation from Colorado. Dad and I went to visit him. He was lying sick or weak in a bed. He had gotten in a tussle with one of the nurses over something. Maybe he wanted to smoke his cigar. He was extremely angry with her, and when we came in he was reprimanding her in the Dutch language. She didn't have the foggiest idea of what he was saying. I would not want to translate what he was saying. But my dad admonished him and told him he must be submissive to the will of God and must be thankful for the help he was getting there. Rich subsided into an unwilling silence and then everything went well. At the end of the visit my dad had the misfortune to read Psalm 139, which ends as you will remember, "Do not I hate them, O Lord, that hate thee?" When my dad came to that text, Rich said, "Amen." I think he had that nurse in mind (laugh).

CK: Yes, we would visit Newhouse quite often over there too, and the main issue was that he wasn't allowed to smoke. So he would sneak outside to smoke (laugh).

CK: Lynn Wells remembers seeing Richard in his wooden shoes and with his big pipe.

DE: I don't remember wooden shoes, although he had a lot of artifacts in that trailer and pictures of himself when he was in some gymnastic group in the Netherlands. It looked like circus uniforms. There were five or six guys who made a pyramid with Rich on the top of the pyramid, probably because he was the smallest of the bunch. He would show me those pictures.

CK: Do you know anyone who has pictures of Rich?

DE: I wondered what happened to his belongings when he died, because I had given him some Dutch books that I had come across in the Netherlands that I really wanted for myself, and I would still like to have them. I think there were a couple of volumes of poetry by an outstanding Dutch poet. I gave those to him, and then when he died I don't know what became of those books. None of his other friends or relatives would have any ability to read those books. If I were to look for those pictures (he had them in a picture book), I would investigate with the Kuiper family. Maybe one of the sons would have gotten them. That would be the first place to investigate.

CK: I don't know of any pictures of him other than the one of Rev. Ophoff, Korhorn, De Jong, and him in the fiftieth anniversary book of Hope church.

DE: Yes, that picture of his gymnastic team was quite different, and he was quite proud of it. He showed me that album more than once. His trailer was under the apple tree right near Tanis' barn. I was to milk the cows every night. After I finished I would walk down there often. He was a short fellow. If his chair was on the floor in the trailer and he sat in it, he couldn't see out the window. So he had a platform made, and he put his chair on the platform.

"Richard would sit there like a little lord with his pipe, filling the room with smoke and looking out over the terrain. He had a good view from there looking to the south, north, and east. His back was to the west."

CK: Yesterday my wife and I visited with Donna Moelker, the wife of Jim Moelker. Her father-in-law [John] was quite prominent in Hope church until 1953. He was the clerk of the consistory many times. Do you remember him?

DE: John Moelker, who I remember, also according to my father, was an important man in the church. One way he was a very important member is that he was the only one [of those who started Hope church] who had any money at all. He had money. According to my father, often at the end of the year when Hope church's balance was low he would contribute a hefty amount of money to bail the church out.

John had a large family. He had a son John, who up until 1953 was a member of Hope church. He lived down Kenowa near where Gord Terpstra lives now. John had a son Gordon who was my age. We went to Hope school together and graduated from the ninth grade together in the early summer of 1953. The split actually happened after we graduated together from Hope school. Then all of the Moelker families separated from the Protestant Reformed Churches, including Gordon's father, John. So, of course, Gord left with his father. But Gord and I kept in touch. We had been good friends through our grade-school days. I went to Loveland and he went into the service, but we wrote each other.

Gordon came back to the Protestant Reformed Churches some years ago, and this bears on the significance of Hope church. Gordon was a member of Hanley Park Christian Reformed Church. His children became of catechism age, but that church did not have catechism for the children of the church. Gord went to the minister with that. The minister told him that he would check with the consistory. Later he called Gord on the telephone and said, "We don't do that, and we are not going to do that." Gord thought his catechism instruction at Hope church under Rev. Heys was so important that he called the consistory of Hope church and said, "My church will not educate my children in catechism. May I send my children to your catechism classes?" Hope church said the children would be welcome. Gord looked at his wife, who also was Christian Reformed, and said, "If our church won't teach catechism to our children but Hope church will, what are we doing in this church?" That was the occasion of their coming back to the Protestant Reformed Churches. It is a testimony of Hope church and its emphasis on catechism. All kinds of powerful influences go out from the church. Sometimes we don't think about that.

CK: Did you know that your grandfather, Charles, left Hope church for a period of time?

DE: Yes, he had an old mother [Jenny] living with them who was the spiritual power in that family, by the way, for better or for worse. My father said she did a lot of teaching of the grandchildren (more so than the father even). Not reflecting badly on his father, she was a spiritual power in the family. Also in 1924 she was very firm that the family must remain with G. Ophoff and the Protestant Reformed Churches.

She couldn't understand English very well so they went to Roosevelt Park Protestant Reformed Church where there was Dutch preaching. They went there until Jenny died, and then they came back to Hope.

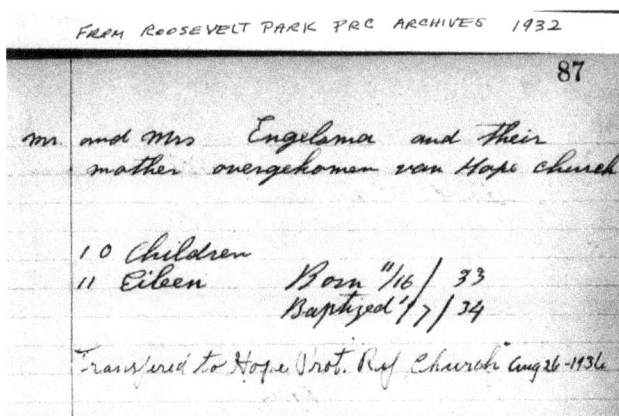

Record of the return of the Charles Engelsma family to Hope church

I wish I knew more about that whole history. Charles, my grandfather, was a young man of eighteen or nineteen in 1900. He and his older brother, George, immigrated to the United States and ended up here on the southwest side of Grand Rapids. That was because in those days in the Netherlands they were starving to death. So for economic reasons they came here. After he got here he settled on the farm where Kenowa ends at the

Grand River and earned enough money to bring his mother here. She must have been a widow by that time. I don't think she came here with her husband. Then in the providence of God Charles joined Hope Christian Reformed Church, and that is how we are in the Protestant Reformed Churches today. His older brother, George, started there, but he had a farm on O'Brien Road. Mainly for that reason he joined the Netherlands Reformed Congregation. So there is a large contingent of Engelsma families in the Netherlands Reformed congregations who are all descendants from George.

CK: Do you know how or why Charles ended up in River Bend?

DE: No, I do not know. I suspect that he had experience with farming in the Netherlands and that land on Kenowa was undeveloped. I have an idea that he homesteaded it. The United States' government let people own land for a small amount of money if they would farm it for a number of years. The farm was about one hundred acres and a lovely sight, really. So farming is what he did his whole life. I remember staying there as a boy. He farmed with horses; he never had a tractor. I remember riding with him on the manure spreader pulled by a team of horses.

CK: Back to Richard Newhouse. Did you ever meet his wife?

DE: No, she had died long before I came on the scene. Susie was her name. They had no children.

One of the memories about Richard Newhouse in connection with his life in the church that stands out with me is his conduct during the controversy of 1953. He was a fighter, and he could not always control his temper either. There were passions in those days. I was a boy of thirteen and that controversy was a monumental upheaval in Hope church. Hope church consisted of families who intimately knew each other. When the people visited in those days, they took the children along on Sunday nights. So they knew all the people. They were like our brothers and sisters, so that conflict was devastating to the children in those days.

I remember that in every service I went to I would hear

another harangue against conditional theology. Every minister worked that in somehow. I remember one time Rev. Ophoff preached. Rev. Ophoff was Rich Newhouse's favorite preacher all the way back to 1924. The split hadn't happened yet, but there were members of Hope who were enemies of Herman Hoeksema. After the service Ophoff and Newhouse together (he was in the consistory) came out of the side door of that little, white-framed church building on Wilson Avenue. An older member of the church confronted Ophoff about his sermon, and I was close enough to hear his question. It was about something Ophoff had said in the sermon. Newhouse could sometimes be belligerent and maybe not handle things quite right, but he stuck himself between that member and Rev. Ophoff and exploded in that man's face (laugh) with accusations and condemnations. It was disconcerting to those who witnessed it. But it was obvious to all, and especially to the children, that something was happening there that wasn't right.

That carried over with its passions to some extent to our family gatherings too. The Engelsma family was large, and there was at least one member of the family (a sister of my father) married to a prominent member of First church who was backing De Wolf. The Engelsma family had the custom of gathering for coffee at the home of my grandmother Engelsma who was still living at that time on Riverbend Street. Those meetings were always very pleasant, but at that time they would break up in an uproar. The women would be crying and the men would be loudly clamoring, and that had its effect on the children. We wondered what in the world was going on.

CK: You said your grandmother Engelsma lived on Riverbend?

DE: Yes, she lived in a white house on the south side of Riverbend, which is right across from where a man named Ted Howerzyl used to live. Right across from that lower entrance to the Hope church property. Another white house, a little east of it, closer to the cemetery was where Uncle Jay and Aunt Hannah Bomers lived.

CK: Now going back to this experience in the split of 1953, are there other things you experienced that demonstrated the tension? How about among the children at school?

DE: No. I don't think it ever surfaced among the children. The actual split happened in the summer, so a goodly number of students of Hope school didn't come back in the fall. But then I had graduated in the early summer of 1953 so I really didn't experience that either.

But, you asked about other memories: one memory stands out rather vividly. I remember in the early part of 1953 when everything was hot, Hoeksema preached one Sunday night at Hope church. That was a rarity. He seldom preached at Hope church, Ophoff more often, but Hoeksema had his own congregation so that played a part. Of course, we all knew who he was. When he stepped into the seven o'clock evening service, he came out the door with the consistory. I was sizing him up as he mounted the pulpit. In those days they read the scripture passage before the congregational prayer. He read Ephesians 4, which is a polemical chapter that contains a particular verse that bears very strongly on the doctrinal issue of 1953. As he was reading the chapter (there was no announcement in the bulletin as to what verse he was going to preach on), I said to myself, "That's the text that bears on the controversy of the conditional or unconditional covenant." He prayed, the deacons took the collection, and then Hoeksema mounted behind the pulpit again. He looked over the congregation, and he said this (a virtual quotation): "When I came here tonight it was my intention to preach verse such and such of Ephesians 4 (that was the text that I knew it was going to be) in view of the controversy in our churches. But when I look over this audience and I see so many young people and children, I decided that that would not be fitting, so I am going to preach on a different text." Then he read out of John 10 about Jesus as the good shepherd. I was thirteen at the time. I can remember thinking two things: that is quite a minister who can change his sermon on the spur of the moment, and this man is not the ogre he is made out to be with that kind of consideration for the young people and children in his audience.

CK: Your family moved to Hall Street. Do you remember that?

DE: My parents married in 1938 and lived for a year in an apartment on Crawford Avenue, which is right off Franklin Street near Chicago Drive. A year later they moved out to the Hope area to the house on Hall Street [east of Wilson Avenue], in which the John Kalsbeek family later lived. They lived on Hall Street from 1939 to 1950. Then my father had the opportunity to buy the farm on Kenowa where he had been raised.

CK: Where was your grandmother at that time?

DE: My grandfather died in 1946. She sold the farm almost immediately and moved to that little house on Riverbend that was built for her. Sybil and Eileen lived with her because they were not married yet (Sybil never married). Johanna Bomers lived right next door.

CK: I have to say that Rev. Heys who was at Hope for a rather long time was used by God to keep Hope church in the Protestant Reformed Churches. The split in the church had its sad days and its advantages too. There were men in Hope church who were both prominent and otherwise very good men who I'm sure put pressure on John Heys to go in another direction.

DE: There is an interesting story about Rev. Holwerzyl. It is likely he influenced his relatives at Hope to leave the Protestant Reformed Churches. He was an influential preacher in California at the time. I did not know him then, although I saw him at the meetings of classis and synod that I attended.

I went to Loveland in the middle 1960s. One Sunday night, almost in the front row of our little church building, sat Rev. James Holwerzyl, his wife, and some children. I even remember the sermon I preached that night. It was shortly before the start of school, and we had a little Christian school there. So I would always preach a sermon that I thought was appropriate for Christian education, because Loveland congregation was not raised on Christian schools, and there was a struggle there about that. I preached on Genesis 1:1 that night: "In the beginning God created the heaven and the earth." I preached the sermon and didn't add or take anything away because Rev. Holwerzyl was there. Afterward he said to me, "We are on our way back to California. We have been visiting relatives and this morning we attended a Christian Reformed Church in Fort Collins. The service was such and such, and the sermon was so pathetic that I said to my wife, "We're not going back there again tonight. That is why we are here this evening, which I guess is better than nothing at all (laugh). [He was a member of that denomination, but he couldn't even attend the worship service of his own denomination.] I also make a practice of preaching a Christian school sermon prior to the start of school season. I was wondering what text I would preach on and now I know. I am going to preach on Genesis 1:1 when I get back." I thought to myself afterward (I did not say anything to him), "There's got to be some sourness he had knowing as well as I what the broader picture was."

CK: Well maybe we should call it quits. I don't think I should take up any more of your time. You have to get back to your writing.

## Interview with Dewey Engelsma

Dewey Engelsma is the grandson of Hope charter member, Jantje (Jennie) Engelsma, uncle of Charles Terpstra, and father of Rev. (Prof.) David Engelsma.[5]

CT: What do you remember of the years prior to 1924? I know that you were only a child, but what memories do you have of those years?

Dewey and Dena Engelsma

---

5   Dewey Engelsma was interviewed by Charles Terpstra in 1985.

DE: Prior to Rev. George Ophoff's coming in 1922, I can remember catechism classes in what was then the Hope Christian Reformed Church. There weren't exactly rooms for it in that church, but I can remember sitting around the furnace, and we had some seminary students for teachers. The name of one of them was Medendorp. He was a seminarian, and he taught us in catechism. That brings us up to about 1922, and then I can remember when Rev. Ophoff came.

CT: He was your first minister then?

DE: Yes, Hope was Rev. Ophoff's first charge after graduating from seminary. We were about twenty to twenty-five families strong in Hope Christian Reformed Church, and then Rev. Ophoff took over catechism and everything. I can very distinctly remember him, teaching us catechism on Saturday mornings.

Rev. Ophoff would come to our place on the farm and visit us on Monday mornings, since he wanted to talk with my old grandmother and see how his sermons were coming across. He would sometimes take Richard Newhouse along, because my grandmother always talked in the Frisian language and Richard would translate that to Rev. Ophoff. I recall Rev. Ophoff saying, "What's she saying? What's she saying?" Well, Richard would say, "That's alright, just be calm," and finally, when Ophoff knew that she was happy with the sermon he had preached the day before, he was comfortable. But, being a new minister, he was always a little bit apprehensive about his sermons and how they were coming across to her.

Engelsma farmhouse on Kenowa Avenue

Charles Engelsma family in the summer of 1924,
from left: Charles, Melvin, Sadie, Winnie, George, Sybil, Lena, Jantje

I remember that in church there was a group of young fellows sitting in the back. After the last song was sung, those boys would go out. They didn't wait for the doxology or the benediction; they just walked out. They were, to put it in today's vernacular, tough, young guys. I was a little kid then, and I thought, "Man, when I get that old and can walk out with them that will be something." Of course, I didn't appreciate then how irregular that was, and that it wasn't right and shouldn't have been done. Their parents should have gotten after them.

In any case, I was ten years old in 1924, and I knew there were things happening, but a ten-year-old doesn't get involved in the doctrinal controversies. One Saturday afternoon in the summer a little, Model T coupe drove in the yard, and I happened to be out there. The man in the car said, "Where's your dad?" I said, "He's in the back field working." Then the man said, "Well, can we drive out there?" I said, "Yes." So he said, "Hop in and we'll go out there." There were two men in the car, and we drove out in the field. On the way the car hit a bump, and the driver said, "Why didn't you tell me there was a bump there?" Well, I was scared of who the men were and so forth. Anyway, he said to my father, "You can't have the church building anymore." As it turned out, he was the sheriff, and he came to give my dad and the others the message that they couldn't have the church building anymore.

That happened on a Saturday afternoon, and the next morning the families that stayed with Ophoff met in the schoolhouse across the street. After we moved into the schoolhouse, we never missed a service. Sometime soon afterward, we called ourselves Hope Protestant Reformed Church. No longer were we the Hope Christian Reformed Church. I don't know just how soon, but I guess that after the classis or the consistories decided that their name wasn't going to be the Protesting Christian Reformed Church anymore, but the Protestant Reformed Church. Anyway, we met in the schoolhouse. How the elders were elected, I don't know. Perhaps some of them had been in the consistory. I'm sure Mr. Newhouse was.

CT: So Hope lost some members then?

DE: Oh, yes.

CT: Do you remember who those families were?

DE: Oh, yes. They were the Goeree, Bergman, and Zaagman families. The families that worshiped in the schoolhouse were Newhouse, De Jong, my parents, and my uncle. He wasn't a member of the church, but he came all the time with his children, but not his wife. She was Netherlands Reformed, so he came with some of the children all the time.

CT: Where did the other families go?

DE: They stayed with the Christian Reformed Church and met in the church building, which was across the road from the schoolhouse.

CT: Oh, I see. They kept the building then?

DE: Yes. They struggled on for some years.

CT: Did any of those families come back?

DE: No. After a while that group built a church in Grandville and continued on as Hope Christian Reformed Church.

I recall that between 1924 and 1930 when we were young people, we didn't have any activities in our little group except catechism and church. So one of our members advised that, since our family was one of the bigger families with young people and I was about fourteen or fifteen years old, we should go to Hope Christian Reformed Church. They had a choir, a choral society, and he advised that we go there and sing with them. So we did that for a while, a few of us, but it never worked. There was something about it that we didn't feel at home there. We did go, and I remember going there and singing in the choir, but it didn't work. We knew we were in the wrong place. The advice that man gave us was not good advice. I think that was probably one winter that we did that.

Those few families left in the church had many problems. They were not doctrinal problems, but problems over loaning tools and horses to each other. Someone would borrow someone's horses for a week or two, and when he brought them back, well, the farmer who owned the horses thought that he ought to have a little remuneration for that. And the other would say, "Well, I never used them. They just set in the barn by me." They had troubles over things like that. They had troubles over dividing up a hay field. Those were serious problems. I can remember at least once they had the whole congregation together, the men at least, to try to settle those things instead of having the consistory do it. The whole congregation came together because being only a few families everyone was involved.

During those years between 1924 and 1928 Hope church seriously considered dissolving and joining with Hudsonville. That's in the record, too. And they decided not to by a single vote. So we went on as Hope church. And then it began to grow a little bit. Isaac Korhorn came. They weren't there originally.

CT: Isaac Korhorn wasn't?

DE: No, no. I shouldn't say that. They weren't there in 1916, but they were there in 1921 when Rev. Ophoff came. Then it began to grow a little bit. We got a Miedema family. And then there was a De Jong family for a little while. This was a different De Jong from the other family there already. They were related to that old De Jong who lived here. It was a brother to Jake De Jong on the consistory. He also left sometime in the 1940s.

Then around 1930 we decided that we should get out of the schoolhouse and build a new church. We then built the church on Wilson Avenue, where Hope school is today.

CT: Yes, I remember that church.

DE: Okay. That land was donated. We dug the basement out with horses. There were no tractors then. I suppose there are some pictures of that. I worked there a few days helping dig the basement.

CT: Did the congregation itself build the church, or did they hire someone to do that?

DE: Lou Bergman built the church. John [Arend J.] Kuiper, the father of the John Kuiper who is presently in Hope church [now in Grace Protestant Reformed Church], made two additions to the building. The church was built in 1931, which was about the same time Wilson Avenue was completed and the bridge in Grandville was being built. Prior to that we could never get to Grandville. We did have a boat in the river. We went to Jenison quite often for small grocery orders or for tobacco for my dad.

CT: Would you go back just a little bit? Hope lost Rev. Ophoff in that time, right? He left for Byron Center?

DE: Yes, he went to Byron Center in 1929.

CT: Do you have any other memories of his pastorate in Hope church?

DE: Well, I have a lot of memories of Rev. Ophoff. He was very, well— for lack of a better word—amusing sometimes. I loved the man, but when I was in my younger days some of the things he did were really funny. He just couldn't get to places on time, and he lived right next to the church. He couldn't get to church on time.

After we lost the property, Rev. Ophoff moved to the west side of Grand Rapids. The church rented a house on Watson or Watkins Street, I forget. But that was worse, because quite a few Sunday mornings we would be waiting. Nine-thirty would come, and no Ophoff. I remember one man, John Kuiper's grandfather, who was kind of a watchdog on time. When it got to be nine-thirty or a few minutes after, he would walk through the door in the schoolhouse that went down to the basement and open the door of the consistory room and say, "It is time, boys. Don't wait for the preacher any longer." So the "boys" [elders] came up to the sanctuary, and one of them would begin the service. Sometimes we would get up to the reading of the law, or even the congregational prayer, and Rev. Ophoff would come in. He grunted a little bit, and he and the elder would have a few words of whispering to let Ophoff know how far along the service was. Then Rev. Ophoff would take over, and the elder would walk down to his seat. That happened not a few times.

CT: Did he preach in Dutch at that time? One service or both?

DE: Yes, there was one Dutch service and one English service.

CT: Did the young people and/or children have any trouble understanding the preaching?

DE: Everyone attended both services. But, oh yes, we had trouble with the Dutch. When we built the new church, my father heard rumors that they wanted to make both services English. We had an old grandmother, my father's mother, who just couldn't understand one word of English. My father said to the elders, "I hear that as soon as the church is built, it's going to be all English services." But they said, "No, we don't think so." Of course, they didn't really know either. But that's what happened. And then from 1932 to 1936, about four years, we joined Roosevelt Park Protestant Reformed Church.

CT: Really? You mean you attended both services at Roosevelt Park?

DE: Yes, we transferred our membership.

CT: I see. Was that also because you were without a pastor for quite a while at that time?

DE: Yes, we were without a pastor. But everything was in English, and my grandmother had to have something, so we joined Roosevelt Park church.

CT: Was your family the only one that left or did other families leave too?

DE: We were the only family. I went to church three times a Sunday for a long time, because the morning and evening services were English, and the afternoon service was in Dutch. I took my grandmother and parents to the Dutch service in the afternoon and stayed there myself, because my father didn't drive. That's when I really learned the Dutch.

CT: Who was the pastor at Roosevelt Park?

DE: Rev. Kok was the minister the whole time we were there. When my grandmother died in 1936, we went back to Hope.

Then Rev. De Wolf was called, and he came. We had a good, prosperous time under De Wolf's preaching. De Wolf was a good preacher—then, at least. He was a good, young preacher, and the people who came to hear him said, "You're not going to have him for too long here." Well, we didn't either, because he stayed for four years. In 1941 Rev. Heys came.

But before Heys came we had seminarians. We also had a lot of reading services over the years, even in the Hope church on Wilson Avenue. There were a lot of readings, and I can remember Newhouse and old Jake De Jong on the pulpit.

CT: Did those elders also teach catechism?

DE: Yes, they taught catechism. I can remember that John Moelker did a lot of catechism teaching. I forgot to mention that he also was a member of Hope Protestant Reformed Church. When we went to the schoolhouse in 1925, he was there too. He had a large family, ten children. So soon those young fellows were getting married, and brought their wives in, and the church was growing a little bit.

By the way there was also a Haggerty family in our church. Not the husband—he was Roman Catholic—but the mother and children were Protestant Reformed, and they always came to Hope church. The father didn't mind. I guess he was not too staunch. So there were people in our church by the name of Haggerty, too.

Well, through marriages and so forth the church began to grow a little bit. And that made us decide to build a new church. Well, anyway, we were up to Rev. De Wolf's leaving and Rev. Heys' coming.

Rev. Heys was in Hope for about thirteen and a half years. My wife and I were married in 1938, and at that time we made the seventeenth family in Hope church. I can remember that Dena wasn't very old. She was seventeen, and I can remember going with her to Hope's consistory for her to make confession of faith when De Wolf was our minister.

CT: Where was Dena from? What church did she attend?

DE: She came from First Protestant Reformed Church.

CT: Did you ever go there with her to church?

DE: Yes.

CT: Do you remember hearing Rev. Hoeksema?

DE: Yes, but not very often, because Dena moved to our area. She worked for Gerald and Jean Korhorn. They had a grocery store on Leonard Street, and she worked for them. She babysat and they ran the store. That's how I met her.

During Rev. Heys' ministry everything went well. Those were the beginning of the war years, too. I think I became a deacon when I was twenty-nine, if I remember. And then I became involved. A deacon at that time sat in on all the meetings. Hope church was small. It had three elders and two deacons, so we had combined consistory meetings as the Church Order allows.

We were married then, of course, and we received the *Concordia*, the paper that Classis West produced. We read and found out that things were not good in the Protestant Reformed Churches. Then, too, there was that whole episode of Rev. Kok's and Rev. De Jong's trip to the Netherlands. We knew what was happening.

We saw people in action in Hope church. I suppose that sometimes people get a little radical when things don't go fast enough, but there were people in Hope church who thought that we ought to boot them out right away. Of course, you can't do that in the church situation just because you feel that way. You have to hear them out. But in our own church it was easy to observe that things were not right.

Some consistory members were not happy where they were or with the way things were going. They had already sided with the other side. During the service you could see them sitting with their heads down and never looking at the preacher. I knew something wasn't right. But they kept on serving in the consistory, even then, and went along with the decisions, but I knew something was awry.

Once Rev. Hoeksema preached in Hope church, and afterward he visited at our house. He had noticed those men, and he asked, "How come there are a couple of men in the consistory who don't ever look up?"

In 1953 we were forty families strong, for Hope had steadily grown. But we lost approximately fifteen families to conditional theology. That brought us down to about twenty-five families, and that was a sad day. But those were the best years for me. Now I'm not saying that I don't like growth, for I certainly like to see a church grow, and that had proved to be a great blessing in Hope church.

Twice [by the mid-1980s] Hope church has established daughter churches. But the best time in Hope church for me was when the membership was about thirty-five families. I liked that; I knew everybody, all the children. And I'm sorry to say, maybe it's because of my age, that I can meet some of our younger people, and I don't know whether they're members of Hope church or not. That's not so good.

CT: I don't like that either. I prefer a smaller church.

DE: But 1953 was a difficult time in Hope church. It really was. We were fortunate that the people didn't leave all in a group. For that reason Hope didn't have any litigation. There was no organized opposition in the consistory. The people left one by one. So we didn't have any problems in that respect. But there were some difficult times in the consistory. I was in the consistory quite a bit at that time.

CT: As an elder?

DE: As an elder, yes. And it didn't really get all settled until 1962 or 1963. It took that long for some of them to leave. And all the while when there are two factions, or elements, in your church, even if there are only one or two families or persons, it's not peaceful, that's all. It comes out. And pretty soon the last one had to leave too. At first he was 100 percent with us, but gradually for some reason or other he became disenchanted with Hope church. He made a terrible mistake, and he knew it too. A few years later he knew he had made a terrible mistake, and he wanted to come back. He realized what so many others realized, too.

CT: So the people were aware of the doctrinal issues, and it wasn't just a case of dissatisfaction with the size of our churches?

DE: Yes. Now I don't know whether the ministers or even some elders were dissatisfied with the growth of our churches in general. I think they were, but in Hope at least that wasn't the case. In Hope I think they were just looking at the leaders and what they were saying, and were sympathetic. But I don't think that everyone really understood the issue.

CT: Would you say that De Wolf had quite a following then among the people?

DE: Yes, Rev. De Wolf was popular. There's no doubt about that. He was a popular man, well-met and articulate.

CT: Did Rev. Heys bring out the issues in his preaching to the congregation?

DE: He sure did bring them out in his preaching. Rev. Heys was a good leader, and he kept on top of the issues. He set them forth plainly, too, so that we knew what the differences were. By the grace of God, Hope survived that controversy. Hope was not nearly as hard hit as some of the other Protestant Reformed churches. As I said, Hope lost fifteen families. That was difficult enough, but it wasn't as bad as First church and Second church [Southwest] and some of the other Protestant Reformed churches.

So we went on after 1953, and started to grow again. And it went rather fast. Building Hope school brought people in.

CT: Perhaps you don't want to answer this, but concerning the people who left, did they simply pull their papers out or was there discipline involved on the part of Hope's consistory? What did they do?

DE: I wasn't in the consistory all the time. I had my turns out.

CT: But were you in at the time that controversy was going on?

DE: Yes, at least some of the time. But, no, there wasn't any discipline. How you can explain that, I don't know, except I think it's something like this. There were people who were not happy with us, but they didn't exert themselves. They didn't set forth or articulate what they believed, at least not in public. And they simply came to the point where they asked for their papers. They were questioned, of course, in the consistory room, and they said that they just wanted to leave because they were going to side with so and so. At that point there is no room for discipline, except that they did it themselves. But they were admonished. One man came to request his papers from the consistory, and he foolishly said something like this: "Well, we've heard long enough in Hope church what God does; let's hear once what man has to do."

CT: Did you attend any of the classical or synodical meetings? Do you have any recollections of that?

DE: Yes, I did. I attended the classical meeting where the split actually took place. That was when classis had to decide whether or not De Wolf was guilty of heresy. Many of his supporters were there. They were all given time to speak, and that's the first time I ever saw a microphone in our meetings. I think the classis meeting was held in Fourth Protestant Reformed Church.

CT: Did the classis get recorded then?

DE: Well, no. They did that just so everyone could hear the speakers, because the building was packed. But that's where the division actually came, and that is where the struggle for the property of First church started too. I can remember going to that classis.

I also remember going to the classis where Rev. Richard Veldman broke with Fourth church. That was kind of interesting. I worked at Keeler Brass, and I was quite friendly with a Christian Reformed man. Every Monday morning we would get together and talk about what was going on. Well, one particular Monday he said, "Well, I have to go to classis tomorrow night where one of your preachers is going to be examined." I said, "What?" And he said, "Yes, Rev. Rich Veldman." He was still with the Protestant Reformed Churches. No one had ever heard that he was leaving. I said, "No, you're kidding." He said, "Yes, Rev. Rich Veldman is going to be examined by our classis tomorrow, because he wants to come to the Christian Reformed Church." Rev. Herman Hanko was our preacher at that time, so I got right on the phone after that and called him. I said, "Rev. Hanko, do you know that I was just told that Rev. Rich Veldman is going to be examined by the Christian Reformed classis tomorrow in Ada?" He said, "You're kidding; that can't be true." Then I said, "I was told that." And it was really true. That's how he left. He never even told his consistory.

CT: In 1953 did Rev. Heys and Mr. Newhouse draw up the minority report that was eventually adopted by classis?

DE: Maybe Rev. Heys was in on it, but the elders were Richard Newhouse from Hope church and Pete Lubbers from Hudsonville church. Three ministers had the majority report, which stated that De Wolf was sound. But Rich Newhouse and Pete Lubbers had the minority report, and they were against De Wolf's statements. And classis sustained their report. The ministers said that De Wolf's statements could be interpreted rightly. One of the ministers later capitulated when De Wolf plainly said regarding the majority report, "That isn't what I meant."

CT: Can you go on to talk about after 1953 and then about trends from then until now?

DE: Well, we had another little episode around 1962 when Rev. Veldman left. We had an elder in Hope church who was not happy with the way Rev. Veldman was treated. I think sometimes that from a personal viewpoint there was mistreatment. There always is. I guess you can't avoid it. Personalities can cause this. But basically Rev. Rich Veldman caused it all because of his shenanigans. He would not come out and defend 1953 in our favor.

We had an elder in Hope church who was 100 percent Protestant Reformed, we thought. He would nail Rev. Veldman after a sermon and say, "Why didn't you bring in this and this?" And Rev. Veldman said, "I think that's better to be left alone." Well, the strange thing is that after Rev. Veldman left, this man didn't like the way classis treated Rev. Veldman, and consequently he went over to his side. This elder took Veldman's position, and he had to be admonished for his support of Veldman. So he left, and that was really the end of it.

After that controversy, and with Hope school being built and so forth, Hope church began to grow rapidly. The church building couldn't be expanded anymore, so we decided to build a new church. That wasn't easy either, because there were quite a few who were against that. Things were prospering, and building was booming. Costs were going up and some of them said, "No, we mustn't build; we have to wait until building supplies get cheaper." It's a good thing we built, because they didn't get any cheaper.

I think that having been in Singapore gives me a more critical look at our churches. If the young people in Singapore have shown us one thing, it's this: they are living much closer to God than our general population in the Protestant Reformed Churches. That's at least what we consider to be true; we can't read the heart. They are spiritual; they seem to be able to cast the world out. I remember one day we were driving by a polo stadium, one of the biggest stadiums in Singapore. I said to one fellow, "Do you keep up with the sports in Singapore?" He said, "No, God delivered us from all of that."

I argued with Rev. Vos once at classis about television. He had a television. He said he got it just for the ballgames. I said, "Rev. Vos, even that's pagan." Well, he didn't appreciate that much. I like ballgames myself, but let's be honest, that's all.

I discussed the whole matter of sports with some of the leaders at Covenant Christian High School in connection with basketball games in school. And I said to this one fellow, "Now you tell me one thing and that's all. That will satisfy me. Does Christ approve of it? Would he come to one of our basketball games and sit there and say, 'This is great?'" Well, he said, "I can't answer it right now." So I let it go a whole summer. Last fall when the games started again, I said, "Did you come up with an answer to my question?" He said, "What was that again?" Well, I told him. Then he said, "Yes, I think he would." Mind you, that's what he said. There was another coach standing there, and he said, "I won't tell you." Well, that's what I mean. It seems like we can have it and no one is criticizing it, but it certainly bodes trouble for us in the future. Worldliness is going to overcome us from within.

CT: Finally, would you care to comment on your feelings about having a son in the ministry in our churches?

DE: Well, I would like to comment, first, that as far as my wife and I are concerned we are undeserving. We had nothing to do with this, and we have nothing to boast of that we have a son in the ministry. That I can say for sure. We are happy and thankful. We never pushed that; it was his own decision, although I suppose there were times we had mentioned that he should think about what he wanted to do, as we said to all our boys. But we knew quite early that he was thinking about it. Even when he was a little boy, he liked to stand on the steps and conduct services most of the afternoon, usually communion services with some of his sisters as his audience. But we are sure happy and thankful that at least one of our sons was called to be a minister, and we keep in close contact, of course.

I can remember one incident when he was going to Calvin College. He would come home and talk about what he had in school. He had Professor De Vries for one of his classes, and he taught that the world was thousands, if not billions, of years old. David would come home with that and tell us all about the professor's proof. Of course, we would try to argue against that. Well, one night—I will never forget—he was in the bedroom next to us, and we were talking back and forth, and I said to him, "Well, maybe this De Vries is right after all." I wanted to get his reaction. David said, "Don't you start talking like that!"

David used to go to seminary in the morning and take one class with Rev. H. Hoeksema. One night he came home and said that in five minutes Hoeksema overthrew everything Professor De Vries had taught him in six weeks.

CT: I want to thank you for your time and input into this interview. It has been very profitable for me, and I'm sure it will be of benefit to the project we are working on.

DE: There's just one more thing I would like to say, and that has to do with some of the trends I see. I think that what doesn't look good for our churches is that we don't want to call a spade a spade anymore. Little by little we are letting down the bars on certain issues. I even detected that concerning divorce and remarriage when I talked with certain leaders in our churches, who said that maybe we shouldn't exclude certain people who are remarried on the basis that they weren't the guilty party. One of them, in fact, said, "Our churches have never taken a stand on that." Well, there are a lot of things our churches never took decisions on. We never took an official stand on whether unions are right or wrong, on movies, and so on. But these are all wrong, and we must maintain our principles. We don't need all kinds of decisions, but we must not let go of our stand or our churches will be finished. That's my concern.

CT: I agree with you wholeheartedly. Thank you for your help.

## A Teenager during the Depression Years

### *Dewey Engelsma*

My first teenage year was spent as an eighth-grade student in the same one-room public schoolhouse where the Hope Protestant Reformed congregation assembled for their worship services on the Lord's day. Our family had been members of this small, rural church from its origin during the 1924 "common grace controversy." Throughout the years 1929 to 1936 we had been without a minister and, although several calls had been extended, it wasn't until 1936 that we received our own pastor. He accepted the call with a yearly salary of $900–truly a Depression-day wage. It was barely enough for an existence, let alone a living.

When the year 1929 with its economic disaster crashed upon the nation, I was nearing my fourteenth birthday, and my formal education had been concluded. By today's standards it would be labeled a meager education; and rightly so, for the eight grades with some fifty or sixty pupils were taught by one teacher.

There wasn't a party to celebrate my graduation, but I was the recipient of a gift. A horse and cultivator were passed along to me, indicating that I had passed my "Shibboleth." I had crossed the ford, and it was time for me to begin a man's work. For you see, my parents were farmers, and relatively poor even before the Depression years, as they cared and provided for the needs of their eleven children. Now their financial struggle was intensified as they bent their backs to keep from losing the farm. These efforts became a daily battle as the returns for their farm products not only continued to decline, but some produce even became worthless.

How well I remember one such occasion. I was selected to make the early morning (2:30 a.m.) safari to the local wholesale market with the strawberries that had been picked the previous day. I found the market flooded with berries, for the harvest that June had been plentiful, but the buyers were few. Several hours later, and with daylight arriving, the disgusted farmers began to pack up and leave. I became desperate and sold the whole load to the lone buyer at 25¢ a crate. I was sick to my stomach as we made the transaction, for that price would hardly pay the cost for the sixteen containers. But neither could I force myself to dump the berries into the Grand River, as some of the growers had threatened. Upon arriving home I told my father the circumstances of the deal. He estimated that the eight of us had worked that whole day for the sum total of $1.50. Well, that was the last of berry picking for the season. The younger children were glad and didn't hide the fact either. We older ones were a bit more sensitive to the heartache and despair of our father and mother as they watched that bountiful red-ripe field shrivel and go to waste.

Incidents such as that were multiplied during the long, lean years and have made a lasting impression on me. Because the last forty years have been years of prosperity and affluence, the majority of this generation's teenagers find it next to impossible to visualize, let alone sympathize, with the lifestyle of the Depression years and its lack of what is currently deemed a necessity.

Beside the daily barn chores of milking, feeding, and cleaning, there was the seasonal fieldwork of plowing, harrowing, haying, cultivating, grain cutting, potato digging, and the never-ending berry and bean picking. If ever a thirteen-, fourteen-, or fifteen-year-old boy is expected to hold up his end, it is in the bean and berry patches. And let me clue you, my brothers and sisters (especially my sisters) were not hesitant to let me know exactly what was demanded of me.

It was also the duty of the teenage son to provide water for the multitude of household tasks. The water had to be carried by the tons of gallons from the spring, which was at least a block away from the house. And it didn't matter, be it blizzard or blistering heat, the call was continually, "Water!"

Also to me, the boy just out of knee britches, was given a third name. Besides my given name and water boy, I responded to wood boy (really in the Frisian dialect it has a much nicer sound). It was, "Don't forget the wood, young one." How could I forget? I had already spent day after day after day at the opposite end of the crosscut saw, cutting down the trees and trimming off the limbs with the ax, after which the wood was sawed into stove-length pieces to be hauled on the sleigh and stacked up beside the barn. Here is where insult was added to injury: "Scrounge around for some kindling too." So the wood was brought in again to be greedily devoured by the huge, kitchen range. That apparatus surely had an insatiable appetite.

No, it wasn't quite all work and no play. We had our fun, too, during many an evening and noon hour while the horses rested. (Horses must have their rest periodically.) But I often did wonder, "And what about me?" We played either softball or baseball, depending on which type of ball we possessed at the time. All the balls we found lodged in the debris along the banks of the river. The bats were either a wagon wheel spoke or a taut, straight tree limb. Yes, even the fielder had his mitt. This was the one item that required a bit of know-how in order to protect our hands and fingers. Whenever I tell my children how we improvised, every single child goes into gales of uproarious laughter and their remarks border on disbelief. But to me it was a serious business to get the "mitt" to fit just right. I would take a burlap sack, fold it into a tight square and tie each corner with binder twine. If with precision and care, the twine was tied just taut enough; a perfect pocket was formed, which was my goal. My brother and I spent many hours using our homemade equipment. The aged grandmother who lived with us was of the opinion that we were "wasting" our lives by our frequent participation in this sport, which she considered to be simply worldly pleasure. According to her, my father should see to it that we were in the house and learning the scriptures.

## Regarding "A Teenager during the Depression Years"

### *Prof. David J. Engelsma*

The one-hundredth anniversary book committee asked me why and for whom my father wrote "A Teenager during the Depression Years." I do not know the answer to those questions. But all the details of his account of his life as a youth on the farm are familiar to me, having heard them from my father more than once.

It is literally true that when Dewey completed the last day of class in the eighth grade, held in the old schoolhouse that stood yet in my memory at the corner of Riverbend and Kenowa, on the west side of the junction, his father, Charles Engelsma, picked the boy up from school and told him, "Now you cultivate with the horses. You are finished with school."

Only thirteen or fourteen, Dewey was at that time small for his age. When he took up the reins of the horses, standing behind the cultivator, he could barely see over the top of the handles of the cultivator. But he cultivated.

The family was very poor. As my father's account relates, all eleven children worked, and from a very young age. The social police of our day would punish parents who required such work of their children. The family was typical of the few families that made up Hope Protestant Reformed Church in the late 1920s and 1930s.

My father told me that a mitigating factor of their poverty was that, as a farm family, they always had enough food in those years of the Great Depression. His father and mother gave food to other members of Hope church who had need. Sometimes those members would simply appear on the farm, asking for eggs and milk, because their cupboards were empty.

The matter of getting water to the house for the drinking, bathing, and cooking needs of the large family should not be overlooked or minimized. The house had no running water. My father underestimated the distance of their only source of water—a free-flowing spring—from the house. It was a good two or three blocks from the house. Every day, the children had to carry pails of water from the spring to the house.

I know because when my father bought the family farm, on the southern extremity of Kenowa Avenue, for himself, his wife, and his children in 1950, the spring was still flowing. Indeed, it is to this day.

Dad's reference to the crosscut saw brings back vivid memories. He kept it. When I was a lad of eleven or twelve, he and I used it to cut down trees and saw them into manageable chunks for the furnace in our home on Hall Street.

Upon his death, I inherited the saw, since I was the only brother who had ever used it. Today it hangs conspicuously on a wall in my garage. What tales it could tell, if it could speak! What a tale of the difference between life in 1929, or in 1950, and life in 2016, it testifies to silently simply by existing!

I confess amusement at my father's story of his homemade ball glove. As my brothers will attest, my father and mother both inherited, or otherwise possessed, the thinking of my father's aged grandmother, Jennie, who by all accounts was a spiritual woman. Ball playing to her was a waste of time, worldly, and a threat to spirituality. Her grandsons, including my father, vexed her soul by their enthusiasm for playing ball. How my parents, who shared Jennie's view of ball playing, likewise vexed their souls at the interest their sons had for ball-playing! But my father never in those days told us of his own love of ball, to the sorrow of his godly grandmother.

## Interview with Prof. Herman Hanko

Professor Herman Hanko was Hope's pastor from 1955 to 1963. In 1968 he accepted the synod's appointment as professor in the Theological School of the Protestant Reformed Churches, and from that time to the present he and his wife Wilma have been members of Hope.[6]

Prof. Herman Hanko

AC: What year was your oldest boy born?

HH: Ron was born in 1954. He was over a year old when I was ordained in Hope church. Neal was born in 1956, the day after the tornado hit Standale. After the tornado hit we went to live with my parents. In fact, we could not get to our house for a week, because the whole area was roped off by the National Guard to prevent looting. The baby was born the day after, so my wife was in the hospital. The classis started meeting the day after the tornado hit, so I was at classis.

AC: It is interesting to read through society minutes. The Mr. and Mrs. Society was formed at the end of the pastorate of Rev. Heys. He may have led the first few meetings before he took a call. Then apparently after you accepted the call but before you were

6    Professor Hanko was interviewed by Aaron Cleveland on July 6, 2015.

ordained, you led the society, because you are listed for a few meetings as a candidate.

HH: I had been called, and I accepted the call, but I had not been examined by classis.

AC: So you led the society before your classical exam, and were known as Mr. Hanko before and then as Rev. Hanko, starting in October 1955 when you were ordained in Hope. The society made it through about Revelation 19 before you took the call to Doon.

What are your memories of going from a large city atmosphere of First church to the small country atmosphere of Hope church? In other words, you were used to worshiping in a big, somewhat impressive First church, and then you came to this little…What was the atmosphere of worship in Hope church? I don't know what that building looked like, but it must have been different for you too, if you came from city people at First church to a bunch of farmers at Hope church.

HH: I don't recall anything significant. Maybe for my wife it was a bit strange, since she was born and raised in First church. When my father was the minister in Oaklawn, Illinois, for ten years most of the members were farmers. We moved from Oaklawn to Montana, where most of the people were farmers. I worked on a farm in Oaklawn for six or seven of the ten years we were there, and I worked on a farm in Montana during the years I was there. I was used to country life. And Hope was not that countrified. Wilson was a major thoroughfare; Standale was a short distance away, and Grandville was a short distance away in the other direction.

AC: Was Wilson paved in 1955?

HH: Yes.

AC: Do you have any distinct memories of preaching in the Wilson Avenue church?

HH: The auditorium was much smaller than the Ferndale building. It had a small narthex by the front door about as big as a closet. It had a window and window sill, on which the men would lay their cigars that burned marks into the window sill. The stairs to the basement were to the south of the pulpit. Right to the south of the pulpit was the organ and just ahead of the organ was the door to the basement. There were two flights of steps to the basement. In the basement there were a big catechism room to the left, a kitchen just to the right of the catechism room, and a smaller room on the north side of the building. We had catechism in there too if the class was not large. That was used as a school-room for a while too. Jesse Dykstra taught there when Hope school was crowded. It was adequate.

AC: Where was the consistory room?

HH: The consistory met in the large catechism and society room.

AC: Before the service the consistory met downstairs, then came up the stairs, and appeared by the door near the organ? Very similar to what we have today?

HH: Yes, right.

AC: Did the Wilson Avenue church have a balcony?

HH: Oh, man, no (laughter)! It didn't have pews either. It had individual seats. It became too crowded so a piece was added on to the west side. It probably increased the size of the auditorium by only three or four rows. It was not nearly enough, and it was much too late. By the time I left, the auditorium was crowded again. They had to do something else.

AC: That must have been a regular discussion, because you were not gone even two years and the new church was built.

HH: We also held Young People's Society in the auditorium, although the other societies—Mr. and Mrs. Society and Men's Society and Ladies Aid—were held in the big room downstairs.

AC: I've heard that after leading the Young People's Society or during the break you would share a cigarette with the young people.

HH: Oh? It could be; I don't recall. I smoked at that time, but I rarely smoked cigarettes. I smoked a pipe.

AC: This is another story I've heard. In the earlier days some of the older children or teenagers would sit separately from their families during the worship services.

HH: I remember that from the Oaklawn congregation where my father was a minister and where we lived for ten years. Sometimes the kids would misbehave, and my father made them sit with their parents. He told those parents, "You have to make those older boys sit with you." The same thing was true in First church. A whole bunch of boys sat in the back balcony, and they played cards back there. They finally hired a deputy sheriff (laugh) from the congregation to keep order back there.

But I don't recall that that was the case in Hope. I think maybe once in a while. The problem was that in the early years of the churches we had no covenant view to speak of. A result of the 1953 controversy was an emphasis that the worship services were the gathering of believers and their seed. Parents began to insist that their children sit with them. There were exceptions once in a while as there are now. I don't remember any problems with that in Hope.

AC: Did Hope have Dutch services?

HH: Hope did not have Dutch services when I was there. I don't know if Hope did in its early history.

AC: I've seen the archives of the Men's Society of Hope church from 1922. The book was half in English and half in Dutch. I was pleasantly surprised to find half of the book in English. I found names such as Richard Newhouse and G. Ophoff.

AC: Is the order of worship now the same as it was in the 1950s?

HH: Basically, yes. When I first came to Hope, the worship services began with the doxology, as many of the Protestant Reformed churches still do today. Hope starts with the salutation and votum, then the benediction and doxology. I like the way Hope does it, because it is more biblical to begin with God's speaking: "Beloved congregation in our Lord Jesus Christ." I think Hope does it the right way.

AC: I read your series of articles in the 1980s on "Our Order of Worship" in the *Standard Bearer*. There you made the same point. I think Hope is one of the few churches that begin with the salutation and votum.

HH: The order of worship in the Protestant Reformed Churches generally is the same order of worship that Calvin had in the church in Strasbourg, with only minor differences. The congregational prayer was at the end of the service and there was a special element for confession and forgiveness of sins.

AC: Calvin was against instrumental accompaniment?

HH: Yes.

AC: In 1969 the consistory limited the offertory to psalter numbers and psalter variations. In 1992 the consistory made clear that all music before, during, and after the worship was to be from the 434 numbers of the psalter. Was the playing of questionable hymns a problem during your pastorate or after that?

HH: I cannot remember that it was. While I was minister in Hope from 1955 to 1962, there was no offertory. The collections were taken during the singing of the third psalter number after the congregational prayer.

AC: Before the scripture reading?

HH: No, scripture was read before the congregation sang the second psalter number. It was an innovation to read scripture after the congregational prayer. The order in the morning service was after the first psalter number to read scripture and then the law. The second psalter was a response to the law. Then came congregational prayer, and during the third psalter the collection was taken.

I remember discussing in consistory whether or not to change that. One elder remarked, "We had better not change it, because Rev. Hanko needs all the time he can get, and he goes overtime already." The trouble was that it was true.

AC: Would you say that the behavior and reverence of the worshipers are similar to what they were sixty years ago? It seems to me that when I go to church the atmosphere is very reverent.

HH: I agree. Yes, it always has been. I think there is one difference: the listening to the sermon is not as intent as it was during the early days. The people are not as intellectually and spiritually involved in the sermon as they used to be. When I was first in Hope, after almost every worship service, I would talk to people who had questions about the sermon. Remember, Wilma, you would sometimes get a little disgusted because I would be outside of church talking about the sermon, and we were supposed to be going on company?

AC: So as soon as you walked out of the church door, you had people come to you?

HH: Yes, not usually criticizing, but they had questions and wanted to talk about certain points I had made in the sermon. That does not happen anymore. Not only that, but I don't think people's attention spans are as long now as they used to be. People would go home, as some did—not necessarily in Hope—and write out the whole sermon. I would like to see someone do that today. I remember my father telling me that while he was the minister in Hull he preached on the doxology of Hannah. Over ten years later when we were on our way to Montana, we stopped in Hull for Sunday. Dad was asked to preach. He didn't have any sermons with him, so he preached a sermon that quickly came to his mind.

AC: He had a photographic memory, right?

HH: Not really; he had a good memory, but he worked hard on his sermons. After the service in Hull that Sunday, a lady said to him,

"Reverend, you preached that sermon when you were the minister here, but you changed the introduction today." Dad said, "She was dead right." Now where do you hear that today? He said there was a lady in Doon who sat on the edge of the seat and she never took her eyes off of him. After the sermon was over, she could repeat almost verbatim the whole sermon. That's the difference.

AC: Do you think that part of that is that during your early ministry we had just gone through the fires of 1953? When you go through controversy people get a renewed zeal for the truth, and they are glad to hear the truth.

HH: Yes, but television has also destroyed the ability to listen. Listening used to be an art, and people would become personally involved in the preaching. It was almost as if there was a conversation, although the audience was silent, between the minister and the members in the congregation. There was a strong rapport; nobody moved or said anything. The rapport between them was so strong that if it was broken, it was quickly evident. Suddenly I sensed that the audience was not listening, because of a siren or some other noise outside.

[After sharing a short story about Rev. Schipper and family visitation, the discussion returns to the effects of television viewing upon our ability to listen to sermons.]

HH: Television gives information in ten-second bites. When you see and hear at the same time, you don't learn to listen. How do you suppose that from Adam to Moses, two thousand years, the whole of the knowledge of the truth was passed on from fathers to children? You could never do that today.

I don't mean to say that people don't listen. There are some, I suppose, whose thoughts are miles away. People listen, but there is no wholehearted personal involvement in listening. It's like Jesus' parable of the four kinds of soil, where the word falls on the ground, but as soon as it falls it is gone. People hear the word and understand it, but they are not involved in thinking, "God is speaking to me. I had better listen, because I want to know what he says." And with heart, mind, soul, and body one is involved in listening. That does not happen much anymore.

Another aspect of the same thing is that people cannot stand silence. They cannot be just by themselves, meditating and thinking profound thoughts or whatever for any length of time. They are scared to be alone with their own thoughts. That is because their heads are pretty empty; their own thoughts aren't worth much. So those things have changed. Our culture has changed those things dramatically.

Dad told about a time when Dr. Hepp came to the United States from the Netherlands. He lectured in Sioux Center, Iowa, on the topic of the devil. The church where he spoke was packed. People were hanging from the chandeliers and sitting in the window sills. Hepp had his audience so completely in his grip that at a certain point when he spoke about the defeat of the devil, he stopped and said, "We are going to sing Psalm 68:1 ['Let God arise, let his enemies be scattered']." The church just about blew apart with the singing, the windows were rattling, and the lights were swaying. When the singing was done, Hepp continued with his speech. The people had been involved with their whole being. You don't just do that automatically; you have to learn to listen.

AC: We are bombarded today with so much useless information that you need the wisdom to shove 99 percent of it out of the way to get to the useful information. You're right, too, if we don't get what we want to hear in the first five or six seconds, we tune out.

HH: That is why when I taught in the seminary I told the students, "You have to make your sermons as well-crafted as you can. Make them a work of art; make them so that the people are forced to pay attention. You do that by your language, words, and emphasis. Otherwise, you will lose the people. Just to preach a sermon, no matter how brilliant, is not enough today. Ministers must formulate the sermons so that they hold the interest of the audience. That is extremely difficult to do. But that's part of our culture. The result is that people do not think for themselves. When I used to preach at Hope, there were men in the audience who made their own sermons while I was preaching. They had their own themes and divisions. Once in a while someone would say to me, "Dominee, I think my theme and divisions are better than yours" (laughter). They would tell me what their theme and divisions were, and sometimes they were better.

AC: You didn't take offense at that?

HH: No, they were not enemies. They were involved in the sermon.

AC: Maybe by 1955 most of the fallout of 1953 was past.

HH: There was one thing that struck me when I came to Hope. I sensed it almost immediately. The time had come to change the emphasis in the preaching. Prior to my coming there probably was not a sermon preached in which conditional theology was not lambasted. To be honest, the people (they were good people) were sick and tired of it. I thought to myself, "What the members of this congregation need now is to put the controversy behind them and to move forward and take the doctrines, which we cherish and for which we fought, and develop them further." I considered that to be my main task at Hope.

There were people who were ready to leave the church because they were so sick of hearing conditions lambasted in every sermon. They did not want conditions, but as one man said to me in Dutch, which would be loosely translated as, "We heard conditions until we were driven out of our minds" (laughter).

AC: Did you preach on the Heidelberg Catechism in the morning or evening?

HH: In the morning services.

AC: What were some of the sermon series you preached at Hope?

HH: I preached series on John the Baptist, Elisha, Matthew 24, 1 Peter, and the parables, which was later published in the book *Mysteries of the Kingdom*. I don't remember any others, but I always preached series, because I think that is the only way to preach.

AC: Do you see diligent series preaching as a necessary part of Reformed worship that is pleasing to God and edifying to the congregation?

HH: I have found series preaching to be the most effective kind of preaching, first, because it forces the minister to preach on texts that otherwise he would not preach on. Second, the minister is forced to preach on the whole counsel of God, although Heidelberg Catechism preaching is a great assistance in that. Third, people may not necessarily remember a given sermon on a text, but they will remember a series on a book of the Bible. Although they will not be able to pinpoint every sermon, they remember the chief teachings of a book. That to me is important.

AC: I will say that too. I remember best those books of the Bible that I studied systematically verse by verse in Bible society. You taught church history in seminary. Has series preaching been a tradition in the Reformed churches since the time of the Reformation?

HH: I don't know.

AC: We know John Calvin preached series.

HH: He preached right through books. He had a different method of preaching though. He preached analytically. He went through a chapter of the Bible and explained each clause and phrase according to the order of the text.

Calvin succeeded, but I can't preach that way. If I try to preach analytically, I forget about and do not make clear the connections between the whole book and a given text and between the text and the contexts. I preach all bits and pieces. So I've never been able to succeed. He could, but then he was Calvin, who was a much more brilliant preacher.

AC: From about 1983 to 1985 you wrote a series of twenty-one articles in the *Standard Bearer*, in which you went through the various elements of Reformed worship. In your judgment are the order and elements of worship as we practice them in the

Protestant Reformed Churches as consistent as they possibly can be with the regulative principle of worship?

HH: We practice the regulative principle of worship.

AC: One thing I don't completely understand. We sing for the most part from the psalter, the psalms, but we don't do that because of the regulative principle. What is the main reason we are not quite an exclusively psalm-singing church?

HH: I don't think it can be proven from scripture that the worship services have to be limited to the psalms. I would love it if that could be done, but I've tried and I can't do that. Even the well-known passages in Colossians and Ephesians do not refer to worship services. And the mention of hymns there does not refer to hymns as we know them either.

AC: It refers to different kinds of psalms, right?

HH: Yes. My objection to the singing of hymns is this: Invariably in the history of the church the introduction of hymns is a part of apostasy. When I was still a minister I was on a committee to study the matter of psalmody.

AC: You were. I think it was 1962–63.

HH: Okay. The committee did a pile of work on that and handed in a couple of hundred pages of material on the history of psalm singing. To the surprise of the committee, every time hymns were introduced into the church the next step was apostasy. There were no exceptions. That is a practical reason, but it is an important one. The Schilder people, the liberated churches in the Netherlands, are way off the rails today because they introduced into the worship services, among other things, what they call "evangelical songs." So apostasy was the committee's chief reason. I think that was the idea of the fathers at Dordt when they included specific hymns in article 69 of the Church Order.

AC: What was the push in the history of the Protestant Reformed Churches for the introduction of hymns in the early 1960s? I know the Hoeksemas were not opposed to them.

HH: There was some misunderstanding there. There was a movement in the churches, which I could support, to include in worship songs based on other parts of scripture. For example, Habakkuk and Job are written in poetry. There is in scripture much poetry and doxological sections, such as the last verses of Romans 8. The idea was that if the musicians in the churches would make songs of those parts of scripture, they could profitably be added to the psalter. The whole matter was discussed in the *Standard Bearer*, and right away those who were pushing for hymns jumped on that. The matter came to synod. I was at that synod and remember very well the remarks indicating that people were using that idea as an excuse to introduce hymns. Synod felt that we have to be careful and voted the whole business down.

AC: So what started out as putting almost direct quotations of scripture to music turned into a plea for hymns. That makes it more understandable.

HH: That scared the synod out of its collective mind.

AC: Do our distinctive doctrinal beliefs, mainly our rejection of the well-meant offer and our holding to an unconditional covenant, have a direct impact on our worship?

HH: Yes, they do.

AC: The main thing concerns the preaching. I cannot separate the idea that if you believe in a well-meant offer of the gospel, that will not only affect how the minister preaches, but also how you sing and pray.

HH: I agree with that. The truth of God's absolute sovereignty and that all glory belongs to him comes through in our worship and in the singing of the psalms. That is one of the main objections against singing hymns. There are good hymns, but very few hymns are theocentric; most of them are wrongly Christocentric. That is not the psalms; they center in God.

AC: We talk of the preaching as being Christocentric. Isn't it more accurate to say that the preaching should be theocentric?

HH: No, the preaching should be Christocentric because it concentrates on God's revelation of himself in all his virtues in Jesus Christ, which puts the emphasis on God's revelation of himself. I think that is proper, just as our prayers must be for Christ's sake. I would insist on that. But most hymns never get around to God.

AC: A few years ago I paged through a hymnal and looked at it from the viewpoint of sin. In the entire hymnal I found only four references to man's sinfulness. That is not the psalms, which emphasize man's sin in relation to God's covenantal faithfulness.

HH: The psalms are a biography of the Christian's spiritual life in all of his pilgrimage in sorrow, grief, disappointment, trouble, danger, happiness, and joy. It's all there. My dad used to say, "When you are a child you like the historical parts of the Bible. When you are a mature adult you like the doctrinal parts of the Bible, but when you are old you go to the psalms." There is truth to that.

AC: Is preparation for the Lord's day different today than what you remember as a youth? Has the development of technology and transportation changed our behavior regarding Sabbath preparation and observance? I bring this up because I think a part of the Lord's day worship is more than just Sunday.

HH: In my home (I think that was true in most homes), by suppertime on Saturday everything had to be finished. No one went away after six o'clock on Saturday night. We had to stay home and get ready for Sunday. We couldn't gad around. It had to be almost an emergency before we could go away on Saturday night. My mother had the potatoes peeled, the roast was on the stove (although not cooking yet), the shoes were shined, and the floors were mopped. Everything was ready so a minimum had to be done on Sunday. No staying in bed Sunday morning, but up bright and early to get ready to go to church. No putting our Sunday clothes on the last minute, but getting in the mood to worship.

AC: So there was a noticeable hush of activity on Saturday night?

HH: Oh, yes, especially as teenagers we were not too happy about some of those rules. No Saturday night dating either. No programs on Saturday night. No playing outside on Sunday.

AC: How about out West?

HH: Out West it was more lax regarding the Sabbath in the afternoon and evening because many churches had the worship services in the afternoon. Then the farmers had to do chores—cows to milk and pigs to feed—so the Sabbath was over more or less in the afternoon. Even in Doon there was not much visiting on Saturday night.

AC: Do you see any current threats that corrupt our worship?

HH: One of the dangers of the churches in general, that includes Hope, is a lack of understanding our doctrine. That is true of some more than others, but there is a whole generation that has come up that is not strong in the knowledge of the truth and are unable to define it. That worries me. Let me give you an example of that. When I first came to seminary in 1965, the young men in seminary knew what they believed, understood it, and could defend the truth. I could ask the men questions and they could answer them. But they could also ask me questions, and we would get involved in discussions. I would ask them, "Do you believe this and why?" They could answer the question. I said, "You are wrong." Then they would defend their position, which was what I wanted them to do. They knew how to think theologically. After I had been in seminary about ten or fifteen years, that was gone. I would get students to whom I would say, "What is the answer to this question?" They would give a stock answer. Then I would ask another question that challenged their answer. They said, "Oh, I am sorry I was wrong. I didn't mean to be wrong." That is not the point. Defend your answer. They couldn't do it.

AC: You were testing them. What was the reason for their inability?

HH: They were not taught to think. That is the problem in societies too. It is hard to get a discussion going in societies because no one knows how to think. If you challenge someone's position, he or she is lost.

AC: I like it in Bible society when there is a friendly disagreement; not to say, "You're wrong; I'm right."

HH: One has to be able to demonstrate why he believes what he believes. We can't do it anymore.

AC: Why is that?

HH: Because people do not think theologically. They do not themselves ask questions about what they believe. Why is unconditional theology important? Well, we believe that God does everything. Okay, prove that. What do you mean that God does everything? Then you ask another question, and they are at their wits end; they don't know where to go. Perhaps people are not spending enough time studying to understand their faith. People do not know how to think; they are not taught in the schools—in grade school, high school, and college. That is not true of everyone, but that is one thing that really bothers me. We were taught to think. If one took a stand, he'd better be able to defend himself or his idea was not worth a hoot. It was not worth considering. The teacher would say, "If you can't defend what you stand for, don't bother us with your ideas."

AC: Now that you say that, I am wondering if in our churches people think that if Professor so-and-so said it, or Reverend or Elder so-and-so says it I take it hook, line, and sinker, and don't put it to the test of scripture.

HH: Yes, and one doesn't know why it's right.

AC: I am not saying that I have to show disrespect to those in authority, but I believe that as a man in the pew I should be able to take what a minister says in the pulpit to scripture, and it better pass the test of scripture and the confessions. That is not disrespect of the preaching or the offices.

HH: When I first came to Hope and taught the essentials in Reformed doctrine catechism class, that was one of the most enjoyable experiences of my ministry. It was a class of good kids, who in a way were unusual. We would spend at least two weeks on a lesson and barely get it finished. I asked questions in class in connection with the subject, and everyone in the class was in a position to answer what I asked. If they could not, I kept after them until they realized I meant business. They had discussions and debates in class, and I didn't say anything for thirty-five minutes, except just to referee the debate among the kids.

Once when two elders visited, the class was debating something with regard to the intermediate state. The debate was hot and heavy. I could see that one of the elders was on the edge of his seat just itching to say something. I stopped the debate and said, "We will let Elder so-and-so speak, because he wants to say something." He said what he thought had to be said and what he thought was right. Then the kids started arguing with him. He loved it and did not consider that disrespectful. Afterward he came to me and said, "I have never been in a catechism class like this before." Those kids learned to think.

Now, even in seminary, you lecture on something and ask, "Does anyone have any questions?" Nope, no one has any questions. "Well, why don't you have any questions?" "Well, we don't know anything beyond what you said." "It's about time you find out a little bit more."

Many of the kids in the essentials catechism class attended Unity Christian High School in Hudsonville, which at that time was teaching the period theory. We spent six weeks on the lesson on creation. Finally, I said, "That is the way it is." I gave them a test on which I asked, what is your view of creation? One person wrote the correct answer, but added in the margin the standard argument in Unity: "I believe in six-day-twenty-four-hour creation, but it really doesn't make any difference whether one believes that or the period theory, because it doesn't have anything to do with salvation." So I wrote in the margin, "It has this much to do with your salvation, that if you don't change your mind on this, I will not let you make confession of faith." I hadn't even said, "Amen," and there was that person in the front saying, "You mean that? You mean you would not let me make confession of faith if I considered the period theory a possibility?" I said, "I would not let you make confession of faith." He looked at me and said, "Wow!" When they made confession of faith, I asked everyone in that class, "What do you believe concerning creation?" They all answered properly. Then I asked, "Why do you believe that?" I could see their faces fall. They had to think because we had not discussed that in exactly that form. Some were sweating. Kids don't know how to think. That is all there is about it. I think television, again, is to blame for that.

## Interview with Roger Kamphuis

Roger is the son of Henry and Ann Kamphuis. The Kamphuis family came to Hope from Grand Haven Protestant Reformed Church around 1962.[7]

Roger Kamphuis

JK: What were the names of your parents?

RK: They were Henry Kamphuis and Angeline Kamphuis.

---

7    Roger was interviewed by Jeff Kalsbeek in September 2015.

JK:  When did they come to Hope church?

RK:  Well, I was talking to my sister [Phyllis King] a little bit about that today. She said that around 1962 we moved into the area.

JK:  Before that they were members of First church?

RK:  No, before that we were in Grand Haven Protestant Reformed Church.

JK:  Were you living at home, yet, when they moved?

RK:  Yes.

JK:  How old were you when the family came here?

RK:  I took driver's training in Grand Haven High School at sixteen years old. I went to the Christian school in Grand Haven for, I think, three or four years. Of course, I went to kindergarten in the public school.

JK:  So you were in your late teens when you came to Hope church?

RK:  Yes, I must've been about seventeen to eighteen years old.

JK:  You went to Hope school when you were still in Grand Haven?

RK:  Yes, my sister, Phyllis, would drive us from Grand Haven to Hope. We didn't really drive alone; we drove with Rev. Lanting and the Lanting children.

JK:  Because he was the minister out there?

RK:  Yes.

JK:  And they drove to the school?

RK:  Some children mentioned to Rev. and Mrs. Lanting, "Do you know in our school [Grand Haven] that they're praying for Billy Graham?" Rev. Lanting said, "Henry [Kamphuis], we've got to get our children out of there and get them to Grand Rapids." Rev. Lanting said, "I'll be willing to drive if we can take turns driving back and forth from Grand Haven to Grand Rapids." So that's what we did. Phyllis was at an age where she could drive, so therefore she was driving us back and forth for a while.

JK: So you're a year or two younger than Phyllis?

RK: Yes, I'm about a year younger than her. Right now I am seventy, and she is seventy-one.

JK: How did your parents become members in the Protestant Reformed Churches?

RK: My dad and mom came out of the Reformed Church of America—Harlem Reformed. That's between Holland and Grand Haven. They lived in West Olive, Michigan. So my dad moved to Grand Haven, then he got to talking to Rev. Vanden Berg, who was the Protestant Reformed minister in Grand Haven. Therefore, my dad became convinced that he had to get out of the Reformed Church of America.

JK: When you came to Hope church, did you move into this house [1511 Ferndale] right away?

RK: No. We moved into Grand Rapids, later we moved on Riverbend.

JK: So when you came here and you became members at Hope with your parents, who was the minister?

RK: It was around the time I got drafted in 1964. The minister would have been Rev. Veldman.

When I did get drafted I was very frightened, because I had never wanted to join the military. But when I received my papers to go to Detroit, Rev. Veldman met with me. He said, "Rog, don't you worry about it. A lot of our men in Hope church will have to go into the service." He said, "We are, as a congregation, praying for you; therefore, when you have God on your side all is well." But I was very thankful that I did not end up like Mike Engelsma in Vietnam. When I got drafted, I had basic [training] in Fort Knox, Kentucky. After that I was shipped over to Fort Sill for artillery.

JK: So you were in the artillery division?

RK: Yes, and that was a huge deal to go to Vietnam. But when we were in training, our general at that post said, "I'm going to keep your division right here in the States, and you're going to train people to go to Vietnam." So we had to help people learn how to load those great big guns and how to do everything. After a couple of months, we had to get on a train to go to Houston, Texas, and the state fair. We stayed in a nice hotel for about three weeks and put our gun in the show and told people about it. They would ask how far it would shoot, and I would tell them, "It will shoot thirty miles." In fact, at Fort Sill we only shot it thirty miles one time. We shot it more than that, but very short landings. Then the one time they wanted to know how far it would actually shoot, we learned that it did thirty miles. So therefore we shot from the one end of Fort Sill to the other end of the post. When General Brown found out that the missile was going directly over his head, he put a stop to it. He was afraid with a short field that the thing would drop on him. He said that wouldn't be too good. So he put a stop to that kind of training. In Oklahoma there are mountains so we'd get the gun there, lock it down into the ground, and we'd shoot into the mountain.

JK:  So that was your target practice.

RK:  Yes. The old guns had a lot of recoil. They'd back that gun down deep into the ground and then have them shoot it.

JK:  Okay. What other things do you remember about Rev. Veldman? You had him for only a couple years.

RK:  Well, he was a very serious man. I guess you could say a very humble person. I did enjoy him for sure. In fact, I really liked all the ministers that we have had. I just figured that when God sends a minister, he's there until God tells him to leave. That's God's work for him to do; therefore, he's to stay there until God's set time.

JK:  Did the church seem different when you got back from the Army? Was there much change?

RK:  Not too much, no.

JK:  Were there other men from Hope church in the service at the same time?

RK: Yes, Clare Kuiper, I think he had to go in, and like I said, Mike Engelsma. Now I don't know about Chuck Kalsbeek, was he drafted too at that time?

JK: Chuck, Cal, and Clare were in the reserves.

JK: Do you remember Rev. Van Overloop's time as Hope's minister?

RK: I don't remember much. I think he was the first one to live in the new parsonage.

JK: Do you remember anything about the transition from the old church to the new church?

RK: I did take quite a few pictures of the new church as it was being built. I think I gave them to different people in the church for the fiftieth anniversary of the church. At that time we lived right behind Hope school, and I would walk to the church and take pictures.

JK: What happened to the old church?

RK: Well, I think that it just sat there for a while. Eventually Hope school bought it and then tore it down for the parking lot.

JK: So that was right where the school parking lot is now?

RK: Yes.

JK: What did you do for work?

RK: I got out of Hope school at eighth grade, and I went to work for Wells Orchard. But that, of course, was only a seasonal thing. So then Dick Eerdmans got me into Eerdman's Publishing Company. I was a book packer. They had many orders come in, books going to Indiana, Washington, wherever. After that Dewey Engelsma got me into Keeler Brass, and that's where I stayed for forty-one years doing plastic injection molding.

JK: Did you have any issues with the union in Keeler Brass?

RK: Well, at least four or five times the workers took up a union vote. Every time it was voted down. There were many who wanted the union in the worst way, but there were enough other people there to vote it down, so the union never made it.

RK: At one time Keeler Brass tried to get people to work on Sundays. That was a no-no for me. The consistory of Hope church wrote a letter for me saying that I would not work on the Sabbath day. I gave Keeler the letter, and the boss said I was free from working on Sunday.

JK: So at that time companies would allow some to not work on Sunday.

RK: Right, I guess if you had good religious affiliations, they would have that letter in their files.

JK: Companies don't do that anymore today. It's either you work on Sunday or you don't work at all.

RK: Right, yes. That's why I think many of our people have their own businesses.

JK: A lot of our people were forced to do that.

RK: Yes. My dad too was always self-employed with his watch and clock repair business.

JK: So at Keeler, it was really the unions and Sabbath observance that you had to face.

RK: Yes.

RK: When I took my breaks I could have my prayer before my meal like I always did, and I would always have my *Standard Bearer* there, which I read. I usually was the only one there.

JK: Did your father and mother remain members at Hope until they passed away?

RK: Yes, they enjoyed it too; especially living so close to church. I can remember my mom looking out the front window and watching the church. She would see the Klamers come in first. Then she would know it was time to walk to church. That's still what I do today. I see Jim Huizinga pass, then pretty soon Jim Schimmel.

JK: Then you know it's time for you to go.

RK: Yes. Sometimes I'm about the third one in church. I thank the Lord constantly for preserving me. I'll never leave the church because we need that preaching. We're not living in really joyful times, although we can be joyful because we're people of God.

## Interview with John Kuiper

John Kuiper's parents were members of Hope almost from Hope's beginning. John was also a member until he left in 1994 to be a charter member of Hope's daughter congregation, Grace Protestant Reformed Church.[8]

John Kuiper

Jeff:   Who were your father and mother?

John:  My father was Arend Kuiper, and my mother was Bernice Alders.

Jeff:   What was their relationship to Hope church?

John:  My dad became a member of Hope church somewhere in the teens, when they built the church on the corner of Riverbend and Kenowa. The church is gone now. My dad talked about

---

8    John Kuiper was interviewed by Jeff Kalsbeek in October 2015.

helping to build it. In the 1924 split we lost the church to Hope Christian Reformed Church, who, in turn, closed it down when the congregation moved to Grandville.

Jeff:  Was your dad living with his parents at the time, or was he already married?

John:  He didn't marry until 1929 or 1930, so he was a single man.

Jeff:  So he went to Hope when it started in 1916. Was he there with his parents?

John:  When they first came from the old country, they went to Walker Christian Reformed. Later on, or vice versa, they went to Jenison Christian Reformed. He crossed the river with the ferry. In the winter they walked across on the ice. They lived by Fennessy Lake, so when the new congregation was formed at Hope, they attended.

Jeff:  How did your father and mother meet? Were they both members of Hope church?

John:  No, I don't remember exactly how they met. My mother moved from Iowa when she was thirteen years old and became employed as a babysitter. Later on she was a maid for Lindsey, the popular lawyer, and she stayed in maids' quarters when she was seventeen years old. When she was nineteen, she married my dad. Rev. Hoeksema married them in First church.

Jeff:  Now you said your dad was a farmer, but did he also help build the original church?

John:  It was a volunteer thing. That's how they were...all helped as they could. I thought he said he was about seventeen years old when he helped there. He was born in 1902 or 1903, so he had to be in his late teens. He was a farmer until he got married, and then he went to school in Ohio for car mechanic. Then the Depression came, so he jumped around to different jobs because there wasn't any work. He became a carpenter around the 1940s. He was a carpenter at Herpolsheimer's, a big department store in downtown Grand Rapids. He built the displays.

Jeff:  Can you relate some of your experiences as a boy in the life of the church?

John:  On Sunday nights after services, we would have Bible discussions in people's homes. I was around six years old. The ladies would be in the kitchen, and the men would get into big debates in the living room. The Korhorn, Engelsma, Newhouse families, and others. That's when Rich Newhouse's wife was still alive.

Jeff:  It was at different people's houses after church?

John:  I think so, I remember going quite often to Charles Engelsma's house. One thing that has always stayed with me is the singing of Dutch psalms afterward. In those days nobody had a whole lot of money. Hope was quite poor, but they had their close fellowship in the Lord.

Richard Newhouse's Dutch psalm book

Jeff:    Your father left Hope and the Protestant Reformed Churches sometime after 1953, right?

John:  He left a little later, I think in the 1960s.

Jeff:    As a young man, what was that like for you?

John:  Not very good. It was tough because although he knew the issues, he never informed me too much about what the issues were. It was between him and the consistory. But he did tell me this: "Don't leave the Protestant Reformed Churches. Stay there." I stayed.

Jeff:    What do you remember about Mr. Newhouse?

John:  He was fair. I was a deacon and enjoyed serving with him because he was straightforward. He could say in a few words what some guys would take one hundred words to say. Rev. Herm Veldman was the same way.

Jeff:    Do you remember anything of what Newhouse did for work?

John:  My grandmother lived on Logan Street. Down the street toward Eastern, he [Newhouse] had a grocery store. We kids used to walk down there, and she [Mrs. Newhouse] would give us candy. I think he did some farming later on. When he retired, he moved in a trailer by Tanis [on Burton Street]. For a while he lived with the Korhorn family.

Jeff:    What about Mrs. Newhouse?

John:  She was not very healthy, I know that. I remember one Sunday she passed out in church, and he carried her out. After she died, he lived with the Korhorn family on Kenowa Avenue.

Jeff:    I heard a story about him. When he lived with the Korhorn family, one morning he was on his way to the grocery store or something. He started the car to warm it up, then he went back into the house and got interested in a book or something, and the car ran until it was out of gas.

John:  Another story told to me: One Sunday Rev. Ophoff was supposed to preach for us in Hope. It got to be nine-thirty, then later and later, but no Ophoff. I think it was Rich Newhouse or another of the men who rode down Riverbend up to Butterworth and found him on Butterworth with his car out of gas. Ophoff was like that. He would drive to First church to teach in the seminary, then walk home, forgetting he took his car. The next morning he would go to the garage and find no car.

Jeff:   Yes, an absent-minded professor.

John:   The one incident I do remember involved Tony Langerak. I was in the consistory room when it happened. We were going to get up to pray, and he said, "I'm all done." We were flabbergasted. It was terrible, that was the worst scene I've witnessed in church.

Jeff:   What do you remember of Ted and Anna Kievit?

John:   They were best friends of my folks. As kids we went there quite often. We visited them very often on Sunday nights. After we were married we went there quite often, too. They were nice; they were good people. She was a good lady; she was outspoken, but she'd do anything for anybody. Some thought that Mr. Kievit slept in church. He didn't sleep. We would go to their house after church, and he could relate the whole sermon to us. He was always a quiet man, didn't say a whole lot, although my dad and he used to talk a lot. They got along good. We kids loved going there. I would come in the back door and look and see what she had in the cupboard.

They were good friends with Rev. Herman Hanko also. She even went out to Iowa to help them out with one of the babies I think. She always helped people. She also did a lot of sewing and knitting.

She was a nice lady. I remember one time, I was probably four or five, and my dad was in consistory. My mother was at home, so we children were sitting alone, and misbehaving during the service. On the way home, my dad had to pick something up from the Kievit's house. Mrs. Kievit came outside, and I got bawled out by Mrs. Kievit. I'll never forget that.

"After Ted Kievit's death, on nights when my dad had consistory meetings, my mother and I would visit Mrs. Kievit and
play dominoes." —Cal Kalsbeek

Jeff:  She wanted you to be reverent in church.

John:  Yes. Professor [Rev.] Hanko, did something similar. Rev. Hanko
had four little boys. One Sunday his wife was at home, and the
boys sat by themselves. I remember Rev. Hanko, told them right
from the pulpit, "Boys, settle down!" He stopped the sermon
and gave them a sermon.

    Yes. I remember, Mr. Kievit well. My dad picked him up
quite a bit. He was always in Men's Society and being active,
but he was always in the background. Sometimes some of those
people are more of an asset than others who want to be known.

Jeff:  What do you know about Maynard and Alice Veenstra?

John:  They went to Creston church for a number of years. Eventually
they bought a house on Luce Street by 8th Avenue. That's where
the family grew up. He had twelve children, I think. Alice, his
wife, went to Hope as a child, since she was a Korhorn. I did
things with Ira [Maynard's son] later on after I got out of the
service. Many of those guys had been in the service and went to
Germany, while I ended up going to Korea. A lot of us didn't get
married right away because we were in the service.

Jeff:  When the Miedema boys went in service, were they at Hope
church?

John:  Yes, Ken was in Korea. He was wounded there. They took him
off the line, and then he was a truck driver and hauled supplies.
Harold was in charge of piling up the dead bodies. That was a
pretty rough job. What a job for a young man!

Jeff:  Do you have any memories of Rev. Heys?

John:  Yes, he was our minister when I was in Korea, so I received
letters from him. He was a mild-mannered man. We lived in

Wyoming, so he used to pick us up on 28th Street. He was teaching catechism, I think, before he became a minister at Hope. Around 1941 I think they came.

Jeff: Do you remember anything about when Rog Kooienga was in his accident?

John: Yes. Was that in 1959? We weren't married very long, I think, before that happened.

Jeff: Was that a tough time for the congregation?

John: Yes, it was a tough time for the family too. I think he had made a delivery. He had two or three of his boys with him. He worked for Rodenhouse, and I think he had made a delivery to Muskegon, and the accident happened on the way back. I don't know if somebody wandered into his lane or what, but after the crash he never really recovered.

Jeff: There were a couple of Howerzyl families. What do you remember about them before they left the Protestant Reformed Churches in the split of 1953?

John: Ted was a carpenter, and Eno owned the Riverbend Body Shop.
My dad was building Tony Langerak's house on Hall Street. Dad was laid up, something to do with sciatic nerve, and he couldn't get up to do anything. He said to me, "John, [I was only nineteen or twenty years old], I don't know what I'm going to do. You're going to have to get somebody to help you." I think Ted Kievit and Dick Kooienga help me. I was not a carpenter yet; I had to learn. We got the roof on the house, got it closed in, and the family moved into the basement.
My dad was a good friend of Tony and others who used to go to Second church in Wyoming. Our family went there for a short time because we didn't have transportation. We only had one car, but we had bus service to Second. For catechism I rode my bike, but if the weather was bad I took the bus. Maybe that's why I hate buses to this day.

Jeff: What are your memories of 1953?

John: I didn't know what was going on because I was in the service. A minister isn't going to write to servicemen about such
things. He wrote more about spiritual things. I imagine that
was rightly so. Why would he send me all that kind of information? So I never really knew what was going on. Fact is, when
you're in the front lines, you know very little about even the
politics of war. You're doing your job, and just trying to stay
alive. Such things change your perspective. I would say you're
in more of a state of reality. That's what I'm afraid of today;
a lot of people aren't going to see the reality. I look at many
people, and they have their heads in football or other things
and don't take any interest in what's going on around them—
just living in fantasyland and going to church on Sunday. Your
grandpa [John Kalsbeek] wasn't that way. He took an interest in what was going on. I remember talking to him about
important things. That's what I always liked about him. He was
more of a realist.

John Kuiper on duty in Korea

Jeff:  What was it like growing up in the Hope area?

John:  One memory is that when I was a kid, we lived across from Fennessy Lake. That whole farm there was our grandpa's farm. We lived below the hill. My cousin, Jim Kuiper, came over to our house in the winter with an old Model T. On the east end of the lake there was a place where we could put boats in. We'd come sailing right down on the ice in that Model T and we'd spin around on the lake. Of course the ice was pretty thick.

Jeff:  What was it like growing up as a teenager at Hope church?

John:  I remember picking raspberries when I was eight or nine years old. We picked raspberries for Mrs. Kievit and did little jobs. My dad always had a small truck farm so we kids started working on the farm early on. Then when I got into high school, ninth grade, I got a job working for Pete Huizinga in the greenhouse. I worked there for three years through high school. I would go there from school. I would start at four o'clock and work till six every day. Then on Saturday I had to haul the clinkers out with a wheelbarrow, and that took about four hours. So I worked that way all through high school. In the summer I did some harvesting. In the winter I worked in the greenhouse. He raised a lot of cut flowers—carnations and mums.

Jeff:  Was Fred Huizinga's dad, John, a farmer too?

John:  Yes. He pedaled produce door to door. Later on, he bought the farm in Allendale. I think that was his mother-in-law's place. That's where Grand Valley State University is now. Their whole farm was taken up with the college.

Jeff:  Growing up, did you have Young People's Society?

John:  Yes, we sure did. I remember either in catechism or society some boys played a trick on Rev. Heys, secretly putting a thumbtack on his seat. Rev. Heys had a good response. He sat down on it, then, of course, he got up suddenly and informed the kids, "I will not stay on that point any longer."

Jeff:    Who was the minister when the new church on Ferndale was built?

John:    In 1965 we built the church. Our minister was Rev. Veldman. He advised, "Don't make this church any bigger than capacity for eighty-five families." He said, "That's a good size." I think he was right.

## Interview with Harry Langerak

Harry Langerak is the oldest child of Anthony and Jean Langerak, who became members of Hope church in 1948 when Harry was six. He went through Hope school from first through ninth grade and taught for five years at Hope school and forty years at Covenant Christian High School. He married Evelyn Kamps in 1964, the year he began to teach. They have two sons of Hope—William and Nathan—in the gospel ministry in the Protestant Reformed Churches. [9]

Harry Langerak

JK:    Would you tell me the names of your dad and mother?

HL:    Anthony Langerak and Jean Battjes.

JK:    How did your dad and mother come to the Protestant Reformed Churches?

---

9    Harry Langerak was interviewed by Jeff Kalsbeek in September 2015.

HL: They had a lot of contact with Protestant Reformed men through my dad's dry cleaning business. The men were from Second Protestant Reformed Church and from Hope. A. J. Kuiper is a name I remember. Those men talked to my dad about our view of the covenant. He was attracted to the unconditional covenant view versus the conditional covenant view and to the assurance of salvation versus the doubt and anguish of the Netherlands Reformed. He began to attend Hoeksema's Heidelberg Catechism classes.

JK: I understand he was Netherlands Reformed at the time?

HL: Yes, both my dad and mother. I was baptized in the Netherlands Reformed Congregation, as were my brothers, Don and Ed.

JK: You couldn't have been very old when that was happening.

HL: I was about five years old when we went to Second church when Sebastian Cammenga was the minister.

At the time my dad was trying to operate a dry cleaning business out the basement of our house. There were pressing and dry cleaning machines in our house across from Wyoming Park High School. The officials of the township required him to have a separate building before he could continue his business. Then he went in partnership with Henry Lotterman for a while.

Shortly thereafter Henry Lotterman and his sons took over the building in Wyoming Park, and my dad bought property for a dry cleaning business in Standale. He was one of the first businesses in Standale. It was a small shop with only a dry cleaning machine and a pressing machine.

JK: People took their clothes there and he took care of them?

HL: Yes, shirts and everything. He had routes around the countryside on which he picked up clothes at people's homes. When the business moved to Standale, my dad bought five acres from Ted Kievit on Hall Street. We moved next door to Mr. and Mrs. Kievit when I was about eleven.

JK: What do you remember about them?

HL: I have fond memories of growing up next door to them. We had
the run of the five acres not only, but we also played in Roberts'
tree farm across the street. We trapped muskrats and mink in the
swamp to the north of Dad's property. Mr. and Mrs. Kievit had to
put up with a family of nine children. That was, I'm sure, a major
adjustment for them, because they had only one daughter. Our
family borrowed implements and did not always return them
in a timely fashion. We used their water because our well was
not working when we moved into our house. We did help them
shuck corn and feed the chickens. They probably could have told
many stories about our family—not always good ones either. But
in Christian love they dealt with us as fellow saints.

When Mr. Kievit needed meat, he took a chicken, tied its legs
to a rope between two trees, cut its throat, and left it hanging
with its wings flapping. That was a very fascinating wonder to us
children who had never seen that done. When my mother needed
eggs, we would get them from Kievit's back porch and put the
money on a chair.

Mrs. Kievit worked for my dad's dry cleaners as a seamstress,
mending rips in clothes, stitching broken seams, and sewing on
buttons.

I remember that she began most of her sentences with the
Dutchism, "Bye."

JK: What year were you born?

HL: I was born on April 13, on Easter Sunday, 1941.

JK: A few months later World War II broke out.

HL: Yes, December 7, 1941.

JK: Did you go to Hope school when it started?

HL: Yes, Hope started in 1947. I had attended kindergarten in the
public school in Wyoming. Hope had no kindergarten, so my
first-grade class was the first to go all the way through to the
ninth grade at Hope.

JK: What do you recall about Rev. Heys? You only had him for a couple of years before he left.

HL: He was my catechism teacher and I remember that we had to learn our questions. But as far as his storytelling I don't recall that he was a particularly dynamic teacher. I just remember him as a catechism teacher. My brother Don recalls that Rev. Heys was a good storyteller. One Saturday when we lived in Wyoming, Dad wasn't going to drive us to catechism because of the snowy weather. Don raised such a fuss about not being able to go to catechism that Dad relented and drove us to catechism.

I would say Rev. Heys was a likeable man, and my dad enjoyed him as a preacher. I know that because he never really talked a lot about the minister. I think if he didn't appreciate him, Dad would've talked a bit about it with my mother. Other than that I don't recall a lot of my early years under Rev. Heys.

JK: Do you recall that things were more proper back then? I notice in the 1952 picture of the church picnic that the ladies wore dresses. Were there no pants back then?

HL: Ladies wore dresses or skirts with blouses. Even when we went to catechism we at least wore our school clothes. We didn't dress down; if anything we dressed up. I recall that I only had jeans to wear to school. Jeans were not an issue at Hope school then. When Covenant started jeans or denim were not allowed.

JK: Even when I was going through Covenant we couldn't wear denim.

HL: As you can see from the picture, even some of the girls wore dresses to the picnic, but the boys wore jeans or shorts.

JK: Do you remember anything about Rev. Heys on the pulpit?

HL: He was a good preacher from the standpoint of a kid.

JK: You could be engaged?

HL: We listened to him carefully, and I enjoyed him as a kid would enjoy him. I don't remember what his content was.

JK: You were just a kid, but did you notice any change or emphasis in his preaching as the controversy of 1953 took place?

HL: I don't remember, but I recall that there was tension. My dad read the *Concordia* and talked a little about the issues going on in the churches. We would have people over to visit. Some of them left Hope church, not immediately but as time went on.

JK: Did you have Bible societies at that time in Hope church?

HL: Yes, there was Men's Society, Ladies' Aid, and Young People's. I babysat for my parents so they could attend society. My parents went together, although the societies were separate. There was no Mr. and Mrs. Society at that time. There was a Choral Society, to which my mother and my dad both went. Later Hope Heralds started and Dad sang in that.

JK: What affect did the controversy in 1953 have on your mom and dad? Do you recall that they talked about it?

HL: My dad was a very staunch supporter of Hoeksema. In fact, even when certain ministers came as pulpit supply, he was upset that they didn't talk about certain things in the sermon, kind of avoiding some of the issues. I think Rich Veldman was one of them.

JK: So he could notice that something should've been said, and it wasn't said. And Heys evidently wasn't that way, otherwise you would've known about it.

HL: That's what makes me think that he definitely preached about the unconditional covenant.

JK: I had heard that Rev. Heys brought it out. He led the congregation through 1953.

HL: Yes, right up to it and until he left in 1955. He went to Iowa, because the churches in the West were pretty hard hit by the split.

JK: Yes, they lost a lot of ministers. What about your friendships? You were probably eleven or twelve at the time. Did any of your friends and their families leave at that time?

HL: Yes they did. I can remember Neil Moelker was a good friend of mine.

JK: What was his dad's name?

HL: Neil. He owned the D & M Metals in Standale with either a relative or a brother. That family left as did a good many of the Moelker families.

JK: Did they stay in Hope school or did they leave the school too?

HL: They eventually left. The first year of the split a lot of them stayed. Some of them even stayed later. Two of Rev. Blankespoor's children stayed for a year or two. The Howerzyl children stayed for quite a while.

JK: So those Howerzyl boys and this Moelker boy, those were your childhood friends?

HL: Yes.

JK: Were there any other friends who you associated with around the Hope neighborhood?

HL: The Kuiper, Kalsbeek, Engelsma, and Kooienga children.

JK: So you knew the Kalsbeek family?

HL: I knew them from school. I started school with your Uncle John. Yes, I had a lot of friends who stayed in Hope church.

JK: What can you tell me about the Rev. Mensch family? I don't know a whole lot about them. He came to Hope from out West. I read Mr. Rau's little story about him and that he came to our seminary, wanting to be a minister. They said he couldn't because he had abandoned his charge out there.

HL: He attended the Protestant Reformed seminary first and was ordained a minister in the German Reformed churches. I don't know a lot about that controversy, but the congregation didn't like his preaching, so they made it pretty tough on him. A lot of it stemmed from his love for the unconditional covenant. He left those churches and came back to Hope and wanted to become a minister in the Protestant Reformed Churches. That was in the late 1950s.

JK:  So then he tried to become a minister in the Protestant Reformed Churches and they didn't allow him?

HL:  Yes, but later Rev. Lubbers went there as the Protestant Reformed home missionary. Isabell and Forbes were two churches that came out of that German Reformed background.

JK:  What do you remember about Mr. Newhouse?

HL:  He lived with the Mensch family for a while. Mr. Mensch owned, or rented, the farm on Kenowa that Charles Engelsma and later his son, Dewey, had owned. Rich Newhouse worked on that farm. Then the farm had to be sold. I remember going to the auction with Jake Kuiper in a rumble seat of a Ford Model A or something like that. Old cars attracted people even back then.

JK:  So then Newhouse, he just always worked on the farms of Tanis and Mensch?

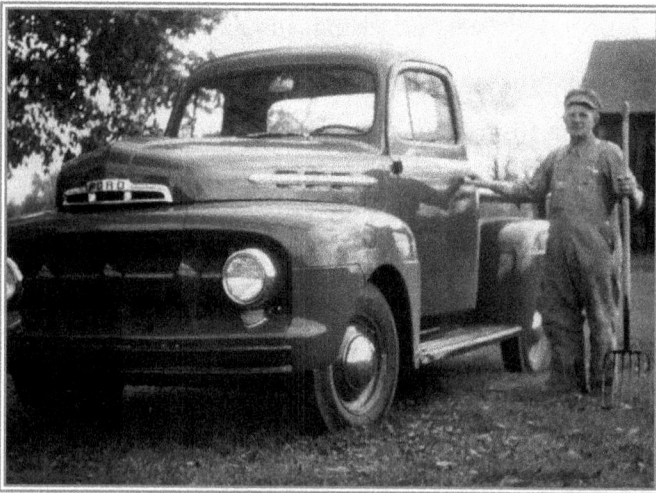

Richard Newhouse on the farm

HL:  I think he had a store at one time in Grand Rapids. His wife helped him in that. And then she died.

JK:  Do you remember her?

HL: I do not. I wasn't born into Hope church so I didn't know a lot of the early people except as I played with their kids and associated with them. I don't remember all the details. Mr. Newhouse was often an elder. In 1953 I did not recognize him as the stalwart who stood and opposed the statements of De Wolf. That escaped me. I just went with the flow. But my dad was a staunch supporter of Hoeksema in that and opposed the conditional covenant theology.

I hung out with John and Cal and particularly Chuck, your dad. Cal was a little younger so I didn't do a lot of hanging around with Cal, but he hung around with us when we would take him with us.

JK: Did you work in your dad's shop?

HL: I did. I first worked for a couple of years in the muck on Dick Kooienga's farm—cutting celery, topping onions, and cutting my fingers a few times. I had a scissors with springs that I had to be very careful when using it. When the boys were not using their scissors, they threw them into the ground. My brother, Don, was careless and threw the scissors into his leg. We played war in the barn with Rog and Don Kooienga, tossing pieces of celery at each other.

JK: Evidently that was when Rog wasn't looking.

HL: No, Rog was in on it. He could make a piece of celery really sting. But anyway, those were fun times. Then I worked for my dad in the shop in the summer and after school until I was about fifteen or sixteen.

JK: You went to Unity Christian High School?

HL: Most of the neighborhood kids went to Unity. Unity's bus came to the Hope area, and we would all get on by Hall Street and Wilson.

JK: Rev. Heys left, and Rev. Hanko came to Hope right out of the seminary?

HL: Yes, he became my minister in 1955.

JK: Hope had lost families in the 1953 split, but a couple of years later it seemed like it had been growing quite a bit.

HL: Hope lost about ten to fifteen families. Then Rev. Hanko came and stabilized things. Hope grew rather rapidly under Rev. Hanko. A lot of people came from different areas.

JK: Do you think the school had something to do with that? People wanted to move closer to school?

HL: Yes, I think that had a lot to do with it.

JK: Was the area around Hope all farmland then?

HL: Yes. Originally Isaac Korhorn owned most of the land from Riverbend to about where Covenant is today. Howard Fenske bought that land and plotted it for houses. Members of Hope church knew Fenske quite well, so the church was able to buy property on Ferndale for the church and parsonage.

I remember Hanko's ministry quite well. He showed good leadership. Later when I was on the Federation Board for the young people, I had conversations with him about the work of the young people.

JK: So you were coming into your own as a mature member of the church when he was your minister?

HL: Yes, I served on the Federation Board for a few years, first as assistant treasurer and then as president. The year I married, 1964, was the last year of my term as president, so the vice-president took over my responsibilities, although I attended the young people's convention that year as a married man. That's when I started teaching at Hope school too.

JK: Where did you go to college?

HL: Calvin. Issues like evolution were coming into Calvin College, starting with the period theory under Prof. John De Vries. He was a dynamic professor, a very powerful and popular man who had worked on the atomic bomb. He wrote the book called *Beyond the Atom*.

*A message from our President*

Dear Young People:

For the last time it is my privilege to welcome you to a convention. It is my hope and confidence that again your expectation of enjoyment and edification will be realized. The theme is especially appropriate to us as covenant youth, for Holiness should be our trade mark. During these convention days, we will discuss, debate and listen to how Holiness applies to our twentieth century lives. Especially on Thursday, we will be able to contribute and benefit through the intercourse of our own ideas. This new aspect of our convention is to be commended as providing the possibility of an extremely worthwhile convention. Your attitude to and participation in it will help determine its value. Let's show that we can share our thoughts as well as have fun; that we can ask questions and seek answers, as well as attend an outing.

As we return home, we must have impressed upon us the duty of Holiness through the Grace of God, this Holiness will be ours.

Yours in Christ,

Harry Langerak

1964 *Beacon Lights,* message to the young people

There was only one man at Calvin, Professor Monsma, who taught creation. He was referred to as "the old man upstairs." De Vries frequently poked fun of him.

In the late 1950s and early 1960s, Rev. Herman Hoeksema wrote editorials in the *Standard Bearer* that refuted the period theory. De Vries knew there were Protestant Reformed students in his class. He called them out, "So you oppose me, huh?" We got in on the ridicule.

JK:  Do you remember any members of Hope church who fought in Korea?

HL:  Yes. A. J. Kuiper was building our family's house on Hall Street, and his son, John, received a notification to get his physical for the draft. It was sobering for a young kid of ten or eleven when that notice came and when John had to report for basic training and then active duty. My mother sent gifts to him as a soldier on the front lines.

JK: So you graduated from college. Were you married before you graduated or afterward?

HL: I had nine hours of college to complete when we got married. I took a contract from Hope school for half time. Part of it was practice teaching. I taught for five years at Hope and then went to Covenant Christian High School at the beginning of its second year. I taught there until I retired. Because I taught all of the government courses, I taught all the kids that went through Covenant until I retired, because government was a required course for seniors.

JK: When you married, did your wife come to Hope church?

HL: Yes. She came from First church. We were ready to start a family in Hope church.

JK: Who was the minister after Rev. Hanko?

HL: Rev. Veldman.

JK: Did he marry you?

HL: No, Rev. David Engelsma married us. He was a boyhood friend. We had a church wedding in First church. Hope's consistory served as the consistory, and Reverend Engelsma was the minister.

JK: Was it on Sunday?

HL: No. Getting back to church weddings [as in article 70 of the Church Order] had to evolve a little bit. When I went to Hope's consistory to ask for approval of my arrangements for a call to worship for a church wedding in First church, with Rev. Engelsma as the officiating minister, and Hope as the supervising consistory, Rev. Veldman was a little upset with those arrangements. I can understand that now, looking back. I was rather presumptuous to ask for an official call to worship on a weekday. It was kind of a learning process, let's say. I think that's when a lot of the rules began to be made in Hope church. Today, if someone wants a church wedding, ideally it must be solemnized during a Sunday worship service. And the service must be held in our church building. These were good changes.

JK: Rev. Veldman was your minister when you got married? He had some quirks, from what I understand.

HL: "That's the way it is" was a common Veldman expression at the end of his sermons.

JK: Did he wear tails then?

HL: Oh, yes.

JK: Were there any other ministers who wore the long tails?

HL: Rev. Lubbers did for a good part of his ministry. Hoeksema, I remember H.C. Hoeksema. A coat with long tails was pretty standard preaching attire in the1950s and into the 1960s. At some point it began to phase out. Then the attire changed to black or very dark suits.

JK: Evidently that was a thing the Dutch ministers did. It was a respect thing maybe for the ministers to dress a little differently.

HL: I think it went partly with the territory; it was expected if you were a minister. You wore these starched collars, a white shirt, and a coat with tails.

JK: So the minister was set apart even in his dress?

HL: Yes, very definitely. I remember Rev. Veldman in particular. He also stood at the bottom of the steps in front of the congregation, and prayed before he went up on the pulpit.

JK: That, too, was a visible picture of his seeking the Lord's blessing before he mounted the pulpit.

JK: When you look back, do you think the ministers were thought of differently, too? Were they held in more respect or esteem? Or did they carry themselves in such a way that even the children were scared of them, whereas maybe that's not so true today?

HL: Yes, even Rev. Heys. I remember that wherever he went he wore a white shirt, pants, and a tie. I think that was kind of a symbol of respect. I can't conceive of wearing a white shirt with a tie to a picnic. I don't know if that was a matter of respect for fellow saints or if that was the custom. Some things we did by custom, and today it is hard to explain why they were the custom. So I don't know whether it was a matter of respect, but I think a minister was quite a bit more reserved. I remember being shocked when Rev. Vos started playing ball with us at school picnics and calling somebody "Kaline" and another "Harvey Kuenn."

JK: Do you think our unconditional covenant view played a part, or was it just culture where the ministers became more part of the people than set apart?

HL: I think it was part of our culture. I remember going to a Christian Reformed church with my cousin. I thought the minister was Roman Catholic because he wore a long robe, and then it shocked me later when Professor Hoeksema started wearing a robe and then justified it in the *Standard Bearer*. I think he tried to get other ministers to go along with him, but robes were hot. I don't think we had air conditioning at the time, so it was a counterproductive attempt to change to robes.

JK: There was no air conditioning. All the big fans went on during collection—sounded like airplanes going through the auditorium. All the little fans were on the sides. Everybody wanted to sit on the side to get a little air.

HL: I remember the Sunday ritual when I started to be the janitor. The big airplane fans were placed in the corners in the back, so they would face the middle and get the air in the middle going. And the side fans had to be started by pushing the buttons with a coat hanger.

JK: Was Rev. Veldman the minister when your dad left?

HL: Yes. He had known Veldman for a while and didn't appreciate him.

JK: Did you get the sense that Veldman was different from Hanko in a certain way, that he told it a little bit more how it was?

HL: Well Rev. Veldman was older, and he had gone through a lot in his ministry. He was the first minister to suffer the consequences of being opposed to a conditional covenant when he was deposed from the ministry in Hamilton.

JK: It is a little ironic that your dad and Rev. Veldman did not see eye to eye, because they both loved the Protestant Reformed view of the covenant.

HL: They did, but my dad was upset with how Rev. Rich Veldman was treated. I think my dad even began to change some of his theology, too. He went to the Christian Reformed Church, which teaches a conditional covenant. He knew that, but that was also where Rich Veldman went.

I remember the Sunday morning Dad informed the family that he was leaving Hope church. Dad wasn't sure where I stood, so he said, "Harry, what are you going to do?" I said, "I'm going to stay." I left the house in a huff and didn't treat him very well, because he was leaving Hope church and had informed us on a Sunday morning.

JK: You had no prior inclination?

HL: No. It was a shock to us and to a lot of people. My dad was an avid reader, and many of the young people came to our house to sit around and talk with him about books he had read, theology, and things like that. But my dad was kind of vocal when he complained, and perhaps many people thought, "Oh, that's just Tony," but he did leave. I was hoping not; I thought about what would happen to the family. I asked my mother to keep me informed about where he was. I never talked to him personally about it. That's the one thing I regret.

JK: During Rev. Kortering's time at Hope did you become a deacon?

HL: I don't think so. I became a deacon under Rev. Van Overloop's ministry.

JK: Do you remember anything special about the church on Wilson? Growing up was it just your church?

HL: I remember going there and flying around after the worship services, but the land was a sandbur patch, so it wasn't the most convenient place to fly around. It was not grassy or anything, there was a little grass in between the two trees that were in front of it. I remember going up the front, cement steps and entering a cubbyhole-sized room. The parking lot was unpaved—just gravel and sometimes plain sand. When it rained the grounds were muddy, and cars got stuck if they were parked behind the church. It was the bare necessities of a church. It was all wood—white, overlapping, cedar siding.

JK: Did you have to go up the steps to get into the main part?

HL: Yes, after the cement steps and passing through the small room under the belfry, which had no bell, there was another set of steps to enter the auditorium. No concern in those days for handicap accessibility!

JK: Where did the minister, elders, and deacons come from when they walked in the auditorium?

HL: They came in a door in the front, and the minister stepped up onto the platform. Off to the south side was the organ.

JK: That was in a time when nobody had much money. What was the lighting? Just big chandeliers up there?

HL: Hardly chandeliers. They were cords hanging from the ceiling with a fixture on the ends. The seats were wooden, folding chairs strung together on boards. There was an aisle down the middle and an aisle on each side. Later the center aisle was eliminated and softer, individual seats were installed.

JK: When was the new church built?

HL: It was finished in 1965.

JK: So right around when you got married it was being built?

HL: We were hoping it would be done so that we could get married in it.

JK: Are there any other things that stick in your mind about the congregation at that time?

HL: The Hope church ball team was started in the 1960s.

JK: A softball team?

HL: Yes. Kalsbeek-De Jong plumbing helped fund it with Gib Schimmel, Heyboer Heating, and other businessmen from Hope church. They gave us hats and printed shirts with "Hope" on the front and the names of the sponsors on the back. Mel Engelsma was the first manager, David (Prof.) Engelsma was the pitcher, and Rog Kooienga was the catcher. He was a very good catcher, one of the few that could catch Engelsma.

"Blue Church titlists—Calvin College basketball player, Dave Engelsma was the key performer with his fine pitching as Hope Protestant Reformed won the city recreation department's Blue Church league softball crown. Team members are back left: Tom Heyboer, Larry Howerzyl, Arie Griffioen, Dave Engelsma, Roger Kooienga; front: Gerald Kuiper, Harry Langerak, John Kalsbeek, Wayne Lanning; missing: George Engelsma, Don Kooienga, Roger King" (*Grand Rapids Press* [September 13, 1959]:41).

JK: He must've been pretty good, because I understand nobody could hit Engelsma very well.

HL: That's right. We won the championship the first year.

JK: I remember a picture of the team. Did other churches have teams or was it kind of a city league team?

HL: It was a city league team.

JK: It wasn't like church leagues?

HL: No, we didn't have a church league. That's when we started a golf team, too. A lot of the guys joined it. I don't know if they still have it going yet.

JK: How many terms did you serve as a deacon?

HL: I think it was two terms, and then I became an elder. And then I don't remember how many terms. I think I turned down a nomination once. I went to Dewey Engelsma and said, "Does a man have the right to turn down a nomination?" "Well," he said. "I haven't, but it shouldn't be that you have to use me as criteria."

JK: Did you have to go, like today, in front of the council?

HL: Yes. It was orderly.

JK: Do you have any recollection of certain saints in the church who really had a difficult life but remained faithful?

HL: Well, I guess when the Den Boers came, I looked at the burden—two adults with special needs, Adrian and Cornelius. They came from West Leonard Christian Reformed Church, and I thought, "It's got to be tough handling those two boys." When the boys were growing up there was no school for special needs children, not even the public school had one. I was amazed at what they knew, what their parents had taught them. The boys lived at home with their parents 24/7, on a little farm on a gravel road, and they played in the little round barn on their property. Adrian got so upset when cars roared by the house that he'd get up and holler at people.

I also remember what Lou Kooienga went through after Rog had the accident—the burden she had raising five boys.

JK: What was that like with Rog, they probably didn't know right away how much he was going to recover?

HL: They knew he had brain damage almost immediately. He was a deacon at the time. Later after he recovered somewhat he continued to be a deacon until his term of office expired. I remember him, taking collection in the white church. I don't remember if he came to deacons' meetings, but he came in with the deacons and took collection with them.

JK: That must have been a traumatic experience for the whole church.

HL: Oh it was. He and Lou and the boys lived in a little house by an oil company. There were three or four little houses, and he rented one of them. The boys from the ball team went to see Rog once in a while. He had to be fed. Then he had to learn to feed himself.

I also remember Mel (Engelsma) going through agony and pain due to rheumatoid arthritis. He was in constant pain.

JK: Do you remember anything about Isaac Korhorn?

HL: He was at home lying on a hospital bed and was incapacitated for some reason. The young boys of Hope church took turns taking the sermon recordings in the back of church. The boys brought the recordings to Mr. Korhorn so he could listen to the sermons. He had a raspberry patch. He hired some neighborhood kids to pick raspberries. I picked raspberries for him. He was in the elders' bench for quite a while.

JK: What do you remember about the Vietnam War?

HL: The draft was still in effect during the Vietnam War. But one could bypass the draft by signing up for the Army Reserves for six months of training.

JK: Which my dad did.

HL: There was a bit of controversy whether it was right to bypass the draft by signing up for the reserves.

JK: So those older men like my dad and your age, they bypassed it mostly. But the younger ones, like Larry Koole and Mike Engelsma, it seems that they were drafted.

HL: Yes, by that time we had hashed over that whole issue, and it was felt that one should wait for the draft. I was deferred as long as I studied to be a teacher. Then I was declared ineligible for the draft because I was a teacher.

JK: Do you remember any issues with the labor unions, where men struggled with the labor unions?

HL: I remember a number of votes taken at Steelcase to organize Steelcase, and the union was always rejected.

JK: And a lot of our men worked there.

HL: Dexter Lock became unionized, and life became miserable for our men who worked there. Finally, the men quit.

JK: When do you think it was more and more accepted to work on Sunday? There must've been a time when Christian Reformed and Protestant Reformed people didn't work on Sunday.

HL: There was a time in our local history when businesses closed on Sunday. I think probably thirty-five years ago this began to change rather substantially; today it is accepted that businesses stay open on Sunday.

JK: I know even from my time that a lot of the young kids worked in grocery stores, stocking shelves and packing and carrying out groceries.

HL: Well I did that at Stanton's Food, but he closed on Sunday.

JK: Evidently places like Great Day were not open on Sunday either because our kids worked there. My grandpa always shopped at Great Day because the store was not open on Sunday. He thought he would give that store his business because he appreciated that.

HL: The Sabbath is not sacred any more.

JK: Do you remember any time at Hope where all the kids didn't sit with their families?

HL: There was a time when the older kids sat in the back of the white church. The congregation received some pastoral letters from the consistory, and there began to be an emphasis on going into church as a family and sitting as families not as a bunch of individuals. I don't know when it came about, but the transition was probably before we moved to the Ferndale church building.

JK: When you think about those who had a big effect on the congregation during your lifetime, can you name a few men and women who had a big spiritual effect on the church?

HL: Hope was a church in transition. You have to remember that there were a lot of people who moved into the neighborhood that first didn't go to Hope church. They gradually came into Hope church. I just remember Jake Kuiper being a very active member of Hope church. He was often a deacon; he was a Sunday school teacher; for years he duplicated the sermon tapes and mailed them to contacts of the Reformed Witness Committee; and he was the janitor for most of the years I can remember that Hope church had a janitor. Jake's wife was very active for many years on the catering committee with her sisters, and she sang in the Choral Society.

Jake and Nelo Kuiper

Dewey Engelsma was very much involved as a leader at Hope church. Dave Meulenberg served as an elder and was very instrumental in giving a lot of direction. I remember Jay Bomers as an elder, but he died quite young. John Dykstra and his wife came to Hope church very early in my history as a young person. I think of Rich Bloem who was instrumental in the Choral Society and the Hope Heralds.

JK: So even in the organic life of the church, different people did different things.

HL: Right, they all took a part in it.

JK: Are there any humorous things you remember?

HL: I remember when Rev. Ophoff would preach. Kids see the quirks, and Rev. Ophoff could move the pulpit. He pounded on it, and we kids watched the glass of water move over to the edge of the pulpit. We wondered if the glass was going to fall off. I don't remember if it ever fell off, but I remember watching that glass of water move.

Rev. Hoeksema preached for Hope around 1953. As a kid, you're very conscious of the leadership. He was the leader, and we respected him for that. He walked into the auditorium and up on the platform and looked around and noticed many children. When it was time to preach, he said, "I've changed my sermon. I see a lot of children and young people here. I was going to preach on a controversial text [related to the conditional covenant controversy], but I'm going to preach on another text." We children were astounded that he could go on the pulpit and make a change in his text and sermon. The next day in school we mentioned that to our teacher, Miss Reitsma, because we thought the man had to study to make a sermon, and it never dawned on us that he could change a sermon when he went on the pulpit. But we didn't know Rev. Hoeksema.

JK: What do you remember about the church picnics?

HL: The church picnic was always called the Sunday school picnic. It wasn't the church picnic, because the Sunday school teachers put it on. If you were a Sunday school teacher, you were put on the picnic committee. Later when the church became larger, a committee from the congregation arranged the picnic.

JK:  Did everyone bring their own food?

HL:  Yes, it used to be that way.

JK:  They would set it all out, and it was a potluck?

HL:  I don't think it was a potluck. Moms took food in a basket for the family. After we were married, I remember a lot of people picked up Chick'n Lick'n. Ballgames were the key. There would be a rip-roaring ballgame with the old men—married versus the unmarried. Everybody joined in, and it was quite interesting.

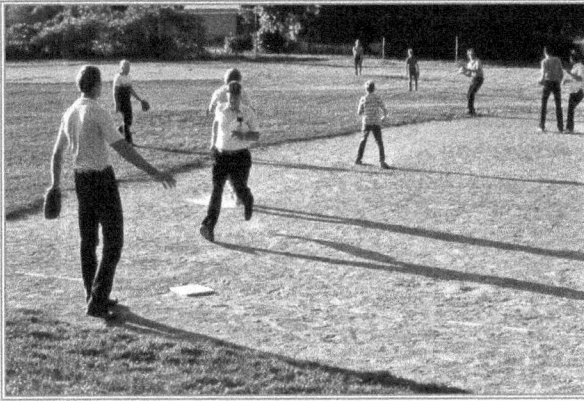

Ballgame at the church picnic with young and old participating

JK:  Today it's not the rip-roaring softball game with the older men anymore, but the young people play ball. I think there was a time where it was hard to get the young people to come to the church picnics, but more and more the parents urged their older kids to come to the supper.

HL:  I would say that there was a time where the young people kind of faded out of the picture for a while. I think that's all coming back, making the church the center of our family and social lives. I think that's a good emphasis. We need a little social time together as a church as well as the institutional time.

JK:  Do you recall any particular changes in the church's history?

HL:  One change that comes to mind is the nursery. When Rev. Van
Overloop came to Hope there was no nursery. He and his wife
had a couple of children too young to sit in church, and so did
a few other families. About four or five of these young families
decided to help the minister and his wife and themselves too.
One of the parents (the men too) would babysit the children
each Sunday morning in the parsonage. That usually worked out
well, until one particular Sunday when my wife was caring for
about seven or eight little ones. Near the end of the service, she
went upstairs to get the Van Overloop baby out of the crib and to
change a diaper. When she returned to the family room, the little
boys and girls were busily removing the ashes from the fireplace
and putting them in dump trucks, which they intended to run
through the house. There was quite a mess on the children and
the carpet to clean up before Reverend and Sue got home!

Later the consistory granted permission to use a catechism
room in the basement of church for a nursery. That was a good
change. It encouraged parents to bring their young children to
church each Sunday, with the result that parents now think about
training their children to sit in church at an earlier age than in
earlier years.

Another important change is that the elders are taking a more
active role in the life of the congregation. Ministers used to do
everything in the church, making and printing the bulletins,
visiting the sick and shut-ins, and doing many other pastoral
labors. Hope has moved in the direction where elders take on
more responsibilities so the minister can spend more time with
the word, preparing sermons and catechism lessons. Our congregation has accepted this transition well. But that change has come
gradually as our congregation grew larger. The elders see that
they are a very important part of the work in the church. Our
elders and deacons are very busy people in the church. When the
men are called into the offices they must realize their importance

in the life of the church. They can't sit back and watch things happen; they have to take an active part in the church life. Our congregation must understand that the minister can't be everything to everybody. He has a particular and important work to do. Preaching and teaching are his main calling.

JK: Are there concerns for the congregation that you see as you look into the future?

HL: Marriages today are under attack in the world and in the church. We must maintain the scriptural principle that the bond of marriage is for life. In dating the young people must understand their calling to seek mates who are one with them in the faith and determine to be faithful to each until death.

## Interview with Donna Moelker

Donna Moelker is a daughter-in-law of Hope charter member, John Moelker. Her son, Tom, and his wife, Bonnie, currently operate Moelker Orchards. The Moelker family was part of Hope Protestant Reformed Church until 1953.[10]

MICHIGAN
CENTENNIAL FARM
OWNED BY THE SAME FAMILY
OVER ONE HUNDRED YEARS
THE HISTORICAL
SOCIETY OF MICHIGAN
Sponsored By: CONSUMERS ENERGY

Moelker Orchards on Kenowa, just west of Riverbend, that Donna and her husband, Jim, managed for years.

---

10  Donna Moelker was interviewed by Cal and Linda Kalsbeek on June 4, 2015.

CK: Your family went with Rev. Hoeksema in 1924?

DM: Yes, we went to First church then, but there was no church on the corner of Fuller and Franklin then. I don't really know where they worshiped at first.

CK: How long were you at First church?

DM: I was there until I married Jim [Moelker, son of John Moelker] and came here [Riverbend area]. Before that I didn't know there was a Hope church. I married Jim in 1946, and he was going to Hope Protestant Reformed Church.

CK: Was Jim's dad still alive at that time?

DM: Oh yes, John was going to Hope Protestant Reformed Church too. I think they all were, except some of his family who lived downtown. They were Christian Reformed. A girl who lived next door to us was Christian Reformed. It bugged her that we stayed with the Protestant Reformed Church. Then we had Rev. De Wolf. He got to be a good friend of the family. We babysat his kids and gave him produce and fruit when he was minister at Hope. So when they had that split, Jim and our family went with him. Then we went to Beverly in Wyoming. They dissolved, and then we went to Hope Christian Reformed Church in Grandville.

CK: Your father-in-law had the farm on Kenowa when you married Jim, so when did you get it?

DM: After he died, he had made arrangements that Jim would have first choice, because he was running it. Of course, the kids all said, "That's not fair; that place is a gold mine" (laugh). Jim said, "Help yourself; you buy it. I'll do something else." Jim was also working at General Motors. The farm was going downhill, so we needed extra income to make a go of it. But all the kids said, "No." They didn't want the farm. So we had it, and then when Tom got married, I sold it to my son, Tom.

John Moelker's farmhouse on Kenowa

CK: Jim's dad, John, was a prominent member at Hope church for many years. Often times he was clerk of the consistory. He was looked up to. He had a large family didn't he?

DM: There were ten children. Jim's parents came through Ellis Island. After they married, they lived on what is now Breton Road. Somehow they ended up with this land from the government. The land that the school [Riverbend] is on was part of our farm. The bell at the farm's bakery was the bell from that old one-room schoolhouse.

CK: Did your father-in-law, John, ever relate any stories about life here?

DM: Not that I remember. He retired and spent most of his time in Florida and came back in the summer. He had a stroke and died, but I can't remember when. He lived with us for a while, but he never said much. Although he did mention that Indians came up to the house from the river.

CK: He was on the school board of Riverbend school, I think.

DM: They needed some land for the school, and we gave some of our farm. That is why our farm curves around it. They also got some

land from another neighbor. They had it recorded that if Grandville didn't use it for a school anymore then they may not sell
it, but must give it back to the donors. They can't find the other
donor, so the school just sets there, and it is going to ruin. It is
used for storage.

CK: The old church [on the corner of Kenowa and Riverbend] was
still there when you were going to Hope church on Wilson. What
happened to it?

DM: It was torn down, and the house that is there today was built
on the foundation of that church. Grandpa was very busy with
the church and they were brought up that way, to be involved.
Church was one of the things you did not skip. If you were not
there, you would get a visit the next day or a call saying, "Where
were you?"

CK: Yes, I looked at some of the consistory minutes from way back, and
they record a lot of visits by the consistory to people who were not
in church for a week or so. The elders would check on them.

CK: Do you remember Rich Newhouse?

DM: Oh yes! He lived with the Ike Korhorn family for a while on
Kenowa. He had a little grocery store in downtown Grand Rapids. We would buy groceries there. Then he came out here. So he
must have gotten rid of his store and moved out here. They were
relatives of my mother-in-law somehow. I remember his wife
wore a dress that came way to the ground, and her hair was tied
in the little knot in the back of her head.

CK: Do you remember the Charles Engelsma family?

DM: Yes I do. They had a lot of children too: Mel, Dewey, Sybil,
Johanna, Eileen... I met my husband on a date with Mel Engelsma
and his girlfriend [Grace].

CK: How about Jacob and Jacoba Zaagman?

DM: Yes, I remember they lived right on Wilson across from the cemetery. They had a little tiny house set back there and a ton of kids.

She used to bring them to Riverbend school with her car, and there were kids sitting on the fenders (laugh) and on the hood. That's how they went to school. They lived in that house. One of the girls married a Bergman.

CK: Is there anything else that comes to mind when you think of the years you were at Hope Protestant Reformed Church?

DM: I remember taking communion in one cup. One member was concerned that he had to drink out of the cup after a woman of the congregation who was wearing lipstick. He said, "She drank with 'dirty lips.'"

CK: Well, Donna, I think we will end the interview with that. If other memories of interest come to mind, please let me know. Thank you.

## Interview with Gerald and Clara Van Den Top

Clara is the granddaughter of Isaac Korhorn, an elder who was deposed from Hope Christian Reformed Church in 1924. Clara and Gerald were members of Hope Protestant Reformed Church and became charter members of Hope's daughter, Grace Protestant Reformed Church.[11]

Gerald and Clara Van Den Top

11   Gerald and Clara Van Den Top were interviewed by Jeff Kalsbeek in September 2015.

CV: I was baptized at Creston Protestant Reformed Church. Dad was a deacon there. We left Creston because he heard that the Hope people were putting up a Protestant Reformed Christian school. He felt that Protestant Reformed education was so important. We moved to Luce Street. I was glad we could go to Hope, because we could worship with Grandpa and Grandma Korhorn and with Uncle Rich Newhouse—Dad's closest friend. I thought the world of my Grandpa; he was a quiet, mild man, but he stood up for the truth. Grandma's name was Henrietta.

JK: Tell me about your dad. What was his name?

CV: Maynard Veenstra. He became a member of Hope in 1948.

JK: How did he get into the Protestant Reformed churches?

CV: His parents were Christian Reformed. My dad started going to First Protestant Reformed Church. Grandma Veenstra couldn't speak English. I remember Dad saying, "I always took my parents to the Dutch services in First church at Fuller and Franklin."

JK: He met your mother somewhere in there, right? What was your mother's name?

CV: Alice Korhorn.

JK: Did your grandpa Korhorn always live in the Hope area?

CV: Years ago, Grandpa owned all the land on Wilson Avenue where the old church was—the church I loved, the little, white one. Where Hope church is now was pasture land of Grandpa Korhorn. In 1946 he gave an acre of land for a future Christian school, which is now Hope school.

When we were dating, we went to the white, wooden church. We had catechism in the basement with Rev. Heys. We sat at tables. He would walk back and forth through the whole hour of catechism while he was teaching us. Even when he asked us our questions, he didn't look at us; he just walked back and forth. That was just him, week after week after week. I wanted him to look at us, but he would just go back and forth. We knew our catechism. My dad always asked us every Friday night, and we had better know it. I had a little bit of fear of Rev. Heys, and I know I shouldn't have, because Dad, in front of his children, talked so highly of all our ministers. I thought, "Why did I fear?" I think it was because I wanted him to smile, and he didn't.

I remember Rev. Heys spoke at my ninth-grade graduation from Hope. I'll never forget when he looked at all of the graduates and said, "Young people, you are the future church." I felt so grown up, and yet I felt that my dad, Uncle Rich, and Grandpa were the staunch ones; we will never be like them. Then Rev. Heys said, "You will be mothers and fathers someday. Some of you will be elders and deacons." Wow, he just put it all before us, and we weren't ready for all that yet. But in a way I felt grown up; that was a beautiful night. I don't know if they are that serious today at graduations. Rev. Heys called us young people, and that makes you grow up too. We were just kids.

JK: Do you know how your mother and your father met?

CV: My mother was the organist in Hope church.

JK: So your dad went to Hope church then?

CV: He was attending; I don't think he was a member. My mother played the organ, and he saw her. I guess that was the beginning. Alice was the first organist in Hope. She was just the average organist, nothing like organists are today.

JK: Can you think of any other childhood remembrances of Rev. Heys?

CV: I never saw him without a white shirt and a tie. Even to all the picnics, he wore a white shirt with either a bow tie or a long tie. Mrs. Heys always went to church with a hat on. I don't remember her with a bare head. I appreciated that as a child, because Rev. Heys was different from the rest of us. He was our minister. It's a high appointment to be a minister, and I respected him for that. You could always see that he was a minister in his actions. Now-a-days ministers dress like we do, but in my younger days it was different.

JK: There are pros and cons there. I think about that too; yes, more and more with our doctrine of the covenant we want to have friendship with one another, but at the same time the minister's office has to be respected.

CV: We did respect it. My dad was an elder in Hope church and president of Hope's school board. During that time the third and fourth classrooms were added to the school.

JK: Wow, what a busy man.

CV: Yes, he was one busy man. He was capable, but I don't know if it was all so good.

JK: That makes someone really busy, but the congregation was much smaller, so there were less men. Evidently they didn't have that unspoken rule that school board members are not asked to be on the consistory.

CV: Maybe shortly after that it changed, I don't remember, but my dad was always really involved. Those were the good old days.

JK: What was it like in Hope school, just a four-room school, right?

CV: It was nice; everybody got along; everybody played together. My favorite teacher was Miss Alice Reitsma. She was so fair; she treated everyone alike. I really appreciated that, because one girl was picked on quite a bit, and Miss Reitsma treated her just like she treated the rest of us.

JK: And you could pick that out as a child? I suppose children look for that. They don't want the teacher to play favorites in any way.

CV: I'll never forget the Bible tests. Everyone had to answer a certain amount of questions, but there were always a couple of extra ones on the bottom for the older students. I was one of the younger ones, so I didn't have to answer the extra questions. My sisters, Ann and Helen, had to answer those questions.

JK: Did you begin school at Hope?

CV: I went to Creston Christian first. At age nine I went to Hope. All the Veenstra kids went to Hope school the first year it opened.

All eight of us were in school at one time. My mother had all of us within a year of each other. A lot of little Veenstra kids in Hope school! Jay graduated the first year, Ira the second year, Ann the third year, Helen the fourth year, June the fifth year, and me the sixth year, and then Hazel and Merle graduated. We lived two and a half miles from school. We walked to and from school every day and to and from catechism on Saturday mornings.

JK: We humor our kids that we walked five miles up hill and then five miles up hill to get home again. But you actually did it. What did you do in winter? Did you have to walk then?

CV: Oh, yes.

JK: You walked in blizzards?

CV: I don't remember ever not walking.

JK: Your mom bundled you up?

GV: You occasionally got a ride from some people.

CV: Not for catechism, but one man in our area would occasionally go by in the afternoon and bring us home.

JK: Back then people usually had one vehicle per family, and the Dad had to have it to get to work. Was your dad a farmer?

CV: No, he worked in different factories, and he was a custodian in the Grand Rapids school system.

JK: In the 1950s there was a push for unions to come in the factories, and a lot of men had to find other jobs. Was that the case with your dad?

CV: No, he worked at Irwin Seating and another factory, but there were no unions. I'm not sure if Dad had to quit because later the union came in. He worked in more than one factory. The Grand Rapids Public school system must have been unionized, but he was never part of a union.

JK: They must've allowed him to be conscientious objector.

CV: I remember when Choral Society started in Hope. My sister, Helen, and I joined choir at the same time. Hattie Lanning was the director. She did a good job. The Choral Society went to First Protestant Reformed Church to record songs for the *Reformed Witness Hour* radio broadcast. I thought that was unique. I remember Sundays; we all had to sit down and listen to the *Reformed Witness Hour.* When the Choral Society sang that was a part of me.

JK: Tell me a little bit about Rich Newhouse. You called him Uncle Rich.

CV: Yes, he was over all the time for coffee with my grandpa and grandma. He had a store for a little while near First church with Uncle Bert [Korhorn] and Aunt Julia.

JK: Was that like a farmers' market? Did he sell produce?

CV: No, he had a grocery store. He closed that and moved closer to Grandpa Korhorn in the Hope area. He lived with Grandpa and Grandma after his wife died. I never knew Aunt Susie. They could not have children. He moved out of Grandpa's and Grandma's house and into a trailer after Grandpa passed away, because I think people were unhappy with his living with Grandma. Uncle Rich was always in the consistory. He was such a wonderful man.

GV: I think your grandpa and Rich got along very well, but I think your grandma and Rich didn't always hit it off real well. One thing I remember about Rich Newhouse is every Sunday morning when he would come to church, right by the door he had his little brick on which he would set his cigar, and when church was over, he would reach up, get his cigar, and light it up again.

CV: Many people talked to Uncle Rich and my grandpa and asked them for advice. God gave them both knowledge and wisdom. They were so good for the church. I so respected them. I felt so bad when Grandpa died, but I guess I wasn't supposed to because he's in a better place. But when you're younger, you want all those good ones to stay.

GV: They basically were uneducated men.

CV: They were, every one of them, but God gave them much wisdom; so education doesn't necessarily give wisdom.

JK: The fear of the Lord gives wisdom. So that bears that passage out then. It's not the educated. During those years, did you visit on Sunday nights with other families?

CV: Yes, my parents did some visiting on Sunday night with Mr. and Mrs. Miedema and Fred and Alice Huizinga. Fred was a little younger, but they were very good friends.

JK: Did they leave you kids home?

CV: When we were little kids, Mother and Dad didn't do much visiting. They were very content being home.

JK: They had to be there to take care of you.

CV: Yes, they never would get a babysitter.

JK: The 1953 schism happened when Rev. Heys was at Hope. What was that like?

CV: I remember hearing Rev. De Wolf at First church, where he said that all you have to do is believe on the Lord and be saved. I don't remember exactly how he said that, but it was basically that we could do that on our own. We all know that we are totally depraved. My dad talked about the controversy a bit. There was another problem that started in 1947. Schilder convinced some people of his view regarding the covenant, and there was discontent. Some weren't happy with Hoeksema. I think about Schilder, putting his views among our people, and then with Rev. De Wolf, almost going back to the things that happened in 1924.

I couldn't hang around with kids anymore that I used to because my dad said their parents knew better. To me it was a very, very sad time, because I always thought those parents knew better; they know our salvation is all of grace and that they can't do anything apart from the Lord's working.

I think Rev. De Wolf would have fit right in with the Christian

Reformed in the split of 1924. It was just a sad time for the church.

JK: And in Hope church you could feel that there, too, but Hope had a faithful minister who got the congregation through.

CV: We had Rev. Heys, who guided us through. He was very good. I remember catechism classes. I remember feeling sorry for him because some of the boys were naughty.

I remember as a young girl the celebration of the Lord's supper in our congregation. There was a change in the partaking of the wine. They went from the one large cup, which all the confessing members drank from, to individual cups. In the Bible and in the form for the Lord's supper we read this: "The cup of blessing which we bless is the communion of the body of Christ." It speaks of one cup, not many cups, and that bothered me as a child. Some ladies said, "Well, if I had a cold, I'd give it to you if we drank out of the same cup." That's true, I guess, but I'd rather have the cold. I remember yet today when that happened. I can't say it bothers me anymore; I'm used to it. But as a child that really, really bothered me. I always liked to laugh and have a good time, but the church was very important to me, and that was a very serious thing because my Lord is everything to me. I wanted everything to be done right, and I still do today. I'm not one for change even now.

JK: I would like to ask you a little bit about Rev. Hanko's time at Hope.

CV: He came in 1955. He was an energetic minister. The church really grew a lot under Rev. Hanko. Rev. H. Hanko married us. We were married in 1958. We went to his study, Gerald and I. We asked him if he would marry us. He said, "No, I can't." My heart sunk, and I asked him, "Why not?" Then he didn't say anything, and all at once he started to laugh. He said, "You know why I can't marry you? It's my birthday that day." But he ended up marrying us on his birthday. I was scared to go there in the first place, and then he said, "No, I can't marry you."

JK: So how did you two meet?

CV: I went to a young people's convention in Doon, Iowa. The conventioneers stayed in houses then. I stayed with Gerald's cousin, Minard Van Den Top.

JK: Gerald, did you live in Michigan then?

GV: I moved to Michigan for the winter.

JK: It happened often that Iowa boys came to work in Michigan. My dad-in-law, Henry Hoekstra, did the same thing.

GV: I came to work at Keeler Brass during the winter and went back in March when the farmers were ready to do the field work. During the years 1955–1957 there was a drought in Iowa, so there were no jobs available. Everyone was looking for work. My cousins in Grand Rapids found jobs at Keeler Brass for me and my brother, Gerrit.

JK: So then you must've stayed here when you got married.

GV: Yes, for two or three years. Then we went to Iowa over Christmas to see my parents. When I was there, I heard about a farm for rent near Rock Rapids. I said to Clara, "I'm going to check with that guy if I can rent that farm, because I really want to be a farmer." That was my first love. So, I went to see him, and before I left his house, he had rented the farm to me.

JK: So you moved back to Iowa?

GV: Yes. We farmed there eight years. In 1968 I had just sold a big yard of fat cattle, and I said to Clara, "Let's run to Michigan to see your parents for a week before school starts." While we were in Michigan, I purchased a farm in Coopersville.

JK: Who was the minister in Hope then?

CV: Rev. Kortering was at Hope.

JK: Were you in Hope when Rev. Veldman was the minister?

GV: Yes. "That's the way it is." That was Rev. Veldman.

JK: He must've never changed, because I can remember as a boy we had a two-year vacancy, and he preached the catechism sermons, and that's what he said at the end of the sermons.

GV: Yes, and then he would take his glass of water, bottoms up.

CV: The preaching is different than what it used to be though. I remember Rev. Schipper would pound on the pulpit. We thought he would break it.

GV: Yes, we milked a lot of cows at that time, so we always had the front seat in church. He hit the pulpit so hard he scared our kids.

CV: When I was a teenager, the older boys never sat with their parents in church. When they got to be a certain age they sat in the back row. I remember one boy wanted to sit in the back seat, but if there wasn't room, he would sit in another seat as close to the back as possible. He slept through every sermon. One time he sat next to me, and he slept so soundly that his head hit my head.

JK: I think a lot of that is changed because we have a better understanding of the covenant. The children are members of the covenant; they're not converted later in life.

CV: I think it's important to sit by your parents, there's no reason you have to sit by yourself. When you think of your life and how God gave us wonderful parents and wonderful preachers, we should be the happiest people on this earth. We have everything if we have the Lord.

JK: Well the difficulty is to live by faith. You get busy with stuff, things go wrong during the day, and soon you're not thinking about that anymore.

CV: Yes and then your sins rise up against you and you're not so happy.

JK: What was your mother like, was she like your dad, or was she different from your dad?

CV: She was very different; day and night difference. My dad was definitely the head of the house. My mother was very quiet. And that was good. My dad was not loud either, but when Dad spoke, we listened.

JK: He commanded respect, then.

CV: Oh yes. Well, when you're a kid Dad couldn't do anything wrong. He was just a good dad. Dad and Mother both got to be ninety-six years old.

CV: When I was a little girl, I liked Uncle Rich and Grandpa Korhorn to come over and visit. Bedtime was 7:30. That did not mean 7:40; that meant 7:30! Dad would say, "All right children, say goodnight." We all went upstairs. The living room was below my older sisters' bedroom, which had a large register. I would go into their room and through the register I could hear Dad and Grandpa and Uncle Rich discuss religion. I would do that every time they came over. I wanted to hear what they had to say; it was so interesting. Grandpa didn't say much, he was a soft-spoken man. But Dad and Uncle Rich would really go after each other, and I thought they didn't like each other. The discussions were good, but they didn't always agree.

Mother would bring coffee, and then everything would be fine. Then I went to bed because I didn't care anymore. It seemed like every time they came, they always got in a good biblical discussion just when it was bedtime. I remember lying on the floor there with my ear on the register for a long time.

GV: Newhouse and old Korhorn, were opposite. That's why they were such close friends.

JK: Newhouse was more outspoken.

CV: Oh yes.

JK: And your grandpa would...

CV: just smile.

GV: When Grandma and Rich got into it, that was a different story.

CV: They liked each other at the end. Those are a lot of good memories.

JK: Gerald, what was it like for you,

Maynard and Alice Veenstra

coming from the Netherlands Reformed? Did you understand the Protestant Reformed doctrine?

GV: Not really, but I learned a lot real quickly.

JK: Did that doctrine of doubting whether you're saved affect you as a child?

GV: Oh yes; I was affected for years.

CV: If you're taught for twenty years that you have to see a vision or whatever, it would stick with you.

GV: The hardest thing for me was taking communion. In the Netherlands Reformed church you really have to know when you were converted and when you had an experience before you could take communion. There were maybe eighty or one hundred members in the congregation, and only six or eight people took communion. They were the only spiritually strong ones—some of the elders and men like that. The Lord's supper was kind of a tearjerker; it was quite a thing.

We got married and became members at Hope church, and the first Sunday we had communion. I thought, "Okay this is going to be quite a thing here." I was sitting in the same row with a lady with bright lipstick and painted fingernails, and she took the wine glass. I thought, "Do I take it, or do I run? What is going on here?" We were so used to being in Iowa with all the plain farm people. That's the way we are.

CV: I can remember Rev. Heys saying years and years ago at Christmas time that we ought to know when we drive by somebody's house what life they're really living. I couldn't believe he said that. That was just when the Protestant Reformed families were beginning to bring the worldly decorations, such as the Christmas tree and others, into their homes. He was very much against that, as we are against it yet today.

JK: He was making a point.

CV: John Kalsbeek was a real asset to Grace church. He did not want to go back to Hope. I sat right by him in church, and I said, "John we really feel bad that you're leaving us." But due to his age he had to go back to Hope where his family could keep a close eye on him.

He was a beautiful example. I will never forget the time two brothers sat right behind him, and one brother watched Mr. Kalsbeek sing the whole psalter number. I thought, "John, if you only knew what a beautiful example you are." John came to me later and said, "Clara I don't know why God is keeping me here. I feel like my work is done." Of course, he knew it wasn't done. I said, "I understand where you're coming from." Then I told him about the two boys in church. Their parents were having problems with them. I said, "The one boy watched you sing and praise your Lord through all those verses. That's why you're here, God is using you."

JK: He probably needed to hear that.

GV: He was a nice, humble man.

JK: I had a lot of lunch hours with him. I'd go to his house every day to eat lunch with him, so he had a positive effect on me too.

CV: Oh, I bet he did. He was very good for Grace church, but he was good for Hope church too. You never want men like that to leave your church.

John Kalsbeek Sr.

## Interview with Lynn Wells Jr. and Lynn Wells Sr.

While the Wells were never members of Hope church, they have been a prominent family in the Riverbend area who had contact and interaction with members of Hope even before Hope's organization. After explaining our purpose in doing the interview, we focused our questions on what they remembered about members of Hope and the contact they had with them.[12]

---

12  Lynn Jr. and Lynn Sr. were interviewed by Cal Kalsbeek on May 21, 2015.

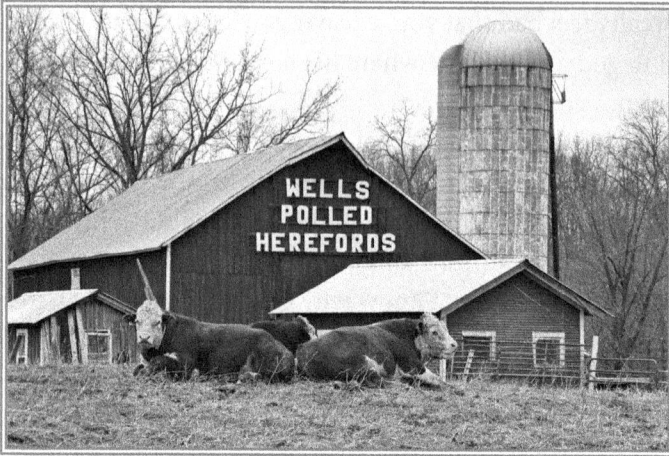

The farmstead of Lynn and Maxine Wells Sr. is located
where Begole Street dead-ends near the Grand River.

CK: Do you remember Charles Engelsma and his son, Dewey?

LW: I remember Charles so well. We would always see him walk to
church. On Saturday the kids would all walk to catechism. I
remember those days real well. Charles was the best ice skater
I ever saw. We used to skate on the bayou [near the Engelsma
farm]. He could stroke at least twenty feet…just beautiful.

CK: Did you get to know his wife and his mother?

LW: I saw them but I did not know them. The women didn't get out
much. I don't know if Charles' mother spoke English.

CK: I know Charles' mother did not speak English. We know that
when Hope church stopped having Dutch services, Charles and
his wife went to another church for a while for the sake of his
mother who didn't understand the English. Earlier you mentioned that from time to time Charles would send something
back to his family in the Netherlands. Tell us about that.

LW: He would send things back as sort of a general care package.
Dewey mentioned that they sent cans of loose tobacco. They did
that for a while. And then they got a letter from the Netherlands

thanking them for their packages, but asking if they would send cigarettes instead of loose tobacco? That made Dewey's dad so mad he never sent another box to the Netherlands (laugh). I guess he thought they should appreciate what they got instead of asking for something different.

CK: You [Lynn Wells Jr.] applied for a job at Keeler Brass, and I understand Dewey helped you get that job?

LW: Yes, I applied for the job there. I knew Dewey worked there, and I put his name down as a reference. So he pulled strings a little bit I guess to get me in there. Eventually I began to work in his department in the paint room.

CK: What do you remember about Rich Newhouse?

LW: I remember he had fancy, painted, wooden shoes. When he walked up here [on Burton Street], and down Kenowa he always wore wooden shoes. He had a great big pipe with a lid over the bowl. I don't know whether he worked for the Tanis farm or if he just rented from them. But I remember him, walking around with his flower-painted, wooden shoes. I do remember seeing him at the Coopersville livestock sale. He had Holstein cows. He would bump the cows with his knee to see if they had been bred. If they were, he could get the cow and the calf. So he was a bit shrewd then and a good buyer. I think he had a meat market in town.

A woman at Peppermill Grill [in Standale] told us a story about Richard: He and a certain Rob were friends, you know, but they didn't necessarily agree. Rob would cuss occasionally (or quite a lot). As soon as he did, why Richard would turn around and leave. They evidently discussed religion, and Richard had a low tolerance for profanity. He would leave, but at another time Richard would pick up the conversation.

CK: Where did he live?

LW: In my [Lynn Jr.'s] memory he lived in a trailer right behind the Tanis house [on Burton Street].

CK: Do you remember anything about Ted and Anna Kievit who lived in a house on Hall Street where Newhouse had previously lived?

LW: Yes, I knew them quite well. Anna would always say, "That's what Ted say." She came over when Ma was in the hospital to straighten the house out when the kids were born. She apparently would do that around the neighborhood. She would hear you had a child and would come and straighten the house out after it had been neglected for a few days.

CK: There was a De Jong family that was a part of Hope church early on. Do you remember them?

LW: They lived up on Riverbend just a little across Wilson (east side); the first house on the grade. He was a farmer, but he also had another job.

CK: What do you remember about Ike Korhorn?

LW: I remember the family lived on Kenowa a little south of Riverbend. The Korhorn families were related; brothers (Cornelius and Ike) I think. They were famers, and they had dairy cows. Ike used to do painting and wallpapering. He did that at our house, I remember. I think he also worked part time in the plaster mines. He always seemed to me to be a pretty old, shriveled-up guy, but he painted. A lot of people worked in the mines. Pat's [Lynn Jr.'s wife] grandpa worked in the mines. [Arf, arf, arf, answered the dog.] He walked from out by Sand Creek, worked his shift in the mines, and then walked back home. That kept him out of trouble, no doubt (laugh). No time for much else.

CK: What about the Moelker family?

LW: They were pretty much fruit farmers, and they had Holstein cows. He [John Moelker] was on the Riverbend school board. The State of Michigan made a law that the school must join a high school district…I must stop and think…Rex Roberts, John Moelker, and my dad, Louis Wells, were on the school board. When the school had to join a high school district, we had to vote whether we would join Grandville or Kenowa Hills. We voted to join Grandville.

CK: Are there any other memories you have about members of Hope church?

LW: I [Lynn Wells Jr.] remember Eileen Engelsma (Terpstra). When my oldest boy was about ten or eleven years old, he got up early before daylight one Sunday morning to go look for deer (he didn't carry a gun or anything). It was kind of a snowy, frosty morning. While he was coming back home, he slipped and fell and hurt his arm. I didn't think too much of it at first, but when I looked at it, it had a big lump on the side, and he couldn't move it to get his shirt off. So we realized he had broken it. Then we got him in the car to take him to the emergency room. We got up to Eileen's house, and we ran out of gas. My mom and dad were gone, so I couldn't get a hold of them. I tried Grandpa John, and he was out in Allendale. I called everybody I could think of, but couldn't get a hold of anyone. After looking at the boy's arm, Eileen said, "Just take my car." She had no idea who I was any more than I realized who she was at the moment. She said, "My brother is coming to take me to church, so just take my car and bring it back when you are done with it." So I finally did. My boy was in the hospital for a week. I brought the car back when I was done with it, but I always thought that was really something that she would let a total stranger take her car.

There is also the story about Mildred Korhorn, [daughter of Cornelius] who got whacked by the swing. She was on the swing on the playground (at Riverbend school) that the school board had decided to fix up. There was a teeter totter, a merry-go-round, and a couple of swings. We would swing and see how high we could go. All of a sudden there was a scream, and we noticed that Mildred had walked right into the swing I was on, and it hit her in the head. She bled like crazy. Someone took her home and told Mrs. Korhorn that Mildred got hit with a board. Mrs. Korhorn drove over to our house to get my mother and questioned her whether I had hit her over the head with a board. We said it was the swing board.

I also remember Neil Korhorn's wife, Florence. She drove around the neighborhood real fast.

CK: If you have no further memories of the members of Hope, we will end our interview with fast Florence. Thank you for your willingness to participate in this interview.

# Chapter 8

~⁓_◯◯_⁓~

# MEMORIES OF
# THE TORNADO OF 1956

## Editor's Introduction

Article 2 of the Belgic Confession answers the question regarding the means by which God is made known to us. The first of the two means recorded in that article of our faith is "by the creation, preservation and government of the universe; which is before our eyes as a most elegant book, wherein all creatures, great and small, are as so many characters leading us to contemplate the invisible things of God, namely, his power and divinity."[1]

At times this speech of our Lord in his creation is impossible to ignore or forget: the F5 tornado that devastated western Michigan on April 3, 1956, was one such event. Without question that tornado led many in western Michigan to contemplate the power of God.

While Hope church was about a mile away from the path of the tornado, it did directly affect many of Hope's members. This chapter relates accounts of the experiences of members of Hope and others on that historic day.

---

1    Belgic Confession 2, in *Confessions and Church Order*, 24.

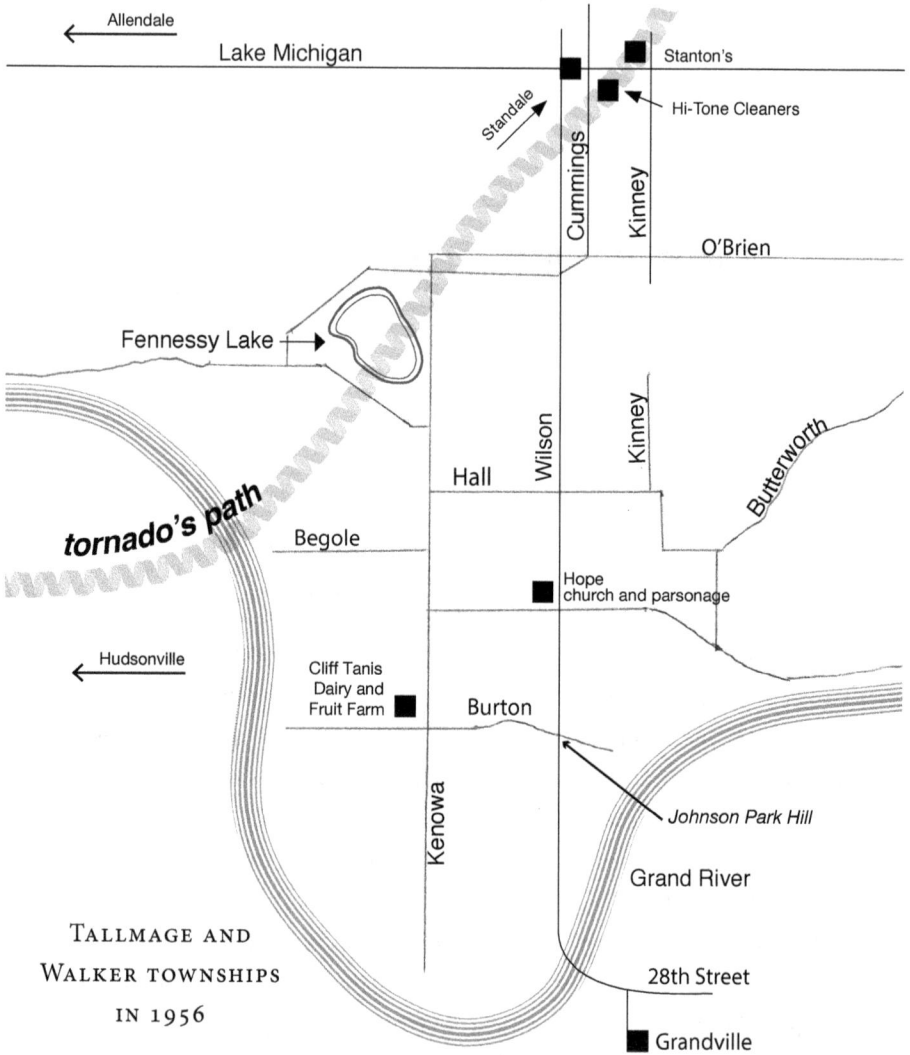

The F5 tornado—the most powerful and deadly kind—dropped out of the sky four miles southwest of Hudsonville, staying on the ground for forty-eight miles while traveling northeast toward Hudsonville, over the Grand River and Fennessy Lake, through the business district in Standale, into Walker, on to Rockford, and ending just north of Trufant.

Photos by *Herald* photographer, George Davis, as he looked west as the tornado headed toward and struck Standale.

## Memories of the Great Tornado

### *James Huizinga*

And we know that all things work together for good to them that love God, to them who are the called according to his purpose.
—Romans 8:28

It was said to be the strongest tornado ever to hit the State of Michigan. Rated an F5, the Hudsonville-Standale tornado created a forty-eight-mile path of destruction from Vriesland in Ottawa County to Trufant in Montcalm County, killing 17 people and injuring 340 more. My father was one of those injured.

It happened on April 3, 1956. The day was warm, too warm. The sky was an eerie, yellow color. We kids played ball in the driveway with our shirts off. We didn't know much about tornados, but we would soon learn.

The Huizinga family lived in Allendale on an eighty-acre farm that would become the location of Grand Valley State University. Our upstairs window faced east, in the direction of Standale. I remember hearing a train-like rumble off to the south. As my gaze shifted to the east, I saw a huge, funnel cloud. Instinctively, I knew it was a tornado, and I casually wondered if it had done any damage. We found out later that night that it did.

When my brother, John, came home around ten o'clock that night, we learned that a tornado had indeed struck Standale, virtually leveling the entire business district. John had been getting an oil change at the Gulf gas station in town.

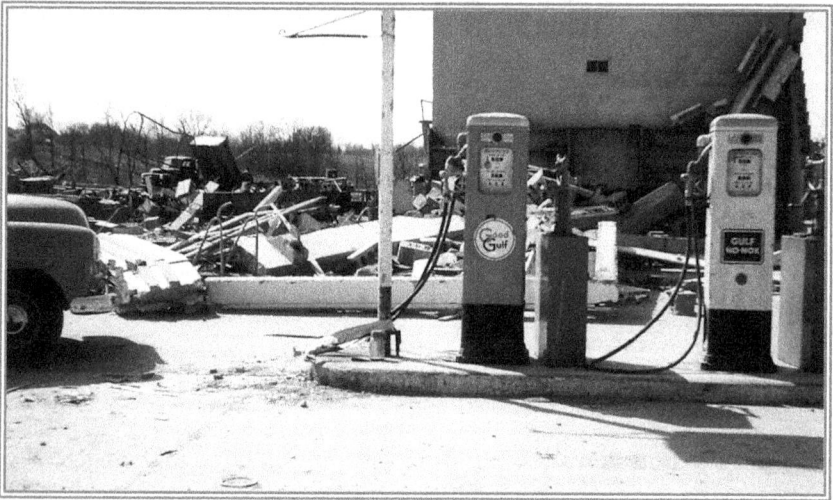

The Gulf gas station turned to rubble.

John told us that he and some others had pulled an old man out from under a truck and helped him into an ambulance. We found out later that John had failed to recognize that man as his own father, one of the grim ironies of that frightful night.

Dad had stopped at Stanton's store to buy a newspaper. Upon seeing no one in the store (everyone had sought shelter in the basement), Dad left a nickel on the counter and grabbed a newspaper. When he stepped outside, he knew he was in trouble. A swirling mass of blackness and debris was bearing down on him. Instinctively, he crawled under his truck to escape the fury of the storm. Dad was blown, truck and all, a considerable distance from the store. Crawling under his truck apparently gave him some protection from the wind and may have saved his life.

"My parents had a grocery store, Stanton's General Store on the corner of Lake Michigan Dr. and Kinney Road. Our house was right behind the two stores on Kinney. It was around 6:30 when...the weatherman...announced that there was a tornado coming towards Standale and everyone should take shelter immediately...Our house had no basement so we ran to the grocery store...We could see the funnel cloud coming straight towards us. The tail was moving back and forth and everything in its path was being sucked up into it. The tail never left the ground and we could see buildings exploding into debris... There was no basement in the grocery store either so we all decided to run to my grandpa's general store as it had a basement. As we were crossing the parking lot the stores across the street were being sucked into the tornado. We ran into the store and down in the basement just as the tornado hit... [and] ripped the store off the foundation...Then the tornado was past us...It was so quiet you could hear a pin drop...We were covered with mud and water as the tornado had sucked up Fennessy Lake and deposited it on Standale. We crawled out of the basement pushing away rubble as we went up the stairs. We were all in shock as we came out of the basement. Not a building was left standing. The two stores and our house were all gone. All of Standale was gone. All we could do is look around in silence and survey what had happened."[2]
—Pat Higgins-Spangenberg

At home we had a problem. We didn't know where Dad was. He hadn't come home that night. I remember worrying all day at school the next day, but when school was out, I found out that my dad was in Butterworth Hospital. He was pretty banged up with wounds to his leg, hand, and head. Thankfully Dad's wounds were not fatal. God had spared his life.

---

2  http://www.weather.gov/grr/1956TornadoOutbreakEyewitnessVT, accessed March 9, 2016.

Standale at Lake Michigan and Kinney turned to rubble by the tornado.

I don't remember much about my dad's hospital experience except one thing. When the nurse asked him if he wanted anything to drink, he said, "I'd like a glass of beer." Unfazed, the nurse came back with a cold glass of beer and a smile. That kind of service probably wouldn't happen today.

By the grace of God, Dad was able to leave the hospital after a few days and was able to carry on his normal life's activities. But the tornado experience was something our family would never forget. Our family was thankful for the kindness shown to us by the members of Hope church; we truly experienced the communion of the saints at that time.

As far as I know my dad was the only member of Hope church to be directly affected by the tornado. I believe that Hudsonville Protestant Reformed Church had more casualties. Rev. Gerrit Vos, who was the minister of Hudsonville church at the time, put the tornado in its proper perspective.

John Huizinga

Our village received a very special visit by the Lord Christ. It was a visit of the Majesty on High. What we really received is a little foretaste of the end of the world.

God came to us, and He roared...It sounded as though a thousand express trains were traversing the sky.

His footsteps were seen; He walked from the southwest to the northeast...everyone was aware of His august presence. And we were afraid...

Oh yes, no one can dispute it: God walked among us; His Christ paid us a special visit; He left desolation, death, pain and misery...

Yes, I do know that the tornado came so that the wicked will have no excuse in the day of His final coming. I know too, that this tornado came as a sign of His final coming so that the church might take courage and know that her deliverance is nigh. But I also am persuaded that the tornado came to shake the church awake, to direct us to His more beautiful Voice of the Gospel, to remind us of His daily and nightly Presence among us.

The church was crowded Sunday morning. And they tell me that such was the case even in other churches in our village. The tornado calls us to a rededication, to a reconsecration. For God says, "Be still, and know that I am God: I will be exalted among the heathen, I will be exalted in the earth." God desires to be exalted. And, let us never forget it, He will be exalted. Therefore He walked through our town...And even the dogs saw Him and trembled. And he was exalted...

God was seen for a few minutes. He was clothed in black, the black swirls of dust, muck, trees, planks, and bodies of men and animals. We saw Him for a few minutes such as He will be seen again in the clouds of darkness of the final tempest, the final tornado of the last Day...[3]

---

3  Gerrit Vos, "Visited by Majesty on High, *Standard Bearer* 32, no. 14 (April 15, 1956):313–14.

Birth pangs that remind us that the day of the Lord is near. As I'm writing this, I'm reminded that the things that happen to us personally almost always have significance for the larger body of believers. Such was the case with the great tornado of 1956.

"In 1956 the telephone lines were all party lines with four or five families on a line. Each party had its own particular ring. Sometimes curious people would lift their receivers and listen in on their neighbors' conversations. When the tornado went through the neighborhood, I lifted the receiver to call Hi-Tone Dry Cleaners, my dad's shop in Standale, to check if my brother, Don, was safe. Upon lifting the receiver I heard Mrs. Kievit say, "Standale's been leveled by a tornado!" That caused me some panic. Later I found out that Don had crawled for safety under the check-in table in the front of the shop. After the roof of the shop lifted and settled again, Don thought the tornado had passed. He began to crawl out from under the table, and a rock flew through the shop window."
—Harry Langerak

Louis Bonema's store next to Hi-Tone Dry Cleaners was turned to rubble.

"After the tornado hit we went to live with my parents. In fact, we could not get to [the Hope church parsonage on Wilson] for a week, because the whole area was roped off by the National Guard to prevent looting. Our second son, Neal, was born the day after the tornado." —Prof. Herman Hanko

# April 3, 1956

## *Prof. David J. Engelsma*

They stood on the knoll of the farmyard—the farmer and his sixteen-year-old helper, a high school senior—and watched it come in the southwestern sky.

It was early evening on April 3, 1956.

All of nature about the farmyard was suddenly, mysteriously still before the roaring monster approaching a few miles distant. Not a bird chirped; not a cow in the nearby barn uttered a sound or rattled its stanchion; not a leaf on one of the apple trees in the orchard surrounding the farmyard stirred.

An unearthly, ominous, green pallor colored everything—the color of impending death and destruction.

The young man[4] had been milking the twenty cows of the Cliff Tanis Dairy and Fruit Farm, just west of Kenowa Avenue on Burton Street, in the area southwest of Grand Rapids, Michigan, known as River Bend. The farmer was eating supper with his family.

The milking would remain unfinished until later that fateful night. For the easy-going farmer ran into the barn, crying as he came, "A tornado! A tornado!"

---

4   The "young man" is David J. Engelsma, a native of western Michigan, having been born in Grand Rapids and having grown up in River Bend. Hundreds of times over the years, after April 3, 1956, to the present day, when in spring and early summer the dark clouds roll in from the southwest and the air becomes sultry, he has gone outside to scan the skies, dreading to see a funnel. He is glad he saw the tornado of April 3, 1956—three times. He hopes he never sees another.

Now the two of them watched it from the farmyard. It had probably just completed its devastation in Hudsonville and was on the way,
through what is now Georgetown, to a river-crossing a scant mile
northwest of the farmyard where the two stood enthralled.

The tornado roared across the Grand River and Fennessy Lake.
Witnesses observed the funnel turn colors as it moved over the water and
a spectacular display of electrical sparks as high tension wires were ripped apart.

For years tornadoes had held a special fascination for the young
man. Throughout his grade-school years at the little, country school a
couple of miles north of the farmyard, when he had finished his assignments he would wander to the bookshelves at the back of the room.
From the set of encyclopedias, he would invariably pick out the volume
*T*. In this volume was the gripping painting of a Kansas farmer and his
family fleeing for their storm shelter before a funnel bearing down on
them. The young man had studied this small painting for hours. Fear
was on the faces of the family. The painting left doubt whether the terrified couple and their young children could make it to the shelter, or
whether they would escape if they did. There was the same sickly green
tint to the painting that the young man now saw, not on the page of a
book, but in the air. Irresistibly drawing the attention and transfixing
the imagination was the looming tornado, falling out of the billowing,
black heavens upon a frightened, defenseless earth.

The reality was all the picture suggested, and more—much, much
more.

The painting that had fascinated the young boy was
John Steurat Curry's *Tornado over Kansas*.

The tornado was huge, monstrously huge. It was not the slender, curved, even graceful cloud of the painting. It was hardly a funnel. Rather, it was an enormous, squat column, nearly as wide at its bottom as at the top. Its top was not high. The reason was the lowering mass of black cloud from which the tornado descended.

Nor was its color the almost attractive gray of the tornado of the painting. Instead, it was a deep and fearsome black—the black of the third horse of the Apocalypse.

One element of the tornado the painting could not express, and for this the young man was altogether unprepared: the sound. It was a roaring, as though creation had found a voice.

The voice sounded from on high. It reverberated from the earth beneath. It echoed in all directions, especially in that toward which the tornado was moving, which, to the young man, was directly through the farmyard. As creation is vast, so its voice is loud. The volume, unbearable at a distance, increased as the tornado came on. It was the voice of fury and power.

The response of the young man was not so much fear, although he was afraid, as awe—awe as before Jehovah God of Israel come to judge the wicked world in the wrath of his holiness.

He did not cower before it, although he had immediately made up his mind to take flight at high speed. But it captivated him. He marveled at it with a wonder foolishly bordering on admiration. He was determined to hold out on his farmyard vantage point until the last possible moment—seeing, hearing, feeling.

Fifty years later,[5] the memory is vivid and detailed. The tornado-scene of April 3, 1956, is as distinct as the painting on the page of the encyclopedia. There are the low, red out-buildings to the right; the barn a little farther off; the teenage boy in jeans and a tee shirt, with a container of salve for the chapped teats of the cows in his back pocket; Cliff on his left; the ghastly hue of nature; and the great, black, vertical cloud filling the southwestern sky, coming on inexorably like Death and Destruction.

Although the event would prove that the tornado was to pass the farmyard a little more than a mile to the northwest, on its appointed path to Standale, it seemed to the young man, as it seemed to the unexcitable farmer, that the farmyard was the bullseye at which the tornado aimed.

"I'm going down the basement," Tanis said. "Come with me."

Hunkering down before the approaching storm appealed to the young man not at all. Deliberate exposure of oneself to that fury and power, basement or no basement, was simply unthinkable.

Flight and escape alone made sense.

The young man had the means at hand. He owned a 1953 Ford hard-top convertible. The stick-shift could do sixty or better in second gear. He knew that, because going sixty in second gear through Grandville recently, in order to let the twin glass-pack mufflers sound off when he let up on the gas pedal, had cost him a hefty fine, as well as a stern lecture from Police Chief Schipper in the presence of the young man's frowning father. The car was parked in the farmyard.

Tanis ran for house and family. The young man sprinted for his car.

They stopped simultaneously, struck by the same thought. Charlie!

---

5    "April 3, 1956," was first published in *Beacon Lights* 65 (June 2006).

In a converted chicken coop on the edge of the orchard just beyond the farmyard, in the direction of the tornado, lived Charlie, a sixty-year-old drifter who worked at odd jobs about the farm. His main task was trimming the apple trees during the winter months. That is, Charlie worked when he was not drunk, which was much of the time. He was drunk that evening. Responding to the pounding on his door and the shouts, "Charlie, wake up; a tornado is coming," the bewildered sot stumbled out of the chicken coop. His gray hair was matted. The old shirt and pants in which he had been sleeping the sleep of the drunken were wrinkled and spotted. He was barefoot.

In his stupor Charlie had not the faintest idea of the impending peril. He never looked in the direction of the tornado. But one thing registered through his fog. From the look on the faces and the sound of the voices of his would-be deliverers, it became clear to Charlie that he must take immediate action to avoid real, though unknown, disaster.

At that point Charlie made his second mistake of the day. He chose to flee with the young man, rather than to seek shelter with the farmer in the basement of his house.

With Charlie in the back seat and the young man's blond German Shepherd in her accustomed spot on the passenger seat, the young man fled before the roaring tornado, which by now, he was convinced, was heading east on Burton Street behind him, and not very far behind him at that. His route was east on Burton Street, across Kenowa Avenue—the divider between Kent and Ottawa counties—to Wilson Avenue and safety.

Now fear reigned—sheer, naked fear. It commandeered the accelerator. The young man floored it. He was doing fifty when he crossed the intersection of Burton Street and Kenowa Avenue. The intersection had neither yield nor stop sign in those days. Besides, it was a blind intersection. Had another car entered the intersection at that moment, the tornado would have been the cause of several more deaths than those that actually resulted.

As the car raced across Kenowa Avenue, every spring snapped. Neither Burton Street nor Kenowa Avenue was paved in 1956. Both of the gravel roads were deeply rutted. An earlier spring thaw had been followed by freezing temperatures. April 2 had been cold. April 3 saw a dramatic rise in temperature. The thermometer rose rapidly to 80 degrees. This clash of cold and heat explained the tornado, weather-wise.

The breaking of the springs did not slow the car down. But it did make a wild ride wilder as the car leaped from rut to rut.

From the farmyard on Burton Street to Wilson Avenue are half a mile and a couple of minutes. The trip was quicker that evening. When Charlie set out from the farmyard, he was dead drunk. When the car stopped at Wilson Avenue, Charlie was stone-cold sober, if only temporarily. Terror had done it, not of the tornado, but of the ride. When in answer to Charlie's demand for an explanation of the hair-raising ride the young man said, "Tornado," Charlie responded with what may have been the most heartfelt words he had ever spoken, "D—, I rather die in a tornado."

Stopping was foolish. If the tornado had been following him, as the young man supposed and as might very well have been the case, it would have caught him there, and Charlie would have had his druthers. In fact, stopping gave the young man his second magnificent view of the tornado.

At the point where Burton Street crosses it, Wilson Avenue is high. It is the top of Johnson Park hill. The spot afforded, and still does afford, an excellent view down its straight length northward, past the muck fields at Hall Street, to the intersection of Wilson Avenue and Lake Michigan Drive, a distance of about three miles. The intersection of Wilson Avenue and Lake Michigan Drive was the western extremity of the little town of Standale, which extended eastward on Lake Michigan Drive a half-mile or so.

From the top of Johnson Park hill, looking about to discover the relationship of the tornado to himself, the young man saw the tornado crossing Wilson Avenue a little south of Lake Michigan Drive. It would make its way virtually down Lake Michigan Drive from west to east through the Standale business district.

It was massive. With the low-lying cloud-bank that was its base, it did not dominate the northern horizon; it obliterated the northern horizon. Almost three miles away and moving away from the young man, it was still threatening—heart-shrinkingly threatening. Strangely, the tornado was gray in color now, even whitish on its fringes. It was not as sharply outlined as it had been, though it was still unmistakably a tornado. High up its side, debris could be clearly seen—apparently large sections of lumber, indeed whole buildings.

Another man, who had also stopped to view the tornado, remarked, accurately as it turned out, "There goes Standale."

The main business section of Standale, centered on the corner of Kinney Avenue and Lake Michigan Drive, was devastated.

Then the young man did something that puzzles him to this day. With Charlie in tow, he drove his sagging car south on Wilson Avenue into Grandville. The only conceivable explanation is that an irrational fear of the tornado moved him to put as much distance between it and himself as possible. Irrational, at that point, because he knew that tornadoes in general and this one in particular traveled from southwest to northeast. The tornado was not going to make a U-turn up Wilson Avenue.

No one who saw and heard the tornado at close quarters that evening would have criticized the young man for continuing his flight, or would even have had difficulty understanding his reaction.

The decision to keep running enabled the young man to get his third, clear look at the tornado. He stopped at the intersection of 28th Street and Wilson Avenue in Grandville. Today the intersection is large and busy. Both Wilson Avenue and 28th Street are busy, four-lane streets. The I-196 expressway adds to its traffic. In 1956 Wilson Avenue and 28th Street were two-lane roads with little traffic. There was no expressway. On the north side of 28th Street, at the junction with Wilson Avenue, was a little, two-pump Standard Oil station. There, with the attendant and a few others, the young man had another good view of the tornado. By this time it was north of Grand Rapids, having skirted the city on the west. Likely, it was in the vicinity of Alpine Avenue.

The tornado was farther away now. In addition, it was framed in a much broader horizon—the entire northern sky, stretching away both to east and west as far as the eye could see. As a result the tornado appeared smaller. It now had the perfect shape of a funnel. There was even a slight curve to its form. The top of the tornado was much higher in the sky than it had been when first the young man saw it. Once again the tornado was black. Oddly, its tip seemed not quite to reach the ground.

He watched it out of sight on its way to Rockford. Charlie did not get out of the car.

His fear abated the young man returned to the farm. The farmer and he had to milk the rest of the now impatient and noisy cows by hand and in the light of a lantern. There was no power.

It was the farmer's suggestion that they drive into Standale to see the destruction.

In the farmer's pick-up they got as far north on Wilson Avenue as a few blocks south of Lake Michigan Drive. There the police had added their barricade to that of felled trees caused by the tornado as it came across the road. Backtracking, the two turned up O'Brien Road to Cummings Avenue and took Cummings Avenue as far as the wreckage strewn by the tornado allowed. The two then walked through the fields into what had been Standale. They came onto the edge of the little town near the intersection of Cummings Avenue and Lake Michigan Drive. They crawled on hands and knees the last distance to avoid detection.

What met their eyes was utter devastation. Standale was no more. More accurately, Standale was rubble.

Here was the effect on man and his works of the fury and power sensed earlier. Adding to the eerie atmosphere of desolation were the sea of floodlights bathing the ruins and the flashing, multi-colored lights of a fleet of emergency vehicles as men and women went about to recover the dead and rescue the injured.

---

## Community Wiped Out
### Fast-Growing Standale Is Now Pile of Rubble

Standale never had a chance. It didn't even make the Michigan map.

The bank that was ready to open is loaded with rubble instead of dollars.

Two blocks of stores on both

### Crews Fight
### Power Lack

---

### Thousands of Homes Darkened in Storm

Thousands of homes not directly in the path of the tornado which struck Tuesday night were darkened by resulting power failures, Gordon Carson, Consumers Power Co. division manager, reported.

He said 200 men from Muskegon, Battle Creek, Alma, Hastings, Flint and Lansing joined 300 local crewmen in speeding restoration

sides of M50 are either flattened or so badly damaged that reconstruction must start from the ground up.

Its residential area of an estimated 100 homes had been reduced by one-fifth. Unofficial damage is over the million-dollar mark, not counting the human suffering and misery.

It took 10 years to build the town from a four-corner outpost to a thriving community with a population of more than 500, on the outskirts of Grand Rapids.

Today it is virtually gone, wiped out in five minutes of devastating destruction that left only the brick fire hall as a reminder of community living. Twenty-nine stores are damaged or wrecked.

Bulldozers Wednesday plowed through the wreckage depositing junk piles of automobiles on the sides of the highway.

State police, civilian defense volunteers, telephone linemen and news reporters were the only occupants of the town.

What was left of Standale had been taken over by "foreigners" on a mission of mercy.

*Grand Rapids Press*, April 4, 1956

---

Standale was rubble with two notable exceptions. These exceptions fixed for the first time in the young man's mind the problem of divine providence, which, as a Calvinist, he believed as firmly as he now believed the existence of tornadoes.

A little to the west on Lake Michigan Drive from where the two crouched in the underbrush, across Wilson Avenue from each other were two notorious dens of iniquity. One was the Vista Drive-in Theater. The other was a "beer garden." Among the Dutch Reformed in the Riverbend area in 1956, these two blots on the landscape had roughly the same reputation that the French Quarter during Mardi Gras has with Christians in New Orleans today.

Neither of these blots had been removed. Neither had been touched. The tornado had spared them both. *Providence* had spared them both. By a few hundred feet!

While honorable grocery stores, department stores, other businesses, and even residences were demolished and scattered, and their upright inhabitants killed or maimed, the Vista Theater and the unsavory tavern were passed by. The denizens of the tavern were as safe and sound as if they had been in a storm cellar in Kansas.

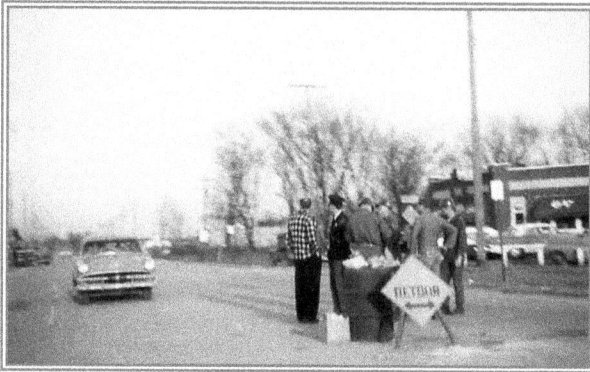

The German Village tavern on the right was unscathed.

"The vagaries of capricious nature," explains the naturalist, although the explanation would not have calmed his heart, had he looked left and right and up and down Lake Michigan Drive that dreadful evening.

A severe test of faith for a sixteen-year-old Reformed believer, who had from childhood sung Psalm 104 with all his heart: "He rides on the clouds, the wings of the storm, / The lightning and wind His mission perform."[6]

On some future April the third, when the grandchildren have grown up a little, around six o'clock in the evening, the young man, now fifty years older, plans to gather with his grandchildren on the knoll of the farmyard where once he watched the F5 tornado of 1956. The farmyard remains much as it was then, although Charlie's chicken coop is gone. He will assemble also as many of his children who fail to escape the call to meet, shamefully using every excuse imaginable to avoid hearing the "tale of the tornado" yet again.

There, on the scene, he will try to describe the indescribable.

---

6    No. 285:1, in *The Psalter*.

He will advise them not to attempt to outrun a tornado, as he himself did, but to find shelter in a basement. His advice, however, will go further (for the problem of providence that troubled him as he lay in the rain and darkness along Lake Michigan Drive fifty years ago by no means destroyed his faith): the ultimate refuge from the wrath of Jehovah God expressed a little in an F5 tornado is the cross of Jesus Christ.

And the ultimate hope of men and women concerning such violent storms is not earlier detection and warning, although these are much to be desired. Comes the day when the Lord Jesus will say to the creation that now groans and roars in its fury and power, but also in its hope, "Peace, be still."

## The Creation Groaned That Day

### *Calvin Kalsbeek*

I was ten years old on that Tuesday, April 3, 1956. It had been a typical day at Hope school. I was wearing a pair of Wrangler blue jeans, which had to stay clean enough for me to use for the rest of the week, and my amazingly adaptable Red Ball Jets (tennis shoes). Back then technology involved in the tennis-shoe-making industry had evolved to the point that just one pair of tennis shoes was good for playing basketball, field hockey, marbles, softball, baseball, football, soccer, boxing, and volleyball. Ice hockey was the only sport in which my faithful Red Ball Jets failed me. It's no wonder that mud rooms (if you had one) were less congested back then; but I digress.

It had been a very hot and muggy day at school, but that was about to change. It wasn't long after supper, around seven o'clock, that Dad excitedly yelled, "Come outside, you gotta' see this!" So out we came, and see it we did, from our home on Hall Street just east of Wilson Avenue. Dipping out of the yellowish sky was a dark funnel cloud carrying with it an F5 tornado. It must have been just west of the Grand River when we first saw it, and it appeared to us that we were directly in its projected path. While Mom was urging us to head for the basement, we continued watching it, spellbound, as it gradually turned northward missing us by about a mile. As it drifted out of sight, I can still hear Dad saying, "I would guess it didn't go any further north than Standale." As usual, Dad was right; actually it passed right through Standale.

"The tornado went right across Fennessy Lake and sucked all the mud and dumped it in Standale. The Huizinga boys helped put their dad on a gurney. He was so muddy; they did not even know it was their dad. He was right in the middle of the tornado, and the kids didn't even recognize him. We saw things flying through the air almost like a flying carpet. We later found out it was a metal roof off a building in Hudsonville. That is how much wind there was. Tanis' house got twisted off the foundation. The tornado skipped us [Moelker Orchards on Kenowa] and hit Goodale's house." —Donna Moelker

A ride through Standale today reveals no evidence of the 1956 tornado. But some scars in the creation remain, as is the testimony of many trees along the river just north of Begole Street. The s-shaped trunks of those trees that I saw on my walks to the river were at first a bit puzzling to me. It was obvious that many years ago the trees had fallen over. Yet with their roots still in the ground they once again began reaching upward toward the sun. But, I wondered, why were there so many in the same area? With further reflection and investigation the cause became clear: the creation groaned there that day in April 1956, only to leave evidence of God's continuing faithfulness even to his creation as it along with God's church await final deliverance.

Trees that were knocked down, only to rise again.

*Part Two*

# The Foundation
## of Hope's
## Spiritual House

# Editor's Introduction
## to Part Two

We could be charged with extreme negligence had we excluded part two in *A Spiritual House Preserved*, which commemorates Hope church's one hundred years as a Reformed congregation of our Lord Jesus Christ. Actually, it can be argued that this is the most important part of the book, because what is recorded in the other two parts would not be there were it not for the church's foundation as related in the three chapters of this section.

A congregation where Christ is absent is not a church. Only where Christ is present and visible, as represented in his threefold office of prophet, priest, and king, does his body, the church, exist. The first chapter of part two, "Hope's Ministry through the Offices of Prophet, Priest, and King," not only records the biblical and confessional requirements of the offices of minister, elder, and deacon, but it also demonstrates from the one-hundred-year life of Hope church, the work of the Spirit of Christ through the officebearers in her midst.

Further demonstrated is that Hope's worship of God has from her beginning in 1916 to the present (2016) remained faithful to the principles of Reformed worship revealed in the word of God. Never in her one hundred years has the question been asked, how do we think God wants to be worshiped? Rather Hope's worship has been molded by scripture's answer to the question, how does God demand to be worshiped? That explains why the present members of Hope would have felt very much at home in the worship services of her early years.

For God to be worshiped as he demands in his word, worshipers are necessary—worshipers who function in the office of believer, worshipers who willingly bow "their necks under the yoke of Jesus Christ; and as mutual members of the same body, serv[e] to the edification of the brethren, according to the talents God has given them."[1] Without

---

1   Belgic Confession 28, in *Confessions and Church Order*, 60.

such members, life in the church at best would be plagued by turmoil and strife and at worst would be nonexistent. The third chapter of part two sets forth Hope's one-hundred-year insistence that her members do, indeed, pattern their lives after their Lord's perfect example.

Part two is of utmost importance for the Hope church of tomorrow. It is certain that apart from Christ's presence in her midst, from worship that is God honoring and from members who live thankfully, there will be no hope for the Hope of tomorrow.

Appropriate and fitting in this connection is the following excerpt from a sermon by Prof. H. Hanko entitled "Walking in the Old Paths":

> The word comes always to the church, "Stand in the ways. Ask for the old paths, where is the good way, and walk therein."
>
> Stand, first of all. Stop, the text means to say. Stop. Just for a moment quit your pell-mell racing so you take time to reflect on where you are going and what you are doing.
>
> Do that as individuals. We all have to do that sometimes as individual people of God. We all have to take the time out in the course of our busy lives, just simply to stop to reflect, to ask ourselves the questions: Where are you going? What is the purpose of your life? What direction do you want to take?
>
> Congregations must do that too. Oftentimes, congregations will use anniversaries to do that. That is a good idea, too. The people get together to commemorate an anniversary in the history of their congregation. It is a time of reflection and a time of meditation, and a time when the congregation mutually together says, "The Lord has brought us hitherto on our way. Ebenezer. Now where are we going? What is our path for the future? What is the direction we want to take?" Pause. Don't be so wrapped up in all of the hurly-burly of time that you never have any time to ask, to evaluate, your congregation and its state.[2]

2  "Walking in the Old Paths," a sermon on Jeremiah 6:16 preached by Prof. Herman Hanko in Hope church on the evening of November 7, 1993.

*Chapter 9*

# Hope's Ministry through the Offices of Prophet, Priest, and King

## The Minister as Prophet

*Rev. David Overway*

Christ Jesus our Lord rules in grace over his church by his word and Spirit. He does so through the special offices of the church, by which he administers his word to his beloved people and cares for them powerfully and graciously.

One of the special offices that Christ has given to his church is the office of the minister of the word. Through this office Christ himself cares for his church by speaking to her as her prophet and teacher. The Heidelberg Catechism instructs us that Christ "is ordained of God the Father, and anointed with the Holy Ghost, to be our chief Prophet and Teacher, who has fully revealed to us the secret counsel and will of God concerning our redemption."[3] That Christ is prophet means that he is anointed of God; therefore, he knows the mind and will of God and reveals the same by proclaiming it unto God's people (Isa. 61:1–3; Luke 4:16–20).

Our Lord is pleased to speak to his church through men. Therefore he has instituted the office of minister through which to do so. He appoints certain men, anoints them with his Spirit of prophecy, and calls

---

3   Heidelberg Catechism A 31, in *Confessions and Church Order*, 95–96.

Rev. David Overway

them to be his servants, his prophets among men, with the promise that he will qualify them and equip them to perform their callings. When they do, he speaks through them words of salvation to his church.

The calling of ministers is, first, to "faithfully explain to their flock the Word of the Lord."[4] The word "faithfully" is important. The minister must explain the word exactly as it has been revealed in the scripture and as the Lord, by his Spirit, gives the minister to understand it. He must be able to say to God's church, "I have not shunned to declare unto you all the counsel of God" (Acts 20:27). The minister must not add his own thoughts or the thoughts of other men to God's word. Nor may he take anything away from God's word to make it more pleasing to sinners. The minister must take the prophet's oath and say with the prophet of old, "As the LORD liveth, even what my God saith, that will I speak" (2 Chron. 18:13). It follows, then, that the minister must give himself to the careful and thorough study of God's word that he may know what God would have him speak.

And then he must "explain" that word to God's people, opening up to them what their Lord would have them to know. He must do this especially in the preaching and in many other circumstances. The office of minister, then, is primarily a teaching office. Whereas the elders must focus on ruling the church and the deacons must bring mercy, the minister teaches God's people the word of God.

This calling to teach includes applying the word. In speaking about the minister's calling to bring the word to God's flock, the ordination form says, "Apply the same as well in general as in particular to the edification of the hearers; instructing, admonishing, comforting, and reproving, according to everyone's need; preaching repentance towards God and reconciliation with him through faith in Christ."[5] The minis-

---

4    Form for Ordination (or Installation) of Ministers of God's Word, in ibid., 284.
5    Ibid., 284–85.

ter must bring the word to the particular congregation that he is called to serve, and he must do so in light of her particular needs as a unique body and as those needs are manifest at a particular time.

This is also why the form adds, "And refuting with the Holy Scriptures all schisms and heresies which are repugnant to the pure doctrine."[6] The minister must also guide and protect the flock with regard to false doctrines that arise and the schisms that accompany them. These are always present, either threatening the church from without or from within. But these various false teachings that threaten the church change from one time to another, so the minister must apply the word as the present circumstances require. His goal must be to proclaim the truth, but always as it stands antithetically over against sin, schism, and false teachings.

The second important duty of the minister is to lead the congregation in prayer. The ordination form lists this as the second duty of ministers, while article 16 of the Church Order mentions it first. It is clear that this is a very important part of a minister's work. He must not only preach, speak to the congregation on God's behalf, but he must also pray, speak to God on the congregation's behalf. Even as God himself speaks to his people through the minister's sermon, so the congregation speaks to God through the minister's congregational prayer. It is thus through the minister's labors that God and his church enjoy blessed covenantal fellowship with one another.

The third duty of ministers, according to both the ordination form and article 16 of the Church Order, is to dispense, or administer, the sacraments—baptism and the Lord's supper. In administering the sacraments the minister holds before the congregation the assurance that "the whole of our salvation depends upon that one sacrifice of Christ which he offered for us on the cross."[7] While God gives faith in his Son and teaches his people through the minister's preaching, God strengthens that faith as the minister dispenses the sacraments.

The final duty that belongs to the minister is to watch over the

---

6   Ibid., 285.
7   Heidelberg Catechism A 67, in ibid., 108.

congregation and to rule over her together with the elders. Church Order article 16 puts it this way: "to watch over his brethren, the elders and deacons, as well as the congregation, and finally, with the elders, to exercise church discipline and to see to it that everything is done decently and in good order."[8] That this work also belongs to the office of minister follows out of the reality that the minister is also an elder (1 Pet. 5:1). Even so, the emphasis on the prophetic nature of the minister's office is still maintained, since the main way he carries out his calling to rule the congregation is by his preaching and teaching the people the word of God.

Although there is a calling to rule that belongs to the office of minister, it is also true that the word *minister* means "servant." The man who occupies the office of minister is a servant of God and of his Lord (master) Jesus Christ. He must care for the congregation in obedient service to the Lord (Phil. 1:1; 2 Tim. 2:24; 2 Pet. 1:1).

His motive to care for God's flock in devoted service to him is, first, thankful love for God in Christ. He personally knows God as the God of his salvation—the God who elected him, rescued him from sin and destruction, brought him unto himself, and showed him the secrets of his love. In addition, the minister's mighty, loving Savior has said to him in his heart and through his church, "I call you now to serve me as my prophet among my people." That call, being as irresistible as any of God's gracious calls, brings out of him the response, "Truly, with all my heart, in love and thankfulness to thee, I will. By thy grace, I will." To put it another way, Christ says to him, "Lovest thou me?" And he responds, "Yea, Lord; thou knowest that I love thee." And Christ replies, "Feed my sheep" (John 21:15–17).

In connection with his love for God, the minister is also motivated by love for God's people. He loves them because they are the precious possession of his God; they are the beloved flock of Christ. The minister loves them with the very love of the Great Shepherd who gave his life for them. This same love Christ puts in the heart of the minister by his Spirit

---

8    Church Order 16, in ibid., 386.

who has anointed the minister. He loves God's people as their pastor, their undershepherd, to whom the Great Shepherd has entrusted them. Then the minister serves God in Christ in love for him and in love for his flock, willingly serving the God who first loved him and then gave him the privilege to serve God in his church. The minister serves God, seeking through his labors the glorification of God, who so wonderfully loves him and all his people.

The duties and labors of Hope's minister at the present time include, but are not limited to, the following. The most important work of a minister is preaching, so the main work of the minister centers on that calling. This means preparing sermons each week, preaching twice most Sundays and for special services. Since a minister cannot do this great work of preaching, or any of the work of the ministry, in his own strength, he must spend devotional time communing with the Lord, meditating on his word, and seeking God's face in prayer. In order to keep developing as a preacher and to be fresh, personal study and continued reading are also necessary for this work.

Although the sermon is the central element of the worship and requires the most time in preparing for worship, the minister also prepares to lead the congregation in the other elements of worship. Attention must be given to preparing to lead the people of God in congregational prayer and choosing fitting psalter numbers for congregational singing.

Catechism instruction for the children and youth is an important part of the official ministry of the church. The minister teaches six classes, while an elder or seminary student teaches one. In addition to preaching the word in the catechism classroom, as it is adapted to the specific ages of the students, the minister prepares lessons and tests and grades the tests.

Leading some of the Bible study societies of Hope church is another responsibility of the minister. He usually leads three per season and accompanies the societies on various outings, such as caroling, banquets, and other activities for fellowship.

The minister is president of the council and consistory and chairs each meeting—the regular monthly meetings and any special meetings. He is a member of the consistory's pulpit committee, an advisor to the Reformed witness committee, and a member of the council's Myanmar committee.

The minister shares with the elders in the work of visiting and counseling members of the congregation. This includes the regular family visitation and visits to the sick, the hospitalized and shut-in, the aged, the dying, the widows and widowers, and others who need comfort. At various times individuals or couples need counseling from the minister due to various struggles in their lives. The minister also meets several times with couples before marriage to give pre-marriage counseling. He also meets several times with those who intend to confess their faith to make certain that they are well prepared and able to confess their faith with knowledge and conviction.

Various other duties are also part of the calling of a minister. He will officiate at weddings and conduct funerals. He and an elder will serve three times a year as delegates to classis. Occasionally he will give a speech for a chapel for one of the Christian schools, a meeting of the PTA, or at some other venue. He also continually keeps in touch with members of the congregation—officebearers and others—by sending and answering emails and texts and by phone communication.

In addition, the minister must make the needs of his family a great priority, as he owes them a double duty as members of the congregation not only, but also as his wife and children.

As weighty and many as the responsibilities of a minister are, we must remember that God cares for his people. He cares for them through the diligent and faithful labors of the minister as his prophet. God uses and blesses those labors to the dedication and preservation of his church. It is God, then, who is to be praised for giving God's prophets, his ministers, to us as a congregation and for using them to care for us, bless us, and preserve us throughout our history for one hundred years.

## Catechetical Instruction at Hope

### Calvin Kalsbeek

As part of the official ministry of the church of Jesus Christ, catechism is a responsibility of the office of prophet, thus this section is included here.

## A Little History

Catechism instruction for new converts and the youth of the church has a long and illustrious history in the church of Jesus Christ. It was exercised from the very beginning of the New Testament church, as is evident from many places in the book of Acts. There it is recorded that instruction preceded baptism, admission into the membership in the church, as well as admission to the Lord's supper (Acts 2; 8:26–39; 10; 16:30–32).

> "In view of the fact that brother Medendorp will serve us as student for the summer months, it is decided to conduct two catechism classes: Wednesday evenings for the young people above sixteen years; and Sundays, after the afternoon service, for married members, especially for those who as yet have made no confession of faith" (June 2, 1919, consistory minutes, article 3).

Although catechism instruction languished in the Roman Catholic Church during the Middle Ages, the reformers gave it new life. Luther, Calvin, and other reformers even prepared catechisms for the instruction of the children of believers. Consider too that one of the stated purposes of the Heidelberg Catechism was "that the youth in the churches and schools may be piously instructed in such Christian doctrine."[9] This attitude toward the importance and need for catechetical instruction flourished in the Reformed churches as they developed in their understanding of God's covenant of grace with believers and their children in the line of generations.

While detractors have long labeled catechetical instruction as "brainwashing," we would agree, without shame, that by means of this instruction we do indeed indoctrinate the church's children; and that

---

9    Thea B. Van Halsema, *Three Men Came to Heidelberg* (Grand Rapids, MI: Baker Book House, 1982), 50–51.

for good reason: the church knows the truth as revealed in scripture and seeks to impart that truth to the next generations. In the process the church reaps a bountiful harvest of children and young people who know the truths of scripture, embrace those truths, and live lives that demonstrate love for them.

In his seminary notes on catechetics, Herman Hoeksema opined:

This instruction should not only be doctrinal, but also spiritual and practical. The purpose of this instruction must not be lost sight of, i.e., to lead the children of the covenant to the conscious confession of faith. The instruction, therefore, should be adapted unto this purpose. It should show to the children of the covenant the way in which they may expect the assurance of faith and of their personal part in the salvation of God in Christ; and it should encourage and admonish them to walk in that way.[10]

"As we love our children, catechize them! It is vitally important for the covenant of God with his people, a very means by which He realizes, maintains, and perfects it. Let us make this more concrete, more personal: Catechism is one of the main means by which God enters into friendship with our children and gets their friendship for Himself."[11] —David J. Engelsma

### Official Ministry of the Church of Jesus Christ

So serious and important is this work that the Reformed churches made catechism a part of the official ministry of the church. As such it is the preaching of the gospel and therefore a means of grace to the church's children and young people. Consequently the task of providing this instruction falls upon the minister and elders of the church. Not only is this confirmed by the fact that catechism teaching is the second duty

---

10  Herman Hoeksema, *Catechetics*, unpublished syllabus, 38.
11  David J. Engelsma, "Catechism," *Standard Bearer* 73, no. 21 (September 15, 1997):487.

expressed in the call letter a Protestant Reformed minister receives, but also each year the church visitors of classis inquire of each consistory: "Does the consistory see to it that catechism classes are regularly conducted? Does the consistory determine the material for instruction? And does it see to it that the classes are regularly attended?"[12] Further, the church visitors ask the minister and deacons in the absence of the elders: "Do they [the elders] at set times attend the catechism classes to see how they are conducted and attended; and do they assist the minister when the need requires it in catechizing?"[13]

## Hope's Response

Affirmative responses to those questions are the result of serious, continuous, and diligent efforts on the part of faithful ministers and elders. Interestingly, concern to carry out the work of catechizing their children was expressed by Hope's founders from the very beginning; even before they were organized as a congregation. During their first meeting in January 1916 in the home of Richard Newhouse, article 2 records their reasons for desiring the establishment of a mission station in River Bend. The second reason was that "it would be advisable, in order that the children and the mature adults could be taught catechism."

> "A motion was then made for the elders to visit the catechism classes as much as possible" (June 3, 1923, consistory minutes, article 10).

For one hundred years the consistories of Hope church have been following in those footsteps of her founders. At present 166 of Hope's catechumens are active and growing spiritually somewhere in the following catechism curriculum:

---

12  Questions for Church Visitation…to the Full Consistory, in *The Church Order of the Protestant Reformed Churches and Constitutions of Standing Synodical Committees, Rules and Regulations, By-laws, Forms, Declaration of Principles* (2010 edition), 133.

13  Questions for Church Visitation…to the Minister and the Deacons in the Absence of the Elders, in ibid., 135.

| Class | Material |
|---|---|
| Kindergarten and first grade | *Old Testament Bible Stories I* (simple edition) |
| | *Old Testament Bible Stories II* (simple edition) |
| | *New Testament Bible Stories* (simple edition) |
| Second and third grades | *Old Testament Bible Stories I* (revised edition) |
| | *Old Testament Bible Stories II* (revised edition) |
| | *New Testament Bible Stories* (revised edition) |
| Fourth and fifth grades | *Old Testament History in Brief* |
| | *New Testament History for Juniors* |
| Sixth and seventh grades | *Old Testament History for Seniors* |
| | *New Testament History for Seniors* |
| Eighth and ninth grades | Heidelberg Catechism: Lord's Days 1–26 |
| | Heidelberg Catechism: Lord's Days 27–52 |
| Tenth and eleventh grades | *Essentials of Reformed Doctrine*: Lessons 1–15 |
| | *Essentials of Reformed Doctrine*: Lessons 16–30 |
| Twelfth grade and post-high school | Belgic Confession |
| | Canons of Dordt |

"In many of our churches, the duration of catechism is far too short, viz., little more than half a year. It should run from September through May."[14] —Herman Hoeksema

At the same time Hope's elders and minister are active in this work. In part that involves obtaining the instructional materials and planning for a year of instruction. In addition the consistory must plan a calendar for the instructional year, and even though Rev. Herman Hoeksema would be disappointed in our "short" instructional year, Hope schedules thirty weeks of instruction. After each five weeks of regular lesson material, a review test follows. The elders are busy also with the responsibility of exercising supervision over the catechetical instruction, which is done in part by scheduling a team of elders to visit each class four times a year. However, the bulk of this blessed work is the instruction given by Rev. Overway, and on occasion the elders, in the classroom.

Great has been the fruit of one hundred years of faithful catechetical instruction. It could be convincingly argued that Hope's thriving as a fruitful church of Jesus Christ based on Reformed principles, is due in large part to her sound, systematic catechizing of her children and youth.

The following reflection about a childhood friend who left Hope church with his father in 1953 bears on the significance of catechism in Hope church. Gord was a member of a Christian Reformed church. "His children became of catechism age, but that church did not have catechism for the children...Gord went to the minister [and] the minister told him that he would check with the consistory. Later he called Gord...and said, 'We don't do that, and we are not going to do that.' Gord thought his catechism instruction at Hope church under Rev. Heys was so important that he called the consistory of Hope church and said, 'My church will not

---

14   Herman Hoeksema quoted in David J. Engelsma, "'Feed My Lambs!'—Command to Catechize," *Standard Bearer* 65, no. 20 (September 1, 1989):463.

educate my children in catechism. May I send my children to your catechism classes?' Hope church said the children would be welcome. Gord looked at his wife...and said, 'If our church won't teach catechism to our children but Hope church will, what are we doing in this church?' That was the occasion of their coming back to the Protestant Reformed Churches."
—Prof. David Engelsma

In an age when many churches struggle to maintain the membership of their youth, Hope's young people continue to come, even to evening worship services. Clearly the Lord has blessed and continues to bless Hope's faithful catechetical instruction: instruction that is a blessing to Hope church and at the same time hands over to the coming generations the precious Reformed faith.

## The Blessings of the Office of Elder
### *Prof. Herman Hanko*

### *The Origin of the Office*

Strange as it may seem, the three offices in the church of Christ trace their origin to paradise. Because the whole creation was made by God and because he loved his great work, he created Adam and appointed him as the caretaker of his world. God gave Adam authority to rule over the creation so that, by his rule, the creation was used for God's glory.

This authority came in the form of God's giving to Adam an office in the creation, with three parts to it: the prophetic, priestly, and kingly aspects. All three were necessary. Adam was a prophet who knew God personally and covenantally, and he was obliged to speak of God in the creation and to any generations born of him and his wife, Eve. Adam had to hold the priestly office, because all the creation had to be used for God's glory by dedicating it to God. And the kingly office was necessary because in it Adam was given the right, the authority, to do with the creation what he had to do to accomplish his calling.

To be an officebearer in God's world required that Adam be created with body, soul, and spirit, and that he be created in the image of God in knowledge, righteousness, and holiness: knowledge to be prophet, righteousness to be king, and holiness to be priest.

### God's Purpose Realized in Adam's Fall into Sin

But Adam rebelled against God and was deposed from his office. He had to be. How could a man who hated God serve as God's representative in God's creation?

Adam lost his office as representative of God and he lost God's image. Adam did not change as a creature with body, soul, and spirit. But all of these being corrupted he could no longer serve God: he must serve Satan. Instead of the image of God, he now bore the image of Satan. He was no longer a son of God but a child of the devil (John 8:44). What was formerly the truth of God was now the lie of Satan; what was once the holiness of God was now the corruption of sin; and what was once righteousness was now unrighteousness.

Nor did Adam any longer serve as an officebearer in God's world. As prophet he now spoke the lie; as priest he represented Satan's foul wickedness; and as king he worked to make God's world the kingdom of Satan.

God did not despair because of Adam's treachery; nor did God figure out another plan to rescue what he could from the ruin Adam brought on the creation. God's creation was so precious to him and so important in his eternal plan to glorify his name that he provided an officebearer in Adam's place, the Lord Jesus Christ. Christ had all the necessary qualifications to take Adam's place: he was like us in all things, except sin; he was the officebearer with supreme authority to do the will of God; he not only bore the image of God (Heb. 1:3), but also he was God in our flesh (v. 2). God in Christ did what Adam failed to do, but also never could do. God redeemed mankind and the creation through the blood of his only begotten Son.

But Christ was on this earth for a very short time: thirty-three years out of over six thousand, for other than bearing God's just wrath against sin, Christ works all God's purpose from heaven, where he is exalted at God's right hand. So God saved a church in Christ, as representative of God's cause in the world. Christ is the second Adam, not as the head of the human race but as the head of the church, elected by God eternally, redeemed by Christ's blood, and destined to live in the new creation with God, much, much more blessed than anything Adam knew.

### The Office of Elder in the Old Dispensation

While the Old Testament scriptures are not clear on the office of elder, they are clear on the offices of priest and king. Nevertheless, while it seems as if the office of elder was poorly defined, there is mention of it throughout the whole history of the nation of Israel.

From the time men began to call on the name of the Lord (Gen. 4:26) to the beginning of the nation of Israel in Egypt, the three aspects of the one office Adam held seemed to have been held by the patriarchs, or the heads of clans. The patriarchs are frequently mentioned as receiving the word of God as prophets, offering sacrifices as priests, and ruling over their families along with their descendants.

It is presupposed in Exodus 3:16 and 4:29 that while Israel was in Egypt there was a body of elders who received the word of God from Moses. While this may be a reference to the heads of the families or tribes, there is also mention in Exodus 24:9–11 of a body of men who accompanied Moses to the top of Sinai, where they all saw God and ate and drank with him.

Also while Israel was at Sinai, Moses, at Jethro's advice, chose a body of men who were to assist him in judging the people. That may have been a fairly large number of men: rulers of ten, of a hundred, and of a thousand. But later on, in the wilderness at the time Israel revolted against God in their lust for meat, God commanded Moses to take seventy of those men to form a special council of rulers who would also possess the Spirit whom God had given Moses to rule over the people of Israel (Num. 11:16–25). The body of elders continued to function during the forty years of wandering, during the conquest of Canaan, and during the time of decline when judges ruled. Scripture mentions them repeatedly.

When judges ruled in Israel and when the monarchy was established, the body of elders continued, but their relationship to the judges and kings was not always clear. It may have been the elders from whom Rehoboam sought advice when some of the tribes asked to have their burden of taxation eased (1 Kings 12:1–15). It seems as if sometimes the elders functioned as rulers under the kings, but when tyrants and evil kings ruled, their work may have been very limited.

When Judah went into captivity in Babylon, the captives apparently organized a body of elders. Ezekiel 8:1 mentions such a body; Ezekiel was a prophet to the captives and not a prophet in Jerusalem. Upon the return of Judah to Canaan after seventy years of captivity, once again a body of elders was present in the nation (Ezra 10:8, 14).

Because Israel was a theocracy, the body of elders was responsible for the enforcement of all the law of God, including dietary, social, and religious laws. In other words, the elders were responsible for the enforcement of both governmental and political law, plus religious and ecclesiastical law. But such is not necessarily true of nations today. Some in post-Reformation times thought of the Netherlands or Scotland as a theocracy, but that was a sad mistake. The old dispensational nation of Israel was a type of the church of the new dispensation in which Christ is the sole ruler.

Sometime after the captivity and before the birth of our Lord, that body of elders became the Sanhedrin of Jesus' day, the body that hated Christ and ultimately crucified him. It was also in the Sanhedrin that Stephen and Paul were tried (Acts 7, 23). The church over which the elders ruled had become apostate.

### The Effect of Pentecost on the Office of Elder

A momentous change came to the church with Pentecost. First and most important was the exaltation of Jesus Christ. His exaltation was the full realization of all God's work of salvation. It was the fulfillment of all the types and shadows of the law, which had pointed ahead to

Christ. It was the climax and full accomplishment of everything God had given Christ to do to pay for our sins and establish the church and the kingdom of heaven.

For our purposes, the important part of Pentecost was the pouring out of the Holy Spirit on the church by the second Adam, the Lord Jesus Christ. He was all that the first Adam was and infinitely more. While remaining God himself, he was like us in all things, except sin. That is, he was truly Christ, the anointed of God, to be what Adam could never be—the true prophet, priest, and king.[15]

While Adam was officebearer in the earthly creation, Christ is officebearer in both the earthly and the heavenly creation. While Adam revealed God by his actions and speech, Christ reveals God as God himself and is thus a far superior prophet. While Adam was dedicated to God and put in Eden to consecrate the earthly creation to God, Christ redeems both the earthly and the heavenly creation to God by reconciling it to God (Col. 1:20) in the perfect work of his atonement. While Adam could and did (for a short time) rule over God's world in the name of God, Christ is exalted to rule in such a way that he carries out all the decrees of God's counsel and is crowned as Lord of lords and King of kings. He rules his church, not only to tell them what is right and what is wrong in God's sight, but also to enable them to do what is right and to run away from what is wrong.

However, a strange thing happened at Pentecost. Not only was Christ exalted as prophet, priest, and king, but also by pouring out his Spirit on the church he made every one of his people a prophet and priest and king. I hope we understand what that means. It means that the offices of minister, elder, and deacon are embodied in every believer: men and women and aged and young (Acts 2:17–18, quoting Joel the prophet).

---

15  Heidelberg Catechism Q&A 31 in *Confessions and Church Order*, 95–96.

### The Office of Elder in the Apostolic Era

God also created the special office of apostle in the church. The unique characteristic of this office is that it combines the three offices of prophet, priest, and king, or in the new dispensation of minister, elder, and deacon. These three distinct offices developed organically from the apostolic office as the new dispensational church took up its own work.

The office of deacon arose out of the need to care for the widows (Acts 6). The office of elder arose as a necessary office to rule over the congregations. James was an elder in the church of Jerusalem (Acts 15:13), and Paul ordained elders in the churches he organized (Acts 14:23; 20:17). When the number of churches grew, ministers were trained to occupy the office of preachers (1 Tim. 4:14; 2 Tim. 2:1–2).

By the end of the apostolic era, the churches of the new dispensation throughout the ancient world were firmly established as congregations that manifested in the world the cause of Christ, the chief and only officebearer in the church. Christ's presence in his threefold office was guaranteed through the church's minister, elders, and deacons.

These offices carried on the offices present in the typical dispensation of the Old Testament church. They were the wonderful means God used to bring Christ, the second Adam, to the everlasting church of which Israel was a picture.

### The Office of Elder in the New Dispensational Church

The offices, including the office of elder, were preserved in the new dispensational church for almost two centuries, and elders were present at the great ecumenical synods. During the days of Augustine, the elders in North Africa refused to obey papal decrees on doctrinal matters. But by the end of the third century the office of elder was gradually weakened, and the weakening continued until the office was lost altogether, usurped by bishops, archbishops, and the bishop of Rome. This was accompanied by the church's denial of the office of believer. These offices were not recovered until the Reformation.

We owe Luther a debt for recovering in the church the office of believer, and we owe Calvin a debt for restoring biblical church government. Calvin developed a large share of biblical church polity while he was laboring in a refugee church in Strasbourg. The church government practiced in Reformed churches was further developed in countries where the Calvinistic Reformation became dominant, especially Scotland and the Netherlands. Reformed church government was also practiced in France until persecution all but obliterated the Reformed church in that land.

As Reformed church government developed alongside Presbyterian church government, it became evident that both systems placed their emphasis on the office of elder. The word *presbyter* actually means "elder," and Presbyterian church government is church government under the rule of elders.

Various differences separate the two systems. One difference is that Reformed church government holds to three offices in the church—minister, elder, and deacon—while Presbyterian church government holds to two offices—elder and deacon—and the office of elder is divided into teaching elders and ruling elders. Nevertheless, both hold to a distinction between teaching and ruling elders, for even Reformed church polity believes that ministers are also elders.[16]

### Problems in Reformed Church Polity

One question of crucial importance in Reformed church polity is the relation between the office of believer and the special offices in the church. This has especially plagued Reformed churches. In many churches the office of elder is gradually pushed out of the consistory room, with the result that the body of elders becomes a board of trustees and the minister becomes a local pope. I recall a vivid example of this when we were touring the Crystal Cathedral, and I asked a guide whether the elders engaged in supervision and discipline. His answer was no, due to the fact that the congregation was highly transient and

---

16  See the Form for Ordination of Elders and Deacons, in ibid., 290–94.

the minister was a powerful man, respected worldwide. He ran the church.

The Reformed system of church government is unique because it is biblical. It is not a democracy; it is not like anything found in the world. Soon after the 1953 schism when First Protestant Reformed Church took the issue of the rightful owners of the church building and name to court, those who had left the Protestant Reformed Churches argued in court for an independent church. As various Protestant Reformed leaders attempted to explain to the judge what Reformed church polity actually is, he finally shook his head and said he had never heard anything like it, nor could he understand it. This is not surprising, for the relation between the office of believer and the office of elder is a delicate balance that can only be maintained when everyone in a congregation seeks only the good of the congregation and not personal gain.

The office of believer is primary and fundamental. The special offices in the church arise out of the office of believer. Although the special offices are ultimately responsible to Christ, they are also responsible to the congregation. The special offices receive their authority from Christ through the congregation. Officebearers are required to answer in the affirmative this question when they are installed: "I ask you, both elders and deacons, whether you do not feel in your hearts that ye are lawfully called of God's church, and consequently of God himself, to these your respective holy offices?"[17]

At the same time, these people who hold basic authority under Christ in the church are obligated to live in submission to their officebearers, especially the elders. Various passages in the New Testament scriptures admonish saints to obey their elders, but none so strongly as Hebrews 13:17: "Obey them that have the rule over you, and submit yourselves: for they watch for your souls, as they that must give account, that they may do it with joy, and not with grief: for that is unprofitable for you."

Those with fundamental authority in the church must submit to the authority of their elders. Yet while I cannot describe here how that

---

17  Ibid., 292.

works out in the practical life of the church, it works well and receives God's blessing when both the body of believers and the elders bow together before the authority of Christ, the head of the church.

To maintain the delicate balance between the members of the congregation, each of whom holds the office of believer, and the elders who are commanded to rule over the congregation, it is important and necessary that believers function in their office. This consists of the following duties that are solemnly placed on them.

All the work that Christ assigns the three special offices is and must be performed by the believers also. They are to speak the word of God as their minister does. They do not officially preach as ministers, but they teach with the word God has given them. They teach their children; they admonish and bring the word to fellow saints. They occupy various positions in the organic life of the church where they speak God's word. And they witness constantly to those outside the church of their faith and salvation.

Further, they actually preach through the minister. Paul admonishes the saints in Colosse to say to their minister Archippus, "Take heed to the ministry which thou hast received in the Lord, that thou fulfill it" (Col. 4:17). The congregation functions in this way in its work through the special offices. The officebearers must be conscious of this and recognize it.

The members of the congregation exercise among themselves what the elders and deacons do officially. Members rule over each other by admonishing each other (James 5:19–20; Gal. 6:1–3) and initiating discipline when necessary (Matt. 18:15–17). They bring the word to fellow saints in times of distress and trouble, and they encourage and comfort each other. God's people help each other, bring gifts to the needy, and show their love for Christ and fellow saints by their gifts and words.

The members of the congregation do all these things through the offices of elder and deacon as well.

In the actual work of the officebearers, God's people function in the office of believer. They suggest names for officebearers when new ones must be elected. They approve or disapprove of nominations. They vote at congregational meetings. They approve or disapprove of discipline exercised by the elders. They approve of the rule of the elders, although usually this approval is done by their silent agreement. But they do have the right to disapprove and must exercise that right when necessary. Yet the elders always have the final authority, and the believers must submit to that authority, for it is submitting to the authority of Christ.

The same delicate balance is present in denominational life. The balance between the authority of the broader assemblies (classes and synods) and the authority of an autonomous local congregation is difficult to maintain, and I have seen and experienced the denomination swing from emphasis on one position to emphasis on the other.

### The Qualifications for the Office of Elder

The scriptures consider the special offices in the church to be so important that they give the church qualifications for these offices. The qualifications for the office of elder are found in 1 Timothy 3:1–7. We need not mention them here, for many books are available in which these qualifications are discussed and explained.

It is easy for a body of elders to nominate for office men who lack these qualifications. Some elders, in their consideration of men to nominate, may propose a man for purely sentimental reasons. They may argue that a certain man has a great deal of influence in the church and society and can give the church a better reputation to make drawing others into the church easier. They may suggest a name because a man may be new in the congregation and election to an office would make him feel more at home. They may suggest a person who has held other positions in the church and has made notable contributions to the life of the church. None of these considerations or any similar ones will do; Christ determines who are qualified.

In considering this matter of qualifications it is interesting and important to read 1 Timothy 3:1: "This is a true saying, If a man desire the office of a bishop, he desireth a good work."

The word "bishop" here is another name for elder. The New Testament use two words to describe the office of elder. One is *presbyter*, which means "aged one." This term is a relative term: one need not be past seventy or eighty years of age to be an elder, but nevertheless, age is important. To rule in the church of Christ requires experience in living as a dedicated member of the church. Experience is important for with experience comes wisdom. And much wisdom is required, for the salvation of souls lies in the hands of the elders. First Timothy 3 requires that one qualification be "not a novice" (v. 6), which is the qualification of a "presbyter" or "old one."

*Episcopos* is another name for an elder and is the one used in 1 Timothy 3:1. It means "overseer" and defines the work of the elder. An elder oversees the life of the congregation in which he works. He oversees that life in all its many aspects.

Second, the desire to be an elder is in itself a qualification. Whatever may be the reason for not wanting to be nominated, one who must be persuaded to leave his name on nomination is not qualified. Sometimes it happens that someone with false modesty refuses to permit his nomination with the plea, "I do not have the qualifications for the office." It always strikes me as a bit ironic that a young man who aspires to the office of minister is qualified only if he wants the office so earnestly that he goes four years to college and four years to the seminary to attain his goal, and he is encouraged by his fellow saints. But some men are reluctant to become an elder and hang back, waiting to be persuaded. That should not be so in the church.

### The Calling of Elders

The Church Order of the Protestant Reformed Churches sums up the work of the elders in two articles. Article 16, speaking of the calling of ministers, says also that the minister, "with the elders…exercise church discipline and…see to it that everything is done decently and in good order."[18] Article 23 says:

> The office of the elders, in addition to what was said in Article
> 16 to be their duty in common with the minister of the Word,

---

18  Church Order 16, in ibid., 386.

is to take heed that the ministers, together with their fellow-elders and the deacons, faithfully discharge their office, and both before and after the Lord's Supper, as time and circumstances may demand, for the edification of the churches, to visit the families of the congregation, in order particularly to comfort and instruct the members, and also to exhort others in respect to the Christian religion.[19]

Scripture makes clear that the office of elder has a long, noble, and God-directed history that dates back at least to the beginnings of the nation of Israel in Egypt and also carries on the office Adam held in paradise, the office of king. It is also clear from scripture that the chief calling of the office is to exercise rule over the church of Christ. Presbyterians rightly call their elders ruling elders. To rule is to have authority over others. To possess authority is to be given the right to determine for those over whom rule is exercised what is right and what is wrong. Rulers also have the authority to insist that those whom they rule must accept their determination of right and wrong upon penalty of discipline.

Because the rule of elders is under Christ, who has given them authority, their determination of right and wrong must be according to the scriptures, where the will of Christ for his church is found. This rule is over the whole congregation. It is over each member; it is over the minister; it is over the deacons; it is over the other elders.

Ministers sometimes forget this. They assume to themselves authority above the elders. The elders may not permit this. Once a decision is made by the elders, the minister must accept it and implement it without further argument or debate.

Thus all three special offices bring the word of Christ. This too is in keeping with Old Testament laws. While the priests brought the word in their work and might not intrude on the other offices, and the kings brought the word in their work, the office of prophet was shared by all three offices. So it is in the new dispensational church.[20]

---

19 Church Order 23, in ibid., 388.
20 The Church Order provides for disagreements between members of the congregation and members of the special offices. Every decision made by an ecclesiastical assembly

The rule of the congregation by the elders must not be limited to deciding on controversial matters; this is, in the normal life of the congregation, a secondary obligation. The elders must exercise their authority in teaching, encouraging, comforting, and strengthening the members entrusted to their rule. They are shepherds (1 Pet. 5:1–4). They must take care of the sheep and the lambs. They must care for every need the flock may have.

But their calling is to bring the word of Christ. They are limited to that. They are not psychiatrists or problem solvers. They are not doctors called to diagnose diseases. They are not close friends with some in the congregation with whom they hold special personal relationships. Their one calling is to say to the congregation, "Thus saith the Lord." They are servants of Christ and must say, in Christ's name, what Christ says. The well-being of the congregation is in their hands, and their responsibility is to see to it, in obedience to Christ, that everything in the life of the church is done decently and in good order.

To their work therefore belongs supervision of the worship services and of the mission activities of the congregation. They regulate the organic life of the congregation in her Bible study groups. They are responsible for the instruction of the children in catechism classes. They must inquire carefully into the spiritual well-being of each member and of each family on family visitation. They must see to it that the deacons do their work according to the injunctions of scripture. Individual elders must make themselves open to any member who seeks from them spiritual direction related to various problems one might have. They must insist on a monthly report from the minister if he is accustomed to making pastoral calls.

Above all, upon them falls the responsibility of seeing that sound doctrine prevails in the entire congregation and in the whole of the life of the church under their supervision. The elders must therefore be

---

is settled and binding, but if someone disagrees with such a decision, he has the right to show that the decision is contrary to the word of God and/or the confessions. If the matter cannot be resolved, one may bring the position he has taken to classes or synods to be adjudicated there.

fully acquainted with the scriptures, the confessions, and the Reformed doctrinal heritage of the church of Christ.

They must insist that the minister preaches the whole counsel of God, as Paul claimed to have done in Ephesus as he described it in Acts 20:18–27, and they must be able to say to the elders what Paul said to the elders in Ephesus:

> Take heed therefore unto yourselves, and to all the flock, over the which the Holy Ghost hath made you overseers, to feed the church of God, which he hath purchased with his own blood. For…grievous wolves enter in among you, not sparing the flock. Also of your own selves shall men arise, speaking perverse things, to draw away disciples after them. Therefore watch, and remember, that…I ceased not to warn every one night and day…I commend you to God, and to the word of his grace, which is able to build you up, and to give you an inheritance among all them which are sanctified…I have shewed you…how…ye ought to support the weak, and to remember the words of the Lord Jesus,…It is more blessed to give than to receive. (vv. 28–35)

They must see to it that no heresy is allowed to creep into the church through the instrumentality of various organizations that belong to the organic life of the church. They must be sure that each member holds fast to the great doctrines of the church of all ages.

At the same time, the elders must see to it that the saints under their care not only hold to sound doctrine, but live it as well. Here is where rebuke, admonition, and warning become an important part of their work. Paul condemns men in the church for holding to false doctrine and warns them of God's anger in sending them a spirit of delusion, because they love not the truth (2 Thess. 2:10). One who loves the truth also lives the truth. Repentance is essential for the spiritual well-being of the saints, and insistence on repentance is part of the work of elders.

The work of the elders is great and important.

### The Blessings of the Office of Elder

The blessings of the office of elder are many and great and are of utmost importance in the life of the church.

The most important blessing is the presence of Christ in the congregation. While what I say now is true of all the special offices in the church, it is primarily true of the office of elder. Christ withdraws his Spirit and presence from the congregation that is unfaithful. Unfaithfulness in a congregation is the responsibility of the elders, but so is faithfulness. A church may call itself a church, but if it is unfaithful, it is despised by Christ, who leaves such a congregation to its own self-imposed destruction.

When Christ is present in a congregation, the congregation is a lively and exciting place to be. Saints dwell together in unity and exercise their callings in the office of believer. Going to church to worship is a joy. The congregation stands at the forefront of sister churches in the defense of the faith and of a Christian walk. It is a place where parents want their children to be taught in catechism, to make confession of faith, and to find a church home when they are of age. It is a church where the elders are held in high esteem and encouraged in their work.

It is a congregation blessed by God.

2016 consistory back from left: Cal Kalsbeek, Steve Langerak, James Koole, Jonathan Engelsma, John Van Baren, Joel Minderhoud; front: David Moelker, Rev. David Overway, David Jessup, Daniel De Meester

# A Year in the Life of an Elder

*Joel Minderhoud*

The labors of an elder can be not only significantly challenging and time consuming, but also richly rewarding and blessed. A glimpse into a sample year in the life of an elder can help illustrate what is involved in the labors as well as the blessings that accompany them.

The labor begins in earnest during the first week of January following the installation service. As a rule, on the first Wednesday of January, the council meets briefly for its annual organizational meeting in which officers for the council and consistory are elected and the regular standing committees are assigned. By the end of that relatively short meeting every elder is assigned some committee work, whether on a consistory or a council committee.

Following the organizational meeting, the elders gather for a lengthy consistory meeting. In this meeting the elders hear reports from elders who have been working on specific cases of discipline or other such work. Elders are assigned to districts, in order to develop a closer relationship with the members of the congregation. Every member has an elder from whom he or she may seek spiritual guidance. Visits to widows and widowers are reported, and the annual schedule of visits is assigned. The annual theme and text for family visitation are adopted at this meeting, and elders are reassigned to standing committees that deal with discipline cases.

Elders are also encouraged to let their names stand for possible nomination to synod. This nomination will occur at the next meeting of Classis East on the second Wednesday of January. To that end, pertinent issues on the agenda for classis are discussed at this meeting, and delegates are approved by motion. The meeting ends in a word of prayer, and the brethren return to their homes.

The following week is the January meeting of Classis East, which one elder (by rotation) will attend with the pastor. Depending on the agenda, the meeting may last only until lunchtime, but it could extend into the evening or even reconvene another day.

On the third Wednesday of January the entire council reassembles to conduct its monthly business. The length of the council meeting varies, depending on the issues that need to be discussed. Some of these matters include building or expansion projects, nominations for elders and deacons, labors in Myanmar, and budget-related discussions.

During the month of January, elders acquaint themselves with the members of their districts and inform them to call on the elders in time of need or if they need spiritual advice. This is an important labor of the elder—in part because it helps to free the pastor from much of this work and gives him time to dedicate to his labors of preaching and catechetical instruction.

During this month and throughout the year, an elder may need to make various visits to the sick, parents of newborn children, and the like. Some preparation regarding an appropriate passage of scripture and corresponding words of encouragement is needed prior to these visits. These visits generally are very positive and blessed experiences for both elders and those visited.

In February, meetings continue at least twice a month (one for consistory and one for council), as they will throughout the year. The family visitation schedule is adopted, and the elders will typically visit three families each night they go out. In the next month or so the elder will probably make a total of nine visits to different homes in the congregation on three separate nights. Bringing encouragement and instruction to the families of the congregation and seeing the work of the Spirit in the lives of the members is also a very enjoyable part of an elder's work in the congregation.

Depending on the discipline workload, an elder and a partner may need to make one or two discipline visits to an individual each month. Depending on how the labor goes, these monthly visits may continue for several months. These visits weigh heavily on the elder, as sin must be addressed. The elders pray for wisdom and positive fruit on their labors. Such visits often are followed up with a meeting between the elders to plan future visits.

Also in February the elders begin to make visits to the various Bible study societies and catechism classes. This will likely occupy two more nights this month. It is time well spent, as the elders see the work of the Spirit among the congregation as the members of the congregation discuss the word and are taught the blessed truths of scripture.

Throughout the catechism season, catechism classes need to be taught in the pastor's absence. Sometimes seminary students are available, but there are times when an elder needs to teach a class. This requires a significant amount of preparation and consideration regarding how to bring the truth to a specific age group (a much different approach is used with second and third graders than in the Heidelberg Catechism class with eighth and ninth graders). Although at times challenging, it is a blessed work. To work with God's children and to be immersed in the word is a rich and rewarding experience.

As April approaches the work of the previous three months begins to cycle again. Another round of family visitation is on the horizon. Visits to the elderly and others in the district continue on an as-needed basis. Routine committee meetings (building, program, and so on) continue to occur at least once a month. Additional committee work takes place depending on the needs in the congregation. These same cyclical activities are repeated four times a year.

For the summer months, the visits to the Bible studies and catechism classes cease, only to be replaced by Sunday-school visits. By August, the council will begin the process of making nominations for elders and deacons. During the next three months, the council meetings grow longer as nominations for officebearers and budget matters are discussed and decided.

Intermixed throughout the year are the joyous occasions of having the young people appear before the consistory to make confessions of their faith, as well as fathers who make arrangements for baptisms of their children. In addition, throughout the year the consistory may receive letters from members of the congregation regarding various issues or requests that require its attention.

The work of an elder is a busy labor, involving many nights of the month. It is a weighty labor—dealing with discipline; overseeing the preaching and catechism instruction; and bringing spiritual instruction to members of the congregation. The nature of that work requires the elder to be immersed in the word. He must study scripture in order to bring an appropriate word, whether of admonition, encouragement, or instruction. It is a work that requires much time in prayer. The elder recognizes that the required work is accomplished by the Holy Spirit, not by the elder's strength, or might, or worldly wisdom. Therefore, the elder prays often for grace to do the work—strength, patience, wisdom, and godliness. Above all, the spiritual nature of the work draws the elder closer to God and to the sheep with whom he labors. In these ways the work of an elder is a very spiritually rewarding and blessed work.

## Committee Work for the Consistory

### Daniel De Meester

The consistory is a body of ordained elders, called of God to labor and shepherd the flock of Jesus Christ. They are called of God through the congregation itself; therefore, the members of the congregation choose who will watch over them, although God governs their desires to choose whom he has determined will serve in the special office. The elders therefore can have confidence that God himself has chosen them to work among the flock and can believe that God will work through them for the benefit of the flock.

There are two classes of committees, standing committees and special committees. The standing committees of Hope's consistory address issues and concerns of regular occurrence, whereas special committees are formed to accommodate work of a more temporary nature, such as discipline work or hardship cases. It is true, however, that some special committees in our past have been of a substantial duration.

The committee opens every meeting with devotions, striving to have appropriate devotions for the situation. The devotions lead into the work that has to be accomplished, and the committee members must be mindful of the events of the meeting so they can prepare a written report for the consistory. The report has to be detailed and truthful, so the consistory can accurately know what is transpiring and can therefore give pertinent advice to the committee and to the person being helped.

It is necessary then that those receiving the help of the committee pay special heed to the advice given. It may be that the person the committee is helping has his or her own train of thought as to the dilemma, with scriptural grounds, but if the advice of the committee and therefore of the consistory is different, that person should heed the advice of the committee believing that God is working through the office of the elder.

## The Differences between Council and Consistory
### Tom De Vries

Each month a bulletin announcement appears, informing the congregation that the council or the consistory will meet during the coming week, the first Wednesday of the month for consistory and the third Wednesday for council. Unless a person is a special officebearer or has business with the council or consistory, that announcement is probably quickly read and readily dismissed. Therefore, the differences between the duties of each group may not be readily apparent to all who read the bulletin.

The consistory consists of the nine elders and the pastor. Simply put, their work is directly concerned with the three marks of the true church: preaching, church discipline, and administration of the two sacraments. The council is composed of all three special offices: elders, deacons, and pastor. Their work is all of the remaining business of the church that is not specific to the work of the elders or the deacons.

In the early years of Hope church the term *council* was unknown to the members. That is still true of the small churches in the Protestant Reformed denomination. At one time, Hope had only three elders and two deacons. Deacons were considered members of the consistory; they had full voice in all the consistory's decisions, including matters that now pertain strictly to the elders. Their vote was counted, for instance, in matters concerning discipline. As the church grew, there became sufficient men, elders and deacons, to work each in the area specific to their office.

A good way to understand how each of these two groups carries out its responsibilities is to look at how the individual committees of consistory and council do their work.

### Consistory

The consistory has five standing committees and likely, at any time, has at least one special committee. These committees answer to the entire consistory, and their work must be approved, usually at monthly meetings, by the entire consistory.

The communion committee of two elders takes care of purchasing wine and bread for the communion service, sets up the table for the Lord's supper, and cleans the trays and linens when the service is over.

The program committee also consists of two elders. They are responsible for reviewing all materials that will be used in programs in Hope church. They also supervise the organists and oversee the maintenance of the pianos and organ. All newsletters and materials distributed within the church must meet their approval.

Three elders, vice-president, clerk, and assistant clerk, directly oversee the worship services and catechism classes. They must find pulpit supply when the pastor is absent and recommend catechism materials and instructors.

One elder and three men from the congregation make up the seminary student aid committee. They collect and distribute funds to seminary and pre-seminary students of our congregation who are in need.

One elder and five men from the congregation are on the Reformed witness committee. This committee distributes Protestant Reformed material to those in the local area and to those outside of our churches. Requests for literature or a sermon CD from those viewing the Hope church website and other contacts are referred to this committee.

Special committees exist for the time it takes the men to accomplish their work. The committee usually consists of two elders. They are appointed for the most difficult work of the consistory, that of discipline. They may finish their work in a couple of months, or committees could last for several years.

## Council

The council has seven standing committees.[21] They also report their activities for the previous month at each meeting and seek approval by the entire council.

The building committee consists of three men of the council, with one being an elder. Any council member with any knowledge of construction is sure to be a member of this committee. The committee oversees the work of the janitor and of the head usher. It sees to the maintenance of the church building, the grounds, and the parsonage. The committee is also responsible for arranging reservations for usage of the church building.

> In September 1929 this committee recommended that the congregation purchase five acres on Wilson Avenue for $200. In March 1930 it was decided to spend $2,095 for constructing the new church building.

The general fund treasurer, benevolent fund treasurer, and vice-president of the council compose the budget committee. This committee prepares the yearly budget that is brought to the annual congregational meeting for approval. The men consult with the pastor, janitor, and church secretary to discuss the needs of each to be sure

---

21  In June 2015 a new standing council committee was formed: the protection and security committee. This committee has the following responsibilities: to clarify further our distinctive beliefs in our by-laws related to membership and building use, for example, to limit our liability in light of increasing hostility toward those who desire to remain faithful to God's word; to establish policies and protections related to the nursery to protect our church from allegations of any type of child abuse while under the watch and care of church member volunteers; to consider means to protect the physical property and persons during worship services.

they are adequately cared for and that their needs are included in the proposed yearly budget. They must also consult with any emeritus minister in our congregation, so that a report can be made to the next synod concerning their needs.

The collection schedule committee is composed of one elder and one deacon. They devise a schedule for all of the special collections and recommend any changes in the schedule from the previous year.

The collection schedule prepared by this committee for 2016 and approved by the council is as follows:

Sunday morning collections are for the general and benevolent funds. Catechism collections for 2016 are for Wingham PR Christian School.

| | | |
|---|---|---|
| January | 1 | (New Year) PR Scholarship, PR Church in Myanmar |
| | 3 | Hope PR Christian School, Reformed Witness Committee |
| | 10 | Covenant Christian High School, *Reformed Witness Hour* |
| | 17 | Free Christian School (Edgerton), Special Education |
| | 24 | Covenant Christian School (Lynden), Berean PR Church (Philippines) Books |
| | 31 | Genesis Christian School (Lacombe), PR Seminary Students |
| February | 7 | Hope PR Christian School, *Beacon Lights* |
| | 14 | Covenant Christian High School, *Reformed Witness Hour* |
| | 21 | Trinity Christian High School (Hull), Special Education |
| | 28 | Emeritus Fund, PR Church in Myanmar |
| March | 6 | Hope PR Christian School, Domestic Missions |
| | 9 | (Prayer Day) Free Christian School (Edgerton), Foreign Missions |
| | 13 | Covenant Christian High School, *Reformed Witness Hour* |
| | 20 | Special Education, Providence PR Church Building |
| | 25 | (Good Friday) *Perspectives in Covenant Education*, PR Church in Myanmar |
| | 27 | Covenant Christian School (Lynden), PR Church in Myanmar |
| April | 3 | Hope PR Christian School, Reformed Witness Committee |
| | 10 | Covenant Christian High School, *Reformed Witness Hour* |

| | | |
|---|---|---|
| | 17 | Hope PR Christian School, *Beacon Lights* |
| | 24 | Special Education, Covenant of Grace PR Building (Spokane) |
| May | 1 | Hope PR Christian School, *Standard Bearer* |
| | 5 | (Ascension Day) PR Emeritus Fund, Covenant Christian School (Lynden) |
| | 8 | Covenant Christian High School, *Reformed Witness Hour* |
| | 15 | Hope PR Christian School, PR Church in Myanmar |
| | 22 | Special Education, PR Seminary Students |
| | 29 | PR Scholarship Fund, PR Church in Myanmar |
| June | 5 | Hope PR Christian School, Foreign Missions |
| | 12 | Covenant Christian High School, *Reformed Witness Hour* |
| | 19 | Special Education, Heritage PR Church Building (Sioux Falls) |
| | 26 | Genesis Christian School (Lacombe), Domestic Missions |
| July | 3 | Hope PR Christian School, Free Christian School (Edgerton) |
| | 10 | Covenant Christian High School, *Reformed Witness Hour* |
| | 17 | Hope PR Christian School, Reformed Witness Committee |
| | 24 | Special Education, PR Church in Myanmar |
| | 31 | Reformed Witness Committee, *Perspectives in Covenant Education* |
| August | 7 | Hope PR Christian School, RFPA Books |
| | 14 | Covenant Christian High School, *Reformed Witness Hour* |
| | 21 | Domestic Missions, PR Church in Myanmar |
| | 28 | Genesis Christian School (Lacombe), Special Education |
| September | 4 | Hope PR Christian School, Sunset Manor |
| | 11 | Covenant Christian High School, *Reformed Witness Hour* |
| | 18 | PR Scholarship Fund, PR Church in Myanmar |
| | 25 | Genesis Christian School (Lacombe), Special Education |
| October | 2 | Hope PR Christian School, Domestic Missions |
| | 9 | Covenant Christian High School, *Reformed Witness Hour* |
| | 16 | Hope PR Christian School, Reformed Witness Committee |

23  Covenant Christian School (Lynden), Special Education

30  Faith Christian School (Randolph), Heritage PR Church Building (Sioux Falls)

November  6  Hope PR Christian School, Foreign Missions

13  Covenant Christian High School, *Reformed Witness Hour*

20  Free Christian School (Edgerton), Special Education

24  (Thanksgiving) *Standard Bearer,* PR Church in Myanmar

27  Covenant of Grace PR Building (Spokane), PR Church in Myanmar

December  4  Hope PR Christian School, Sunset Manor

11  Covenant Christian High School, *Reformed Witness Hour*

18  Foreign Missions, PR Church in Myanmar

25  Trinity Christian High School, (Hull), Special Education

31  (Old Year) Genesis Christian School (Lacombe), TBD

One council member and one member of the congregation oversee the church library. They read or review all new books for the library, supervise the work of the librarian, and find ways to improve the library.

Four men of the congregation, not necessarily council members, make up the audio-visual committee. These men operate the audio, video, and duplicating equipment in the church. They also make recommendations to the council for use of new technologies, such as bringing live-streaming of sermons into the homes of the elderly.

The Myanmar committee is composed of at least one elder, one deacon, and the pastor. This is a very busy committee, especially in light of the trips that our men have made to Myanmar in the past several years. They assist the Protestant Reformed Churches in Myanmar with spiritual guidance and instruction and also find the means to assist these churches financially.

The transportation committee, which consists of two deacons, arrange for the transporting of members of Hope who are unable to drive to church.

In addition to the standing committees, there is a welcome committee that consists of an elder and a deacon. By rotation each elder and deacon is assigned a month to be on this committee. The function of this committee is to meet with newly married couples, those who have recently made public confessions of faith, and new families that have joined Hope church. This committee was established in April 1972.

The work of the special officebearers often goes unnoticed. All goes well in the congregation of Hope because of the work done by men who give countless hours to the welfare of the church. The Lord has blessed us greatly; his face has shone upon us for one hundred years. Much of that blessing has come to us through the work of men in the past that can now be seen in our congregation in the present. We live with one another in peace; we hear our Lord speak to us from week to week through our pastor. Our elders have been watchmen on the walls of Zion; our deacons have been a blessing in the distribution of the mercies of Christ to those who have need. May the Lord continue to bless our congregation for many generations to come through the work of our faithful special officebearers; may we remain stalwart in the truth until the Lord's return.

## The Council and Its Meetings

### Daniel Kalsbeek

By definition the council is an advisory, deliberative, or legislative body of people formally constituted and meeting regularly. Another definition is an ecclesiastical assembly. At Hope church the council is made up of nine elders, six deacons, and the minister. The minister serves as the chairman of the council. In the absence of the minister, the elected vice-president assumes the chairing of the council meetings. The council differs from the consistory in that the consistory is comprised of the duly elected and installed elders of the church and the minister of the church.

What does the Bible say about the council and counselors? Wise King Solomon was familiar with counselors, as the following texts illustrate.

"Without counsel purposes are disappointed: but in the multitude of counsellors they are established" (Prov. 15:22). "Where no counsel is, the people fall: but in the multitude of counselors there is safety" (Prov. 11:14). "For by wise counsel thou shalt make thy war: and in the multitude of counsellors there is safety" (Prov. 24:6). "If one prevail against him, two shall withstand him; and a threefold cord is not quickly broken" (Eccl. 4:12).

The church council serves a vital role in the oversight and management of the church.

The full council has a scheduled meeting once a month. The minister opens the meeting with devotions and prayer, and the council sings a psalter number. The minutes of the previous meeting are read by the clerk and approved by the council. An agenda, prepared by the clerk, is closely followed during the council meeting. The various committees of the council present reports of their committee work. If a committee has any recommendations these are also presented, discussed, and voted on. The concept minutes are read at the end of the council meeting. When a motion is made, supported, and voted on to adjourn the meeting, the meeting is concluded. The council members by alphabetical rotation of their last names close the meetings in prayer.

The Hope church council meets with the church visitors of the Protestant Reformed Churches, two senior ministers from Classis East, once a year to discuss the well-being of the congregation.

The council's various committees work together, allowing for a harmonious, orderly, and structured church. With God's blessing resting on the work, this is the end result of a council's working in unity.

May God continue to bless the council of Hope Protestant Reformed Church by providing men who know the truth, desire the pure preaching of the truth, and have a love for the congregation of believers. Having been preserved in the truth for one hundred years, we have confidence that God will continue to preserve us until the coming of Christ.

# Duties of the Officers of Council and Consistory

*Joel Minderhoud*

Each January the council (elders and deacons) has an organizational meeting in which officers are elected. The officers have special duties to help ensure that all things are done in decency and good order. There are five officers: president, vice-president, clerk, assistant clerk, and general fund treasurer. Their duties are as follows.

## President

Historically, the president of the consistory and the council is the pastor. The primary duty of the president is to direct and to chair all the consistory and council meetings. This requires a working knowledge of the Church Order and of the rules for the orderly conduct of meetings (*Robert's Rules of Order*). It is surprising how often discussions arise about the proper way to proceed in a meeting. For example the following questions might arise: Can discussion take place on this motion? What is a substitute motion? When is it appropriate? The orderly running of a meeting is the key to a successful meeting and proper decisions.

The president leads the confessions of faith and directs the questions to the young people. The president also leads when the church visitors visit the council and as a representative of the council answers many of their questions.

## Vice-President

The vice-president performs the role and duties of the president in the president's absence. This is a great responsibility especially during a lengthy vacancy. With the clerk and assistant clerk, he serves on the pulpit committee. The pulpit committee has the important work of writing the sermon evaluations of the pastor's preaching for the consistory. The men also are responsible to obtain pulpit supply for preaching and catechism instruction when the pastor is on vacation or has classical appointments.

## Clerk

The clerk's chief duty is to maintain proper records of the council and consistory meetings.

In preparation for each meeting, in consultation with the president, the clerk prepares a detailed agenda for the meeting. He also begins to prepare the concept minutes. Knowing the agenda, the clerk can write portions of the minutes, so that during the meeting the matters on the agenda can be dealt with efficiently. During the meetings the clerk fills in the concept minutes with the official details and decisions of the meeting.

After the meeting the clerk goes through the minutes, corrects errors, prints a copy of the minutes, and files it. At the next meeting these minutes will be read to the consistory and council members again for their final approval.

Between meetings the clerk writes and sends any necessary correspondence. This includes letters to men nominated for special offices, letters to other consistories with membership records to transfer membership, and letters to individuals or consistories regarding decisions made by the consistory or council in a particular matter.

The clerk must also file all supplements (correspondence and committee reports). The consistory files and the membership records must be kept orderly.

### Assistant Clerk

The duties of the assistant clerk include overseeing the bulletin and ensuring that it contains the necessary and correct information and that the information meets the guidelines established by the consistory. He prepares all the schedules for the consistory—family visitation schedules, widow and widower visiting schedules, and so on. During the meetings, he reads aloud all correspondence and committee reports to the council or consistory members so that the clerk can focus on keeping accurate minutes of the meetings. Also, he performs the duties of the clerk in the clerk's absence.

### General Fund Treasurer

The duties of the general fund treasurer center around the finances of the congregation. Sometimes the work of the general fund treasurer is confused with the work of the benevolent fund treasurer. The benevolent fund treasurer is a deacon who oversees the money for the poor. That fund is a matter not for the council, but for the deacons only.

The general fund treasurer, typically a deacon, but not necessarily, is responsible to maintain orderly records of the finances of the congregation. This includes making sure that the synodical assessments, pastor's salary, and other church-related expenses, such as utilities and building repairs, are being paid.

Each month the general fund treasurer gives a detailed report to the council regarding receipts and expenses of the previous month. In recent years the payment of bills and the preparation of detailed financial reports are done by an organized and capable member of the congregation (business manager). This has been an excellent asset to the general fund treasurer, freeing him from mundane accounting duties. It is important to note that the business manager does not have access to the benevolent fund records and therefore has no knowledge of those who receive benevolent help.

The general fund treasurer also serves on the budget committee and has the task of producing the annual budget and presenting it to the congregation after approval by the council. Although the general fund treasurer plays a key role in producing the budget, after it is approved by the council, it is the council's budget. When he presents the budget to the congregation, it must be clear to all that concerns over the budget must be tempered by the fact that sixteen men approved the budget.

## What Officebearers Need to Know
### John Van Baren

There are a few things that you are not taught in school. Perhaps the assumption is that you will figure them out soon enough on your own.

From my experience, things as basic as balancing a checkbook, how taxes work, and a home mortgage are three things that you will figure out on your own.

My goal is to point out a few things that nobody has told you—things that you need to know as an officebearer in the church of Jesus Christ. Thankfully, between home, Christian schools, and catechism instruction, you have learned the principles needed for spiritual oversight. However, there are some things that can be pointed out regarding how to be an effective officebearer. So, to tell the things nobody told you, I will write a few sentences about different observations I have made over the years.

### Regarding Good Order

Get a copy of *Robert's Rules of Order*. An abridged version, such as *Robert's Rules for Dummies*, is best in my opinion. You should know the basics, so the meetings proceed without confusion. The following are important for good order: always have a motion on the floor before things are discussed and submit the motion in writing, so specifics are understood by all. Furthermore, this often prevents hours of useless discussion on the topic.

For regularly scheduled meetings the clerk will always provide an agenda. It is important to have an agenda so nothing is forgotten. It will include old business, new business, committee reports, and perhaps tabled motion(s).

### Discussion Considerations

Discussion is an important topic. Each member is entitled to present his opinion on a motion on the floor. If the discussion strays, and it will; the chair should remind the body of the motion on the floor, or a member can make a "point of order" to direct the discussion back to the motion where it belongs.

The wisdom of many is better than individual wisdom. An individual member is entitled to his opinion, but there is wisdom in many counselors. "Without counsel purposes are disappointed: but in the multitude of counsellors they are established" (Prov. 15:22). I have come to a meeting knowing a certain topic was going to be discussed. I had my opinion on the topic and was quite assured of it. After the topic was discussed by the body, my mind turned completely around to a different opinion.

In order to take part in the discussion, it is important to present one's viewpoint clearly and concisely, without rambling. I have found it helpful to jot down a few bullet points I wish to present and to refer to them as I state my views. This helps me not to forget things and to be concise.

### Committee Work

Always, always, always provide a written report of your committee's work. The written report should be given to the clerk, so he will not have to ask how you want that proposal worded. Also give copies of the report to each person for reference during discussion of the report. Written reports will have two sections. The information section should include when the committee met, where it met, who attended the meeting, and a summary of the discussion. The second section is comprised of the committee's recommendations, for the body to adopt, with the grounds on which each recommendation is based.

Finish your committee work. For example, if you are on the building committee and have three quotes for some repairs, discuss the quotes at the committee level, pick one, propose it, and as grounds state why you picked the one you did. "We have the funds" is never a good ground.

Always have grounds for a proposal. This removes ambiguity, which may occur during a meeting, but will most certainly be evident years after a meeting when the minutes are combed for earlier decisions. Grounds will remove the "why in the world did they decide that" factor.

If possible, submit a committee report in advance of a meeting. Then points of discussion can be thought of in advance and thereby help the efficiency of the meeting. Committee reports can be easily distributed by electronic means, so use them effectively. However, if sensitive and confidential issues are in committee reports, distribution by email is not a good idea. Always assume that all your emails will be read by others than the specific copied recipients.

For all issues some discussion is needed. A good leader will recognize when discussion is needed. When discussion becomes too lengthy, he will refer the issue back to the committee with instructions to reformulate its proposal.

At the end of the meeting, the clerk will read the minutes. Some of us use this time to put away our paperwork and organize our documents. Resist this practice. Listen to the minutes to make sure they are accurate as you understood them. There are always a few corrections and clarifications that are necessary. When someone comes back to the minutes in a month or a year, that clarity will ensure the decisions made earlier are understood later.

### The Place of the Church Order

The Church Order is important. Keep a copy handy for reference. Some councils and consistories make a practice of reading through the Church Order and discussing it. I think that is a good idea. There are many important and interesting items you need to know. The Church Order is the constitution that has guided the Reformed churches since the Synod of Dordt in 1618–19. The current Church Order is available in two green books: *The Confessions and the Church Order of the Protestant Reformed Churches*, a hard cover book, and a ringed binder, *The Church Order of the Protestant Reformed Churches*. Both are published by the Protestant Reformed Churches and are available from the bookstore in the Protestant Reformed seminary. Also recommended is the *Church Order Commentary* by Idzerd Van Dellen and Martin Monsma. Copies of this book are available at the Protestant Reformed seminary and as a ebook from the Reformed Free Publishing Association.

As specified in the Church Order, the council will be visited annually by "at least two of her oldest, most experienced, and most competent ministers" appointed by classis.[22] The council will be asked questions from a specified list of questions. These questions are found in the

---

22  Church Order 44, in *Confessions and Church Order*, 394.

forms section in the ringed binder. Review these questions before the specified meeting and take a copy with you to that meeting.

### Policies and Practices

A policy in practice at Hope church is to finish the meetings by 11:00 p.m. This is a good practice, as decisions regarding the church demand the attention of alert officebearers. In addition, most of the men have day jobs, and they need a night of reasonable sleep. A motion regarding finishing the business or reconvening on another date is usually automatically put on the floor at 11:00 p.m.

When does something need congregational approval? Do expenditures of a certain dollar amount need its approval? I remember one time when it was proposed to spend a "significant" amount of money, and the following comment was made: "Mr. Chairman, I think this expenditure exceeds the spending cap rule adopted by previous councils." But, nobody knew what the cap was. Was it $500, $1,000, or $5,000? The clerk extensively and exhaustively went through all the old minutes and found that no such policy had ever been adopted. Some Protestant Reformed churches have such a figure, which is probably a good thing. But the other side is that if an item is in the budget, spend the money. If the furnace needs to be replaced and there is money in the major building maintenance fund, get it done, because the money has been set aside for that purpose, and the men have been elected to make those decisions. If the congregation needs a new organ, but no funds have been established to replace it, that is a different story. Bring a proposal to the congregation for approval.

Some guidelines should be followed in the nomination of officebearers. The council places an announcement in the bulletin before nominations are made. The congregation, exercising the office of believer, is encouraged to bring names to the council for consideration. Just a mention to one's district elder should get the name presented at the meeting and put on the board for consideration. In an effort to be consistent, Hope's council established the following written guidelines regarding the nomination process:

1. Open nominations
   a. Open nominations from the floor (council members call out names of men they think to be qualified to serve in the office of elder or deacon).
   b. Council members should come to the meeting prepared with names of men they believe meet the qualifications for the special offices.

2. Close nominations
   a. Close nominations by motion.
   b. Be sure not to close nominations too quickly to give all men sufficient time to suggest men for the special offices.

3. Discussion of nominees
   a. Give opportunity for the council to discuss the strengths of men on nomination
   b. For example:
      i. A council member may feel that a specific man has more gifts than another and express this to the council;
      ii. or a council member may feel that although a specific man has the gifts for the special office, he may serve better as a deacon for various reasons;
      iii. or a specific man may be qualified but may not be able to serve because of a specific family situation and requests that the council consider this when voting.
   c. This is not the time to bring up sins or other matters for which a man should not serve. That is done *after* the voting to save the man from unnecessarily having matters made known (if he is not nominated no one would need to know about them).

4. Vote
   a. Vote to obtain a nomination to present to the congregation (each council member votes by private ballot, double the number of men needed to fill the out-going

officers' positions. For example, six names are needed for three retiring officers.

   b.  Ballots may contain less than the required number of names.

   c.  The assistant clerk shall keep a record of the gross list of names and of the number of votes each man has received. If a man who received a majority vote declines his nomination, the gross list will be used to select a replacement.

5. Council approbation

   a.  Once a double slate of men who have a majority of votes from the council is selected, the chairman obtains a motion to approve those men for nomination and to present those names to the congregation. At this time a period of discussion occurs where opportunity is given to express why a man should not be nominated. For example, he is involved in a particular sin; the consistory is working with him on an issue; or he does not have the necessary qualifications.

   b.  If it is necessary to remove a man from nomination (removed by majority vote), another man shall be selected by majority vote from the original gross list of names.

6. Letter of nomination

   a.  The clerk sends letters to men on nomination, giving them at least two weeks to consider the nomination. If they cannot serve they must come to a council meeting (regular or special) to explain why they cannot serve. The council should be open to having special meetings to expedite the nomination process.

   b.  The letter shall include a request that nominated men respond to the clerk that they did in fact receive the letter (prevents the danger that a nominee is not informed because a letter was lost in the mail).

    c.  If a man is removed from nomination by majority vote of the council, a replacement must be chosen from the original gross list that the assistant clerk has. The replacement must obtain a majority vote from the council. This replacement shall be given at least two weeks to consider the nomination.

7.  Nominations for deacons follow nominations for elders
    a.  Council is to begin the nominations for the special offices by August with the elder nominees.
    b.  As soon as the elder nominations are filled, the council is to begin the deacon nominations. Deacon nominations must begin at the October council meeting regardless if the elder nominations are filled.

8.  Publication of nominations
    a.  Names of both elder and deacon nominations are to be published to the congregation at least two weeks before the congregational meeting and sooner if possible.

## The Deacons' Fundamental Work

### Rev. Douglas Kuiper

Deacons in Reformed churches are expected to perform various duties. The members of the church see the deacons taking collection and know that the deacons care for some of the church's financial affairs. As a result, one of the deacons is often made the bookkeeper of the church. Often it falls to the deacons to prepare a budget for the coming year. Perhaps they are asked to organize the church picnic or serve as the building committee of the church. In small churches, necessity may require them to assist the elders in their work; in larger churches in which the elders and deacons meet separately, the deacons still meet with the elders as a council, to oversee matters that pertain to the earthly affairs of their church.

None of these is their fundamental work, however. Some of the activities mentioned above, such as being bookkeepers or members of the building committee, could be profitably assigned to other members of the church, especially in a larger congregation. Other activities, such as assisting the elders, are permitted by the Church Order adopted by Reformed churches at the Synod of Dordt, 1618–19. Still other activities, such as overseeing the general finances of the church, naturally fall to the deacons, because these men (if they are the kind of men God's word in 1 Timothy 3 requires deacons to be) are respected men who can be trusted with the monies of the congregation.

But what is the fundamental work that God gave deacons to do in the church of Jesus Christ? With which members of the church particularly must this work be concerned? And how should this work be carried out?

### The Reformed Confessions

The Church Order of the Protestant Reformed Churches in America, which is considered a minor confession and is generally the same church order as that adopted by Dordt, speaks directly to the fundamental work of the deacons.

Article 25 reads:

> The office peculiar to the deacons is diligently to collect alms and other contributions of charity and, after mutual counsel, faithfully and diligently to distribute the same to the poor as their needs may require it; to visit and comfort the distressed and to exercise care that the alms are not misused; of which they shall render an account in consistory, and also (if anyone desires to be present) to the congregation, at such a time as the consistory may see fit.[23]

While article 25 speaks of the fundamental duties of the diaconate within the congregation with which they are connected, article 26 speaks of the cooperation of the deacons with other agencies or diaconates in other congregations:

---

23  Church Order 25, in ibid., 388.

In places where others are devoting themselves to the care of the poor, the deacons shall seek a mutual understanding with them, to the end that the alms may all the better be distributed among those who have the greatest need. Moreover, they shall make it possible for the poor to make use of institutions of mercy, and to that end they shall request the board of directors of such institutions to keep in close touch with them. It is also desirable that the diaconates assist and consult one another, especially in caring for the poor in such institutions.[24]

Two questions asked every year in every church at church visitation underscore the fundamental duties of the diaconate. In the absence of the deacons, the church visitors must put these questions to the minister and elders: "2. Are they diligent in the collecting of the alms, and do they faithfully realize their calling in the care and comfort of the poor and the oppressed? 4. Do they administer the finances wisely, in consultation with the minister and the consistory?"[25]

Article 30 of the Belgic Confession is entitled "Concerning the Government of, and Offices in the Church." Among the listed duties of officebearers is this: "that the poor and distressed may be relieved and comforted, according to their necessities."[26] While the article does not expressly state that this is the duty of the deacons in particular, Reformed churches have always understood the article to mean that.

The Form for Ordination of Elders and Deacons speaks in two places of the work of the deacons. In the first part of the form, in which elders and deacons are instructed as to the nature, origin, and work of their office, we read:

From which passage [Acts 6, Romans 12:8, and 1 Corinthians 12:28] we may easily gather what the deacons' office is, namely, that they in the first place collect and preserve with the greatest

---

24  Church Order 26, in ibid.
25  Questions for Church Visitation...to the Minister and Elders in the Absence of the Deacons, in *The Church Order of the Protestant Reformed Church* (2010), 136.
26  Belgic Confession 30, in *Confessions and Church Order*, 64–65.

fidelity and diligence the alms and goods which are given to the poor; yea, to do their utmost endeavors that many good means be procured for the relief of the poor.

The second part of their office consists in distribution, wherein are not only required discretion and prudence to bestow the alms only on objects of charity, but also cheerfulness and simplicity to assist the poor with compassion and hearty affection, as the apostle requires (Rom. 12, and 2 Cor. 9). For which end it is very beneficial that they do not only administer relief to the poor and indigent with external gifts, but also with comfortable words from Scripture.[27]

After the vows are made, the minister exhorts the officebearers to diligence in their work. To the deacons he says, "And, ye deacons, be diligent in collecting the alms, prudent and cheerful in the distribution of the same; assist the oppressed, provide for the true widows and orphans, show liberality unto all men, but especially to the household of faith."[28]

### Scripture

That these statements regarding the work of the deacons are based on scripture, the confessions have made clear.

Acts 6, the passage that speaks of the institution of the office of deacon, shows that the duty of those first deacons was the care of the widows in the daily ministration. The church supplied food to its poor widows every day, in order that they might eat. This work the apostles had been doing, for they knew it was important to care for the poor widows. Yet it became apparent that the apostles were not able to do justice to that work, as well as their own fundamental task of prayer and the ministry of the word. So deacons were appointed to care for the widows in their need.

Romans 12:6–8 speaks of the work of pastors, elders, and deacons

---

27 Form for Ordination of Elders and Deacons, in ibid., 292.
28 Ibid., 293.

in the church. This work is spoken of from the viewpoint of the office-bearers as members of the body of Christ, serving the body as a whole. We read, "Having then gifts differing according to the grace that is given to us, whether prophecy, let us prophesy according to the proportion of faith; or ministry, let us wait on our ministering: or he that teacheth, on teaching; or he that exhorteth, on exhortation; he that giveth, let him do it with simplicity; he that ruleth, with diligence; he that sheweth mercy, with cheerfulness." Especially the references to giving and showing mercy apply to the work of the deacons.

"God hath set some in the church, first apostles, secondarily prophets, thirdly teachers, after that miracles, then gifts of healings, helps, governments, diversities of tongues" (1 Cor. 12:28). The Form for Ordination of Elders and Deacons interprets the word "helps" as applying to the office and work of the deacons: "speaking of helps, [the apostle] means those who are appointed in the church to help and assist the poor and indigent in time of need." While this connection between the word "helps" and the work of the deacons might not seem obvious to the English-speaking person, the fact is that "helps" has the particular meaning of aid or assistance given to one in need. To understand this, remember that in his farewell speech to the elders of Ephesus, Paul said, "I have shewed you all things, how that so labouring ye ought to support the weak, and to remember the words of the Lord Jesus, how he said, It is more blessed to give than to receive" (Acts 20:35). The noun "helps" in 1 Corinthians 12:28 is translated in its verb form "support" in Acts 20:35. The help of 1 Corinthians 12:28 is that of assistance to those in need, which brings to mind the work of the deacons.

The ordination form also refers to 2 Corinthians 9:7: "Every man according as he purposeth in his heart, so let him give; not grudgingly, or of necessity: for God loveth a cheerful giver." This passage speaks not so much to the deacons in particular as to the members of the church as a whole. But it is true that the cheerfulness required of every child of God as he gives for the relief of the poor and other causes of the kingdom must also characterize the deacons as they distribute the mercies of Christ.

### Conclusions

On the basis of these passages from the Reformed confessions and scripture, we draw the following conclusions about the work of the diaconate.

First, the proper work of the diaconate is limited. It is limited in its objects. The work of the diaconate seeks the benefit of the poor, sick, widows, and those in the church with other particular needs. The office of deacon in the New Testament church was instituted because of the need of the poor Grecian widows (Acts 6). The mercy shown to the poor in their need can also be shown to the sick or to others with needs. In other words, the work of the diaconate is limited to those in need of mercy. So Paul in Romans 12:8 speaks of those in the church who show mercy.

Because the fundamental work of deacons is limited with respect to its objects, it is also limited in its scope. It is limited to showing mercy upon those in need, and therefore also to doing whatever is necessary to obtain the earthly means (money or otherwise) for helping those in need.

Second, although the work of the deacons is limited, it is not minor or relatively unimportant. This work is important because our love for God and fellow saints requires us to have compassion on the poor and needy. It is also important because in this work the deacons function as officebearers of Christ, picturing the work he performs in showing mercy to his people. In fact, through the deacons Christ himself actually does bestow mercy.

Third, the work of the diaconate is primarily spiritual. Because the deacons are Christ's instruments to show mercy to his people, the Holy Spirit works spiritual blessings through them. Accordingly, the gifts they distribute, while certainly including the material gifts of money or food, must also include the spiritual gift of comfortable words from scripture.

Fourth, because the fundamental work of the diaconate, although limited, is important, the deacons must give themselves to that work with diligence. This is the general point of Romans 12:6–8, in which specific application is made to the deacons: "He that giveth, let him do it with simplicity...he that sheweth mercy, with cheerfulness." Those whom God has placed in positions of service in the church and those to whom God has given gifts to carry out that work must be diligent in carrying out their work.

Let every faithful church pray that God gives us deacons who are diligent in their care of the poor and needy, and who are ready to bring to those poor and needy not only material gifts, but also words of comfort from the scriptures. Having such deacons, the church may know she is blessed of God, through Christ!

2016 deacons back from left: Daniel Van Uffelen,
Brad Duistermars, Alex Kalsbeek; front: Brian Kalsbeek,
Vance Grasman, Jonathon Kamps

## The Office of Mercy: The Deacons at Hope

### *Alex Kalsbeek*

The book of Acts records the beginning of the office of deacon. The apostles had to focus on the work of preaching the gospel, so they did not have time to care for the widows and the poor. They appointed seven men to do the work, among whom was Stephen, the first martyr.

Things have changed dramatically in the following two thousand years, but the calling of the office of deacon has not changed—deacons today, Hope's deacons, still care for the widows and the poor. This is no surprise. Jesus promised us that we would have the poor with us always.

He did not promise this as some sort of curse or punishment. It is a blessing. If there were no poor in the church, there would be no need for the congregation to give. We give in order to show our thankfulness for what God has given us. God provides a need in the congregation in order for the congregation to show its thankfulness.

The deacons' work is also distinct from the work of the elders. The deacons' office is an office of mercy. While it is true that the minister and the elders must also be merciful, the focus of the deacon's office and work is mercy. The deacons seek out those in need and help them—first those in the congregation, and then those outside of it. Oftentimes we think of the help of the deacons as purely financial; it is also spiritual. The deacons must always bring scripture when they bring help. While some of us are in need of financial or physical assistance, all of us are in need of spiritual help. The deacons bring this spiritual help as officers of mercy, just as Christ, our merciful high priest, filled our great spiritual need of salvation from sin.

The office of deacon is a separate and equal office to that of minister and elder. It is important not to think of the office of deacon as the first step of church office, necessary before one can become an elder. A man does not need to be a deacon before he is an elder, nor does a man necessarily become an elder after he has served as a deacon. God gives different men different gifts—some he gives the gift of leadership, others he gives a merciful heart. Although those who serve in the offices of deacon and elder have different responsibilities in those offices, as members of the council the deacons have as much right (and responsibility) as the elders to have their opinions heard at council meetings. Their voices are just as important as everyone else's. This, of course, can be a little intimidating for a young deacon at his first meeting with men his father's age who have served many years in office. It need not be, but often it is.

The work of the deacon is often very practical. Sometimes a family needs help with how to budget its money. The deacons may provide financial assistance for a time, but they also teach the family how to develop and follow a budget, thus to gain control of its finances and no longer to need financial assistance from the deacons. In some congregations a deacon is appointed by the council as the church treasurer. This is true in Hope church. A deacon serves as the general fund treasurer who oversees the finances of the church.

The deacons meet officially as a body every month. They also often discuss their work, primarily the work of the committees on which they serve. This can be after a church service when they count the money from the collections or by phone or email.

The monthly official deacons' meeting always has an agenda. This keeps the meeting focused and prevents late meetings. After opening devotions, the various committees give their reports. There might be a report from a welcoming committee. There are always reports from the committees who visited those in need, consisting of the text that the deacons brought and the amount distributed. The deacons then discuss the requests for aid for the coming month. The agenda always gives the deacons an opportunity to bring up for consideration those who might require financial assistance, and someone volunteers to contact them. When the official meeting ends, the visiting elder closes in prayer, and the deacons count the money from the general fund and benevolent fund offerings from the month before.

Five of the deacons serve as officers: the chairman, the vice-all, the secretary, the benevolent fund treasurer, and the general fund treasurer. The general fund treasurer is really an officer of the council, since the council oversees the general fund. The man serving in this position gives his monthly report to the full council, rather than only to the diaconate.

The chairman leads the diaconate meetings. He opens with devotions, oversees the discussion, and keeps things moving and on task. One of his duties is to assign committees to the various diaconate cases. These committees normally consist of two deacons; the chairman reassigns these committees every six months.

The vice-all fills the position of any officers who might be absent for a meeting. For example, if the chairman is sick the night of the meeting, the vice-all takes his place and leads the meeting. The vice-all also has the responsibility of recording the general fund contributions received in the budget envelopes. He also sends out statements at the end of the year for tax purposes.

The essential duty of the secretary is to carry out all of the administrative tasks of the diaconate. He records what goes on in the deacons' meeting and decisions that the deacons make on the different aspects of their work. This record is important. If questions ever come up concerning decisions that the deacons made earlier, the secretary can look back through the record, or minutes, and figure out what the deacons had determined before. The secretary also gathers all the committee reports for each monthly meeting and neatly organizes those reports. This makes the meetings go smoothly. The deacons have the material in front of them to make informed, wise decisions. The secretary is also responsible for all correspondence. He receives the letters sent to the diaconate and writes the letters for the diaconate. A final duty of the secretary is putting together schedules. He schedules visits with the widows of the congregation, meetings with new members of the congregation, and elder visitors to the monthly deacons' meetings.

The benevolent fund treasurer keeps track of the benevolent fund of the church. When the diaconate decides to distribute the mercies of Christ to someone in need, the benevolent fund treasurer is the one who signs the check. The committee assigned to the one in need will give that person or family the check when they bring the word. Having one man oversee these monies keeps things orderly. It is less likely that two deacons will each expect the other to subtract a check from the balance and then overdraw the account because neither did. One man is responsible for keeping track of those numbers. The elders also check to make sure that he is doing his job correctly. Near the beginning of the year, the outgoing elders look over his books to make sure he is keeping an accurate account of the money in the benevolent fund.

While all of these offices are important, it is good to remember that these men, first of all, hold the office of deacon. These offices within the diaconate are only there so that the deacons can do their work decently and in good order.

We are thankful that God has given faithful men to Hope church who can serve in the office of deacon. It is our prayer as deacons that he will continue to raise up men—men with merciful hearts—to collect and distribute the mercies of Christ. It is our prayer as deacons that God will continue to give thankful hearts to the congregation of Hope church, so that her deacons will have mercies of Christ to distribute. And it is our prayer as deacons that God will continue to bless Hope church with those who have need of the mercies of Christ, so that we can show our thankfulness by giving—even as we have been given.

## Our Duty to Honor Jesus Christ
### *Ronald Koole*

Parents who love the church of Jesus Christ desire their children to develop a deep appreciation and respect for the special offices in the church, namely, minister, elder, and deacon. Godly parents desire their children to honor these offices and to honor and respect the men who are called to occupy these offices in the instituted church. To accomplish this goal, parents need to be vigilant to foster these attitudes throughout their children's lives and to instruct their children according to their level of understanding from infancy to adulthood.

Parents begin this instruction when the children are very young by teaching them about God. Already in infancy, children must be taught to reverence God and spiritual things. The children must be taught by word, example, and discipline to be attentive and reverent during family devotions. They must fold their hands and close their eyes when father prays or when they learn simple prayers at the end of father's prayers or before they go to sleep at night, because they come into the presence of God, and God is to be worshiped and feared for he is holy. Parents should begin teaching their young children about the wonderful works of God by telling and reading Bible stories to them so they develop an awe of the power and majesty and works of God, who made and determines all things.

We follow here the biblical example of the instruction of Timothy, whom Paul states learned the holy scriptures already as a child.

Apart from this attitude toward God and spiritual things fostered by instruction and applied to the heart of the child of God by the Spirit of Christ, there will not grow an appreciation and honoring of the offices of Christ as the children grow up. Reverence for God and spiritual things comes first.

While children are being taught to reverence and love the Lord at a very young age, they must as they become a little older be instructed concerning the truth of the church. They must be taught that the church is the universal body and bride of Christ, made up of all the elect, who are gathered by the Spirit and word of Christ from the beginning to the end of time. This church is so loved by the Lord that he sent his Son, Jesus Christ, to suffer and die to save all of his people from their sins. God loves his church, and so must we and our children. Parents must teach their children that it is the greatest privilege, far outweighing all earthly possessions and circumstances, to be a living member of God's church.

As the children are being instructed and increase in their knowledge of biblical history, they are to be shown that in the Old Testament God gathered his people, the church, out of his chosen nation of Israel. There God was present in the tabernacle and temple, and he revealed himself and his word through the offices of prophet, priest, and king. With the dawning of the New Testament came the prophesied spread of the church to the Gentiles and the gathering of that church throughout the nations.

Through the work and writings of the apostles and especially of Paul, God clearly revealed in the New Testament scriptures that Christ by his Spirit manifests himself in the instituted congregation of believers. Christ is our chief prophet, our only high priest, and our eternal king. Within the newly instituted churches of the New Testament, Christ's Spirit guided the apostles to ordain ministers, elders, and deacons and laid out the work and qualifications necessary for these offices, so that those chosen to occupy these offices might carry out the work of Christ necessary for the salvation of his elect.

We must make very clear to our children that there is no salvation apart from membership in a faithful and true instituted church of Jesus

Christ. Every believer is obliged to place himself under the authority and care of Jesus Christ, who is present only in the true church. Our children and young people must be taught that this involves earthly sacrifice and a setting of priorities. They must be taught that church and spiritual things must be first in their lives. This must be clearly demonstrated by the lives and examples of father and mother. The godly home must leave the children with no doubt in their minds that the things of the church of Jesus Christ come first at whatever cost.

This means that the lives of the family and each member of the family revolve around the church. This begins with proper observance of the Sabbath, by frequenting the house of the Lord for worship twice each Lord's day, and proper preparation for the Sabbath already on Saturday evenings. In the church the voice and word of Christ is spoken, and where Christ speaks, there the child of God must be.

This also has implications for instruction in catechism. Our children and young people need to be taught that the time the officebearers set for catechetical instruction is the time parents make sure their children are there and know their lessons well. Social and entertainment time must always be subject and secondary to church and spiritual instructions. This is honoring Christ, who through the officebearers calls God's people to worship and who oversees this proper attitude by setting spiritual things as first priority in the lives of God's people. It must then be made very clear to our children that under no circumstances may the believer withdraw himself from the true church of Christ. Salvation depends on membership in a true church of Jesus Christ.

Parents will show their young people that the church of which they are members demonstrates the marks of the true church by preaching pure doctrine, properly administrating the sacraments, and overseeing the lives of God's people with faithful church discipline. Because these marks are present in the Protestant Reformed Churches, we establish our memberships there.

Christ is present in the true church in the saving power of his three-fold office. Christ through the offices of minister, elder, and deacon preserves true religion, propagates true doctrine, and provides for the poor and distressed. In the church the children of God are well provided for through the work of faithful officebearers, who see to it that all things are carried out in good order and decency. Christ's church remains the ground and pillar of the truth. This will determine the proper attitude God's children, young and old, must have toward the threefold office of Christ in the church.

Christ, who is our chief prophet, speaks his word to us through the preaching and teaching of the ministers of the gospel. Scripture teaches that through faith worked by the preaching we shall through Christ inherit eternal life. The minister is also an elder who exercises Christ's rule over our lives, and he watches for our souls. Those ministers who are faithful are worthy of double honor, and we must reverence Christ by holding the minister in highest esteem.

Christ calls and qualifies men to this office through the church, and our children are to receive these men with all gladness and to hold them in highest esteem. The apostle Paul says about those who are sent to preach, "How beautiful are the feet of them that preach the gospel of peace, and bring glad tidings of good things!" (Rom. 10:15). We receive their preaching not as the word of a man, but as the word of God. With this attitude taught and held to in our homes, the peace of God enters our homes.

Christ, who also is our only king, rules over us in the church not only through the minister of the word, but also through the office of elder. Elders are called to be watchmen on the walls of Zion. These men are called not only to see to it that the truth is preached and the people of God are being fed by faithful preaching, but they must also guard God's people from the spiritual dangers and false teachings from without as well as within the church. These men too are called and qualified by God through the church. Because they are servants of Jesus Christ, we must give ourselves willingly to their inspection and government. So serious is this rule over the lives of the members of the church that the scriptures teach that what the church through her elders (teaching and ruling under the authority of Christ) binds on earth is bound in heaven (Matt. 16:19; 18:18). So the ruling elders who serve faithfully are also worthy of double honor by God's people, who view them as the servants of God.

One of the ways that the elders exercise supervision over the lives of the congregation is by conducting annual family visitation. This provides fathers an opportunity to teach their children about the care and supervision of Jesus Christ over their homes through the elders. Fathers should take time to read and discuss the theme passage announced for the visit and to prepare the family for the elders' visit so that a profitable hour around God's word can be enjoyed. Parents need to see to it that the young people are home and set that evening's visit as a priority in their lives. Again, fathers must demand that spiritual things and the church are first in the life of the child of God.

"A particular family visitation many years ago remains vividly in my mind. A beloved elder, Dewey Engelsma, gave wise advice to this then young mother with two small children. He said to me, "Yes, reading Reformed Bible stories to your young children is a good way to teach them biblical truths, but read the Bible to them too. It may seem to you that they are too young to comprehend what it is saying, but never underestimate the working of the Holy Spirit in their young hearts."
—Brenda (Langerak) Bomers

Christ, who is our only high priest, demonstrates his mercy and loving care for us through the office of deacon. The deacon's calling is to collect and distribute alms and goods to the poor and objects of charity in the congregation with compassion and hearty affection. Always these alms are to be accompanied by the word of God.

Children must be taught to be cheerful givers. Because giving is contrary to our natures, instruction and training are necessary especially as the children grow a little older and take on jobs. Fathers must see to it that the children give to the causes of Christ and give liberally and willingly. God loves the cheerful giver. And if the Lord sends need and poverty to the family, fathers must not be ashamed but show the children that Christ is mercifully providing through the office of deacon and they must be thankful.

God provides a yearly opportunity for fathers to give further instruction regarding how Christ is present in the three offices. Each year nominations and elections are held for the offices of elder and deacon. Fathers do well to use this opportunity to read passages during family devotions that teach the qualifications required of the men who are nominated to serve in these offices. Discussion about these qualifications will increase the children's knowledge about these offices, as well as teach them that through proper elections held at congregational meetings, Christ chooses the men whom he would have serve in his church.

Fathers should even speak privately about the men on nomination to their confessing sons who will cast votes at the congregational meeting. Votes must be cast for those men who most clearly exhibit the spiritual qualifications spoken of in the scriptures. Election of officebearers is serious business and one that must take place with much thought and prayer.

But it must not be thought that teaching our children and young people should take place only on special occasions such as family visitation or election of officebearers at annual congregational meetings. One of the outstanding means God uses to teach our children to appreciate and honor officebearers is through prayer. Fathers must pray often in family devotions, not only for the church of Jesus Christ in general, but also specifically for the minister, elders, and deacons. They must teach their children to do so also. Petitions must be made to God that he will grant the officebearers wisdom, courage, and discretion to carry out their respective offices. The prayers should petition God to give his grace to these men as they deal with sinner saints so that they do not become weary in well-doing. We can be assured that God hears these prayers and not only grants these requests to the up-building of the officebearers, but also uses parents' instruction and prayers to prepare many of our sons to someday serve as God's servants in the church.

To that end, we as parents must give special encouragement and instruction to our sons. We do not know if our sons will be called to serve as officebearers in the church, but we must encourage them to prepare themselves if the Lord so determines to use them. We may instruct our sons to desire to serve in the special offices in the church. In 1 Timothy 3:1, Paul wrote to Timothy, "If a man desire the office of a bishop, he desireth a good work."

In order for one to serve well as an officebearer, he must have a love for the truth. Sons must be encouraged to read sound Reformed literature. This includes the churches' periodicals such as the *Beacon Lights* and the *Standard Bearer*. Also included are the books published by the Reformed Free Publishing Association and other books of a spiritual and doctrinal nature. Knowledge is also attained through diligent study and preparation for catechism and society life. Attendance at church-sponsored lectures and conferences also aids this preparation. Qualified officebearers must be knowledgeable in the scriptures so that they can bring God's word to bear on the needs of God's people. That takes preparation and study already when our sons are maturing young men. When sons demonstrate special gifts of intellect and spirituality, they must be instructed to prayerfully consider the ministry of the gospel.

The church needs preachers! The church needs qualified elders and deacons! Pray that the Lord of the harvest will continue to provide the church with men to carry out his work through the offices of minister, elder, and deacon, and that we and our children highly esteem those called to serve Christ and his bride, the church, in these offices.

# Chapter 10

$\sim\!\!\sim\!\!\odot\!\!\odot\!\!\sim\!\!\sim$

# REFORMED WORSHIP
# AT HOPE

*Aaron J. Cleveland*

God very commonly takes on the character of a husband to us. Indeed, the union by which he binds us to himself when he receives us into the bosom of the church is like sacred wedlock...[Eph. 5:29–32]...The more holy and chaste a husband is, the more wrathful he becomes if he sees his wife inclining her heart to a rival. In like manner, the Lord, who has wedded us to himself in truth [cf. Hos. 2:19–20], manifests the most burning jealousy whenever we, neglecting the purity of his holy marriage, become polluted with wicked lusts. But he especially feels this when we transfer to another or stain with some superstition the worship of his divine majesty, which deserved to be utterly uncorrupted. In this way we not only violate the pledge given in marriage, but also defile the very marriage bed by bringing adulterers to it.[1]

Such is the seriousness of the pure worship of God according to the great reformer John Calvin, in his explanation of the threatening words of the second commandment. God visits the "iniquity of the fathers upon the children unto the third and fourth generation" (Ex. 20:5) of

---

1    John Calvin, *Institutes of the Christian Religion*, ed. John T. Mc Neill, trans. Ford Lewis Battles, Library of Christian Classics (Philadelphia: The Westminster Press, 1960), 2.8.18, 20:385.

those who pollute his worship by introducing false doctrine and what is not commanded in his word.

## Some History

The worship of Hope Protestant Reformed Church has been maintained for one hundred years in the midst of the fires of doctrinal controversy. Shortly after organization in 1916, Hope church and her pastor, Rev. G. M. Ophoff, figured prominently in the rejection of the theory of common grace and the well-meant offer of the gospel in the early 1920s.

"I think of Rev. Ophoff. You know he stood there on Classis West and they wanted him to sign the three points. And you know what he said to them, don't you? We kind of smile and smirk a little bit and we talk about melodramatic. He told them, 'You can shoot me out of a cannon—I won't sign the three points.' The Grand Rapids Press got a big joke out of it. 'Ophoff Prefers Death' were the headlines…Alright, let 'em smile, let 'em smirk. I tell you he meant it. And that's why there's a Hope Protestant Reformed Church today. He knew what he believed and he would die for it."[2]
—Prof. Herman Hanko, recounting the stand of Rev. Ophoff on the floor of classis and connecting his rejection of the three points to the very existence of Hope church today.

This rejection of false doctrine and the proclamation of God's sovereign, particular grace in the salvation of the elect and the antithesis between the church and the world served as God's means to preserve the pure worship of God in the congregation of Hope.

Again in the early 1950s, when the false doctrine of a conditional covenant crept into the denomination, only in the way of rejecting this manifestation of Arminianism injected into the covenant was pure worship maintained. If anyone doubts the connection between sound

---

2  Herman Hanko, "Men for the Times" (sermon on 1 Chronicles 12:32–33 preached in Hope Protestant Reformed Church, Walker, Michigan, on July 9, 1995).

doctrine and the pure worship of God, one only needs to notice how worship has changed over the past decades in our mother church, the Christian Reformed Church. Nearly every aspect of her worship has been corrupted. The regulative principle of worship is both ignored and dismissed.

It is reason for gratitude to God that he continues to preserve true worship in our midst in the way of being governed by the regulative principle. The *biblical* basis of the regulative principle is the second commandment: "Thou shalt not make unto thee any graven image, or any likeness of any thing that is in heaven above, or that is in the earth beneath, or that is in the water under the earth: thou shalt not bow down thyself to them, nor serve them" (Ex. 20:4–5). The *confessional* basis of the regulative principle is the Heidelberg Catechism's explanation of the second commandment: "that we in no wise represent God by images, nor worship him in any other way than he has commanded in his Word."[3] The *traditional* basis of the regulative principle can be found in the writings of those men of the Reformed tradition, including Zacharias Ursinus (an author of the Heidelberg Catechism), Gijsbert Voetius (delegate to the Synod of Dordt), and John Calvin.[4] The significance of the regulative principle will be explained later in this chapter.

## Worship Defined

The starting point in examining worship at Hope is understanding that worship at its heart is fellowship with God. James A. De Jong defines Reformed worship as "a prescribed, corporate meeting between God and his people, in which God is praised and his church is blessed."[5] Professor Hanko, in defining the spiritual nature (John 4:24) of worship, writes, "We must worship God in such a way that we consciously enter into God's presence, consciously enjoy fellowship and communion with

---

3   Heidelberg Catechism A 96, in *Confessions and Church Order*, 125.
4   David J. Engelsma, "The Basis of the Regulative Principle of Worship," in David J. Engelsma, Barry Gritters, Charles Terpstra, *Reformed Worship* (Grandville, MI: Reformed Free Publishing Association, 2004), 6–12.
5   James A. De Jong, *Into His Presence* (Grand Rapids, MI: Board of Publications of the Christian Reformed Church, 1985), 13.

Him, consciously enter into conversation with Him. We must worship God with our hearts and minds and wills and emotions."[6]

It is important to remember the "corporate" aspect of worship. As individuals we worship God in our private devotions. As families we worship God when we gather around the table to read and discuss a portion of his word, sing praises to his name, and offer our prayers to him. However, these are not corporate worship. De Jong writes, "Our definition of worship as a corporate meeting refers precisely to the officially called and supervised worship of the one, holy, catholic, and apostolic church." These four adjectives "are usually reserved for the organized, instituted congregation of believers."[7] Following the lead of this definition, Hope church, a local manifestation of the body of Christ, called to worship by her elders, gathers morning and evening on the Lord's day to have intimate, covenantal fellowship with God under the supervision of the elders.

This officially called and supervised worship of God has a threefold purpose. The chief purpose of corporate worship is the glorification of God's name. "The Anglo-Saxon word from which we get our word 'worship' is *weorthscipe*, which is what worship is: declaring the *worthiness* of God. Psalm 95:3 says it well, 'The Lord is a great God, and a great King above all gods.'"[8] Writes Professor Hanko regarding this "most fundamental purpose of worship,"

> This...could bear a bit of emphasis. From a certain point of view, we have made worship man-centered. We have done this by going to church and leaving church with the question in our mouths: What benefit can I get out of going to church? We are concerned about ourselves and what is of value to us. We even ask each other this question sometimes: Did you get anything out of the sermon today? And elders sometimes set this question on the foreground when on family visitation they ask: Are you blessed through the preaching?

---

6    Herman Hanko, "Our Order of Worship," *Standard Bearer* 60, no. 2 (October 15, 1983):45.

7    De Jong, *Into His Presence*, 14.

8    Barry Gritters, *Public Worship and the Reformed Faith* (Byron Center, MI: The Evangelism Society of Byron Center Protestant Reformed Church, 1990), 4.

These questions may, of course, be asked. And there ought to be spiritual blessing in the worship of God. But it is not the most important thing. The chief question is: Have we gone to church to praise and bless our God, Who alone is worthy of all praise. Perhaps it is because we have become so man-centered that worship services also become man-centered. If we go to bless the Name of God, the blessing to us will come.[9]

In the way of properly worshiping God, we will experience that we are edified, especially as we sit under sound preaching. This is another important purpose of our gathering for corporate worship. The Canons of Dordt speak powerfully of the necessity of being diligent in attending to the means of grace.

As the almighty operation of God, whereby he prolongs and supports this our natural life, does not exclude, but requires, the use of means, by which God of his infinite mercy and goodness hath chosen to exert his influence, *so also the before mentioned supernatural operation of God by which we are regenerated in no wise excludes or subverts the use of the gospel, which the most wise God has ordained to be the seed of regeneration, and food of the soul.* Wherefore, as the apostles and teachers who succeeded them piously instructed the people concerning this grace of God, to his glory, and the abasement of all pride, and in the meantime, however, neglected not to keep them by the sacred precepts of the gospel in the exercise of the Word, sacraments, and discipline; so, even to this day, be it far from either instructors or instructed to presume to tempt God in the church by separating what he of his good pleasure hath most intimately joined together. *For grace is conferred by means of admonitions; and the more readily we perform our duty, the more eminent usually is this blessing of God working in us, and the more directly is his work advanced*; to whom alone all the glory, both of means and their saving fruit and efficacy, is forever due. Amen.[10]

---

9    Hanko, "Our Order of Worship," *Standard Bearer* 60, no. 3 (November 1, 1983):55.

10   Canons of Dordt 3–4.17, in *Confessions and Church Order*, 170; emphasis added.

Finally, in gathering together for worship on the Lord's day, we experience the communion of the saints. On Sunday the individual members gather together as a body. Prof. Barry Gritters describes this purpose of our worship.

> In the fellowship of worship, believers pray together for their life as a body, offer united homage to their king, support the cause of God's kingdom in the world, listen collectively to the word that they preach through their pastor. This fellowship (and the fellowship *after* the official service) cements the bond of love among them, serves to encourage each in his calling, and supports the witness that they give to the community.[11]

How many of us can remember conversations we have had with fellow saints after the worship services, not only about how the sermon was a comfort to us, but how that word must have been a comfort to the afflicted brother or sister we are talking to. How many of us remember watching fellow saints, coming to church week after week, each time a little more weak and frail because of the ravages of age or disease, and God worked in our heart the desire to bring a comforting word to them. We received in return their assurance that God was working all things for good in their lives. God's glory, our edification, and fellowship with members of the body of Christ are all purposes of corporate worship.

Over the one hundred years of worshiping at Hope, very little has changed in the worship services. All of the *elements* of worship remain the same. We have essentially the same order of worship that we did one hundred years ago. The consistory has approved changes only in the *circumstances* of worship. At the time of this writing, the clerk of the consistory, Elder David Moelker, examined the consistory minutes from 1921 to the present, looking for consistory-approved changes to our worship. All of the typewritten minutes of the changes easily fit on two pages. This is as it should be. We have a precious liturgical heritage that has stood the test of time and should not be quickly tinkered with.

---

11 Gritters, *Public Worship and the Reformed Faith*, 8.

Professor Hanko explains why we ought not to lightly cast aside the liturgy of our fathers:

> We are part of the church of the past and we trace our ecclesiastical and theological roots back to that church of the past. We have a tradition, after all; and that tradition includes not only our doctrine—although that most importantly—but also our liturgical heritage. And our liturgical heritage includes not only our liturgical forms, but also our order of worship. We ought never to cast all this lightly aside. Our fathers, after all, were much more sensitive to proper worship of God than we often are; they were called upon to develop their liturgy over against Rome and to worship under the pressure of persecution. They knew what they were doing and why they were doing what they did.[12]

## Preparation for Worship

Proper and God-pleasing worship on the Lord's day begins with preparation. We too narrowly limit preparation if we talk only about our Saturday evening and Sunday morning activities before worship. The authors of the Heidelberg Catechism, in the second half of their explanation of the fourth commandment, write, "That all the days of my life I cease from my evil works, and yield myself to the Lord, to work by his Holy Spirit in me; and thus begin in this life the eternal sabbath."[13] Rev. Herman Hoeksema, in his explanation of the fourth commandment, refers to the life of the "Christian sojourner" as "his Sabbath life." In part his description of this life reads as follows:

> He lives the Sabbath life. Hence his whole life is a Sabbath-life: a ceasing from sin and an entering into the rest of God's perfected covenant.
>
> But in this world his life is a sojourner's Sabbath. He still sojourns in Babylon, and in Babylon the people do not know

---

12  Herman Hanko, "Our Order of Worship," *Standard Bearer* 59, no. 17 (June 1, 1983):393.
13  Heidelberg Catechism A 103, in *Confessions and Church Order*, 128.

the Sabbath of the Lord our God. They are aliens to the very idea of the Sabbath, the rest of God's tabernacle. We need not be surprised therefore that in the world people devote the first day of the week to the pursuit of earthly and worldly things. Especially on the Sabbath all that is in the world, the lust of the flesh and the lust of the eyes and the pride of life, becomes emphatically manifest.

This is all the more reason that the Christian sojourner, living his Sabbath life in the world, where he feels that he is a stranger, where he meets with Babylon's opposition and reproach, where all things tend to draw him downward and make it difficult for him to live his life of rest, longs for the day of the Lord, the weekly Sabbath that the Lord in his great mercy provided for him, and insists on keeping it holy.[14]

Living within the sphere of the church and participating in the congregational life of the church throughout the week is one of the main ways that we come properly prepared for our worship on the Lord's day. It is not the case that during the week we live our lives in separation from the church, occupying our minds and time with only "worldly" cares and endeavors. If this is true, as experience teaches us, we simply will not come to church prepared.

We, as Christian sojourners, also live our Sabbath lives *within our homes as families* throughout the week. We make time daily for the reading and study of God's word. We fellowship as families around the word. We read good Reformed literature. Throughout the week we make a conscious effort to keep our homes safe havens from the "Babylonian" entertainment and philosophy that surrounds us.

*Personally*, we are engaged in a fierce battle against our own sins and enemies. At times this can be exhausting, especially when walking as sojourners puts us into direct conflict with those who oppose

---

14 Herman Hoeksema, *Love the Lord Thy God: An Exposition of the Heidelberg Catechism*, Triple Knowledge Series 8 (Jenison, MI: Reformed Free Publishing Association, 2015), 308.

a godly, antithetical walk. Sabbath life means that we must deny ourselves, take up our cross, and follow Jesus, finding our way very narrow in this world. When we live daily in the heat of this battle, aware of the constant threats to our spiritual well-being that surround us and in the end are "so weak in ourselves that we cannot stand a moment,"[15] it is inevitable that we will come prepared to worship God.

This is the idea of Psalm 27, the text that Hope's elders chose for family visitation in 2015. David cried out, "One thing have I desired of the Lord, that will I seek after; that I may dwell in the house of the Lord all the days of my life, to behold the beauty of the Lord, and to inquire in his temple" (v. 4). That desire of David arose from within him because of his helplessness in the face of his enemies. They surrounded him, tormented him, and threatened his certain destruction. David's only safety was dwelling in the "house of the Lord" and hiding in "his pavilion" and "tabernacle" (vv. 4–5). God very really uses the afflictions and tribulations of this life to prepare us for worship and to work within us a desire to come weekly to his house. He uses that worship as a means to strengthen that Sabbath life within us as we live as pilgrims and strangers in the Babylon of this world.

## Diligently Frequenting the House of God

The pinnacle of our Sabbath life is coming to church Sunday morning. We all come, young and old, individuals and entire families, both parents and all of their children; even when that means getting to church thirty to forty minutes before the service begins in order to sit together as a family. The Form for the Administration of Baptism eloquently states why we include young children in our worship.

> For when we are baptized in the name of the Father, God the Father witnesseth and sealeth unto us *that He doth make an eternal covenant of grace with us, and adopts us for His children and heirs,* and therefore will provide us with every good thing, and avert all evil or turn it to our profit...Since then baptism is

---

15   Heidelberg Catechism A 127, in *Confessions and Church Order,* 139.

come in the place of circumcision, *therefore infants are to be baptized as heirs of the kingdom of God and of his covenant.*[16]

Our children are included in God's covenant, and this requires them to be present at the worship of God, not only to sit under the preaching, but also to actively participate in the worship. We are reminded of Jesus' response to the chief priests and scribes at their displeasure with the children's praise of Jesus in the temple: "When the chief priests and scribes saw the wonderful things that he did, and the children crying in the temple, and saying, Hosanna to the son of David; they were sore displeased, and said unto him, Hearest thou what these say? And Jesus saith unto them, Yea; have ye never read, Out of the mouth of babes and sucklings thou hast perfected praise?" (Matt. 21:15–16). We greatly minimize the work of the Holy Spirit when we underestimate our children's ability to understand the preaching and to respond in heartfelt worship of God.

Lord's Day 38 reminds us that proper Sabbath observance requires that we, "especially on the sabbath, that is, on the day of rest, diligently frequent the church of God."[17] This means that we worship together not only in the morning, but also in the evening. Further, that we "diligently frequent the church" means that gathering for worship is a *weekly* activity. Prof. David Engelsma has the following to say regarding this:

> This aspect of obedience to the Fourth Commandment is threatened today. There are leaks in the dike. There are those who attend only infrequently, missing entire Sundays or consistently missing one of the services every Sunday ("oncers"). There is the growing practice of missing the worship services, now and then, because they interfere with our pleasures, e.g., our vacation-plans. The Lord's Day is completely forgotten. It is used for traveling or for sightseeing, just as though it did not belong to the risen Christ, but to ourselves. The strange notion is found in the Church that the Fourth Commandment may be broken occasionally. Men suppose that, if they remember the

---

16  Form for the Administration of Baptism, in ibid., 258–59; emphasis added.
17  Heidelberg Catechism A 103, in ibid., 128.

Lord's Day 51 weeks of the year, they are warranted in forgetting it one week. What would these same people say if others would adopt this thinking in regard to the commandment against stealing, or the commandment against murder?

"But the Lord's Day gets in the way of my pleasures," says the man determined to enjoy his weekend vacation. Yes, the Law of God has a way of doing this. Throughout the Old Testament, the Sabbath-Commandment "interfered" with Israel's pleasures; and for this reason they broke it (cf. Isaiah 58:13 and Amos 8:5). May we bend and twist the Law to suit our pleasures? Or are we to plan our lives according to the law and find our pleasure in doing what it says?

Our would-be vacationer persists, "But I work hard during the year, and I need some rest." To be sure, we need rest; and this needed rest is the rest of the Lord's house and the Lord's Word.[18]

## The Regulative Principle of Worship

Needing that rest, we gather twice on the Lord's day for worship—worship that is governed by the *regulative principle* of worship. Earlier in this chapter the biblical, confessional, and traditional bases of the regulative principle were explained. Now we will take a more in-depth look at how the regulative principle governs worship at Hope church.

The regulative principle is essentially the second commandment. While the first commandment tells us *whom* we are to worship, the second commandment establishes the *manner* or the *how* of the worship of the one true God. This understanding of the second commandment is confirmed by the Heidelberg Catechism's explanation of it: "that we in no wise represent God by images, *nor worship him in any other way than he has commanded in his Word*."[19] God determines how he will be worshiped; we do not. We find the directions for our worship of him *in his word*.

---

18  David Engelsma, *Remembering the Lord's Day* (South Holland, IL: The Evangelism Committee of South Holland Protestant Reformed Church, 1992), 9–10.
19  Heidelberg Catechism A 96, in *Confessions and Church Order*, 125; emphasis added.

As obvious as this may seem, one of the warnings we must take from a study of church history is the frequency with which the church departed from the true worship of God. The Old Testament is a sad chronicle of one corruption after another of true worship. Remember Aaron's golden calf, the strange fire of Nadab and Abihu, Gideon's ephod, the golden calves set up in Dan and Bethel...and the list goes on. New Testament church history is no better. By the end of the Middle Ages the worship of God had been so corrupted that true worship could scarcely be found on the earth. The vast and powerful Roman Catholic Church was mired in superstition and idolatry, and God's people had nowhere to gather as a church to worship him in spirit and in truth.

By means of the Reformation of the sixteenth century God opened the way for his people to again worship him as he has commanded in his word. God raised up men such as John Calvin to expose the false worship of the Roman Catholic Church and to lead the Reformation churches to a greater understanding of the principles of proper worship. Maintaining the pure worship of God is a theme that consistently runs through the writings of Calvin, especially his *Institutes*.

In his treatise *De necessitate reformandae Ecclesiae* (The necessity of reforming the church), Calvin writes of his high regard for the proper worship of God:

> If it be asked, then, by what things chiefly the Christian religion has a standing existence amongst us, and maintains its truth, it will be found that the following two not only occupy the principal place, but comprehend under them all the other parts, and consequently the whole substance of Christianity, viz., a knowledge first, of the right way to worship God; and secondly of the source from which salvation is to be sought. When these are kept out of view, though we may glory in the name of Christians, our profession is empty and vain.[20]

Calvin understood well the sad condition of fallen man. "Every one

---

20 John Calvin, quoted in Carlos Eire, *War Against the Idols: The Reformation of Worship from Erasmus to Calvin* (Cambridge: Cambridge University Press, 1986), 198.

of us is, even from his mother's womb, a master craftsman of idols."[21] About man's mind Calvin writes,

> Each man's mind is like a labyrinth, so that it is no wonder that individual nations were drawn aside into various falsehoods; and not only this—but individual men, almost, had their own gods. For as rashness and superficiality are joined to ignorance and darkness, scarcely a single person has ever been found who did not fashion for himself an idol or specter in place of God. Surely, just as waters boil up from a vast, full spring, so does an immense crowd of gods flow forth from the human mind, while each one, in wandering about with too much license, wrongly invents this or that about God himself. [22]

Fallen man possesses a tremendous proclivity to idolatry and the corruption of the worship of God. In Isaiah 65 God accuses his people, through the prophet, of their sin of corrupting his worship. Calvin has the following comments on verse 7:

> He glances at one kind of sin, under which, by a figure of speech in which a part is taken for the whole, he describes also the rest of their sins; for he means by it the whole of the revolt by which the people withdrew from the true worship, and devoted and gave themselves up to strange gods. This is the utmost verge of iniquities; for, when the fear of God has been taken away, we can have nothing sound or healthy in us. Thus he points out the source of all evils, which ought to be the more diligently observed, because men are highly pleased with themselves, and think that they deserve great praise, when they worship God according to their own fancy, and do not understand that nothing is more abominable in the sight of God than pretended worship, which proceeds from human contrivance. Beyond all doubt, the people desired to be acceptable to God by "offering

---

21  Ibid., 208.
22  Calvin, *Institutes*, 1.5.12, 20:64–65.

incense on the mountains;" but it is not from the purpose of their mind, and from their intention, as they call it, that we must judge of their work. In preference to all men, we must listen to the voice of the Lord, who testifies that he is greatly dishonoured, that we may not endeavour to defend ourselves by pleading our intention, which will render us doubly guilty before God.[23]

Calvin is very careful to point out God's severe displeasure with man's "will worship." The regulative principle, that we worship God only as he has commanded in his word, stands in sharp contrast to worship according to the good intentions and precepts of man. Calvin writes very sharply against "will worship" in his *Institutes* under the heading "Perverse worship an abomination to God."

Many marvel why the Lord so sharply threatens to astound the people who worshiped him with the commands of men [Isa. 29:13–14] and declares that he is vainly worshiped by the precepts of men [Matt. 15:9]. But if they were to weigh what it is to depend upon God's bidding alone in matters of religion (that is, on account of heavenly wisdom), they would at the same time see that the Lord has strong reasons to abominate such perverse rites, which are performed for him according to the willfulness of human nature. For even though those who obey such laws in the worship of God have some semblance of humility in this obedience of theirs, they are nevertheless not at all humble in God's sight, since they prescribe for him these same laws which they observe. Now, this is the reason why Paul so urgently warns us not to be deceived by the traditions of men [Col. 2:4ff.], or by what he calls…"will worship," devised by men apart from God's teaching [Col. 2:22–23]. It is certainly true that our own and all men's wisdom must become foolish, that we may allow him alone to be wise. Those who expect his

---

23  John Calvin, *Commentary on the Book of the Prophet Isaiah,* trans. William Pringle (Grand Rapids, MI: Baker Book House, 1998), 4:385.

approval for their paltry observances contrived by men's will, and offer to him, as if involuntarily, a sham obedience which is paid actually to men, do not hold to that path.[24]

The true worship of God is *spiritual*. Jesus said to the Samaritan woman in John 4:23–24, "But the hour cometh, and now is, when the true worshippers shall worship the Father in spirit and in truth: for the Father seeketh such to worship him. God is a Spirit: and they that worship him must worship him in spirit and in truth." Calvin comments on these two verses:

> But the first inquiry which presents itself here is, Why, and in what sense, is the worship of God called *spiritual*? To understand this, we must attend to the contrast between the spirit and outward emblems, as between the shadows and the truth. The worship of God is said to consist *in the spirit*, because it is nothing else than that inward faith of the heart which produces prayer, and, next, purity of conscience and self-denial, that we may be dedicated to obedience to God as holy sacrifices.
>
> What it is to *worship God in spirit and truth* appears clearly from what has been already said. It is to lay aside the entanglements of ancient ceremonies, and to retain merely what is spiritual in the worship of God; for the *truth* of the worship of God consists in *the spirit*, and ceremonies are but a sort of appendage. And here again it must be observed, that *truth* is not compared with *falsehood*, but with the outward addition of the figures of the Law; so that—to use a common expression— it is the pure and simple substance of spiritual worship.[25]

Another implication of the regulative principle as "implied by the second commandment is that it is a service of the Word: the Word *read*, the Word *preached*, the Word *sung*, the Word *prayed*, and the

---

24 Calvin, *Institutes*, 4.10.24, 21:1203.
25 John Calvin, *Commentary on the Gospel according to John*, trans. William Pringle (Grand Rapids, MI: Baker Book House, 1998), 1:161–64.

Word *signified and sealed*."[26] The word may never be pushed out of our worship services. Nor may we, in the name of maintaining Reformed worship, allow that word to be dishonored by preaching a god, singing of a god, and praying to a god who is not the God of scripture. There are many "Reformed" churches where the regulative principle is for the most part maintained but where a universal, resistible grace is preached. The congregations sing Arminian hymns that extol the decisive will of man and the begging and pleading of a god who waits for man's decision. The ministers lead the congregations in prayer to a god whose desires are frustrated by the wills of men. The regulative principle and sound doctrine go hand in hand. The result of maintaining the regulative principle apart from sound doctrine is worship displeasing to God.

The regulative principle dictates six essential elements in our order of worship. These elements are congregational singing (Col. 3:16), prayer (Mark 11:17), scripture reading (Acts 13:15), the preaching of the word (Acts 15:21; 1 Tim. 4:13), the administration of baptism and the Lord's supper (Acts 2:42; Lord's Day 38), and offerings (1 Cor. 16:1–4).

## The Prelude

As those who are members of Hope church know, arriving well before the worship service begins is normal, especially for large families. Frequently one has thirty minutes to sit in the pew before worship begins. Usually ten to fifteen minutes before the service, the organist (or pianist) plays a prelude. Professor Hanko makes the following observations about the prelude:

> The purpose of this is to establish by music a spiritual atmosphere for worship, to put the congregation into the mood for worship, to assist the people of God in meditating upon their presence in the house of God...It ought to be understood at the outset that there is a great deal of music which is inappropriate for this organ (or piano) prelude. I have been in worship services where music was played during this prelude which

---

26 Engelsma, *Reformed Worship*, 7.

was altogether out of keeping with the nature of the worship service. I have heard hymns played which are far from being Reformed and are sometimes downright Arminian. I have heard spirituals played, the words of which are not expressive of biblical truths. I have heard patriotic music played which is secular. I have heard classical music played which, while good enough in itself, is not fitting for a worship service. It is clear that such music has no place in the congregational gathering for worship and detracts from, rather than adds to, the worship of God. (We might add that the same thing is true of the music played during Offertory.)[27]

In the history of Hope church, the consistory has taken a few decisions relating not only to the prelude, but also to music played during the offertory and postlude. At its September 14, 1983, meeting, the consistory decided that only psalter numbers were to be played before and after the service. At the next meeting on October 12, the consistory modified its decision by allowing variations of psalter numbers to be played. At the November 11, 1992, meeting, the consistory decided to clarify that the allowed music before, during, and after the worship service is to be taken from the 434 numbers of the psalter that the Protestant Reformed denomination has used since its beginning.

A couple of minutes before the service begins, the door in the front of the sanctuary by the organ opens. First through the door is the oldest elder, followed by his fellow elders in descending age as they walk to the elders' bench. The deacons follow, each taking his seat with his family across from the elders. During this time, the minister has walked through the door on the platform in the front of church, setting his Bible and notes on the pulpit and then usually sitting in one of the chairs to pray before the service begins. Perhaps some will remember Rev. Herman Veldman, walking through the door by the organ, stopping at the bottom of the platform steps to pray, and then ascending the steps to the pulpit.

---

27  Herman Hanko, "Our Order of Worship," *Standard Bearer* 60, no. 9 (February 1, 1984): 201–2.

## Elements of Worship

### *Salutation, Votum, and Benediction*

After the minister and officebearers have finished their silent prayers, the organist ends the prelude, the sanctuary falls silent, and the entire congregation rises to its feet. Now the worship service has begun. The service begins with three important but often minimized elements: the salutation, votum, and benediction.

The minister recites the words of the salutation, "Beloved in our Lord Jesus Christ." Next follows the votum, "Our help is in the name of the LORD, who made heaven and earth." The votum is the last verse of Psalm 124. Then the minister raises his arms and pronounces the benediction: "Grace, mercy, and peace be granted unto thee from God our Father and from Jesus Christ our Lord, through the operation of the Holy Spirit, Amen."

It is proper to begin a worship service with the salutation, votum, and benediction. As Professor Hanko observes:

> It is more in keeping with our doctrine to preserve this order [beginning with salutation, votum, and benediction before the doxology]...We believe in the truth of sovereign grace... As applied to the worship service, this means that our speech to God is always a response to God's speech to us. God says, according to Psalm 27:8, "Seek ye My face"; and our hearts respond, "Thy face Lord will we seek." The order here is important. It is not only the order of command and obedience to that command; it is also the divine order of sovereign grace. God's word, "Seek ye My face," is the sovereign power within us by which we are able to say, "Thy face Lord will we seek." This divine order ought to be preserved in the worship service. God speaks first, always, in the work of salvation. Our speech is the response to His voice.[28]

---

28  Herman Hanko, "Our Order of Worship," *Standard Bearer* 61, no. 2 (October 15, 1984):34.

### Doxology

In response to the salutation, votum, and benediction, the congregation sings the doxology, "Praise God from Whom All Blessings Flow." This is a fitting way for the congregation to respond in praise to God. All blessings come from God, especially the blessings needed to properly worship God.

The question may be asked, are doxologies expressly commanded in scripture as a part of worship? Professor Hanko answers this question:

> While there is no specific injunction in Scripture to include such doxologies in the worship service, it is clear that such songs of praise are often found in Scripture both in the Old Testament and in the New. Not only are many of the Psalms and songs recorded in the Old Testament specific songs of praise, but there are similar passages in the New Testament, such as Romans 11:33–36, 16:27, 2 Corinthians 1:3, Ephesians 1:3ff., 1 Timothy 1:17, and several which can be found in the book of Revelation.[29]

It is also interesting to note that singing a doxology at the beginning of the service is of "comparatively recent origin."[30]

> "I remember the time, when I was younger, that very few, if any, of our congregations began with a doxology. There is no rule here, and the people of God have freedom in this matter."[31]
> —Prof. Herman Hanko

The consistory minutes reveal that from time to time decisions were taken to change which doxologies were sung at the conclusion of the morning and evening services.

### Congregational Singing

At the conclusion of the opening doxology, the minister announces the first psalter number to be sung. Clearly congregational singing is

---

29  Ibid., 33.
30  Ibid.
31  Ibid.

one of the important *elements* of proper worship. Three questions arise regarding singing in worship. Why *congregational* singing? Will there be *accompaniment* to the singing? *What* will be sung?

There is biblical warrant for *congregational* singing. Both Ephesians 5:18–19 and Colossians 3:16 speak of singing in fellowship with other saints. In our singing we are "teaching and admonishing one another" (Col. 3:16). We are also responding as a body in praise and dependence upon God. Remember, worship is covenantal fellowship and communion with God. That we would remain silent and put this privilege in the hands of a soloist or choir is an idea that we would find "abhorrent." Professor Hanko writes,

> Not that there is no place for choirs in the life of the people of God; singing is an important part of the life of the people of God, and they find a particular delight in joining with fellow saints in choir singing. But choirs have no place in the worship service. One does not come to the worship service to be entertained, but to worship. And...this...is the worship of the congregation. The congregation must speak to God. When choirs sing this is impossible.[32]

What about accompaniment? It is important when discussing accompaniment to the singing that we distinguish between an *element* of worship and *circumstances* related to that element. The regulative principle demands congregational singing. Whether we stand or sit while singing, whether we sing three psalms or five, and whether we have organ or piano accompaniment or no accompaniment are circumstances attending to the element of singing. The church has freedom in connection with these circumstances. Professor Engelsma writes, "There are *circumstances* attending worship as well as the elements themselves, and one reduces the regulative principle to an unworkable principle, if not to absurdity, if he attempts to apply it to every detail of worship. The New Testament church has liberty

---

32 Herman Hanko, "Our Order of Worship," *Standard Bearer* 60, no. 20 (September 1, 1984):467.

in Christ to arrange the details of her worship, and this liberty is important."[33]

The Reformed organist who plays during the worship service understands the principles of worship. The organ accompaniment is secondary to the congregational singing and in service of it. The worship service is no place for an organ recital or any playing that detracts from or overpowers the singing congregation.

"The Huizinga family often sat in the front row of church, and that was no different the Sunday Rev. Veldman came to preach. There we were—front and center in the first pew. When the congregation rose to sing, I enthusiastically joined in, singing from my own psalter, although I was not yet old enough to read. After sitting down, imagine my surprise when Rev. Veldman, from the pulpit, pointed straight at me and announced, 'Now look at that little girl singing so beautifully! We should all sing like that!'"
—Sue (Huizinga) Grasman

*Psalm Singing*

Finally, the most important question is, what will we sing? The Church Order of the Protestant Reformed Churches prescribes this: "In the churches only the 150 Psalms of David, the Ten Commandments, the Lord's Prayer, the Twelve Articles of Faith, the Songs of Mary, Zacharias, and Simeon, the Morning and Evening Hymns, and the Hymn of Prayer before the sermon shall be sung."[34] The Church Order does not demand exclusive psalmody. Obviously our opening doxology, "Praise God from Whom All Blessings Flow," is not found in the psalms. Occasionally we sing the Lord's prayer, or perhaps the Song of Mary. We do allow for certain hymns, but they are sung rarely, almost never. But the question remains, why do we sing versified psalms almost exclusively?

---

33 Engelsma, *Reformed Worship*, 15.
34 Church Order 69, in *Confessions and Church Order*, 400.

Sometimes it is mistakenly assumed that we are a psalm-singing congregation and denomination because the regulative principle demands this. The history of the Protestant Reformed Churches proves this not to be true. Professor Engelsma recounts this history.

> There are other reasons than the regulative principle for singing the Psalms at church, virtually exclusively. From 1959 to 1962, the Protestant Reformed Churches considered becoming a hymn-singing denomination. The occasion was an overture from one of the churches to the synod of 1959 to change Article 69 of the church order to include many more hymns. In response to this overture, the synod of 1960 moved to change Article 69 to read: "In the churches only the 150 Psalms of David shall be sung, *as also such Hymns which are faithful versifications of the Holy Scriptures*, in each case the General Synod being the judge" (emphasis added). This motion was not then adopted, but was referred back to committee for further study. The result was lively debate in the churches until 1962 when the issue was finally decided by the synod. The debate was carried on in the *Standard Bearer*, in private discussions, and annually at the synods of 1961 and 1962. The conclusion was a decision by the synod of 1962 defeating the motion to open up the worship services to hymns.
>
> The significant thing about the debate is that neither the friends nor the foes of hymns in worship argued on the basis of the regulative principle. The regulative principle simply did not figure in the discussion.[35]

While Rev. Herman Hanko was pastor at Hope, he served on the study committee that reported to the synod of 1962 on the matter of hymns.

"When I was still a minister [1962–63], I was on a committee to study the matter of psalmody. The committee did a pile of work on that and handed in a couple of hundred pages of

---

35  Engelsma, *Reformed Worship*, 21–22.

material on the history of psalm singing. To the surprise of the committee, every time hymns were introduced into the church the next step was apostasy. There were no exceptions. That is a practical reason, but it is an important one."[36]
—Prof. Herman Hanko

The reasons for psalm singing can easily be multiplied. John Calvin wrote in the preface to the *Genevan Psalter*,

What is there now to do? It is to have songs not only honest, but also holy, which will be like spurs to incite us to pray to and praise God, and to meditate upon his works in order to love, fear, honor and glorify him. Moreover, that which St. Augustine has said is true, that no one is able to sing things worthy of God except that which he has received from him. Therefore, when we have looked thoroughly, and searched here and there, we shall not find better songs nor more fitting for the purpose, than the Psalms of David, which the Holy Spirit spoke and made through him. And moreover, when we sing them, we are certain that God puts in our mouths these, as if he himself were singing in us to exalt his glory. Wherefore Chrysostom exhorts, as well as the men, the women and the little children to accustom themselves to singing them, in order that this may be a sort of meditation to associate themselves with the company of the angels.[37]

Professor Hanko gives many compelling reasons for singing the psalms in our public worship.

The Psalms express all the truths of the Christian faith as found throughout the Scriptures. There is not one doctrine in all God's Word which is not expressed in the Bible's Psalter. Thus the Psalms can be used for confession of the truth in song. The

---

36  Herman Hanko, interview by Aaron J. Cleveland on July 6, 2015.
37  John Calvin, preface to the *Genevan Psalter*, "Why the Choice of the Psalms," http://www.ccel.org/ccel/ccel/eee/files/calvinps.htm.

Psalms also are thoroughly God-centered. This is, in my judgment, one of the chief differences between the Psalms and most
free hymns. Most hymns tend to be at best wrongly Christ-cen-
tered, and at worst man-centered. But this is not true of the
Psalms which begin and end with God. They are ideally suited,
therefore, for praise and adoration. Further, the Psalms are,
more than any other book in the Bible, a spiritual biography
of the Christian in all his life in the world, in his battles and
struggles, in his grief and joy, in his longings and desires, in his
temptations and victories. It is not an exaggeration to say that
there is no single experience in the life of the Christian which
is not described in the Psalms.[38]

It is also interesting to note that several times over the years Hope's
consistory has made decisions regarding the singing of psalter numbers during the service. On September 10, 1959, the consistory took a
decision to sing an appropriate number after baptism. At its January 11,
1978, meeting, the consistory decided that after baptism the congregation would stand to sing verse 5 of psalter 425. At the January 12, 1977,
meeting, the consistory decided to sing verse 8 of psalter 428 after public
confession of faith. These traditions continue to the present day.

### Reading of the Law

During the morning service, after the first psalter number has been sung,
the congregation is seated and the service continues with the minister's
reading the ten commandments. The reading or singing of the law has
been a part of Reformed liturgy since the days of Calvin. In Calvin's day
the law was sung. Remember, article 69 of the Church Order allows for
the singing of the ten commandments. At the June 7, 1921, meeting of
Hope's consistory, a decision was taken to read the law during the morning service and to read the Apostles' Creed during the evening service.

A couple of questions arise when considering the reading of the law
during the worship service. First, is the reading of the law a demand of the

---

38   Herman Hanko, "Our Order of Worship," *Standard Bearer* 60, no. 17 (June 1, 1984):393.

regulative principle? Second, what is the purpose of reading the ten commandments during worship? Professor Hanko answers both questions:

> This particular element in the liturgy of the worship service does not have direct Scriptural sanction. The inclusion (or exclusion) of the reading of the law, therefore, is not absolutely required, and the determination concerning whether or not it should be included lies in the area of Christian liberty. The decision to include it must be decided on other grounds than direct Scriptural injunction.
>
> What purpose does the reading of the law serve? The answer to this question will determine both whether it should be included, and, if it is included, what place it should occupy in the order of worship.
>
> Our fathers have maintained that the purpose of reading the law is threefold: 1) It is read to remind us of God's absolute sovereignty over our lives; 2) It is read to serve as a mirror for our misery—according to the teaching of our Heidelberg Catechism in Lord's Day 2: "Whence knowest thou thy misery? Out of the law of God"; 3) It is read to remind us of the truth that the law is the rule of gratitude of God's people who have been delivered from sin through the blood of Christ—according to the teaching of our Heidelberg Catechism in Lord's Day 32–44, where the detailed discussion of the law of God and its significance for our lives is placed under the general subject of "gratitude."[39]

### Recitation of the Apostles' Creed

During the evening service, after the first psalter number, the congregation remains standing and recites the Apostles' Creed in unison. Until 2014 the congregation was seated while the minister read the creed. It is interesting to note that at its February 24, 1971, meeting, the consistory took a decision with grounds not to recite the Apostles' Creed in unison.

As the reading of the law is not expressly commanded in scripture,

---

39  Herman Hanko, "Our Order of Worship," *Standard Bearer* 60, no. 15 (May 1, 1984):342.

so also the recitation of the Apostles' Creed is not expressly commanded. At the time the scriptures were being written, creeds had not been formulated. Whether or not we make use of creeds in our worship is a matter of Christian liberty.

What reasons do we have for reciting the Apostles' Creed during our evening service? What about the other creeds, such as the Nicene Creed, which occasionally are read during special worship services? Again, Professor Hanko gives the answer to these questions when he writes that "the unity of the church of Christ is a unity of *faith*."

> This faith which unites the church must come to verbal expression: "For with the heart man believeth unto righteousness; and with the mouth confession is made unto salvation" (Rom. 10:10). When the church comes together in worship—when in a worship service we have an earthly manifestation of the body of Christ—then nothing could be more in keeping with this characteristic of the church than that she together confesses her faith.[40]

### Congregational Prayer

After the Apostles' Creed has been recited and the second psalter number sung, the congregation again is seated and the sanctuary becomes silent. Now it is time for the minister to lead the congregation into the presence of God in prayer.

John Calvin gives biblical warrant for the importance of congregational prayer during worship.

> Moreover, that the common prayers of the church may not be held in contempt, God of old adorned them with shining titles, especially when he called the temple the "house of prayer" [Isa. 56:7; Matt. 21:13]. For he taught by this term that the chief part of his worship lies in the office of prayer, and that the temple was

---

40 Herman Hanko, "Our Order of Worship," *Standard Bearer* 60, no. 16 (May 15, 1984):368.

set up like a banner for believers so that they might, with one consent, participate in it. A distinctive promise was also added: "Praise waits for thee, O God, in Zion, and to thee shall the vow be performed" [Ps. 65:1, Comm.]. By these words the prophet intimates that the prayers of the church are never ineffectual, for God always furnishes his people occasion for singing with joy.[41]

Later, in talking of the use of the tongue, Calvin writes,

Moreover, since the glory of God ought, in a measure, to shine in the several parts of our bodies, it is especially fitting that the tongue has been assigned and destined for this task, both through singing and through speaking. For it was peculiarly created to tell and proclaim the praise of God. But the chief use of the tongue is in public prayers, which are offered in the assembly of believers, by which it comes about that with one common voice, and as it were, with the same mouth, we all glorify God together, worshiping him with one spirit and the same faith. And we do this openly, that all men mutually, each one from his brother, may receive the confession of faith and be invited and prompted by his example.[42]

We must remember that worship is consciously entering into conversation with God. Through prayer we speak to God as the minister leads the congregation in prayer. Professor Hanko writes of the elements that ought to be included in every congregational prayer. Each prayer ought to be "adapted to leading the congregation consciously into the presence of God." This means that the congregation knows "that our only access to the throne of God's grace is through the blood of our heavenly Mediator, Jesus Christ our Lord." "Thanksgiving and praise" must be brought to God for all he has given us, and he "alone is worthy of all praise and glory."

Further, in congregational prayer we must confess our sins, not only

---

41  Calvin, *Institutes*, 3.20.29, 21:892–93.
42  Calvin, *Institutes*, 3.20.31, 21:894–95.

as individuals, but also as a congregation, recognizing our corporate responsibility. In confessing our sins, we must seek forgiveness. The congregational prayer must include "the needs of the congregation in the hour of worship," asking "grace for the minister" and that the congregation may submit to God's word. Because of suffering, persecution, discipline, poverty, and various threats that face the congregation, "the minister must be spiritually sensitive to these needs and bring them before God." Also aware that the congregation is part of a denomination and part of the church of God scattered over the whole world, the minister must remember in the congregational prayer the needs of "the whole of Christendom."[43]

## Offerings

When the congregational prayer is finished, the minister announces the causes for which offerings will be collected, and four deacons rise to distribute the collection baskets. That offerings are to be included in the worship is plain from a number of scriptural passages. Perhaps the most memorable Old Testament passage is Exodus 25:1–9, where God commanded Moses to take an "offering" of the people in order to gather the necessary items for the construction of the tabernacle. Later God commanded Moses to tell the people, "Let neither man nor woman make any more work for the offering of the sanctuary. So the people were restrained from bringing. For the stuff they had was sufficient for all the work to make it, and too much" (Ex. 36:5–7).

During the days of King Josiah of Judah, the temple badly needed repair. "At the king's commandment they made a chest, and set it without at the gate of the house of the Lord. And they made a proclamation through Judah and Jerusalem, to bring in to the Lord the collection that Moses the servant of God laid upon Israel in the wilderness" (2 Chron. 24:8–9). Offerings were still collected in the same manner during Jesus' time (Mark 12:41–44).

The apostle Paul instructed the Corinthian church to take collections "for the saints" on the "first day of the week" (1 Cor. 16:1–4). These

---

43    Herman Hanko, "Our Order of Worship," *Standard Bearer* 62, no. 1 (October 1, 1985):9. All of the quotations relating to congregational prayer are taken from this article.

collections for poor saints in Jerusalem (Acts 11:27–30) were to be taken on the day that the New Testament church gathered in worship. In the Form for Ordination of Elders and Deacons the minister exhorts the congregation to "provide the deacons with good means to assist the indigent." The rich are urged to "be charitable" and "give liberally."[44] Obviously these references to giving refer to collections for the benevolent fund that are taken in Hope church during the Sunday morning worship services.

Because these collections are taken during the worship services, our giving is an act of worship. Perhaps some may argue that giving to the poor is the only cause to which we should give during the worship service. Professor Hanko answers this objection:

> Sometimes a distinction is made between giving to the benevolent fund [and] giving to support the church, which is usually done by the "budget"...Only the giving for benevolence is really considered *giving* in the true sense of the word, while giving for the other causes of God's kingdom is considered as bills which we are obligated to pay in the same way as we are required to pay for our groceries or car repairs or home repairs. But the Scriptures make no such distinctions. Everything which is contributed for the cause of the gospel and for the purpose of the advancement of the kingdom of Christ as manifested here in the world is considered giving. This is especially clear in the Old Testament where the tithes which were brought by the people were used for the support of the priests and Levites, for the needed repairs of the temple, for the purchase of sacrifices, etc., as well as for the care of the poor.[45]

Over the years, Hope's consistory has taken a number of decisions relating to incidental matters of the offertory. At the January 6, 1923, consistory meeting, a decision was made to have a silent offertory. At

---

44  Form for Ordination of Elders and Deacons, in *Confessions and Church Order*, 293.

45  Herman Hanko, "Our Order of Worship," *Standard Bearer* 61, no. 4 (November 15, 1984):81–82.

the August 10, 1926, meeting, it was decided to discontinue silent collections. Professor Hanko recalls that during his first pastorate in Hope that "collections were taken during the singing of a Psalm. So far as I know, this practice was common throughout the churches. But this has changed so that now almost all, if not all, of our churches have what is called 'Offertory.'"[46]

## Scripture Reading

After the offertory and the singing of another psalter number, the congregation is seated and the minister announces the passage of scripture from which he will read. Not reading the Bible during the worship service would be unimaginable to us. However, this was the case prior to the Reformation, when the Roman Catholic Church dominated. The reformers saw to it that scripture was returned to the central place in the worship of God.

> The Reformers found that the early church followed the pattern of the synagogue in reading the Scripture *lectio continua*, that is, sequential readings, picking up each week where one left off the previous week, with the exhortation or sermon arising out of the reading (Neh. 8:5–8ff.; Luke 4:16–27; Acts 13:14; 15:21; 1 Tim. 4:13; cf. Acts 5:42; 6:2, 4). The apostle Paul wrote, "Until I come, give attention to the public reading of Scripture, to exhortation and teaching" (1 Tim. 4:13). [Quotation from the NASB]
>
> "The public reading" is literally "the reading." Apparently the practice of reading Scripture was widely known and could be referred to in this general way. "Exhortation and teaching" follow upon the reading. The Reformers found further *lectio continua* reading and preaching in the works of Origen (c. 185–c. 254), Augustine (343–430), Chrysostom (c. 347–407), Jerome (c. 343–420), and others.[47]

---

46  Ibid., 82.
47  Terry L. Johnson, *Tributes to John Calvin: A Celebration of His Quincentenary*, ed. David W. Hall (Phillipsburg, NJ: P & R Publishing Company, 2010), 125.

It is no accident that a large open Bible sits on the pulpit in Hope's sanctuary. Nor is it an accident that the pulpit is front and center on the platform in the front of church. This is as it should be. God's word is central in our worship and determines every aspect of our worship.

For all of our history as a congregation and denomination we have used the King James Version of the Bible. Rev. Wilbur Bruinsma gives two of the most important reasons that we insist on using the King James Version:

> There are two reasons we believe the King James Version is faithful and accurate. First, it is based upon what is known as the *Received Text*. The *Received Text* is based on hundreds of manuscripts that were "received" or approved by the church for centuries. Yet, with the exception of three or four modern versions of the Bible, all modern translations of the Bible are mostly based upon 10 to 20 percent of these manuscripts that omit or change thousands of words in the Bible. This is one reason we believe the King James Version is faithful and accurate. It is based on the majority of the old Hebrew and Greek manuscripts.
>
> The second reason...is that the translators of this version were committed to "verbal inspiration." This terminology simply means that God moved holy men to record word for word in the Bible exactly what He had chosen to make known to us. Because the translators of the KJV believed in verbal inspiration, they were careful in their attempt to make, as much as possible, an accurate translation of all the words found in the original languages.
>
> The vast majority of modern versions are translated by men who believe that God only inspired the thoughts of men but not the words they wrote. In other words, they believe that men recorded in their own words their inspired thoughts. For that reason, these translators have no problem adding or subtracting words from the Bible, or worse, rewording an entire phrase or sentence to express what they think the writers of the Bible meant. This has resulted in many inaccuracies, omissions, and even doctrinal errors in the translation. Since our churches

maintain the truth of verbal inspiration we believe the King James Version truly remains a faithful version of the Bible.[48]

### The Sermon

During the morning service, after the minister has finished reading scripture, he reads the portion of the Heidelberg Catechism on which he will base his sermon. During the evening service, after a passage has been read and the particular text on which the sermon is based is reread, the minister begins his sermon.

Without question, the preaching of the word is the central element of our worship. Through the preaching God meets with us and speaks to us. Professor Hanko writes,

> I want to emphasize the point that when the gospel is preached in the midst of the church of Christ, a profound miracle takes place. This needs emphasis lest we fall into the error of making light of the preaching and considering it of only relative value to us.
>
> At the very heart of this miracle of preaching lies the truth that through the preaching God comes to meet with His people in covenant fellowship…
>
> God comes to His people in the preaching of the Word to dwell with them in covenant fellowship. He speaks to His people through Christ and by the Spirit of Christ within their hearts. And, in this speech of God to His people, there is the fullness of the unity of the covenant. God's people listen; and listening, they bow in worship and respond in praise and in prayer confessing their God as the God of their salvation. The covenant comes to realization in these worship services where God's Word is preached.[49]

---

48  Wilbur Bruinsma, "Why We Read from the King James Bible" (Pittsburgh, PA: Protestant Reformed Fellowship of Pittsburgh, n.d.), unnumbered pages.

49  Herman Hanko, "The Importance of Preaching," *Standard Bearer* 43, no. 18 (July 1, 1967):414.

## Children Present

It is important that old and young, including little children, be present in the worship services to hear the preaching of the word. The Form for the Administration of Baptism lists three biblical passages that emphasize God's covenant with parents and their children. First, in Genesis 17:7 we read, "I will establish my covenant between me and thee *and thy seed after thee in their generations* for an everlasting covenant, to be a God unto thee, and to *thy seed after thee*" (emphasis added). Second, the Form refers to Acts 2:39: "For the promise is unto you, and *to your children*, and to all that are afar off, even as many as the Lord our God shall call" (emphasis added). Third, reference is made to Mark 10:13–16. Jesus said to his disciples who had "rebuked" parents who tried to bring their children to him, "Suffer the little children to come unto me, and forbid them not: for of such is the kingdom of God." Jesus then proceeded to take the little children "up in his arms, put his hands upon them, and blessed them."

We ought never to minimize how the Holy Spirit works in the hearts of our children through the preaching of the word. Perhaps most of us have very early memories of our parents bringing us to church.

> "My earliest memory of an unusual worship service is the preaching of Prof. George Ophoff as a guest minister on a Sunday morning. Such was his vehemence in preaching that, as a small boy of a few years old, I was terrified. Ophoff reduced me to tears on my father's lap."[50] —Prof. David Engelsma

Professor Engelsma also recalls the time Rev. Herman Hoeksema came to preach at Hope church during the height of the controversy of 1953. This was a rare occurrence, because Rev. Hoeksema almost never preached at Hope. The congregation expected Rev. Hoeksema to address the controversy over the covenant in his sermon.

---

50   David Engelsma, email message to Aaron J. Cleveland on May 30, 2015.

In those days, the order of worship was the reading of Scripture before the congregational prayer. The chapter was Ephesians 4. Verse 14 of the chapter reads: "That we henceforth be no more children, tossed to and fro, and carried about with every wind of doctrine, by the sleight of men, and cunning craftiness, whereby they lie in wait to deceive." Although there was no announcement of the text in the bulletin (Hoeksema was a visiting preacher) and although Hoeksema did not reveal his text before reading the chapter, I knew without any doubt, as did everyone else in the audience, the text he intended to preach—verse 14, a warning against being carried about with every wind of doctrine, that is, the doctrine of a conditional covenant.

After the congregational prayer, the collection, and the singing of another psalm, the remarkable, memorable thing happened. Hoeksema came to the pulpit, looked us over, and said this: "I had intended when I came here tonight to preach on verse 14 of Ephesians 4, because of the present serious troubles in our churches. But I have changed my mind. There are so many children and young people in the Hope congregation that I have decided that my sermon on Ephesians 4:14 would not be fitting. Therefore, I am going to preach a different sermon."

Whereupon he read a brief passage from John 10 and preached a sermon on Jesus as the good shepherd. There was not a word in the sermon about conditions, or a conditional covenant…

In the midst of struggle over everything he believed, worked for, suffered for, and built, he showed a shepherd's concern for the children and young people of the Hope congregation.[51]

## Preaching as a Command

As a result of the Protestant Reformed Churches' rejection of the theory of common grace, our view of the character of preaching is vastly different than that of most Reformed churches. In the first point of common

---

51   David Engelsma, "I Remember Herman Hoeksema: Personal Remembrances of a Great Man (4)," *Beacon Lights* 63, no. 1 (January 2009):21.

grace, the Christian Reformed Church, and all those who subscribe to its version of common grace, maintains what the first point calls "the general offer of the Gospel." Herman Hoeksema defined the general offer of the first point thus: "In the preaching of the Gospel God is graciously inclined and bestows grace upon all the hearers. Or, still more briefly: The preaching of the Gospel is grace to all."[52]

In 1953 one of Hope's elders, Richard Newhouse, figured prominently in the rejection of a conditional covenant. Included in that rejection is the denial that the preaching of the gospel is a general promise on God's part to save all men. The well-meant offer of 1924 and the general promise of 1953 are intimately related. Both have to do with the character of preaching. Both make faith a condition. In the words of Professor Hanko, "Both, in making faith a condition, also make faith the work of man. God, in the work of salvation, depends upon man's choice to believe."[53]

When the preaching is viewed as an offer and not a command, the content of preaching is affected. The history of our mother church in the decades following 1924 proves this point. Professor Hanko writes,

> The Christian Reformed Church is in the throes of a controversy at present [1967] concerning the content of the preaching. But this controversy has a long and sad history which began in 1924. Then the Christian Reformed Church spoke rather emphatically of the character of the preaching, and insisted that the preaching was (as far as its most formal aspect was concerned) an offer. It was described as a general and well-meant offer to all who came under it. This is a key modification of the true essence of preaching; and it is not surprising that over the years the content has been altered culminating in the controversy raging today. The content has become (completely in keeping with the idea of "offer") a statement on the part of

---

52  Hoeksema, *Protestant Reformed Churches in America*, 322; see also Herman Hoeksema and Herman Hanko, *Ready to Give an Answer: A Catechism of Reformed Distinctives* (Grandville, MI: Reformed Free Publishing Association, 1997), 77–78.

53  Hoeksema and Hanko, *Ready to Give an Answer*, 198.

God in which God expresses His desire to save all men. This is implied necessarily in an offer. And it ought not to surprise us a great deal that the swirling debate which goes on today in that church has its roots in 1924. The content of the preaching is an expression of God in which He speaks of His love for all men, a love which is revealed in a universal cross of Christ upon which cross Christ died for all men...

It is essential therefore that we take a sharp and uncompromising stand against all this to preserve our heritage.

Indeed the character of the preaching determines the content. In the preaching God comes to His elect people through Christ and by the operation of the Spirit. He comes to work salvation through the preaching—a salvation which He has determined for them from all eternity and which is accomplished on the cross. Sovereignly He works accomplishing His purpose so that He faithfully gathers, defends and preserves His church unto the end of time.[54]

That God throughout our history has preserved in our midst a proper understanding of the character of preaching, and in that way the proper content of preaching, ought to move us to profound gratitude to him. God has used faithful preaching from the pulpit of Hope church to gather believers and their seed over many generations. That we continue to hear faithful preaching is a manifestation of God's covenantal faithfulness.

## Distinctive and Polemical Preaching

Within the sphere of the covenant, the preaching of the word from week to week must be both "*distinctive*" and "*up-building*." Prof. Homer Hoeksema writes about these two attributes of preaching:

a.  It cannot proceed on the basis that all children are elect and regenerated.

---

54  Herman Hanko, "The Importance of Preaching," *Standard Bearer* 43, no. 18 (July 1, 1967):415.

b. Preaching must be so distinctive that through it the elect are converted and strengthened, while the reprobate cannot remain but will reveal themselves as haters of the truth of God and His Christ.[55]

When preaching is distinctive, God uses it as one of the keys to open and shut the kingdom of heaven.[56] Rev. Hoeksema understood this well during times of controversy in his pastorates. His daughter writes of his pastorate at Fourteenth Street Christian Reformed Church.

I can understand now something he used to say about the preaching of the word being one of the keys of the kingdom: it was a matter of strengthening the faith of some and of being uncompromising in the preaching of the truth, so that the preaching was so unpalatable that the opposition would leave. The preaching would be strong, even stronger as the objections increased, so that he would "preach them out of the church"— or they would change and believe the truth that was preached. That is what happened at Fourteenth Street: the strong became stronger; the weak left. It was the exercise of the keys of the kingdom.[57]

Distinctive, polemical sermons are part of the history of worship at Hope church. Professor Engelsma recalls the tense church services during the early 1950s:

My vivid memories of unusual events in worship and in connection with worship stem from the early 1950s when the Protestant Reformed Churches were in the throes of a serious internal controversy, which would issue in schism in 1953. I was eleven in 1950, but the memories of that time and its events are clear and powerful to this day.

---

55  Homer Hoeksema, *Dogmatics Outlines, Locus 5: Ecclesiology*, chap. 6 (Grandville, MI: Theological School of the Protestant Reformed Churches, 1975), 2.

56  Heidelberg Catechism Q&A 83, in *Confessions and Church Order*, 118.

57  Lois E. Kregel, *Just Dad: Stories of Herman Hoeksema* (Jenison, MI: Reformed Free Publishing Association, 2014), 41–42.

Sermons were polemical. Drilled into the head and heart of an eleven-year-old boy was that the doctrine of a conditional covenant and salvation is false doctrine, and that the churches were threatened by this doctrine. Many sermons, perhaps most, contained at least a warning about a conditional covenant.

At the height of the controversy in early 1953, Professor Ophoff preached in Hope church a fiery sermon on the unconditionality of the covenant. After the conclusion of the service, members of the congregation who were not so sure of the heretical nature of the doctrine of a conditional covenant and who disliked such a strong sermon against the conditional covenant attempted to address Ophoff on the church grounds, outside the building. Standing in front of Ophoff (I can visualize the scene still), like a guard, was the little elder, Richard Newhouse. Newhouse took up the defense. Ophoff remained silent.[58]

## Heidelberg Catechism Preaching

The tradition at Hope church is that the morning sermon is based on a Lord's Day of the Heidelberg Catechism. Article 68 of the Church Order requires that "the ministers shall on Sunday explain briefly the sum of Christian doctrine comprehended in the Heidelberg Catechism, so that as much as possible the explanation shall be annually completed, according to the division of the catechism itself for that purpose."[59] Heidelberg Catechism preaching has been a Reformed tradition since the Synod of Dordrecht in 1618–19 adopted the Church Order. In times of apostasy, churches abandoned the principles of church government set forth in the Church Order. During times of reformation, such as the Secession of 1834 and the reformation of 1886 led by Abraham Kuyper, "the Church Order of Dordrecht was reaffirmed."[60] Obviously, faithful weekly catechism preaching will be found in churches that affirm the Church Order and that are faithful to Reformation principles.

---

58  David Engelsma, email message to Aaron J. Cleveland on May 30, 2015.
59  Church Order 68, in *Confessions and Church Order*, 399.
60  Introduction to the Church Order, in ibid., 376.

The question is often asked, should the minister base his catechism sermons on certain texts and passages of scripture or on the Catechism itself? Throughout the history of the Protestant Reformed Churches a consistent answer to this question has been given. Perhaps it is best summarized in the writings of Rev. Hoeksema and his son Prof. Homer Hoeksema, both teachers of homiletics in the Protestant Reformed seminary for many decades.

> In view of the fact that increasingly this practice [Catechism preaching] is neglected in many churches, and in view of the fact that many ministers try in various ways to evade this duty, it is not amiss that we stress that the minister must preach on the Heidelberg Catechism itself, and must in his preaching expound the Catechism. He must not preach on a text from Scripture and merely refer to the Catechism in the course of his sermon. He must not merely preach on the truth on which the Catechism touches in a particular Lord's Day. But he must preach on the Catechism itself. He must read the Lord's Day as he reads his text before the sermon, and then he must proceed to preach a sermon on that Lord's Day. Anything less than this cannot properly be called Catechism preaching...The minister must not forget to leave the impression with the congregation that even in Catechism preaching he administers the Word of God. This is not the place to argue the question whether Heidelberg Catechism preaching is indeed ministry of the Word. Here we proceed on the assumption that it is undoubtedly ministry of the Word. But we make the point that this ought to be explicit in the preaching. It is a good custom, therefore, that at the beginning of the sermon the minister quotes a few pertinent texts and points the congregation to them as the basis of the instruction contained in the particular Lord's Day on which he is preaching.[61]

---

61  Herman Hoeksema and Homer C. Hoeksema, *Homiletics* (Grandville, MI: Theological School of the Protestant Reformed Churches, 1975), 42–43.

Faithful, weekly Heidelberg Catechism preaching is a great blessing in the church of Christ. First, when the Catechism is properly preached, "we may be assured that the whole counsel of God is preached and no doctrines are forgotten. Ministers are forgetful and one-sided, and, if they are not required to preach on the Heidelberg Catechism, many doctrines would be left untreated."[62] Regularly we hear in the preaching an explanation of all the important doctrines of scripture. In hearing these doctrines regularly, our doctrinal heritage is passed on from one generation to the next.

Second, Catechism preaching is an expression of our oneness with the church of all ages. "We and our children must recognize that our fathers believed, lived, and confessed the same truths we do. There is one Christ Jesus, one God, one faith, and one church of Christ in all ages of time and found in all the world. The Heidelberg Catechism holds before us that one faith!"[63]

Third, we are living in the days of the great "falling away" that precede the rise of antichrist (2 Thess. 2:3). Churches that once stood firm upon the Reformed confessions are now openly hostile to them. Catechism preaching has long been lost among them. Their youth are no longer catechized. Their members grow up doctrinally illiterate. Why is this? Because God has not given them "the love of the truth" (2 Thess. 2:10), they have rejected the preaching of sound doctrine. Upon this darkening background of apostasy we ought to be thankful that God continues to use the means of Catechism preaching to preserve us in a love of his truth.

## Series Preaching

Another practice that emerged from the Reformation was that of preaching through whole books of the Bible. As mentioned earlier, the reformers found *lectio continua* (reading scripture in sequence over a period of time) in the writings of the early church fathers. Out of the

---

62  Marvin Kamps, *Heidelberg Catechism Preaching: Our Reformed Heritage* (Wyoming, MI: Southwest Protestant Reformed Church Evangelism Committee, 1987), 12.

63  Ibid., 13.

sequential reading of scripture arose the sermons. Both Calvin and Zwingli regularly preached through whole books of the Bible. Today this is referred to as "series preaching." There are advantages to both the pastor and congregation in this method of preaching.

For the pastor the advantages are:

First, after having selected a book to preach, one's work is determined for the next several weeks, and maybe for more than three or four months, thus eliminating much wasted time and frustration. Secondly, it would give opportunity for in-depth study of the particular book in the light of all Scripture. Thirdly, it would help the pastor to understand better the historical redemptive character of Scripture.[64]

The benefits for the congregation include:

First, the congregation would have opportunity to study the book and the particular passage throughout the week. I believe that home Bible study, by the head of the house, is a must, especially in our day of gross apostasy. Second, the congregation would learn very well the unity of Scripture, as one book is expounded in the light of all of Scripture; and they would be exposed concretely to the developmental character of revelation. Third, they would better come to understand the concept of organic inspiration, as God's use of the "secondary author" would constantly come into focus in the explanation of the book...

It should be obvious that to preach through long historical books of the Old Testament should not be attempted in one long endeavor. Yet one can treat sections of these books very profitably.[65]

As well as series preaching, in a large congregation such as Hope, many opportunities arise for the pastor to preach on various passages

---

64  Marvin Kamps, "Series Preaching," *Protestant Reformed Theological Journal* 24, no. 2 (April 1, 1991):7.

65  Ibid., 7–8.

of scripture. When the sacrament of baptism is administered, the pastor has a good opportunity to preach a sermon focused on the rearing of covenantal children. Before the sacrament of the Lord's supper is administered, preparatory sermons focused on self-examination are preached. During the evening services after the Lord's supper, applicatory sermons are preached, giving the pastor the opportunity to preach on the sanctified walk of the believer who has been washed in the blood of Christ. The occasion of public confession of faith gives the pastor the opportunity to preach on passages related to our antithetical confession and walk in the midst of this sinful world. During different times of the year, for example Christmas and Easter, passages telling of Jesus' birth and suffering can be expounded.

## The Sacraments

Intimately connected to the preaching of the word is the administration of the sacraments, holy baptism and the Lord's supper. The Heidelberg Catechism makes the inseparable connection between the preaching and the sacraments. The Holy Ghost "works faith in our hearts by the preaching of the gospel, and confirms it by the use of the sacraments." The sacraments "more fully declare and seal to us the promise of the gospel." "The Holy Ghost teaches us in the gospel, and assures us by the sacraments."[66] It is obvious from these quotations that the sacraments are to be administered along with the preaching of the word during the corporate worship of the church on the Lord's day.

Article 56 of the Church Order states, "The covenant of God shall be sealed unto the children of Christians by baptism, as soon as the administration thereof is feasible, *in the public assembly when the Word of God is preached.*"[67] Regarding the Lord's supper, article 64 of the Church Order states, "The administration of the Lord's Supper shall take place only where there is supervision of elders, according to the ecclesiastical order, *and in a public gathering of the congregation.*"[68]

---

66  Heidelberg Catechism A 65–67, in *Confessions and Church Order*, 108.
67  Church Order 56, in ibid., 397; emphasis added.
68  Church Order 64, in ibid., 399; emphasis added.

The sacraments are properly administered only when joined with the preaching of the word, in the public gathering of the congregation, and under the supervision of the elders. All three of these requirements must be met. Rev. Ophoff writes,

> Also the administration of the Lord's Supper and the official preaching of the gospel by teaching ministry instituted by Christ are inseparable, and this for two reasons. As baptism, so the Lord's Supper, it is a dead symbol and therefore by itself mute. It only speaks with the gospel as preached imposed upon it. Secondly, Christ instituted in His church the teaching ministry for the edification of His people, the establishing of His covenant among them and the gathering of His church. Now the gospel as officially preached and the administration of the Lord's Supper are the divinely ordained instruments for the achievement of this purpose. Hence, the two belong together and are inseparable. Therefore if the official preaching of the gospel must take place on the meetings for public worship, then also the official administration of the Lord's Supper.[69]

The preaching of the word that we hear from week to week is in perfect harmony with the contents of both the baptism and Lord's supper forms. Sovereign election and reprobation is preached. Just as the preaching proclaims that election governs the covenant, so does the baptism form. Professor Engelsma writes,

> The form makes plain that election governs the covenant with regard to the salvation of the children of believers. For one thing, the salvation of infants can be ascribed to nothing else but God's gracious election. Infants are not only incapable of performing any act upon which their salvation might depend (they are completely oblivious to what is happening in the administration of the holy sacrament), but are also by nature guilty and totally depraved. God saves our infants according to

---

69  G. M. Ophoff, quoted in "Supervision in the Lord's Supper," *Standard Bearer* 38, no. 2 (October 15, 1961):44.

his covenant promise, which is founded exclusively upon his eternal election.

Election governs the covenant in this important respect, that election determines and accomplishes God's reception of the infant children of believers unto grace in Christ, that is, the salvation of these infants, in their infancy.

It is certainly nothing in the children themselves that determines their salvation in the covenant, for they are "partakers of the condemnation of Adam."

It is certainly no condition performed by the children that determines their salvation in the covenant, for when they are received by God again into grace in Christ, they are *infants*.[70]

Just as the preaching of the word along with Christian discipline is used by the elders to guard the table of the Lord, so is the preaching in harmony with the Lord's supper form. In the preaching the command of Christ goes out proclaiming that "those who under the name of Christians maintain doctrines, or practices inconsistent therewith, and will not, after having been often brotherly admonished, renounce their errors and wicked course of life," are "forbidden the use of the sacraments."[71] The Lord's supper form assumes faithful preaching and discipline. All of us are familiar with the long list of sins in the form that make one, "according to the command of Christ and the apostle Paul,"[72] an unworthy partaker of the Lord's supper.

In Hope's history, the consistory has made a number of decisions relating to the administration of the Lord's supper. At its January 6, 1923, meeting, the consistory decided that the examination part of the Lord's supper form would be read the Sunday before communion. How long this practice continued is not recorded. In 1952 the consistory brought a proposal to the December 10 congregational meeting to have individual communion cups. At the meeting an amendment was

---

70  David Engelsma, *Covenant and Election in the Reformed Tradition* (Jenison, MI: Reformed Free Publishing Association, 2011), 34–35.
71  Heidelberg Catechism A 85, in *Confessions and Church Order*, 119.
72  Form for the Administration of the Lord's Supper, in ibid, 269.

moved to leave the choice and quality of the set purchased to the judg-ment of the consistory. The amendment carried as well as the motion to institute individual cups.

At the January 1953 consistory meeting, a decision was made to read scripture or sing a psalter number during the distribution of the bread and wine. At the September 10, 1959, meeting, a decision was made to include pouring out of wine as a part of the communion service.

## Public Confession of Faith

Another event that takes place from time to time during our wor-ship services is public confession of faith. We may question why this is incorporated into the worship service. There are two reasons. First, as article 61 of the Church Order states, no one may be admitted to the Lord's supper unless he or she has made public confession of the "Reformed religion."[73] Public confession of faith is very much a part of the elders' supervision of the Lord's supper. Upon approval of the consistory, when confession of faith is made in the presence of the con-gregation, all of the members of the church know that the confessing individual is a worthy partaker of the Lord's supper.

Second, when we read the three questions asked at public confes-sion of faith, we immediately see that they are eminently suited for the public worship of God. All of us as individuals must answer yes every time these questions are asked of those making public confession. I must answer yes that I believe that I belong to this "Christian church" because I believe this church teaches the "true and complete doctrine of salvation." I must answer yes that I adhere to this doctrine, I "reject all heresies repugnant thereto," and promise to lead a "new, godly life." I must answer yes that I will submit to "church government" should I become delinquent.[74] In answering yes to these questions, those mak-ing public confession, along with the entire congregation, worship God.

---

73  Church Order 61, in ibid., 398.
74  Public Confession of Faith, in ibid., 266.

## Conclusion

Having completed an examination of the various elements of our worship, there are a couple of attributes about worship worth noticing. First is the *simplicity* of our worship. There is nothing "showy" that draws our attention from the pure worship of God. Our sanctuary is plain (ugly, some may argue), with no stained glass windows, ornate decorations, or physical symbolism. Our order of worship is uncomplicated and free from the clutter of ceremonies, performances, and empty rituals not commanded in God's word.

Closely related to this is the *reverence* that characterizes our worship. Throughout the whole service there is the awareness that we are in the presence of God. The best behavior of old and young, including little children, is exhibited. Joking and laughter are out of place. Solemn orderliness prevails.

In Ecclesiastes 5:1–2 we read, "Keep thy foot when thou goest to the house of God, and be more ready to hear, than to give the sacrifice of fools: for they consider not that they do evil. Be not rash with thy mouth, and let not thine heart be hasty to utter any thing before God: for God is in heaven, and thou upon earth: therefore let thy words be few." That we, as insignificant creatures of dust, have the privilege to truly worship the holy God of heaven and earth is a gift of his grace. In his covenantal faithfulness he has given us the gift of the public worship of him. John Calvin, commenting on David's grief at being denied access to the tabernacle (Ps. 84:2–3), writes that David's "trouble, vexation, and sorrow" are "surely...because believers have no greater help than public worship, for by it God raises his own folk upward step by step."[75] Perhaps we cannot know the bitterness of being denied the privilege of publicly worshiping God, as David was, until we have actually experienced it.

How seriously do we take this gift of being able every week to gather with fellow saints to worship God as he has commanded in his word? Can we, from the heart, sing the fourth stanza of psalter 380,

---

75   Calvin, *Institutes*, 4.1.5, 21:1019.

entitled "Remembrance of Church Privileges"? "Yea, let my tongue, I pray, all silent be, / If I do not alway remember thee; / If I prefer not thee, though in thy grief, / Above all other joys my very chief."[76]

The church fathers of Hope were willing to suffer for righteousness' sake in order to maintain true worship. Our first pastor, Rev. Ophoff, refused to sign the three points of common grace. He and many members of our congregation lost their place in the Christian Reformed Church, lost their place of worship, and suffered financial hardship. By their refusing to compromise doctrinally, pure worship was maintained.

In 1953 one of our elders, Richard Newhouse, played a key role in defense of God's unconditional covenant of grace and the condemnation of a general promise in the preaching of the gospel. This stand involved suffering on the part of many members of Hope congregation. Families were divided, friendships were broken up, and financial sacrifice was required. By God's grace, our spiritual fathers showed themselves "worthy" of Christ (Matt. 10:32–39).

As we continue to go forward as the congregation of Hope Protestant Reformed Church and as we desire to bring to God pleasing worship, let us remember Jesus' promise to his disciples in Matthew 10:32–33, 38–39.

32. Whosoever therefore shall confess me before men, him will I confess also before my Father which is in heaven.
33. But whosoever shall deny me before men, him will I also deny before my Father which is in heaven.
38. He that taketh not his cross, and followeth after me, is not worthy of me.
39. He that findeth his life shall lose it: and he that loseth his life for my sake shall find it.

---

76  No. 380:4, in *The Psalter*.

Congregation of Hope after a morning worship service in April 2016

Members in alphabetical order are assigned to worship in the basement each week.

What we all knew is confirmed: John Van Baren will do whatever it takes
to get a good picture. Thanks to some excellent photo editing, the ladder on which
John stood to take the pictures of the congregation has disappeared.

Chapter 11

─────⟨ෙ⟩─────

# The Responsibilities
# and Privileges of
# Membership at Hope

*Jeffrey Kalsbeek*

I have manifested thy name unto the men which thou gavest me out of the world...and they have kept thy word. And the glory which thou gavest me I have given them; that they may be one. —John 17:6, 22

## The Meaning

GOD POSSESSED HIS CHURCH IN CHRIST FROM eternity. This church on the earth he continues to gather through time and history, by the mighty working of the Spirit of Jesus Christ, purposing to reveal himself as glorious. The church then is not brought into existence by men. God gathers his elect, uniting them to Christ and placing them in the earthly institution for the one great purpose that they "should be to the praise of his glory" (Eph.1:12).

This being the nature and purpose of the church explains why she is referred to as the bride of Christ. The bride is the "glory of" her husband (1 Cor. 11:7). The bride is also loved by her Husband. Her consciousness of his free, unconditional, and faithful love also stands in the service of the Bridegroom's glory.

Scripture often describes the church by another term, the body

475

of Christ. The organism has Christ as its one common life-principle. Directed by its Head, the congregation is equipped for the calling to show forth his glory. Christ's life flows into the members of his body by means of faith, and the invisible elect church becomes visible by its fruit, resulting in glory being given to Christ.

God's determination to use Hope congregation for this purpose is the explanation for her being given one hundred years of faithful existence. By showing his glories in the congregation, the Lord is faithfully keeping his promise to Christ: "I have made a covenant with my chosen, I have sworn unto David my servant, thy seed will I establish forever" (Ps. 89:3–4). Faithfulness to Christ means faithfulness to his people, who are his body. This is often true despite their unfaithfulness. In their own unique way the many failures, such as murmuring, doubts, sinful deeds, thanklessness, and pride, manifest another glory of God—his faithfulness in maintaining and strengthening such a people. "The Lord hath done great things for us; whereof we are glad" (Ps. 126:3).

There is a relationship between one's being brought into the invisible, universal body of Christ by faith and his or her membership in a church on earth. Elect members of Christ's body are sovereignly brought into such an earthly institution. Whether born into the congregation or gathered in adulthood, they recognize the presence of Christ and become convicted of the need and value of membership in his body manifested on the earth. By faith there is conviction that this is God's intention. "All those who...do not join themselves to it, act contrary to the ordinance of God."[1] His spiritual body comes to manifestation by his people's membership in instituted congregations. Christ's work brings individuals into an organism—his body. Christ, in speaking to Peter regarding the building of Christ's church, revealed the necessary and inseparable relation between membership in the church and one's place in heaven: "I will give unto thee the keys of the kingdom of heaven; and whatsoever thou shalt bind on earth shall be bound in heaven" (Matt. 16:19). Christ makes plain that his kingdom and the instituted church are synonymous.

---

1    Belgic Confession 28, in *Confessions and Church Order*, 61.

For the elect child of God, membership in the congregation is very really fellowship with Christ. This is an aspect of God's salvation of his people. While election and redemption are God's saving of his children from *without*, salvation *within* is his work by the Holy Spirit to personally unite them to Christ so there is a consciousness of Christ and an active seeking of him. Christ is found and experienced where true preaching is proclaimed. It is his voice. In Romans 10:13–14 the Lord reveals that he has tied salvation to this earthly means within the sphere of church membership: "Whosoever shall call upon the name of the Lord shall be saved...how shall they hear without a preacher?" Christ's work of salvation reaches even further when he sovereignly places his elect in the earthly institute. Paul, addressing a local, instituted congregation declared, "Now hath God *set the members* every one of them in the body, as it hath pleased him" (1 Cor. 12:18; emphasis added).

Membership must be in a true church. After recognizing the voice of one's Savior and Husband, love desires to be where his voice is most clearly heard. The Lord has not placed us in any church. He has given us *Reformed* church membership. On the basis of scripture and the confessions, we believe, and desire to confess with others of like faith, the sovereignty of God in the salvation of sinners by God's grace alone. We believe in God's particular grace, which follows from his sovereign grace. We believe in God's sovereignty over all things, from the rise and fall of nations to each hair of our heads. We recognize that this institute is where Christ has set his name.

Along with this Spirit-worked knowledge comes a zeal for the church as she is manifested in the earthly institution. There is a desire to abide in the truth and to continue to experience God's friendship while loving the covenantal people of God. There is a sense of urgency in representing his cause and rejecting the kingdom of man. Profound gratitude, revealed by devotion, characterizes those who have been so blessed. The products of God's grace manifest his glory. The brightness of his attributes shine through in great splendor.

## The Importance

Most important in church membership is manifesting the glory of God as his representatives on the earth who are joined to the church militant. The Lord ensures this by drawing, with irresistible grace, his elect into this church. One hundred years of elect believers' exercising membership in Hope congregation is a visible testimony to the power of God's grace. On display is the fulfillment of God's covenantal promise to call his children out of Satan's kingdom, by working enmity against it, and to bring them into the kingdom of his dear Son. This important testimony not only explains why an instituted church is unceasingly assaulted by Satan and his fallen angels, but also is the reason "the gates of hell shall not prevail against it" (Matt. 16:18).

Due to our frailty the Lord also purposed membership in the church as the important means of preservation. Being characterized as sheep emphasizes that we are weak, foolish, often fearful, and spiritually vulnerable. Spiritual power comes from our Shepherd who provides his word and Spirit by means of officebearers. This is given also by the mutual exhortation and encouragement of fellow saints.

Importantly, God's covenant is experienced in the way of church membership. Just as a wife enjoys the blessings of her husband by abiding with him in the home, so enjoyment of the blessings of salvation comes through one's active membership in the congregation. There we experience our Husband, "God with us," Immanuel.

The importance of church membership needs emphasis in the present day due to its being minimized or even disparaged as sectarian. The spirit of the age shows disregard for church membership. This is manifested in doctrinal ignorance, disinterest in the goings on within the church, absence of faithful Sabbath observance, evil speaking against officebearers, and leaving the church due to personal grievances.

The Spirit of Christ is not like this and does not produce such members. Where the Spirit is working, there will be a desire to abide in the truth, a love for the covenantal people of God, respect for officebearers as Christ's servants, and proper spiritual resting on the Sabbath.

Abraham Kuyper is representative of the Reformed's regard for church membership: "You may not be indifferent about the visible church... The invisible church is contained within the visible, and flourishes only when the visible grows."[2]

Membership in a Reformed church is a blessing of great importance, and one that a believing child of God does not take lightly. It is where God covenants with his children and assures them that his bond of love will never be broken. This profoundly affects the child of God in every area of life. The "certainty of perseverance...is the real source of humility, filial reverence, true piety, patience in every tribulation, fervent prayers, constancy in suffering and in confessing the truth, and of solid rejoicing in God."[3]

## God's Glories Manifested (Evidences)

The history of any true church's membership is a realization and recounting of the glories that God has determined to manifest through the particular congregation. Praise be to the dominion of our Lord Jesus Christ!

### Hardships and Struggles

The Lord's customary way of realizing his covenant in history is by means of struggle. This more than any other way has served to manifest the amazing zeal and love for God of which so many members of Hope congregation have given evidence. This is consistent with the church's depiction as a body. The body of Christ is exercised in order to develop the strength of faith and ardent love. Without exercise a body becomes weak and unhealthy.

Very early in the congregation's history, members recognized the spiritual blessings given to them and considered them precious. Less than ten years after her beginning and after much financial sacrifice, the members experienced the events of 1924 in the common grace

---

2   Abraham Kuyper, *The Implications of Public Confession*, trans. Henry Zylstra, 6th ed. (n.p.: Federation of Protestant Reformed Young People's Societies, 1989), 65.

3   Canons of Dordt 5.12, in *Confessions and Church Order*, 175.

controversy. The congregation had recently become self-supporting, but the members were to face the realization that their church membership constituted more than merely an earthly association. Their conviction with regard to God's particular grace worked in them a willingness to lose the stability of the Christian Reformed denomination for an unknown way. This meant that their being members of the body of Christ was a treasure of greater value than being members of a financially stable Christian Reformed denomination. "For where your treasure is, there will your heart be also" (Matt. 6:21). They did not retain the building for which they had spent their meager earnings, but sought first the "kingdom of God, and his righteousness" (v. 33) and looked past the immediate hardships to the honor of God and the spiritual welfare of their generations.

We are the recipients of their decision taken only eight years after Hope's beginning. John Calvin wrote regarding the spiritual principle the founding members set down: "We are not to think at all of our own interest; we must set [God's] glory before our eyes, and keep them intent upon it alone."[4] With membership in a true congregation, one's ease is not a consideration and is not promised. What *is* promised is the privilege to have a part in manifesting God's glory. Throughout Hope's history as a congregation, "church militant" became more than a mere concept.

There were similar circumstances in the 1953 schism that took place throughout the Protestant Reformed denomination. As told by members who experienced it, Hope was a small and close-knit congregation. They had cooperated in starting a school in 1947 with very little financial means. Then theology of a conditional covenant was supported by some in the congregation, even prominent families, along with warnings against it in sermons by Rev. John Heys. There was much dissention. The reaction of one young boy is most likely representative.

---

4   John Calvin, *Institutes of the Christian Religion*, trans. Henry Beveridge (Grand Rapids, MI: Wm. B. Eerdmans Publishing Company, repr. 1966), 3.20.35, 2:184.

"I was grieved and fearful because of those developments. I watched in horror as men of the church shouted at each other after church." —David Engelsma

An older son of the congregation had been on the battlefield of Korea during the year leading up to 1953. He returned, as he relates, "eager for some peace and tranquility at home." He was sorely mistaken.

"My father [Arend Kuiper] suggested that I visit the classis in order to understand the issues, which I did. Afterward, I told my father that I felt I had come from one battle into another. I witnessed the church disintegrating." —John Kuiper

As is the Lord's way, the members who were preserved in the truth of the unconditional covenant grew in spiritual vigor and discernment by means of the struggle. Just fifteen years earlier, Rev. H. De Wolf had been Hope's pastor. In the early 1950s he was a pastor in First Protestant Reformed Church in Grand Rapids, Michigan, where he was bold to publicly preach conditional covenant theology, touching off a series of events that led to the eventual split of the churches.

He was warmly regarded by many at Hope as a dear friend.

One member of Hope said, "Though we loved him, we could not follow a man. We had to follow God's word."

Internal strife that does not lead to specific splits, as in 1924 and 1953, is also a congregation's experience of hardship and struggle. There are circumstances of weak, sinful officebearers who scatter the sheep, as well as grievous disagreements and disunity within a congregation. During such trials the truth that the congregation is a complete manifestation of the body of Christ is a principle that upholds believers.

When church membership is taken seriously, one does not quickly leave a congregation and seek membership in another congregation that enjoys peace, but will remain and endure the painful times as well as the pleasant ones.

### Doctrines Developed and Maintained

Membership importantly involves the maintenance and development of certain doctrines for the purpose of manifesting the glory of God, who "predestinated us...to the praise of the glory of his grace" (Eph.1:5–6). This being the purpose makes clear why a well-meant offer of the gospel is rejected as perversion. If some avail themselves of an "opportunity" or a "condition," *they* receive the glory. God's elect have been predetermined to manifest *his* glory.

Jesus is present where the true preaching of the gospel is proclaimed. His might is on display for all to see in the regenerated, believing hearts of his chosen people and by God's judgment upon the reprobate wicked. Proper content in the preaching also assures a church's members of Christ's presence. Only where the true doctrines are preached and loved, will membership truly experience Christ and manifest him as glorious. There is urgency then for the members of Hope to know and to love the doctrines handed down to them.

Defending and maintaining God's truth works development of it. By bringing the truth more clearly to light, his glory is revealed to a greater extent, which is the ultimate purpose. That a strong, faithful confession brings glory to God is expressed in a versification of Psalm 48:13: "Mark her defenses well... / That ye her *glories* may unfold."[5] Other noteworthy doctrines developed in the Protestant Reformed denomination of churches and consequently upheld by Hope congregation were God's covenant of grace, the unbreakable bond of marriage, and the antithesis. Instead of a succession of persons (popes), the Lord gives a succession of doctrines to a true church built on the apostles' foundation.

---

5    No. 133:2, in *The Psalter*; emphasis added.

According to one member of Hope, Rev. John Heys once remarked, "People say we need more practical rather than doctrinal preaching. I say it is practical to know doctrine."

One is unable to live a Christian life unless it is based on and motivated by the true doctrines revealed by God to his beloved church. Having an awareness of salvation is one thing. Acute knowledge of the specific way God has accomplished our salvation, results in commitment of heart to bless and praise him forever.

### Children Included

Membership in the church is comprised of believing parents and their baptized children. This is based on God's inclusion of children in his covenant. Baptism is the sign of entrance into God's covenant. Elect infants have entered into the covenant in every sense except for the consciousness of it. The Lord ordained his elect into certain families with normally at least one believing parent. He uses the parents' examples and instruction, backed by discipline, to work conscious faith in the child.

Hope congregation has maintained this glory of God. Covenantal children are saved unconditionally, never influenced by some act of the child in later life.

During the pastorate of Rev. Heys a conditional covenant was being maintained within the Protestant Reformed denomination so that the truth expressed in the first question asked of parents in the baptism form was disregarded. Wonderfully, still today, parents are able to confess about their infants: "they *are* sanctified in Christ, and therefore, *as members* of his church, ought to be baptized."[6]

Older members can remember a time when worldly, wild, young people were tolerated. Evidently this was acceptable in some families. At one time in Hope's history, the older children sat as a group in the

---

6    Form for the Administration of Baptism, in *Confessions and Church Order*, 260; emphasis added.

back pews of the auditorium. Due to rowdiness during a worship service, the minister stopped his sermon and spoke to those failing to act with reverence. Soon after that all children sat with their families. The truth that the covenant is with believers and their seed is important knowledge. Parents began to take more seriously how their children lived and to hold them accountable as children of God.

"I remember one time, I was probably four or five, and my dad was in consistory. My mother was at home, so we children were sitting alone, and misbehaving during the service. On the way home, my dad had to pick something up from the Kievit's house. Mrs. Kievit came outside, and I got bawled out by Mrs. Kievit. I'll never forget that." —John Kuiper

"I remember one Sunday morning many years ago. The ushers seated five of our small children and me in the 'prized' seats of Hope church—the chairs along the side wall in the front of the sanctuary. Since I was not fond of being on display to the whole congregation, I sighed under my breath and hoped for the best. It was not to be. Right off the bat, each child decided he needed his own psalter, and before I could stop them, one after the other bounced off his chair to retrieve a psalter from the stash behind the wall around the piano. With some stern looks, order was restored. During congregational prayer my son on the left dropped a piece of candy, and as it noisily bounced along the tile floor, the candy-less child began to sob. Not long after the sermon started, I heard a sneeze to my right. To my complete horror that son, with his face turned to the congregation, looked at me with a string of mucus hanging from his nose. I had no tissues with me that morning, and I don't remember what happened next. The minister was well into his sermon, and I did a mother's head check to see if the kids were behaving. Son number four had removed his shoe, and while propping his little leg on his lap, he was attempting to squeeze all of his toes through the one small hole he had found in his sock. He was managing quite well, completely oblivious to his audience and conveniently just out of my reach. This experience, as humiliating as it was, has given me the opportunity to encourage other young mothers who now have the privilege of sitting in those 'prized' seats with their little children." —Brenda (Langerak) Bomers

Unlike during the first decades of Hope's history, secular society now disparages children as detriments to self-advancement. In 1973, with a decision upholding abortion as a legal right, the United States approved the murdering of its most vulnerable citizens. Faith in God's covenantal promise is the power to bring forth children. Believing parents are the willing means God uses to bring forth and to gather his elect children throughout history. Through them the glory of a zeal for God's covenant shines. Families with many children give evidence of God's provision of faith and love. Where love for God wanes, love for his children wanes as well.

Sunday school (December 2015)

Young people (December 2015)

## Christian Education

Christian schooling is based on the truth that God continues his covenantal friendship with *families* and commands parents to nurture their children so they know God and have the ability to use all of the creation ordinances in his service. In seeking to faithfully rear their children, parents in the congregation found Christian Reformed schools inadequate in developing the children as friend-servants of God. The late 1940s, when Hope Protestant Reformed Christian School became a reality, were not prosperous times; but for the members of Hope building a school where the children could be taught a distinctly Protestant Reformed worldview was a great priority.

Even the children had to make sacrifices.

When asked to describe how the change to a small Protestant Reformed school affected her, a former student quipped, "I remember not liking it because I was the only girl in my class." —Eileen (Engelsma) Terpstra

Another student recalls, "My father [Maynard Veenstra] moved the family to a house on Luce Street when Hope school started, because he determined it absolutely necessary that we attend a Protestant Reformed School. We walked two and a half miles to school (and catechism) and then back home again in all kinds of weather." —Clara Van Den Top

Throughout the congregation's history many examples of great personal sacrifice for the sake of Christian schooling have been observed. Members have uprooted their families, left steady employment, and struggled financially for a number of years for the privilege of paying Christian school tuition.

One such struggling family felt responsible to help pay for a building project of additional classrooms at Hope school, but the family funds were exhausted. The father took out a bank loan in order to contribute to the financial drive.

### *Honoring the Marriage Ordinance*

During the first decades of the Protestant Reformed denomination, Rev. Herman Hoeksema uncovered again the gospel truth regarding the unbreakable covenant and its application of a lifelong bond of marriage.[7]

Hope congregation had no instances of divorce, and this "new" truth was never debated or argued. For the members of Hope it went without saying that marriage is for life. Prof. David Engelsma, who was raised in Hope during that time, offered this reason: "A sound, solid church of Christ simply lives the Christian life, especially with

---

7   Herman Hoeksema, *The Unbreakable Bond of Marriage* (Grand Rapids, MI: Sunday School of the First Protestant Reformed Church, n.d.; repr. 1969). For Hoeksema's recovering the doctrine of the unbreakable bond of marriage and its relationship to the covenant of grace, see also David J. Engelsma, *Marriage: The Mystery of Christ and the Church*, 3rd ed. (Jenison, MI: Reformed Free Publishing Association, 2015), 137–149.

regard to its fundamental aspects, as a healthy human lives the normal earthly life, rather than debating it, arguing about it, or studying how to live it."

Strong and faithful marriages are *the* symbol of God's covenant with his bride. This implies an important calling, since much is required with regard to the marriages of those who have received much. Just as glorious are members who have remained faithful when a spouse has sinfully abandoned them. They are a means to shine light on the truth of God's unbreakable, unfailing covenantal love for his bride. Their lives of hardship and self-denial are an inspiration to the following generation, but especially their lives glorify the faithful God. They give clear testimony that the promise-keeping God brings forth covenantal children who keep their vows to God, without regard to the cost.

Observable during the century of Hope's existence, as other denominations have capitulated to the world's acceptance of divorce and remarriage, is that the witness of God's unbreakable marriage bond has been ostracized. This reproach has served to isolate the congregation and her sister churches and is often the reason interested persons have turned away from membership in Hope congregation. The cost is too high when it involves family and relationships, especially when other "conservative" churches will embrace them without repentance manifested by turning from sin. This isolation is not due to the congregation's lack of love for others, although this is often the accusation. Such disparagement increases the temptation "to be loving" by tolerating divorce and remarriage in families or speaking of lifelong marriage as a mere Protestant Reformed distinctive, leaving the impression that it is not fundamental. This brings no glory to God. The lifelong, unbreakable bond is the truth of the gospel, a glory and development of God's covenant, now known nearly throughout the entire world. Churches that know but refuse to join in confessing and living according to it are without excuse.

In the ninety-ninth year of Hope's existence, the United States Supreme Court, expressing the will and wisdom of man, decreed the legalization of same sex "marriage." Attempts to change the immutable ordinances of God are futile, but the effects upon his church in the world are severe. The institution of marriage has been assailed for some time already, as indicated by society's condoning of adultery, divorce, remarriage, and abortion. A sanctified, believing family manifests the reality of God's everlasting covenant with his elect: "Behold, I and the children whom the Lord hath given me are for signs and for wonders in Israel from the Lord of hosts, which dwelleth in mount Zion" (Isa. 8:18). Demanding that everyone not only recognize, but also condone sodomite "marriage" will be a culmination of Satan's effective campaign to eradicate the earthly, glorious sign of God's covenant or at least to distort it so that it will be unrecognizable.

### Submission to Authority

Church membership is submission to our Lord and master, Jesus Christ. This glory has been manifested within members of Hope congregation.

In the sphere of labor, this showed itself in submission to employers and fair treatment of employees. It became more evident as the percentage of men who worked farms decreased. The 1950s brought a number of members into conflict with labor unions.

By being conscientious objectors when a union was organized, some men were able to remain in their places of employment. One business owner made a promise to two of his employees who were members of Hope, "If you're willing to pay the dues, I will see to it that they go to the charity of your choice." Both men chose Hope school. The school began to receive payments, but that soon ended, and the men soon sought new employment. Often when men remained employed as conscientious objectors, there was still harassment that was effective in convincing them to seek other employment to avoid the union's tactics. A fellow employee, explaining his reasoning for joining the union to John J. Dykstra, said, "I like it for the ability to swing a bigger hammer." Hope's pastor met with the union boss from Detroit, in order to find a way for a member of Hope church to remain employed. The union man would have none of it. He declared that the beliefs of that member were neither Christian nor patriotic and stated, "The unions are the ones who obey the laws and truly care about the people." Union tactics and antagonism resulted in many members' beginning their own businesses in order to earn a living. The Lord has clearly blessed those endeavors.

Though often a lone voice, the conviction to honor the employer was no small testimony. Respectful, obedient employees (servants) bring an added beauty to the church's confession. "Exhort servants to be obedient...that they may adorn the doctrine of God our Saviour in all things" (Titus 2:9–10). This was substantiated by an individual who remembered, some fifty years later, the member of Hope church who had refused to remain employed by that boy's father when the shop became a union shop. Evidently it made a lasting impression on the boy so that the member's name and church affiliation never left him even in adulthood. That God blesses not only a strong conviction against ungodly unions, but also a humble manner when witnessing, became apparent to one member who recounted that her father, in visits with his Christian Reformed friend, repeatedly brought up the evils of union membership. That man eventually left his union job.

Some men were able to remain in their places of work, as the union was voted down in certain instances. Dewey Engelsma was employed for many years at Keeler Brass. At various times the employees, including men from other Reformed churches, strongly pushed the company to unionize. At meetings to unionize, Dewey vocally appealed against the union, giving witness that the issue was the Christian life, which meant submission to the employer.

Submission to authority in the sphere of government has manifested itself in members of the congregation as they lived as good, upright citizens in their communities. Acknowledgment that Christ places certain people in positions of authority reveals itself in proper honor and respect for those individuals. This respect is not dependent on that person's worthiness, but on Christ's appointment.

This was on the foreground when fathers and mothers saw their sons off to the military in obedience to the country's law during WWII and then again in the following wars.

Although members recall the sadness and uncertainty as sons of the congregation were drafted, when the Vietnam War became a source of public demonstrations and defiance, there was no participation by the young members of Hope church.

George Engelsma in uniform with his brother, Melvin

### Faithful Church Attendance

Church membership has always been viewed as synonymous with faithful church attendance. This was evidenced at the outset by Hope's early consistory minutes.

> Visited Mr. and Mrs. _____ about attending church (July 5, 1921, article 2).

> Mr. and Mrs._____ [were] visited and urged to attend church more regularly (December 5, 1922, article 3).

> A motion [was] made and accepted to advise full members of the church as to their obligation toward the church (November 6, 1923, article 5).

These minutes are the consistory's recognition of the covenantal demand of Hebrews 10: "Let us draw near with a true heart…*not forsaking the assembling of ourselves together*, as the manner of some is" (vv. 22, 25; emphasis added). Another aspect of God's glory is revealed in this. The Lord is faithful in exhorting and calling to himself, through his officebearers, his elect children. Elders recognized that a spiritually healthy member desires to attend faithfully, while spiritual sickness shows itself in a disregard for the church and its official worship.

Such a commitment of the members to be concerned about their faithful attendance is rooted in the knowledge that God fellowships by means of speech. Already in the garden of Eden that was God's way: "And they heard the *voice* of the Lord God walking in the garden" (Gen. 3:8; emphasis added). God fellowships with Christ, and through Christ, with his bride each Sunday where the truth is audibly proclaimed.

"When Ike died, Mrs. Korhorn came to church faithfully every Sunday. She lived to be in her nineties. And she never stopped coming to church that I can remember. She'd come in with a hat on all the time." —Donna Dykstra

A consistory decision in 1987 was the culmination of this care and concern for members' faithful attendance, when the issue of some who left the worship services for extended periods of time manifested itself.

1.  The consistory should send a committee to those in the congregation who are absent for extended periods of time. These committees should:
    a.  Inquire as to the reasons and circumstances of their absence.
    b.  Explain from scripture and the confessions the calling to be active in the life of the congregation.
    c.  Emphasize that a leave of absence from the congregation, although permissible as such, may before God be taken only to enable and equip the member better to serve God in the church. Examples of this could be a leave of absence for the sake of education as well as for health.
    d.  Warn against making liberty in this matter a license to sin.

Grounds:
    a.  Belgic Confession, articles 28–29; Heidelberg Catechism, questions and answers 54–55, 103;

1 Corinthians 12; and Romans 12:5–8, which teach that we must be active, living members in a local congregation which bears the marks of the true church.

b.  Galatians 4:1–11; Galatians 5:1; Acts 15:10; and Matthew 23:4, which teach that we are not only free in Christ from the power of sin to serve the Lord in the church as living, active members, but also we are free in many instances to determine before God how this service in the church is to be carried out specifically by us.

c.  Galatians 5:13–14 and 1 Peter 2:16, which warn against making our liberty in Christ a license to sin.

2.  The consistory should require those leaving for an extended period of time to inform the consistory of their plans. If possible the consistory should place these members under the temporary care of a closer sister congregation during their absence.

3.  The consistory should apply discipline to those only who obviously have little or no regard for fulfilling their calling in and towards the local church. In this connection, the consistory ought to take into consideration:

a.  The reason for an extended leave of absence. Is it merely for the sake of selfish pleasure or is there some God glorifying purpose?

b.  Where those absenting themselves from the congregation attend church during their absences. Are they attending another Protestant Reformed church or a church of another denomination?

c.  The fact that some in the church will tend to turn liberty into a license to sin. This the church may not allow.

Ground: Church Order, articles 74–77; 1 Thessalonians 5:14; and 2 Thessalonians 3:6, 14 require discipline for those who are unruly and have no regard for the commandments of God.

This decision was reiterated with a 1997 letter to the congregation entitled "The Privileges and Responsibilities of Membership in the Local Church." After defining what the local church is, the letter explained that the church is "not a mere collection of individuals... but a church, the Body of Christ having design and purpose, in which each individual elect child of God is a living member." After listing the privileges of membership, the letter listed a member's responsibilities, giving scriptural and confessional references, such as, "Hebrews 10:25 instructs us that we must not forsake the assembling of ourselves together...A member of the body [who] is missing...cannot be of service to the body." Finally, instruction was given regarding the principle of Christian liberty, which is "primarily deliverance from the power of sin and the power to walk according to God's laws through the inner working of the Spirit,...freedom from the precepts of the Mosaic law,... freedom from the legalistic precepts of men...[to] use not for an occasion to the flesh, but by love to serve one another."

A common refrain from the older members has been, "Our congregation has been blessed with strong elders." The decisions regarding faithful attendance are a demonstration of that. Members flourish where faithful preaching is backed up by consistories that rule on the basis of scriptural principles. Members have healthy awe and peace of soul, experiencing Christ's rule over them. Where pragmatic decisions are made or important issues ignored, membership suffers.

Fellowshiping with the Lord is not merely outward. The elect believer is fundamentally a new person at the moment of conscious faith. Carnal considerations cannot and will not separate the believer from Christ. There is no casualness, but a willingness even to forsake all to experience worshiping him.

This has been noticeable with regard to aged saints whose physical conditions give sufficient reasons to stay home, yet they take up the physical challenge for the opportunity to worship. This is the more striking when in the present day there is the ability to listen to or even watch the service online.

When questioned about this, one such infirmed saint expressed, "The older I get, the more I realize how much I need to be near God."

Alvin Rau and Betty Bloem

Gordon and Eileen Terpstra

John J. Dykstra and Rod Brunsting

Martin and Emma De Vries

Marge Kamps

Prof. Herman and Wilma Hanko

Nettie De Vries, Joanne Bomers, Lou Kooienga, Eileen Terpstra

The believing soul longs for closeness, and nothing in this earth is closer to our loved One than in church with fellow saints during the worship services. "Unto you therefore which believe he is precious" (1 Pet. 2:7). Though less than ideal for the healthy child of God, modern technology is profitable for the shut-in.

This principle longing for the Lord's house also explains why there is not a desire to pursue occupations that demand even legitimate

Sunday work. The believer has no desire to be absent from corporate worship, and if in such a situation, he or she will do whatever is possible to avoid missing worship services.

Eileen Terpstra remembered some early technology that was utilized at Hope church. Her mother, Lena Engelsma, lived across the street from church, but was a shut-in. A wire was buried to the house, so Mrs. Engelsma could hear the sermons at home.

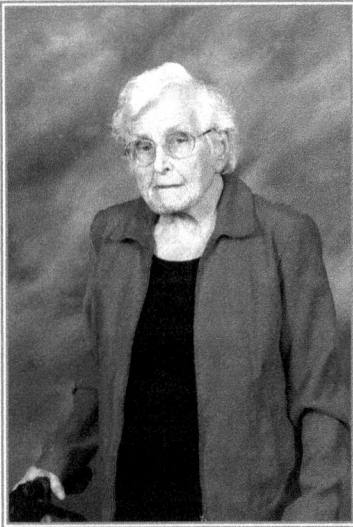

Anna Elzinga (deceased March 2, 2016)

Phyllis and Alvin Rau

Alvin Huizinga

Alice Huizinga

Though there was recognition of God's authority when the nation's government drafted young men into military service, Hope congregation has understood that the same is not true if one seeks to join the military today. In such a case where there is no draft, the Lord does not call a believer to leave the fellowship, being absent from the church and its worship. Such an individual who leaves his God-given membership, forsaking the spiritual battle station next to his fellow members, is no hero and is worthy of no admiration.

### *Organic Life*

Membership implies a body that is more important than individual interests. God's salvation of his children is personal but never individualistic. The Spirit of Christ so works within believers, that they understand membership not as a way to receive, but as the way to give for the "advantage...of other members."[8]

Anne Buiter and her mother, Thea Buiter

Anne Buiter, as a special needs child of God, has brought special things to Hope congregation. It is now customary that all newborn children must pass through the adoring arms of Anne soon after their first worship service. Anne continues to love the children as they grow. She has for many years helped the Sunday school teacher in the preschool/kindergarten class each summer. Not just children, but also adult members of the congregation are liable to receive a hug from Anne on any given Sunday.

---

8    Heidelberg Catechism Q&A 55, in *Confessions and Church Order*, 104.

Anne is well-known for making birthday and anniversary cards for every member (with plenty of stickers included). For many years she had the task of finding all the individuals and handing them their cards. The addition some years ago of mailboxes in the narthex has made her mission less laborious and the cards proliferate. Such a saint, who is uninhibited and harmless as a dove, is a reminder of one aspect that will be part of the coming perfected church of Christ.

This desire for the body's welfare, the Spirit accomplishes by giving diversity of gifts. "There are diversities of gifts...but the manifestation of the Spirit is given to every man to profit withal" (1 Cor. 12:4, 7). The Spirit works the *same* thing in all members (faith in Christ as Lord). He also works *differently* in each member, with regard to the measure of spiritual gifts, "dividing to every man severally as he will" (v. 11). The Lord's purpose is not to work envy and strife, but to promote unity in the body "that there should be no schism in the body; but that the members should have the same care one for another" (v. 25). As with a human body, so in the body of Christ, instead of competition there is working together for a common purpose. Instead of merely receiving, there is a conscious giving for the body's welfare.

John J. Dykstra experienced this in the 1950s when his wife Josephine was in a serious automobile accident. Many fellow members can relate to what John learned. "When you experience difficulties, you begin to speak of your church-family, rather than of your congregation. Because you feel this truth so much more." —John J. Dykstra

The Spirit's gift of love (1 Cor. 13) makes for a vibrant organic life in the congregation that reflects the glory of Christ. Love is the sacrificing of one's own interests for the sake of another that is precious. Love forgoes all of one's liberty and privileges for the highest good of the church. Christ's love shed abroad in our hearts is the basis of Hope church's organic life. Each member has something they must give for the whole. Each member lacks necessary gifts that are given only through the other members.

However, self-interest manifests itself in isolating oneself and developing prejudices against fellow members, which are then used as excuses to be unloving.

One member recalls conducting a school financial drive with Richard Newhouse soon after joining Hope. At each house the family greeted him as "Uncle Rich." "Wait a minute, they can't all be related to Rich Newhouse," the new member finally recognized.

A closely knit congregation it was, being composed of thirty to forty families. Sunday night visiting between members, with their entire families, was the norm for many. The fellowship always ended with the impassioned singing of Dutch psalms. Those who were children at the time, relate the experience with deep affection. Such warm reflection on this delightful concord among members is understandable. Nearness to God always unifies. Observance of good works and love between members manifests that there is power in the speech of God. This honors and brings glory to him.

"On Sunday nights after the services, we would have Bible discussions in people's homes. I was around six years old. The ladies would be in the kitchen, and the men would get into big debates in the living room." —John Kuiper

As when a human body suffers then heals, so in the congregation there is no discarding of a penitent member who causes grievous hurt through shameful sin. There is healing. Similar to the human body, healing is not always a quick, easy process. This does not imply a lack of forgiveness or absence of love in the congregation, but reveals how destructive our sins against one another often are: "A brother offended is harder to be won than a strong city" (Prov. 18:19). God's mercy to restore one who has fallen is a manifestation of his glory that is almost beyond words to describe.

## Discipline

Mere outward membership does not constitute fellowship with God. In salvation God glorifies himself by working holiness in confession and in conduct. The importance of faithful discipline is that it glorifies Christ, manifesting who he is. During a conference in Hope, one speaker put it this way: "Christ takes away sin. This will be in the way of repentance and covering, followed by an upright life, or by impenitence and exposing, which is followed by removal from the congregation. Discipline stands in the service of a member's holy life."[9]

Sin is the barrier that has been removed by Christ so that there can be fellowship with God. Where there is impenitence, the barrier remains. The church must deal with members who live in sins of conduct and/ or confession. As a final remedy the church is instructed in Matthew 7 to cease preaching to such an individual. An impenitent person is compared to a dog or a pig that has no regard for what is precious (Christ) and is unable to perceive what is of true value. "Give not that which is holy unto the dogs, neither cast ye your pearls before swine, lest they trample them under their feet, and turn again and rend you" (Matt. 7:6).

Faithful preaching will eventually expose hypocrites. Like physical death, spiritual death manifests itself as grotesque and often with foul behavior without repentance. Deplorable lives and calloused impenitence of some former members raises the question why such things can happen in a true church of Christ. As with Moses' speech to Pharaoh, the closer an unbeliever is to the truth about God, the harder his heart will become.

It is a heart-rending experience when a family member is not blessed with repentance. As one mother expressed it, "It would have been less painful to lay my child in the grave."

---

9    "The Covenant of Grace as Manifested in the Marks of the True Church," July 2012.

In such cases faithful church membership includes the responsibility to have true concern for the impenitent individual, although he is no longer a member in the congregation. Any contact with such a person always includes admonishment. Importantly, there is no fellowship any longer, recognizing and praying for the Lord's discipline to work repentance. "If any man obey not our word...note that man, and have no company with him, that he may be ashamed. Yet count him not as an enemy, but admonish him as a brother" (2 Thess. 3:14–15). For the Lord's companions, there is another consideration: "Whosoever...will be a friend of the world is the enemy of God" (James 4:4), and "He that loveth father or mother...son or daughter more than me is not worthy of me" (Matt. 10:37).

The testimonies of saints who have repented and returned to faithful membership in the church are that the experience of being apart from God and his people was an instrumental means in turning them. There is a principle reason for this. The covenantal relationship is disparaged by one's refusal to live according to the rules of God's house. If this one is an elect child of God, the bond is not destroyed, but the warm friendship can no longer be enjoyed. God is pleased to use the experience of this disruption to bring his own children to repentance.

The opinion of one such person is, "Those who I thought were the hardest on me, were the ones who really cared about me."

Discipline also occurs by "mutual censure," as fellow members care for and watch over one another. Countless members have a story of another's seeking them out to admonish or to encourage them to walk uprightly. How many have repented at the "first step" of discipline will never be known, but membership in a true church with the aid of fellow saints cannot be overestimated.

All such active discipline is a recognition of, and faithfulness in maintaining, God's glorious truth regarding the mighty, effectual power of his Spirit. A member who partakes of God's glory is always transformed. Conversely, "if any man have not the Spirit of Christ, he is none of his" (Rom. 8:9).

### Persecution

Unlike many children of God throughout history, bodily persecution has been almost nonexistent in the life of the members of Hope church. There are signs that this will not be the case for long, as the darkness intensifies, making membership in a true church more costly than before.

The most outward form of persecution has been threats, slander, and the closing of potential job opportunities. The pressure to conform to or to participate in the world's sins has thus far closed an increasing amount of jobs as being off limits, but has not prohibited Hope's members from being able to buy and sell. This is not to minimize the pressure to conform to this world. No one by nature desires to stand out as abnormal. To have "ceased from sin" (1 Pet. 4:1) is not normal earthly life, and consequently there is suffering in the flesh prompted by those who "think it strange" (v. 4). The reaction of contempt "because Christ's life has become so manifest in us that others see us as belonging to Christ" is the driving force of persecution.[10] This too will serve to magnify the Lord's grace as persecution will fail to accomplish the desired purpose. "The workers of iniquity /...shall not triumph in their pride, / Or drive my soul from Thee."[11]

### Sanctification/Holy Lives

Membership of elect believers in a true church is God's work of creating fellowship between believers and Christ by destroying one's natural fellowship with Satan. "You...were dead in trespasses and sins...and were by nature the children of wrath, even as others. But God....hath quickened us together with Christ" (Eph. 2:1–5).

Holiness was the purpose for our election and re-creation in Christ, as 2 Timothy 1:9 states: "Who hath saved us, and called us with a holy calling....in Christ Jesus before the world began." Rather than holiness being something that must be endured, it is a benefit to be enjoyed.

---

10  Herman Hanko, *A Pilgrim's Manual: Commentary on 1 Peter* (Jenison, MI: Reformed Free Publishing Association, 2012), 244.

11  No. 94:6, in *The Psalter*.

Since Christ captures the hearts of his people, to live in holiness is not drudgery but a delight. Service to God as a labor of love especially serves to bring glory to God. The wife's beauty tends to the glory of her divine Husband: "being filled with the fruits of righteousness, which are by Jesus Christ, unto the glory and praise of God" (Phil. 1:11).

Church membership, which is the means of abiding in Christ, is essential for sanctification. Being in Christ by faith has an empowering effect on the child of God and is pictured in the vine. "As the branch cannot bear fruit of itself, except it abide in the vine; no more can ye, except ye abide in me" (John 15:4). There is personal experience of the favor and blessing of God. Knowing our Father's and Husband's love, we love him in return.

With knowledge also comes thankfulness. There is no greater motivation to holy living than gratitude. John Calvin speaks of this: "Wherever God hath made himself known, his perfections must be displayed...which fill us with admiration, and incite us to show forth his praise."[12] Such praise is, in essence, a noticeably antithetical life. Preservation for one hundred years is in harmony with the faithfulness in this regard of early parents of Hope church. The well-known history of Judges makes this perfectly clear. Thankful, consecrated lives with the establishment of the antithesis within their homes resulted in another generation's knowing the Lord. Parents reared their children, and they had living, personal, fellowship with God in Jesus Christ.

Nearness to God was illustrated to one elder who visited a member in the hospital, still groggy and lying in bed after an operation. Relates the elder: "I proceeded to read a psalm while he was lying there, with wife and children by his bedside. I must have paused between verses, and when I did, he began to speak slowly, picking up where I had stopped and finishing the rest of the psalm."

---

12  Calvin, *Institutes of the Christian Religion*, 3.20.41, 2:188.

Profound gratitude along with urgency in living and teaching the antithesis are the only way. It is the well-worn path, as old as God's covenant, and is the way of life for believing families. The present generation of Hope's membership experiences the beckoning of new paths. Besides the new doctrines that question whether Christ is truly the only way, there are new paths of Christian living. Rather than a spiritually strenuous, selfless life, there is a new path of pursuing ease and carnal pleasure. It is supposed that a Christian can walk on the road of conforming to this world rather than being transformed. Instead of the old path of enmity between seeds, a new way to heaven allows the traveler to have pleasure in those who commit sins, find humor in sin, or sing of sin. Some insist that the path of pitching one's tent toward Hollywood will be free from any personal or family consequences.

However, the old paths, wherein is the good way, promise that "ye shall find rest for your souls" (Jer. 6:16). God does not bless his people *because* they walk in the proper paths, but he blesses them *in the way of* these paths. The promise and command were incentives for those early families in Hope who remained faithful, and they are incentives for us today.

A holy life, consecrated to God, is the stamp of genuineness God uses to bring others into the membership of his church, in almost every instance. A life of dedication to God, within the church and while living in this world, is true and effective witnessing, even to unbelievers, "that…they may by your good works, which they shall behold, glorify God" (1 Pet. 2:12).

> As one member put it, "Finding strength in the word and putting faith into practice during the course of our everyday lives is a powerful witness."

Lack of holiness is detrimental to God's glory, as others observe the individual is a farce and conclude that the teachings of his church are worthless.

A verbal witness often follows a godly life, as others observe and then ask of the hope within us.

> One member attributes his family's place in Hope church to such witnessing: "Due to his dry cleaning business, my father had a lot of contact with Protestant Reformed men. They talked to him about the Protestant Reformed view of the covenant. He was attracted to the unconditional covenant view versus the conditional covenant view and to the assurance of salvation versus the doubt and anguish of the Netherlands Reformed [where he was a member]. He began to attend Hoeksema's Heidelberg Catechism classes."
> —Harry Langerak

> "In 1952 our dry cleaner, Tony Langerak, came to our home on O'Brien Road to pick up dry cleaning. He saw the *Standard Bearer* on our kitchen table. Tony said to my wife, Marilyn, 'It is your duty to join the nearest Protestant Reformed church.' Marilyn told him that we had visited, but no one spoke to us. 'Well!' he said, 'I will fix that.' He arranged a visit with his wife and Mary Howerzyl. Marilyn did not want to go alone, so she called Kay Van Dyke to go with her. The result of that meeting was that we joined Hope church." —John N. Dykstra

Klamer family back from left: Verna, Vicky, Valerie;
middle: Vern, Barb; front: Brenda, Vonda, Brent, Bruce

Vern and Barb Klamer, who joined Hope with their young family said, "It all started in the 1960s when the Christian Reformed Church and schools were deteriorating, and we knew that we had to do something. But what could we do? We began by sending our oldest child to Covenant Christian High School. Then we realized that we should be consistent with church and school. A friend from the celery co-op, who had left the Christian Reformed Church and joined the Protestant Reformed Churches a few years earlier, invited us to join him at the evening service in Southeast Protestant Reformed Church, where in the providence of God Rev. Marinus Schipper preached a sermon on "The Church of Laodicea." He called those who belonged to an apostate church to come out from among her and join a true church of Jesus Christ. That word of God was powerful and timely for us. It was obvious to us that the Christian Reformed Church was apostatizing in its preaching and catechism teaching. Before we arrived home from church that night, we had made the decision: we had to leave the Christian Reformed Church. But which congregation should we join? Another person we talked to suggested that we check out Hope Protestant Reformed Church, so we thought we would try it. When we got to church, we saw how full it was. We decided that if we were going to join we would have to come early to get a seat! There was a little trepidation about joining Hope, because the congregation was without a pastor and had

Barb and Vern Klamer

called a seminary graduate to be its next minister. Our past history with the seminary students the Christian Reformed Church produced was not good! Thankfully, we were never disappointed when a seminary graduate became the new minister at Hope! We have been truly blessed by the preaching at Hope and have experienced God's blessing in our generations!

The congregation as a whole, manifesting herself as the bride of Christ, gives an unmistakable witness. Preaching that distinguishes Christ will be backed up with the upright lives of her membership with no toleration of unholiness. Others will observe a church that is devoted to her Lord. "Whoso offereth praise glorifieth me: and to him that ordereth his conversation aright will I shew the salvation of God" (Ps. 50:23).

Preservation in holiness serves to manifest another glory of God: "that they proceed not to extreme and desperate impiety is not owing to any innate goodness in them, but because the eye of God watches for their safety, and his hand is stretched over them."[13]

A fitting tribute to and desire for God's exaltation is sung after each morning service. "Blest be His great and glorious Name / For evermore, Amen. / And let His glory fill the earth / From shore to shore. Amen.[14]

---

13  Ibid., 3.24.10, 2:249.
14  No. 196:2, in *The Psalter*.

*Part Three*

# The Blessings

## of a

# Spiritual House
# Preserved

# Editor's Introduction to
## Part Three

Jesus Christ is the head of his church. As her head, he cares for his body's spiritual needs by placing prophets, priests, and kings in her midst. As her head, he leads his church to worship him in the way that "he has commanded in his Word."[1] As her head, he works, by his word and Spirit, in the members of his body the desire to join a true church and to be living members thereof.[2]

Where Christ has built his spiritual house on that firm foundation, the Lord is pleased to bless the dwellers in that house. He does that by sending his Spirit of truth to live in the local manifestations of his body. Hope's one-hundred-year history clearly demonstrates an abundance of blessings experienced as a result of the Spirit's work.

Although the chapters in part three relate an aspect of Hope's history as recorded in part one, the focus of part three will be from the perspective of Hope blessings throughout the years as a spiritual house preserved by God's grace.

---

1   Heidelberg Catechism A 96, in *Confessions and Church Order*, 125.
2   Heidelberg Catechism A 54, in ibid., 104.

## Chapter 12

~~~⸙~~~

# Hope Church in Communion
# and Fellowship

## Editor's Introduction

Unquestionably the focal point of a Reformed congregation's life is her worship of God in the divine worship services. True this has been for Hope from her beginnings in 1916. This aspect of the church's life is called the institutional life of the church. As such, it is ordered by the Church Order and governed by the consistory.

The societies of the church, however, flow out of the organic life of the church. While the consistory does exercise supervision over every organization in the congregation, the consistory has nothing to do with a society's establishment or internal affairs. These societies lie in the area of the office of believer. The apostle John says about believers, "Ye have the unction from the Holy One, and ye know all things. But the anointing which ye have received of him abideth in you, and ye need not that any man teach you: but as the same anointing teacheth you of all things, and is truth, and is no lie, and even as it hath taught you, ye shall abide in him" (1 John 2:20, 27). Because this is true, it is possible for believers to get together as a society to study God's word and mutually instruct and edify one another.

Throughout the one hundred years of her existence, Hope's members have actively promoted and participated in this aspect of the life of the church. Presently there are ten such opportunities in the organic life of Hope, and even though participation is voluntary, attendance is excellent. Read on for a taste of the office of believer in action at Hope.

## Men's Society
### *Gary Nienhuis*

The purpose of the Men's Society is stated in article 3 of its constitution. "The object of this society shall be to study the Word of God as found in the Scriptures, to promote an earnest Christian life among its members, to increase their mutual acquaintance and benefit its members in their spiritual life and faith."

For almost one hundred years the society has been conducted about the same. The meetings start with the singing of a psalter number and prayer. The men discuss a book of the Bible, going verse by verse, for about an hour. After a short business meeting, there is discussion of a topic for a half hour, and then the meeting is closed with prayer.

From the available minute books, it can be determined that in the last seventy-five years, the men have studied Ephesians, 1 Peter, Daniel, Genesis, James, Revelation, Acts, Romans, 1 Corinthians, and 2 Corinthians.

In the early 1940s for the after-recess portion of the meeting, the men wrote papers that answered various questions, such as, Why was the lineage of Christ so adulterous? Why must the Christian pray? Does prayer change things? Was Jesus God on earth? Why did Satan approach Eve instead of Adam? Why is marriage not a sacrament? Why is Heidelberg Catechism preaching necessary? and many other pertinent and interesting questions. Later for the after-recess discussions the men wrote papers on various scriptural and timely topics, such as, war, the blessing of Ishmael, the Civil Rights Movement, heart transplants, preparation for the end times, Jehovah's Witnesses, the Battle of

Armageddon, and many others. After recess the society has also studied the Canons of Dordt, Compendium, Belgic Confession, Church Order, liturgical forms, and the Declaration of Principles, using the "Brief Commentary on the Declaration of Principles of the Protestant Reformed Churches."[1]

From its beginning in 1922 until the present, the society has remained true to its purpose in the study of the word of God. Beginning with Genesis in 1922, the society has studied scripture and the doctrines of the Reformed faith, such as the covenant, grace, salvation, revelation, inspiration, the unity of the church, and her battle for sovereign grace in the covenant.

Men's Society (2016) back from left: David Moelker, David Kamps, Hank Vander Waal, John Buiter, Michael Engelsma, Rod Brunsting; middle: Gary Moelker, Ernie Medema, Harry Langerak, Harry Rutgers, Jim Huizinga, Jonathan Engelsma; front: Roger Kamphuis, Clare Kuiper, Gary Nienhuis, John N. Dykstra, John Streyle, Ken Dykstra, Cal Kalsbeek, Ron Koole

---

1    Engelsma, *Battle for Sovereign Grace in the Covenant*, 221–267.

## Ladies' Aid Society, Ruth

*Sherry Koole, Helen Medema, LeAnn Streyle*

Looking into the history of the Ladies' Society at Hope church, we dug into the minute books dating as far back as were made available to us. Since we were unable to obtain the first book of minutes, we are left to wonder, "Were there just two societies way back in the beginning, one for the men and one for the ladies?" We ask this because the first book of minutes we reviewed (1937) shows that there were young and old, single and married, and even widowed women found sitting around the discussion tables at society. Baby gifts were given to many of its members, while today's society consists of many who are grandmothers and most who are well beyond childbearing years. Also back then, the ladies met on Mondays and the men on Tuesdays, so that the children in the homes could be cared for by one of the parents. In time things changed so that both groups met at the same time, on the same night, but in different rooms. This practice is still held today—both societies meet every other Tuesday beginning at 7:30 p.m.

The women of the society formulated a constitution that still governs the society today. The name of the society is the Ladies' Aid Society, Ruth of the Hope Protestant Reformed Church and its purpose is "to study the Scriptures, to promote an earnest Christian life among its members, to increase their mutual acquaintance, and benefit the church and the poor."

The society joined the League of Eastern Men's and Ladies' Societies of the Protestant Reformed Churches. This league was later opened to all adult Bible societies of the Protestant Reformed Churches in western Michigan. The league held meetings at regular intervals, at which time beneficial programs and speeches were given to stimulate and further the mutual interests and welfare of the societies, thereby better equipping the members to take up their places in the world. The league disbanded in 2012.

An interesting find in our research was that in the beginning and early years our society was also a fundraising group of women. On a regular basis they would have a sewing, craft, or rug making night *after* their regular society meeting was finished for the evening. They would spend $10 at different times on materials for those projects and between meetings the materials and sewing machine was stored in the home of Mrs. Kievit. Those rugs and other items were sold at area sales, bazaars, and auctions. Other means of fundraising were hamburger fries, hostess suppers, plastic demonstrations, and handkerchief sales.

The ladies used the money raised to "benefit the church and the poor." Baby gifts were given to new moms, and cards and planters were given to sick members of the society. The society covered the costs of welcomes and parties for new ministers and their families. The ladies sent boxes of clothing to the Netherlands, Canada, and Korea. They purchased psalters and Bibles for the Jamaican mission field. They assisted in buying an organ for the church, a piano for the young people, collections plates, psalters, and water pipes in the church basement. They helped purchase needed supplies for the church kitchen, but the buying of a new stove had to be put on hold due to a shortage of oil during World War II.

When in 1948 they were asked to pay for refreshments at the dedication of the newly formulated Hope Protestant Reformed Christian School, they readily agreed. The cost of those refreshments? A total of $5! Makes one wonder what was served and how many people attended. Later they also gave several monetary gifts to the school board to use as it saw fit.

After Hope Protestant Reformed Christian School opened its doors, we read little of anymore fundraising being done by the society. Likely many of the women became members of the newly formed Hope School Mothers' Circle. The after-society-sewing-and-craft nights came to an end. Instead, the women took collections for different causes at different times. They also continued with society dues, which we still do today. Dues have doubled over the years, from 15¢ per meeting in the beginning to $5 per year today.

In the 1960s the ladies were once again active in their giving. They sent packages and goodie boxes to the young servicemen from Hope church during time of war. The minute books mention many thank-you letters being read from those young men. It is interesting that several of those men are still members at Hope. They and their wives are not only the older members, but also are very near to being the elder generation. They are now members of the Men's Society, and their wives are members of the very society that sent their husbands goodies during wartime.

Society life today is much the same as it was in the early days, with only a few minor changes taking place through the years. In the early years the minister of the congregation was the president. Over time things changed. Today nominations for president and vice-president can be made from male members of area Protestant Reformed churches, which allows for ministers, professors, seminarians, candidates for the ministry, as well as others to lead the society. Meetings still begin with singing from the psalter and opening prayer by the president, followed by Bible discussion and the reading of the minutes. In the early years discussing of various topics and asking and answering questions took place after the minutes and before closing devotions. This is no longer done, and the society members spend a longer period of time in the study of God's word, followed by reading of the minutes, business, psalter singing and prayer.

And that brings us to the main purpose of our society—the main purpose of any Bible society—the study of God's word. Through the years the ladies have studied books of the Bible from both the Old and the New Testaments. One year they studied various passages from scripture dealing with their discussion of women of the Bible: Eve, Sarah, and Rebekah. Just recently the society finished a ten-year study of the book of Genesis.

Society life can be very enriching for the child of God. We have learned a lot in our reading of many years of the society's minutes. Those women had a love for the truth and a love for each other. We found it rather interesting and touching to read that many of them would come

a half hour to forty-five minutes early so they could socialize beforehand. Silent roll call was taken and still is today. Many of those women
had two, three, and even four consecutive years of perfect attendance.
But one woman—Mrs. Maynard Veenstra—had twelve (or was it thirteen?) years of never being absent! Oh, to bring back that kind of zeal
for the study of God's word!

We end with a note given to our society just a couple of years ago.
It was a resignation letter from one of our members. Although resig-
nations are not something we usually enjoy receiving, this one moved
many of us to tears, both of sorrow and joy.
This resignation came from one whose membership spanned seven decades in the Ladies'
Aid Society! Her resignation was worded as
follows:

Dena Engelsma

> To Hope Ladies' Aid Society,
>
> Due to age and my present medical con-
> dition, I am resigning from the society.
> After 70 years of attending, sometimes
> hesitantly—and then, too, even reluc-
> tantly—still always after returning home, I
> have found that the mining of the jewels of
> truth found in the Scriptures have always
> proved to be a blessing in my life. So I pray God's continued
> blessing upon your society.
>
> United in Christ,
> Mrs. Dena Engelsma

Her prayer is also our prayer. That God bless our society and all the
societies of Hope church until he comes again on the clouds of glory to
gather the whole of his church unto himself.

Ladies' Aid Society, Ruth (2016) back from left: Deb Vander Waal, Evelyn Langerak, Rose Rutgers, Brenda Engelsma, Carol Nienhuis, Althea Brunsting, Bonnie Moelker; middle: Dan De Meester (president), LeAnn Streyle, Helen Medema, Sherry Koole, Carol Schimmel, Gladys Koole, Carol Tanis; front: Betty Bloem, Jan Kuiper, Thea Buiter, Floretta Engelsma, Kris Moelker, Linda Kalsbeek, Marilyn De Vries, Barb Huizinga

# Mr. and Mrs. Society
## (Senior Adult Bible Study Society)

### Aaron J. Cleveland

On the evening of October 19, 1954, the Mr. and Mrs. Society of Hope church met for the first time. Rev. John Heys was elected president, and Fred Huizinga was the vice-president. Ann Griffioen was the secretary; John Dykstra was the treasurer; Gilbert Schimmel was the vice-secretary/treasurer.

The society chose to study the book of Revelation. Bible study began at 8:00 p.m. and continued to 9:00 p.m. After a fifteen minute recess, the society had after-recess discussions on various topics. At that first meeting Rev. Heys was appointed to write a constitution that would eventually be approved by the consistory. The society chose to have an annual membership fee of $1 per couple. Mr. Jay Bomers closed that first meeting with prayer.

So began the Mr. and Mrs. Society. Since that beginning sixty-two years ago much has changed. The Mr. and Mrs. Society had an eleven-year history. Because of the steady growth of the Hope congregation, another society was needed in order to accommodate this growth. In the fall of 1965, the Senior Mr. and Mrs. Society was formed, while the Mr. and Mrs. Society continued on as the Junior Mr. and Mrs. Society. Today, both of these societies have removed "Mr. and Mrs." from their names and are known as the Senior Adult Bible Study Society and Junior Adult Bible Society.

In researching the history of the Mr. and Mrs. Society, I found that those days, in many respects, were much different than the days in which we live. The minutes of the society reveal this. Let's take a look at some of the highlights of the history of this society.

By the next meeting, Rev. Heys had already written a constitution. On November 30, 1954, the society approved it and sent it to the consistory. At the December 14 meeting, Rev. Heys reported the consistory's approval of the constitution. Also at that meeting Rev. Heys appointed what was known as the "sick and delinquent visiting committee." Mr. and Mrs. Gib Schimmel and Mr. and Mrs. Arie Griffioen first served on that committee. Any members who were sick or had missed more than two consecutive meetings received a visit from that committee, which then reported their visits to the society. Delinquent members were required to have adequate reasons as to why they were unable to attend. It is also worthy to note that the society chose to study the book, *History of the Protestant Reformed Churches*, for their after-recess program.

At the April 5, 1955, meeting, Rev. Hong of Korea "spoke on the living conditions and the suffering of the church in his native country." In the fall of 1955 a new season began. Rev. Heys had taken a call and the society asked Candidate Herman Hanko to preside as president "after he is installed as pastor of Hope Church." Rev. H. Hanko continued to lead the society for the next eight years until he took the call to Doon,

Iowa. Beginning in October 1955 the society studied the Declaration of Principles after recess. Occasionally, the regular after-recess discussion was set aside for special topics. On January 24, 1956, the minutes read, "The film *Precious Jewels* from Children's Retreat was shown to us by Mrs. Bodbyl." On the evening of April 17, 1956, Gib Schimmel, Fred Huizinga, John J. Dykstra, and Jay Bomers had a roundtable discussion on the Christian Labor Association. The October 16, 1956, minutes read, "The society discusses the question of 'Tricks or Treat' on Halloween."

On February 19, 1957, Gordon Terpstra (a Korean War veteran) showed pictures of life in Korea. He was unable to complete his program because the bulb in the projector burned out. Thankfully, the society allowed him to finish his presentation at the next meeting. At the meeting of September 24, 1957, the society passed a motion to give $100 from the treasury to the expansion fund of Hope school.

Regular after-recess discussions included the three points (beginning in 1958) and the Church Order (1959). Some of the occasional departures from the regular after-recess topics included a roundtable discussion on Free Masonry conducted by John Dykstra, Tom Heyboer, Roger Kooienga, and Gordon Terpstra (March 3, 1959). One after-recess debate I would have liked to witness was on the topic of smoking on April 28, 1959. Marilyn Dykstra took the stand against smoking, and Ray Ezinga and Gib Schimmel took the position in favor of smoking. On the evening of November 10, 1959, John J. Dykstra presented an after-recess paper on "Teaching our Children to be Reverent."

The February 7, 1961, meeting of the society was held at the Children's Retreat where "Mr. Lanning took the society on an interesting tour." A collection of $14.50 was taken for the Children's Retreat.

Occasionally, the society held combined meetings with other Mr. and Mrs. societies. On the evening of March 21, 1961, they met with the society of Southwest Protestant Reformed Church. A quartet of John N. Dykstra, John Kalsbeek, Roger Kooienga, and Herman Van Dyke sang a couple of numbers, and Arnold Dykstra presented a paper on the subject "Federal Aid to Private and Parochial Schools." In the fall of

1961 Dale Mensch presented a paper on "Fallout—Its Danger and Our Protection."

On April 17, 1962, the society completed its eight-year study of the book of Revelation. In the fall of 1962 the members chose to study the gospel of John. Three after-recess papers are worth noting. On December 11, 1962, John Besselsen presented a paper on the topic "Should We Hire and Pay Babysitters on Sunday?" On February 5, 1963, Ray Ezinga presented a paper on the topic "Should Marriage and Church Membership be Allowed between the Negro and the White?" Certainly the times were different then. On the evening of March 27, 1963, during a combined meeting with the Mr. and Mrs. Society from First Protestant Reformed Church, Louis Elzinga presented a paper on "Social Drinking."

In the fall of 1963 Rev. Herman Veldman became the new president. The secretary for that season, Mary Beth Lubbers, records the details of a combined meeting with the Mr. and Mrs. Society of Southwest Protestant Reformed Church. Following the Bible study there was a brief recess. "Small chatter, some scholarly dialogues, but mostly heavy smoking prevailed."

In the fall of 1965 a Senior Mr. and Mrs. Society was formed. The Mr. and Mrs. Society continued on as the Junior Mr. and Mrs. Society. At this point, the history of the Senior Mr. and Mrs. Society becomes difficult to recount. To the best of my knowledge, no minutes of the society exist from that time until the late 1990s. For whatever reason, they are missing.

Over the past few decades, leaders of the Senior Adult Bible Study, as it is called today, have included Professor Hanko, Professor Dykstra, Rev. Slopsema, Alvin Rau, Calvin Kalsbeek, Rev. Laning, Ronald Koole, Harry Langerak, Joel Minderhoud, and Rev. Overway.

Over the past several years the society has studied the life of David as found in 1 and 2 Samuel and 1 Kings. Other books studied include Judges, John, 1 Timothy, 2 Timothy, Psalms, Hosea, and presently Ephesians. The practice of having an after-recess program was discontinued by society vote a few years ago. Bible study is conducted from 8:00 p.m. until 9:30 p.m. A time of fellowship and refreshment follows.

On most alternate Tuesday evenings during the Bible study season you will find the society room filled to capacity. These gatherings of saints to study God's word are evidence of his covenantal faithfulness. "Wherefore comfort yourselves together, and edify one another, even as also ye do" (1 Thess. 5:11).

Senior Adult Bible Study Society (2016) 7th row from left: Rebecca Overway, Rev. David Overway, Valerie Van Baren, John Van Baren, Brian Kalsbeek, Jen Kalsbeek; 6th row: Carla Langerak, David Langerak, Tim Bomers, Vonda Jessup, Tamara Kalsbeek, Daniel Kalsbeek; 5th row: Rachel Morris, Jon Hop, Joel Langerak, Brenda Bomers, Michael Bosveld, Shari Bosveld, Terri Brunsting, Ryan Brunsting; 4th row: Tricia Kamps, Jori Langerak, Daryl Bleyenberg, Valerie Minderhoud, Julie Schwarz; 3rd row: Dan De Vries, Angie De Vries, Dawn De Vries, Mindy Bleyenberg; 2nd row: Chuck Doezema, Steve Langerak, Joel Vink, Jeffrey Kalsbeek, Aaron Cleveland, Vance Grasman; 1st row: Heidi Doezema, Brenda Langerak, Barb Vink, Mary Kalsbeek, Molly Cleveland, Susann Grasman

## Junior Adult Bible Society
### Susann Grasman

The Junior Adult Bible Society of Hope Protestant Reformed Church was formed in 1967 under the original name of the Junior Mr. and Mrs. Society. The purpose of starting that society was to study the word of

God as found in the Bible, to promote an earnest Christian life among its members, to increase their mutual acquaintance, and to benefit its members in their spiritual life and faith.

Since its beginning in 1967, the society has enjoyed studying a variety of books of the Bible under the direction of many different leaders. Samplings of the books are Genesis, Philippians, Romans, James, and Revelation. The society also enjoyed discussing many topics for the after-recess portion of society, such as psalm singing, the Church Order, signs of the times, cults, and the family. The society has been led by Prof. Herman Hanko, Marinus Kamps, Rev. James Slopsema, (Rev.) William Langerak, Prof. Russell Dykstra, Rev. David Overway, and the current leader, Gary Nienhuis. These men have capably led the society through the green pastures of God's word.

When the first constitution was adopted in 1967, society dues were 50¢ per couple at each society meeting. This was changed in 1976 when the dues were raised to $7 for the entire society season. The dues were raised again in 1984 to $15. Currently the dues are $20 for the society year. The dues are used for expressions of sympathy when a member loses a loved one in death and also to present a gift of appreciation to a speaker at the conclusion of the society season.

In 2009, desiring to include more members of Hope church, the name of the Junior Mr. and Mrs. Society was changed to the Junior Adult Bible Society of Hope Protestant Reformed Church. This past society season, 2015–16, the society was comprised of thirty-six members: seventeen couples and two single members. These members, led by Gary Nienhuis, recently completed their society season where they enjoyed a lively and profitable discussion of the book of Genesis, followed by an after-recess discussion of the Church Order.

The junior adults are active in both their society and in the life of Hope church in many ways. They are responsible for stocking and caring for the nursery. Each society season they also host a progressive dinner for the elderly saints. This highly anticipated evening is enjoyable for all, as the society members invite the elderly to church to enjoy a home-cooked meal along with fellowship and communion. The night is truly a blessing for the young and old, which is a testament to the society's dedication to promoting an earnest Christian life among its members, one that also benefits those members in their Christian faith.

Junior Adult Bible Society (2016) back from left: Gary Nienhuis (president), Luke Bomers, Sydney Bomers, Kelly Langerak, Jeremy Langerak, Chris Overway, Matthew Overway, John Cleveland, Tom Huizinga; middle: Bennett Meyer, Don Lotterman, Brent Tanis, Matthew Rutgers, Ashley Cleveland, Rich De Meester, Kristin Huizinga; front: Sara Meyer, Hillary Lotterman, Sara Schipper, Erin Rutgers, Nelle De Meester, Iva Lim

## Young Adults' Society
### *Laura Huizinga*

While Hope church has held societies for the young people and married members, for many years there was not a society for the young, single adults of the church. This changed in the early 2000s when the Young Adults' Society was formed. This society was formed in order to give those "in between" Senior Young People's Society and Junior Mr. and Mrs. Society a society home and place in society life.

Rev. David Overway is the current leader of the society, which meets twice monthly on Sunday nights after the evening service. Previously, the society has been led by Gary Nienhuis, Cal Kalsbeek, our former pastor, Rev. J. Laning, and Aaron Cleveland.

Presently the society is studying the New Testament book of Romans. Over the past few years they have enjoyed studying books of the Bible, such as, Malachi, Philippians, and 1 Timothy, as well as good Reformed literature, including *When You Pray* and *Mysteries of the Kingdom*, both written by Prof. H. Hanko.

These young adults are active in the church, as well as with each other. Together they enjoy outings and activities, such as, bowling, game nights, and mall scavenger hunts. A plan to organize a sing-along with the elderly saints of Hope church is currently in the works. This activity is sure to be enjoyed by the young and old alike.

In 2016 the society numbers twenty-five to thirty young adults who enjoy studying God's word together and who are always looking for and welcoming new members who are interested in joining them as they serve God in Hope church.

Young Adults' Society (2016) 4th row from left: Peter Koole, Cody Bomers, Tyler Koole, Chad Jessup, Nathan Jessup, David Koole, Caleb Koole; 3rd row: Joel Rau, Jesse Kamps, Matthew Streyle, Jared Bosveld, Patrick Streyle, Adam Streyle; 2nd row: Jason Koole, Emily Langerak, Lydia Koole, Annica Bosveld, Laura Huizinga, Emily Hop, Jesse Bomers; 1st row: Rev. David Overway, Monica Koole, Brianna Langerak, Sara Doezema, Rose Doezema, Katherine Doezema

## Monday Night Class

### *Jeffrey Kalsbeek*

The Monday Night Class had its origin in the church's youth. It began with a group of young adults and an equally youthful minister who matched their energy.

The group and their new leader's youth was observable even by the starting time of this society. After the last catechism class on Monday night, the class began their discussions at 10:00 p.m., when most adults are having their first thoughts of retiring for the night.

Rev. Ronald Van Overloop, newly ordained into his first charge in October of 1972, was asked by a group of Hope's young people to lead a Bible discussion class. They were single, young men and women who had recently made confessions of their faith. They were no longer in Young People's Society, but also did not fit in the Mr. and Mrs. societies. In January 1973, the consistory minutes record approval for Rev. Van Overloop to lead this new class. Rev. Van Overloop remembers, "I was asked by the young people who had made confessions of their faith, if we could have a regular meeting." He recalled that "it was a very interesting class with a lot of discussion." And also "my love for and appreciation of young people was developed through that experience."

From its origination as members from Hope's congregation, the group began evolving into a class for any west-Michigan young adult to attend. Most likely, the addition of attendees' friends first caused it to expand beyond Hope church's young adults. One former attendee counted at least six marriages related to attending the class. This is a delightful evidence of God's stamp of approval. Incidentally, this is still happening on a denominational scale today, as many marriages are a result of meeting at the various young adult retreats that are held every so often. Young adults manifest themselves as committed to marrying in the Lord, unwilling to look elsewhere. Importantly they seek one with an interest in spending time discussing God's word. Considering this, it is not surprising that one of the early studies with Rev. Van

Overloop was *Marriage: The Mystery of Christ and the Church*, authored by a minister in Loveland, Colorado, Rev. David Engelsma.

The class continued leaderless when, in 1977, Rev. Van Overloop was allowed by Hope's consistory to spend eight months ministering in New Zealand. When he accepted the call from South Holland Protestant Reformed Church to be missionary in Birmingham, Alabama, in 1979, the group determined to keep meeting. Two seminary students attempted to keep the class going. One was a young seminarian, Barry Gritters, who remembers, "We suggested to the consistory that we study the thirty or so pamphlets that Professor Hanko had written on the covenant. We began discussing them until the group got so small, we thought it would die. That's when we decided to ask Professor Hanko if he would take it over. He did, and that was that."

Prof. Herman Hanko led the Monday Night Class for many years. At one point, there were inquiries from married couples who were interested in coming to the Bible study. The group, along with Professor Hanko, decided against this because they wanted to keep the class geared for single adults.

One individual remembered studying Matthew 5–7 and 24–25. "These chapters took us a number of years and we had lively discussions. This was because Professor Hanko was open and willing to entertain many broader subjects and questions that came up in the course of our discussing. It took a while before we got back to the chapter we were studying. This resulted in many interesting discussions on any number of topics, which added a real zest to the overall class." After the class ended for the evening, Professor Hanko didn't always get a reprieve. But he was up to the task. As one recalls, "When the class was smaller, afterwards a group of us would head to the Rainbow Grill, and Professor Hanko would come along with us, where we would smoke and continue to discuss various subjects. Later, as the class began to grow, we stayed at Hope church for coffee together there, and Professor Hanko stayed around, and we had more lively discussions. We had Professor all to ourselves, could ask him any question, and he was willing to discuss it."

Another interesting dimension to the class was the attendance of quite a number of single adults from outside the Protestant Reformed Churches. This brought questions, with the resulting discussions, that otherwise would not have been considered.

Another former participant states, "The Monday Night Class has always been an important part of the life of young adults in the Grand Rapids area, in my estimation." Professor Hanko himself affirms that the class was a help to him. He authored the book *When You Pray* after studying the subject of prayer with the class. In its preface he relates, "We spent nearly two years—a total of over sixty meetings...I owe the Bible class a debt of gratitude."[2]

Upon retirement, Professor Hanko asked Prof. Russell Dykstra, then a member of Hope congregation, to become the new leader of the Monday Night Class. Professor Dykstra, similar to Professor Hanko, is not averse to taking a few weeks to discuss a particular issue that comes up in the class, before getting back to the scriptural passage of study. With his involvement on the committee of contact, Professor often informs the class of what the denomination is doing around the globe and gives presentations on his trips to other lands. In addition, seminary students have given presentations on their internship labors, which give young adults a perspective of the catholicity of the church, otherwise unknown.

## Young People's Society
### *Susann Grasman*

The Young People's Society of Hope Protestant Reformed Church was organized on August 29, 1937. Rev. Hubert De Wolf was the leader, and the book of Philippians was chosen for the first discussion topic. Dues were set at 10¢ a person. The members of that young society numbered eight: John Dykema, George Engelsma, Melvin Engelsma, Sybil Engelsma, Evelyn Kievit, Henreitta Korhorn, James Kuiper, and Elizabeth Moelker.

---

2    Herman Hanko, *When You Pray: Scripture's Teaching on Prayer*, (Jenison, MI: Reformed Free Publishing Association, 2006), xii.

One of the first orders of business for those young people was to request a piano for the church. In 1938 the consistory granted their request "with the understanding that the organ retains its place." A piano was soon purchased and paid for with a $5 donation from the Men's Society and the Ladies' Aid Society and with the Young People's Society contributing $30.

Early leaders of the society who followed Rev. De Wolf were Rev. J. Heys, Rev. H. Hanko and Rev. H. Veldman.

When controversy came to the Protestant Reformed Churches in 1953 it deeply affected the Young People's Society. This is clearly seen in the minutes, which state: "at the start of the 1953 society season a motion was made and supported to discuss each week for our after recess program the present controversy in our churches, both politically and doctrinally."

God was with his people at Hope church through the split of 1953, and Hope church continued to grow. This was true of the Young People's Society as well, as the society was becoming too large. In 1968 the society officially split into two groups—that of a senior society and a junior society. This continues to the present time, as the young people continue to meet together for an hour after the morning worship service to study God's word and to enjoy Christian fellowship together. God's faithfulness over the generations is clearly seen as what started as a small group of eight, young saints seventy-eight years ago has grown into a senior society of twenty-nine and a junior society of nineteen in 2015.

As societies these young people of Hope maintain an active role in the church in many different ways. They participate in the annual Sunday school program by performing a special number and annually host a fall singspiration, a winter soup supper, and an ice cream social after the Good Friday worship service.

A highlight of the year for both the young and old is always the annual Christmas caroling, when the young people visit and sing with the elderly, sick, widows, and widowers of the congregation. These visits by the young people are always met with many thanks, appreciation, and love and are looked forward to throughout the year.

Cornelius Den Boer with carolers in December 2004, back from left: Ben
Laning, Mike Cnossen, Grant Streyle, David Koole, Ben Rau; middle: Rachel
Koole, Phillip Koole, Jordan Koole, Luke Bomers, Sara Kamps, Carolyn
Cleveland; front: Joel Minderhoud, Cornelius Den Boer, Missy Van Baren

Praise the Lord for his covenantal blessings seen in the youth of
Hope Protestant Reformed Church!

Senior Young People's Society (2016) back from left: Ryan Brunsting, Dustin
Nienhuis, Jared Minderhoud, Derrick De Vries, Caleb Rutgers, Jacob De
Vries, Samuel Bomers, Kyle Doezema; middle: Elyssa Schwarz, Jacob
Cleveland, Lydia Kamps, Zachary Koole, Caitlyn De Vries, Aaron Langerak,
Larissa Langerak, Richard Van Baren, Rachel Rutgers, Hannah Kalsbeek, Ellie
Jessup; front: Rev. Overway (leader), Melanie Terpstra, Kara Minderhoud,
Rebecca Hop, Katelyn Bosveld, Megan Vink, Taylor Schwarz, Josie Doezema

Junior Young People's Society (2016) back from left: Kyle Lotterman, Eric Doezema, Jacob Kamps, Nathan Minderhoud, Isaac Jessup, Luke Koole, Justin Cleveland; middle: Justin Bosveld, Joseph Overway, Alec De Vries, Nathan Van Baren, Roseanna Bomers, Nicole Hop, Megan De Vries; front: Mr. Brian Feenstra (leader), Cole Kalsbeek, Nathan Cleveland, Derek Koole, Leah Rau, Sarah Kalsbeek, Madeline Langerak

## Eighth-grade Bible Study Class
### *Jeffrey Kalsbeek*

As with almost all Bible study groups, this class's inception arose out of the organic life of the congregation, not the institute.

Don Lotterman noticed a need and took it upon himself in 1980 to lead a study for the eighth graders. With the last Sunday school class being seventh grade, and the Junior Young People's Society beginning with ninth graders, Don's desire was to have a class that would in some way prepare eighth graders for the new experience of society life.

Preparation and learning how to study and discuss the scripture has been the focus of the eighth-grade class ever since. The eighth graders are transitioning from being taught in a lecture format to discussing scripture in a group setting. They learn to read and meditate on the Bible in order to enter Young People's Society equipped to be productive members.

Some of the early class attendees remember Don's peculiar habit of cleaning out his ears with his car keys during discussion. This is a reminder to all society leaders that if kids remember nothing else, they will have your idiosyncrasies engraved in their memories. His strong personality and affable nature were endearing to the eighth graders in his classes.

When Don began to become heavily involved in the group that had formed to become the eventual sister church of Grace, he asked Jeff Terpstra to lead the class. Jeff led the class for the next twenty years, with one respite of three years, which was filled by Tim Koole. Jeff remembers that Don had the class become acquainted with all aspects of society life, including taking minutes and having officers. This has since been discontinued in favor of the main object that the class learns to study and discuss the scriptures. Hebrews 11, the parables of Jesus, and the Judges, have been frequently studied passages.

When Jeff Terpstra concluded his time as leader in 2014, Jeff Kalsbeek was asked to continue the class. The class meets after the morning worship service for twelve to fifteen weeks from October to February.

Eighth-grade Bible Study Class (2016) back from left: Mr. Jeffrey Kalsbeek, Emily Rutgers, Kamryn Jessup, Evan Langerak, Calvin Cleveland, Owen Kalsbeek; front: Anna De Vries, Katherine Morris, Trevor Minderhoud, Ethan Vink, Alicia Brunsting

# Discussion Groups
## Calvin Kalsbeek

One aspect of Hope's life of communion and fellowship dates its beginning to the time of Rev. Van Overloop's ministry in the middle 1970s. While most of Hope's societies are very much age specific, the goal for Discussion Groups was to provide a spiritually uplifting setting that would cut across age barriers and be conducted in a somewhat informal setting.

To accomplish this the meetings take place after the evening worship services on the second Sunday of the months of October, November, January, February, March, and April, and the participants are divided into small groups that meet in the members' homes. A significant change was begun in 2015 to accommodate participants who require handicapped accessibility. Consequently the groups now divide into small groups and meet in the church basement.

Subjects of discussion and the division into groups are planned by two couples from the membership and are subject to the approval of the consistory. Discussion outlines on a variety of subjects have been used. Here is a sampling of the topics discussed: "Are You Married to Television?" "Christian Recreation," "Our Obligation to the Slow Learner," "The Christian and Suffering," "The Sabbath Day and Its Observance and Preparation," "Self-Examination," "The Signs of the Times," "The Place of the Single Person in the Church," "Christian Stewardship," "The Role of Parents in Sunday School," "Facing Temptation," " The Way Movement," "Bible Translations," "Public Worship," "What Does the Scripture Teach Us about Angels," "The Devil and Demons," "The Christian and Organ Transplants," "Raising Covenant Children," "Addressing God in Prayer," "The New Age Movement," "Euthanasia," "Post-millennialism," "Union Membership," "The Internet, the Family, and I," and "Personal Witnessing." On occasion discussion groups have discussed books and pamphlets. A few examples are *The Fruit of the Spirit* by Rev. Richard Smit, *Studies in Philippians* by Rev. Carl

Haak, and *The Shadow of the Cross: Studies in Self-Denial* by Walter J. Chantry.

While Discussion Groups continue to be a spiritually edifying forum for fellowship at Hope, it has for various reasons lost some of its cross-section-of-the-congregation flavor. At the present time (2016) about thirty members participate and the pamphlet, *The Doctrine of God* by Rev. Houck, is the subject of discussion.

## Sunday School
### Susann Grasman

The Sunday School of Hope Protestant Reformed Church was begun in order to instruct the youth of the congregation in the word of God and all matters pertinent to it. The Sunday school works under the jurisdiction of the consistory of Hope church. The elders visit the classrooms regularly each season. The Sunday school also follows a constitution written in 1964.

The first recorded meeting of the Sunday school teachers was held in February 1953 in the home of Richard and Betty Bloem. The first order of business for that meeting was to elect the following officers: John Kuiper, superintendent; Sybil Engelsma, secretary; Richard Bloem, treasurer; and Jacob Kuiper, vice-superintendent. The beginning balance on hand for the Sunday school in 1953 was $42.40. At that time the Sunday school met from September through June and used *Our Guide* Sunday school papers. These papers were first published by South Kent News and cost Hope church $75. This was paid for by church collections until 1967 when collections for Sunday school were eliminated. The cost of the *Our Guide* papers is now a part of the annual church budget.

Early on the Sunday school was also in charge of planning the Hope church (Sunday school) picnic. The teachers were responsible for the games, while their wives were in charge of prizes and gifts. This was changed in 1964, when a committee from the congregation was formed to plan the annual church picnic. This first committee consisted of Mr. and Mrs. Peter Koole, Mr. Joe King, Mr. Arnold Dykstra, and Mr. Marinus Kamps.

The Sunday school Christmas program, given by the Sunday school children on Christmas morning after the worship service, has always been a highlight for the congregation. In the early days practices were held starting in November on Friday evenings from 7:15 to 9:00. Each teacher was responsible for his or her section of the program. Starting in 1965 a candy bar and an orange were given to each Sunday school student. Although each student still receives M&M's and oranges, practices are now held on Sunday mornings after the worship services, and the Sunday school now appoints a separate committee to plan the Christmas program.

A pin system was introduced in 1969. Each Sunday school student who capably recited his or her merit work was given a pin. Parents were invited to the first session of the season to witness a special presentation were these pins were given out. Although the pin system is no longer in use, a $5 gift certificate to the Reformed Book Outlet is awarded to all students who recite merit work.

Currently, the Sunday school meets after the morning worship services from 11:15 to 12:00 during the summer months of June, July, and August. *Our Guide*, now published by the Protestant Reformed Sunday School Association, is the teaching material used. The teachers, led by Superintendent Jon Rutgers, meet every other week for an hour to discuss the lessons for the upcoming two weeks.

The membership of the Sunday school in 2016 was 99 students, consisting of preschool through seventh grade. With thanksgiving to God, the purpose of the Sunday school in Hope church remains the same as it was in the early days of the congregation as the teachers continue to instruct the youth of the congregation in the ways of the Lord and in the light of his word.

Sunday school teachers back from left: Jonathan Rutgers, Luke Bomers, David Rutgers; front: Anne Buiter, Linda Kalsbeek, Laurel Lotterman, Annica Bosveld, Alyssa De Vries, Lynn Oosterhouse

Preschool back from left: Chase De Vries, Levi Cleveland, Walter Langerak, Jared Cleveland, Oliver De Meester; front: Cara Kalsbeek, Brooklyn Huizinga, Sonya Minderhoud, Lillian Rutgers, Ella Miersma, Aubrey Rutgers

Kindergarten back from left: Tyler Tanis, Daniel Langerak, Dean Langerak, Colton Huizinga, Evan Cleveland, Caleb Schipper; front: Ondra Kalsbeek, Gwenyth Overway, Ruby Van Uffelen, Jane Duistermars, Sarah Brunsting

First grade back from left: Lydia Minderhoud, Harry Langerak, Jakob Rutgers, Eli Miersma, Graham De Meester, Ava Cleveland; front: Alanna Kalsbeek, Leah Kalsbeek, Sara De Vries, Jenna De Vries, Laura Cleveland

Second grade back from left: Ian Cleveland, Joseph Oosterhouse, Benjamin Overway, Levi Overway, Roy Doezema, Jeremy Rutgers; front: Raquel De Vries, Ava Langerak, Madison Schwarz, Annika Kamps

Third grade back from left: David Langerak, Liam Kalsbeek, Stefan Rau, Nicholas Oosterhouse, James Cleveland, Dirk Van Uffelen; middle: Michael Cleveland, Myles Miersma; front: Eloise Langerak, Mona De Meester, Avery De Vries, Emma Bosveld, Clair Kalsbeek

Fourth grade back from left: Isaac Cleveland, Jonathan Bomers, Owen Langerak; front: Lindsay Minderhoud, Elaine Doezema

Fifth grade back from left: Eli Langerak, Caleb Kamps, Jeremy Langerak, David Cleveland, Joel Hop; middle: Toby Van Baren, Ethan Cleveland; front: Emma Van Uffelen, Michelle Langerak, Eleanor Duistermars (Caleb Cleveland missing)

Sixth grade back from left: Brendan Langerak, Jedd Kalsbeek, Russell Van Baren, Levi Klamer, Lydia Miersma; front: Grace Kalsbeek, Emma Minderhoud, Claire De Vries, Jessica Morris, Sally Doezema, Callie De Vries

Seventh grade back from left: Austin Koole, Joshua Bosveld, Joel Rutgers, Chet Doezema, Zachary Schwarz, Jake Van Uffelen, Josiah Bomers; front: Caroline Duistermars, Elena Overway, Rachel Langerak, Leah Hop, Hannah Kamps, Allison Terpstra, Stephanie Langerak

## Hope Heralds

### Susann Grasman

Hope church is, and always has been, a singing church. This is evident throughout her history in many ways, one of which is the Hope Heralds. The Hope Heralds, a male chorus, was formed with the purpose of singing praises to God. This service of praise originated a few years before its formal organization when four men of Hope church formed a male quartet in order to herald God's praises in song. Wanting others to share in their enjoyment and service they expanded prior to 1960 to an octet comprised of Richard Bloem, John N. Dykstra, Melvin Engelsma, John Kalsbeek Jr., Roger Kooienga, Gerald Kuiper, Don Langerak, and Harry Langerak. This octet continued to grow, as David Meulenberg, Herman Van Dyke, Merle Veenstra, and John Besselsen joined the group in January 1960.

In February 1960 those twelve men selected the Hope Heralds as a name to characterize the purpose of their chorus. Soon a constitution was adopted and in October 1961 the constitution received approval from the consistory of Hope church, giving formal existence to the Hope Heralds as an organized entity.

In the years that followed, the Hope Heralds praised God's holy name with the singing of psalms, hymns, and spiritual songs. They have sung for society gatherings, seminary convocations and graduations, residents of retirement homes, young people's programs, and for many recordings for the *Reformed Witness Hour*.

The Hope Heralds has also ventured out of west Michigan to perform concerts in Canada, Indiana, Illinois, Iowa, and Wisconsin. These road trips have given the choir opportunities to share God's love and grace through song.

However, the choir's main focus is, and always has been, to sing for the retired saints in the Grand Rapids, Michigan, area. In doing so, the men have found that wherever they sing, one of their songs touches a heart in a way that God's providence arranged for that particular person. That is a humbling way to express the Lord's grace and mercy to those who may be hurting or struggling in one way or another!

For many years the chorus performed under the direction of Gerald Kuiper. Before him both Richard Bloem and Clare Kuiper served as directors. The current director, Dan Van Dyke, has directed the Hope Heralds since 1998. Gerald Kuiper's daughter, Karen Daling, the latest of six persons to serve as pianist, has accompanied the choir for the past thirty-two years (she started in 1984). Prior to Karen's service, Jake Kuiper, Lois Schipper, Bonnie Moelker, Bill Langerak, and Bonnie Kuiper all served as accompanists.

"We have grandpas, dads, and sons singing together—generations of men—and they do it out of the joy of their hearts to praise God! It is amazingly beautiful, seeing the blessings of the covenant experienced in such a wonderful way. It is invariably something that is mentioned when we speak with the saints in the retirement homes after our concerts, which we do! We never file out and leave as soon as the concert is done, but we mingle with the audience and talk with the people for a while. It is always special and moving to sing for people, some of whom are obviously deep in the stages of Alzheimer's disease, and to see them suddenly singing the words along with us! Music is a very powerful pathway of praise to our God, and it embeds itself in our hearts. This recall that the older saints gain for a few moments is an evidence of that fact."
—Karen (Kuiper) Daling, accompanist for Hope Heralds

Today, the Hope Heralds with Dan Van Dyke as director enjoys steady growth as men who desire to praise God with their voices continue to join. The chorus consists of between sixty-five and seventy men of all ages. The youngest member this past season was fourteen and the oldest was nearly eighty. Together these men are a blessing to the saints they sing to as they praise God in song![3]

## Choral Society of Hope Protestant Reformed Church

### Susann Grasman

Singing has always been an important part of the Christian's life, and this is true for the members of Hope church as well. Desiring to praise God with music, a male chorus from Hope church was formed in 1948. Originally an eight-member group, or octet, these men formally organized in 1949 with Eno Howerzyl as president, Dewey Engelsma as vice-president, and Richard Bloem as secretary. The all-male octet met faithfully each Thursday night to sing, accompanied by Mrs. John (Hattie) Lanning. Soon the chorus group was asked to give special numbers at various events, including Hope school's 1950 PTA meeting and also at the twenty-fifth anniversary celebration of the Protestant Reformed Churches, which was held on March 10, 1950.

On January 14, 1952, with a strong desire to include more members of Hope church, the male chorus officially reorganized as the Choral Society of Hope Protestant Reformed Church. During its first year, the Choral Society consisted of twenty-two members and was first directed by Mrs. John Lanning and accompanied by Miss Sybil Engelsma. The dues were set at 25¢ per week, and concerts were given twice a year, typically at Easter and Christmas. In 1956 the Easter concert had to be cancelled due the after effects of the 1956 Standale tornado.

---

3  From the beginning and long into its illustrious history, the Hope Heralds was Hope church's men's choir and thus under the supervision of Hope's consistory. Over the years many from other congregations have joined the heralds, resulting in a membership numbering over sixty-five, of which a small number are members of Hope. Consequently at present the Hope Heralds is an organization independent of consistory oversight. The group has maintained the name Hope Heralds, not because of its ties to Hope church but because their message of hope continues. —Editor

Over the years, the Choral Society was led by many capable and enthusiastic directors, including Mrs. J. Lanning, Richard Bloem, Jacob Kuiper Jr., Clare Kuiper, Gerald Kuiper, Roland Peterson, Dan De Meester, and Dan Van Dyke. Many talented accompanists also faithfully served the choir, including Sybil Engelsma, Marilyn King, Terri Garvelink, Mary Veenstra (20 years), Bonnie (Bylsma) Kuiper, Linda (Kuiper) Corson, and Karen (Kuiper) Daling.

At each concert the choir normally took a collection, with the proceeds generously given to a worthwhile kingdom cause, such as the Protestant Reformed schools throughout the United States, the *Beacon Lights* and *Standard Bearer* magazines, Protestant Reformed scholarship fund, and once toward the purchase of a piano for Hope church.

After struggling to fill its ranks for a few years, the choir disbanded in 1995, thus ending forty-seven years of singing praises to God. However, as the Choral Society presented a special number at both the fiftieth- and seventy-fifth anniversary celebrations of Hope church, it is fitting that a choir has been formed to sing at the one-hundredth anniversary celebration. We look forward to hearing the "Choral Society" once again in June 2016.

One-hundredth anniversary choir

# Catering Committee
## *Linda Kalsbeek*

Hope's catering committee has contributed much to the fellowship and communion of Hope.

I have been a member of Hope church for over forty years, and as long as I have been a member the catering committee has played a part in the life of the church. I remember the older women (at that time I thought they were the older women, now they would not seem old) prepared the food, and the younger women came to church later to serve the food. The catering committee has changed over the years, but the service to the church has not changed. The women still serve meals as needed at church functions, prepare food for the meetings of classis and synod hosted by Hope church, and serve at gatherings after funerals.

Some things have changed regarding how the catering committee functions: no longer is it a task for just a few women, rather it includes most of the women of the congregation, serving together, taking turns, and working together to make the work less time consuming.

## 2016 Catering Work Groups

*Voluntary permanent chairwoman
The first person listed is the chairwoman for that group.

| Work Group 1 | Work Group 2 | Work Group 3 |
|---|---|---|
| Tresa Koole | Bonnie Moelker | Deb Vander Waal* |
| Tamara Kalsbeek | Helen Medema | Carolyn Cleveland |
| Vonda Jessup | Melinda Bleyenberg | Connie Meyer |
| Mari De Vries | Cheri Rutgers | Pam Engelsma |
| Laura Huizinga | Valerie Minderhoud | Terri Brunsting |
| Katlyn Tanis | Kelly Langerak | Rachel Morris |
| Jori Langerak | Kate Van Uffelen | Dawn De Vries |
| Gladys Koole | Rose Rutgers | Heidi Doezema |

| | | |
|---|---|---|
| Carol Schimmel | Kristin Huizinga | Katelyn Vermeer |
| Grace Lotterman | Valerie Van Baren | Angie De Vries |
| Brenda Engelsma | Fred Engelsma | |

| Work Group 4 | Work Group 5 | Work Group 6 |
|---|---|---|
| Cori Hop * | Elaine Rau * | Brenda Bomers * |
| LeAnn Streyle | Althea Brunsting | Marcia Miersma |
| Sherry Koole | Beth Grasman | Carol Nienhuis |
| Karla Kamps | Ruth Oosterhouse | Barb Huizinga |
| Sharon Kamps | Carla Langerak | Carol Tanis |
| Jo Klamer | Mary Kalsbeek | Brenda Langerak |
| Sue Grasman | Shari Bosveld | Tricia Kamps |
| Lydia Koole | Nelle De Meester | Julie Schwarz |
| Lynette Oosterhouse | Laura Rutgers | Tabi Feenstra |
| Tami Cleveland | Ashley Cleveland | Linda Kalsbeek |
| Erin Rutgers | Rebecca Overway | Sara Schipper |

Clearly, having different work groups responsible for the catering requires careful planning. While some fine tuning of this system has been necessary, the result is a smooth system functioning under a written set of guidelines.

The chair and co-chair of the work group will work together and call all of the members of their group to tell them that they need to work a certain function at a certain time. A work group member who is unable to work when her group comes up is responsible for finding her own replacement.

The chair and co-chair decide on the food that is needed, order and/or shop for it, and have it all organized for when the work group arrives. Assignments regarding what needs to be done and who will be doing it are then made.

The work group will prepare punch (no red), coffee, fix buns, prepare dinner, and whatever else needs to be done for the function. For each function that is served, coffee and paper products (plates, napkins, and utensils) must be purchased. Styrofoam cups are in the kitchen. The remaining products and food will be given to the family who was served.

Food purchasing will be done with a debit card from the catering account by the chair of the work group. Debit cards are available from Mary Kalsbeek or Melinda Bleyenberg. If you are purchasing from Gordon Foods, Melinda also has a discount card for it.

The work group chairman must count how many people were served and fill out the appropriate funeral or dinner form for record keeping. (These forms are in the catering committee's binder in the church kitchen in the drawer underneath the telephone.)

A bill for food and supplies (along with the $25 fee, see below) must be given to the renting party. The chairman must keep receipts of food purchases and submit them along with the payment from the party that was served to Melinda Bleyenberg.

In case of a funeral, the funeral home will ask for a food bill. They will write a check to Hope church for the food amount and (generally) include a $50 honorarium donation. Return all receipts, debit card, and check from the funeral home to Mary or Melinda.

In the event that Hope church hosts classis and synod, the catering committee will contact the appropriate work groups, with one group working each day that the body needs to be served. The chairpersons from each work group will meet together to plan the menu for the days/week. The work groups may enlist the help of the ladies of the congregation to provide baked goods for coffee time.

With the exception of funerals, a $25 fee must be charged to each party that we serve. (Funerals are not charged this fee due to an honorarium donation…from the funeral home.) This fee is for miscellaneous supplies for the kitchen, such as, coffee and cups, cream and sugar for society, council and consistory meetings, salt and pepper, towels, table coverings, cleaning products, and replacing utensils and other necessary kitchen items (updated March 2016).

Some things have not changed. One is the catering committee's sumptuous meal of roast beef, mashed potatoes, and various vegetables, and another is the recipients of the committee's meager profits: Protestant Reformed seminary students.

A few typical responses to Hope's catering services follow:

"We take this opportunity also on behalf of synod, to extend hearty thanks for the [catering] service. I'm sure you have been thanked by individual members of synod, but we think that service as timely, efficient, and friendly as yours deserves also this more formal expression of appreciation. Be assured that your efforts were not lost on the synod of 2014."—Don Doezema, stated clerk

"Thank you for catering lunch and breakfast to our hungry group at the 1993 PRTI Convention. The food was delicious, the portions substantial, and the service impeccable. We teachers aren't an easy group to please, but you did it!"—Dirk Westra, secretary of the Protestant Reformed Teacher's Institute

Ladies of Hope church, thank you for the services you perform on behalf of the life of the church.

*Chapter 13*

# SONS OF HOPE
# IN THE GOSPEL MINISTRY

## Editor's Introduction

Then the word of the LORD came unto me, saying, before I formed thee in the belly I knew thee; and before thou camest forth out of the womb I sanctified thee, and I ordained thee a prophet unto the nations. Then said I, Ah, Lord GOD! behold, I cannot speak: for I am a child. But the LORD said unto me, Say not, I am a child: for thou shalt go to all that I shall send thee, and whatsoever I command thee thou shalt speak. Be not afraid of their faces: for I am with thee to deliver thee, saith the LORD. Then the LORD put forth his hand, and touched my mouth. And the LORD said unto me, Behold, I have put my words in thy mouth. —Jeremiah 1:4–9

THE LORD'S CALL TO THOSE HE WILL have serve his cause in the gospel ministry comes to each individual in God's way and in God's time; few in as dramatic a fashion as revealed in this account of God's call to the prophet Jeremiah. Nevertheless, no matter the circumstances, in each case his call is just as real, serious, and irresistible. God will have his spiritual house preserved, and that in large part through the preaching of the word.

No congregation may boast in the sons God has called to the gospel ministry from her midst, but the fact that she has those sons is evidence of God's good pleasure to use that congregation to rear, nurture, and prepare some to take up this high calling. Hope thanks God for his covenantal faithfulness in calling eight of her sons to serve in the gospel ministry. Hope thanks these sons for their willingness to share their stories in this chapter: stories which follow in chronological order according to their dates of ordination.

## Prof. David J. Engelsma

### *Thanks to Mother Hope on Her One-Hundredth Birthday from a Grateful Son*

It is right that a son honor his mother.

It is especially necessary that a son honor his mother if she has been a good mother.

He honors her by being thankful to her and expressing his gratitude.

Hope Protestant Reformed Church in Walker, Michigan, is my spiritual mother, and she has been a good mother.

To her I am grateful.

I welcome this splendid opportunity publicly to express my gratitude.

Into Hope I was born and baptized as a son of the congregation in 1939. My parents were members of the congregation. My father's parents, Charles and Lena Engelsma, and grandmother, Jennie Engelsma, as well as my father as a little child, Dewey Engelsma, were founding members of the congregation when she was organized as a Christian Reformed church in 1916. God kept my father's family faithful to sound Reformed doctrine and life during the schism in the congregation in 1924, occasioned by the Christian Reformed Church's adoption of the false doctrine of common grace. Thus they were part of the small, insignificant, despised band of poor farmer folk that made up one of the three congregations that formed the Protestant Reformed Churches in 1924–26.

When my earthly mother, Dena (Koole) Engelsma, married my father in 1938, she joined Hope from First Protestant Reformed Church in Grand Rapids, of which her parents were charter members.

Both my father and my mother were members of Hope when they died. Both were translated into the church triumphant from this institution of the church militant at their death.

Hope Protestant Reformed Church, her thinking, and her way of life are my spiritual DNA, by the mysterious working of the Holy Spirit of truth.

But the Spirit uses the truth to make one truly a child of a true church. That truth was especially the instruction in catechism for about eleven years by Rev. J. A. Heys and then for about four years by Rev. H. Hanko. Under Rev. Hanko I made public confession of faith and thus became a full, confessing member of Hope Protestant Reformed Church and of the visible church of Jesus Christ on earth on October 27, 1957.

All the while, of course, I was also nurtured by the preaching of the word twice every Lord's day by Heys and Hanko. Diligent attendance of the worship services of the church—twice every Sunday and rigorous observance of every special service—was as much an unquestioned part of our family's life as eating regularly every day and as sleeping every night. I distinctly remember sermons of sixty or more years ago and the spiritual impressions they made upon my soul. For example, at an Old Year's service, when I was a young teenager, perhaps thirteen, Rev. Heys pointed to the clock on the north wall of the church auditorium (with my mind's eye, I can see that clock and the minister pointing to it as clearly as though I were sitting in that worship service at this moment), inexorably moving toward midnight of the last day of another year, and drove home the point that thus the life of every one of us—thirteen-year-old teenagers as well as their parents and grandparents—was moving continuously to death, judgment, and eternity. Whether I then thought of the truth in precisely those terms, the truth that came home to me in that service was that life without Jesus Christ, life lived without hope in the resurrection, life lived in disobedience to the will of God, life lived outside the church is utter vanity—empty, worthless, hopeless, foolish.

The sound instruction and godly discipline at home—realities and powerful influences—were founded on the confession and teaching of the truth of the Reformed faith by the church.

Therefore, I heartily acknowledge my indebtedness to mother Hope in the words of John Calvin in his *Institutes* concerning the role of the church institute in the salvation of her members, particularly her members who are children and young people.

> There is no other way to enter into life unless this mother [the visible church] conceive us in her womb, give us birth, nourish us at her breast, and lastly, unless she keep us under her care and guidance until, putting off mortal flesh, we become like the angels...Away from her bosom one cannot hope for any forgiveness of sins or any salvation.[1]

Hope's prominent role in my life extended also to my marriage. I married a daughter of the congregation, whose family were also long-time members from Hope's early days. Her father, John Lanning, served often with my father as elders of the congregation. Both were members of the first board of Hope Protestant Reformed Christian School in the early 1940s, before the school was instituted. She was Ruth Lanning. Such was Hope's role in our wedding that this son and this daughter of the church married in a worship service of the congregation.

Memories of life with mother, from my childhood and youth, abound.

The earliest are not all pleasant. My very earliest memory is of great distress at church. During a Sunday morning service, in the small, white, wood-frame building on Wilson Avenue, long since destroyed, as a very small lad I buried my head in my father's lap and cried. I was afraid of the visiting minister. He roared, as it seemed to me, and pounded the pulpit vehemently. Prof. George M. Ophoff was the visiting preacher, and he was a loud and lively speaker. In later years, I recognized in his

---

1    Calvin, *Institutes of the Christian Religion*, 4.1.4, 21:1016.

pulpit presence what was said of the Scottish reformer, John Knox, in only slightly different words: he shouted, came near to pounding the pulpit to splinters, and seemed about to fly out of the pulpit upon the congregation, probably upon one terrified little boy.

The struggle and division in the churches in the early 1950s, culminating in schism in the denomination and in the loss of almost half of the small Hope congregation made a deep impression on a boy of twelve to fourteen years old. Former friends argued angrily on the church grounds after the services. Family gatherings that had always been peaceful and joyful broke up in shouting and tears.

In that controversy over the covenant, resulting in the denominational schism of 1953, when I was an impressionable fourteen, Hope stood fast on the old paths of sovereign grace. She was a good mother in those dangerous days. She protected her children. She did not scatter them and their generations into the winds of false doctrine, along ways that forsook the Reformed faith, and unto apostatizing churches.

On behalf of ourselves, as well now of our children and grandchildren, my wife and I are thankful to mother Hope.

Prof. David and Ruth Engelsma and their children and grandchildren

Influential as Hope church has been in my life, it was not the church that first put the thought of the ministry of the gospel into my mind.

That influence was a gifted, unforgettable teacher in Hope Protestant Reformed Christian School, Miss Alice Reitsma.

She was the one who took an eighth- or ninth-grade schoolboy, whose interests at that time ran largely in the direction of farming, fast-pitch softball, and ice hockey, aside one afternoon and, with green eyes flashing with intensity, exhorted him to consider the gospel ministry as his calling from God. This exhortation first put the thought in his mind, a thought that never entirely left, but rather became stronger with the passing years, until the thought became a conviction.

Out of that extra-curricular instruction by the teacher in a good Christian school was born, in the power of the Holy Spirit, an active ministry of some forty-five years—twenty-five years as pastor of two churches, Loveland, Colorado, and South Holland, Illinois, and twenty additional years as professor of theology at the Protestant Reformed seminary, with sixteen years as editor of the *Standard Bearer* magazine thrown in for good measure.

Nevertheless, in regard to the call to the ministry, Hope church played her significant role. She had preached and encouraged the establishment in 1947 of the Protestant Reformed Christian school that the boy attended and at which Miss Reitsma taught.

The remembrance is vivid—although the events took place more than sixty-five years ago—of the men of Hope church, all of them working men and none of them with any experience in laying bricks and constructing a school building, putting up the school building with their own hands, Saturday after Saturday, and night after night after working all day at their jobs. They labored in the deep consciousness of the covenant of God with them and in sacrificial obedience to their calling at the baptism of their children.

The board minutes of the beginning years read: "Pay men who work on the school building $1 per hour." "Each member must fulfill a total of two days donated labor in periods of one-half day or more at a time."

These memories helped to fix in the soul of a son of such a church and of such members the necessity of good, Christian schools, as this necessity is declared and decreed in article 21 of the Church Order of Dordt: "The consistories shall see to it that there are good Christian schools in which the parents have their children instructed according to the demands of the covenant."[2]

Eternity will reveal how powerful, how widespread, how great, and how continuing from generation to generation is the influence for good in the kingdom of God, now on earth and one day in the kingdom of God in the new world, of Hope Protestant Reformed Church, a faithful, spiritual mother of what is now a very large family in God's Israel.

Out of that small, insignificant, despised band of poor farmer folk on the southwest side of Grand Rapids, of whom nothing could have been expected for the kingdom of Christ, God (who delights to make something out of nothing) has brought forth, and is still bringing forth, a multitude of his own elect, redeemed, and sanctified children, to live and reign with Jesus Christ over all things in the new world, to the everlasting praise of their heavenly Father.

Dear mother, on your one-hundredth birthday your children rise up and call you blessed (Prov. 31:28).

### A Brief Account of the Ministry of a Son of Hope Church

In the fall of 1960 a son of Hope Protestant Reformed Church in what is now Walker, Michigan, and what was then known as the Riverbend countryside, south and west of the city of Grand Rapids, began his training for the ministry of the gospel in the Protestant Reformed Churches. The theological school was the very small seminary of these churches.

This young man, only twenty-one years of age, was the first of the sons of Hope to aspire to the ministry, to study at the seminary, and three years later to graduate from the seminary and to be ordained into the ministry of the gospel in the Protestant Reformed Churches.

---

2    Church Order 21, in *Confessions and Church Order*, 387.

The young man was myself.

I wonder now whether the Rev. Prof. Herman Hoeksema did not reflect upon my entering seminary, and then upon my ordination into the ministry, that there was something fitting about the events. Well did he know that the little Hope congregation was one of only three churches that had founded the Protestant Reformed Churches in 1924–26, and one of only two churches that persevered in this union. Well did he know also that the Engelsma family was one of the few families that made up the Hope congregation in those early days. Nor was he ignorant of the fact that my mother was a Koole, a family that were charter members of Hoeksema's own First church in Grand Rapids.

God's covenantal work of salvation in the generations of believers includes not only personal salvation, but also the calling of sons of Reformed believers to the office of the ministry, as also to the other offices in the church, and the calling of sons and daughters of Reformed Christians to the position in the kingdom of Christ of Christian schoolteachers.

This covenantal working of God, in the end, is the explanation of the role of Hope church in my call to the ministry. My conviction of my call was, with one notable exception, not a dramatic, datable occurrence. Rather, it was the slow, steady, secret, spiritual, mysterious working of the Spirit upon my soul, from early childhood on. The means of the Spirit was the ordinary means of the weekly preaching of the gospel, including, importantly, catechism classes. The Bible history and doctrine that were the content of the catechism instruction made the truth of God and his Christ live in my soul as reality and of utmost importance. By these means, over the years, the Spirit bound upon me that I was called to be a minister.

I do not minimize, much less exclude, in the matter of my sense of the call to the ministry the pervasive influence of a godly, Reformed home, with which God blessed me richly. This influence too owes much to the true church, which preaches the covenantal home and family.

Even though the call was not a dramatic, "experiential," datable voice from heaven, never have I doubted, even for a moment, the reality of the call, not even when, at times, the carrying out of the call in the work of the pastoral ministry pressed me to the wall. In fact, on the contrary, like the assurance of salvation itself, the conviction of the call to the ministry has become stronger with every passing year.

"With one notable exception."

There was one exception to the rule that the sense of call was gradual and ordinary. When I was an eight- or ninth-grade student at Hope Protestant Reformed Christian School in the early 1950s, the dynamic, gifted, remarkable teacher and principal, Miss Alice Reitsma, whom I respected greatly with a respect tinged with fear, took me aside on one occasion to admonish me, with authority, to consider the ministry as my calling from God. This admonition pursued me throughout the course of my continuing studies at Grand Rapids Christian High School and then at Calvin College, until in my second year at Calvin I determined with certainty, and announced, that I would give myself to the ministry of the gospel.

Without any implication of foolish comparisons, I have always specially appreciated the account of God's use of Pastor Farel in his call of John Calvin to the ministry in Geneva. The fiery Farel was bold to lay the call to the ministry upon the conscience of a hesitant Calvin as the very call of God.

I am grateful that sometime after I had definitely decided on the ministry, perhaps during the years I was a student in seminary, I paid a visit to Alice Reitsma, then dying of cancer, to inform her of her role in my call to the ministry and to thank her for that role, as well as for all her lively, solid, Reformed instruction at Hope school.

The three years of my seminary training were, by every human standard, not only exceedingly ordinary, but also deficient.

First, the classroom and other physical features of a postgraduate school were absurd. The classroom, indeed the *entire school*, was one, very small room in the dark basement of First church. There was no library whatsoever, save for the oddity of a large, red-bound set of *The Lives of the Popes*, of all things (into which someday I must dip, just for old time's sake). My reading and research for three years had to be done in the library of Calvin College. Fortunately, that library was nearby.

There were two—*only* two—professors, teaching all the courses of a Reformed seminary curriculum. Herman Hoeksema taught dogmatics and the New Testament subjects. Homer C. Hoeksema taught church history and all the Old Testament subjects, including Hebrew grammar. The subjects that fell outside these two main categories, for instance, catechetics and what today is called pastoral theology, the two men divided between themselves.

Twice a week, the venerable Gerrit Vos, pastor of the Protestant Reformed church in Hudsonville, drove in, officially to teach me Dutch and unofficially to teach also certain practical aspects of the ministry that he thought I should know. One such piece of practical wisdom was, in the words of Vos, "Remember, Davey, you can lead sheep; you cannot drive them."

A third deficiency of my seminary experience was that for the first two years I was the only student. Two professors, or two and a half, if Vos is included, for just one student! The third year, the student body doubled with the enrollment of one other student.

Strange as the size of the student body was to me, who had just spent four years at Calvin College, the student body of which numbered about four thousand and which, therefore, offered camaraderie, it must have seemed unusual also to Herman Hoeksema. Years later, I learned that often after a morning session at the seminary, he would return home to his wife to discuss with her the progress of Hoeksema's "*ooilam*" (*ooilam* being the Dutch word in 2 Samuel 12:3 for the "one little *ewe lamb*" in Nathan's rebuke of David for his taking of the wife of Uriah). Anecdotes of my seminary years, I have related in a series of articles entitled "I Remember Herman Hoeksema," in *Beacon Lights* (October 2008 to December 2009) and will not repeat here.

One, however, deserves repeating. Herman Hoeksema did not restrict his instruction to the academic. Nor did his instruction concerning the broader life of the student have any regard for the student's preferences or circumstances. Hoeksema strongly advised against (virtually forbade) marriage by the student while in seminary ("harmful to your studies"). But equally strongly he advised (virtually exhorted) marriage prior to entrance upon the pastoral ministry ("to be unmarried as a pastor is dangerous"). That this prohibition and exhortation gave the seminarian only four months to obtain acceptance by a fair maiden, arrange a wedding, and marry, to say nothing of a honeymoon, bothered Hoeksema not at all, if it even entered into his mind. It was simply the right thing, and one could carry it off, if he put his mind to it. He had.

Looking back on the instruction and training of those three years some fifty-odd years later, I know the instruction and training to have been, not only adequate to prepare a man for the ministry, but also superb. Instruction in dogmatics by a Herman Hoeksema was the best theological education God could give a man in those days. "Nonpareil" is not an exaggeration.

Homer Hoeksema's instruction in Old Testament subjects—history and exegesis—as well as his insightful teaching of church history and his incisive explanation of the Church Order of Dordt, were excellent. Again and again in the pastoral ministry, when making sermons on Old Testament passages and in guiding consistories in handling cases with decency and in good order, I have had occasion to remember that instruction with gratitude.

This reflection on my seminary instruction says nothing yet about the chief benefit of that instruction: being taught to preach. All of the instruction was directed toward good preaching. But the practice-preaching sessions were special. In them the critique concerning both the content and the form of the first floundering efforts was thorough, sharp, learned, and eminently helpful. One emerged, painfully, a potentially capable preacher (as precious metal emerges from a fiery furnace, a *very* fiery furnace).

A general, though fundamental, blessing of my seminary training was the forming of the conviction that the Reformed faith of the creeds, the three forms of unity, is the pure and glorious gospel of the Bible; that the confession of the Protestant Reformed Churches is the distinctively orthodox expression and development of the Reformed faith; and that

David J. Engelsma (August 1, 1963), ordained in September 1963 in Loveland, Colorado

it is the calling of these churches and of every minister in them not only to teach it positively, but also vigorously to defend it against all its adversaries.

I did not graduate from the instruction of my seminary professors with the impression that Protestant Reformed ministers are to show themselves "nice guys" to the departing Reformed community of churches and to the churches that oppose the Reformed faith. Seminary did not teach me to smile engagingly at all times upon all and sundry. Tolerance of false doctrine, particularly regarding the sovereignty and particularity of grace and regarding the unconditionality of the covenant, was not tolerated, much less advised.

Because of the very real danger, also to ministers and congregants in the Protestant Reformed Churches, that the essential polemical nature of preaching, indeed of one's entire ministry, be lost, or deliberately rejected, probably from the false notions of "love" and "ecumenicity" that prevail today, I defend this aspect of my seminary training by appeal to John Calvin, surely an authority regarding what constitutes Reformed preaching and ministry.

Describing his own ministry, Calvin declares, "Complaints [against false doctrines], we make in our daily sermons."[3] The reformer explains, to the exposure of those preachers who are all positive sweetness and light, as also of those members of the church who support the "positive preachers": "It were flagitious perfidy if, while they [the enemies of the gospel] defame the eternal truth of God, we should in a manner betray it by our silence!"[4] I would add: "with a sweet smile on our face."

---

3    John Calvin, "Antidote to the Council of Trent," in *Tracts and Treatises*, ed. and trans. Henry Beveridge (Edinburgh: Calvin Translation Society, 1851), 3:39.
4    Ibid., 3:54.

That polemical preaching and teaching are necessary for the building up of the church, Calvin affirms in another place: "Then only do pastors edify the Church, when, besides leading docile souls to Christ, placidly, as with the hand, they are also armed to repel the machinations of those who strive to impede the work of God"[5]

In addition, one may read for himself the polemical nature of Calvin's preaching in his published sermons, any of them.

As for the actual ministry that Christ has given me, I served two Protestant Reformed congregations as pastor for a total of twenty-five years. The first was in Loveland, Colorado, from 1963 to 1974. The second was in South Holland, Illinois, from 1974 to 1988. Those years, from 1963 to 1988, in the pastoral ministry, were the best years of my ministry. Not the easiest, or always the most pleasant, but the best.

In 1988 with no small reluctance, I yielded to the appointment by the synod of the denomination to the Protestant Reformed seminary. There, I taught dogmatics (systematic theology), the Old Testament subjects, and, with the other professors, preaching for twenty years, from 1988 to 2008.

Prior to retirement according to the rules of the seminary, therefore, I served actively in the ministry of the gospel in the Protestant Reformed Churches for forty-five years. This activity included delegation to many meetings of Classis West and many (forty-three) sessions of synod, as well as membership in a goodly number of trouble-shooting (in the hope of trouble-solving) special committees of Classis West.

My work on behalf of Classis West consisted also of functioning as the clerk of the classis for nearly the entire time that I was a member of Classis West, some twenty-five years. In those days the agendas were usually thick and heavy (because of troubles in various congregations, but that is another story). The record, as I recall, was an agenda of four hundred-odd pages. My wife and I (a minister's wife is a help to her husband in ways she never dreamed of when she took the vow, and a good thing too, or the young woman might be frightened into declining his

---

5   John Calvin, "Reply...to Letter by Cardinal Sadolet," in *Tracts and Treatises*, ed. and trans. Henry Beveridge (Edinburgh: Calvin Translation Society, 1844), 1:29.

proposal) ran off the agendas (which my wife had laboriously typed on stencils) on an ancient mimeograph machine. It belonged in a museum already in 1965. Into that antiquated beast, we had to pour ink (and out of it the ink would often drip on to everything in its vicinity). I enlisted the entire family in the labor of compiling the pages in the proper order and then stapling the pages into individual copies of the agenda. Around and around the large table we would walk, one after the other, adding one page after the other, in proper order, to compose the copies of the agenda.

Unknowingly, Classis West remains indebted to three or four of our older children for their labors in putting together the agendas. Or, unwittingly, the children contributed freely to this work of the kingdom.

I was glad that Classis West met only twice in the year, simply on account of the miserable, time-consuming, and ink-splattering work of publishing the agenda.

Regardless of the agendas and in spite of the burdensome work of the classes that these agendas involved, the meetings of Classis West were, in the main, the most enjoyable and edifying denominational gatherings of my ministerial experience. There was good fellowship among ministers and elders who were for the most part widely separated from each other geographically. There was oneness not only in the faith, but also in the resolve to protect and promote the kingdom of Christ by deciding all cases in light of scripture, the creeds, the Church Order of Dordt, and the Reformed tradition.

There was no pushing of private agendas, no unecclesiastical conclaves of a few prior to the assembly, deciding issues beforehand, and, if such shameful behavior ever surfaced, the majority of delegates refused to connive at this disgraceful conduct. In deciding on issues and cases, there was no respect of persons.

Most of the time I taught in the seminary, I was also, by appointment of my colleagues, editor of the (unofficial) magazine of the denomination, the *Standard Bearer*. To the magazine, I had contributed regularly for many years prior to my becoming editor. Writing, therefore, came to be a prominent aspect of my ministry.

Nor was my work in the ministry limited to the sphere of the

Protestant Reformed Churches. With several theologians in other Reformed denominations of churches, I was a founding and board member of the Dutch Reformed Translation Society, whose main purpose, since accomplished, was the translation of the entire dogmatics of Herman Bavinck into English.

Since my emeritation (retirement) in 2008, I have busied myself with continuing to write for the *Standard Bearer*; with the writing of books for the vitally important Reformed Free Publishing Association; and with preaching and lecturing as opportunities presented themselves.

Little did that eighth-grade farm boy in the hinterlands southwest of Grand Rapids realize to what God was directing him by the admonition of his Christian schoolteacher. Little did the youthful graduate of the Protestant Reformed seminary in 1963 know to what labor, on and off the pulpit, God was sending him.

But this, that boy and youthful graduate is convinced of, in 2016, at the age of seventy-seven, after fifty-three years in the office of the ministry: he has been

Prof. David and Ruth Engelsma in their retirement years

privileged, having been called and God empowered, and faithful; and Hope Protestant Reformed Church has been his good mother, giving birth to his ministry and to his spiritual life.

## Rev. Kenneth Koole

I graduated from the Protestant Reformed seminary in 1977. The first semester of my seminary career in the fall of 1973 was the last semester the seminary used the basement of First church. The second semester in the spring of 1974 the seminary moved to its new structure on Ivanrest in Grandville. My first year in seminary was also Professor Decker's first year as a seminary professor.

In the fall of 1977 I took the call to the Protestant Reformed church in Randolph, Wisconsin, and moved there with my wife Pat (Rau), who was a daughter of the Hope congregation, together with our newborn son, Justin.

Pat, Rev. Koole, and Justin

We served four years in Randolph. Two more of our children, Bruce and Catherine, were born during that time.

In 1982 we took the call to Hope Protestant Reformed Church in Redlands, California, where we served for seven years. During that time the Redlands congregation built its present edifice on Brockton Avenue and vacated its old church building on Lagonia Avenue, another structure the men of the Redlands congregation had built in the 1930s. Our youngest child, Audra, was born in Redlands.

In 1989 we took the call to Faith Protestant Reformed Church in Jenison, Michigan, where we served for thirteen years.

In 2002 we took the call to Grandville Protestant Reformed Church, where we presently serve.

During my teenage years in Hope church during the 1960s, I began to consider the call to the ministry. My family, the Peter Koole family, did not become members of Hope until the early 1960s. Prior to that the family's membership was at Creston Protestant Reformed Church, which disbanded in 1962 due to its small size, the aftermath of the split of 1953 from which it never recovered.

Hope church played a role in my considering the gospel ministry, in particular through two of its ministers. The first was Rev. H. Veldman, whose preaching was of an apologetic style, sharply refuting error—that of the Roman Catholics and the Arminians in particular—which engaged my mind and led me to see the importance of the logical consistency of one's doctrinal system and thinking. Then came Rev. J. Kortering, under whose instruction I learned the essentials of Reformed doctrine. He was thorough in his instruction and demanding in his tests, as all his catechism students will tell you. In my senior year in high school, he invited me up to his study (in an upstairs room in what is now the home of Hope school's administrator) and asked me whether I had ever considered the ministry of the gospel. Hearing that I had, he encouraged me to continue to think strongly in that direction. His encouragement served as the seed that midway in my college education would help me decide to move in the direction of preparing for the gospel ministry.

Indeed, with gratitude to God I can testify that Hope church with its members and consistory had a great impact on my spiritual development and nurture in my formative years. As well it was used by God to provide me and our churches with my wonderful wife, Pat, who has been of inestimable help to me in my ministry as well as benefiting every congregation where I served.

God be thanked!

And may his Son, our Lord Jesus Christ, continue to prosper and preserve the Hope congregation in the years ahead.

—Rev. Kenneth Koole

Rev. and Mrs. Kenneth Koole (2016)

## Rev. Ronald Hanko

I still think of Hope Protestant Reformed Church as my "home" church. I've been a member there twice, and my parents are still members there, along with a sister and her family.

My father took the call to Hope in 1955, the year after I was born, and we were there until 1963 when I was eight years old and in the third grade. In 1963 my father took the call to the Protestant Reformed church in Doon, Iowa, and we did not return to Hope until 1968 when I was thirteen years old and in the eighth grade. My father was then professor in the Protestant Reformed seminary.

We, first my family and then my wife and I, were at Hope church until 1979.

Hope's consistory approved my application to enter the seminary. We were married in Hope church, and Hope looked after us during our pre-seminary and seminary days.

Ronald Hanko at his seminary graduation with his father,
Prof. Herman Hanko, and his grandfather, Rev. Cornelius Hanko

I was ordained in 1979. We moved to Wyckoff, New Jersey, and I became the minister of the Covenant Protestant Reformed Church there. We were in Wyckoff from 1979 to 1985, when we moved to Houston, Texas, and a new pastorate there. From Houston we moved to Ballymena, Northern Ireland, where I was missionary and minister from 1993 to 2001. In 2002 we moved to Lynden, Washington, and that is where we now live.

It has been over thirty-five years, therefore, since we left Hope, and we no longer know many of the younger families and members, but whenever we are in Michigan we try to get back "home" to Hope for at least one worship service. When we are back in Hope, though many things have changed, it seems in another way that things have not changed, since some of the present consistory members are sons and grandsons of the men who served us so faithfully.

My first memories of Hope are of the old church on Wilson Avenue in front of Hope school, and of the old parsonage, now the home of the administrator of Hope school. I remember, too, many of the old members of the congregation, some of them founding members and all of them now in glory. My clearest memories, though, are of the present church and parsonage. When we returned to Hope in 1968, the new church had been built and the new parsonage was under construction. My brothers and I played at the construction site.

Our ministers during those years from 1968 to 1979 were Rev. Jason Kortering and Rev. Ronald Van Overloop. Our first three children were baptized by them.

Rev. Ronald Hanko, minister of Lynden Protestant Reformed Church

We are very thankful for the years we were members of Hope and for the many ways in which we were blessed there.

We pray that God will continue to preserve his church there and make the congregation a blessing to many others.

—Rev. Ronald Hanko

## Prof. Russell Dykstra

### Years before Seminary

My life has been very much intertwined with Hope congregation. Baptized by Rev. John Heys, most of my childhood was as a member of Hope (with a two year intermission in Creston Protestant Reformed Church). I brought my bride to Hope from First church. Only two of our nine children were baptized in Hope, but six made confession of faith there. We inhabited Hope's parsonage for two different periods for a total of two years. We were members of Hope in the seminary (student) years, later as pastor, and then as seminary professor. All in all, Hope church has been a formidable force shaping my life in many ways.

The earliest memories are those of a small and quiet catechumen (five or six years old), with a young Rev. Herman Hanko teaching in the church basement of the Wilson Avenue building. He graphically described (he does not know any other way of teaching) the suffering of Jesus on the cross. Not only does that memory of his description linger, but I can still see his long arms stretched out and his hands almost reaching to the ceiling in the basement. My next concrete memory is of the Sunday when it seemed that everyone was weeping because Rev. Hanko had accepted the call to far away Doon.

I wish I could say that those memories of the then Rev. Hanko were provoking me to consider the ministry, but that was not the case. From the age of ten I focused on but one vocation, namely, teaching, and a Christian school teacher I would be.

My early memory of the worship service is also less than inspiring. It is the memory of hats: ladies hats of feathers, lace, and netting, some with wide brims, all making it virtually impossible to catch even a glimpse of the preacher. I am thankful that hats went out of style in the Protestant Reformed Churches.

Other memories? Congregational meetings. Hope was Dutch, really Dutch. Every line item was up for scrutiny and debate. Why was the heat budget up $20? What about the janitor's wage? Supplies? Even "miscellaneous" could be debated. However, a strange phenomenon in Hope's thinking never ceased to amaze me. Hope congregation was the most generous congregation imaginable. Every fall (for years), the congregation approved a budget that included a line item for some $10,000 for the small, struggling congregation in Wyckoff, New Jersey. At the same time (more than once), the men voted down proposals to put up curtains on the windows in the back of the sanctuary—a proposal grounded partly on the problem of the blinding sun in the minister's face for a few weeks every year. The curtains would cost $60, installed. But at one such meeting, one member gallantly offered to buy the minister a pair of $5 sunglasses. Unforgettable!

I had no inkling in those days, how much of Hope's generosity we would experience later in life.

As such, nothing in my early years in Hope overtly directed me toward the ministry. For years I managed to put the idea of being a preacher out of my mind. Conviction with regard to the call came after a few years of teaching, and that partly through serious conflicts that focused my attention on the ministry.

Yet, God was using Hope to prepare me for that office. I had excellent preachers and pastors as examples, the Rev. H. Hanko, Rev. H. Veldman, Rev. J. Kortering, and Rev. R. Van Overloop. I also observed many outstanding elders and deacons in those formative years. Those men were wise, stable, and balanced overseers of the church. They never sought the praise of men. They were godly, but never gave a hint of being "righteous overmuch." They were committed heart and soul to the Protestant Reformed churches and schools, and unbending with regard to the truth, and yet they were not radical in their views of other Reformed Christians.

### Our Seminary Years

Carol and I left Hope in 1976 to teach in the new Protestant Reformed school in Hull, Iowa. We left Hope with one child; we returned four years later with four. The Lord convicted me of the call to the ministry, and we returned to western Michigan for seminary. We were facing six years of schooling—two years of college courses and four at the Protestant Reformed seminary. School tuition, house rent, food, clothes, and utilities—where would the money come from? It came from working part-time jobs, our family, aid from the Protestant Reformed Churches, and a generous amount from Hope. Since the congregation was vacant when we moved back to Michigan, the consistory generously allowed us to stay in the parsonage for the cost of the utilities until a minister accepted a call. We stayed there for about five months.

During the entire six years, Hope was very gracious to us and demonstrated Christian love beyond compare. Carol still jokes that if we had been given a baby girl during that time, she would have been named either Hope or Charity, for that is how our needs were supplied to a large degree.

## The Ministry

The Lord called us to the pastorate in Doon, Iowa, in 1986, and we moved to Doon with joy.

Minister-elect, Russell Dykstra, receiving his classical diploma from Classis West in 1986

It felt a bit like coming home after the four years of teaching in Hull, Iowa. The years in Doon were very good ones for us and the entire family. The church had over sixty families and supported well its own three-room school established in the 1960s. There is something special about the closeness of a one-church- and a one-school-arrangement. The people share one life—activities, work, sorrows, and joys. The church members are close. And the minister and his family are welcomed with open arms into their community. We all—pastor, wife, and children—thrived in Doon.

The work in Doon included the ordinary work of a minister—making and preaching sermons, teaching catechism, hospital visits, pastoral work. It embraced many joys—births and baptisms, confessions of faith, weddings, school graduations, and much good Christian fellowship. And there were sorrows—youth who forsook their instruction and left for other denominations, families who drifted away, and the deaths of dear members. Of the funerals at which I officiated, a few are noteworthy. The first funeral in Doon was conducted before I was ordained. Another time, I had two funerals in one day—the circumstances of the deaths were simply too different to consider combining the funerals.

Although every ministry has joys and sorrows, the time in Doon contained decidedly more joy than sorrow. The children enjoyed the church and the small town. God led our oldest to her life's mate out of the nearby Hull congregation.

Looking back, I can see that our life in Hope was forming attitudes and thinking that would be good for the ministry. That starts with the

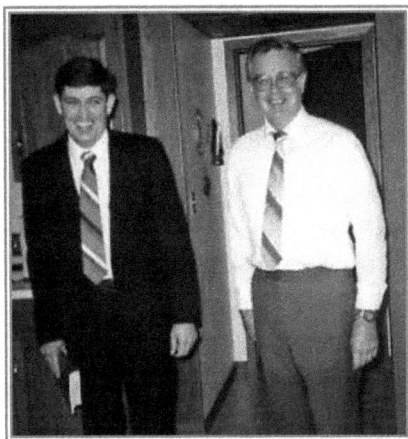

Rev. Russell Dykstra with his dad, Arnold Dykstra

high regard for elders. I did not struggle with the elders' being the rulers in the church and being my authority in the ministry. That is the way I was raised.

In addition, for all its conservatism, Hope was an outward-looking congregation. She was interested in the church world outside of the Protestant Reformed Churches. The congregation had a genuine and serious interest in missions and was well represented at evangelism lectures and rallies, as well as at special presentations on missions. She was willing to share her minister with Reformed believers in far-away New Zealand for nine months. The churches recognized Hope's interest in those matters and repeatedly appointed Hope the calling church for missionaries. Later Hope was the calling church for the minister-on-loan to the sister churches in Singapore.

Those positive attitudes certainly had some effect on my thinking and interest in evangelism and mission work. In the work of local evangelism, the congregations of Doon, Edgerton, and Hull banded together. One notable venture was a Bible study for students at Dordt College jointly led by Chester (Skip) Hunter, another former member of Hope, and me. The study thrived with many youth from the Protestant Reformed Churches and other conservative churches, and we were privileged to have groups of college students in our home from time to time.

A second new activity was a radio program produced in Sioux Center, Iowa. It was a half hour, call-in program hosted by Jim Regnerus and me on Sunday evenings (Doon's second worship service was at 2:00 p.m.). We chose our weekly topic, chose three Protestant Reformed people to call in questions on the topic, and hoped that other listeners would call in their comments and questions.

God also gave me opportunity to work on the foreign mission committee, which broadened my perspective on the church of Jesus Christ. Elder Henry Bleyenberg and I were the first to venture into Ghana. We well remember the tense feelings—landing in the strange land, the soldiers with machine guns, and entering a world where we were usually the only white faces in sight. We knew we were a long, long way from the cornfields of Iowa. My second trip for the foreign mission committee was a visit to the Evangelical Reformed Churches in Singapore. What a joy to preach to and visit with the saints there so many years ago and to experience the catholicity of the church.

All in all, the Lord taught me much in Doon. In trials and busy weeks, I learned that his grace is sufficient. God made it plain what a blessing faithful elders are to the minster, to say nothing of the blessing to the congregation. I learned to give the rule of the church over to the elders, into whose capable hands God entrusts his church. The great value of the covenantal school was reinforced in my mind. And I learned that God's people are found over all the earth.

Accepting the call to Hope in 1995 meant coming home and yet, obviously, much changed. I was now her pastor.

The congregation received us well. One of the issues with which I struggled in considering the call from Hope was Jesus' warning about a prophet not being honored in his own country. I was returning to my "own country." However the congregation was quite different from the Hope where I grew up. Most of my generation had gone to one of the three daughter congregations: Faith, Grandville, or Grace. Few of my relatives remained. I believed that Hope had a high enough regard for the minister that a lack of honor for one's own countryman would not be a problem. That was confirmed by our experience there. The congregation gave due respect to the office and received the preaching and instruction well.

Certain events in a congregation can strengthen a bond between a pastor and the congregation. Deaths, personal struggles, and pastoral counsel. In the providence of God, little of that happened in our short ministry in Hope.

And short the pastorate surely was. The year after we came to Hope, the synod of the Protestant Reformed Churches appointed me to the seminary. It was more than a shock to me. When I came to Hope, I had assumed that I was not even eligible for such a call, since the Church Order requires that a minister not be called for a year after accepting a call. Synod apparently did not believe that rule applied with synodical appointments to the seminary.

Rev. Russell Dykstra

Convicted of the call of Christ to that new labor, I bid farewell to Hope after only eight months. At my request, we never had a formal farewell. For another year we lived in the parsonage during which time I preached the Heidelberg Catechism and taught the catechism classes. When seminarian James Laning accepted Hope's call in 1997, we moved a couple of blocks and gladly continued as members.

Living in that area was a blessing: within walking distance of the church and the schools. Only after all our children were out of the home did we consider moving, and that was given significant impetus from another young family who desired the same benefits we had enjoyed. With the purchase of a new home within walking distance of Faith Protestant Reformed Church, our latest stay in Hope came to an end. But the memories and the effects remain with us, and will, all our days.

We thank God for Hope church and pray that God will continue to keep her faithful.

—Prof. Russell Dykstra

## Rev. Douglas Kuiper

God has been pleased to put me into the ministry of the word and sacraments in the Protestant Reformed Churches. I began my ministry in Byron Center, Michigan, in November 1995.

I served in Byron Center until I took the call to Randolph, Wisconsin, in December 2001. I served in Randolph until June 2012, and am currently serving in Edgerton, Minnesota.

To prepare me for this work, God caused me to be born to my covenant parents, Clarence and Janice (Lotterman) Kuiper, and to be baptized into a faithful and Reformed church, Hope church. I was a member there from the day of my baptism, November 23, 1969, until my transfer to Byron Center in 1995. Although I did not realize it at the time, God was preparing me for the ministry by the faithful Reformed preaching and catechism instruction of Hope's pastors, as well as their pastoral work from which I directly benefitted at times.

My first memories of Hope church are vague, but they regard Rev. Van Overloop, teaching catechism and greeting young children after the worship services. My formative years were during the pastorates of Rev. Flikkema and Rev. Slopsema, so my memories of them are more vivid. During their pastorates I learned that the pastor is one who cares for his sheep, and who opens his study door when they knock or ring the doorbell. To this day, as opportunity arises, I try to get the young people of my congregation to understand that it is fine to stop by my study to talk to me if they need to.

Other memories include singing in the choir, teaching Sunday school and catechism at Hope, church picnics, and attending the congregational meeting at which the congregation decided to enlarge the narthex and put bathrooms on the main floor. As a little boy I remember my parents' taking us children to a nursing home to visit an old man. Later I understood that he was Rich Newhouse.

Grandma (Nelo) Kuiper
and Rev. Douglas Kuiper

God used various factors to convince me that I must begin preparing for the ministry, but three members of Hope are worthy of mention. One was Dewey Engelsma, who spoke to me privately in the church basement, encouraging me to consider whether that was God's will for me. Another was Ann Daling: "Doug, you sure talk a lot; you should be a minister." Her comment was spontaneous, not premeditated as was Mr. Engelsma's, but it stuck with me, because I had been wondering whether that was God's will for me. The third was Professor Hanko. I visited him, in part because I knew him as a member of Hope, and because that was during the vacancy between the pastorates of Rev. Flikkema and Rev. Slopsema. My recollection is that I went to him for some advice regarding whether to study to be a minister or to be a Christian school teacher. Every argument I used against studying for the ministry, he turned on its head; and every argument I used for studying to be a teacher, he used in support of studying for the ministry.

While I was studying, the congregation supported me with prayers and gifts and encouragement. Particularly the congregational prayers and the annual food drive made an impression on me. In seminary I was single and lived at home, so I had little need; by contrast, other members of Hope who were in seminary had families. Yet the people of Hope remembered me with their gifts. That struck me. And Eileen Terpstra and Kathy De Meester spoke with me almost weekly about how my studies were going and encouraged me in them.

Kuiper family (2015) back from left: Ryan, Daniel;
front: Jared, Teresa, Rev. Douglas Kuiper, Sarah

Although I still know many members of Hope, I've certainly lost touch with the congregation as a whole, and much has changed in the twenty years since I've left. I'm thankful that we both continue to share the same love for the Reformed faith and godliness.

God has always preserved his church throughout history; he has preserved Hope from Satan's attacks many times over the last century; may he preserve you and your generations in his truth and love until Christ comes again.

—Rev. Douglas Kuiper

## Rev. William Langerak

Our family rejoices with you in celebrating the one-hundredth birthday of our spiritual mother, and we are thankful to be part of the memories.

This chapter, "Sons of Hope in the Gospel Ministry," reminds us of scripture's high estimation of Hope Protestant Reformed Church and the great calling given her as mother. "Jerusalem which is above is free, which is the mother of us all" (Gal. 4:26). Of course, this appellation applies not strictly to Hope, but to the one, universal, holy, and true church of the Lord Jesus Christ everywhere and at all times. And we ministers are not her only sons. All believers are her children. Commenting on this passage, John Calvin reminds us of the blessed privilege of having such a mother.

> The heavenly Jerusalem, which derives its origin from heaven, and dwells above by faith, is the mother of believers. She has the incorruptible seed of life deposited in her by which she forms us, cherishes us in her womb and brings us to light. She has the milk and the food by which she continually nourishes her off-spring....Certainly, he who refuses to be a son of the Church desires in vain to have God as his Father. For it is only through the ministry of the Church that God begets sons for Himself and brings them up until they pass through adolescence and reason manhood. This is a title of wonderful and the highest honor.[6]

---

6   John Calvin, *Calvin's New Testament Commentaries: Galatians, Ephesians, Philippians, and*

Langerak family (2015) back from left: Jared, Jason,
Rev. William Langerak, Justin, Stephen; front: Will, Charlotte, Lisa,
Karen, Katrina, Alex, Dorothy, Jessica

It has been thirteen years since our family left Hope for Southeast Protestant Reformed Church. Like a virtuous woman, Hope certainly nurtured and prepared me and my family for our future callings.

William and Karen Langerak, receiving congratulations from
Prof. R. Decker after William passed his synodical exam in
2003 and was declared a candidate for the gospel ministry

I cannot think of any particular incidents at Hope that personally moved me to enter the ministry. But one matter stands out as highly influential on me. By God's providence I learned under what seems an

Colossians, trans. T. H. L. Parker and John W. Fraser, ed. David W. Torrance and David E. Torrance (Grand Rapids, Michigan: Wm. B. Eerdmans Publishing Co., 1974), 87–88.

unusually large number of different officebearers with varying personalities, gifts, and experiences. Seven different men were my pastors.
Only the one who baptized me I do not recall. The rest I remember
well their faithful service, especially counsel, society leadership, catechism instruction, leadership, and preaching. Plus there were a myriad
of guest ministers, professors, and seminary students who preached
during the numerous times, some lengthy, when Hope was vacant.
And elders filled in. That is where I learned that elders are very capable
not only as rulers, but also as teachers. I also learned that no matter
the servant, Hope church brought the sincere milk of the word. Then
there was influence of a wide breadth of fellowship. Our lengthy stay at
Hope plus the size of the church gave grand opportunity to make many
friends and interact with many more than only one's peers, although
regrettably I did not always take that opportunity.

A regret I have is that, being a minister's family, we are unable to
return home more frequently than we wish, especially to see the ongoing nurture of all the other sons and daughters of Hope, our spiritual
siblings. With you, and the church of God everywhere, we give humble
thanks to our heavenly Father for such a blessed mother (Prov. 31:28).
—Rev. William Langerak

## Rev. Nathan Langerak

### Memories of Life in My Mother's House

I left Hope church when I married my wife Carrie. I lived my adult
life mostly in other congregations: first at Trinity Protestant Reformed
Church, then at Crete, where I am the minister.

I have some memories of Hope as a young man. I can recall my first
congregational meeting and a lengthy and spirited debate about a new
light for the parking lot. As a teenager I remember that Rev. Laning's
catechism instruction was accompanied by the faint twangs of the piano
strings that vibrated from his deep, powerful voice. It was a combina-
tion of my age and his instruction, but I remember learning Reformed

doctrine then. It was exciting to me. I remember with great pleasure Professor Hanko's Monday Night Class, where I met my wife, and the discussions and instruction were good too.

As a son of Hope church, though, my memories of Hope are like a child's for his pleasant home life or of his mother. My memories of Hope are not colored by the experiences of adulthood in the church but by the oddities and pleasantries that make up the experiences of any child. I remember them, too, as a child with the details running together and the order mixed up.

I remember Sunday school. I can still sing psalter number 60, stanza 3 from memory. It was the Sunday school theme song every year. I savored the Wilhelmina peppermints that Elder Klamer gave to me every Sunday when I sat on my dad's lap in the council room before the worship services and the lemon drops that I got in the parking lot after church from one of the ladies. It made me feel special when those members interrupted their own conversations to take notice of the little boy tapping them on the side and to hand him a piece of candy.

Rev. Nathan Langerak, graduated from seminary and was ordained in Crete Protestant Reformed Church in 2007

There were many Sunday morning coffees and Sunday night companies with coffee, chicken buns, dessert, and sweet pickle spears of the oddest shade of green, and stacks of fancy cups, shiny silverware, and glass dishes that Mom only used for company. I remember a large silver plate displayed in the church basement that the saints in Singapore had given as a token of thanks. I remember having Cornelius Den Boer over for dinner before

Young Nathan Langerak

church on Sunday night and his polite response when he was offered a second cup of coffee: "No thank you; I'm a one-tupper."

Cornelius Den Boer, enjoying his one cup of coffee
with Michael Cleveland watching

I remember sitting in church. I liked church. I learned in church. I also counted wooden slats on the ceiling and light bulbs in the auditorium. I made hash marks for how many times the minister said "God," "Jesus," and "salvation," and other words Mom wrote down that were supposed to be related to the sermon. But I would surreptitiously draft an army tank and soon turned my doodle into a whole battle scene of swooping planes and fighting men.

I remember peculiar details about the sanctuary. I was awed by the three straight-back, wooden chairs on the pulpit, upholstered in a rusty orange fabric. I wondered why there were three. My eyes inevitably wandered to the scroll that was painted high on the wall behind the minister. I would recite to myself the Bible verse that was on it and tried to copy its oddly painted rolls on my piece of paper. I liked the scroll. It had a comforting familiarity to it. It was peculiarly Hope church. I wondered absentmindedly what it would be like to preach on that pulpit beneath that scroll, and if I did preach whether I would sit in the middle chair or one of the other two, as the visiting ministers did, in what to a boy seemed like an act of deference to the absent shepherd of the church. I was impressed by the two elders, solemnly folding the white tablecloth that covered the stacks of wine cups and bread on the communion table. I thought that table was the most beautiful in the world, and when I cleaned the church with my dad I would polish and buff that table until it had a satisfying, slippery finish.

Unforgettable were the sometimes gutsy, frequently awkward, always entertaining performances that the ushers staged every Sunday. They stalked the aisles, scoured the pews for empty spots, confidently waved whole families into spaces big enough for only half their number, easily brushed aside resistance from a firmly shaken head, and ignored the pleading eyes of the crowded occupants in a pew where the usher had determined to squeeze in just one more. Occasionally, there was the last minute hustle to put up chairs in the empty spaces up front or along the aisles. Tightly packed, everyone sat uncomfortably until they stood up to sing the first psalter number, when there was the inevitable and apparently unconscious adjustment of positions. I wanted to be an usher.

One memorable Sunday night the services of the ushers were not needed. That summer we were meeting in Southwest Protestant Reformed Church while Hope church was being remodeled. It had been an unusually hot summer. That afternoon the sky was a weird shade of yellow. The air was thick and oppressive. We got ready for church as usual. The phone rang, but we thought nothing of it until Dad told us that church was canceled because of a tornado warning. Naughtily, we were in transports of joy. We had heard about a church cancellation before, but it had never happened in our church, and we were quite certain it was never going to happen again. I do not think it has.

Normally, the members gathered every Sunday, fair weather or foul, some early, others very early, still others in the last hectic rush, and a few habitually slipping late into a seat artfully hidden from the prowling ushers. Hope church was pleasant enough to worship in during winter, but during summer the church baked. The side aisles of the church were each lined with about a half dozen, small, blue-bladed and blue-buttoned fans. Those fans normally sat as silent observers of the worship services. When the hot weather came they were pressed into the futile effort to make the inside of church a bit more comfortable. The ritual with the fans always seemed to take place during the singing of the first psalter number, perhaps because the janitor, Jake Kuiper, did it that way; so did Stan Dykstra; and then Harry Langerak did too.

During the song the janitor got up, grabbed a large wooden hanger kept conveniently near him, and quickly made his way down one aisle and up the other, opening windows and reaching up with the hanger to click the fans on high. The still air began to move ever so slightly, and the oscillating fans brought an occasional hot, but welcome draft to take the edge off the heat.

Mainly, though, the oppressive heat and humidity of a Michigan summer Sunday seemed to mock the combined efforts of the fans. Sundays always seemed to be the sunniest, hottest days. I remember being thirsty in church. We children were never allowed to get a drink. The rhythmic movement of the fans, gentle whir of the blades, and sweltering heat weighed heavy on the eyelids. I remember seeing young men slouch low in the pews, prop up psalters on the pews in front of them, and then rest their knees on those psalters. I wanted to put my knee up like that. I tried a couple of times, but my legs were too short, so the psalter fell to the floor, and I almost fell off the pew. When I was finally old enough to reach the pew in front with my knee, I realized that the position was only good for sleeping.

Langerak family (2015) back from left: Caleb, Rev. Nathan Langerak, Sadie; front: Simone, Ethan, Carrie, Noah

At Hope I first consciously remember the Spirit's stirring in me the calling to the gospel ministry. I liked catechism. I liked the stories. I liked learning the truth. After catechism one Saturday morning, Rev. Slopsema told my friend and me to stay after class. I do not remember how old we were. We might have been in the history class for seniors. I was nervous. I did not remember doing anything wrong. After the others left Rev. Slopsema told us that we should consider the gospel ministry. I am sure he said other things, too, but that word never left me and neither have the memories, instruction, guidance, love, and fellowship that I had in Hope church.

Happy anniversary, Mother!

—Rev. Nathan Langerak

## Rev. Joshua Engelsma

Dearly beloved saints of Hope Protestant Reformed Church, greetings in the name of the Son of God, who gathers, defends, and preserves to himself a church chosen to everlasting life!

I write these words to you on October 3, 2015, the one-year anniversary of my ordination and installation into the gospel ministry as the pastor of the Protestant Reformed Church in Doon, Iowa. This makes me the youngest son of Hope to enter the gospel ministry. This occasion gives me the chance to reflect on how God has led me from your midst to this small town nestled among endless cornfields ripe for the harvest.

One of the ways in which God used Hope to mold me was through the excellent instruction I received in catechism. I have vague memories of going to church on Saturday mornings as a boy to be taught by the towering Rev. Slopsema. I recall vividly the engaging lessons of Rev. Dykstra in Bible history. And I remember well the enjoyment of studying Reformed doctrine with Rev. Laning as a young man. All were used by

Rev. Joshua Engelsma

God to ground me in the scriptures and in the truths of the Reformed confessions. In fact, so influential was the instruction that I have yet in my possession all the notes I took in catechism, from the fourth grade until my second year of college.

Another subtler way in which God used Hope to prepare me for the ministry was through her capable, godly officebearers. Through these men God provided a church home where I was spiritually fed and where I grew to love the church of Christ.

God further laid the call to the ministry upon my heart through the preaching of the gospel and congregational prayers. I remember squirming through several sermons preached by Rev. Laning in which he spoke of young men heeding the call to prepare for the ministry. Through these sermons, as well as many congregational prayers offered for the seminary, God worked this conviction in my heart.

I cannot speak of the part Hope played without mentioning the loving support of the congregation as a whole. I experienced that when I was there as a single young man. My wife, Courtney, and I experienced that together after we got married. Together we received that in greater measure as God gave us children and as we continued through college and seminary. There was a steady flow of encouraging words and prayers offered on our behalf that carried us through those years. In addition your financial and material support of us was overwhelming. The baby showers, grocery showers, Christmas gifts, and private gifts were a rich blessing. It brings tears to my eyes still today when I think of all you did for us. From the bottom of my heart, and that of my wife and children, a hearty thanks!

We rejoice with you as you celebrate your centennial. It is almost unheard of in the history of the church that a congregation exists for one hundred years. It is even rarer that a church remains faithful for that length of time by continuing to preach and teach the truth. I do not say that to flatter you, but only to recognize with you the amazing grace of God as he has shown it to our denomination and to you as a congregation. All glory be to him!

But that does not mean that you or any other congregation can rest and be satisfied. As we look back in gratitude for what God has done in the past, we also look to the future. May God grant that you might continue to love and proclaim the gospel of grace in these dark days. And may he bless it to the hearts of your children and grandchildren that generations might arise that know the truth, love it, live according to it, and are willing boldly and unashamedly to defend it.

And before I close I cannot help but add one more thing. My prayer is that through you God might work in the hearts of your sons and grandsons a conviction to prepare for the gospel ministry. And thus through further sons of Hope the gospel might be proclaimed until the coming of the Lord Jesus.

"We give thanks to God always for you all, making mention of you in our prayers; remembering without ceasing your work of faith, and labour of love, and patience of hope in our Lord Jesus Christ, in the sight of God and our Father" (1 Thess. 1:2–3).

In the love of Christ,

—Rev. Joshua Engelsma

Engelsma family (2016) back from left: Caleb, Rev. Joshua Engelsma, Courtney, Jacob; front: Calvin, Noah, Charlotte

Chapter 14

# Daughter Congregations of Hope

## Editor's Introduction

THE BIRTH OF A CHILD IS AN occasion of great joy for a Christian family. Similarly as a congregation, Hope has had three such joyous occasions due to the births of three daughter congregations: Faith in 1973, Grandville in 1984, and Grace in 1995. When these congregations were born, they had 18, 26, and 26 families, respectively.

Presently they are large thriving congregations: Faith with 144 families, Grandville with 94 families, and Grace with 85 families. In fact, Faith has had a daughter congregation of her own: Providence Protestant Reformed Church. Thus it would appear that Hope could claim Providence as her granddaughter. One could speculate on the basis of the statistics in the 2015 *Acts of Synod and Yearbook of the Protestant Reformed Churches in America* that without those timely births Hope would be a megachurch of about 450 families and 1,900 souls.

Speculation aside, Hope is thankful for, and appreciative of, her daughters. She is thankful too for her daughters' willingness to expend the time and energy needed to provide the accounts and pictures of their congregations that follow. The accounts are presented chronologically from oldest to youngest by date of birth.

# Brief History of Faith
# Protestant Reformed Church

July 27, 2015

Dear Hope Protestant Reformed Church,

Greetings to you from Faith Protestant Reformed Church. We rejoice with you in the anticipated one-hundredth anniversary of the organization of your congregation. Such a milestone is certainly reason to give thanks to our covenant God who has blessed your congregation for so many years to be a faithful earthly manifestation of the body of Christ. Not only has God blessed your congregation, but he also blessed us at Faith. As a congregation born out of Hope we can rejoice with you on such an occasion.

Your committee has requested a brief history of our congregation. This task was placed in the hands of a few charter members who then put together the enclosed history. Use it as it seems best in the context of your book. Should you need any clarification please contact us.

May God's blessing continue to shine upon you and the work God accomplishes through your congregation and in the hearts of his people.

Sincerely,
Faith Protestant Reformed Church
Doug Dykstra, clerk

Faith Protestant Reformed Church was organized on February 22, 1973. For several years before that date, there had been talk of the rising need for a new church in the Grandville-Jenison area. Hope church was crowded, Hudsonville church was crowded, even using its basement for worship services (this was prior to any plans for a new building there), and more and more families were moving to the Grandville-Jenison-Hudsonville area. It was thought there was a definite need for a Protestant Reformed witness in that area.

In 1972 three men, Dale Mensch, William Huber, and Irvan Velthouse, approached the consistories of Hope and Hudsonville churches and requested permission to canvass the members of their congregations so they could evaluate the amount of interest in organizing a new church. Prof. H. Hanko was contacted, and he gave much support, guidance, and advice to the committee.

When Classis East met on January 3, 1973, a letter signed by sixteen men was presented, requesting approval for organizing a new church in the area mentioned. The request was granted, and the consistory of Hope church was appointed to be responsible for the organizational meeting.

An informational meeting was held in Hope school on February 1 to answer some questions, to inform the twenty-two interested attendees regarding the proper procedure for organizing a church, and to offer advice and encouragement. Professor Hanko led that meeting.

The organizational worship service was held February 22, 1973, according to article 38 of the Church Order, with Hope's consistory presiding. Professor Hanko preached on "The Church: Pillar of Truth," using 1 Timothy 3:15 as his text. At this meeting the following eighteen families (listed with their previous church affiliation) presented their church papers and became charter members of the new church:

Frank Block—Southeast
Andrew Brummel—Hope
John Hoekstra—Hope
William Huber—Hope

Al Karsten—Hudsonville
William Lafferty—Hudsonville
Dale Mensch—Hope
Don Offringa—Hope
David Ondersma—First
James Rau—Hope
Gerald Schipper—Hope
Herman Schipper—Hope
Clarence Tinklenberg—Southeast
John Van Baren—First
Gerrit Van Den Top—Hope
James Van Overloop—Hudsonville
Irvan Velthouse—Hope
Melvin Yonkman—Hudsonville

Charter members of Faith Protestant Reformed Church

Nominations for consistory members came from the floor, and the following men were installed by Rev. Ronald VanOverloop: Herman Schipper, John Van Baren, and Gerrit Van Den Top as elders and David Ondersma and Frank Block as deacons.

For the charter members and all others present, it was truly a most memorable and edifying experience. The uncertainty of the future and the tremendous responsibility of starting a new church were overshadowed by the great joy of helping to establish one of Christ's churches on this earth. Very helpful and loving support and encouragement was given by the consistory and members of Hope church.

Plans were immediately made for holding worship services in the auditorium of Jenison Christian Junior High School. The first service was held there the following Sunday, February 25. Society meetings and catechism classes were held in a room above the former Union Bank in Jenison. Consistory meetings and congregational meetings, as well as some catechism classes, were held at Deacon Block's home in Jenison.

The congregation was asked to put in the collection plate suggestions for a name for the new church. The consistory then presented three names at the congregational meeting on March 29. From the suggestions of Bethel, Faith, and Jenison, Faith Protestant Reformed Church was chosen.

In August 1973 Candidate Meindert Joostens accepted the call to become Faith church's first pastor. He was ordained and installed on October 5 of that year.

Several parcels of land in Grandville and Jenison were considered as possible future sites for the church and parsonage. At the congregational meeting of October 5, 1973, it was decided to purchase five acres of land on 20th Avenue in Jenison for $13,000. This money had been received from supporting churches upon Faith's organization. After months of study, the feasibility of building a church or even a wing-unit was ruled out until after a parsonage could be constructed and used as collateral toward a future sanctuary loan.

Rev. Joostens and his family moved into the newly constructed parsonage in February 1975.

On November 22, 1977, the plans and proposed financing of the new sanctuary were unanimously passed at the congregational meeting. Groundbreaking was set for the following April.

Parsonage of Faith Protestant Reformed Church

December 10, 1978, Faith church held the first worship service in its own sanctuary. In six years' time, from February 1973 to February 1979, Faith church grew from nineteen families to sixty-eight families and witnessed fifty-two baptisms. After beginning with only fourteen children in catechism classes, by 1979 there were seventy-four.

Since 1979 the church building has experienced many changes. As the congregation continued to grow, an addition was built in 1992, adding more seating in the sanctuary, a wing of society rooms, larger bathrooms, nurseries, a kitchen, and a large fellowship hall.

Church building of Faith Protestant Reformed Church

The following seven pastors have served at Faith church:

Rev. Meindert Joostens (1973 to 1978)
Rev. William Bruinsma (1978 to 1984)

Rev. Wayne Bekkering (1984 to 1989)

Rev. Kenneth Koole (1989 to 2002)

Rev. Ronald Cammenga (2004 to 2005)

Rev. Andrew Lanning (2006 to 2012)

Rev. Clayton Spronk (2014 to the present)

At organization in 1973 there were eighteen families and seventy-one total members. At the end of 2014, there were 144 families, with 617 total members. There are seven charter families and eight charter individuals remaining at Faith.

As a congregation, we give thanks to the most gracious Lord who has guided us and granted us so very much through forty-two years. The physical growth of the congregation has been above expectations and very humbling to the charter members. On June 18, 2008, an organizational service was held for Faith's daughter congregation, Providence Protestant Reformed church. At that meeting twenty-six families and one individual were present as charter members. Eight of those families came from other Protestant Reformed congregations. But, far more important than that is the spiritual growth the congregation has experienced. We have labored together through joys and sorrows, which has knitted us closer together in the true communion of the saints. We only pray that we can continue to serve God well, both internally by the pure preaching of the word and externally by being a witness of this word in our community.

"Enter into his gates with thanksgiving, and into his courts with praise: be thankful unto him, and bless his name. For the Lord is good; his mercy is everlasting; and his truth endureth to all generations" (Ps. 100:4–5).

## Brief History of Grandville
## Protestant Reformed Church

Grandville Protestant Reformed Church was conceived in 1983 as a daughter church of Hope church. Because of that, most of her charter members came from Hope. After a poll was taken in Hope, her consistory decided that there would be enough interest to go ahead with birthing a daughter church. Hope brought that request to the January 1984 meeting of Classis East of the Protestant Reformed Churches.

By God's providence on January 11, 1984, Classis East granted the organization of the Protestant Reformed church in Grandville, Michigan. The consistory of Hope was appointed to represent classis and the churches at the organizational meeting. That meeting was held on February 9, 1984, with a divine worship service led by Prof. Herman Hanko. He preached on 1 Timothy 3:15: "the church of the living God, the pillar and the ground of the truth."

Rev. Richard Flikkema, pastor of Hope church, chaired the business portion of the service. At that time, the heads of households and individuals presented their membership certificates, the chairman read the names, and declared the church officially organized. There were twenty-six families, fifty-three communicants, and a total membership of 116 souls.

*Mr. & *Mrs. Phil Baas and family
*Mr. & *Mrs. Tom Bodbyl and family
+Miss Diane Brenner
*Mr. & *Mrs. Bruce Bomers and family
+Mr. Warren Busscher
*Mr. & *Mrs. Ron Corson and family
*Mr. & *Mrs. Don De Vries and family
*Mr. & *Mrs. Herm De Vries and family
*Mr. & *Mrs. Dennis Dykstra
*Mr. & *Mrs. Jon Engelsma and family
*Mr. & *Mrs. Neal Hanko and family
*Mr. David Harbach
*Mr. & *Mrs. Paul Harbach
*Rev. & *Mrs. Robert Harbach
*Miss Amy Huisken
*Mr. & *Mrs. Jon Huisken and family
*Mr. & *Mrs. Dan Huizinga and family

*Mr. & *Mrs. Pete Kamps and family
*Mr. & *Mrs. Steve Kerkstra and family
*Mr. & *Mrs. Dan Key and family
*Mr. & *Mrs. Dave Kregel and family
*Mr. & *Mrs. Daryle Kuiper and family
*Mr. Henry Kuiper
*Mr. & *Mrs. Gordon Ondersma and family
*Mr. & *Mrs. Rich Peterson and family
*Mr. & *Mrs. Jim Reitsma
*Mr. & *Mrs. John Schipper and family
*Mr. & *Mrs. Jan ten Haaf and family
*Mr. & *Mrs. Chuck Terpstra and family
*Mr. & *Mrs. John Van Baren and family

* denotes confessing member; + denotes baptized member

Voting for elders resulted in Jon Huisken serving for three years, Richard Peterson serving for two years, and David Harbach serving for one year. Voting for deacons resulted in John Van Baren serving for three years and Tom Bodbyl serving for two years. As appointed moderator from Classis East, Rev. Flikkema also chaired the first consistory meeting held on February 14, 1984. Jon Huisken was elected as vice-president, Richard Peterson as clerk, David Harbach as assistant clerk, Tom Bodbyl as treasurer, and John Van Baren as assistant treasurer.

After organization Hope gave the Grandville congregation a generous gift of $80,000 to help the congregation meet its needs to become an established church. The weekly budget at that time was $25 for the general fund and $5 for the building fund. We had more children than adults in the early history of Grandville church. Worship services were held in the auditorium of Grandville Public High School, which is now Grandville Public Middle School, on Wilson Avenue in Grandville. The council met in a small hall off the main hallway prior to each worship service.

At the first congregational meeting of Grandville Protestant Reformed Church, on March 13, 1984, Rev. Jason Kortering was chosen to receive our first call to come over and help us as pastor. He accepted the call in April 1984 and was installed on July 1, 1984. He, his wife, Jean, and two daughters, Carol and Ellen, lived in a rented condo in Grandville until the parsonage was built.

Grandville's church property at 4320 40th Street was purchased in July, 1985, and construction was begun immediately on the parsonage, which was completed in 1986.

Grandville's church building under construction

Groundbreaking for the construction of the church building occurred July 10, 1989, and the dedication service was held in the new church sanctuary on March 27, 1990.

Rev. Kortering remained our minister until he accepted the call as minister-on-loan to the churches in Singapore in 1992.

Rev. Kortering was followed by Rev. Audred Spriensma, who accepted the call in that same year. He pastored Grandville church until he accepted the call to be missionary to the Philippines in 2002. We then called Rev. Kenneth Koole, who accepted and became our minister that same year. He remains Grandville's minister at present.

Rev. and Mrs. Jason Kortering

In 2012 Grandville congregation called Rev. Andrew

Lanning to be minister-on-loan to the Covenant Evangelical Reformed Church in Singapore, and upon his acceptance of the call he was installed in October 2012. In October 2014 Rev. Lanning accepted the call to become the pastor of that church.

We at Grandville Protestant Reformed Church have been greatly blessed by God's guidance over the thirty-one years of our existence, and perhaps Rev. Kortering's words at the groundbreaking ceremony express it best: "Let us go forward with courage and confidence in God's blessing as we stand together for the great task which he has given to us as a church, the ministry of the gospel for the gathering of Christ's church from within and without."

## Brief History of Grace
## Protestant Reformed Church

How well we remember services in Hope Protestant Reformed Church—services filled to overflowing every Sunday and everyone taking turns to sit in the monitor room in the basement. Because of this, Hope's consistory sent out a survey to see if there was enough interest in forming a daughter congregation. So it was that in January 1994 a meeting was held in the basement of Hope church to discuss the possibility and feasibility of forming a new congregation. More meetings followed and our group sent a request to Hope's consistory that we begin holding services in the Standale area.

On June 5, 1994, we began separate services in the Grand Valley Orthodox Christian Reformed Church on the corner of 8th Avenue and Lake Michigan Drive. We had to work around Grand Valley's services, which were 9:30 a.m. and 5:00 p.m. We met at 1:00 in the afternoon and 7:30 in the evening. For our first service Rev. Slopsema, pastor of Hope church, preached on Matthew 16:18. His theme was "The Building of the Church." He preached on how Christ works in us and through us, and because he builds we will be greatly blessed. With hearts filled with joy, how well did we sing with Barb Feenstra accompanying us on the organ.

Our pulpit was always supplied by either visiting ministers or seminary students. Rev. Peter Breen consented to preach three Sunday evenings each month for us. Two elders and one deacon from Hope church came to each service to "watch over us" as we were yet members of Hope church.

By October 1994 our group had grown to twenty-two families and a committee of three was appointed to work toward organization. They were Larry Meulenberg, John Kuiper, and Gerald Van Den Top. In February 1995 our group requested permission from Hope church's council and Classis East to organize. When Classis East met in First church in Grand Rapids, Michigan, on May 10, our request was granted. It was at this time that Don Lotterman resigned his office of elder at Hope church, as he saw the need of a daughter congregation. He, along with Roger King, did much of the "footwork" for the beginnings of Grace church.

In February 1995 Hope's council proposed to the congregation the support of $140,000 for the Standale group. At the congregational meeting this proposal passed.

Charter members of Grace Protestant Reformed Church

Organization as a church took place on Thursday evening, July 6, 1995. The front thirteen rows on one side of Hope church were reserved for the families taking part in the organization. We all walked down the aisle together as a group. Rev. Breen preached on "Preaching as a Means of Grace," using 1 Thessalonians 2:13 as the text. Rev. J. Slopsema conducted the business part of the organization. The officebearers elected were: John Kuiper, Don Lotterman, and Gerrit Van Den Top as elders and Gerald Dykstra, David Hanko, and Gilbert Schimmel as deacons. This was an event that we will remember, and may it be told to future generations. We began Grace church with twenty-three families and nine individuals, totaling fifty-five confessing members and fifty-two baptized members.

Our first building committee went right to work looking for suitable land to purchase for a church building. In February 1996 they sent a proposal to the council to consider buying land on the corner of Leonard and 14th Avenue and also renting a house for our first parsonage. Both were approved at the congregational meeting held February 26, 1996.

God continued to richly bless us by providing us with our first minister, Rev. Mitchell Dick. On April 21, 1996, Rev. Slopsema led the congregation in worship and installed our new minister. How thankful we were to our gracious God for giving us Rev. Dick to feed the flock with spiritual food from Sunday to Sunday.

God in his wisdom chose a different path for us to go. In December 1997 the congregation of the Grand Valley Orthodox Christian Reformed Church decided to disband and offered to sell the Grace congregation its church, property, and parsonage.

Church and parsonage of Grace Protestant Reformed Church

Grace's council proposed to the congregation to accept the offer and also to purchase 2.4 acres of land directly to the north of the church property. Those proposals passed at the congregational meeting on January 7, 1998. Already in March the sanctuary had to be enlarged. That was accomplished by removing an existing interior wall behind the pulpit area, which gave the auditorium quite a few more rows of seats.

The church bulletin of February 7, 1999, informed the congregation that it had received the final installment of money that our mother church pledged to us. How thankful we were for her generous gift, for her help and encouragement, and her many prayers offered on our behalf.

Because of membership growth, in 2001 a large addition was put on the church building. Along with more members came more Sunday school classes, societies, and larger catechism classes.

Rev. Dick was with us for twelve years and was released as our pastor in June 2008. The period of time without an undershepherd was very short.

Rev. Ronald Van Overloop

Rev. Ronald Van Overloop accepted our call to come over and help us. We witnessed his installation on November 23, 2008, as our second pastor. How thankful we are for his God-given ability to make plain the truth of the scriptures.

By the grace of God our congregation has grown spiritually, so also in numbers. According to our directory, we now have eighty-five families, sixteen individuals, with a total number of souls being 339.

We are thankful for our church, our mother church, and above all, to God. Great is his faithfulness! And may his faithfulness inspire us to be faithful to him (Lam. 3:23). —Clara Van Den Top

Chapter 15

# BLESSINGS OF HOPE'S PARTICIPATION IN GOSPEL OUTREACH

## Editor's Introduction

HOPE'S HISTORY HAS BEEN CHECKERED WITH NUMEROUS and varied efforts to honor the Lord's command to preach and baptize. This chapter will focus on those efforts as they have been directed toward an audience outside the Protestant Reformed denomination.

Through her Reformed witness committee, Hope has conducted this work on a local level beginning in the mid-1950s and continuing to the present.

In the early 1970s the synod of the Protestant Reformed Churches decided that Hope should be the calling church for a mission station in Houston, Texas. From 1974 to 1979 Hope's council carried out that work through its missionary, Rev. Robert Harbach. After Houston was organized in 1977 as Trinity Protestant Reformed Church, Hope sent Rev. Harbach to Victoria, British Columbia, where he labored until his emeritation in 1982, at which time the mission in Victoria was discontinued. In 1979 Rev. Steven Houck accepted Hope's call to serve as missionary to Lansing, Michigan. After three years of Rev. Houck's faithful labor, the Lansing field was closed for a lack of positive fruit.

Designated as the denominational calling church for a "minister-on-loan" in the early 1990s, Hope sent Rev. Jason Kortering (1992 to 2002) and Rev. Arie den Hartog (2002 to 2005) to serve the Evangelical Reformed Churches in Singapore in that capacity. The Covenant Evangelical Reformed Church in Singapore is a sister church of the Protestant Reformed Churches today as a consequence of that faithful labor.

During their time in Singapore, Rev. Kortering and Rev. den Hartog established contact with Rev. Titus and the Protestant Reformed Churches in Myanmar. Instrumental Rev. Kortering and Rev. den Hartog were in getting Hope's council involved in working with the Myanmar churches since 2006, where Hope continues to labor to the present.

In the rest of this chapter those who labored in the capacities outlined above will flesh out what has been briefly listed above.

## Reformed Witness Committee of Hope Church

### *Matthew Overway and Rick Van Baren*

Jesus Christ gave his church the following parting instruction:

All power is given unto me in heaven and in earth. Go ye therefore, and teach all nations, baptizing them in the name of the Father, and of the Son, and of the Holy Ghost: teaching them to observe all things whatsoever I have commanded you: and, lo, I am with you alway, even unto the end of the world. Amen. (Matt. 28:18–20)

The primary way the church institute follows this calling is by the public preaching of the gospel every Lord's day.

The preaching from the pulpit, however, is not the sole means to teach the gospel to all nations. With this in mind the consistory of Hope church some sixty years ago organized a committee to help the church institute "teach all nations." The committee has been made up of officebearers and men chosen by the council to assist the church with this work. Names that have been mainstays to Hope church have filled this roster: Kuiper, Langerak, Engelsma, Kamps, Koole, and Reitsma to list just a few.

Sometime in the mid-to-late 1950s the first committee was organized. Its mandate was to disseminate the truths of Hope Protestant Reformed Church. Its first name was the pamphlet committee.

One of the early struggles for the committee was to determine how *that* committee would "teach all nations." Initially there was investigation into radio broadcasts in several places around the United States and the world. That would have been work similar to the *Reformed Witness Hour* radio broadcast of First Protestant Reformed Church. However, the committee soon decided to direct its attention to a different way.

The way chosen by the committee to teach all nations was the distribution of pamphlets written by Hope's minister. The message of the pamphlets was to be a truth or doctrine as set forth distinctively by the Protestant Reformed Churches. The committee wanted to send out a pamphlet about every other month.

The first topic chosen to be a witness to all nations was the covenant. The title of that pamphlet series was *The Covenant Witness*. Because the committee had chosen that way to "teach all nations," the name of the committee was changed to the covenant witness pamphlet committee.

The first author of those pamphlets was Hope's pastor at the time, Rev. Herman Hanko. His series, which focused on the covenant, was much later included in his book *God's Everlasting Covenant of Grace* published in 1988 by the Reformed Free Publishing Association.

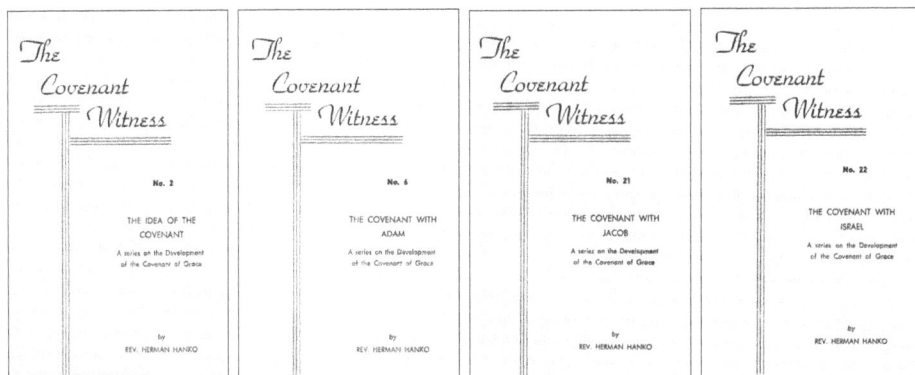

The
Covenant
Witness

No. 2

THE IDEA OF THE
COVENANT

A series on the Development
of the Covenant of Grace

by
REV. HERMAN HANKO

---

The
Covenant
Witness

No. 6

THE COVENANT WITH
ADAM

A series on the Development
of the Covenant of Grace

by
REV. HERMAN HANKO

---

The
Covenant
Witness

No. 21

THE COVENANT WITH
JACOB

A series on the Development
of the Covenant of Grace

by
REV. HERMAN HANKO

---

The
Covenant
Witness

No. 22

THE COVENANT WITH
ISRAEL

A series on the Development
of the Covenant of Grace

by
REV. HERMAN HANKO

The second author for that pamphlet series was Hope's minister, Rev. J. Kortering. His area of focus was eschatology. Shortly after he finished his series entitled, *A Study in Eschatology,* sometime in the late 1970s or early 1980s, the covenant witness publishing effort ended.

With the end of publishing the covenant witness pamphlets, the name of the committee needed to be updated, so it was changed to the Reformed witness committee.

At the beginning of the committee's publishing efforts, the readership was primarily members of Hope church and some outside contacts. However, through persistent work of the members of Hope church the mailings grew rapidly to four hundred and even to over five hundred mailings every other month.

Many responses from around the world were solicited and recorded. Some responses were positive and others were negative, but it was clear that God was blessing that work, small though it seemed. Sometimes the readers of that series would request more information, and other pamphlets and literature were sent to them.

During the early 1980s there were several people in the Allendale area who were interested in the truths of the Protestant Reformed Churches. The Reformed witness committee, under the direction of the council, started a class led by Professor Hanko. That class helped transplant some of our current members into the membership and fellowship of the Protestant Reformed Churches.

In the late 1990s and early 2000s the committee sponsored lecture series by Protestant Reformed professors. Most notably Professor Hanko did the lion's share of those lectures. The lectures were on various topics from the antithesis to God's revelation.

As time passes and technologies change, the ways available to proclaim God's truth change as well. New technologies, such as the tape player and soon after the compact disc, made it affordable and easy to record and replay sermon messages. The Reformed witness committee took advantage of those technologies and began sending audio versions of sermons to people on its mailing list.

Now with the advent of digital technology the committee is trying to use these new means to "teach all nations." The committee has developed and is actively trying to improve the website of Hope church. Recently, in co-sponsorship with Georgetown Protestant Reformed Church, an app for the Protestant Reformed Churches has been developed. The committee is actively pursuing and brainstorming new ways to use this powerful tool to teach all nations.

All of this work is very important. It can be slow, frustrating work at times. But there is always fruit—to some a savor of life unto life and to some a savor of death unto death—for God's word always has its effect. By God's grace Hope church has been used to teach his word to all the nations, and his people are being gathered.

We are thankful for all the work put in throughout the years by all the members of this committee. But most importantly we thank God and Jesus our Lord for giving Hope church the opportunity to serve our Lord in this great calling to teach all nations!

Reformed witness committee (2016) back from left: Rick Van Baren, Luke Bomers, Dan De Vries, Brad Schipper; front: Rev. David Overway, Matthew Rutgers, Joel Minderhoud

## Mission Work by Rev. and Mrs. Robert C. Harbach, 1974 to 1979

*Philip R. Harbach*

### Houston, Texas

In June 1974 Dad and Mom left Kalamazoo, Michigan, to take up domestic mission work in Houston, Texas, having been called to that field by Hope Protestant Reformed Church. On June 7 they moved into an apartment in the Hedwig Village area about eight miles west of downtown Houston. That new endeavor required a number of life adjustments. Some loneliness was involved, as that was the first time the family was separated and the children were living twelve hundred miles away. Dad and Mom needed to adapt not only to apartment life, moving in with twenty-four cartons of books, but also to the local fire department located just across the way from their bedroom window. A loudspeaker would blare the incoming call and sometimes even the address of the fire; then followed a good blast of alarms and sirens. The Katy freeway, less than one thousand feet away, had its shocking moments. Dad's letter of October 17, 1974, to the congregation of Hope church opened with his typical descriptive and graphic prose.

> My most immediate impressions of Houston are of its freeways. Advanced far beyond "clover-leafs," we how have "spaghetti bowls" merging into merges, bending and curving off into straightaways with at least five lanes one way... "Drive Friendly" is a typical Texas road sign motto, but no matter how carefully one drives, the freeway rarely affords friendly experience. Cars mass over the winding strip of concrete like so many ants scrambling pell-mell over the serpentine coils of a monstrous fire-breathing dragon. Even in the quiet and relative safety of our beds, the dragon's roar is a ubiquitous witness that it never sleeps. The tire on an oil tanker blew out. The driver jumped to safety before the vehicle overturned and

then experienced numerous dying and death-dealing convulsive explosions, which punctuated the screaming of police and fire sirens. A pall of black smoke darkened the night sky over the writhing dragon. The ants on its back clotted for miles.

Then he gave several examples of objects' flying off vehicles ahead and various near misses. And then he wrote, "By now you're saying, 'What's this got to do with mission work in Houston?' To ask the question now is to answer it. Visiting here, you'd be shown around on the quietest and most beautiful lanes and drives. Not much would you see of that ominously buzzing, snapping, tail-lashing, fire-belching dragon."

My sister, Jan, and I first visited Houston in the late summer of 1974. Meeting and visiting with the people was most enjoyable. Memorable destinations included San Antonio, Galveston, the Busch Gardens, and the San Jacinto monument. Church services were held in a room at a community club so one could see people in sports attire and carrying tennis rackets walking by the windows.

Mom played the piano to accompany the singing in the worship services even though she could not read music. She played everything by ear. She was always nervous about that. One man in the group, Mr. B, teased her about that and once said that someday there will be a symphony conductor in the audience, and he will be so impressed he will give you a good offer. Well, a visitor showed up for the Easter afternoon service and afterward Dad introduced the visitor to Mom, saying he was a symphony conductor! Mom said, "I nearly dropped over, thinking about my banging away on the piano and all the mistakes I made." Dad did not tell Mom before the service in order to keep her from being even more nervous. Mom told this to Mr. B and the whole group had a good laugh. "Many a true word are spoken in jest," Mom said. The conductor had spoken to her saying, "You have a gift; use it for the Lord."

Unexpected deaths are always a shock and a hard blow to a small group. In early 1975 Don Slabbekoorn died of a heart attack at age thirty-five. His widow, Faye, later moved back to Michigan. Still, there were the joys in the work, seeing members, especially the young couples, really enthusiastic about the group and learning more about the Reformed truth and children really loving catechism classes. Dad closed a letter in May 1975 with "So we continue to labor here, and do so with joy and satisfaction, knowing that the Lord has a people here who love His truth."

Dad loved birding and would go to the marshlands near the coastal areas loaded down with spotting scope, binoculars, camera, and field guides. He kept a written record of sightings of different species. Letters to us kids would often include detailed accounts of the location and circumstances of his observation of unusual birds. In the first ten months in Texas he had added fifty-two species to his personal list.

The bulletin of Hope church for June 8, 1975, noted that Pastor Van Overloop with elders Kooienga and Huizinga had visited Houston and reported that about ten families attended the worship services. Six families and two individuals were considered to be the core group. Based on the report, Hope's council decided organization could take place early in the fall, pending approval of the mission committee of the Protestant Reformed Churches. The Houston Sunday bulletin of August 24 noted that the group had voted to send a letter to the mission committee requesting organization.

However, the group did experience difficulties common to mission fields. Some who were thought to be committed and trusted members of the group later becoming antagonistic and eventually left the group. Some said they did not want to give up dancing, movies, and rock music. To some the Church Order was too strict; one Sunday service was enough. Some said they never really could accept our stand on divorce and remarriage. By late 1975 two families had left the group.

There was also the difficulty of finding existing Protestant Reformed literature to hand out when going door to door that was not over the heads of the average person outside the Protestant Reformed Churches. Dad wrote a newsletter, the *Calvinist Contender*, advertising the services, midweek Bible study, where to get literature, and what the Protestant Reformed Churches believe.

In the summer of 1975 we had a family vacation in a rented trailer on the beach in Galveston. A cousin from Pennsylvania joined us. As the water temperature was eighty-five degrees, it did not afford a great relief from the blazing sun.

That was the year Ima Hogg died at age ninety-three. She was the daughter of Governor Hogg. Mom wrote that women from the group told her over lunch that Texas Governor Hogg, who really wanted a son, had named his first daughter Ima and the second Ura. However, it turns out that the story about Ura is a legend. But Ima Hogg was real. She never married but she was a well-known philanthropist who contributed greatly to the culture of Texas and founded the Houston symphony.

Dad wrote in October 1975 that he had been reading and studying the works of Jay Adams and that he could use what he learned in his pastoral work on the mission field. "I only wish there had been material like this 35 years ago! But there was not."

In late 1975 Dad reported that two families had left and a third was planning to move away, leaving the group with four families. By January 1976 Dad said that since he had been in Houston the group lost about twelve souls. "We find our souls very sad." One Sunday morning there were eighteen people plus two visitors from South Holland.

Dad wrote to Hulda Kuiper and her sixth-grade class in early 1976:

Blooming shrubbery is gorgeous and there are more wild-flowers than I've ever seen or identified in my life up North. I wish I could take you all by bus or caravan to Galveston Island and show you there the myriads of magnificent marsh, shore, pelagic and water birds, and a shore nook where you could swim, wade and look for unusual shells.

Dad and Mom were in Michigan for three Sundays during June 1976 and also attended synod, which was to deal with the issue of baptism on the mission field. The council of Hope church and Dad had asked the mission committee to request that the 1975 synod appoint a study committee to clarify the issue. The study committee reported to the synod of 1976 and advised synod to declare that the mission-ary has the authority to baptize. Synod decided to put the issue to the churches for discussion for a year with a view to a decision by the synod of 1977. Dad reported to the mission committee and Hope's council in July 1976 that synod's "let's wait" decision was disappointing to the group because three families had unbaptized children. Dad believed the decision was a hindrance to mission work and was very difficult to explain to people he met.

By September 1976 four more families were joining the group, three from a Presbyterian background.

An "independent Presbyterian" minister saw the Protestant Reformed mission group's advertisement in the paper and came to worship with the group. He also visited Mom and Dad at their apart-ment and took with him some Protestant Reformed literature. He worked up a sermon on the absolute sovereignty of God, but his group rejected it. He encouraged the people to study the three forms of unity, but they rejected that also. At his next service, he had only his wife and one other man to preach to. A few weeks later some were slowly coming back.

Around January 1977 a letter requesting organization was sent to Hope's council and the mission committee. On February 15, 1977, the group was organized as Trinity Protestant Reformed Church. At least three children were baptized shortly thereafter.

In April 1977 the Houston consistory had a local lawyer draw up an incorporation document. He was told to communicate with law-yer Jim Lanting of South Holland Protestant Reformed Church, but instead the Houston lawyer wrote the document on his own. Dad said it was "full of ERA principles, women's lib thinking, and anti-Reformed individualism. If we get stuck with this document, our Reformed struc-ture will be destroyed, our freedom denied, and nothing and nobody in our church here protected." Later they got a copy of a document from Hull Protestant Reformed Church and patterned a new draft after that "most excellent document."

## Victoria, British Columbia

Dad and Mom returned from Houston to Grand Rapids in May 1977. They left later that month for an investigative trip to Canada, north of Lynden, Washington. By that time Rev. Dale Kuiper was pastor of the Lynden Protestant Reformed Church. A group of Christian Reformed people in Victoria, British Columbia, who were dissatisfied with conditions in the Christian Reformed Church were listening to the radio broadcasts of Lynden church and were using Protestant Reformed tapes and literature from Lynden church.

Dad and Mom returned briefly to Grand Rapids to make further arrangements for the work in Victoria, where they arrived again in late August 1977. It was difficult finding a furnished apartment. It took almost a month; meanwhile they rented a hotel room by the week. Space for books in the hotel room was tight, so some cartons of books stayed in the car trunk. Not knowing how long the stay in Victoria was to be, they kept the apartment on Taft Street in Wyoming, Michigan, and most of Dad's books were there. Victoria was his "workshop," but his tools were thousands of miles away. He often felt "like a workman without his tools." Several times he asked me to send him a book after he described to me its exact location not only in what bookcase, but also on what shelf and "fourth book from the left side."

The first worship service was attended by about four families out of the seven that had been contacted. The midweek Bible study meetings were attended by only two couples, but the discussion was very intense and enjoyable. Another two couples who had initially shown some interest in wanting a Protestant Reformed minister to work there later expressed that they likely would not leave the Christian Reformed Church mainly for social reasons, even though they were not happy in that church.

One might be tempted to think that all things are the same in Canada and in the United States. But Dad and Mom felt rather lonely in a different country with different postal and banking systems, long waits for checks to clear, long waits for mail to arrive from the States, and special delivery mail delivered with the regular mail. The bank told them there was a lot of stealing by the postal system. Being on an island makes for longer travel time to visit the mainland (Lynden). Canada had recently switched to the metric system so they had to adapt to that. People in the apartment on the other side of the bedroom wall often partied all Saturday night when Dad needed his rest for preaching on Sunday.

Their meeting place in Victoria was in a room at the Holyrood House, a "Scotia Dining Lounge," which referred to the Holyrood Palace in Edinburgh, Scotland; "rood" being a type of Roman Catholic cross.

As to the surrounding environment, Dad wrote, "It certainly is a breathtakingly beautiful place." The apartment was only a couple of blocks from the Lime Bay waterfront where one could spot seaplanes flying in and out, barges loaded with lumber, and railway boxcars. Off in the distance were the mountains of mainland Canada and Washington State.

In October 1977 both Dad and Mom went to Beacon Hill Park and drove along Dallas Road to various bays and points and saw a wonderful variety of birds, and Mom helped him identify some. Mom usually did not accompany him on birding trips. Commenting on his birding, he wrote, "It's too much to keep to myself...Such recreation does refit one for his work. What a glorious creation the mighty Creator has made! How beautiful heaven must be!" And later referring to views of the Olympic Mountains, as seen across the Strait of Juan de Fuca from Beacon Hill Park, "It's too much—I can't express the glory of God in His own magnificent creation!" A whole paragraph described the bird species seen in a bay area seven miles from the apartment. "Wonderful hard work. And wonderful stimulating recreation!"

Also that month Dad wrote, "After a gloomy, wet, rainy day, we had another delightful midweek meeting. This time we studied the names of God for 1-1/2 hr. We had a wonderful time of fellowship in the truth again, and also talked about more newspaper advertising and ways to contact others. These 2 families do delight in learning Reformed truth—their children too!"

On January 5, 1978, he wrote, "It does, admittedly, get lonely out here. We're in another country, on an island, away from loved ones... True it is lovely in this place and we do enjoy the most blessed fellowship with the Lord our Redeemer and with a few of His people."

In early 1978 Dad started conducting a Bible study every two weeks in Abbotsford, which is on the mainland, thus requiring a ferry boat trip each way. He still tried to communicate with those of the original group who were going back to the Christian Reformed Church, even though it was filled with entertainment and a serious lack of knowledge of Reformed truth and the scriptures. He commented,

It is an honor to represent the Protestant Reformed cause, especially in these days of apostasy...We see how much the Lord has given us—such pure Truth. Yet the work is like running into a stone wall! How ignorant people in the Reformed community are! No catechism until 12 years old! A young mother finds *A Triple Breach* so terribly hard to read and understand! The lessons of the *Essentials of Reformed Doctrine* [catechism book] are "a bit much."...They are just not *taught* in their churches. They have about 90% prejudice, 4% knowledge, and 6% lethargy and apathy. And there (here) am I, so *hungry* for God's Word, and I have to strive and strive with sickening deadheads who cannot leave their sinking ships (apostate church and profane world) because they are preoccupied triflers! Still, for an old guy...it is good to be busy in the Lord's service. We send, by His grace and providence, the Word in preaching, teaching, by the "Calvinist Contender," by news ads (in 3 papers) and by pamphlets, etc.

Yet a little later he wrote that he enjoyed leading the Bible study in Clearbrook (Abbotsford). He had been reading Berkouwer and Bavinck. "An evaluation of Herman Bavinck (as compared to Herman Hoeksema): The former is like sunlight irradiating a barrier of clouds, while the latter is like a sunbeam which shines through the clouds, the most brilliant straightedge to earth!" Regarding William Hendriksen,

Dad wrote, "I enjoy his volume on 1 Timothy. Naturally, I make my preaching on this book more Reformed and more relevant than either Lenski or Hendriksen. But these commentators do get one deeply into the task of exegetical preaching!"

Dad wrote in March 1978,

> Tremors! Earth tremors! So they tell me. Couldn't tell by me. But Sunday, during the pastoral prayer, there was an earth tremor (reminds of Acts 4:31), which shook the building, after which the building creaked (so said one). It happened while I was in my prayer mentioning the Rider on the white horse with the bow of victory and who rides on conquering and to conquer. See the Revelation 6 *context* too! Anyway, the Lord is coming! The psalms in the 90s say not that He shall come, but that He *comes* (is *on the way*).

In the fall of 1978 around the time of my parents' thirty-fifth wedding anniversary, I visited Victoria. We took in some magnificent destinations, such as the Englishman River Falls, Qualicum Falls, and Butchart Gardens, which had a moving fountain system with multicolored lighting at night. Two Rypstra brothers took me on a day hike in the beautiful Sooke Mountain area.

On March 13, 1979, Dad wrote that Elder Huisken and Rev. Van Overloop had visited the field. They had discussed Dad's applying for emeritation on the basis of article 13 of the Church Order: "by reason of age."[1] Dad's time allowed by the Canadian government was to expire in October, and he much preferred to leave earlier than that to avoid driving back over mountain passes in deep snow. So he asked for emeritation by July and recommended that the mission committee and synod send a student to continue the work until another man was called. However, of the three families in the group, one was planning to move to Lynden, another stopped attending, leaving only one family. In light of that, synod 1979 decided to conclude full-time work in Victoria in August 1979.

---

1   Church Order 13, in *Confessions and Church Order*, 385.

Rev. and Mrs. Harbach (1984)

Although the Victoria field was closed, one significant fruit of that work was that a young man from that group in Victoria, Richard Smit, became convinced of God's calling him to the ministry, which ministry has continued to be blessed today.

## The Lansing Mission

*Rev. Steven Houck*

The mission in Lansing, Michigan, began as a Bible study conducted by the Kalamazoo Protestant Reformed Church. In July 1978 the pastor began holding midweek Bible studies with four families of the Charlotte, Michigan, area. As interest grew the mission committee of the Protestant Reformed Churches became involved in the work. In January 1979 the mission committee, in conjunction with the consistory of the Kalamazoo church, began holding worship services for those families. At first retired ministers, seminary professors, and students conducted the worship services. In June 1979 Candidate Steven Houck was asked to labor with the group.

By 1979 the meeting place had changed from Charlotte to East Lansing, and four families had become six families. In June of that year, the

Rev. Steven Houck (2015)

synod of the Protestant Reformed Churches decided to declare Lansing a mission field and to put it under the care of the council of Hope Protestant Reformed Church. Synod also instructed Hope church to call a missionary for the Lansing field. The congregation called Candidate Houck. He accepted the call and was ordained as missionary on September 19, 1979. Professor Hanko conducted the installation service.

The Houck family rented a home in Haslett (not far from East Lansing).

Duplex in Haslett where the Houck family lived

The mission group rented the University Seventh Day Adventist Church building located in East Lansing at 149 Highland Avenue. This building was well suited for a meeting place.

The Houck family with part of the Lansing mission group, standing in front of the University Seventh Day Adventist Church building

Since the Seventh Day Adventists met on Saturday, the mission group had the building all to itself on Sunday. The group had two worship services on Sunday as well as several catechism classes. A Bible study was held every Wednesday. Missionary Houck also conducted a Bible study class on the campus of Michigan State University. The core group of that Bible study was comprised of Protestant Reformed students who attended the university. However, these students invited other students of Michigan State University to attend the meetings. It was a unique and interesting Bible study. Sometimes the discussions were very lively.

The Houck family (1980) back: Rev. Houck; middle from left: Elizabeth, Carolyn; front: Nathaniel, Sarah, Joel

The labors in the Lansing mission centered on the distinctive doctrines of the Protestant Reformed Churches. In the preaching, as well as in the Bible studies, the doctrines of sovereign grace were emphasized. That is the heart of the gospel. God sovereignly and unconditionally saves his elect people. That is what the people of Lansing, Michigan, needed to hear. The Protestant Reformed doctrine of the covenant was often the subject of discussions. Marriage and divorce, as well as labor union membership, were brought up on many occasions. Members of the mission group who attended the worship services and Bible studies on a regular basis heard these doctrines. Many visitors at the worship services also heard these great truths. Some received the word with open hearts. They loved the word and were very happy to hear the word. They grew in the grace and knowledge of our Lord Jesus Christ. For other people the word was a stumbling stone. It was a rock of offense. They hated the word. Most people do not want to hear that God, in his sovereignty, elects and reprobates. They do not want to hear about man's depravity or that God loves only his elect people. They do not want to hear that Christ died for his elect people only. On one occasion while Rev. Houck was preaching, a man in the audience continually shook his head, no. He did not like what he heard. On another occasion, four Seventh Day Adventists attended the worship service. Evidently they wanted to know what those renters believed. In the middle of the sermon, they all got up and walked out. That is the nature of the preaching. It is a two-edged sword that softens the hearts of the elect and hardens the hearts of the reprobate.

Because East Lansing is only about eighty miles from Walker, there was a close relationship between the mission field and the calling church. Representatives of the council of Hope church and the mission committee visited the field on a regular basis. Their counsel and advice were invaluable to the young missionary. Other members of the Hope congregation also gave much encouragement to the missionary, his family, and the mission group. The Lansing mission welcomed many visitors from Hope church who came to Sunday worship services. There were even visitors who occasionally attended the Wednesday Bible study meetings. Those visits were especially encouraging to the Houck family when there were family sicknesses, hospitalizations, and other problems. This close relationship made the Houck family feel that they belonged to the Hope congregation. They experienced not only the support of the congregation, but also the communion of the saints.

After three years of labor in Lansing, Michigan, the field was closed in June 1982. That was a sad time for the members of the mission group. They did not want the mission to close. However, both the Hope council and the mission committee agreed that there was not enough positive fruit to continue. Even though there was spiritual growth among many of the members, some did not agree with the Protestant Reformed Churches on key issues. Even though many visitors attended at various times, the group lost members rather than gained them. The organization of a church seemed unreachable.

Men from Hope church who moved the Houck family after the mission was closed from left: Bob Huizinga, Jim Langerak, Roger King, Clare Kuiper

The closing of the Lansing mission, however, did not mean that the work had been for nothing. The word of God always accomplishes God's eternal purpose. It never returns to him void. The word of God was preached and taught in Lansing, Michigan, and it did accomplish God's purpose. Many who had never heard the gospel of grace were exposed to that gospel. There was a witness of God, Christ, and sovereign grace in Lansing, Michigan. Many learned much and developed in their Christian lives. Only God knows the full extent to which he used the preaching, the Bible studies, the lectures, the pamphlets, the radio broadcasts, and the personal contacts. Even today God may be using those things to influence others. What we do know is that it was and is all for the good of God's cause and kingdom, and ultimately for the glory of his great name.

# Labors in Singapore from
# August 27, 1991, to September 5, 2002

*Rev. Jason and Jean Kortering*

### Preparing to be Minister-on-Loan

Technically my labors as minister-on-loan began on July 1, 1992. Inseparably connected with that work was our six-month stay in Singapore prior to that.

The contact committee of the Protestant Reformed Churches asked us to go to Singapore. The immediate need was the difficulty in Covenant Evangelical Reformed Church, which had a no-vote-of-confidence motion on the floor of its session. In addition to that, the assignment was to assess the possibility of the Protestant Reformed Churches' assisting the Evangelical Reformed Churches in doing mission work and theological training.

To do that work the session of Covenant church requested a special committee from First Evangelical Reformed Church to advise Covenant regarding its pastor. I had to meet with both the session of Covenant church and that committee, make an evaluation of the problems, give a possible solution, and propose that to the sessions of First church and Covenant church. That process took about four months. Untold meetings went into the wee hours of the morning. After all that work, the sessions of both churches adopted the advice of the special committee that Covenant should release its pastor under article 11 of the Church Order. It was a time of great tension—a young denomination of churches had to make hard decisions, the pastor was humble to receive the decision of the sessions as from the Lord, and by the time the six-month stay was finished, things had settled down and we could leave with the assurance that it "seemed good to the Holy Ghost, and to us" so to decide (Acts 15:28).

During all that time, I preached twice in Covenant church and functioned as pastor in the hurting congregation. I gave a lecture each Thursday evening to address such things as church government and mission outreach. I became a hurting man, exhausted physically and emotionally drained. My Crohn's disease flared up and my heart arrhythmia became scary. I visited a local Indian doctor and got some help. On the way back to Grandville, Michigan, Jean and I wondered if I had permanently damaged my body.

What did we face when we returned to the States? We faced the call to be minister-on-loan to Singapore. At the same time I also had the call to be missionary to Northern Ireland and the call to stay in Grandville, a congregation that we loved deeply. I recall saying to Jean, "The Lord has to guide the call to Singapore. I need the help of doctors to determine if my health allows it." Amazingly, the heart doctor said, "No problem, your problem is easily treatable with medication." We went to the urologist, who said, "No reason you can't work in Singapore; we have just the medication for you." We vacillated. Was that medical information good news, or did it make the decision more difficult? To my amazement, after all we had experienced in Singapore, the Lord led me to accept the call to be minister-on-loan. We both had peace with that decision. Our family supported us as well.

### Tension between the Protestant Reformed Churches and the Evangelical Reformed Churches

The best indication of the tension was during our stay prior to my being minister-on-loan. Two professors from Kampen in the Netherlands lectured in the Dutch language on the subject of the covenant. The two lectures were translated into English. When I raised concerns about the lectures, I was told that I could have my say and give a lecture in response. This I did. The question for me was, why did the Singaporean churches allow and want those lectures when they knew they came from men who sharply differed with the Protestant Reformed Churches on the doctrine of the covenant? I was fully aware of that prior to accepting the call to be minister-on-loan.

When a Dutch expat family, who was liberated in its theology, left Singapore, the tension subsided a bit. But always there was a certain discontent with the Protestant Reformed Churches. It came out at book sales: Protestant Reformed literature was not always displayed and sold. It came up in my teaching, which was questioned by some. I was even asked if that was the view of the Protestant Reformed Churches or my personal view. As time went on I was asked to give lectures on subjects relating to the well-meant offer and common grace. Not everyone appreciated or agreed with those lectures.

God in his wisdom raised a question within the Evangelical Reformed Churches in Singapore about divorce and remarriage. There was difference among them regarding whether the Westminster Confession is right or the Protestant Reformed Churches are right in their interpretation of scriptural passages regarding divorce and remarriage. I observed as the subject was discussed within the Singaporean churches and placed by classis in the hands of a study committee that an opportunity arose to express openly their opposition to the Protestant Reformed Churches. The churches became polarized on that question and eventually a split took place. The split was not clean-cut on any specific issue, but those who did not appreciate the Protestant Reformed Churches could then openly oppose them by supporting divorce and remarriage.

Obviously, that made my work as minister-on-loan difficult. As ministers learn with every pastorate, there are many wonderful things that take place, but if there is one particular difficulty, it gets the lion's portion of attention. The support and help of Hope church as my calling church was extraordinary. Let me explain.

As we worked in Singapore, and it did take time to understand what the issues were and what was really going on, I was concerned that there were two ways to deal with those issues. The first was to force the Evangelical Reformed Churches to face their differences with the Protestant Reformed Churches and immediately to call the Singaporean churches to account. That view was held by some. The second way was to work pastorally with the churches, that is, to continue the pastoral work among them—teach at every opportunity, preach the gospel as I was burdened to do, teach the truths of the Reformed faith in every prebaptism class, lecture as I had opportunity, and refer the members to good books and literature no matter what some men thought about the Protestant Reformed Churches.

The difference between those two methods was that forced confrontation would be easiest in the sense of dealing with the issue and bringing it to an end, but the danger would be to force a decision on a church not mature or ready to deal with it. A pastoral approach would allow the Holy Spirit to work in the hearts of the people and in God's time to bear fruit. My thinking was that if there had to be a split, let God arrange the events and timing according to his good pleasure. Meanwhile, it taxed my patience beyond measure.

My gratitude to Hope as my calling church is that the council supported my thinking and actions. That was so helpful to me, as I did not have to argue with my calling church, and I could focus on those in Singapore who differed. Looking back, it is quite remarkable how much "room" Hope gave me to work on those issues and did not interfere with burdensome questions. I thank God for that to this day.

### Missions and Theological Training

Missions and theological training was the enjoyable and exciting part of the labors in Singapore.

Rev. and Mrs. Kortering with members of the Singaporean churches

Preaching in a congregation that at almost every service had uncon-
verted people seeking salvation was mind altering for me. Meeting with
many of those people and having the opportunity to teach them with a
view to baptism was energizing. Opportunities for local missions were
seemingly endless.

Within a month of arriving in Singapore, I had the opportunity
to join Pastor Mahtani on a trip to India to explore mission outreach
there. Understandably Hope said, "Too soon, settle down in Singapore
and maybe later." But that was not acceptable to me, for opportunity
knocked at the door and I had to go along. Hope relented. That trip was
eye-opening for me; it was a big-time culture shock, but it prepared me
for many trips that followed.

The door was opened to work with two churches in Myanmar.

"In 1997 the synodical emissaries to
Singapore from the committee of
contact and Hope's council—Prof.
Robert Decker and myself—with our
wives met Rev. Titus, a minister from
Myanmar. Rev. Kortering taught
Rev. Titus the Reformed faith, which
he loves and preaches in Myanmar
today." —Harry Langerak

That was followed by individual pastors in India who became convicted of the
Reformed faith. It was obvious that the Lord was giving us opportunity
to work in those two countries by means of local men who were growing in their conviction of the Reformed truth.

That raised the inevitable question, how can we train those men to
be good Reformed pastors? The individual pastors represented many
other pastors and church members who were scattered throughout the
country. The great need of the hour was theological training for present
and future pastors.

That led to the formation of the theological training committee. At first its focus of interest was on the training of pastors to serve in the Evangelical Reformed Churches in Singapore. That was soon abandoned because of the ease and appreciation of the theological training available in the Protestant Reformed Churches. The Evangelical Reformed Churches concentrated on a school for the training of third-world pastors. Professor Hanko spent six months with us in Singapore to draw up a curriculum and program of instruction for that purpose. A beautiful catalog was printed for the Asia Reformed Theological School. Paulraj of India was the first student to complete a course.

I will never forget the burden for the Evangelical Reformed Churches that I felt when we left Singapore in 2007.[2] The split in the churches was just taking place. We wondered whether there would ever be a church that survived. Would all our efforts for the theological school be for nothing? We prayed mightily for Rev. den Hartog who was in the middle of all that unrest.

And look what God has done. It was in his way, in his time, and in his use of the right men for the right moment that God preserved his church. We can believe that God has much work for the Covenant Reformed Church in Singapore. It is obvious that Rev. Lanning is doing well and is richly blessed.

### Family and Conclusion

Children are so precious to family and church. Even though our children were all married and had their own homes, just to say good-bye to all of them was so painful. We had to be convinced that God's call to work took precedence over our call to nurture our extended family.

---

2    Although Rev. Kortering retired from the active ministry in 2002, he and his wife returned to Singapore on numerous occasions for extended periods of time in the years following. They traveled to Singapore in late 2006 and early 2007 at the request of the session of Covenant Evangelical Reformed Church in Singapore and with the approval of the contact committee of the Protestant Reformed Churches. During that stay, the Evangelical Reformed Churches in Singapore were in the process of adopting a decision to dissolve: a decision that took effect on June 30, 2007 (*Acts of Synod and Yearbook of the Protestant Reformed Churches in America 2007*, 83–85).—Editor

Hope church and the Protestant Reformed Churches met part of that need by providing for our return to the United States every year. What a blessing that was to us.

Jean and I worked as a team in Singapore. Many times we would sit by the kitchen table and discuss what her visit with one of the women ought to focus on. What was the issue? What Bible passage would be helpful? How should she pray? In most Asian cultures a male is not accepted to meet individually with another female. We tried doing some of those visits together, but that was even difficult. There were weeks that Jean made more "pastoral calls" than I did, simply determined by marriage and family issues.

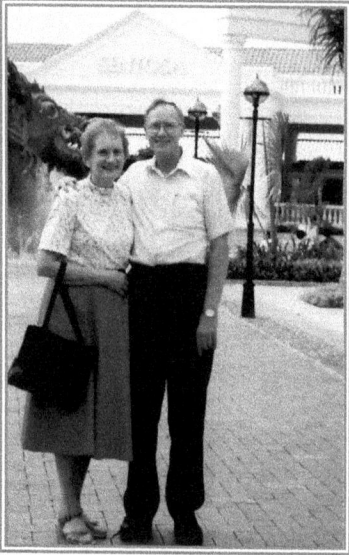

Rev. and Mrs. Kortering

We grew in our love for each other and in our spiritual life of understanding. In that way Jean never felt like I was called to the work but she was not. We were both called, and we had to work and pray together.

That work humbled me personally. Nothing made me aware of the need of the Holy Spirit in my work as when we worked with unbelievers who sought faith, when we saw the terrible consequences of sin and unbelief in the individual and family, and when we recognized that the only way of deliverance is by conversion and faith. Only God can give what is necessary, and only God can make the change so desperately needed. What a blessing to experience that in ministry; it enriches our faith, strengthens our prayer life, and teaches us to look heavenward for every need.

Thanks, Hope church, for our family visits every summer. Thanks for working closely with the contact committee so we could work together in peace and harmony. Thanks for your weekly prayers and personal letters.

To God alone be all the glory.

# Labors in Singapore
## from January 2002 to April 2005

### *Rev. Arie den Hartog*

My first term of service to Singapore began as foreign missionary of the Protestant Reformed Churches in 1979. I served there for seven eventful and exciting years. Two of our seven children were born in Singapore during those seven years. Most of them had some of their schooling there.

As missionary I experienced the great joy of witnessing the conversion of many young people from Buddhism to Christianity. I taught several successive catechism classes, which led to the baptisms of large groups of young people at once and the establishment of the church of Jesus Christ among his people in Singapore. As the young people grew up and found each other in the Lord, I had the privilege of officiating at many weddings.

Two young men were trained in the Theological School of the Protestant Reformed Churches in the United States and became the first native pastors of the recently instituted church. A second Evangelical Reformed church, Covenant, had its birth. It would be easy for me to write a book about the blessings of the Lord during those seven years.

We returned to Singapore fifteen years later in answer to the call of Hope Protestant Reformed Church and served as minister-on-loan from January 2002 to April 2005 under the supervision of Hope. Then we took only two of our children with us.

Of course, many things had changed during our absence from Singapore. The country had become ultra-modern and had a very prosperous economy and a population of more than three and a half million. Modern high-rise apartment buildings covered the island, some as tall as twenty-five stories. The city center had become impressive with its towering buildings, shopping centers, some even with major underground levels, and with the most unique architectural designs imaginable. Singapore had an extensive subway system that made it possible to rapidly travel all over the island in modern trains. Many of the young people who were added to the churches during our time in Singapore as a missionary had become highly educated and were well established in lucrative, distinguished careers. We were awed by some of the beautiful private apartments that the members of the churches lived in. Many of the couples for whom I had officiated at their marriages had children, some already in their teens. A denomination with two congregations had been formed. First Evangelical Church in Singapore had more than three hundred members.

It was a joyous and memorable event to be greeted at the airport on our arrival by so many dear saints with whom we were so well acquainted and with whom we still had deep bonds in love for the gospel and its truth that had been established in our earlier stay.

As minister-on-loan I would have the position of serving both First and Covenant congregations, though regretfully I did not serve on the session of either one of them. The church over the years had developed in her faith. Some of the members had lost their original zeal, being preoccupied with their careers, and they were no longer able to give the time and energy to church activities that they once had given. Christians had been added from other denominations, some of whom had spent several years studying overseas, especially in England and Europe, and being in Reformed and Presbyterian churches. Along with the influx of those new members came variations of doctrinal perspectives that would lead to some controversy in years to come.

During the years as minister-on-loan I was given opportunity to preach in both congregations of the Evangelical Reformed denomination. This happened almost every Lord's day. The fellowship among the saints in both congregations was blessed.

When we came to Singapore there was the newly started theological school called Asian Reformed Theological School. My predecessor, Rev. Jason Kortering, had done a lot of very good work to get the school off the ground. A few of the students came to the school from foreign countries, including a student from India and a couple from Myanmar. The school would not have met the standards of most seminaries in the United States, but I trust that it served a purpose in the providence of God at that time to help equip young men for service to the Lord. It was an interesting experience to prepare for teaching the courses there. I had to review many things from my seminary days. One is greatly helped in understanding a subject by the demands of having to prepare for teaching it to others.

During my three years as minister-on-loan in Singapore, I was heavily involved in teaching seminars for church leaders in the country of Myanmar. My passport has stamps of the seven times I traveled to Myanmar. Each stay there was for three weeks. Most of my work involved teaching men from various churches at a seminar. Instruction was given in many subjects of the Reformed faith. Classes usually had around forty men in attendance. All of the lectures had to be translated into both the Burmese language and the Chin dialect in order to be understood by the students in attendance.

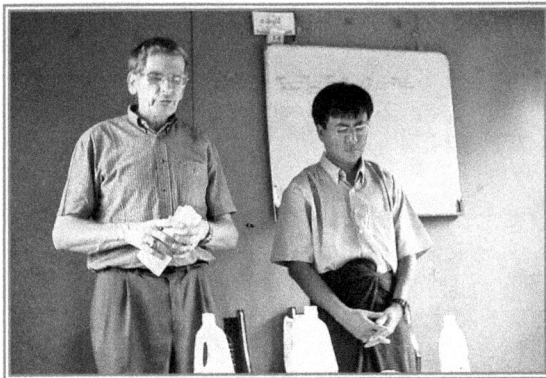

Rev. den Hartog teaching a class in Myanmar;
Rev. Titus serving as the translator

Not all of the students were at the seminars for the right reasons, but some showed themselves to be sincere men of God who were greatly interested in learning the deeper things of the Reformed faith.

Our stays in Myanmar were exciting and filled with many unusual events, far too many to be related here. We wrestled hard with administering benevolence in a desperately poor country where those who were part of the churches could not even afford basic medical care. This greatly aggravated sicknesses and diseases and even led to the sorrow of the untimely death of some who were members of the churches. There was in our hearts often a deep feeling of sadness because of inability to render much greater help to those in need. Several "self-help projects" were established so the members could support their churches and contribute to the many benevolent needs. Great complications were faced; some proved to be dishonest, and most of the projects failed.

The most lasting legacy of my many weeks of work in Myanmar is the continued existence of the Yangon Protestant Reformed Church in Myanmar, of which Rev. Titus is still the faithful pastor.

Home of Rev. Titus and place where the
Yangon church meets for worship

Women from the church in Myanmar with the wife and children
of Rev. Titus and two members of the church in Singapore

In Singapore my wife and I were involved in many labors in leading Bible study groups, some of which met in our home. There was a great deal of pastoral work with individual saints of God who struggled with various aspects of Christian living.

During our last year in Singapore the two churches struggled with some doctrinal controversies in their midst. A practical and very significant controversy involved maintaining the biblical teaching on marriage in the churches. The result of those controversies was the sad breakup of the two congregations in Singapore and the dissolution of the denomination. Some might say that differences regarding faithfulness in marriage should have been tolerated to avoid the division. I maintained that very important practical truths of Christian living, as well as their doctrinal and biblical bases, were at stake. Controversy causes pain and sorrow and division. The Lord rules over all of them for the preservation of his true church.

Hope Protestant Reformed Church was a great help for us in the years of our service in Singapore and Myanmar. We were thankful for several visits of elders and Hope's minister to help and support us in the work and to encourage members of the church there in times of controversy and divisions.

In spite of divisions, the bond of love between us and those who faithfully love the Lord and his truth abides. We rejoice that the church of Jesus Christ is gloriously catholic, called and saved and preserved in the nations of the world. As long as she is still on earth she still has many imperfections.

When I received a call from several churches in the United States at the end of our stay in Singapore, I accepted the call of Southwest. We wrestled hard with the will of the Lord and the situation in the Singaporean churches when we left. Even today we think about whether we should have stayed longer and tried even harder to help and encourage. We are thankful for having been used by the Lord as much as we were.

After some years we are greatly thankful to God, especially for Covenant Evangelical Reformed Church. She remains steadfast to the Reformed truth and is growing deeper in her love for and commitment to the precious Reformed faith, of which I had the great privilege of being one of the earliest ambassadors. We are thankful for the deepening appreciation of the truth of God's gracious covenant with his people in Covenant. Knowledge and commitment to the blessed truths of God's covenantal grace gives the members of the church a solid basis for strong and faithful Christian marriages. This in turn gives great hope that a strong and faithful church of Jesus Christ will continue in the years to come.

May the Lord also according to his purposes heal the breaches brought by disagreement over the truth of his word and cause the unity of the church to be restored for the glory of the Lord.

## Hope's Mission Work in Myanmar

### Calvin Kalsbeek

Hope church has not been deaf to the Lord's command to his New Testament church: "Go ye therefore, and teach all nations, baptizing them in the name of the Father, and of the Son, and of the Holy Ghost: teaching them to observe all things whatsoever I have commanded you: and, lo, I am with you alway, even unto the end of the world (Matt. 28:19–20)." Evidence of this is clearly seen in Hope's work in Myanmar.

### Background to Hope's Work in Myanmar

In 1 Corinthians 3 the apostle Paul laid his finger on what had transpired regarding the gospel message that had been brought to the saints in Corinth: "I have *planted*, Apollos *watered*; but God gave the *increase*" (v. 6; emphasis added). This process also aptly describes the progress of the Reformed faith in Myanmar.

Prior to Hope's involvement in 2006, the Evangelical Reformed Churches in Singapore were *watering* Reformed seeds in Myanmar largely through the labors of Rev. Kortering and Rev. den Hartog, Protestant Reformed ministers-on-loan. They were working with Rev. Titus and the Protestant Reformed Churches in Myanmar. They were providing spiritual advice and regular training seminars in Yangon. In addition, they were providing assistance in the form of benevolence and financial aid for some orphanages.

Left to right: Jemima, Certe, Jeanette, Rev. Titus, Joanna, Josiah, Moyte

In 2005 there was a split in these churches because a man named Daniel convinced a significant part of the group to follow him instead of Rev. Titus. When the Evangelical Reformed Churches were slow to act in support of the group led by Rev. Titus, he and his elders began to distance themselves from the Singaporean churches.

In 2006 the internal struggles in the Evangelical Reformed Churches over the matter of divorce and remarriage became the occasion for Rev. Titus and the Myanmar churches to break off their relationship with the Evangelical Reformed Churches and to pursue a direct relationship with the Protestant Reformed Churches.

When the Evangelical Reformed denomination dissolved in 2007, Rev. Kortering made known to several Protestant Reformed churches in the United States that the needs of the Protestant Reformed Churches in Myanmar were no longer being met by the Singaporean churches and encouraged some action to remedy that situation. At that point Hope's diaconate began asking questions regarding the situation. Rev. Kortering and the Protestant Reformed committee of contact made known the nature of the work that needed to be done, much of which was outside the proper work of the deacons. Consequently, Hope's deacons brought the matter to Hope's council. After considerable investigation, the council decided to take up the work of *cultivating* the Reformed seeds that had been planted and watered in Myanmar.

Hope's subsequent contact with the contact committee of the Protestant Reformed Churches revealed that the committee did not believe the work of establishing a relationship with the Protestant Reformed Churches in Myanmar and the financial work associated with it fit within the scope of its constitution. Consequently, Hope's council sent a letter to the 2007 synod informing synod of Hope's plans to work with the Protestant Reformed Churches in Myanmar. Regarding that the *Acts of Synod* read as follows:

A.  Information: Hope's council has taken a decision to assist the Protestant Reformed Churches in Myanmar (PRCM) by providing them with spiritual guidance and instruction and by assisting them financially. Hope's council informs synod of this in the event synod should disapprove, because it recognizes that it is unusual for a congregation to assist a denomination of churches in a foreign country.

B.  Recommendation: That synod approve of Hope's council taking on this work with a view to helping the PRCM progress to the point that the Contact Committee should be involved. Grounds:

1.  Hope is willing to do this work.

2.  That which this work requires (interaction on a more personal level, mentoring a pastor, and benevolent help) is not part of the work of the CC according to its constitution.[3]

Synod adopted that recommendation.

### Hope's Work in Myanmar

Initially Hope's council needed to address whether or not it would continue the "self-help projects" begun by the Evangelical Reformed Churches in Singapore. The council concluded that the projects would be difficult, if not impossible, for the council to manage from half a

---

3    Article 43, in ibid., 32.

world away. The council also believed that those projects would distract Rev. Titus from his primary calling to preach the gospel. Consequently, Hope's council decided to move in the direction of providing some financial support for Rev. Titus so he could devote himself totally to the ministry of the word.

Congregation of the Protestant Reformed Church of Yangon

Following Paul's language in 1 Corinthians 3, Hope has been, and currently is, *cultivating* that which was *planted* and *watered* by others. This can be seen also in Hope's work in Myanmar over the past eight years. Recent delegations have built upon the faithful labors of earlier ones. Delegations have been sent by Hope to provide spiritual instruction not only, but also to set in place technological equipment, and instruction on how to use it, so that spiritual development can take place even when delegations are absent from the field.

In March 2009 Hope sent its first of five delegations to Myanmar. Rev. James Laning, Rev. Arie den Hartog and Elder John Van Baren went with the primary goal of getting to know the people of Rev. Titus' congregation. This led them to put together a picture directory of the congregation. Rev. Laning and Elder Van Baren went to Myanmar again in December 2009, and Elder Van Baren and Deacon Henry Vander Waal went in November 2014.

Reports of more recent delegations demonstrate that significant progress has been made in Hope's purpose of advancing the cause of the Reformed faith in Myanmar. Elder David Jessup, Deacon Jonathon Kamps, and John Van Baren went to Myanmar in early November of 2014. The primary goal of the delegation was to establish what Hope's council had believed to be true, namely, that the Protestant Reformed Church of Yangon was a properly instituted church and that the office-bearers were lawfully called and installed. Utilizing the Questions for Church Visitation and discussion of the Church Order with Rev. Titus and the officebearers of the Yangon congregation, it became clear to Hope's delegation that what the council had from the beginning believed to be true was indeed true. As a result, upon the delegation's return to the States the council took a formal decision recognizing that the Yangon church, of which Rev. Titus is the pastor, is a properly instituted church and that its officebearers are lawfully called and installed.

Left to right: Elder Kyaw (Papa), Rev. Titus, Deacon Timothy, Elder Soe Thine

Five months later, in March 2015, Hope sent another delegation to Myanmar. Rev. David Overway and Elder David Jessup were sent by Hope's council to provide instruction on the doctrine of the covenant and the creeds as requested by the council of the Protestant

Reformed Churches in Myanmar. Additional instruction was provided concerning how to design and manage a church budget and the necessity of establishing and maintaining proper church membership. It is interesting to note that the Yangon congregation took the matter of church membership so seriously that it reaffirmed its membership by formally making public confession of faith. That visit confirmed to Hope's council that its continuing goal of assisting the Myanmar churches to grow in the Reformed faith and church government is progressing well.

Hope's labors over the past eight years in Myanmar have made it clear to the council and congregation that Rev. Titus is a faithful undershepherd to the flock under his care in Myanmar. This is demonstrated by his regular preaching of the Heidelberg Catechism, his faithful instruction of the children and youth of his congregation, his work of translating Reformed writings and the scriptures into Burmese, and his obvious desire to develop and lead his congregation in the Reformed faith.

### A Look to the Future

It is abundantly clear to Hope's council that while our labors in Myanmar have been blessed by the Lord, there is much work for the council to do yet. Its future goals regarding this include, first, keeping regular contact with the Protestant Reformed Churches in Myanmar by means of at least one visit each year; second, working toward arranging to have Rev. Titus receive some training in the United States regarding the practical aspects of the ministry and the functioning of Reformed churches; third, assisting the Myanmar churches in organizing new congregations and forming a functioning Reformed denomination of churches in Myanmar; fourth, working with the foreign mission committee of the Protestant Reformed Churches in the calling of a missionary to labor in or near Myanmar.

It is our prayer as we go forward in the watering and cultivating of the Reformed faith in Myanmar that our faithful covenant God will continue to bless our labors there.

Chapter 16

HOPE AND
CHRISTIAN EDUCATION

### Editor's Introduction

THINK IT NOT STRANGE THAT A FAITHFUL church of Jesus Christ
has a strong interest in Christian education. Hope's interest is not and
never has been for the church to establish, own, and operate Christian schools. Her history demonstrates her support of the principle of
*parental* (parent-owned-and-operated) schools, rather than *parochial*
(church-owned-and-operated) schools.

Nevertheless, Hope is and always has been committed to honoring
article 21 of the Church Order of Dordt: "The consistories shall see to
it that there are good Christian schools in which the parents have their
children instructed according to the demands of the covenant."[1]

Chapter 16 presents Hope consistory's active support of Christian
education in accordance with the requirements of article 21.

Hope church's support of Christian education is further demonstrated by the many members who have devoted themselves to teaching
in Protestant Reformed schools. The list below of current members of
Hope church who have taught, are teaching, or are preparing to teach
confirms this.

---

1  Church Order 21, in *Confessions and Church Order*, 387.

| Name | Place | Dates |
|---|---|---|
| Annica Bosveld | Studying at Grand Valley State University for elementary education | present |
| Shari Bosveld | Heritage Christian School | 1990 to 1992 |
| John Buiter | Adams Christian School | 1956 to 1957 |
| | Hope Protestant Reformed Christian School | 1957 to 1960 |
| | Hope Protestant Reformed Christian School | 1962 to 1996 |
| Alyssa De Vries | Completing secondary education program at Grand Valley State University | 2016 |
| Marilyn De Vries | Free Christian School | 1968 to 1972 |
| Nathan De Vries | Hope Protestant Reformed Christian School | 2015 to present |
| Tom De Vries | Loveland Protestant Reformed Christian School | 1962 to 1964 |
| | Free Christian School | 1967 to 1972 |
| | Loveland Protestant Reformed Christian School | 1979 to 1989 |
| | Hope Protestant Reformed Christian School | 1989 to 2009 |
| | Adams Christian School | 2015 to present |
| Richard De Vries | Mount Vernon Christian High School | 1989 to 1995 |
| | Adams Christian School | 1995 to 1997 |
| | Covenant Christian High School | 1997 to present |
| Susann Grasman | Hope Protestant Reformed Christian School | 2002 to present |
| James Huizinga | Adams Christian School | 1967 to 1971 |
| | Covenant Christian High School | 1971 to 2012 |
| Alex Kalsbeek | Heritage Christian High School | 2007 to 2013 |

| Name | Place | Dates |
|------|-------|-------|
| Calvin Kalsbeek | Adams Christian School | 1973 to 1982 |
| | Covenant Christian High School | 1982 to 2011 |
| Gladys Koole | Hull Protestant Reformed Christian School | 1978 to 1979 |
| | Hope Protestant Reformed Christian School | 1979 to 1982 |
| Ronald Koole | Hull Protestant Reformed Christian School | 1979 to 1986 |
| | Loveland Protestant Reformed Christian School | 1986 to 1995 |
| | Heritage Christian School | 1995 to 1996 |
| | Hope Protestant Reformed Christian School | 1996 to present |
| Harry Langerak | Hope Protestant Reformed Christian School | 1964 to 1969 |
| | Covenant Christian High School | 1969 to 2009 |
| Joel Langerak Jr. | Studying at Calvin College for secondary education | present |
| Gayle Lotterman | Covenant Christian High School | 2014 to 2015 |
| | Heritage Christian School | 2014 to 2015 |
| | Hope Protestant Reformed Christian School | 2015 to present |
| Helen Medema | Hope Protestant Reformed Christian School | 1966 to 1969 |
| | Hope Protestant Reformed Christian School | 1990 to 2008 |
| Joel Minderhoud | Covenant Christian High School | 1995 to present |
| Julie Schwarz | Heritage Christian School | 1992 to 1997 |
| Daniel Van Uffelen | Heritage Christian High School | 2001 to 2011 |
| | Covenant Christian High School | 2011 to present |
| Helen Veenstra | Hope Protestant Reformed Christian School | 1953 to 1954 |

Past, present, and aspiring teachers at Hope back from left: James Huizinga, Alex Kalsbeek, Tom De Vries, Annica Bosveld, Gladys Koole, Gayle Lotterman, Dan Van Uffelen, Cal Kalsbeek, John Buiter, Harry Langerak, Joel Langerak Jr; front: Marilyn De Vries, Helen Medema, Alyssa De Vries, Shari Bosveld, Julie Schwarz, Susann Grasman, Joel Minderhoud, Ronald Koole

## Mother Hope and the Rearing of a Son in Hope Protestant Reformed Christian School

### *Prof. David J. Engelsma*

This son of Hope Protestant Reformed Church was eight years old when Hope Protestant Reformed Christian School began educating the children of Hope church in the fall of 1947. He was entering the fourth grade.

With other boys and girls who were members of Hope church, I attended the Christian Reformed school in Jenison, Michigan, for three years—grades one through three. Upon the institution of Hope school in 1947, I became a student there from grades four through nine. I graduated in the early summer of 1953. My teachers were Miss Jessie Dykstra, Miss Della Vander Vennen, and then Miss Alice Reitsma in grades seven through nine. These teachers signed my report cards.

My last year at Hope was 1953, the year of the schism in the Protestant Reformed Churches. Good friends in church and school disappeared in the summer of 1953. Some I have never seen again—a regret. From time to time, I give thought to suggesting a Hope school reunion of all who attended, or graduated from, the school in or prior to 1953.

### Birth of the School

With regard to the forming of Hope school, the first reference in the minutes of Hope church to the movement to establish a Protestant Reformed Christian school for the children of Hope church is dated in May 1943. At that time there was already a "board of the Protestant Reformed School Society." The consistory of Hope decided to "give the board our moral and financial support." The consistory also decided to take three collections a year for the proposed Protestant Reformed Christian school. In addition, the offering at the worship service on Christmas Day in 1943 was designated for the as yet nonexistent school.

During the years 1943 to 1946, Hope church took collections for both Jenison Christian School and for the Protestant Reformed school, which was in progress. In May 1947 Hope's consistory discontinued taking collections for Jenison Christian School and designated all Christian school offerings for Hope Protestant Reformed Christian School.

Showing exemplary gratitude for the Christian instruction the Jenison Christian School had given the children of Hope, the consistory of Hope in 1946 permitted the Jenison school board to canvass the Hope congregation for funds to purchase a new school bus, even though plans were well under way to establish a Protestant Reformed Christian school.

Indicating the zeal of the members of Hope church for Protestant Reformed Christian education of their children, the consistory minutes of April 1938 include this cryptic decision: "A motion to comply with the request to distribute the questionnaire for our Christian *high school*" (emphasis added). Already some nine years before the establishment of a Protestant Reformed Christian grade school, there was interest in Hope church for a Protestant Reformed high school. This was some thirty years before the institution in the Grand Rapids area of Covenant Christian High School in 1968.

The commitment of the members of Hope church to Protestant Reformed education of their children already in 1942 or 1943 and their establishment of the school in 1947 are striking and especially commendable in view of the small size of the Hope congregation in those years. In 1943, by which time a school society and board had already formed, Hope church consisted of merely approximately fifteen families. When the school began in 1947, Hope was only twenty-four families, with a total membership of 112 souls.

Despite her small size and limited financial resources, Hope was the first congregation in Michigan, indeed in all of the territory of Classis East of the Protestant Reformed denomination, to establish a Protestant Reformed Christian school. Only Redlands, California, in all of the Protestant Reformed denomination formed a Protestant Reformed Christian school earlier than Hope.

Hope School board (c. 1950–51) comprised mostly of members of Hope church; back from left: John Lanning, Melvin Engelsma, Dick Kooienga, Joe King, G. Ten Elshof, Gerrit Moelker; Ted Howerzyl, Gary Korhorn, Maynard Veenstra, Dewey Engelsma, John Kalsbeek Sr.

Hope's strong concern and willingness to sacrifice for a school are the more fascinating in view of the fact that most, if not all, of the members of the church had very little formal education. My father was typical. He had only an eighth-grade education in the small, dingy, one-room school at the corner of Riverbend Drive and Kenowa Avenue. One teacher taught all eight grades, with the help of a strong stick to encourage both good behavior and diligent study. Upon my father's graduation from this primitive institution of learning, my father's father put an end to my father's schooling, so that young Dewey could plow the fields behind a team of horses in the farm country of River Bend.

HOPE AND CHRISTIAN EDUCATION 643

It is doubtful that Mr. Richard Newhouse, original president of the Hope school board, had had even eight grades of education in the Netherlands, whence he had emigrated to the United States.

## Grace in the Birth

Rejection of common grace played a powerful role in the establishment of Hope school. The fathers and mothers of Hope church were convinced that the worldview of common grace—which became the worldview of the Christian Reformed schools by decision of the Christian Reformed synod of 1924 in place of the worldview of the antithesis of scripture and the Reformed confessions—deeply and adversely affected Christian schools and education. I note in passing that it is highly unlikely that those fathers and mothers ever used the sophisticated term *worldview*, although they had a good grasp of the reality. Those members of Hope church were also convinced that the confession by the Protestant Reformed Churches of particular grace, implying the *antithesis*—with which word they were thoroughly acquainted—between the holy church and the totally depraved world, required distinctively Protestant Reformed schools as well as churches.

"Such men and their wives esteemed the education of their children and the other children of the church highly and were willing to sacrifice for their education, if only the education would be Reformed according to scripture and the creeds. That our fathers at Hope church, a congregation of about thirty families, actually began plans to build a school just seems incredible. Did they know what they were getting into? Were they really counting the cost? Was it perhaps a vain dream? Bear in mind that the congregation was composed of mostly ordinary, factory wage earners and farmers. But the decision had been made to build a school no matter what the cost. Our fathers were motivated by the divine mandate to instruct their covenant children." —John Kalsbeek Sr.

Although the words *worldview* and *antithesis* were not used, the "basis" of Hope school in the original constitution, which was adopted by the board in March 1946, set forth the realities of these words: "The training of the covenant child[ren] in the school as well as in the home and in the church must serve to prepare them to follow their lifelong calling to reveal the glory of their God in a life lived from the principle of regeneration by grace."

Even though I was only at the most a third grader at Jenison Christian School at the time, I remember reporting to my parents activities that were strange to me and that my parents frowned on and attributed to the pernicious influence of the theory of common grace. Perhaps the disturbing activities were certain chapel talks or the showing of certain movies. They were certainly not the gross evils arising from common grace that are accepted in Christian Reformed schools today. The staff of Jenison Christian School in the early 1940s, under the supervision of the principal, Peter Bouma, was conservative.

Speaking of Mr. Bouma, some forty-five years after my attendance at Jenison Christian I was asked to give a chapel speech at a Grand Rapids facility for the elderly. Sitting in the front row of the audience was Mr. Bouma, whom I recognized. After the speech, I greeted him warmly, informed him of my relation to him many years before, and spoke with him of my teacher in those primary grades at Jenison Christian, Miss Ann Bolthouse.

Distinct in my memory is a sharp, even heated, debate we Protestant Reformed children had on one occasion with our Christian Reformed bus driver, as he was driving us home after school down Wilson Avenue to the Riverbend area. The issue was common grace. This brings home to me how thoroughly we had been instructed concerning the evils of the theory of common grace already at the young age of seven or eight. We could and did argue the doctrinal issue with an adult. When I reported this exchange to my father that evening, his response was, "We must have our own school."

"Through the passing of the years, the members and especially parents in Hope Protestant Reformed Church had
become very conscious that the doctrinal differences which
had caused denominational separation in 1924 were surely
permeating the various subjects taught in the existing Christian school." [2] —Mr. and Mrs. Dewey Engelsma

At the time the men of Hope church, and the women also, were at
work establishing a school uncorrupted by the theory of a common
grace of God. This work was not only mental and spiritual, but also
intensely physical. Well do I remember the men of Hope church at work
in the spring and summer of 1947 putting up a red brick school building with their own hands. Working men all, and most of them living
from paycheck to paycheck, they devoted their evenings after supper
and Saturdays to the erection of a school building that they would not
otherwise been able to afford. Especially on Saturdays, we small children would accompany our fathers to the grounds of the future school,
the land just off Wilson Avenue, a little north of Riverbend Drive. This
is where the present school, now much enlarged and enhanced, stands.

"I never view the present school without seeing its original,
smaller form—just a few rooms—and the founding fathers
of Hope themselves mixing cement and standing on ladders laying the bricks." —Prof. David J. Engelsma

2    "History of Hope School," in *Hope Protestant Reformed Christian School 25th Anniversary Booklet 1947–1972*, 6.

"We know from the history of Hope school that much of the work in building the school was done by volunteer labor. Zeal for the building reminds one of the Jews' building the wall of Jerusalem in Nehemiah's day." —John Kalsbeek Sr.

"Each member must fulfill a total of two days donated labor in periods of one-half or more at a time."[3]

In those days, the school building stood directly behind the white, frame building that was the place of worship of Hope church. The physical juxtaposition of the two buildings said something, *loudly*, about the close, important relation of church and school.

"Letter received from Hope's consistory asking to use the school's toilet (church's outhouse torn down)." [4]

Those experiences as a child in the actual life of the covenant with regard to the rearing of covenant children are, no doubt, part of the reason I not only have, and never had, any trouble with the strong language of article 21 of the Church Order of Dordt, but I also thrill to this language, and have always preached and exhorted the grand calling of the language: "The consistories shall see to it that there are good Christian schools in which the parents have their children instructed according to the demands of the covenant."[5]

Thus I will be able one day to look my own and my wife's fathers, and the other founding fathers of Hope Protestant Reformed Christian School, in the eye (if we do such things in heaven), as also to give account of my ministry to the Judge (which we must surely do).

---

3   "Gleaned from the minutes of the beginning years," in ibid., 13.
4   Ibid.
5   Church Order 21, in *Confessions and Church Oder*, 387.

## *Humble Beginning*

Education in the new building began in the fall of 1947. There were fifty-two students in grades one through nine. Two teachers taught the children. Miss Jessie Dykstra taught the lower grades. Miss Della Vander Vennen taught the upper grades. Miss Vander Vennen having left for the newly established Adams Street Protestant Reformed Christian School, Miss Alice Reitsma soon became the principal of Hope school and taught the upper grades.

Hope faculty in 1952–53 from left: Agatha Lubbers, Alice Reitsma, Jessie Dykstra

"We can be certain that many prayers, beseeching the Lord's blessing and success for this bold project, were heard. But the founders persisted, believing that the Lord would bless their cause and endeavor." —John Kalsbeek Sr.

A small, humble beginning of the now large, impressive institution that is Hope Protestant Reformed Christian School!

"Yes, we organized a society. We raised funds. We toiled hard to erect a building with two classrooms. We donated time and toil and finances. We struggled with government agencies for permission to build at a time when there was a ban on all but the most necessary building projects. We approached them for the right to buy critical materials when a war denied these to many. We persisted and sought without discouragement to hurdle the unexpected obstacle of being required to have a registered architect or building contractor supervise the building of our school—and that after we had already erected a goodly part of it. We committed the matter of teachers to [God]. But He is the one Who in covenant faithfulness gave us all this and opened the way every time. He kept us faithful and confident. He supplied our every need from the night we organized the society which He put in our hearts to bring into being."[6] —Rev. John A. Heys

How true to the way in this world of the kingdom of God, always and in every form! God loves to make something out of nothing.

### Culture in the Country School

Miss Reitsma especially had influence on the spiritual, educational, and, yes, cultural development of this farm boy in the upper grades of Hope school. The area of Hope church and Hope school was considered the "sticks" in those days by the more civilized inhabitants of the city of Grand Rapids. We knew.

Alice Reitsma brought culture to those "sticks."

By her scintillating teaching, she opened up the wonderful world of study and learning to this student and others.

---

6    J. A. Heys, "Joy of Covenant Faithfulness," in *Hope Protestant Reformed Christian School 25th Anniversary Booklet 1947–1972*, 2.

"Alice Reitsma first initiated the annual all-school programs. I remember the very first one was entitled "Our Only Comfort," with the three divisions of misery, deliverance, and thankfulness. It was rendered in First Protestant Reformed Church at Fuller and Franklin...As one of our ministers remarked to me after the program, "It was so good it made one weep." And I might add that they are still the highlight of the year; still just as inspiring." —John Kalsbeek Sr.

Miss Reitsma introduced her students to the beauty of classical music. Previously, our tastes in music—other than love for the psalter, our songbook at worship on the Sabbath—ran to country music and stopped there. Slim Whitman and Johnny Cash were the peak of our musical mountain. When Miss Reitsma announced that the last period on Friday afternoons would be devoted to listening to classical music, we rough, country boys glanced at each other with scorn disfiguring our faces.

How ignorant we were!

To this day I cannot hear the strains of Verdi's "Triumphal March" from Verdi's *Aida* without being transported back to the little Hope school in the early 1950s on a Friday afternoon, where first I heard the piece, indeed heard *of* the piece, and was moved by it. I see the portable record player on the teacher's desk, with Miss Alice Reitsma presiding over what today would be called "music appreciation hour."

Pronounced was her promotion of literature. I see and hear her still, dramatically reading aloud to the class Longfellow's epic poem, *Evangeline: A Tale of Acadie*, with tears streaming down her cheeks.

Less effective was her effort to apply the Reformed religion, indeed the *Protestant* Reformed religion, to politics. But she made the effort long before the appearance of the Moral Majority or similar religious political movements in the United States. At the time of the presidential election of 1952, when her student was an eighth or ninth grader, Miss Reitsma prevailed upon me (imposed her will upon me would be closer to the truth) to give a speech to the regular meeting of the Hope school PTA urging that association to take the lead in promoting the candidacy of a Protestant Reformed man for the presidency of the United States. (I wonder how that speech was recorded in the minutes of the PTA.)

The man? Her pastor and hero, the Rev. Herman Hoeksema.

I gave the speech. Miss Reitsma had written the better part of it.

Hoeksema was not elected. He did not run. The Hope PTA had not been galvanized into political action by my speech.

When in seminary, some ten years later, I was tempted to inform Hoeksema how close he had once come to the presidency. Wisely, I refrained. Hoeksema was ever critical of Abraham Kuyper's abandonment of the ministry for political office.

### Spiritual Power

And then there was Alice Reitsma's direct and powerful influence upon me, and Hope school's influence through her, to pursue the ministry of the gospel in the Protestant Reformed Churches. One afternoon the vivacious teacher took this young, farm boy aside and admonished him to consider the ministry of the gospel as his calling from God. She did not convince me on the spot. But she introduced the thought, which never thereafter disappeared. God used her admonition, as well as other means, over several years, to convict the boy, then a young man at Calvin College, that he was called to the gospel ministry.

Another student reports that Miss Reitsma's also encouraged and admonished some of her students to become teachers in the Protestant Reformed schools, as is evidenced by what she wrote on this student's ninth grade report card.

Church and school!

Specifically, Hope Protestant Reformed Church and Hope Protestant Reformed Christian School!

More completely, church, school, *and home!*

With regard to church and school, the church was instrumental to produce the school, as article 21 of the Dordt Church Order envisions. The school on its part brought the truth preached and taught by the church to bear upon all the rearing, learning, and living of the covenantal children of the church. Thus the school has been a support to the church.

Whether as a minister or as a soundly Reformed layman or woman, the students of the school, in various degrees, became lively, competent, faithful, confessing members of the church and knowledgeable, strong, courageous citizens of the kingdom of God.

And still are becoming such members and citizens!

By the covenantal grace of God, still powerful and beneficent in and through Hope Protestant Reformed Church after one hundred years!

"There is little doubt that Hope school has been uniquely blessed. And, just as significant, Hope school has been a blessing to our community. Distinctive education must and does produce a distinctive product. Our students are given a heritage, a distinctive view of the whole body of knowledge and experience, which can be acquired in no place other than a Protestant Reformed school."[7] —Jon Huisken

---

7    Jon Huisken, editor's preface, in ibid.

*Chapter 17*

~~~◎~~~

# YOUNG PEOPLE'S CONVENTIONS
# HOSTED BY HOPE CHURCH

**Susann Grasman**

THE ANNUAL CONVENTION IS OFTEN THE HIGHLIGHT of the summer for the young people of the Protestant Reformed Churches. It is always a spiritually beneficial time for all the covenant youth who attend. But the annual convention has not always been an assumed part of our youths' summer plans. For the first fifteen years of the history of the Protestant Reformed Churches, there was no convention, no federation board, and no unifying event that brought all the young people into one place during one time. Each society, separated from each other society, carried on individual activities quite apart from the rest of the other societies. Some societies in the western part of the United States formed a league, but its activities were confined to a limited area, and no societies were united in any way.

Many young people felt a need and desired to have closer connections with their fellow societies. In 1939 South Holland Young People's Society decided to hold something entirely new—a convention of all the Protestant Reformed young people's societies. All societies in the denomination received an invitation asking them to send delegates and visitors to South Holland in August 1939. A tradition was about to begin, one in which the young people of Hope church would eagerly participate.

653

## Eighteenth Annual Young People's Convention
## Held August 5–7, 1958

In 1958 Hope church joined with Creston Protestant Reformed Church to plan the eighteenth annual convention. Per tradition, a debate was held on the subject of "Resolved That It Is Necessary to Believe in a Young Earth." The panel members were David Engelsma, James Jonker, Rev. Bernard Woudenberg, and Rev. Herman Hanko. A keynote of that convention was also a program entitled "This Is Your Life," in which by means of narration, pictures, and actual personalities a history of the Protestant Reformed young people's federation was portrayed. Rev. Cornelius Hanko, first editor of the *Beacon Lights*, Rev. George Lubbers, first convention speaker, Homer Kuiper, first federation board president, and Alice Reitsma, instrumental in the workings of the *Beacon Lights*, were introduced to the young people.

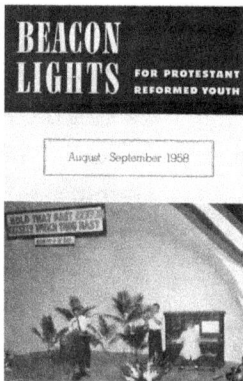

1958 *Beacon Lights* showing special number at the evening mass meeting

1958 convention delegate name tag

"Hold That Fast Which Thou Hast" based on Revelation 3:11 was the convention theme, which was developed in three speeches. The first speech, "Holding Fast to the Truth," was given by Rev. Herman Hoeksema. Rev. Gise Van Baren gave the second speech, "Fighting the Battle of Faith." "Standing unto the Day of Christ," the last speech, was given by Rev. George Lanting.

The convention theme song was psalter 20, "Unshaken Faith Amid Danger": "In God will I trust, tho' my counselors say, / O flee as a bird to your mountain away; / The wicked are strong and the righteous are weak, / Foundation are shaken, yet God will I seek" (v. 1).

The first evening a mass meeting was held in Zeeland City Park.

The next day the outing was held in Long Lake Park in Cedar Springs, Michigan. Although it rained as the conventioneers headed north to Long Lake, marvelously enough the rain stopped when they arrived, and the sun shone the rest of the day. They all enjoyed a treasure hunt, swimming, volleyball, softball, and an excellent supper.

The next morning a pancake breakfast was held in Pinery Park in Wyoming, Michigan. That evening the conventioneers enjoyed a banquet and program, with the theme "Water Wonderland," in First Protestant Reformed Church in Grand Rapids.

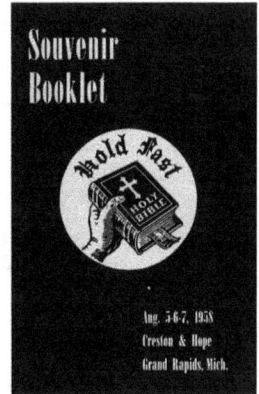

1958 convention booklet

Why was that convention called the eighteenth *annual* convention when the first convention had been held *twenty* years prior? "We did not have conventions for two years during the war," said one of the participants in the convention program, "since the boys were all in the service and gasoline was rationed. No boys, no cars, no convention."

The convention assessments received from the various societies were $978, and the left-over expense at the time the booklets were printed was $37.

"After we have returned to our homes from the convention, we realize even more what a wonderful and extremely valuable thing the convention really is. I know of no other place where we as Protestant Reformed young people can go and feel as much at home or as close to one another as at the convention." —Tom Newhof, president of the federation board

"The convention committee, consisting of Lamm Lubbers, Marybeth Engelsma, Harry Langerak, Mart De Vries, and Delores Mensch deserve credit for making the convention the success that it was." —David Engelsma, vice-president of the federation board

"We thank and congratulate the Hope and Creston societies for the terrific job they did as hosts of the 18th convention and eagerly look forward to the 19th in Oaklawn, Illinois." —Jim Jonker

## Twenty-fourth Annual Young People's Convention
### Held August 25–27, 1964

Protestant Reformed young people from all over the United States came together at Hope church on Tuesday, August 25, 1964, to participate in the twenty-fourth annual young people's convention. The conventioneers were warmly welcomed by the host society of Hope church.

FIRST ROW — (L to R): Anna Lynn Lanning, Lenore Engelsma, Judy Huizinga, Beverly Kamphuis, Sharon Kuiper, Carol Petroelje, Mary Knot.

SECOND ROW — John Kalsbeek, Clare Kuiper, Ed Langerak, Dave Miedema, Rev. H. Veldman, Larry Koole, Ivan Elzinga, Jim Langerak, Harry Langerak.

THIRD ROW — Roger Kamphuis, Gary Moelker, Bob Miedema, Mike Engelsma, Dave Moelker, Rick Huizinga, Al Huizinga, Cal Kalsbeek.

ABSENT — Carol Bomers, Ron Graeser, Dave Hop, Jim Huizinga, Chuck Kalsbeek, Tim Orme.

1964 host society

All conventioneers registered in front of Hope church that afternoon and received badges, booklets, tickets, maps, and lodging assignments. "They were also subjected at that time to some amateur photographers. They all seemed to survive this ordeal with patience and perseverance."[1]

1964 registration

The theme chosen for the convention was "Be Ye Holy," based on 1 Peter 1:15–16. To develop the theme and to provide spiritual guidance, three speeches were given, the first by Prof. Homer C. Hoeksema[2]

---

1   John Kalsbeek, "The Convention in Retrospect," in *Beacon Lights* 24, no. 6 (August–September 1964), 1–2.

2   Rev. Herman Hoeksema had been scheduled to give the "keynote" address at the inspirational mass meeting on Tuesday evening. He always had a great love and concern for the young people of the Protestant Reformed Churches. He was a loved and respected leader, and nearly every year the young people asked him to speak at their convention. Although he was scheduled to speak in 1964, he was unable to do so. His son filled in for him. The Lord took Rev. Hoeksema to glory one year later on September 2, 1965, at the age of seventy-nine.

entitled "Be Ye Holy Personally," followed by Rev. Herman Hanko, speaking on "Be Ye Holy with Friends," and concluding with Rev. David Engelsma speaking on "Be Ye Holy in the World."

The theme song was psalter 321, "The Blessedness of Obedience."

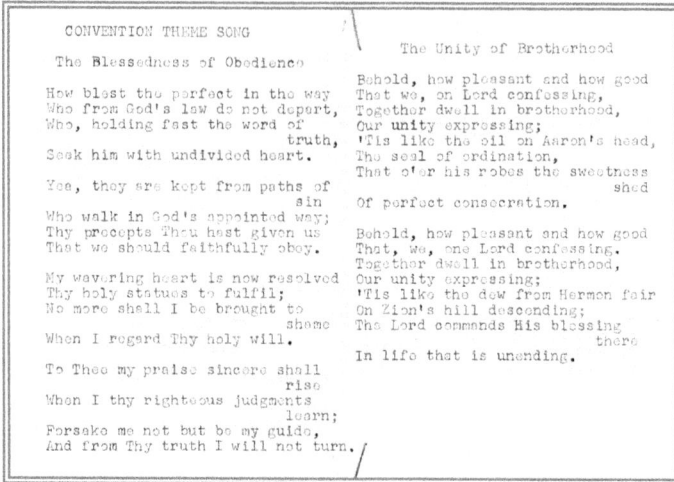

1964 theme song

Pre-convention issue of *Beacon Lights* showing delegate badges from previous conventions

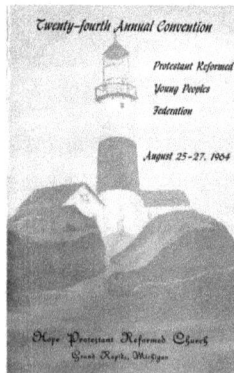

1964 convention booklet

The activities Tuesday evening began with the annual convention picture, which was taken in the gym of South Grandville Elementary School. Unfortunately, that picture did not turn out because the photographer unknowingly used faulty equipment. The picture had to be retaken the night of the banquet in Unity Christian High School.

After the convention picture was taken, the young people and others assembled for the inspirational mass meeting, which began with singing the convention theme song, reading and prayer, and a girls' sextet from the Hudsonville society. Then Prof. H. C. Hoeksema made the following opening remarks to his speech:

> Mr. Chairman, Protestant Reformed conventioneers, parents and friends gathered with us tonight:
>
> It is with rather mixed feelings that I am on the platform tonight—feelings with regret, on the one hand, because I am acutely aware, as you must be, that I am a substitute for one who had well-nigh become an institution on this first convention evening. Both personally, and as far as the federation and the convention are concerned, I regret that I must be here in the place of my father. On the other hand, I am glad, nevertheless, that I may address you tonight in connection with the theme of the convention "Be Ye Holy"; and I will try to be of service to you with respect to the particular aspect of the theme that was assigned to me, that is, "Be Ye Holy Personally."[3]

The next day the conventioneers headed to John Ball Park in Grand Rapids to view the animals, fish, reptiles, and plants in the zoo and to eat a delicious lunch. Swimming followed in Bostwick Lake in Townsend Park. A highlight of early conventions, the East versus West ballgame, was played in Townsend Park. Interestingly, the winning pitcher was Dale Kuiper of the East while Rev. David Engelsma of the West took the loss.

Good food is an absolute must for any successful convention, so day three started with a pancake breakfast in Pinery Park at 8:00 a.m. Everyone returned to Hope church for a debate entitled "Resolved that Christian young people may read secular literature that describes scenes of wickedness."

---

3    H. C. Hoeksema, "Be Ye Holy Personally," in *Beacon Lights* 24, no. 6 (August–September 1964), 8.

After lunch in Hope church, the host society tried a new experiment, "which was found wanting. The reason for the failure was not that the experiment was out of order, but because the young people had no interest. This new experiment was the introduction of discussion groups. Of the more than one hundred fifty conventioneers only thirty-six felt the need to discuss matters pertaining to the kingdom of God. That was a sad incident in an otherwise successful convention.[4]

"I feel that the goal of this convention was sadly missed. When such a few are willing to give only thirty to forty-five minutes of their time for something spiritual, it is a sure indication that something is lacking in our young people. It is a sad thing when ten to twelve cars boldly left the churchyard fully loaded after the occupants had been requested to remain to enjoy spiritual fellowship. One begins to question the right of the Federation to spend over fifteen hundred dollars just in order to entertain our young people. Oh —this entertainment has a place all right, but when it becomes an obsession then one begins to wonder if perhaps our conventioneers have lost sight of the goals."[5] —John Kalsbeek Jr.

The evening banquet, with the theme "Nederlands," was held in Unity Christian High School. The entertainment that followed the speech by Rev. Engelsma was a production called "This is your *Beacon Lights*," a movie whose purpose was to involve the young people in the publishing of their magazine.

Convention costs in the 1960s were much lower than today. The 1963 convention expenses totaled $924.65, while the traveling expenses came to $567. In 1964, the year that Hope hosted, the convention assessments equaled $1,604.50.

---

4  Kalsbeek, "The Convention in Retrospect," in ibid., 6.
5  Kalsbeek, "The Convention in Retrospect," in ibid.

1964 banquet program

"Late Monday afternoon the Edgerton, Minnesota, delegates made their appearances in Grand Rapids. However, they did not come in together because they lost track of each other just outside of Edgerton. The people in the front car somehow thought they were behind so they speeded up; while those in the rear car, thinking they were ahead, stopped. Instead of drawing closer together they drew further apart. A rather foolish way to begin a convention, I think. What is really remarkable is that some of them arrived at all."[6]
—John Kalsbeek Jr.

## Thirty-third Annual Young People's Convention Held August 13–18, 1973

The young people of Hope church chose the theme "Soldiers of Christ" for the 1973 convention. Ephesians 6:11–18 was the fitting text, along with psalter 92, "God Our Advocate and Judge" as the theme song.

Ken Koole, a member of Hope church and president of the federation board, wrote concerning the convention and its theme:

---

6    Kalsbeek, "The Convention in Retrospect," in ibid., 1.

1973 convention booklet

At first glance this convention...may seem to lack uniqueness. Being held in Michigan, it cannot offer...a distinctive geography, such as the Rocky Mountains or the Pacific Ocean, or a structure like the John Hancock Building. The theme...is a common one...It certainly is not original. But look again.

I maintain that the theme is particularly distinctive. Though common, it is unique because of the thought content behind it. Others claim to march behind Christ's distinctive standard but forget that what is emphasized in the antithesis. They would march under a standard that allows for compromise and truce, not under a battle standard. We are called to be not peace negotiators but solders, humble and common soldiers. The distinctiveness lays in the strong stance which we repeatedly, in Ephesians 6:11–18, are commanded to take, which stance the world wants no part of. The gospel is a gospel of peace to the defender and his fellow soldiers, not to the world.

There is an old adage, "Don't judge a book by its cover." So, too, don't judge a convention by its location. A convention is unique not because its location is unique, but because its participants are unique. We are distinctive young people, and if we participate with this in mind, this convention will be a unique as well as a memorable one. May God grant us that strength of purpose.[7]

The speeches, the heart of any convention, were given by Prof. Homer C. Hoeksema, Rev. Marvin Kamps, and Rev. Cornelius Hanko. Professor Hoeksema gave the first speech, "The Enemy in Battle," at the Tuesday evening mass meeting in Hope church. The second mass meeting speech, "The Armor of God," was given by Rev. Kamps. At the Friday evening banquet Rev. Hanko spoke on "The Victory of Faith."

---

7    Ken Koole, "Message from the President," in *Soldiers of Christ, 33rd Annual Protestant Reformed Young People's Convention.*

With lodging being provided by the members of Hope church, the young people ate breakfast in the homes of their hosts. The convention days were filled with spiritual enrichment and fun activities. A sports mixer was held Monday evening in Johnson Park in Walker, Michigan. Tuesday morning began with a business meeting followed by a speech by Jon Huisken on tolerance and discussion groups. The convention-eers were then off to tour the Kellogg's Plant in Battle Creek, Michigan. They returned to enjoy supper in the homes of their hosts before the evening mass meeting.

On Wednesday the young people could be found canoeing down the White River, after which they visited Hoffmaster State Park in Norton Shores, Michigan, where a delicious chicken supper was served by the ladies of Hope. Following supper the conventioneers went to Grand Haven to enjoy the "Grand Haven Water Thrills and Musical Fountain." The night also included a speech on witnessing given by John Kalsbeek.

Thursday morning began with an informative talk on prayer by Hope's elder, David Meulenberg, followed by discussion groups on the same subject. Thursday afternoon was spent in Lamar Park, where the traditional East versus West ballgame was played. The Western guys were victorious over the Eastern guys, while the Eastern girls evened the score by beating their Western rivals.

Unfortunately, a planned Friday outing to North Shore beach was rained out, so the afternoon was spent playing basketball and volleyball in Hope school's gym. Friday evening's banquet was held in the gym of Grandville Christian School, where Judy Swart and Linda Vander Vennen played a flute duet as the special number.

On Saturday morning the conventioneers bid each other, "Farewell."

"Thus another convention had come to an end. Although we had to part with friends and relatives, we retained many happy memories of that week. We can be so thankful that our Lord even provided such an opportunity as this to meet as young people. Thus, the Lord willing, we'll once again

meet each other in covenant fellowship next year in the farm-
lands of Iowa and Minnesota." —Dawn De Jong and Linda
Vander Vennen

## Fortieth Annual Young People's Convention
### Held July 21–25, 1980

The 1980 convention was held on the beautiful campus of Hope College
in Holland, Michigan. Bob Faber, president of the federation board,
welcomed the conventioneers and wrote, "We are indeed blessed with
this privilege…It is a unique opportunity to meet with fellow believers
and discuss matters of faith and conviction. So when we meet with old
friends, establish new relationships, and engage in the activities of this,
let's keep in mind the ultimate purpose of the time. Let's be aware that
through discussion, speeches, and devotions we are able together to
grow spiritually and to mature as Christian young people."[8]

1980 convention booklet

The theme, "Appreciation of the Reformed
Truth," based on Hebrews 10:23, was fitting for
what was to be a spiritually beneficial time for
all participants. The theme was divided into four
parts: foundation, development, admonition, and
application. The hymn, "The Church's One Foundation," was chosen as the theme song.

Breaking with tradition, four convention
speeches were given that year. They were "The
Foundation of an Appreciation of Reformed
Truth" given by Rev. Gise Van Baren Monday evening. The next evening Prof. Herman Hanko spoke
on "The Development of the Truth." "Admonition to Adhere" was the
topic of Rev. Ronald Van Overloop's speech at the Wednesday evening
gathering, and Rev. Meindert Joostens addressed the conventioneers

---

8    Bob Faber, "Message from the Federation Board President," in *Appreciation of the
Reformed Truth, 40th Annual PRYP Convention.*

at the Thursday evening banquet on the topic, "The Application of the Reformed Truth in Our Lives."

The young people attending the convention also participated in discussion groups. Three topics were chosen that emphasized an appreciation of the Reformed truth. The first, "Aspects of the Worship Service," was introduced by Deanne Wassink. The second, "Christian Courtesy," was introduced by Everett Buiter, and Tom Miersma introduced the third, "Confession of Sin."

On Monday morning the conventioneers met at Hope church for registration before continuing on to Hope College. A convention picture was taken on the Hope College campus followed by a speech and a pizza party, at which the young people could have all the pizza and pop they could eat and drink for only $1.90.

Tuesday was spent playing sports on the campus, including a basketball tournament. The night was concluded with an evening speech. The young people spent Wednesday at beautiful Oval Beach in Saugatuck, Michigan, and again ended the night with an evening speech back on campus. Thursday morning discussion groups were followed by the East versus West softball game, and the week ended with a Friday night banquet provided by the college.

> "The 1980 convention was one not soon to be forgotten. The most important thing to me was the Christian fellowship with each other in Christ, which was bountifully given to us."
> —Anna Mae Meelker

> "The convention was nicely arranged so that every day there was free time to swim, play basketball, or racquetball, or just visit with old and new friends. We also had a great time on the beach Wednesday, which turned out to be a bright, sunny day, and a lot of the young people, myself included, went back to Hope looking somewhat like boiled lobster."
> —Gerald Van Baren

"This year, although the convention was smaller than usual, the participation was better than ever." —Grace Hauck

"The speeches…were very meaningful because they were directed especially to people our age. The things that were learned kept being brought up throughout the convention, and this really helped us apply them practically." —Doug Wassink

## Forty-ninth Annual Young People's Convention Held August 14–18, 1989

Going back to a tradition of past convention, willing members of Hope church once again lodged the conventioneers in their homes.

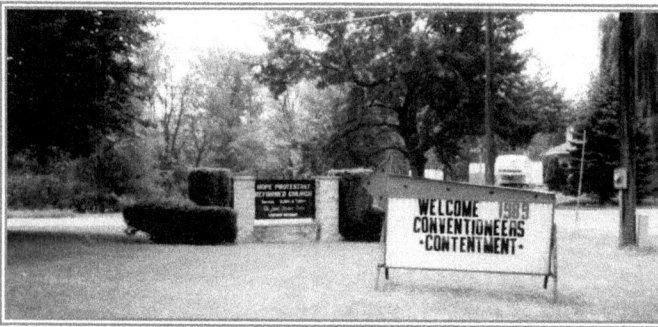

The host societies of Hope welcomed the young people with a large sign in front of church

The host societies of Hope church

Hope church and Hope school served as the host buildings for whenever the conventioneers met as a large group.

The theme for the 1989 convention was "Contentment," based on Philippians 4:11: "Not that I speak in respect of want: for I have learned, in whatsoever state I am, therewith to be content." The theme song, psalter 95 "An Answer to Distrust," was sung many times throughout the week.

1989 steering committee back left to right: Rev. James Slopsema, Hank Vander Waal, Neil Meyer, Cal Kalsbeek, Roger King; front: Doug Kooienga, Deb Vander Waal, Connie Meyer, Linda Kalsbeek, Phyllis King

In accordance with the theme, and following convention tradition, three speeches were given. Prof. Robert Decker spoke on "Contentment in Suffering"; Rev. Barry Gritters spoke on "Contentment in Self-denial"; and Rev. Van Overloop spoke on "Contentment under Authority." Alongside the speeches, three discussion groups took place on the subjects of family communication, stewardship, and the body, a temple of the Holy Spirit.

The first day, Monday, consisted of mixer games, including "animal swat," "lap change," and "slam dunk."

The convention picture, taken at Hope Protestant Reformed Christian School, was followed by Professor Decker's speech and an evening hayride.

1989 conventioneers

Tuesday morning discussion groups were followed by the day's outing to Pleasure Island waterpark in Muskegon, Michigan, where the young people also ate lunch and participated in a vigorous tug-of-war contest. Then they left for supper and volleyball on the beautiful Lake Michigan shoreline at Grand Haven State Park.

Wednesday morning also began with discussion groups and then fun and fellowship in the fieldhouse of Grand Valley State University.

1989 discussion group

That evening after supper and Rev. Gritters' speech in Hope church, all conventioneers enjoyed roller skating and bowling. At 12:00 p.m. they returned to their hosts' homes.

Thursday brought canoeing and then the banquet—a roasted pig in Douglas Walker Park in Byron Center, Michigan. The total cost for the 1989 convention was $12,983.27, a low number due to lodging provided by the members of Hope church. This truly was an uplifting experience, and one that was enjoyed by all.

"If I were giving a grade to this year's convention, I'd probably give it an *E*. An *E* for excellence, and *E* for effort, and an *E* for effectiveness. The hosts who opened up their homes and made us feel welcome are appreciated more than any of us could ever say. This year's convention was one I wouldn't have missed for anything." —Laura Van Dyk

"This was my first convention and it has made a deep impression on me. Back home in New Zealand, I can only dream about having this kind of fellowship and fun with young people of like faith. Having never really had it, I couldn't miss it. After having experienced this convention, I shall miss it very much." —Theo de Klerk

"If I look at the convention overall it was planned well in all areas. The hayride, the canoe trip, and the trip to Pleasure Island, etc. were a lot of fun. I look forward to more conventions in the future as fun as this convention." —Mike Feenstra

## Sixtieth Annual Young People's Convention
## Held June 19–23, 2000

The sixtieth annual young people's convention was unique as it was held in conjunction with the seventy-fifth anniversary of the Protestant Reformed Churches. The campus of Calvin College was chosen as the host location for both the convention and the anniversary, while all speeches were held in Sunshine Ministries on the East Beltline. The theme for that special convention and anniversary celebration was "Living out of Our Heritage," based on Psalm 16:6: "The lines are fallen unto me in pleasant places; yea, I have a goodly heritage." The beautiful words of psalter 27, "God the Highest Good," were all sung many times throughout the special week. The speeches, meant for both the conventioneers and the anniversary attendees, were given by Rev. Jason Kortering, Prof. David Engelsma, and Rev. Carl Haak. The discussion groups, held only for the conventioneers, were based on such worthwhile subjects as life-endangering sports, heavenly and earthly treasures, and the Reformed creeds.

The convention began on Monday with mixer games and a convention picture, both happening on the campus of Calvin College.

The evening was spent playing broom ball and ice skating in Michigan National Ice Arena. Tuesday began with discussion groups and then a trip to Michigan's Adventure in Muskegon followed by Rev. Kortering's speech in the evening. Wednesday morning found the conventioneers in discussion groups and then at a beach day in Grand Haven State Park. Unfortunately, the weather didn't cooperate, as it was cold and rainy. The pizza that was provided however, was very good. The evening was concluded with a speech by Professor Engelsma in Sunshine Ministries. Discussion groups were held on Thursday morning, and then the young people participated in tournament field games at Calvin. The banquet was held at Calvin, and then once again all were off to Sunshine Ministries for a concluding speech by Rev. Carl Haak. The convention ended with an all-night lock-in at Calvin's fieldhouse, and on Friday morning all went their separate ways, thanking God for a wonderful time enjoyed by all.

## Seventy-second Annual Young People's Convention
## Held August 13–17, 2012

The latest convention hosted by Hope church was in 2012. This convention was held at the beautiful Michindoh Conference Center in Hillsdale, Michigan.

Main building of Michindoh Conference Center

Chaperones from Hope church from left: Mike Rau, Jim Schimmel, Tim Koole

Based on the comforting twenty-third psalm, the theme chosen was "Led by the Shepherd." Psalter 53, with the beautiful heading, "The Guardian Care of God," was the familiar and beloved theme song.

Four speeches were given that year. Rev. Martyn McGeown spoke on "The Shepherd." Rev. Andrew Lanning spoke on "The Sheep." Rev. James Laning spoke on "The Relationship." Seminarian Joshua Engelsma spoke on "Only a Boy Named David." The conventioneers also met together for discussion groups on the subjects of church membership and who is on the Lord's side?

After meeting bright and early at Covenant Christian High School for registration, the conventioneers were all bussed to Michindoh in Hillsdale. After all were settled into their cabins, a group picture was taken and all participated in the mixer games that were planned for the afternoon.

Inner tube mixer game

Mixer game building boats

Boat race

Junk pile of boats after the race

The evening speech was followed by an ice cream social and root beer floats.

Tuesday morning began with a speech and discussion groups followed by afternoon tournament games and team events.

Wednesday morning began with a special speech given by then seminarian Joshua Engelsma. The afternoon consisted of tournament finals.

Volleyball skill

The evening game night included Minute to Win It and an ice cream social.

Thursday morning began with a speech followed by discussion groups, team events, mud pit, and broom ball. The banquet theme that evening was "A Garden Party." The night ended with a midnight water slide.

Friday morning began with an awards ceremony and then the buses were off back to Grand Rapids with tired but happy conventioneers, praising God for a profitable and enjoyable time.

## Conclusion

In 1939, seventy-seven years ago, South Holland Protestant Reformed Church hosted the first Protestant Reformed young people's convention. Except for the years 1942 and 1943, when the conventions were cancelled due to World War II, a convention has been held ever since. Hope church has hosted seven of them.

As anyone who has ever been directly

Michael Bosveld, chairman of the steering committee, dressed for the garden party

involved in planning and hosting a convention will attest to and appreciate, conventions are worthy endeavors, but they involve much work, many people, and considerable organization. In fact, it takes years of planning and fundraising for just one convention.

But hosting and planning a convention is a fruitful and blessed work, for although much has changed over the years, such as the type of lodging, increased costs, activities, and the number of attendees, the purpose of the conventions remains the same. An annual convention continues to unify the young people of the denomination, bringing them together with the purpose of serving their Lord and Savior. Although times have changed, the intent of the young people's convention established back in 1939 "to unite all Protestant Reformed young people's societies to work in close unity and [to] secure a sense of solidarity and to seek the mutual edification and development of talents as becomes Christian young people and that we strive to maintain with united front our specific Protestant Reformed character" still rings true in 2016. To God be the glory!

# EPILOGUE

*Calvin Kalsbeek*

GEOGRAPHY SERVES HISTORY. THIS PRINCIPLE OF A Reformed understanding of geography underscores the truth that God in his inscrutable wisdom designed the creation in such a way that it would further the cause of his kingdom, as that cause is realized throughout history. The geography of the land of Canaan demonstrated in a powerful way how God's purpose in the gathering, preserving, and defending of his Old Testament church was served by it.

But that was then. What about now? No less is this true for God's New Testament church. In many instances this aspect of God's providential care for his church is difficult, if not impossible, for our feeble minds to see and understand. The beginning of Hope church is *not* one of them. Reread chapter one to be reminded of the prominent role geography played in God's gathering and preserving of Hope church in the Grand River's bend. Then thank him God it.

It is also true that the world serves the church. This principle of a Reformed understanding of history is seen in the history of the nation of Israel. Most clearly was that evident in the decree of Caesar Augustus "that all the world should be taxed"(Luke 2:1). That decree brought Joseph and Mary to Bethlehem where our Savior was born as prophesied by Micah the prophet.

But that, too, was then. What about now? Many instances in the history of the New Testament church demonstrate this profound truth. In the celebration of Hope church's centennial anniversary we ought to take note of how Hope's beginning was deemed necessary by her founders because of a decree by the Michigan State Highway Department to shut down the ferry that gave them access to church membership in

Jenison. Reread chapter one and be reminded of how our sovereign Friend, in his love for his bride, governs all history (even the seemingly insignificant decisions of state highway departments) for the gathering, preserving, and defending of his church. Then thank God for it.

But do not reread only chapter one. Consider *A Spiritual House Preserved* as a means to follow the numerous examples in scripture of Israel's reviewing her history (Neh. 9; Ps.105) to remind her generations of God's preserving faithfulness. Review the history of Hope and consider God's continuing faithfulness in gathering his church. Review the times Hope had conflict and consider how her officebearers continue to be used by God to defend Hope when she is confronted by false teachings. Review Hope's worship and society life and consider how these continue to serve to preserve Hope in the truth. Review the chapters on Hope's daughters and sons and consider these as evidences of God's covenantal faithfulness and blessings on Hope.

Read and reread *A Spiritual House Preserved* with your children and grandchildren and consider that while times change and technology changes with it, God is unchangeable. Furthermore, consider and believe that in the way of living according to those unchanging teachings of God's word as those truths are set forth in the Reformed confessions, our God will continue to preserve Hope church in the river's bend.

༺⚬༻

# HOPE, GRANDVILLE, MICHIGAN

In the winter of 1916 I received a telephone call from a person living about two miles north of Jenison and about seven miles west of Grand Rapids. He wanted to know whether it would be possible to start a mission in his neighborhood, a rural community where several Christian Reformed families were living. As I had a number of fields under my care and was busy every Sunday, I agreed to come over on Wednesday evenings to preach for them. The man who called said we could use his home as a meeting place. I soon found out that these people were hungry for the gospel message. There were also a goodly number of children at the meetings. The attendance grew, and soon we were compelled to move. A public school hall was used, and soon Sunday services were started.

But when the report of these services came to Classis, there was strong opposition. The argument was that they were located only a little over a mile from Jenison. They could easily go to the Jenison church, across the river. However, this comment overlooked two things: the old ferry, which had plied its way across the river at Grandville had stopped running; the nearest bridge was at Wealthy Street in Grand Rapids, a trip of at least thirteen miles to get to the Jenison church. Also several of the people attending the services were not members of Jenison; some were "nominal" members of churches in Grand Rapids, many had not been attending any church for some time, and several were unchurched. So, after a lot of wrangling at Classis, to which I had become accustomed by this time, Classis finally allowed this to become a mission of our church. During the next summer, student J. Medendorp spent his vacation serving these people. He was instrumental in inducing several families to unite with the new congregation. At the end of the summer, the group gave him a royal gift to show their appreciation, about $500.

I never met a group of people who could accomplish so much with so little money. They watched the Grand Rapids papers for bargains in cement blocks and used lumber and showed a lot of zeal by donating their labor in building their church. The first pastor, George Ophoff, served them from 1917 [should be 1922] until 1924, when he broke away to join the Hoeksema group; he took all but four families with him to form the First Protestant Reformed Church of Grandville [should be Hope Protestant Reformed Church]. Although the attendance was small, services with the members remaining at Hope [Christian Reformed] Church were continued.

A big change was made when a fine new bridge was built over the Grand River. The Hope [CR] people decided to move their services to Grandville, and met in a former Kroger store building. But then, "the fat was in the fire" or, as the Dutch would say, "*Had je de poppen aan het dansen*" ("the dolls began to dance"). Two consistories, Wyoming Park and Jenison, brought a protest to classis because Hope [CR] Church was "infringing on their territory." However, they did not get much support from Classis. In the discussion, it was stated that if this were a mission, we might have something to say about it. Since this is an organized congregation, their move is their business, not ours. If this change is conducive to their growth, they have the right to go ahead, and we should not interfere. History proved this a wise choice, for the church flourished and gave birth to daughter churches later on.[1]

---

1    Brink, "Memoirs of Rev. J. R. Brink," 69–70.

꧁ ⊙⊙ ꧂

# HOPE'S PREORGANIZATIONAL
# RECORD

## River Bend, January 23, 1916

On January 23, 1916, a worship service was held in the home of R. Nieuwenhuis. The service was conducted by Rev. J. R. Brink. At this gathering twenty-one were present. After the service a meeting was held for the purpose of bringing about various improvements regarding ecclesiastical matters in the vicinity of River Bend.

Art. 1. Rev. J. R. Brink was chosen to serve the gathering as its president.

Art. 2. The president inquires if or not it would be advisable and necessary to establish a Mission Station in the vicinity of River Bend. It would be desirable, first of all, since regular worship service attendance in this area is almost impossible in view of the fact that the Walker church, and the Grand Rapids churches are too far distant to make regular church attendance possible. Second, it would also be advisable, in order that the children and the mature adults could be taught catechism. [Catechetical instruction could be given to them.]

Art. 3. After this all was considered and discussed, and the necessity of going ahead had become obvious, it is proposed to proceed, under the blessing of the Lord, to call into being a Mission Station here at River Bend. This proposition was brought to a vote and passed unanimously, to call into being a Mission Station.

Art. 4. C. Bouwman was chosen to serve as secretary; R. Nieuwenhuis, as treasurer.

Art. 5. Since, in this vicinity of River Bend, no suitable building to regularly hold divine services, is available, a committee is appointed. This committee is given the mandate to investigate the cost of a church building, and to find a suitable place (location) where such a building could be erected, to meet there regularly. The committee consists of the following four persons: J. Moelker, T. [Mathys] Van Eeuwen, J. Zaagman, and R. Nieuwenhuis to serve as Building Committee.

Art. 6. Upon the request of Rev. Brink, J. Kuiper closes with prayer after the ones present are asked individually if they have anything else to bring up.

## February 2, 1916

A [divine] worship service under the leadership of Missionary Rev. Brink was held at the home of R. Nieuwenhuis. At this occasion, to hear God's Word proclaimed, twenty-five were in attendance to make use of this opportunity. After the worship service a meeting was held regarding a Mission [Station].

Art. 1. The minutes of the previous meeting were accepted and approved.

Art. 2. A report of the Building Committee. J. Moelker presents a plan for the hopefully soon to be built church building if no suitable location is found elsewhere.

Art. 3. The dementions [sic] of the church building would be 32' x 40', which would be erected as practical as possible for this purpose.

Art. 4. Since brother elders from Walker congregation are present at this meeting, it is suggested by one of those brethren, to join ourselves as a Mission Station of River Bend, with one or the other churches. If we then needed help or support, one could apply to one of those churches. If we would place ourselves under Classis West, we would be acknowledged as a Mission Station.

Art. 5. It is decided to join ourselves as a Mission Station to the congregation of Walker.

Art. 6. As delegates to the Classis, the brethren C. Bouwman and R. Nieuwenhuis were chosen.

Art. 7. After the members were asked if any had anything to bring up to the meeting, upon the request of Rev. Brink, C. Kraai closes with thanksgiving.

w.s. J. Brink, president

w.s. C. Bouwman, secretary

## February 9, 1916

On February 9, 1916, a third divine worship service was held at the home of R. Nieuwenhuis, under the leadership of Rev. J. R. Brink. Fifteen persons were present. After the service, a meeting is held regarding the matter of establishing a Mission Station.

Art. 1. The minutes of the previous meeting were accepted and approved.

Art. 2. It is decided to erect [construct] the church building on land of J. Moelker whereas the Committee was unable to find land that was necessary for this purpose. This land was given gratis by J. Moelker.

Art. 3. It was decided to request Classis for a $300 loan for the newly constructed church building.

Art. 4. It was decided to conduct an English service in the forenoon; a service in the Holland language in the afternoon.

Art. 5. After members were asked if any had anything to present to the meeting, the meeting is closed with thanksgiving by C. Bouwman, upon the request of Rev. Brink.

## April 25, 1916

The meeting held on April 25, 1916, at the home of R. Nieuwenhuis.

The minutes of the previous meeting were accepted and approved. The meeting is opened with prayer by Rev. J. R. Brink and singing of Psalm 25:6.

Art. 1. It is decided, that, since the summer is at hand and the [theological school] gives its students vacation, to have a student here during the next three months regularly. He is to work here in the Mission Station River Bend.

Art. 2. It is decided to request Classis West for permission to be organized as the Christian Reformed Church of River Bend.

Art. 3. As delegates to Classis, C. Bouwman and R. Nieuwenhuis were appointed.

Art. 4. A motion was accepted to take an extra collection [offering] every last Sunday of each month when no more than $1 is contributed.

Art. 5. After members were asked if any had anything to present to the meeting, said meeting is closed by Rev. J. R. Brink.[2]

w.s. J. R. Brink, president
w.s. C. Bouwman, clerk

---

2   This record was translated from the Dutch by Rev. Sebastian Cammenga.

*Appendix 3*

~~~⊙⊙~~~

# HOPE'S ORGANIZATIONAL RECORD

Art. 1. A meeting held June 8, 1916, to be organized as the congregation at River Bend, was led by Rev. J. R. Brink, who opened with prayer.
Psalm 68:10 was sung. A committee from West Leonard [Chr. Ref.
Church] was also present. Rev. Brink presents a short sermon based on
according to the Word of the Holy Scriptures: 1 Peter 2: 4–5.

Art. 2. The following membership [papers] were presented, coming
from the Walker congregation: Chas. Bouwman and wife, confessing members; Adrian Heyboer, confessing member; Richard (Rijtse)
Nieuwenhuis and wife, confessing members; Pieter Ruiter, confessing member; Jan Moelker and wife, confessing members, with eight
(8) baptized children; Jennie (Jantje) Engelsma, nee Batema, confessing member; [Jacob and] Jacoba Zaagman, nee Wagenaar member of
the Chr. Ref. Church, as member[s] by baptism with five (5) baptized
children; Wietse Visbeck, as baptized member from the Walker Chr.
Ref. Church; Johannes Van Dyke, Jacoba Maria Wilhelmina Bating and
four (4) baptized children; the former from the Netherlands Reformed
church and the latter, his wife, from the Reformed Church (*Gereformeerde Kerk*) in the Netherlands. The committee reviews these proofs
of membership, approves, and accepts them.

Art. 3. Voting for members of the Consistory: It is decided to vote
for two (2) elders and one (1) deacon. Chosen as elders are Jan Moelker
and C. Bouwman; for deacon, Richard (Rijtse) Nieuwenhuis, who are

installed into their respective offices by Rev. Brink. J. Moelker is chosen president and C. Bouwman as clerk of the consistory.

Art. 4. It is decided these brethren will serve through the year 1918, and then one (1) elder and one (1) deacon will retire. Candidate Terpstra speaks a few words to the congregation after which the above named brother closed with prayer after we had sung Psalm 122:1. The benediction is pronounced over the youthful congregation by Rev. J. R. Brink.[3]

w.s. Rev. J. R. Brink, president

w.s. C. Bouwman, secretary

---

3    This record was translated from the Dutch by Rev. Sebastian Cammenga.

# Response of Hope's Consistory to the Declaration of Principles

Having studied the Declaration of Principles of the Protestant Reformed Churches which the Synod of 1950 drew up for consideration in our churches we wish to inform Synod that our reaction to this Declaration is as follows:

1. We believe that this Declaration is an accurate presentation of the truth which our churches have always believed and taught concerning the points treated in this Declaration.

2. It is our conviction that Synod should adopt this Declaration. Our reasons for taking this stand are the following:

   a. Although the Three Formulas of Unity are sufficient for the demonstration of the unreformed and unscriptural position of every departure from the truth that has arisen to this day, we believe that this Declaration is nevertheless necessary that we as Prot. Reformed Churches may exhibit ourselves as unitedly standing foursquare upon these Confessions.

      i. The published letter of Prof. Holwerda reveals that both in the Netherlands and in Canada the opinion is held by some that our churches are not agreed on such an important thing as the doctrine of election.

ii. The writings in our church periodicals of the past year reveal that there is a difference of opinion among us as to whether the Confessions teach "Faith as a condition" and "The Covenant of Works."

iii. On the background of these undeniable facts to reject the Declaration, *now that it has been presented for our approval*, would give all those who do not agree with the contents of this Declaration the right to believe:

1. that our churches are willing to expose themselves to a different opinion of election than the one our churches have always believed and taught.

2. that our churches are willing to let the coming generations make use of the term, "Faith as a condition," and that we are willing to expose them to the danger of falling into the belief that man can merit before God and that Christ's coming and work is repair work, which false doctrines are implied in the current theory of the Covenant of Works.

iv. By rejection [of] this Declaration we deny the Committee for Correspondence, if and when they make their visit to the Netherlands, the right to maintain officially anything that is expressed in this Declaration. The Committee will have no right to maintain that our Churches do not believe that the Confessions teach that the promises of the Covenant are for every baptized child. They can only state that this is or is not their own personal opinion.

b. This Declaration is necessary that we may give a clear and honest answer to those who are considering joining one of our churches or of organizing as a Prot. Reformed Church and who ask us concerning the teachings of our churches. Similarly, to seek correspondence with other churches in an honest way, we must inform these churches in unequivocal language what we believe and teach.

    i.   We believe in exercising all love and tact, but we do not believe that it is either love or tact to leave the wrong impression upon others.

    ii.   We are likewise convinced that the truth of Scripture and therefore the Confessions which are based upon the Scriptures never antagonizes a child of God. Therefore we cannot believe that the adoption of this Declaration will close the door to further contact and discussion with the Liberated Churches of the Netherlands. Nor can we believe that this Declaration, which expresses what the Confessions teach, when adopted will close the door to all mission activity among the immigrants.

    iii.  However, having made plain in this Declaration what our churches believe to be the teachings of the Scriptures and the Confessions, we believe that those who understand that this is binding in our churches and still desire to affiliate with us should be allowed to do so when they declare that they are willing to be instructed in this doctrine and promise not to agitate against it.

c.  Since other views such as "common grace" and "the promise of the Covenant blessings unto every baptized child" have been set forth as being taught by *our* Confessions, it becomes our duty before God to declare, as we do in this Declaration, our opposition to these views, calling upon these same Confessions to show that our view of their teachings is the correct one. In

1924 we did not hesitate to refuse to sign a declaration which was a perversion of the teachings of the Confessions because we felt that it was our God-given duty to do so. Dare we now fail to sign this Declaration which maintains the truth of the Scriptures and the Confessions and reveals that God in His grace has given us the light and faithfulness to the truth?

3.    However:

a.    Although we are not eager to lengthen this Declaration, we believe that quotations from the Confessions to show why we condemn the theory of "common grace" would improve the Declaration.

b.    Since, because of our stand expressed in the Declaration, we are often accused of denying the responsibility of man and of teaching a deadly passivism, we believe that the section dealing with this matter should be given more prominence by a somewhat further development of this matter and by calling upon Lord's Day 24 and Article 24 of the Netherlands Confession to show that the accusation that this doctrine makes men careless is entirely false.

w.s. John A. Heys, president
w.s. Dewey Engelsma, clerk

*Appendix 5*

~~~ᎧᎧ~~~

# [Minority] Report of the Committee of Pre-Advice in re Protests of the Revs. H. Hoeksema and G. M. Ophoff against the Consistory of First Church

Grand Rapids Michigan

May 18, 1953

To the Classis East of the Protestant Reformed Churches convening May 19, 1953

Esteemed Brethren:

We, the undersigned, members of the committee appointed to study the protests of the Rev. Hoeksema and the Rev. Ophoff against their Consistory in re its action with the Rev. De Wolf cannot agree with the necessity nor with the contents of the long document which precedes the advice given by the other members of our committee. Neither can we sign the advice that they have drawn up. Instead, as our minority report we present the following:

1. We cannot agree that the Consistory should maintain its former stand that the statement "God promises every

one of you that if you believe you will be saved" is not a concise statement of the truth. In our opinion both the statements which the protestants condemn are literally heretical regardless of what the Rev. De Wolf meant by them, regardless of how he explains them, and regardless of however much we may rejoice that his examination shows that he does not believe the heresy implied in them. We take this stand:

a. because the protestants have clearly shown from the Scriptures and the Confessions that the literal statements are heretical.

b. and because we believe this is necessary for us to state in the light of our past experiences and history with the Liberated Churches who use these Arminian expressions.

2. As far as the making known to the congregation is concerned we believe:

a. that the statements which the Rev. De Wolf himself made at his examination should be announced to the congregation. We have in mind the following: in regard to the expression "God promises every one of you..." this statement found on page 4 of the examination, "I didn't realize that I shouldn't have used the word 'promise' there because of the implications which it might have." And in the regard to the expression, "our converting ourselves is a prerequisite to entering into the kingdom," this statement found on page 23 of the examination, "I will frankly admit that I said more on the pulpit than what I now realize I said. I didn't realize all the implications."

b. The way in which this is to be announced we leave to the discretion of the Consistory—whether by an announcement that is read or by the Rev. De Wolf himself personally—as Art. 75 of the Church Order also allows.

c.  This action we feel is necessary lest a very dangerous precedent be set in our churches that public statements which in
their literal form are heretical are explained in private and
the unskilled in the congregation who never hear the explanation are left to believe all and any of the implications in
the statements. This is all the more so necessary when, as
was the case with these two statements of the Rev. De Wolf,
there was such an abundance of protest made over against
the statements he made.

Wishing you the Lord's blessing,

w.s. R. Newhouse

w.s. P. Lubbers

*Appendix 6*

‿◦◦‿

# ELDERS AND DEACONS
# OF HOPE

Formula of Subscription handwritten in Dutch from the first minute book[4]

---

4   The first time an officebearer is installed into office he is required to sign the Formula
    of Subscription. Hope's officebearers do this by signing their names on the inside cover
    of the minute book currently in use by the council. These lists identify by dates the
    minute book in which the signatures are found.

## Translated Minutes

### *Elders*

Tjark Bouwman
John Moelker
Richard (Rietse) Nieuwenhuis
G. De Jong
Isaac Korhorn
James Kuipers
Henry Vande Kieft
Mathys Van Eeuwen
Cornelius [Korhorn]
John Winkel
John Riddering
J. E. Brink
Charles E. Vanderlaan
H. Van der Malen
Corniel Van der Tuin

### *Deacons*

Rietse Nieuwenhuis[5]
Isaac Korhorn
Bergman
Henrick Goeree
Mathys Van Eeuwen
Cornelius Tuinstra
Jacob Staal
Jacob Goeree
Ed Saagman
Marinus Vugteveen

## Consistory Minute Book
## January 1916 to December 1939

Rietse Newhouse
G. De Jong
Isaac Korhorn
John Moelker

---

5    We are not sure of the reason some officebearers signed the Formula more than once.

John Kuiper
Gerrit Moelker
T. J. Kievit
Gerald Korhorn
Charles Engelsma
Arie Ponstein
Harry E. Bloem
Neil Moelker
Dick Kooienga
John Lanning
John Huizinga
Dewey Engelsma
Eno Howerzyl
Jacob Kuiper
Theodore Howerzyl
Maynard Veenstra
Richard L. Bloem
Anthony Langerak
Fred Huizinga
John Kalsbeek
A. J. Kuiper

**Consistory Minute Book
July 1951[6] to December 1958**

J. Bomers
Peter Petroelje
John P. Miedema
Melvin Engelsma

**Consistory Minute Book
January 1959 to October 1963**

David Meulenberg
Richard Newhouse

---

6    While there is a gap between 1939 and 1951 in the listed minute books, in which the
officebearers signed the Formula of Subscription, this is a complete list of Hope's officebearers. Apparently they continued to place their signatures in the January 1916 to
December 1939 book even though the clerk used another book to record the minutes.
This becomes clear when one considers that some of those who signed the 1916–39
book were not members at Hope until the 1950s.

Dewey Engelsma
Roger Kooienga
John J. Dykstra
John Kuiper Jr.

## Consistory Minute Book
## October 1963 to June 1970

Johannes King
Alvin Rau
Louis Elzinga
Arnold Dykstra
Peter Zandstra
Peter Koole
Gordon Terpstra
Peter F. Knott
John Dykstra
Henry Velthouse
Milo De Wald

## Council Minute Book
## July 1970 to March 1978

Fredrick Hanko
Joseph Van Dyke
Thomas Reitsma
Leon Garvelink
John De Vries
Jon Huisken
Ira Veenstra
Charles Kalsbeek
Herman Van Dyke
Vernon Klamer
David Moelker
Robert Harbach
Donald Lotterman
Harry Langerak
Larry Meulenberg

Carl Potjer
Cal Kalsbeek

## Council Minute Book
## March 1978 to July 1985

John Buiter
Lawrence Koole
John Cleveland
Clarence Kuiper
James Koole
James Huizinga
David Kamps
Neil Meyer

## Council Minute Book
## August 1985 to December 1992

Robert Knott
Marinus Kamps
Martin Daling
James Schimmel
Gary Moelker
Gerald Dykstra
Daniel De Meester
Douglas Kooienga
Robert Vermeer
Steven Langerak
Jonathan Engelsma

## Council Minute Book
## January 1993 to April 2000

Tom Oosterhouse
Harlan Hoekstra
Michael Rau
Bruce Klamer
Jim Koole
Tom L. De Vries
Timothy Bomers

Michael A. Engelsma
Michael Bosveld
Martin De Vries
Gary Nienhuis
Harry H. Rutgers
Jeffrey Kalsbeek
Joel Minderhoud

## Council Minute Book
## May 2000 to September 2011

Richard Peterson
John Van Baren
Eugene Kamps
Jeffrey Terpstra
Mike Lotterman
Jon Hop
David Langerak
David Jessup
Kenneth Engelsma
Jonathon Kamps
Aaron Cleveland
Dan Kalsbeek
Joel Langerak
Jon Rutgers
Brad Duistermars
Henry Vander Waal

## Council Minute Book
## January 2012 to the present

Daryl Bleyenberg
Joel Vink
Vance Grasman
Alexander Kalsbeek
Dan Van Uffelen
Brian Kalsbeek

# Appendix 7

## ORGANISTS OF HOPE

Hope church has had many organists through the years. However, we have found it difficult to name those who played for the worship services before the 1940s. The organists we are able to name are the following:

Alice Korhorn (Veenstra)

Cornelia Korhorn (Kuiper)

Hattie Lanning

Sadie Engelsma

Sybil Engelsma

John G. Moelker

Alice Korhorn

Cornelia Korhorn

Hattie Lanning

Sadie Engelsma

Sybil Engelsma

John G. Moelker

Bonnie Kuiper

Bonnie Meulenberg (Moelker)

Clare Kuiper

Terri Garvelink

Mary Veenstra

Deb Kooienga

Melva Mastbergen

Joan Slopsema

Mary Kalsbeek

Marilyn De Vries

Rose Rutgers

Sharon Kamps

Valerie Van Baren

Rose Doezema

~~~ ⚬⚬ ~~~

# CURRENT MEMBERS OF HOPE WHO HAVE BEEN MEMBERS FOR FIFTY AND MORE YEARS

| Years | Name | Year Became a Member |
|---|---|---|
| 91 | Johanna (Engelsma) Bomers | 1925 |
| 89 | Betty (Korhorn) Bloem | 1927 |
| 80 | Eileen (Engelsma) Terpstra | 1936 |
| 80 | Helen Veenstra | 1936 |
| 74 | Alvin Huizinga | 1942 |
| 72 | James Huizinga | 1944 |
| 72 | Clare Kuiper | 1944 |
| 71 | Lucille (Boogaard) Kooienga | 1945 |
| 68 | Harry Langerak | 1948 |
| 68 | Alice (Vander Loon) Huizinga | 1948 |
| 64 | John N. Dykstra | 1952 |
| 64 | David Moelker | 1952 |
| 63 | Calvin Kalsbeek | 1953 |
| 62 | John J. Dykstra Jr. | 1954 |
| 62 | Kenneth Dykstra | 1954 |
| 62 | Deborah (Schimmel) Vander Waal | 1954 |

| Years | Name | Year Became a Member |
|-------|------|----------------------|
| 62 | James Schimmel | 1954 |
| 62 | Gordon Terpstra | 1954 |
| 61 | Karla (Kalsbeek) Kamps | 1958 |
| 60 | Bonnie (Meulenberg) Moelker | 1956 |
| 59 | Alvin Rau | 1957 |
| 59 | Phyllis (De Wald) Rau | 1957 |
| 58 | Anna (Jacobs) Elzinga (deceased March 2, 2016) | 1958 |
| 58 | Carol (Elzinga) Tanis | 1958 |
| 58 | Roger Kamphuis | 1962 |
| 56 | Prof. Herman Hanko | 1955 (8 years as Hope's minister) then since 1968 |
| 56 | Wilma (Knoper) Hanko | 1955 (8 years as minister's wife) then since 1968 |
| 54 | James Koole | 1962 |
| 54 | Timothy Koole | 1962 |
| 53 | Timothy Bomers | 1963 |
| 53 | Michael Rau | 1963 |
| 52 | Michael Engelsma | 1947 (17-year hiatus to Southeast PR Church) |
| 52 | David Kamps | 1964 |
| 52 | Evelyn (Kamps) Langerak | 1964 |
| 51 | Kenneth Engelsma | 1961 (4-year hiatus to Grandville PR Church) |
| 50 | Brenda (Langerak) Bomers | 1966 |
| 50 | Eugene Kamps | 1966 |

# Appendix 9

*Appendix 9*

# MEMBERSHIP STATISTICS
# OF HOPE

| Year | Families | Year | Families | Year | Families |
|------|----------|------|----------|------|----------|
| 1916 | 7  | 1940 | 12 | 1964 | 60  |
| 1917 | 7  | 1941 | 12 | 1965 | 63  |
| 1918 | 7  | 1942 | 12 | 1966 | 66  |
| 1919 | 12 | 1943 | 17 | 1967 | 76  |
| 1920 | 21 | 1944 | 17 | 1968 | 85  |
| 1921 | 22 | 1945 | 17 | 1969 | 92  |
| 1922 | 23 | 1946 | 22 | 1970 | 92  |
| 1923 | 24 | 1947 | 24 | 1971 | 91  |
| 1924 | 18 | 1948 | 29 | 1972 | 84  |
| 1925 | 24 | 1949 | 29 | 1973 | 87  |
| 1926 | 13 | 1950 | 35 | 1974 | 89  |
| 1927 | 13 | 1951 | 35 | 1975 | 96  |
| 1928 | 11 | 1952 | 35 | 1976 | 104 |
| 1929 | 11 | 1953 | 40 | 1977 | 106 |
| 1930 | 13 | 1954 | 30 | 1978 | 108 |
| 1931 | 13 | 1955 | 34 | 1979 | 97  |
| 1932 | 9  | 1956 | 34 | 1980 | 104 |
| 1933 | 9  | 1957 | 34 | 1981 | 104 |
| 1934 | 14 | 1958 | 43 | 1982 | 103 |
| 1935 | 7  | 1959 | 44 | 1983 | 85  |
| 1936 | 7  | 1960 | 46 | 1984 | 81  |
| 1937 | 16 | 1961 | 47 | 1985 | 84  |
| 1938 | 15 | 1962 | 55 | 1986 | 85  |
| 1939 | 13 | 1963 | 60 | 1987 | 82  |

| Year | Families |
|------|----------|
| 1988 | 87 |
| 1989 | 98 |
| 1990 | 99 |
| 1991 | 104 |
| 1992 | 105 |
| 1993 | 108 |
| 1994 | 113 |
| 1995 | 92 |
| 1996 | 93 |
| 1997 | 95 |
| 1998 | 93 |
| 1999 | 92 |
| 2000 | 90 |
| 2001 | 90 |
| 2002 | 88 |
| 2003 | 87 |
| 2004 | 86 |
| 2005 | 86 |
| 2006 | 88 |
| 2007 | 93 |
| 2008 | 90 |
| 2009 | 92 |
| 2010 | 91 |
| 2011 | 88 |
| 2012 | 90 |
| 2013 | 91 |
| 2014 | 91 |
| 2015 | 88 |

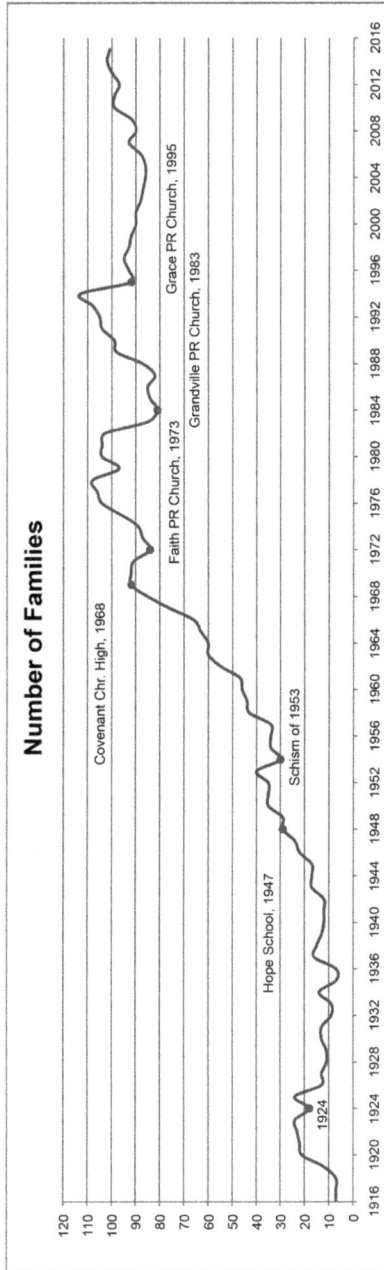

Three main sources were used to compile the above charts. For the years before the first synod of the Protestant Reformed Churches in 1940, the number of families was calculated from information available in the consistory minutes and by counting those who were visited for family visitation. In the instances this method did not work, the number of the previous year was repeated. From 1940 to 1950 the statistics in the *Acts of Synod* were used, however these numbers are usually about 5 to 10 percent high because of synod's method of calculating families (presently three confessing individuals are counted as a family). The most accurate numbers are from 1951 to the present, since those were taken from Hope's church directories.

*Appendix 10*

# THEMES AND BIBLE TEXTS USED FOR FAMILY VISITATION

From the beginning Hope's consistory has conducted family visitation, as required by article 23 of the Church Order, for the purpose of comforting, instructing, and exhorting her members. The list of topics below represents the themes and Bible passages used by the consistory to set the tone for the elders' visits for the last forty-five years.

| | |
|---|---|
| 1971 | Subjection to Authority |
| 1972 | To Know Him is Life Eternal |
| 1973 | Trying the Spirits—1 John 4:1–3 |
| 1974 | Seeking First the Kingdom of Heaven—Matthew 6; Luke 12 |
| 1975 | Seeking the Communion of the Saints—1 Corinthians 12; Philippians 2 |
| 1976 | Antithetical Living |
| 1977 | Proverbs 23:23; Hosea 4:6 |
| 1978 | Living a Sanctified Life |
| 1979 | The Word of Christ Dwelling in Us Richly—Colossians 3:16 |
| 1980 | Continuing in the Ways of Scripture—2 Timothy 3:14–15; Jeremiah 6:16 |
| 1981 | Living a Life of Separation from the World—2 Corinthians 6:14–18; 7:1; Revelation 18:4b |
| 1982 | Christian Stewardship—Ephesians 5:1–16; Luke 21:1–4 |
| 1983 | Communion of the Saints—1 Corinthians 12; Philippians 2 |

1984    The Fear of the Lord
1985    Discipleship—Mark 8:34; Ephesians 5:1-21; 2 Corinthians
        6:11-18
1986    Christian Family in the Present Age
1987-89 Behavior of Love—1 Corinthians 13:4-7
1990    Christian Contentment
1991    Holding the Traditions
1992    Laboring in the Lord
1993    Making Our Calling and Election Sure
1994    Numbering Our Days
1995    Knowing the Scriptures
1996    Watching for the Coming of the Lord—1 Thessalonians
        4:13-5:11
1997    Trusting in the Lord—Psalm 37:3-6; Proverbs 3:5-6
1998    Laboring for the Meat That Endureth—John 6:27
2000    Living in the Last Days—Matthew 24
2001    Covenant Fellowship in the Home and Church—Ephesians
        5:18-6:4
2002    In Everything Giving Thanks to God—1 Thessalonians 5:18
2003    Abounding in the Work of the Lord—1 Corinthians 15:58
2004    Living in Perilous Times—2 Timothy 3:1-5
2005    Meditating upon the Word—Joshua 1:8
2006    Exhortation to Sound Doctrine—Titus 2
2007    Abiding in Christ's Love—John 15
2008    Seeking First the Kingdom of Heaven—Matthew 6; Luke 12
2009    Presenting Yourselves a Living Sacrifice—Romans 12
2010    Redeeming the Time—Ephesians 5:15-16
2011    Begotten unto a Lively Hope—1 Peter 1:3
2012    Covenant Fellowship in Home and Church—Colossians 3
2013    The Whole Armor of God—Ephesians 6:10-20
2014    Living a Life of Separation from the World—2 Corinthians
        6:14-18; 7:1
2015    Dwelling in the House of the Lord—Psalm 27:4
2016    A Spiritual House Offering Acceptable Sacrifices—1 Peter 2:4-5

*Appendix 11*

⁓◦◦⁓

# A Spiritual House

To whom coming, as unto a living stone, disallowed indeed of men, but chosen of God, and precious, ye also, as lively stones, are built up a spiritual house, an holy priesthood, to offer up spiritual sacrifices, acceptable to God by Jesus Christ.
—1 Peter 2:4–5

## Introduction

Beloved people of God in Jesus Christ our Lord, our elders chose 1 Peter 2:4–5 to consider together for this year's family visitation. It's an appropriate text also to consider this year in particular as we celebrate God's graciousness to us in preserving us for the past one hundred years. This is a fitting text to consider as we think of God's preserving care for us as a church, because the text is about the church of Jesus Christ.

The text uses various images to describe the church. It uses the image of a house, which means a temple, a house made of stones. The text uses also the symbolism of a holy priesthood. It uses this image to speak of the church as a gathering of God's people anointed with the Spirit of Christ.

Similar themes are also central themes of the book of Hebrews. As we read through Hebrews, we hear of God's instruction of us with regard to a new temple in Jesus Christ—a new temple, the old having

---

"A Spiritual House" is an adaptation of a sermon preached on January 17, 2016, by Rev. David Overway in connection with the theme for family visitation in 2016.

been done away, and the whole old way of worship having been done away, or fulfilled, in Christ. Now there is a new temple. We also read in Hebrews of the priesthood, of a new priesthood established in Jesus Christ, which is prevalent in the New Testament.

But in 1 Peter 2:4–5 there are those same themes brought out in connection with a rock, a living stone. Although Hebrews brings these things up in connection with that same rock, it does so with different terms and not by using the language of a rock. Peter speaks of a new temple, a new house of God, and a new priesthood in connection with a rock, a living stone, by which he refers to Jesus Christ, our savior. How fitting that is for Peter, named Cephas, which means "a rock" or "a stone." As God's humble, godly, and faithful servant, Peter directs our attention away from himself to the true Rock, our Savior—the true Living Stone, upon whom the church, "a spiritual house," is built.

## Of Living Stones

The spiritual house is made of living stones. Each individual child of God is another stone to build one complete unity—one house, one church. The text refers to the church as the universal body of Jesus Christ, that is, the whole church catholic. The whole church from the beginning of time to the very end of time, gathered throughout all the nations, tongues, and tribes of the world, is one house. Each believer is another stone in that house.

Although this is true, the text speaks of the church as she is *instituted.* For the church as a catholic, universal church is manifested and expressed within the institute. Each instituted church of Jesus Christ—as the Hope congregation—is in itself complete and full not in the sense that it has no need for the rest of the body, but that there is nothing lacking, nothing missing in the church as she is instituted.

So the text also can be taken to explain the church as she is instituted in a local congregation. The text describes the Hope congregation and says we are a house of God. We are the house as we live with God. Each one of us is a stone in that house.

As the text uses the language of a house, we cannot help but think of a family. And certainly that is the intention of the text as well. A family ordinarily is found living in a house. And by virtue of the family's living within that house, we refer to the house as a home, a place where love, relationships, and fellowship exist. Within a home one can find a husband and a wife living together as the home, as the family, the central core of the family. So that, too, is meant as we read that the church is a house. We read of God's living together with his bride, God in Jesus Christ. Christ, the bridegroom, lives with his bride. They live a life of love and unity. That is the church. Let us think of the church not only as the bride, but also as a house of a husband and a wife living together—the bride and the Bridegroom living together in one house, one unity.

Or to look at what is found within a house from another viewpoint: parents and children, father and sons, to use the language of scripture. We find that also in the church. The church is the house of God wherein Father lives with his children, with his sons and daughters, redeemed by him and adopted in his grace.

Those relationships are experienced as friendships. A husband and wife do not really live as husband and wife unless they live as friends. God lives as the bridegroom of his church, his bride, as her friend; and she lives with him as a friend, as the church, the house of God. Father lives with his children as friends. Certainly, he comes with authority; he does not abrogate or put aside his authority to be the friend of his people. He is still the authority within the house; he is still Father. But he is Father as a gentle, compassionate, and understanding friend who is interested in his children. He lives together with them as their friends. And they live together, God and his people, as Husband and wife, as Father and children, as friends, enjoying one another's fellowship.

The church is a place of fellowship. The church is a house of God where God dwells in the relationship of friendship with his people, but where God also reveals himself and speaks to his people, and they hear his voice and speak to him. And warm, loving fellowship takes place between God and his people.

The term "house" not only brings to our minds the idea of a family, but also the idea of a temple. Then our speaking of us as individual members is to be thought of as each of us as another stone in that temple. And God lives within us.

That was the picture of the temple in the Old Testament. When the temple was set up within Israel and Jerusalem, the people would say, "That's where God dwells with us. We live here, and God lives there in the midst of us. God is with us in that temple." God says, "You have the New Testament fulfillment of that in the church." She is now the temple of God. God dwells in her midst, among those stones, among the members of the church. God says, "I will be their God, and they shall be my people, and I will dwell with them." God himself shall be with them, and in reference to the temple, as she will be perfected in the return of Jesus Christ. But that is also true now as the church exists in the midst of this world. God dwells with us here. And we dwell with him. We dwell with him as his temple to worship him, to serve him, and to glorify him.

All of us together, as members of the church, are that house. We are that house. We are that temple. We need to understand that, too. Even those who are younger and have limited understanding need to understand that this building that is around us, above us, and below us is not really the church. We call it the church, but only because it is the place where the church, the people of God, gathers. We are the church. We are the house of God not this building. We are the temple of God not this earthly building.

The text speaks of a house and of a temple made of stones. That is a figure; it does not literally mean made of stones. Then we could not speak of ourselves. The Old Testament temple was made of stones, so God uses that figure and says that the church, the New Testament temple, is made of stones.

The very first stone, indeed the most important stone, is Jesus Christ. We read of that in verse 4: "to whom coming, as unto a living stone." That refers to verse 3, which mentions him as "Lord." He is Jesus Christ our Lord—a living stone, but a stone. We also read of him in verse 6 as the "corner stone": "wherefore also it is contained in the scripture, Behold, I lay in Zion a chief corner stone, elect, precious";

even as in verse 4 he is referred to as "chosen of God, and precious." The references are plainly to Jesus Christ. He is the cornerstone of the house of God, the temple of God. He determines, then, everything about that house. Everything about that temple is traced back to him. He determines the height, the boundary, and the glory of the church. The cornerstone determines it all.

And Jesus is "chosen of God." He is chosen out first, and that is true also according to the picture. If a builder were planning to build some grand building, he would begin with the corner stone, a perfect cornerstone, exactly the one he needs. He would set it in place, and upon that cornerstone he would build everything else. So it is with the house of God. God elected Jesus Christ first, as in logical primacy. Christ is most important. In Christ all the rest of the temple was chosen, out of him all the rest of the temple comes, and upon him all the rest of the house is built.

Jesus is called "a living stone," in verse 4. That is an amazing statement! We do not find such stones in the creation. We could search throughout the whole creation, and we would not find a living stone.

Jesus Christ is referred to as a "stone." But the apostle, under the inspiration of the Holy Spirit, says, "That analogy, that figure, does not fully capture who the cornerstone, Jesus Christ the savior of the church, really is. He is not just a stone but a 'living' stone, a stone who is alive." So it is with Jesus Christ. As a stone he is sound, sturdy, and steadfast, and upon him the whole church is built. Everything that he is determines the church. But he is also alive, crucified but risen, risen with resurrection life, with a mighty life that has conquered death, a life that can never again be touched by death. Everlasting is his life as the living stone.

Because the Cornerstone is living, so are all of the other stones in the building. It is not a building constructed of only a living cornerstone with all the other stones dead, inert, and piled on that cornerstone. But scripture says that all of the stones in the building are living stones. Verse 5 refers to them in the King James Version as "lively" stones. The word is really "living": "ye also, as living stones." Ye are living stones because of your connection to Jesus Christ. As we rest upon him, as we are built upon him, and as we are united to him with a real living bond, his life becomes our life. Christ's life is given to us, and by God's grace we are made spiritually alive with his resurrection life, alive with everlasting life.

We are his body. During his earthly ministry Jesus referred to his body as his "temple." "Destroy this temple, and in three days I will raise it up" (John 2:19). He spoke there "of the temple of his body" (v. 21). Certainly, what is meant first by "body" is his physical body. The text was fulfilled when the Jews destroyed him, and in three days he arose as the Living Stone. "Body" also refers to his church. His physical body is a picture of the full church—the full body of Jesus Christ made up of many members, who would be raised and begin to be established upon his resurrection because he is the living stone.

All of the living stones in the church, all of the members in the church—as they comprise that body, that house, that temple of God—live one life. One life flows from Christ, the living stone, into all the various members of the body, so they live one life. That is the unity of the living stones. That is our unity. We experience and enjoy that. We have one salvation, one life, one Savior. When we discuss the things of God we sense that. We thrill to know and to enjoy that unity—that blessed, blessed unity that we have together through our one life.

That one life is ours even though we are very different from one another. The stones are diverse; yet they have one life. All of that is traced back to the Cornerstone. So it is within an earthly building. One might use various materials and arrange them in different ways so that the building would be composed of walls, flooring, ceiling, windows, and all the different parts of a building. The materials would be diverse, yet all of them together would form one house, one temple—one living house and temple in the case of the church.

What an amazing thing it is that we stand as the house of God, as the temple of God. For by nature we are really very lowly stones, worthless stones unsuitable for building—certainly unsuitable to be hauled out of the dirt and mud and carried over and built upon one another to establish a temple for the living God. But God takes these lowly stones, crafts and makes them into glorious stones, and sets them within that glorious house, that marvelous temple. We are ugly stones, not at all attractive by nature. We are even broken, fractured, and crumbling stones unable to be used. Yet God fits us into the temple, fills us with the life of his Son, and makes us living stones so that he can dwell among us, within us, and we can glorify him as his temple, his house.

The text also refers to the house as "a spiritual house." The temple of God is a spiritual house, first, in its essence. It is spiritual not material. The house is not made of earthly materials as the Old Testament temple was. Now it is a spiritual house realized within the hearts of God's people, and as there is an invisible bond between those people and a bond back to Jesus Christ. It is a spiritual house.

Second, that house is spiritual in its purpose. The church is not in this world with an earthly purpose: to make this world a happier, better place, to serve our communities, to give something back to them to improve their quality of life, to try to redeem the world for Christ, or to establish some kind of Christian impact within various spheres of society. The church is a spiritual house; it has a spiritual purpose, which is the glory of God, the service of God, and the fellowship and communion with her covenantal God.

Third, the church is a spiritual house in its construction. It is not built by earthly forces or by man's strength, or man's wisdom or ingenuity. She is a spiritual house because she is built by the Spirit of Jesus Christ. She is gathered out of all nations and from among all kinds of people by the irresistible, powerful, mysterious, and gracious Spirit of Jesus Christ. That gathering is also by another spiritual means— the word of Jesus Christ, the mighty, effectual voice of Jesus Christ. Through the word the Spirit builds the church.

Fourth, the church is spiritual in its life. It is a living house. But it does not live a natural, earthly life; but as living stones, a living house, it lives a spiritual life. The church's life, as a spiritual life, is a holy life that enables God's people to serve him. That is what spiritual life is, beloved. It is nothing else than that. It certainly can be more than that, but it is not different than a holy life, a life of service. That is seen when we understand the reason the stones are living: they have the life of the Living Stone within them. We have Christ's life in us. And Christ's life certainly was a holy life, a life of consecration, devotion to God, a life that stood over against sin and unrepentant sinners. His life was also a life of serving God. That was the whole goal of his life: "the zeal of thine house hath eaten me up" (Ps. 69:9). This means that the zeal to build God's house was everything to him, it was his all-consuming desire to serve Jehovah by building his house.

## Of Acceptable Sacrifices

Therefore, it is not surprising that Peter switches and changes his figure from a spiritual house to a "holy priesthood" (v. 5). When he thinks of a living stone and of living stones built upon that living Cornerstone, he thinks immediately of a holy priesthood, of people of God filled with the life of Christ, so they *are* holy, and they *do serve* their God as priests.

Old Testament priests served in the temple, the house of God. They were consecrated to God's service. Their lives were to be separate from various earthly affairs and in service to God for the sake of his church and for his glory. They were to do that as holy, as separated from the common, and devoted, or consecrated, to God's service.

In the New Testament, through Jesus Christ, we are all holy priests. Every living stone in the house, every member of the church, is a priest unto God. In fact, this is the goal, or the purpose, God has in mind as he sets up a living stone, builds upon that living stone other living stones, and builds unto himself a temple. His view, or purpose, is to establish a holy priesthood who will serve him. That comes out in the language of the original of the text. No longer will only Levites stand between God and his people, lead the people to God, and make sacrifices for the people for their comfort. But through our High Priest and his one and only atoning sacrifice, we all are now priests, a holy priesthood.

To offer sacrifices was the business of the Old Testament priests. We are now a holy priesthood to offer acceptable sacrifices unto God. We do not make atoning sacrifices. That cannot be. Christ has died to atone for our sins once and for all. All of our sins are washed away. We are perfectly righteous in him. We cannot add anything more to his sacrifice and must not even think such a thought. Yet, sacrifices we offer—sacrifices of service to God, of love to God, of thankfulness to God, and of praise to him.

A sacrifice is something given from one to another. As the Old Testament saint brought his bullock to the temple, handed it over to the priest, and the priest offered the animal and sacrificed it, that offering went from that Israelite unto God. It was given for the praise and glory of God.

The sacrifice was given at some expense, some cost. A sacrifice is not a sacrifice if it is not given at some cost, some expense by the one who gives it. One must bring is own sheep or some other animal, his own sacrifice to God, at his own expense.

But 1 Peter 2:4 does not speak of bulls, goats, sheep, or the blood thereof, but the verse refers to "spiritual sacrifices." That fits with the fact that these sacrifices are offered by the spiritual house of God. They are spiritual sacrifices not physical, such as sacrifices of bulls, goats, or the like. The psalmist David understood the true, spiritual sacrifice required by God of all of his people, which every one of his people offer to him. He spoke of it in Psalm 51, that beautiful psalm of repentance: "the sacrifices of God are a broken spirit: a broken and a contrite heart, O God, thou wilt not despise" (v. 17). That is centrally the sacrifice that we as a holy priesthood must offer, and do offer, unto God: a broken spirit of humble repentance before God. That is what God will not despise; that God will not turn from; that is an acceptable sacrifice unto him. Always remember that. More is meant by "sacrifice" than only that, which we see from other passages. But remember, this sacrifice is required as utterly essential. It must never be set aside in favor of other kinds of sacrifices. Always we must come to God with a broken heart, a contrite spirit, confessing our sins.

We must also offer to him the sacrifice of praise, as we read of it in Hebrews 13:15: "by him therefore let us offer the sacrifice of praise to God continually, that is, the fruit of our lips giving thanks to his name." Say it, beloved. Say thanks unto God. Praise him with your lips. Those are sacrifices that a holy priesthood brings unto God. We do that in worship. God comes and speaks to us in the preaching. We fold our hands, close our eyes, and offer the fruit of our lips, praise and thanks to God in prayer. We rise and hold our psalters, and out of our hearts and lips come the sacrifices of praise and thanks to God for including us in the spiritual house and giving us all the blessings of salvation.

Not only from hearts and lips we offer sacrifices, but also our lives and the activities of our lives as lived in our earthly bodies are to be sacrifices unto God. "I beseech you therefore, brethren, by the mercies of God, that ye present your bodies a living sacrifice" (Rom. 12:1). That is not a sacrifice laid upon an altar and put to death, but it is a living sacrifice coming out of a spiritual life: "a living sacrifice, holy, acceptable unto God, which is your reasonable service" (v. 1). That is the same language as 1 Peter 2:4. Romans 12 spells out what that sacrifice looks like, what that living sacrifice of our bodies and of our lives in the world looks like. As you read through the chapter, you cannot avoid that the sacrifice certainly includes loving one another and serving one another in love. Verse 2 says, "Be not conformed to this world: but be ye transformed by the renewing of your mind." This speaks of our being humble and antithetical to the pride of this world. Pride is the way of the world. God says, "No, do not be that; be humble." Verse 3 says, "For I say, through the grace given unto me, to every man that is among you, not to think of himself more highly than he ought to think; but to think soberly, according as God hath dealt to every man the measure of faith." The way of the world is to think in pride. The way of living stones is to offer to God the sacrifice of humility and to deal with one another by using the gifts that God has given to serve the body, to strengthen, to edify, to encourage, and to build up the spiritual strength of the body. That is our spiritual sacrifice. As Paul sacrificed himself to God for the Philippians, and as he spoke of his labor on their behalf, which he did not mind at all, he counted it "joy" to offer himself as a sacrifice for their strengthening (Phil. 2:17). Let that be the mind, spirit, heart, and life of all of us. As also Paul speaks in Philippians 4:18 of the Philippians' giving to him a sacrifice as a sacrifice unto God, so we give to one another within the church. In that way we sacrifice to God as an act of covenantal service of love unto him.

As living stones, as a holy priesthood, as members of his church, we cannot offer acceptable sacrifices unto God apart from his church, apart from living in his church and among his church, and availing ourselves of the means of grace in the church. But in the church, as members of the church, we live, offering sacrifices unto God as a holy priesthood and living stones.

And those sacrifices, beloved, are "acceptable," which means that the sacrifices are what God receives to himself. That is a delight to us. God does not put out his hand and say, "No, I don't want those sacrifices. They are filthy and stained with sin." But God receives our sacrifices. But more than that, God receives them to himself with pleasure. God delights in the sacrifices offered by his people. That is what "acceptable" means. God receives our sacrifices. All of our life of thankful living before him as a holy priesthood God receives with delight. Good works indeed, if God views them, values them, and receives them with delight! That is an amazing, amazing thought to ponder.

These sacrifices are acceptable and delightful unto God "by Jesus Christ," as cleansed by him (1 Pet. 2:5). He cleanses all the spots and stains of even our best works and purifies them by his perfect atonement, so that God can receive them as acceptable, as delightful unto himself. They are acceptable unto God not only as cleansed by Jesus Christ, but also because they ultimately come from him. They come from Christ, and he is precious unto God.

### Of Precious Foundation

He is not precious unto men as they stand by nature and in sin, men apart from Christ and his grace. Christ as the cornerstone is "disallowed indeed of men" (v. 4). "Disallowed" is a strong word that means rejected, but rejected with knowledge, rejected after a careful examination. The text uses the picture again of builders who look at all the stones, evaluate them, examine them, receive some to be built into the building, and throw aside others as unusable.

That is what the Jews and the leaders of the Jews did with our Lord Jesus. They examined him and his teachings, they listened to his truth and his doctrine, they watched his life, they thought about it, they asked themselves, "Could he be the Messiah? Should we receive him as such? Could he build the church? Could the church be built upon him?" And they decided, "Absolutely not! He stands for everything we hate! He is no good." They disallowed him. They rejected him. And so do many today.

But God did not. To God he is chosen and precious. He is God's only begotten Son in human nature, in human flesh and blood. He was a perfect savior, perfect in his obedience, even in the way of suffering. He perfectly submitted himself to the suffering he must endure to save his people. He was selfless in his life and service to God. He was mighty in his work of salvation and holy in everything he did. Approving him, God set him as the cornerstone of the church, so that now he determines everything about the church, and the whole church is built upon him as the living cornerstone. His resurrection life flows out of him into all of the other stones of the building.

And all of the living stones, receiving that life, strengthened by that life, and empowered by that life say, "Precious! Unto us he is precious!" This is exactly the statement of verse 7: "Unto you therefore which believe he is precious." Precious he is because by him we live. We are living stones placed upon him. Resting upon him and receiving his life as our life, we live holy lives that serve him and that serve God. He is precious because by him we are holy; by him we are a holy priesthood by his Spirit of anointing. By him we offer sacrifices. By him our sacrifices are acceptable unto God.

So, then, to him we come. That is how verse 4 begins: "to whom coming, as unto a living stone." This means we who are built upon him, we who are living stones and rest upon him, we who are a holy priesthood. Again and again we come. Over and over, continuously, we come to him, drawn by his voice and his power, and drawn to him because he is so very precious to us. We are drawn to him, so that from him we can receive the grace and the strength we need to live as a holy priesthood and to offer acceptable sacrifices unto God. Therefore, continue to serve him in that way and to glorify him in that way as a holy priesthood, offering acceptable sacrifices delightful unto God and to the glory of God.

That is the church—the spiritual house wherein and with which God lives. We have all of this because of that precious Cornerstone. Amen.

Father, we thank thee for thy word. We thank thee for the cornerstone, Jesus Christ. We thank thee that from him we receive our life that we might live unto thee and offer sacrifices that indeed are acceptable and delightful unto thee. Father, continue to glorify thyself in us as a congregation. May we know and rejoice to know that we are living stones and that we are thy house wherein we find thy fellowship. And we are thy holy temple built by thee, established by thee, and preserved by thee, in order that we might glorify thee in all of our life. In Jesus' name we pray these things. Amen.

◦◦

# ANNIVERSARY PROGRAM: A SPIRITUAL HOUSE ACCEPTABLE TO GOD

## A Spiritual House: Built by Christ

*Rev. Overway*

Opening prayer and remarks

Read 1 Peter 2:4–5

Read the meditation "A House Built by Christ"

*Audience*

Sing the anniversary theme song, psalter 134:1–3,
"Praise and Trust"

1. Within Thy temple, Lord,
   In that most holy place,
   We on Thy loving-kindness dwell,
   The wonders of Thy grace.
   Men sing Thy praise, O God,
   Where'er Thy Name is known;
   By ev'ry deed Thy hand hath wrought
   Thy righteousness is shown.

2. Let Zion now rejoice,
   And all her children sing;
   Let them with thankfulness proclaim

The judgments of their King.
Mount Zion's walls behold,
About her ramparts go,
And number ye the lofty tow'rs
That guard her from the foe.

3.  Observe her palaces,
    Mark her defenses well,
    That to the sons that follow you
    Her glories you may tell;
    For God as our own God
    Forever will abide,
    And till life's journey close in death
    Will be our faithful guide.

## A Spiritual House: Let All Her Children Sing

### Sunday school

Psalter 250:1, 4–5
"My Hope is Built on Nothing Less"

### Young people and Sunday school

"The Apostles' Creed"
"As the Deer"

### Audience

Sing psalter 247:1–6, "God Our Help and Hope" (second tune)

## A Spiritual House: Learning from Her Past

### Alex De Vries, Nathan De Vries, Cal Kalsbeek

PowerPoint presentation:
"One Hundred Years Ago in the River's Bend"

### John Van Baren, moderator, with Prof. David Engelsma and Prof. Herman Hanko

"Reflections of the Past One Hundred Years"

*Audience*

Sing psalter 375:1–5, "Invitations to Praise"

## A Spiritual House: Offering Acceptable Praise

*One-Hundredth Anniversary Choir*

Psalm 122
"Nearer Still Nearer"
Psalm 84
"In Christ Alone"

### A Spiritual House: Offering a Prayer of Thanksgiving

*Rev. James Laning*

Closing prayer

### A Spiritual House:
### Offering a Doxology of Thanks and Praise

*Audience*

Sing psalter 197, "The Doxology"

1.  Now blessed be Jehovah, God,
    The God of Israel,
    Who only doeth wondrous works,
    In glory that excel;
    Who only doeth wondrous works,
    In glory that excel;

2.  And blessed be His glorious Name
    To all eternity;
    The whole earth let His glory fill.
    Amen: So let it be.
    The whole earth let His glory fill.
    Amen: So let it be.

# Photo Credits

The editor and publisher thank those who gave us permission to reproduce the photographs listed below. Those listed, however, are but a small fraction of the many people and families in the Protestant Reformed Churches who have willingly scrounged through family archives to satisfy our thirst for those precious jewels that significantly add to the treasures in this volume. Thank you for sharing your wealth.

## Chapter 1

Sternwheel steamboat on the Grand River—Grandville Historical Commission

The *May Graham*—Grandville Historical Commission

Ferry crossing the Grand River at Jenison—Grandville Historical Commission

Gridley's hill—Lynn and Maxine Wells family collection

Sand Road—Lynn and Maxine Wells family collection

Walker Christian Reformed Church—Walker United Reformed Church

Blair School—Tom and Bonnie Moelker family collection

Rev. John R. Brink—Calvin College, archives

John Moelker family—Tom and Bonnie Moelker family collection

Minute of Classis Grand Rapids East regarding the organization of Hope—Calvin College, archives

First consistory minutes of Hope church—Hope Christian Reformed Church

Hope church built in 1917—Tom and Bonnie Moelker family collection

Rev. Peter J. Hoekenga—Calvin College, archives

Rev. Jacob W. Wyngaarden—Calvin College, archives

Rev. John Medendorp—Calvin College, archives

## Chapter 2

Hope church and parsonage—Tom and Bonnie Moelker family collection

Hope's deposed officebearers—Reformed Free Publishing Association, archives

Typical farming activities—Gerald Roberts' photo album

Wilson Avenue bridge over the Grand River under construction—Grandville Historical Commission

J. G. Kooistra—Calvin College, archives

## Chapter 3

Richard Newhouse home at 4551 Hall Street SW—*The History of Hope 1916-1991*

Hope church with Universal Car and Service Company signage—Tom and Bonnie Moelker family collection

Corner of Riverbend and Kenowa showing parsonage, church, and Blair School—Tom and Bonnie Moelker family collection

"New Structure to Seat 400"—*Grandville Star* (October 8, 1964)

## Chapter 4

Ralph Janssen—Calvin College, archives

Janssen headlines—*Grand Rapids Press*

"Classis Holds Off Decision in Cases of Two Ministers"—*Grand Rapids Press* (January 22, 1925)

Blair School on Kenowa Avenue—Tom and Bonnie Moelker family collection

Rev. Henry D. Vande Kieft—Calvin College, archives

Klaas Schilder—Protestant Reformed Churches, archives

Rev. Hubert De Wolf— Protestant Reformed Churches, archives

Richard Newhouse—Reformed Free Publishing Association, archives

## Chapter 5

Sand Road—Lynn and Maxine Wells family collection

"Ophoff is Installed by Riverbend Church"—*Grand Rapids Press* (January 26, 1922)

Heys' arrangements of the Lord's prayer—*The Psalter*

Consistory of Hamilton—*Twenty-five Year Jubilee of the Protestant Reformed Church of America 1925-1950*

## Chapter 7

Record of the return of the Charles Engelsma family to Hope church— Roosevelt Park Protestant Reformed Church, archives (1932)

"Blue Church titlists"—*Grand Rapids Press* (September 13, 1959)

John Moelker's farmhouse on Kenowa—Tom and Bonnie Moelker family collection

## Chapter 8

Looking west as the tornado headed toward and struck Standale—George Davis, *The Herald*

The tornado roared across the Grand River and Fennessy Lake— http:// www.weather.gov/grr/1956TornadoOutbreakVrieslandTrufant

John Steuart Curry, *Tornado over Kansas*, oil on canvas, 1929—Collection of the Muskegon Museum of Art, Michigan, Hackley Picture Fund Purchase, 1935.4

"Community Wiped Out"—*Grand Rapids Press* (April 4, 1956)

## Chapter 16

Hope school board (c. 1950-51)—Hope Protestant Reformed Christian School, archives

Men building Hope school and original school building—Hope Protestant Reformed Christian School, archives

Hope faculty in 1952-53—Hope Protestant Reformed Christian School, archives